Fodor's 2008

CAPE COD, NANTUCKET & MARTHA'S VINEYARD

Where to Stay and [E]
for All Budgets

Must-See Sights
and Local Secrets

Ratings You Can Tru[st]

Fodor's Travel Publications   N
www.fodors.com

FODOR'S CAPE COD, NANTUCKET & MARTHA'S VINEYARD 2008

Editor: Paul Eisenberg

Editorial Production: Evangelos Vasilakis

Editorial Contributors: Andrew Collins, Sandy MacDonald, Laura V. Scheel

Maps & Illustrations: David Lindroth, *cartographer;* Bob Blake and Rebecca Baer, *map editors*

Design: Fabrizio LaRocca, *creative director;* Guido Caroti, Siobhan O'Hare, *art directors;* Tina Malaney, Chie Ushio, Ann McBride, *designers;* Melanie Marin, *senior picture editor;* Moon Sun Kim, *cover designer*

Cover Photo (Brant Point Lighthouse, Nantucket): Atlantide Phototravel/Corbis

Production/Manufacturing: Angela L. McLean

COPYRIGHT

Copyright © 2008 by Fodor's Travel, a division of Random House, Inc.

Fodor's is a registered trademark of Random House, Inc.

All rights reserved. Published in the United States by Fodor's Travel, a division of Random House, Inc., and simultaneously in Canada by Random House of Canada, Limited, Toronto. Distributed by Random House, Inc., New York.

No maps, illustrations, or other portions of this book may be reproduced in any form without written permission from the publisher.

ISBN 978–1–4000–1898–7

ISSN 1934–5569

SPECIAL SALES

This book is available at special discounts for bulk purchases for sales promotions or premiums. Special editions, including personalized covers, excerpts of existing books, and corporate imprints, can be created in large quantities for special needs. For more information, write to Special Markets/Premium Sales, 1745 Broadway, MD 6-2, New York, New York 10019, or e-mail specialmarkets@randomhouse.com.

AN IMPORTANT TIP & AN INVITATION

Although all prices, opening times, and other details in this book are based on information supplied to us at press time, changes occur all the time in the travel world, and Fodor's cannot accept responsibility for facts that become outdated or for inadvertent errors or omissions. So **always confirm information when it matters,** especially if you're making a detour to visit a specific place. Your experiences—positive and negative—matter to us. If we have missed or misstated something, **please write to us.** We follow up on all suggestions. Contact the Cape Cod, Nantucket & Martha's Vineyard editor at editors@fodors.com or c/o Fodor's at 1745 Broadway, New York, NY 10019.

PRINTED IN THE UNITED STATES OF AMERICA

10 9 8 7 6 5 4 3 2 1

Be a Fodor's Correspondent

Your opinion matters. It matters to us. It matters to your fellow Fodor's travelers, too. And we'd like to hear it. In fact, we need to hear it.

When you share your experiences and opinions, you become an active member of the Fodor's community. That means we'll not only use your feedback to make our books better, but we'll publish your names and comments whenever possible. Throughout our guides, look for "Word of Mouth," excerpts of your unvarnished feedback.

Here's how you can help improve Fodor's for all of us.

Tell us when we're right. We rely on local writers to give you an insider's perspective. But our writers and staff editors—who are the best in the business—depend on you. Your positive feedback is a vote to renew our recommendations for the next edition.

Tell us when we're wrong. We're proud that we update most of our guides every year. But we're not perfect. Things change. Hotels cut services. Museums change hours. Charming cafés lose charm. If our writer didn't quite capture the essence of a place, tell us how you'd do it differently. If any of our descriptions are inaccurate or inadequate, we'll incorporate your changes in the next edition and will correct factual errors at fodors.com immediately.

Tell us what to include. You probably have had fantastic travel experiences that aren't yet in Fodor's. Why not share them with a community of like-minded travelers? Maybe you chanced upon a beach or bistro or B&B that you don't want to keep to yourself. Tell us why we should include it. And share your discoveries and experiences with everyone directly at fodors.com. Your input may lead us to add a new listing or highlight a place we cover with a "Highly Recommended" star or with our highest rating, "Fodor's Choice."

Give us your opinion instantly at our feedback center at www.fodors.com/feedback. You may also e-mail editors@fodors.com with the subject line "Cape Cod Editor." Or send your nominations, comments, and complaints by mail to Cape Cod Editor, Fodor's, 1745 Broadway, New York, NY 10019.

You and travelers like you are the heart of the Fodor's community. Make our community richer by sharing your experiences. Be a Fodor's correspondent.

Happy Traveling!

Tim Jarrell, Publisher

CONTENTS

MAPS

CLOSE UPS

ABOUT THIS BOOK

Our Ratings

Sometimes you find terrific travel experiences and sometimes they just find you. But usually the burden is on you to select the right combination of experiences. That's where our ratings come in.

As travelers we've all discovered a place so wonderful that its worthiness is obvious. And sometimes that place is so unique that superlatives don't do it justice: you just have to be there to know. These sights, properties, and experiences get our highest rating, **Fodor's Choice**, indicated by orange stars throughout this book.

Black stars highlight sights and properties we deem **Highly Recommended**, places that our writers, editors, and readers praise again and again for consistency and excellence.

By default, there's another category: any place we include in this book is by definition worth your time, unless we say otherwise. And we will.

Disagree with any of our choices? Care to nominate a place or suggest that we rate one more highly? Visit our feedback center at www.fodors.com/feedback.

Budget Well

Hotel- and restaurant-price categories from ¢ to $$$$ are defined in the opening pages of each chapter. For attractions, we always give standard adult admission fees; reductions are usually available for children, students, and senior citizens. Want to pay with plastic? **AE, D, DC, MC, V** after restaurant and hotel listings indicate whether American Express, Discover, Diners Club, MasterCard, and Visa are accepted.

Restaurants

Unless we state otherwise, restaurants are open for lunch and dinner daily. We mention dress only when there's a specific requirement and reservations only when they're essential or not accepted—it's always best to book ahead.

Hotels

Hotels have private bath, phone, TV, and air-conditioning and operate on the European Plan (aka EP, meaning without meals), unless we specify that they use the Continental Plan (CP, with a continental breakfast), Breakfast Plan (BP, with a full breakfast), or Modified American Plan (MAP, with breakfast and dinner) or are all-inclusive (including all meals and most activi-

ties). We always list facilities but not whether you'll be charged an extra fee to use them, so when pricing accommodations, find out what's included.

Many Listings

★	Fodor's Choice
★	Highly recommended
⊠	Physical address
⊹	Directions
⌂	Mailing address
☎	Telephone
🖷	Fax
⊕	On the Web
✑	E-mail
✒	Admission fee
☉	Open/closed times
Ⓜ	Metro stations
▭	Credit cards

Hotels & Restaurants

▦	Hotel
⇖	Number of rooms
⚴	Facilities
❦	Meal plans
✕	Restaurant
⚬	Reservations
↘	Smoking
⌘	BYOB
✕▦	Hotel with restaurant that warrants a visit

Outdoors

⚐	Golf
⚠	Camping

Other

ℂ	Family-friendly
⇨	See also
⊠	Branch address
☞	Take note

WHAT'S WHERE

APPROACHING
THE CAPE

Heading for the Cape from either Boston or Providence, you pass southeastern Massachusetts towns that range from intriguing historic villages to former industrial cities to a handful of bucolic seaside communities with perhaps as much charm as—and far fewer crowds than—the Cape itself. Along Boston's South Shore, the city of Quincy celebrates the legacy of two hometown presidents, John Adams and John Quincy Adams. It's well worth exploring the Adams National Historic Park, which comprises 11 historic buildings. A bit farther south, the region's must-see draw is Plimoth Plantation, a stellar living-history museum in the family-friendly town of Plymouth. If you're approaching from the south and west, Fall River's Battleship Cove provides a floating piece of WWII history, and New Bedford gives a powerful image of the country's whaling days and early industrial era. These cities are both a bit rough around the edges, but these key attractions merit a visit. If you have time to meander, venture off the interstate and pass through the pastoral seafront villages of Westport, South Dartmouth, and Marion, which hark back to the old-time New England pleasures of lobster boils, sugary beaches, and long summer days.

THE UPPER CAPE

The region nearest the bridges is the most suburban and sprawling chunk of Cape Cod as well as the most historic—increasingly, it's also becoming more and more upscale in character, as affluent Boston and South Shore commuters continue to snap up homes in the area's two biggest towns, Falmouth and Sandwich. Many old B&Bs have been turned into private homes, but the infusion of money has also led to a better selection of fine restaurants and shops that remain open year-round. Proximity to the bridges also makes this a relatively more accessible area than the rest of the Cape, and it's handy for short getaways. Along the northern bay side lie the Cape's oldest towns—Sandwich was settled back in 1637. Nearby Mashpee, where more than 600 residents are descended from the original Wampanoags, is one of two Massachusetts towns with Native American–governed areas. The west coast from Bourne through North and West Falmouth mixes residential suburbs with hidden coves and beaches lining the bay, while Falmouth proper is an established year-round community with a particularly strong and fine performing-arts scene. Nearby Woods Hole brims with maritime attractions and is where a ferry chugs year-round to Martha's Vineyard.

WHAT'S WHERE

**THE MID CAPE**	The Mid Cape has a bit of a Jekyll-and-Hyde complex. Along the northern fringes, narrow Route 6A snakes through the peaceful, all-American, colonial hamlets of Barnstable, Yarmouth Port, and Dennis. It's a sophisticated, adult-minded area filled with antiques shops, smart taverns, and romantic B&Bs with creaky floorboards and wavy-glass windows. At the southern end of the area, booming Hyannis acts as a transportation and social hub for a more family-oriented—in some places honky-tonk—patch of seaside fun. It's chock-full of both hip and casual restaurants and galleries and has dozens of motels as well as some charming country inns. Traffic-clogged and rather tacky, Route 28 cuts east from Hyannis into South Yarmouth and West Dennis—the Cape capitals of motor lodges and minigolf courses. In the other direction, though, Route 28 runs west through the more low-key, old-money enclaves of Centerville, Cotuit, and Osterville.
**THE LOWER CAPE**	The Lower Cape is really a microcosm of everything that is Cape Cod. Brewster is a continuation of the subtle, historic charms of Route 6A, whereas Harwich Port and Orleans both see some of the same commercial exuberance—and excess—along Route 28 and other parts of Cape Cod's southern shore. Pristine and lightly developed Eastham is the gateway to Cape Cod National Seashore. And blue-blooded Chatham feels like a cross between the tony sections of Falmouth and Sandwich mixed with the restrained elegance of Nantucket—it's more expensive and conservative than just about any town on Cape Cod. In addition to the Cape, nature lovers can explore remote Monomoy National Wildlife Refuge as well as dozens of inviting ponds and beaches, plus one of the best stretches of the Cape Cod bike path. There's virtually nothing on Cape Cod—opulent inns and resorts, casual lobster shacks, funky galleries, historic lighthouses and windmills—that you won't find in considerable abundance in the Lower Cape.
**THE OUTER CAPE**	The narrow "forearm" of the Cape—less than 2 mi wide between Cape Cod Bay and the Atlantic Ocean in some spots—includes two of the Cape's least-developed areas, Wellfleet and Truro. That being said, Wellfleet fosters one of the most sophisticated and intriguing gallery and boutique scenes in coastal Massachusetts; its discreetly developed downtown is rife with fine window-browsing opportunities. Truro is super laid-back, the quintessence of subdued yet stunningly beautiful seclusion. U.S. 6 hooks around to the

west from Truro and terminates in one of the world's great hubs of bohemian life, Provincetown, which ranks among the nation's leading gay vacation getaways. Increasingly high housing costs, however, have steadily turned Provincetown from quirky to snazzy—bring your credit cards if you plan to visit the town's bevy of high-end galleries, home-furnishing shops, and bistros. But in the end, this entire area represents the Cape of dunes and beach grasses, of crashing surf and scrubby pines—the Cape that most attracts creative minds and seekers of solitude.

MARTHA'S VINEYARD	This fabled island just off the southwest tip of Cape Cod, about 5 mi south of Falmouth by boat, makes for an easy day trip from the mainland but merits several days' worth of exploration if you want a real sense of its allure. The three towns that compose Down-Island (the east end of Martha's Vineyard)—Vineyard Haven, Oak Bluffs, and Edgartown—are the most popular and the most populated. Here you'll find the ferry docks, the shops, and a concentration of things to do and see, including the centuries-old houses and churches that document the island's history. However, much of what makes the Vineyard special is found in its rural reaches, in the agricultural heart of the island and the largely undeveloped lands south and west of the Vineyard Haven–to–Edgartown line known as Up-Island. Country roads meander through woods and tranquil farmland, and dirt side roads lead past crystalline ponds, abandoned cranberry bogs, and conservation lands.

NANTUCKET	A bit smaller than Martha's Vineyard and quite a bit farther from mainland Cape Cod (about 25 mi south of Hyannis), Nantucket is divided into town and country. Town, where the ferries dock, is the center of island activity, with historical homes and inns and boutiques, galleries, and restaurants leading up from the harbor and waterfront. The rest of the island is largely residential (trophy houses abound), and nearly all roads from town terminate at one of the island's teeny (and seasonal) beach communities. Surfside, 3 mi to the south of Nantucket Town, is the island's premier beach (although Jetties also draws a crowd). The Village of Siasconset (known locally as 'Sconset) lies 8 mi to the east of town, past Windswept Cranberry Bog, and has spectacular rose-covered cottages worth a peek.

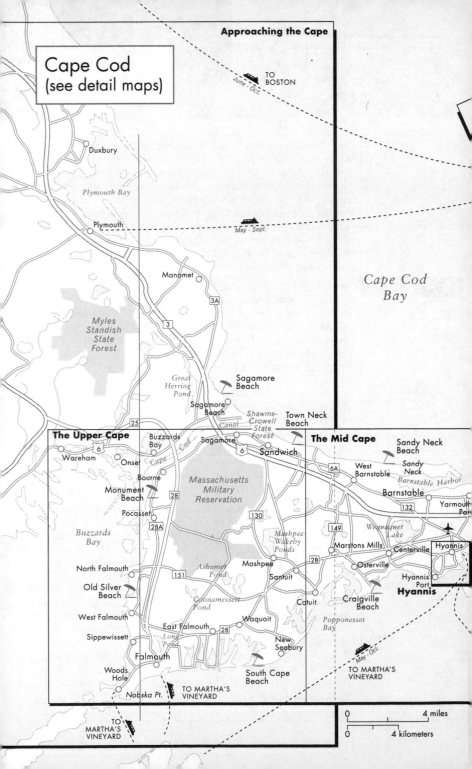

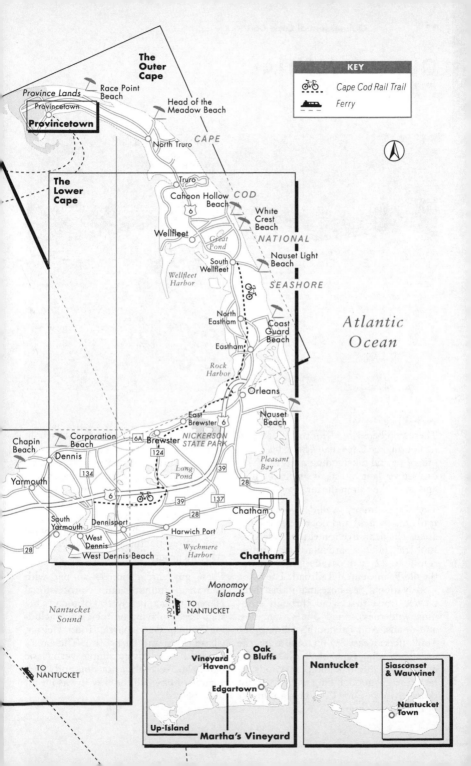

QUINTESSENTIAL CAPE COD

Two-Wheel Drive

There's no better mode of transportation for touring the Cape than a bike. It's along one of several outstanding trails that you can see verdant forests, hear birds chirp, and smell the salt in the air.

The Cape's many well-developed bike trails satisfy avid and occasional cyclists alike. The definitive route, the Cape Cod Rail Trail, offers a particularly memorable ride along 22-mi of paved right-of-way of the old Penn Central Railroad. The Cape Cod National Seashore maintains three bicycle trails that wind through stunning wilderness, amid dunes, marshes, and ponds. And Falmouth's Shining Sea Trail offers an easy 3½-mi route along the coast, providing views of Vineyard Sound and dipping into oak and pine woods. In fact, there's good biking in just about every town on Cape Cod, plus a number of bike-rental shops.

Play Ball!

America's national pastime, baseball, takes on special meaning each summer on Cape Cod. It's here that you can watch the sport in its purest form, without having to deal with pricey tickets, primadonna ballplayers, and riotous crowds. The Cape Cod Baseball League comprises 10 teams and has been going strong since the 1950s, attracting top college ballplayers from around the country.

These guys are talented—on par with midrange minor-league professional players. In fact, nearly 200 of today's big stars began playing on the Cape, including Nomar Garciaparra, Todd Helton, Chase Utley, and Barry Zito. The games are held at relatively simple yet classic ball fields, so grab a hot dog and catch a game of baseball the way it was meant to be played.

If you want to get a sense of Cape Cod culture, and indulge in some of its pleasures, start by familiarizing yourself with the rituals of daily life. These are a few highlights—things you can take part in with relative ease.

Lobster Lovin'

Scores of eateries and markets on the Cape serve lobster, usually the traditional way—boiled whole in the shell with drawn butter—but also in pies, bisques, quesadillas, and omelets. At the Yarmouth House Restaurant, you can order a delicious filet mignon topped with fresh-picked lobster meat and rich hollandaise sauce. Or opt for the standard summer lunch treat, a lobster roll—light lobster salad with just a hint of mayo on a plain white frankfurter roll.

Wherever you try it, don't leave Cape Cod without sampling this revered culinary offering. And if you get a hankering for lobsters once you get home, just call Quality Fresh Seafood in Bourne—they can airmail you a full clambake, complete with a whole lobster ready for steaming.

Seeing the Light

In addition to traditional Cape-style houses, Cape Cod is known for another distinctive architectural type: lighthouses. You'll find them up and down the Cape, some still active, others decommissioned.

Each has its own personality and profile. There's Highland Light in Truro, the Cape's oldest. Eastham's oft-photographed Nauset Light ranks among the most beautiful, and both Chatham Light and Falmouth's Nobska Light afford some of the best views. In Martha's Vineyard, be sure to journey out to Aquinnah Lighthouse, which stands atop a bluff above the beach and crashing surf. It's definitely worth ascending any lighthouse open for tours (several are, albeit with limited hours) to enjoy a magical perspective of the Cape's spectacular landscape.

WHEN TO GO

Memorial Day through Labor Day (or, in some cases, Columbus Day) is high season on Cape Cod. This is summer with a capital *S*, a time for barbecues, beach bumming, swimming, and water sports. In summer everything is open for business on the Cape, but you can also expect high-season evils: high prices, crowds, and traffic.

The Cape, however, is increasingly a year-round destination.

Climate

The following are average daily maximum and minimum temperatures for Hyannis. For local Cape weather, coastal marine forecasts, and today's tide times, call the weather line of **WQRC** (☎ *508/771–5522*) in Hyannis; average temperatures on the islands are similar.

Forecasts Weather Channel (⊕ www. weather.com).

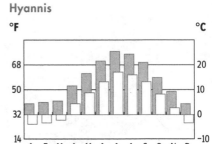

Hyannis

IF YOU LIKE

Beachcombing

Cape Cod has more than 150 beaches, enough to keep beachcombers happy and sandy year-round. Remember, strolling the beach can be just as enjoyable on a winter morning, when crowds are sparse and the surf is intense, as on a sultry summer afternoon.

Bay-side beaches generally have more temperate waters and gentler waves. South-side beaches, on Nantucket Sound, have rolling surf and, though still a bit chilly, are moderated by the Gulf Stream. Inland are dozens of freshwater ponds, many with warm water and sandy beaches ideal for kids. The Cape Cod National Seashore offers the greatest "wow" factor: serious surf, long and wide expanses of sand, and magnificent dunes. Here are some favorite spots to dip your toes into the sand.

The **Massachusetts Audubon Wellfleet Bay Wildlife Sanctuary**, in South Wellfleet, with its numerous adult and children's programs and its beautiful salt-marsh surroundings, is a favorite migration stop for Cape vacationers year-round.

Nauset Light, Coast Guard, Marconi, and Race Point beaches stretch majestically along the length of the Cape Cod National Seashore. Backed by dunes, they are the classic Cape beaches.

Across from the scenic Bass River, the Mid Cape's **West Dennis Beach** is long and wide, with pristine marshland. It's great for windsurfing.

One of the nicest beaches on the approach to the Cape, Westport's **Horseneck Beach State Reservation** stretches for 2 mi and offers access to great kayaking and boating on the Westport River.

Art & Antiques

The Cape's off-the-beaten-path locale and glorious setting helped turn it into a prominent art colony in the mid-19th century. Today, its concentration of art galleries is among the highest in the nation, with everything from modestly priced crafts and pen-and-ink drawings to priceless nautical paintings and contemporary bronzes. The Cape's prosperous history as a shipping and whaling center accounts for its plethora of fine antiques shops. If it's fine artwork and vintage furnishings you're after, this is the place. Here are a few areas worth scouring.

Driving along **Route 6A from Sandwich to Brewster** you'll pass dozens of fine antiques shops and more than a few excellent galleries. Pay special attention as you drive through the village of Dennis. There are also two great antiques auction houses in this area, Robert C. Eldred Co. in East Dennis and Sandwich Auction House in Sandwich.

Historic **Nantucket Town** is worth ferrying to for its abundance of very fine—and pricey—galleries and antiques emporia.

Along laid-back **Wellfleet's Main and Commercial streets**, numerous galleries offer everything from stained glass to nautical watercolors to African carved-wood sculptures. South of downtown, the Wellfleet Flea Market—great for bargain hunting—is held four days a week in summer.

Commercial Street in Provincetown, especially along the stretch in the East End, abounds with high-quality options. Just in the past few years, dozens of new and increasingly prestigious establishments have opened along here.

Ice-Cream Shops

However you spend the day on Cape Cod—whether beachcombing or biking, sailing or sidewalk shopping—break up the action with a sweet treat from one of the region's many distinctive ice-cream shops. Devotees debate the merits of soft-serve versus hard ice cream, and waffle versus sugar cones. And some loyalists frown upon the recent influx of newfangled gelato shops, not to mention restaurants serving such offbeat variations as deep-fried ice cream. Whatever you do, avoid ubiquitous franchise operations, and try to stick with parlors selling homemade ice cream—there are plenty to choose from. Consider the following local faves.

Set in a rustic mid-19th-century barn decorated with a working nickelodeon, Dennisport's **Sundae School Ice Cream Parlor** serves great homemade ice cream, real whipped cream, and old-fashioned sarsaparilla and cream soda (there are additional locales in Harwich Port and East Orleans).

In Chatham, **Buffy's** serves delicious, rich ice cream that you can savor outside beneath a prodigious apple tree. Don't overlook the fresh-squeezed lime rickies and tangy smoothies.

Since 1889, **Hallet's**—a quaint country drugstore in Yarmouth Port—has served tasty and justly famous ice-cream concoctions from its all-marble soda fountain with swivel stools.

Jerry's Seafood and Dairy Freeze in West Yarmouth ranks among the Cape's favorite purveyors of soft-serve ice cream.

Boating Adventures

Given that the Cape is completely surrounded by water, it's no wonder that one of the best ways to appreciate it is from a boat, whether a charter fishing yacht or a nimble kayak. Companies renting all types of boats and offering a wide range of tours and excursions exist all around the Cape, and whale-watching cruises rank among the most popular options. Even just riding one of the region's many ferryboats offers a great chance to enjoy the high seas and wonderful views of the land. Here are a few great ways to take to the water in and around Cape Cod.

Take a boat trip out to **Monomoy National Wildlife Refuge,** a 7,600-acre preserve that comprises the Monomoy Islands, a fragile 8-mi-long barrier-beach area south of Chatham. Several companies offer excursions out this way.

Cruise the Outer Cape on Provincetown's **Bay Lady II Excursion Schooner,** a beautiful 73-foot sailing vessel that heads out for two-hour cruises three times daily. You're welcome to bring your own spirits and snacks for this scenic and peaceful sail.

Book an excursion with **Great Marsh Kayak Tours,** which has offices in West Yarmouth and Barnstable and offers a range of great trips, from fly-fishing runs to sunset jaunts—you can also customize your own itinerary.

Hy-Line, in Hyannis, offers cruises on reproductions of old-time Maine coastal steamers. The one-hour tours of Hyannis Harbor and Lewis Bay include a view of the Kennedy compound and other points of interest.

GREAT ITINERARY

CAPE COD: CLASSIC BEACHES & BUSTLING VILLAGES

Day 1: Falmouth

Begin by crossing the Bourne Bridge and taking Route 28A south through some lovely little towns until you reach Falmouth, an excellent base for exploring the Upper Cape. Here you can stroll around the village green, look into some of the historic houses, and stop at the Waquoit Bay National Estuarine Research Reserve for a walk along the estuary and barrier beach. Take some time to check out the village of Woods Hole, the center for international marine research and the year-round ferry port for Martha's Vineyard. A small aquarium in town has regional sea-life exhibits, and there are several shops and museums. If you have any extra time, spend it north of here in the lovely old town of Sandwich, known for the Sandwich Glass Museum and the beautiful grounds and collection of antique cars at Heritage Museums and Gardens.

Days 2 & 3: Hyannis

The crowded Mid Cape is a center of activity, and its hub is Hyannis. Here you can take a cruise around the harbor or go on a deep-sea fishing trip. There are shops and restaurants along Main Street and plenty of kid-worthy amusements. Kennedy fans shouldn't miss the JFK Hyannis Museum. End the day with a concert at the Cape Cod Melody Tent. Spend your second day exploring the northern reaches of the Mid Cape with a drive along scenic U.S. 6, which passes through the charming, slow-paced villages of Barnstable, Yarmouth Port, and Dennis. There are beaches and salt marshes, museums, antiques shops and galleries, and old graveyards along this route. Yarmouth Port's Bass Hole Boardwalk makes for a particularly beautiful stroll. In Dennis there are historic houses to tour, and the Cape Museum of Fine Arts merits a stop. End the day by climbing 30-foot Scargo Tower to watch the sun set. At night you can catch a film at the Cape Cinema, on the grounds of the Cape Playhouse.

Days 4 & 5: Chatham

Chatham, with its handsome Main Street, is a perfect base for strolling, shopping, and dining. A trip to the nearby Monomoy Islands is a must for bird-watchers and nature lovers. Back in town, you can watch glassblowing at the Chatham Glass Company, visit the Old Atwood House and Railroad museums, and drive over to take in the view from Chatham Light. Spend your second day detouring up to Brewster to check out the eclectic mix of antiques shops, museums, freshwater ponds for swimming and fishing, and miles of biking and hiking trails through Nickerson State Park. Don't miss the Cape Cod Museum of Natural History. On the way north from Chatham, take the less-commercial end of Route 28 to Orleans, driving past sailboat-speckled views of Pleasant Bay. On the way up toward Provincetown, stop in Eastham at the National Seashore's Salt Pond Visitor Center.

Days 6 & 7: Provincetown

Bustling Provincetown sits at the very tip of the Cape, and there's a lot to see and do here. Catch a whale-watch boat and take a trolley tour in town or bike through the National Seashore on its miles of trails. Climb the Pilgrim Monument for a spectacular view of the area—on an excep-

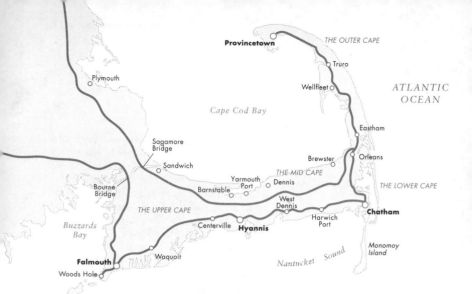

tionally clear day you can see the Boston skyline. Visit the museums and shops and art galleries, or spend the afternoon swimming and sunning on one of the beaches. To escape the crowds, spend a day driving south through sleepy but scenic Truro and then park your car in Wellfleet's historic downtown, where you'll find a bounty of intriguing shops and galleries. Continue a bit south to historic Marconi Station, which was the landing point for the transatlantic telegraph early in the 20th century. It's also worth walking the short but stunning White Cedar Swamp Trail.

Alternatives

On Day 2, hop the ferry for a day trip to either Martha's Vineyard or Nantucket. Both islands offer breathtaking scenery and village centers chock-full of great shops and restaurants. And if you're really keen on exploring either island, consider spending the night. Martha's Vineyard requires a shorter ferry ride and is your best choice if time is tight.

On either your first or final day—especially if you're a history buff or you're traveling with kids—pass through Plymouth, on the mainland just north of Sagamore Bridge, and make a visit to Plimoth Plantation, one of the most impressive living-history museums in the country.

TIPS

1. Keep in mind that traffic leading onto the Cape is particularly horrendous on Friday, and traffic leading off the Cape is rough on Sunday. Try to time your visit to avoid these times, but if you must travel to or from the Cape on these days, cross as early in the day as possible.

2. If you're traveling with kids, you might want to pass on some of the itinerary's more adult-oriented highlights described above—such as shopping in Wellfleet and driving along scenic Route 6A from Barnstable to Dennis—and instead set aside some time in the southern sections of Yarmouth and Dennis, where Route 28 passes by countless amusement centers, minigolf courses, and other kid-friendly amusements.

3. A car is the best way to explore the Cape, but in the busier town centers—such as Falmouth, Hyannis, Chatham, and Provincetown—you can get around quite easily on foot. Plan to park your car at your accommodation and avoid using it except to explore less densely populated areas of the Cape.

ON THE CALENDAR

	The Massachusetts Office of Travel & Tourism offers events listings and a whale-watch guide for the entire state. Also see the events calendar in "CapeWeek," an arts-and-entertainment supplement published every Friday in the *Cape Cod Times*; it's available online at ⊕ *www.capeweek.com*.
WINTER Early December	Many Cape towns ring in the Christmas season in grand style. To take in the best-known celebration, plan an excursion to nearby Nantucket for the annual **Christmas Stroll Weekend** (☎ *508/228–1700*), which takes place the first weekend of the month. Carolers and musicians entertain strollers as they walk the festive cobblestone streets and sample shops' wares and seasonal refreshments. Activities include theatrical performances, art exhibitions, crafts sales, and a tour of historic homes. To avoid the throngs, visit on one of the surrounding weekends (festivities begin the day after Thanksgiving and last through New Year's Eve). Various Cape towns also have **holiday strolls**; call the **Cape Cod Chamber of Commerce** (☎ *508/862–0700*) for a free brochure. Falmouth's **Holidays-by-the-Sea** (☎ *508/548–8500 or 800/526–8532*), held the first full weekend of December, includes lighting ceremonies at the Village Green, caroling at Nobska Light in Woods Hole, a house tour, church fairs, and a parade.
December	Chatham's **Christmas by the Sea weekend** (☎ *508/945–5199*), generally the first weekend of the month, includes caroling, a Festival of Trees, and other special events. The events are part of a monthlong celebration beginning just after Thanksgiving and ending with a lavish First Night celebration, with fireworks over Oyster Pond on New Year's Eve.
SPRING Late April	The weekend-long **Brewster in Bloom** (☎ *800/399–2967* ⊕ *www.brewsterinbloom.org*) greets the spring season with a daffodil fest each year during the last weekend in April. Geared to promote small-town life, the festival includes arts-and-crafts shows, a parade, a spring dance, tours of historic homes and inns, a golf tournament, and a giant antiques and collectibles market.
Mid May	The Green Briar Nature Center and Jam Kitchen in Sandwich holds its annual **Green Briar Herb Festival** (☎ *508/888–6870*

	⊕*www.thorntonburgess.org/herb.htm*), where you can pick up perennials, wildflowers, and dozens of herb varieties. During **Cape Cod Maritime Days** (☎*508/362–3225* ⊕*www.capecodmaritimedays.com*) lighthouse tours, guided shore-front walks, and special exhibits Cape-wide help celebrate the Cape's nautical heritage.
SUMMER June – August	Summer theater, town-band concerts, and arts-and-crafts fairs enliven most every Cape town.
Early June	The **Cape Cod Antique Dealers Association Spring Antiques Show** (☎*508/888–3300* ⊕*www.ccada.com*) at Sandwich's Heritage Plantation is attended by 60 dealers of fine 18th- and 19th-century English and American furniture, folk art, Sandwich glass, jewelry, paintings, and quilts.
Mid to Late June	The **Portuguese Festival** (☎*508/487–0500* ⊕*www.province townportuguesefestival.com*) honors Provincetown's Portuguese heritage with a lively weekend of ethnic foods and crafts, bands playing in the streets, a children's fishing derby, traditional dances, fireworks, and other events. The **Blessing of the Fleet** in Provincetown concludes the Portuguese Festival weekend. On Sunday, a parade ends at the wharf, where anglers and their families and friends pile onto boats and form a procession. The bishop stands on the dock and blesses the boats with holy water as they pass by.
Late June	Falmouth welcomes the **Soundfest Chamber Music Festival** (☎*508/548–2290* ⊕*www.coloradoquartet.com*), including the Colorado Quartet and guest artists. Daily events during the two-week festival include student performances, concerts, master classes, and lectures.
July 4 Weekend	The **Mashpee Powwow** (☎*508/477–0208* ⊕*www.mashpee wampanoagtribe.com*) brings together Wampanoags from North and South America for three days of dance contests, drumming, a fireball game, and a clambake, plus the crowning of the Mashpee Wampanoag Indian princess on the final night. **Fireworks displays** are a part of July 4 celebrations in several Cape towns; Falmouth has one of the most spectacular shows.

Mid to Late July	The **Barnstable County Fair** (☎508/563–3200 ⊕*www.barns tablecountyfair.org*) in East Falmouth, begun in 1844, is Cape Cod's biggest event. The nine-day affair includes livestock and food judging; horse, pony, and oxen pulls and shows; arts-and-crafts demonstrations; carnival rides; lots of food; and appearances by formerly famous performing artists bent on comebacks.
Late July	The Cape Cod Symphony Orchestra sets up at the Mashpee Commons for the first of two annual **Sounds of Summer Pops Concerts** (☎508/539–2345 ⊕*www.mashpeepops.com*).
August	The **Cape & Islands Chamber Music Festival** (☎508/945–8060 or 800/818–0608 ⊕*www.capecodchambermusic.org*), three weeks of top-caliber performances, including a jazz night, is held at various locations in August. The festival also sponsors an off-season concert series; call or check the Web site for the schedule.
Early August	The Boston Pops Esplanade Orchestra wows the crowds with its annual **Pops by the Sea Concert** (☎508/362–0066 ⊕*www.artsfoundationcapecod.org*), held at the Hyannis Village Green at 5 PM. Each year a guest conductor strikes up the band.
	New Bedford's **Feast of the Blessed Sacrament** (☎508/992–6911 ⊕*www.portuguesefeast.com*) is one of the largest celebrations of Portuguese culture in the country. Music, dance, a parade, carnival rides, and traditional foods—particularly the giant *carne de espeto* outdoor barbecue—are all part of the four-day event.
Mid August	The 7-mi **SBLI Falmouth Road Race** (☎508/540–7000 ⊕*www. falmouthroadrace.com*) is a world-class race covering the coast from Woods Hole to Falmouth Heights; to participate, apply by mail the fall or winter before the race.
Late August	The Osterville Historical Society holds its annual **antiques show** (☎508/428–5861 ⊕*www.osterville.org*) on the third or fourth Thursday in August.
Late September	The **Annual Bourne Scallop Fest** (☎508/759–6000) attracts thousands of people to Buzzards Bay for three days of music, parades, carnival rides, and, of course, fried scallops.

	The **Harwich Cranberry Festival** (☎ *508/430–2811* ⊕ *www.harwichcranberryfestival.org*) includes an arts-and-crafts show, a carnival, fireworks, pancake breakfasts, an antique-car show, and much more.
Late October	**Fall foliage.** The leaf season usually peaks around the end of October. Colors might flame a few weeks earlier or later, however, depending on the weather during the preceding months.
Thanksgiving Eve	The **Lighting of the Monument festivities** (☎ *508/487–1310* ⊕ *www.pilgrim-monument.org*) commemorate the Pilgrims' landing, with the lighting of 5,000 white and gold bulbs draped over the Pilgrim Monument in Provincetown. The lighting occurs each night until just after the New Year. A musical performance accompanies the lighting, and the monument museum holds an open house and tours. Other events include dramatic readings of the Mayflower Compact (which was signed in Provincetown Harbor), fireworks, and numerous Thanksgiving-dinner celebrations. Various arts-and-crafts events kick off around the same time and continue through the holiday season.

Approaching the Cape

PLYMOUTH, FALL RIVER, WESTPORT, SOUTH DARTMOUTH, NEW BEDFORD & MARION

WORD OF MOUTH

"[In Plymouth] the 'rock' is not the draw, but the historical actors [at Plimoth Plantation and the Mayflower II] do a great job of bringing history alive. You'll find it absolutely amazing that all those people traveled all those days on that small 'flotation device' in the middle of the Atlantic. It's a great cloudy day activity, or when you've had just enough of the beach!"

—Dreamer2

Updated
by Laura V.
Scheel

IF THE REST OF CREATION isn't streaming toward the Bourne or Saga-more bridges at precisely the same moment, it's quite possible you'll make excellent time reaching one of them while dispensing with the towns along the way. But that doesn't mean you should.

A mix of suburbanized colonial hamlets, low-key yachting enclaves, and riches-to-rags industrial communities enjoying varying degrees of resurgence, the approach to Cape merits more than a pit stop. In the communities that line routes 3, 6, Interstate 495 and the other arteries to the Cape you'll find some of New England's quintessential historic attractions, a handful of bewitching beaches, a few pretty-damn-quaint seaside villages, and passable restaurants and accommodations.

In Plymouth you can see that monument you've heard about since childhood, Plymouth Rock, and walk the decks of the *Mayflower II*. A few miles down the road is Plimoth Plantation, a re-created 17th-century Puritan village where trained staff members vividly dramatize the everyday lives of the first English settlers. Watch them make cheese, forge nails, and explain where and when they bathe (hint: not often). If you have the time, as you leave Boston and pass through Quincy, exit from Route 3 onto the South Shore's slower but infinitely more scenic highway, Route 3A. It runs for about 50 mi down through the South Shore along Massachusetts Bay, from Quincy through Scituate, Dux-bury, and Plymouth and on to Cape Cod Canal. It takes an extra hour to go this way, but it's scenic and you'll avoid Route 3's occasionally vicious traffic jams.

If you're coming by way of Interstate 195, consider stopping in the sea-faring city of New Bedford, a major whaling port in the 19th century. It now delights visitors with the nation's largest museum on the history of whaling. If you have the time, and especially if you're intrigued by the macabre legacy of the 19th century's most infamous trial, in which Lizzie Borden was accused, and acquitted, of dispatching her parents with "40 whacks" of an ax, stop in Fall River, where this riveting drama played out. Fall River has seen better days, but it's also home to the largest collection of historic naval ships and submarines all open for exploration—Battleship Cove. Not far from Interstate 195 and the Fall River–New Bedford corridors, along the coves of Buzzards Bay, you'll find charming seaside towns and sandy beaches, the best known of which is Horseneck Beach in Westport. The pretty villages of South Dartmouth, Fairhaven, and Marion are also worth a stop.

EXPLORING THE APPROACH TO THE CAPE

If you're approaching the Cape by car, you have three key options. If you're coming from metro Boston and points due north, you'll likely approach the Cape via Route 3 (which is a major four-lane, limited-access highway, just like any interstate). If you're approaching from points south and west (i.e., Rhode Island, Connecticut, New York City), you'll likely take Interstate 195, which cuts over from Interstate 95 in Providence. And if you're approaching from central or western Massachusetts (i.e., Worcester or Springfield) or from Vermont, New Hampshire, or Maine, you'll probably take Interstate 495, which cuts down in a southeasterly direction toward the Cape from the Mass Pike.

We've organized this chapter by covering first Plymouth, the region's must-see destination, which lies along Route 3, and then the engaging communities on or near Interstate 195, from the cities of Fall River and New Bedford to the mellow but arresting villages of Westport, South Dartmouth, and Marion. There aren't many notable stops off Interstate 495, but if you're coming that way and are keen on visiting some of the towns in this chapter, you can easily jog northeast to Route 3 or south to Interstate 195. Again, Plymouth is

TOP 5
■ Whale-watch excursions from Plymouth, daily June–Sept., more limited basis in Apr, May, Oct.
■ Canoeing and kayaking on Buzzards Bay, especially the Westport, Mattapoisett, Paskamanset, Agawam, and Weweantic rivers
■ Musical and theatrical events staged Sept.–May at the Zelterlon Theatre in New Bedford
■ Antiquing along U.S. 6 from New Bedford to Buzzards Bay
■ Discovering Plymouth's *Mayflower II* and Plimoth Plantation

the star of the region, and even if you approach Cape Cod from a different direction, it's worth making a day trip back out to America's socalled hometown—it's easy to reach Plymouth from the Upper Cape.

ABOUT THE RESTAURANTS

Like other Massachusetts shorefront towns, the communities approaching the Cape have plenty of seafood restaurants, where you'll find everything from clam shacks to more upscale dining options. In New Bedford and Fall River, which have large Portuguese populations, you can sample traditional Portuguese dishes made with spicy *linguica* (sausage) or *bacalau* (salt cod), and pick up some soft, doughy Portuguese sweet bread to sustain you as you explore.

WHAT IT COSTS				
	$$$$	$$$	$$	$	¢
RESTAURANTS	over $30	$22–$30	$16–$22	$10–$16	under $10
HOTELS	over $260	$200–$260	$140–$200	$90–$140	under $90

Restaurant prices are per person for a main course at dinner. Hotel prices are for a standard double room, excluding 6% sales tax (more in some counties) and 1%–4% tourist tax.

ABOUT THE HOTELS

Plymouth's numerous lodgings include quaint bed-and-breakfasts and chain properties. Choices on the coast are more limited, although the area does have several worthwhile small inns and B&Bs. If you're traveling with children, ask whether they are welcome at smaller properties; and if they are, ask yourself if your family will be comfortable around antique furniture, staircases, and couples without kids.

TIMING

The fair-weather days of autumn make for a good time to visit Plymouth and the surrounding area. The Thanksgiving holiday is filled with special events at Plimoth Plantation, the site of the first permanent European settlement in southern New England in 1620. Heavy traffic is the norm on summer weekends and holidays on all major routes approaching the Sagamore and Bourne bridges. It's not uncommon for bridge backups to extend several miles, tacking on extra travel time.

PLYMOUTH

40 mi southeast of Boston.

On December 26, 1620, 102 weary British men, women, and children disembarked from the *Mayflower* to found the first permanent European settlement north of Virginia. (Virginia was their intended destination, but storms pushed the ship off course. Their first landing site, in Provincetown on the tip of Cape Cod, proved inhospitable; they set sail after spending nearly five weeks there, crossing Cape Cod Bay and ending their journey in Plymouth.) Of the settlers, now known as the Pilgrims, a third were members of a Puritan sect of religious reformers known as the Separatists, so called because they wanted to establish their own church separate from the national Church of England. This separation was considered treasonous, and the group had previously fled to the city of Leiden in the Netherlands seeking religious freedom. After more than 10 years there, they joined with other emigrants to start a new life in the New World.

While in Provincetown, the expedition's leaders drew up the Mayflower Compact, a historic agreement binding the group to the law of the majority. This compact became the basis for the colony's government. After a rough start (half the original settlers died during the first winter), the colony stabilized and grew under the leadership of Governor William Bradford. Two other founding fathers—military leader Myles Standish and John Alden—acquired mythical status via a poem by Henry Wadsworth Longfellow, *The Courtship of Miles Standish*.

Forty miles south of Boston, Plymouth today is characterized by narrow streets, clapboard mansions, shops, and antiques stores. Some commercial names would make the Pilgrims shudder: the John Alden Gift Shop and Mayflower Seafoods. But it's easy to overlook these and admire the picturesque waterfront. The town also holds a parade, historic-house tours, and other activities to mark Thanksgiving.

It's simple to get around Plymouth on foot or via the **Plymouth Rock Trolley** (☎*508/747–4161*); $15 gets you unlimited rides for the day.

Plymouth is dotted with historical statues, including depictions of William Bradford on Water Street, a Pilgrim maiden in the verdant Brewster Gardens, and Massasoit (chief of the local Wampanoag tribe) on Carver Street.

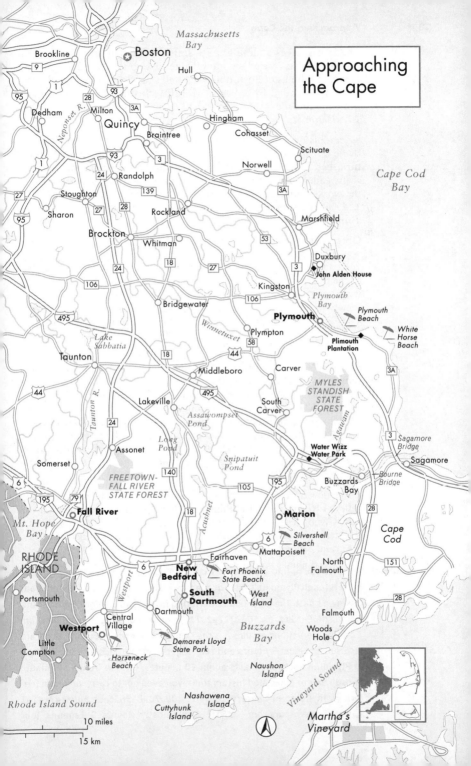

Approaching the Cape

Massachusetts Bay

Boston

Brookline

9

95

1

Dedham

1

95

27

Milton

3A

Quincy

Braintree

Hull

Hingham

Cohasset

Scituate

Norwell

3A

Cape Cod Bay

93

28

93

24

Randolph

139

Rockland

53

Marshfield

Stoughton

27

28

Sharon

Brockton

Whitman

18

27

Duxbury

John Alden House

495

24

106

Bridgewater

106

Kingston

Plymouth Bay

Plymouth Beach

Lake Sabbatia

18

Plympton

58

Plymouth

White Horse Beach

Taunton

44

44

Winnetuxet R.

Middleboro

Carver

Plimoth Plantation

3A

MYLES STANDISH STATE FOREST

Assawompset Pond

495

South Carver

Agawam

3

Sagamore Bridge

Sagamore

Lakeville

Long Pond

Assonet

Snipatuit Pond

Water Wizz Water Park

Bourne Bridge

Somerset

140

105

195

Buzzards Bay

FREETOWN–FALL RIVER STATE FOREST

Acushnet R.

18

Marion

28

6

195

79

Fall River

Silvershell Beach

Cape Cod

RHODE ISLAND

Mt. Hope Bay

Fairhaven

Mattapoisett

North Falmouth

151

Portsmouth

6

New Bedford

Fort Phoenix State Beach

West Island

28

Westport

South Dartmouth

Falmouth

Central Village

Dartmouth

Buzzards Bay

Woods Hole

Little Compton

Westport R.

Demarest Lloyd State Park

Horseneck Beach

Naushon Island

Vineyard Sound

Rhode Island Sound

10 miles

15 km

Cuttyhunk Island

Nashawena Island

Martha's Vineyard

The largest freestanding granite statue in the country, the **National Monument to the Forefathers** stands high on a grassy hill. Designed by Hammet Billings of Boston in 1854 and dedicated in 1889, it depicts Faith surrounded by Liberty, Morality, Justice, Law, and Education, and includes scenes from the Pilgrims' early days in Plymouth. ⊠*Allerton St.*

Several historic houses are open for visits, including the 1640 **Sparrow House,** Plymouth's oldest structure. You can peek into several rooms furnished in the spartan style of the Pilgrims' era. A contemporary crafts gallery also on the premises seems somewhat incongruous, but the works on view are of high quality. ⊠*42 Summer St.* ☎*508/747–1240* ⊕*www.sparrowhouse.com* ✉*$2; gallery free* ☉*Apr.–late Nov., Thurs.–Tues. 10–5.*

Operated by the Plymouth Antiquarian Society, the 1749 **Spooner House** was home to the same family for 200 years; today you can take a guided tour through its restored interior and well-tended gardens. The **Hedge House Museum,** a massive Federal home from 1809, reveals the wealthier side of successful 19th-century living. As of this writing, the society was restoring a third historic property, the **Harlow Old Fort House,** a 1677 gambrel-roofed dwelling, which is slated to reopen for tours in 2008. ⊠*27 North St.* ☎*508/746–0012* ✉*$5* ☉*Early June–early Oct., Thurs.–Fri. 2–6, Sat. 9–noon.*

☾ Like Plimoth Plantation, the *Mayflower II,* a reproduction of the 1620 *Mayflower,* is manned by staff, some clad in period dress, and docents who regularly present demonstrations on board, from knot tying to cooking. The ship was built in England through research and a bit of guesswork, and then sailed across the Atlantic in 1957. In addition to touring the ship, you can peruse the several interesting exhibits on the pier next to it. ⊠*State Pier* ☎*508/746–1622* ⊕*www.plimoth. org* ✉*$8; free with Plimoth Plantation combination ticket* ☉*Late Mar.–Nov., daily 9–5.*

A few dozen yards from the *Mayflower II* is **Plymouth Rock,** popularly believed to have been the Pilgrims' stepping-stone when they left the ship. Given the stone's unimpressive appearance—it's little more than a boulder—and dubious authenticity (as explained on a nearby plaque), the grand canopy overhead seems a trifle ostentatious.

■ SPOOKY WALKS

Whether you're into local lore or creepy tales of the paranormal, walking tours through Plymouth's historic areas are a great way to learn more about the town's past. The most popular offering from **Dead of Night Ghost Tours** (☎*508/866–5111 or 508/277–2371* ⊕ *www.deadofnightghosttours.com* ✉ *$13; reservations required*) is the Twilight Lantern Ghost Tour; there are also sunset cemetery tours and scavenger hunts for kids. The walks meet at Plymouth Rock; each lasts about 90 minutes. Choose from a 90-minute ghostly tour or a narrated history tour—you even get to carry your own lantern—with **Colonial Lantern Tours** (☎*800/698–5636 or 508/747–4161* ⊕ *www.lanterntours.com* ✉ *$15*). The Ghostly Haunts & Legends Tour departs nightly from the John Carver Inn at 25 Summer Street; the history tour meets at 86 Water Street.

Across the street from Plymouth Rock is **Cole's Hill,** where the company buried its dead—at night, so the local Native Americans could not count the dwindling numbers of survivors. Just past the hill, on what was once called 1st Street, is the site of the original settlement; in 1834 the street was renamed Leyden Street in honor of the Dutch city that sheltered the Pilgrims. Look for plaques designating the locations of the original lots.

From the waterfront sights it's a short walk to one of the country's oldest public museums. The **Pilgrim Hall Museum,** established in 1824, transports you back to the time just before the Pilgrims' landing with its exhibition of items carried by those weary travelers to the New World. Included are a carved chest, a remarkably well-preserved wicker cradle, Myles Standish's sword, John Alden's Bible, Native American artifacts, and the remains of the *Sparrow Hawk,* a sailing ship that was wrecked in 1626. ⊠*75 Court St. (Rte. 3A)* ☎*508/746–1620* ⊕*www.pilgrimhall. org* ⊴*$6* ⊘*Feb.–Dec., daily 9:30–4:30.*

NEED A BREAK?

Sample fruit wines—the cranberry variety is particularly refreshing—at the **Plymouth Bay Winery** (⊠*114 Water St.* ☎*508/746–2100*), open March to December, Monday through Saturday 10:30 to 5, Sunday noon to 5. It's a short walk from the *Mayflower II.*

ᗒ
Fodor'sChoice
★
When you see the sign at the entrance of **Plimoth Plantation** welcoming you to the 17th century—take it seriously! Against the backdrop of the Atlantic Ocean, a Pilgrim village has been painstakingly re-created, from the thatch roofs, cramped quarters, and open fireplaces to the long-horn livestock. Throw away your preconceptions of white collars and funny hats; through ongoing research, the Plimoth staff has developed a portrait of the Pilgrims that's more complex than the dour folk pictured in elementary-school textbooks. Listen to the accents of the "residents," who never break character. You might see them plucking ducks, cooking rabbit stew, or tending garden. Feel free to engage them in conversation about their life, but expect only curious looks if you ask about anything that happened later than 1627.

Elsewhere on the plantation is **Hobbamock's Homestead,** where descendants of the Wampanoag Indians re-create the life of a Native American who chose to live near the newcomers. In the **Carriage House Crafts Center** you'll see earthenware, candles, clothing, and other items created using the techniques of 17th-century English craftsmanship—that is, reproductions of what the Pilgrims might have imported (you can also buy samples). There are always a few artisans on hand demonstrating early crafts-making techniques, too. At the **Nye Barn** you can see descendants of 17th-century goats, cows, pigs, and chickens, bred to resemble animals raised on the original plantation. The visitor center has gift shops, a cafeteria, and multimedia presentations. Dress for the weather, because many exhibits are outdoors. Admission tickets are good for two consecutive days; if you have time, you may want to

Portrait of a Pilgrim

At Plimoth Plantation, the living history interpreters you meet are not just quaintly costumed actors. Beyond the bonnets, sweeping skirts, breeches, and cloaks of these folks going about 17th-century everyday business are glimpses and representations of actual, documented Pilgrim residents.

Once an interpreter is assigned their character for the year, the studying begins—role players closely examine primary sources from the 1627 village, learning biographical backgrounds, regional dialects, typical skills, and customs. Associate Director of Colonial Interpretation John Kemp says that this type of training instills "a sense of responsibility to a real person in history. We want every person to really connect with the character they are portraying."

The staff, says Kemp, is a combination of "curious experts and passionate learners." There are those who have a great knowledge of Renaissance foodways, agriculture, and livestock; others have studied 17th-century woodworking, blacksmithing, or military history. It's definitely not your average seasonal job; after all, these "Pilgrims" spend their days creating a world that existed almost 400 years ago. Keep this in mind when you ask them where the bathrooms are—they won't have any idea what you're talking about. —*Laura V. Scheel*

spread out your plantation visit to take in all the sights. ☒ *Warren Ave. (Rte. 3A)* ☎*508/746–1622* ⊕*www.plimoth.org* ☜*$21; $25 including entry to Mayflower II (2-day passes)* ⊙*Late Mar.–Nov., daily 9–5.*

OFF THE BEATEN PATH

John Alden House Museum. The only standing structure in which original Pilgrims are known to have lived is about 10 mi north of Plymouth in the town of Duxbury, settled in 1628 by Pilgrim colonists Myles Standish and John Alden, among others. Alden, who served as assistant governor of Plymouth colony, occupied this house, which was built in 1653, along with his wife, Priscilla, and eight or nine of their children. One bedroom has a "seven-day dresser" with a drawer for each day of the week; the Sunday drawer, which held formal church wear, is the largest. ☒*105 Alden St., Duxbury* ☎*781/934–9092* ⊕*www.alden.org* ☜*Guided tours $5* ⊙*Mid-May–mid-Oct., Mon.–Sat. noon–4.*

WHERE TO STAY & EAT

$–$$$ ✕**East Bay Grille.** A boisterous locals' favorite with subtle nautical decorations (oars, half-model ships), the East Bay looks natty enough for a special occasion but works as a casual family option, too. You'll find a menu here that suits many tastes and budgets, from mammoth lobster rolls and juicy burgers to more substantial fare, such as Chilean sea bass topped with tropical-fruit salsa, and charbroiled steak tips. Also note the several fine salads and the tasty steamed mussels appetizer. There's a popular Sunday brunch, and a pianist performs many evenings. ☒*173 Water St., Town Wharf* ☎*508/746–9751* ▭*AE, D, MC, V.*

\$–\$\$ ✕**Lobster Hut.** This casual, cafeteria-style eatery at the waterfront offers
★ seafood in the classic breaded-and-fried style, plus sandwiches and
luncheon specials. The interior is Formica-basic, but the fish is tasty,
and the water views are excellent. You can eat inside or outdoors on
the patio under a tent. ⊠ *Town Wharf* ☎ *508/746–2270* ▤ *MC, V*
⊘ *Closed Jan.*

¢–\$\$ ✕**Wood's Seafood.** Furnished with a simple counter for ordering fish
and a handful of plastic tables and chairs, this harborside seafood
shack looks authentically and endearingly shabby. If you're looking
for reasonably priced seafood (fried clams, lobster rolls, crab-cake
sandwiches, and assorted fish plates) with a water view, it's a great
choice. You can also buy live lobsters to take with you, or have them
shipped to anywhere in the country. ⊠ *Town Wharf* ☎ *508/746–0261*
▤ *AE, MC, V.*

¢ ✕**The All-American Diner.** The look is nostalgia—red, white, and blue
with movie posters. The specialties are beloved American foods—
Monte Cristo–style egg sandwiches and banana Belgian waffles for
breakfast (served all day) and cheeseburger club sandwiches, chicken-
fried steak, and meat loaf for lunch. ⊠ *60 Court St.* ☎ *508/747–4763*
▤ *AE, DC, MC, V* ⊘ *No dinner.*

\$\$–\$\$\$\$ ✕▣**John Carver Inn.** This three-story colonial-style redbrick building is
steps from Plymouth's main attractions. The public rooms are lavish,
with period furnishings and stylish drapes. The guest rooms are more
matter-of-fact, but the six suites have hot tubs and working fireplaces;
two-room suites have fireplaces and whirlpool baths. The indoor pool
has a *Mayflower*-ship theme and an 80-foot waterslide. At its Hearth 'n
Kettle Restaurant, staff in colonial attire serve a huge selection of pre-
dictable American favorites, including seafood and hearty sandwiches.
In response to the ever-expanding trend toward self-indulgence, the
Inn added the Beach Plum Spa in 2007, a full-service treatment center that includes the very fruit of its name into many of the soothing
potions. **Pros:** Short walk to downtown and waterfront attractions,
well-appointed rooms in full-service hotel, pool is a favorite with kids,
on-site spa. **Cons:** Theme pool is not suited for quiet relaxation (lots of
kids), not for those looking for authentic historic lodging. ⊠ *25 Summer St., 02360* ☎ *508/746–7100 or 800/274–1620* ▤ *508/746–8299*
⊕ *www.johncarverinn.com* ▱ *74 rooms, 6 suites* ⚘ *In-room: DVD
(some), Wi-Fi (some). In-hotel: restaurant, room service, bar, business
services, pool, spa, gym, game room* ▤ *AE, D, DC, MC, V.*

\$\$ ▣**Beach House Oceanfront B&B.** At the end of a long dirt road, this con-
★ temporary gray-shingle home overlooking the Atlantic makes a perfect
hideaway. Although it's only about 10 minutes south of Plymouth center, the house feels like it's a world away. The deck, screened porch,
and living room–dining room with floor-to-ceiling windows all face a
wide expanse of ocean, and steps lead down the cliff to a small private
beach. Inside, the theme is white—from the leather sofas in the living
room to the lace curtains and quilts in the bedrooms. Inquire about
weekly rentals. **Pros:** Water views and beachfront location, serene surroundings, ideal for those looking for a quiet getaway. **Cons:** Not an
in-town location. ⊠ *45 Black Pond La.* ▱ *429 Center Hill Rd., 02360*

☎508/224–3517 or 888/262–2543 ⊕www.beachhouseplymouth.com ⇋3 rooms, 1 suite ⚅In-room: no in-room phones, cable TV (some), Wi-Fi. In-hotel: beachfront, no-smoking rooms, no elevator ▤MC, V ⦿BP ⊘Closed Nov.–late May.

$$ :: Best Western Cold Spring. This neat-as-a-pin motel, about ½ mi from downtown Plymouth, is a good choice for families. Several buildings cluster around the parking areas and a lush green lawn, and inside, the rooms are nicely maintained, if nondescript, with floral bedspreads and sturdy wooden furnishings. Deluxe rooms are a tad more spacious than standard ones, and a few 2nd-floor rooms look out toward the harbor. **Pros:** Good for those wanting no-frills, standard lodging from a chain hotel, popular with business travelers, good bet for those traveling with children. **Cons:** Longish walk to town and waterfront (for small children and/or disabled), not for those looking for a more personalized lodging experience. ⊠188 Court St., 02360 ☎508/746–2222 or 800/678–8667 ⎙508/746–2744 ⊕www.coldspringmotel.com ⇋55 rooms, 3 suites, 2 cottages ⚅In-room: Wi-Fi. In-hotel: pool ▤AE, D, MC, V ⦿CP ⊘Closed Jan.–Mar.

$$ :: Pilgrim Sands Motel. This is the closest accommodation in town to Plimoth Plantation, and one of the few beachfront properties in the region. It's run by a friendly and helpful staff; and while the rooms themselves lack personality and feel a bit dated, they're clean and functional—you're paying more for the location. **Pros:** Directly across the street from Plimoth Plantation, half of the rooms have ocean views. **Cons:** Not an in-town location, no-frills, bland rooms (try to get the water-view ones). ⊠150 Warren Ave., 02360 ☎508/747–7263 or 800/729–7263 ⎙508/746–8066 ⊕www.pilgrimsands.com ⇋62 rooms ⚅In-room: refrigerator, Wi-Fi (some). In-hotel: pools, beachfront, Wi-Fi, no elevator ▤AE, D, MC, V ⦿CP.

$–$$ :: Governor Bradford on the Harbour. The waterfront location here (directly across from the *Mayflower II*) is a big plus. Rooms are motelbasic, each with two double beds, a small refrigerator, and free HBO. A Continental Plan is available from May to October. **Pros:** Great location for seeing waterfront and downtown attractions, kids (under 17) stay free. **Cons:** Rooms lack any kind of character but are clean and functional. ⊠98 Water St., 02360 ☎508/746–6200 or 800/332–1620 ⎙508/747–3032 ⊕www.governorbradford.com ⇋94 rooms ⚅In-room: refrigerator. In-hotel: pool, no-smoking rooms, Wi-Fi, no elevator ▤AE, D, DC, MC, V ⊘Closed late Dec.–Mar.

SPORTS & THE OUTDOORS

BEACHES **Plymouth Long Beach** (⊠Warren Ave. [Rte. 3A]), south of town, has restrooms, showers, and lifeguards (in season). Daily parking fees are $10 weekdays, $15 weekends.

White Horse Beach (⊠Taylor Ave.) is a popular long, sandy beach in a neighborhood of summer cottages, off Route 3A south of Plimoth Plantation. Parking is very limited.

BICYCLING Plymouth's gently sloping terrain and scenic streets make excellent terrain for bicycling. You can rent bikes at **Martha's Cyclery** (⊠300 Court St. ☎508/746–2109).

GOLF Play a fine, challenging 18-hole game at **Atlantic Country Club** (⊠*450 Little Sandy Pond Rd.* ☏*508/759–6644*).

Crosswinds Golf Club (⊠*424 Long Pond Rd.* ☏*508/830–1199*) has great views, a driving range, and 18- and 9-hole course options.

Shoot 9- or 18 holes at **Waverly Oaks Golf Club** (⊠*444 Long Pond Rd.* ☏*508/224–6700*), which also has plenty of practice space.

STATE PARKS **Myles Standish State Forest** (⊠*Cranberry Rd., South Carver* ✛*Exit 5 off Rte. 3* ☏*508/866–2526* ⊕*www. mass.gov/dcr*) has more than 16,000 acres for hiking, biking, swimming, picnicking, and canoeing.

TOURS **Andy Lynn Boats** (☏*508/746–7776*), at Plymouth Town Wharf, runs whale-watch trips June through September; call for their schedule.

Capt. John Boats (☏*508/746–2643 or 800/242–2469* ⊕*www.whale watchingplymouth.com*) offers several daily whale-watch cruises from Plymouth Town Wharf June through early September, and on a more limited schedule in April, May, and early September and October.

> ### LIZZIE BORDEN
>
> It's a famous rhyme of woe: "Lizzie Borden took an axe / And gave her mother forty whacks. / When she saw what she had done, / She gave her father forty-one." And yet Lizzie, the maiden daughter of Fall River's prominent banker, was found innocent of the 1892 bludgeoning deaths of her father and stepmother in the most sensational trial of its time.

FALL RIVER

18 mi east of Providence, 54 mi southeast of Boston.

This fading port and textile-milling center is today a prosaic, mostly industrial town that's en route to the Cape if you're coming from the south and west through Rhode Island. Fall River is home to the impressive nautical museum Battleship Cove and was the site of the infamous 19th-century Borden murders. Otherwise, this once-thriving city—better known today as the hometown of celeb chef Emeril Lagasse—has little to attract visitors.

The best place to learn about the Borden case is the **Fall River Historical Society,** which is packed with Borden memorabilia, including courtroom evidence, photographs, and the handleless hatchet believed to be the murder weapon. The 1843 Greek-revival mansion also contains exhibits on the Fall River steamship line and the city's days as the world's largest cotton-cloth manufacturer. One-hour tours begin on the hour. ⊠*451 Rock St.* ☏*508/679–1071* ⊕*www.lizzieborden.org* 🎫*Tours $5* ⊙*Apr., May, Oct., and Nov., Tues.–Fri. 9–4:30; June–Sept. and Dec., Tues.–Fri. 9–4:30, weekends 1–5.*

If you're strong of heart and stomach, you may want to take in the **Lizzie Borden Bed & Breakfast Museum,** in the Bordens' former home, the site of the murders, which has been transformed into a B&B. Even if you don't spend the night here, you can stop in to see the display of Lizzie-

related items. ⊠*92 2nd St.* ☎*508/675–7333* ⊕*www.lizzie-borden.*
com 🎟*Tours $10* ⊙*Tours daily on the hr 11–3.*

A visit to Fall River can skirt Lizzie Borden's sad saga entirely. The
town's industrial docks and enormous factories recall its past as a
major textile center in the 19th and early 20th centuries.

ᘓ In the past, Fall River served as a port; today the most interesting
nautical site is **Battleship Cove,** a "floating" museum complex docked
on the Taunton River. You can go aboard the 35,000-ton battleship
USS *Massachusetts*; the destroyer USS *Joseph P. Kennedy Jr.*; a World
War II attack sub, the USS *Lionfish*; two PT boats from World War
II; and a Cold War–era Russian-built warship. Also on the grounds is
the wooden **Fall River Carousel,** which was built in the 1920s. Rides
cost 50¢. ⊠*5 Water St., at Davol St., off Rte. 79* ☎*508/678–1100 or*
800/533–3194 ⊕*www.battleshipcove.org* 🎟*$14* ⊙*Apr.–June, daily*
9–5; July–early Sept., daily 9–5:30; early Sept.–Oct., daily 9–5; Nov.–
Mar., daily 9–4:30.

WHERE TO STAY & EAT

$–$$ ✕**Waterstreet Café.** This casually sophisticated café, with exposed brick
and sponge-painted walls, serves hummus and tabbouleh wraps, falafel,
and other Middle Eastern–inspired salads and sandwiches, along with
creative American and Mediterranean specialties such as maple-chipo-
tle char-grilled pork chops or Greek Island Shrimp sautéed with arti-
choke hearts and feta cheese. It's a short walk from Battleship Cove.
There's brunch on Sunday and live music many nights. ⊠*36 Water*
St. ☎*508/672–8748* ⊕*www.waterstreetcafe.com* ⊟*AE, D, MC, V.*
⊙*Closed Mon. and Tues. No dinner Wed.*

¢–$ ✕**T. A. Restaurant.** Fall River has a substantial Portuguese community,
and this modest but excellent eatery serves some of the best examples
of that culture's cuisine in the state. *Alentejana* (marinated pork with
clams and potatoes), garlicky shrimp Mozambique, and baked cod
with onions and tomatoes are among the specialties. A shop next door
sells Portuguese foods and provisions. ⊠*408 S. Main St.* ☎*508/673–*
5890 ⊟*AE, D, MC, V.*

$$–$$$ 🏠**Lizzie Borden Bed & Breakfast Museum.** Could you stand to sleep in
the same house where Lizzie Borden's father and stepmother met a
bloody end? Choose from one of the original bedrooms, some of which
can be combined into adjoining suites, or three rooms converted from
attic space—all are lavishly appointed with fine Victorian pieces. A full
breakfast and a house tour are included, as well as a map of the "Lizzie
Trail" (related sites in the Fall River area). You can also watch videos
about the Borden case. Owners Donald Woods and Lee Ann Wilbur
have restored and rejuvenated the entire property, using fabrics, paints,
and furnishings that more closely resemble how the Borden house
would have looked at the time of its infamy. **Pros:** Great for those with
macabre curiosities, rooms are outfitted with authentic antiques and
accoutrements that really set the tone for the Lizzie story. **Cons:** Attic
rooms must share a bathroom, rooms accessed via steep stairways, not
for those afraid of ghosts. ⊠*92 2nd St., 02721* ☎*508/675–7333*
⊕*www.lizzie-borden.com* ⇱*6 rooms, 2 suites, 3 with shared bath*

&In-room: no phone, no TV, Wi-Fi. In-hotel: no-smoking rooms, no elevator ☰AE, D, MC, V ⌶◎⌶BP ⊗Closed late Dec.–mid-Jan.

WESTPORT

12 mi southeast of Fall River.

As you venture south and east of Fall River, the urban landscape gives way to farm country. You'll pass rows of corn, old stone walls, and pastures of cows and horses. About 12 mi from Fall River, Westport is comprised of farmland and summer homes in a small village and scattered throughout the countryside; it also has one of the area's nicest beaches.

The **Westport Rivers Vineyard and Winery** has earned considerable acclaim for their sparkling, white, and rosé vintages, which they've been producing since the early '90s using grapes they grow on an 80-acre vineyard—the sparkling wines are particularly well regarded. You can sample the wines, and there's a small art gallery above the store with changing exhibits. Free winery tours are offered on weekends, and the winery holds special food-and-wine events and festivals throughout the year. ✉*417 Hixbridge Rd., off Rte. 88* ☎*508/636–3423* ⊕*www.westportrivers.com* ⊗*Tasting room, shop, and gallery May–Dec., daily 11–5; Jan.–Apr., weekends 11–5.*

NEED A BREAK? Traditional baking techniques are still employed at **Butler's Colonial Donut House** (✉*459 Sanford Rd.* ☎*508/672–4600*). Specialties include cream puffs, Long Johns, and a variety of old-time favorites, all handmade with real cream. Rounding out the offerings are tasty pastries and pies.

WHERE TO STAY & EAT

$$–$$$$
Fodor'sChoice
★
✕**The Back Eddy.** Fresh, creatively prepared seafood—such as applewood bacon–wrapped sea scallops with corn-and-tomato succotash, and rare grilled yellowfin tuna with wasabi oil and house-made kimchee—is the specialty at this laid-back waterfront restaurant where some diners arrive by boat and many patrons greet each other by name. The casual, wood-floor dining room is boisterous, with a lively bar scene, and most of the large windows overlook the busy harbor—an ideal place to watch the sunset. Expect to wait for a table. ✉*1 Bridge Rd.* ☎*508/636–6500* ⊕*www.thebackeddy.com* ☰*AE, D, MC, V* ⌓*Reservations not accepted* ⊗*Closed Jan.–Mar. No lunch weekdays.*

¢–$$
✕**Marguerite's.** The scene is pure country kitchen inside this gray-shingle house—from the wooden tables to the cheerful waitresses who circulate with ever-full coffeepots. Diner-style breakfasts and old-time New England specialties, from stuffed quahogs (clams) and chowder to broiled scrod, liver, and onions, and chicken pie, make up most of the menu; the daily specials offer some jazzier flourishes, such as grilled swordfish with lemon-dill butter. It's all fresh and homemade, which has earned this little house a devoted local following. Note that dinner is served only until 8 PM weeknights and until 8:30 on Friday

and Saturday. ⊠*778 Main Rd., Village Commons shopping center*
☎*508/636–3040* ⊟*No credit cards* ◉*Closed Sun.*

$$ 🏠**Paquachuck Inn.** Built in 1827 as a supply house for whaling ships, this wood-shingle building on Westport Point is now a modest, comfortable inn. The wood-floor rooms with exposed beams aren't large, but several have four-poster beds and all offer at least a glimpse of the water. Unfortunately, none has a private bath (the nine rooms share four baths), although one shared bath does have a whirlpool tub, and there's also an outdoor shower. The large, sunny breakfast room with comfy couches leads to a patio and yard—note the three whale vertebrae that are now a garden sculpture. **Pros:** All rooms have water views, simple, attractive lodging in a scenic location. **Cons:** No private baths, rooms on the small side. ⊠*2056 Main Rd., 02791* ☎*508/636–4398* ⊕*www.paquachuck.com* 🛏*9 rooms* 🛆*In-room: no a/c, no phone, no TV. In-hotel: dock, no-smoking rooms, no elevator* ⊟*AE, D, MC, V* ◉� *CP.*

SPORTS & THE OUTDOORS

★ One of the nicest beaches in southeastern Massachusetts, **Horseneck**
BEACHES **Beach State Reservation** (⊠*Rte. 88* ☎*508/636–8816* ⊕*www.mass.gov/ dcr*) draws summer crowds to its 2 mi of sand, with access to kayaking and boating on the Westport River. There are restrooms with showers, and lifeguards in season. Parking is $8 a day from May through early September.

SOUTH DARTMOUTH

4 mi east of Westport.

As in nearby Westport, the South Dartmouth countryside is dotted with farms and summer homes, but residents who work in nearby New Bedford also make their homes here year-round. One of the prettiest spots is Padanaram (pronounced pay-duh-*nair*-um) Village, where Gulf Road and Dartmouth Road meet. Built around the sailboat-filled harbor, it's a little oasis of shops, galleries, and cafés. Nearby, the village of Russells Mills houses one of the region's oldest general stores and a pottery studio.

WHERE TO STAY

$$–$$$$ 🏠**Residence Inn.** This comfortable extended-stay Marriott is near shopping and golf; Horseneck Beach is 12 mi away. The spacious suites have full kitchens, high-speed Internet access, and separate sleeping and living areas; some units have fireplaces. There's a complimentary full breakfast, and you can order in from local restaurants through a delivery service. **Pros:** Good for those who need a lot of space with a kitchen, a favorite for business travelers and families; free, light dinner offered Monday to Thursday evenings (5 to 7 PM). **Cons:** A long drive to the beach. ⊠*181 Faunce Corner Rd., North Dartmouth 02747* ☎*508/990–7725 or 800/331–3131* ⊟*508/747–3032* 🛏*96 suites* 🛆*In-room: kitchen, Wi-Fi. In-hotel: pool, gym, concierge, laundry facilities, laundry service, some pets allowed (fee)* ⊟*AE, D, DC, MC, V* ◉�*BP.*

1

SPORTS & THE OUTDOORS

BEACHES **Demarest Lloyd State Park** (✉*Barney's Joy Rd.* ☎*508/636–8816* ⊕*www. mass.gov/dcr*) may be hard to find, but it's worth seeking out for its long beach of soft, white sand on a sheltered Buzzards Bay cove. Behind the beach is a wooded area with picnic tables and barbecue grills. The bathhouse has restrooms and showers. In season (late May to early September) there are lifeguards, and parking is $8 a day.

SHOPPING

Davoll's General Store (✉*1228 Russells Mills Rd.* ☎*508/636–4530*), established in 1793, sells antiques and collectibles, as well as clothing, deli sandwiches, and a small selection of groceries.

Salt Marsh Pottery (✉*1167 Russells Mills Rd.* ☎*508/636–4813 or 800/859–5028* ⊕*www.saltmarsh.com*) makes platters, bowls, and other unique ceramic pieces decorated with wildflowers.

NEW BEDFORD

15 mi east of Fall River, 50 mi south of Boston.

In 1652, colonists from Plymouth settled the area that now includes New Bedford. The city has a long maritime tradition, which began when it was a shipbuilding center and small whaling port in the late 1700s. By the mid-1800s New Bedford had flourished into a center of North American whaling.

Today New Bedford still has the largest fishing fleet on the East Coast, and although much of the town is industrial, the restored historic district near the water is a pleasant stop. It was here that Herman Melville set some of the opening sections of his masterpiece, *Moby-Dick*.

New Bedford's whaling tradition is commemorated in the **New Bedford Whaling National Historical Park**, encompassing 13 blocks of the waterfront historic district. The park visitor center, in an 1853 Greek-revival former bank, provides maps and information about whaling-related sites. Free walking tours of the park leave from the visitor center at 10 AM and noon in July and August. You can also view an orientation film about American whaling and the New Bedford historic sites; the film is free and is shown on the hour, daily 10 to 3, at the nearby New Bedford Whaling Museum. ✉*33 William St., Downtown* ☎*508/996–4095* ⊕*www.nps.gov/nebe* ☉*Daily 9–5.*

☾ The **New Bedford Whaling Museum,** established in 1903, is the world's
★ largest museum devoted to the history of whaling. A highlight is the skeleton of a 66-foot blue whale, one of only three on view anywhere in the world. An interactive exhibit lets you listen to the underwater sounds of whales, dolphins, and other sea life, plus the sounds of a thunderstorm and a whale-watching boat—all as a whale might hear them. You can also peruse the collection of scrimshaw, visit exhibits on regional history, and climb aboard an 89-foot half-scale model of the 1826 whaling ship *Lagoda*—the world's largest ship model. ✉*18*

Johnny Cake Hill, Downtown ☎*508/997–0046* ⊕*www.whalingmuseum.org* ☜*$10* ⊙*Daily 9–5; late May–early Sept. until 9 on Thurs.*

Seaman's Bethel, the small chapel described in *Moby-Dick,* is across the street from the whaling museum. ⊠*15 Johnny Cake Hill, Downtown* ☎*508/992–3295* ⊙*Weekdays 10–5.*

The **New Bedford Art Museum,** a compact gallery space in the 1918 Vault Building (a former bank), showcases the work of area artists. Included are paintings by 19th- and early-20th-century New Bedford artists Albert Bierstadt, William Bradford, and Charles Henry Gifford. ⊠*608 Pleasant St., Downtown* ☎*508/961–3072* ⊕*www.newbedfordartmuseum.org* ☜*$3* ⊙*Late May–early Sept., Mon.–Wed. and Fri.–Sun. 10–5, Thurs. 10–7; early Sept.–late May, Wed. and Fri.–Sun. noon–5, Thurs. noon–7.*

For a glimpse of upper-class life during New Bedford's whaling heyday, head ½ mi south of downtown to the **Rotch-Jones-Duff House and Garden Museum.** This 1834 Greek-revival mansion, set amid a full city block of gardens, housed three prominent families in the 1800s and is filled with elegant furnishings from the era, including a mahogany piano, a massive marble-top sideboard, and portraits of the house's occupants. A self-guided audio tour is available. ⊠*396 County St.* ☎*508/997–1401* ⊕*www.rjdmuseum.org* ☜*$5* ⊙*Mon.–Sat. 10–4, Sun. noon–4.*

WHERE TO EAT

$–$$$ ✕ **Davy's Locker.** A huge seafood menu is the main draw at this spot overlooking Buzzards Bay. Choose from more than a dozen shrimp preparations or one of several Caribbean-inspired treats, such as swordfish with mango-salsa jambalaya. An almost daunting array of surf-and-turf combos, steaks, salmon grills, lobster platters, and fried seafood plates round out the enormous menu. Ice-cream smoothie cocktails, such as the toasted almond (with amaretto, Kahlua, and vanilla ice cream), make for toothsome desserts. ⊠*1480 E. Rodney French Blvd.* ☎*508/992–7359* ☰*AE, D, MC, V.*

¢–$$ ✕ **Antonio's.** If you'd like to sample the traditional fare of New Bedford's large Portuguese population, friendly, unadorned Antonio's serves hearty portions of pork and shellfish stew, *bacalau* (salt cod), and grilled sardines, often on plates piled high with crispy fried potatoes and rice. ⊠*267 Coggeshall St., near intersection of I–195 and Rte. 18* ☎*508/990–3636* ☰*No credit cards.*

¢–$$ ✕ **Freestone's City Grill.** Housed in an 1877 former bank in the historic
★   district, Freestone's serves soups and chowders, sandwiches and salads, plus scrod casino (topped with seafood stuffing and bacon bits), Asian-veggie stir-fry, and broiled flat-iron steak with Jack Daniel's sauce. Traditional details—mahogany paneling, marble floors, and brass rails—blend with contemporary art. No reservations are taken, but you can call ahead to get on a waiting list for busy nights. ⊠*41 William St., Downtown* ☎*508/993–7477* ⊕*www.freestones.com* ☰*AE, DC, MC, V* ⚑*Reservations not accepted.*

Cuttyhunk Island

1

For a taste of old New England–island magic without the development or crowds of Cape Cod, Martha's Vineyard, or Nantucket, visit bucolic Cuttyhunk Island, which is accessible only by boat or seaplane. Cuttyhunk, which is about 10 mi south of New Bedford, sits at the southwestern end of the Elizabeth Islands, an isolated 16-mi chain extending from Woods Hole and separating Vineyard Sound from Buzzards Bay. The rest of these lovely islands (Noamesset, Uncatena, Naushon, Nashawena, and Pasque) are privately owned and inaccessible to the public. Cuttyhunk was first explored by Bartholomew Gosnold in 1602 and was settled in 1641. In the days of sail, Cuttyhunk served as home to the pilots who guided the whaling ships safely into New Bedford harbor. Today's year-round population is fewer than 100, a living testament to the island's reputation for isolation. In summer, the population swells to several hundred. You'll see very few cars here—golf carts are the vehicle of choice for residents—but there's little need for one. At just 2½ mi long and less than 1 mi wide, Cuttyhunk is easily navigable on foot.

Upon arrival at the dock, you will be surrounded by many boats both large and small. You need not bother to bring much pocket money, as there's little to buy except perhaps some fresh oysters and an ice-cream cone. Outdoor public restrooms are available. A short uphill walk brings you to the center of the island, where you'll be treated to majestic views of Vineyard Sound. Here you will find a small general store, a one-room schoolhouse, a church, a library, a seasonal café, a small museum, and a B&B. An unpaved dirt road leads to the far end of the island, where you can find a pond among pastoral natural surroundings. This is a quiet place where you can truly relax amid peaceful, natural surroundings.

If you want to stay overnight, contact the **Cuttyhunk Fishing Club B&B** (☎ 508/992–5585 ⊕ www.cuttyhunkfishingclub.com), which rents rooms, apartments, and houses from mid-May to mid-October. **Pete's Place Rentals** (☎ 508/992–5131 ⊕ www.cuttyhunk.net/lodging.htm) has a small number of water-view properties available for weekly rentals from late May to mid-October.

The **M/V Cuttyhunk ferry** (☎ 508/992–0200 ⊕ www.cuttyhunkferryco.com) makes the one-hour trip from 66B State Pier to Cuttyhunk daily, year-round (weather permitting). The ferry departs New Bedford at 9 AM and returns from Cuttyhunk at 4 PM (with additional trips on Friday, Saturday, and Sunday); same-day round-trip fares are $30. —By James W. Rohlf

NIGHTLIFE & THE ARTS

On the second Thursday of every month from 5 to 9 PM, New Bedford hosts **AHA! Nights** (☎ 508/264–8859 ⊕ www.ahanewbedford.org), a downtown gallery-night program that highlights the city's art, history, and architecture. Museums and galleries, including the Whaling Museum and the New Bedford Art Museum, have extended hours and offer free admission. Concerts, crafts demonstrations, and other special events are often on the program.

A variety of musical and artistic events are held at the **Zeiterion Theatre** (☎ *508/994–2900* ⊕ *www.zeiterion.org*), a wonderful old building in New Bedford's historic district.

SPORTS & THE OUTDOORS

BEACHES **Fort Phoenix State Beach Reservation** (⊠ *Green St., Fairhaven* ✛ *Off U.S. 6* ☎ *508/992–4524* ⊕ *www.mass.gov/dcr*), the site of the Revolutionary War's first naval battle, has a small sandy beach. Parking is free, and there are restrooms with showers.

MARION

20 mi east of Fall River, 50 mi south of Boston.

Small-town charm pervades the modest village center of Marion, a town that has worked hard to preserve its historic buildings and landmarks. Nineteenth-century and even some earlier homes, many with white-picket fences and well-tended flower gardens, line the narrow streets. The present home of the **Sippican Historical Society,** an integral part of the Town of Marion, was built in 1834 by Dr. Walton Nathan Ellis. The **Marion Art Center** was once the Universalist Church, built in 1833 by a group of people who wanted to start a "new religion" in Sippican Village. **Handy's Tavern,** built in 1812, was a popular place for the seafaring men to gather after their ships docked at the foot of Main Street. What is now the **Marion General Store** was a place of worship from 1799 to 1841.

During the early and mid-1800s, Marion was mainly a home for sea captains and sailors carrying cotton to Europe and cargoes to the Orient, and returning with products from the East. Many of them became wealthy, and some built magnificent homes in Marion, which was also a small shipbuilding community. Today, the year-round community of about 6,000 is tenacious about preserving its historic character and private to the point of not encouraging publicity and shunning tourism. The majority of out-of-towners come to visit children boarding at **Tabor Academy,** a private school for grades 9 through 12 whose campus stretches along a ½ mi of Sippican Harbor, or to attend a high-end antiques show every August. Still, Marion is worth a stop to view the spectacle of more than 700 boats moored in scenic **Sippican Harbor** and to soak up the historical beauty of this hidden treasure of a town.

WHERE TO EAT

$–$$ ✗**Sippican Café.** Historically, Marion has been a one-restaurant town, and when Kathleen and Bob Bost bought and renovated a local breakfast joint, this became the place to go for dinner. Chef Loretta Imbriglio, alumna of the Meridien and the Chatham Bars Inn, delights locals with her light-handed, inventive twists on fresh seafood, beef, chicken, and pasta. Like the place itself, the menu is small but enticing, with three or four specials nightly and even a cheese course. Take note: it's BYOB. ⊠ *167 Spring St.* ☎ *508/748–0176* ⊟ *AE, MC, V* ⊗ *No dinner Sun.–Tues.*

1

¢ ✕**Uncle John's Cafe & Cookies.** Marion's local java joint serves breakfast and lunch, doling out coffee, scones, muffins, bagels, sandwiches, soups, and salads, which you can enjoy at tables or at the counter. Despite its name, the cookie selection is small. ⊠*356 Front St.* ☎*508/748–0063* ▭*No credit cards* ⊘*No dinner.*

NIGHTLIFE & THE ARTS

The **Marion Art Center** (⊠*80 Pleasant St.* ☎*508/748–1266* ⊕*www. marionartcenter.org*)—comprising two galleries; a small, intimate theater; and a studio—offers classes in art, music, dance, and theater arts year-round to both children and adults. Local artists have shows here, and four major theatrical productions are performed each year. In the late 19th century, during Marion's "Gilded Age," many famous writers and artists—including Henry James, Charles Dana Gibson, Sanford White, and the Barrymores—came to the area to share ideas and each other's company.

EN ☾ As you head east toward Cape Cod, a wet-and-wild adventure for the
ROUTE kids awaits at the **Water Wizz Water Park,** with a 50-foot-high waterslide complete with tunnels and dips, a wave pool, a river ride, three tube rides, two enclosed water-mat slides, a children's slide, a pool, miniature golf, and food. The enclosed Black Wizard waterslide descends 75 feet in darkness. ⊠*U.S. 6 and Rte. 28, Wareham* ⊹*2 mi west of Bourne Bridge* ☎*508/295–3255* ⊕*www.waterwizz.com* ⌨*$29* ⊘*Mid-June– mid-Aug., daily 10–6:30; mid-Aug.–early Sept., daily 10–6.*

SPORTS & THE OUTDOORS

BEACHES **Silvershell Beach,** at the south end of Front Street, is open to the public. Facilities include lifeguards and a playground.

SHOPPING

Marion Sports Shop (⊠*290 Front St.* ☎*508/748–1318*) is one of the oldest tennis specialty shops in New England, but the impressive selection of tennis gear at the back of the store is not all it has to offer. Owner Frank Fletcher, a former tennis instructor, also stocks hip clothing lines for both men and women by up-and-coming designers and unusual jewelry and accessories, items procured during his regular buying trips to Manhattan.

APPROACHING THE CAPE ESSENTIALS

To research prices, get advice from other travelers, and book travel arrangements, visit ⊕*www.fodors.com.*

BY BOAT & FERRY

From mid-spring through early autumn, ferries run from New Bedford to Cuttyhunk Island and to Oak Bluffs and Vineyard Haven on Martha's Vineyard, and from Plymouth to Provincetown.

For details, ⇨*Boat & Ferry Travel in Essentials in the back of the book.*

BY BUS

Dattco offers service from Boston to New Bedford. Bonanza Bus Lines runs frequent direct service between Boston and Fall River, as well as service to both Fall River and New Bedford from Providence. From Fall River and New Bedford to the Cape, Bonanza provides service to Bourne, Falmouth, Woods Hole, and Hyannis. Plymouth & Brockton Street Railway buses stop in Plymouth en route to the Cape from Boston. From the Plymouth stop, you can take Plymouth Area Link buses to the town center or to Plimoth Plantation.

Bus Depots Plymouth & Brockton Plymouth depot (⊠ *Visitor's Center Park/Ride lot, Rte. 3, Exit 5, Plymouth* ☎ *508/746–0378*). **Southeastern Regional Transit Authority Fall River Terminal** (⊠ *221 2nd St., Fall River* ☎ *508/679–2335*). **Southeastern Regional Transit Authority New Bedford Terminal** (⊠ *134 Elm St., New Bedford* ☎ *508/999–5211*).

Bus Lines Bonanza Bus Lines (☎ *888/751–8800* ⊕ *www.bonanzabus.com*). **Dattco** (☎ *508/993–5040* ⊕ *www.dattco.com*). **Plymouth & Brockton Street Railway** (☎ *508/746–0378* ⊕ *www.p-b.com*). **Plymouth Area Link** (☎ *508/746–0378* ⊕ *www.gatra.org/*).

BY TAXI

Taxi Companies Central Transportation (⊠ *Plymouth* ☎ *508/746–0018*). **Yellow Cab** (⊠ *Fall River* ☎ *508/674–4633*). **Yellow Cab** (⊠ *New Bedford* ☎ *508/999–5213*).

VISITOR INFORMATION

Tourist Information Destination Plymouth (⊠ *170 Water St., Suite 10C, Plymouth 02360* ☎ *508/747–7533* ⊕ *www.visit-plymouth.com*). **Plymouth County Convention & Visitors Center** (⊠ *32 Court St., 2nd fl., Plymouth 02360* ☎ *508/747–0100 or 800/231–1620* ⊕ *www.seeplymouth.com*). **Fall River Chamber of Commerce** (⊠ *200 Pocasset St., Fall River 02721* ☎ *508/676–8226* ⊕ *www.fallriverchamber. com*). **Bristol County Convention & Visitors Bureau** (⊠ *70 N. 2nd St., New Bedford 02741* ☎ *508/997–1250 or 800/288–6263* ⊕ *www.southofboston.org*). **New Bedford Office of Tourism** (⊠ *Waterfront Visitors Center, Old City Pier 3, New Bedford 02740* ☎ *508/979–1745 or 800/508–5353* ⊕ *www.destination-newbedford.org*).

The Upper Cape

WORD OF MOUTH

"Sandwich is one of the least commercialized towns on the Cape. Heck, we just got our first movie theater a few years back, and there still isn't a fast food restaurant in sight! If you like to shop, you could easily spend some of your days driving along 6A from Sandwich down into Barnstable and even Yarmouth, stopping along the way at dozens upon dozens of antiques stores and unique shops. There are also many nice restaurants along the way."

—klw25

Updated
by Laura V.
Scheel

THE UPPER CAPE HAS NONE of the briny, otherworldly breeziness of the Outer Cape and little of the resort feel of Lower Cape cousins like Chatham. The reason is solidly geographical: The Upper Cape's proximity to the mainland yields slightly less-brutal winters than elsewhere on the Cape and, consequently, a substantial year-round population; the region's beaches are intimate; and more of its attractions—freshwater ponds, conservation areas, and small museums—are inland.

If you're collecting superlatives, the Upper Cape is fertile. Sandwich is the oldest town on the Cape, Bourne was the Pilgrims' first Cape Cod settlement and an important trading area, and the first Native American reservation in the United States was established in Mashpee, which still has a large Wampanoag population and a tribal-council governing body.

Being able to find peace and quiet so close to the mainland and the traffic-clogged bridges is an unexpected and much-appreciated characteristic of the Upper Cape. Sandwich, its village streets lined with historic houses and museums, is remarkably well preserved. Heading east, Route 6A meanders past antiques shops, bed-and-breakfasts, and salt marshes. Falmouth, to the south, is an active year-round community, more suburban than seaside, though its easy-to-reach beaches are popular with families. In the villages of North and West Falmouth, along Buzzards Bay, tree-lined country lanes lead to sandy coves, and in East Falmouth and Waquoit, narrow spits of land jut into marshy inlets; plenty of secluded sites for hiking and walking are yours for the taking. Woods Hole, a small but bustling village on the Cape's southwestern tip, is a center for international marine research; it's also the departure point for ferries to Martha's Vineyard.

EXPLORING THE UPPER CAPE

On the north shore, Sandwich, gracious and lovely, is the Cape's oldest town. Centered inland, Mashpee is a long-standing Native American township in which Native American–owned land is governed by local Wampanoags. Falmouth, the Cape's second-most populous town, is still green and historic, if seemingly overrun with strip malls. Woods Hole, the major port for ferries to Martha's Vineyard, is world renowned for its biological research institutions. Along the west coast, in parts of Bourne and West and North Falmouth, you can find wooded areas ending in secluded coves; the south coast has long-established resort communities.

ABOUT THE RESTAURANTS

Much like the rest of Cape Cod, the Upper Cape's dining scene ranges from basic seafood shacks to contemporary restaurants that draw inspiration from the far corners of the globe—plus everything in between. Overall, the restaurant options tend toward the traditional, with fried clams, baked scrod, and boiled lobster gracing the most popular menus. Restaurants are more widely scattered in the Upper Cape towns—there are few "restaurant rows"—but if you like to wander and check out your dining options, try Main Street in Falmouth Center or Water Street in Woods Hole.

ABOUT THE HOTELS

Sandwich and other towns along the north-shore Route 6A Historic District have quiet, traditional villages with an old-Cape feel and charming B&Bs. Along Route 6A you can also find family-friendly motels, ranging from the modest to the better equipped. Historic B&Bs fill the center of Falmouth, and other small inns line the shore and the neighboring streets of Falmouth Heights. Lodging options are fewer in Bourne and West and North Falmouth, but a few B&Bs hidden away on country lanes provide glimpses of old New England. You can also rent modern town houses and condominiums with extensive resort amenities in Mashpee's New Seabury community.

WHAT IT COSTS				
	$$$$	$$$	$$	$	¢
RESTAURANTS	over $30	$22–$30	$16–$22	$10–$16	under $10
HOTELS	over $260	$200–$260	$140–$200	$90–$140	under $90

Restaurant prices are per person for a main course at dinner. Hotel prices are for a standard double room, excluding 6% sales tax (more in some counties) and 1%–4% tourist tax.

TIMING

Although summer on the Upper Cape is the quintessential New England–vacation experience, the ideal time of the year to visit may be early autumn. You can enjoy the beaches and water activities on Cape Cod Bay, Buzzards Bay, and Nantucket Sound in tranquillity between mid-September and late October, when the summer crowds have left but the weather is still mild. The Bourne Scallop Festival takes place in mid-September for three days.

BOURNE

6 mi southwest of Sandwich.

The town of Bourne includes nine villages—Bourne Village, Bournedale, Buzzards Bay, Cataumet, Gray Gables, Monument Beach, Pocas-

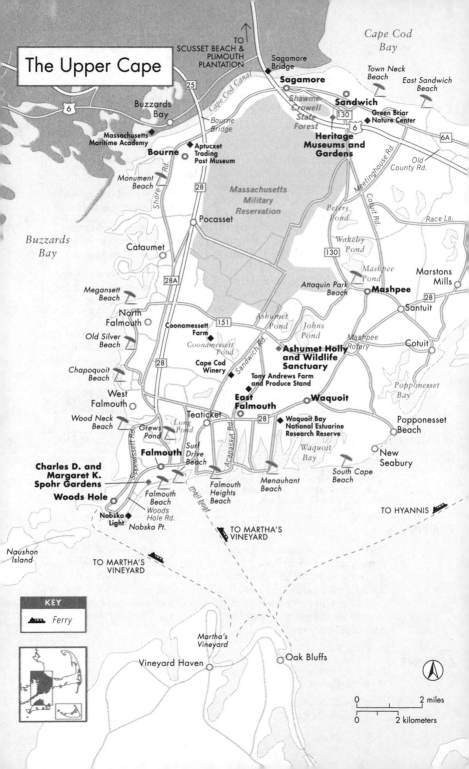

set, Sagamore, and Sagamore Beach—along Buzzards Bay and both sides of the Cape Cod Canal. The villages range from souvenir-shop-dominated commercial districts to bucolic waterfront suburbs. With a mix of year-round and summer residents, the area includes places for learning about the region's marine life and early commercial history, as well as several attractive recreation areas, established and maintained by the Army Corps of Engineers, for biking, hiking, and fishing along the canal.

The Pilgrims established their first Cape Cod settlement in Bourne in 1627, but back then it was still part of Sandwich; Bourne didn't become a separate town until 1884. By that time it had grown into a popular summer colony whose part-time residents included President Grover Cleveland and *Boston Globe* publisher Charles Taylor. Present-day Bourne's maritime orientation was created by the Cape Cod Canal, which opened in 1914. The 17½-mi canal cut the distance for shipping traffic between Boston and New York by 75 mi and eliminated the often-treacherous journey around the Cape. The Army Corps of Engineers took over the canal's operation in the late 1920s and embarked on a project to widen it; the current Bourne and Sagamore bridges were built in the 1930s as part of this project.

☾ The **National Marine Life Center,** on the mainland near the chamber of commerce office, has a small exhibit area devoted to whales, dolphins, seals, and other marine life. In summer there are marine-life educational programs for children and evening lectures about the ocean environment for adults. The center hopes to break ground on an expanded facility for rehabilitating stranded marine animals that will include a marine animal hospital and nursery, eight rehabilitation pools, and additional exhibit space as soon as the necessary funds can be raised. ⊠ *120 Main St., Buzzards Bay* ☎ *508/743–9888* ⊕ *www.nmlc.org* 🎟 *Free, donations accepted* ☉ *Late May–early Sept., daily 10–5.*

On the mainland side, the **Massachusetts Maritime Academy,** founded in 1891, is the oldest such academy in the country. Future members of the Merchant Marines receive their training at its 55-acre campus in Buzzards Bay. The library has nautical paintings and scale models of ships from the 18th century to the present and is open to the public at no charge (hours are extensive but vary widely depending on whether school is in session; call ahead). For a 30- to 60-minute tour of the academy (weekdays only; times vary), call 48 hours in advance. The tours are designed for prospective students and their families but are open to all. ⊠ *Taylor's Point, Buzzards Bay* ☎ *508/830–5000* ⊕ *www.maritime.edu.*

A monument to the birth of commerce in the New World, the **Aptucxet Trading Post Museum** was erected on the foundation of the original post archaeologically excavated in the 1920s. Here, in 1627, Plimoth Plantation leaders established a way station between the Native American encampment at Great Herring Pond 3 mi to the northeast, Dutch colonists in New Amsterdam (New York) to the south, and English colonists on Cape Cod Bay. Before the canal was built, the Manomet River connected Herring Pond with Buzzards Bay (no, scavengers don't frequent it—it was misnamed for the migrating osprey that do), and a short portage connected the pond to Scusset River, which met Cape Cod Bay. The Native Americans traded furs; the Dutch traded linen cloth, metal tools, glass beads, sugar, and other staples; and the Pilgrims traded wool cloth, clay beads, sassafras, and tobacco (which they imported from Virginia). Wampum (beads made from polished shells) was the medium of exchange.

Inside the post, 17th-century cooking utensils hang from the original brick hearth; beaver and otter skins, furniture, and other artifacts such as arrowheads, tools, and tomahawks are displayed throughout. Also on the grounds are a gift shop in a Dutch-style windmill, a saltworks, herb and wildflower gardens, a picnic area overlooking the canal, and a small Victorian railroad station built for the sole use of President Grover Cleveland, who had a summer home in Bourne. To get here, cross the Bourne Bridge; then take the first right from the Bourne Bridge rotary onto Trowbridge Road and follow the signs. Note that the site is also open on holiday Mondays in season. ⊠*24 Aptucxet Rd.* ☏*508/759–9487* ⊕*www.bournehistoricalsoc.org* ⊠*$4* ⊙*May, June, and Sept.–mid-Oct., Tues.–Sat. 10–4, Sun. 2–5; July and Aug., Mon.–Sat. 10–4, Sun. 2–5.*

☾ A break for energetic children pent up in a car for too many miles, **Adventure Isle** has a go-kart track, bumper-boat lagoon, 18 holes of miniature golf, 25-foot Super Slide, batting cages, kiddie rides, laser tag, a roller-skating and blading rink, and an arcade with snack bar. Check the Web site for discount coupons. ⊠*Rte. 28, 2 mi south of Bourne Bridge* ☏*508/759–2636 or 800/535–2787* ⊕*www.adventureislecapecod.com* ⊙*Apr.–Oct., call for off-season hrs; July–early Sept., daily 10 AM–11 PM.*

A short drive northeast of Bourne proper, the village of **Sagamore** straddles the Cape Cod Canal and is perhaps best known for the bridge, completed in 1935, that bears its name. Primarily a small suburban community, the town has several stores for those interested in bargain hunting or gift shopping.

Watch richly colored lead crystal being handblown at **Pairpoint Glass Company,** America's oldest glass factory (founded in 1837). The shop sells candlesticks, vases, stemware, sun catchers, cup plates, lamps, perfume bottles, and reproductions of original Boston and Sandwich glass pieces. ⊠*851 Sandwich Rd. (Rte. 6A)* ☏*508/888–2344 or 800/899–0953* ⊕*www.pairpoint.com* ⊠*Free* ⊙*Showroom weekdays 9–6, Sat. 10–5, Sun. 11–5. Demonstrations May–Dec., weekdays 9–4; Jan.–Apr., call before visiting; demonstration hrs are limited.*

WHERE TO STAY & EAT

$–$$ ✕**Chart Room.** Located harborside at the marina in a former cargo
BOURNE barge, this traditional watering hole has been serving up seafood classics since 1966. Clam chowder, lobster rolls, broiled scrod, seafood Newburg, baked stuffed shrimp—they're all here, as are sirloin steak, broiled lamb chops, and even grilled cheese-and-tomato sandwiches. ⊠*1 Shipyard La., at Kingman Yacht Center, Cataumet* ☏*508/563–*

5350 ⊟*AE, MC, V* ⊘*Closed mid-Oct.–mid May and weekdays late May–late June and early Sept.–mid-Oct.*

$ ✕**Stir Crazy.** Fresh ingredients with lively Cambodian, Thai, and Viet-
Fodor'sChoice namese flavors dominate every dish that graces the menu here (owner
★ Bopha Samms hails from Cambodia). Try the *nhem shross* (an appetizer of vegetables and shrimp) and the refreshing *bar bong* (chilled noodles topped with pork, egg rolls, and coconut-peanut sauce). ⊠*570 MacAr-thur Blvd. (Rte. 28 S), Pocasset* ☎*508/564–6464* ⌦*Reservations not accepted* ⊟*MC, V* ⊘*Closed Mon. No lunch Sat.–Thurs.*

$–$$ ⊞**Wood Duck Inn.** Behind this cozy B&B, a 17-acre working cran-berry bog and acres of conservation land spread out as far as you can see. The small but comfy Cottage Room has lace curtains and a brass bed with a floral comforter, and both suites have a bedroom plus a sitting room that doubles as extra sleeping space. The Garden Suite is done in romantic florals, and the family-friendly Treetops Suite resembles a contemporary apartment in forest green and white; it has a tiny but fully equipped kitchen and sweeping views. The innkeepers deliver breakfast to your door. **Pros:** Privacy assured with individual entrances, no common rooms, and breakfast brought to your room; walk to nearby free summer shuttle to island ferry terminals; beauti-ful pastoral views. **Cons:** Suites accessed only by stairs, credit cards not accepted. ⊠*1050 County Rd., Cataumet 02534* ☎☎*508/564–6404* ⊕*www.woodduckinnbb.com* ⌫*1 room, 2 suites* ⌧*In-room: no a/c (some), kitchen (some), refrigerator, VCR. In-hotel: Wi-Fi, no-smoking rooms, no elevator* ⊟*No credit cards* ⌺*CP.*

$–$$ ✕**Sagamore Inn.** Old Cape Cod traditions with an Italian twist can be
SAGAMORE found at this local favorite, owned by the Pagliarani family since 1963. Pressed-tin walls and ceilings, fans, old wooden booths and tables, lace curtains, and white linen add up to a dining room so casual you almost overlook its elegance. The seafood platter is a knockout, and the chicken potpie and prime rib are substantial. Luncheon specials attract regulars from all over town, and the service is friendly. A cozy, hand-some old bar is under the same roof. ⊠*1131 Sandwich Rd. (Rte. 6A)* ☎*508/888–9707* ⊟*AE, MC, V* ⊘*Closed Tues. and Nov.–mid-May.*

$ ⚠**Scusset Beach State Reservation.** Encompassing 300 acres adjacent to the Cape Cod Canal (there's a fishing pier for anglers), the park has a beach on Cape Cod Bay and 98 RV sites plus 5 tent sites, some wooded. There are cold showers on the beach and hot showers in the camp-ground. ⌧*Beachfront, full hookups* ⌫*103 sites* ⊠*140 Scusset Beach Rd., off Rte. 3 at Sagamore Bridge rotary* ☎*877/422–6762 campsite reservations, 508/888–0859 general information* ⊕*www.reserveam-erica.com* ⊟*MC, V.*

NIGHTLIFE & THE ARTS

The **Army Corps of Engineers** (☎*508/759–4431*), which maintains the Cape Cod Canal via a field office in Buzzards Bay, offers free daily programs in summer, including evening campfire programs on canal-related topics (with marshmallow roasting). Call for program details and locations.

In Bourne, Thursday evening **town-band concerts** (⊠*Main St.* ☎*508/759–6000*) in July and August start at 7 in Buzzards Bay Park.

SPORTS & THE OUTDOORS

The **Army Corps of Engineers** (☎ *508/759–4431*) sponsors guided walks, bike trips, and hikes, including canal and area natural-history walks.

BASEBALL   The **Bourne Braves** of the collegiate Cape Cod Baseball League play home games at **Upper Cape Tech** (✉ *Sandwich Rd.* ⊕ *www.bournebraves.org*) from mid-June to mid-August.

BEACHES   **Monument Beach,** off Shore Road, is a small but pretty crescent of sand adjacent to the town dock, facing Buzzards Bay just south of Bourne Bridge. The beach has a snack bar, restrooms, and a parking lot, which is restricted in season to those with resident permits. From Shore Road, turn right onto Emmons Road just past the old train depot.

Sagamore's **Scusset Beach State Reservation** is a pleasant place for a swim, walk, or bike ride near the mainland side of the Sagamore Bridge. The beach sweeps along Cape Cod Bay, and its pier and canal breakwater are popular for fishing and viewing boat traffic; other activities include hiking, picnicking, and camping. There's a parking fee from mid-April to mid-October. ✉ *140 Scusset Beach Rd., off Rte. 3 at Sagamore Bridge rotary* ☎ *508/888–0859* ⊕ *www.mass.gov/dcr* ✐ *Mid-Apr.–mid-Oct., parking $7* ⊙ *Daily 8–8.*

BICYCLING   An easy, straight trail stretches on either side of the **Cape Cod Canal**, 6½ mi on the south side, 7 mi on the north, with views of the bridges and ship traffic on the canal. Contact the **Army Corps of Engineers** (☎ *508/759–4431*) for information about canal trail access and parking.

FISHING   The Cape Cod Canal is a great place to fish—from the service road on either side—for the big blues and striped bass making their way through the passage seasonally (April through November). You don't need a fishing license for saltwater angling, though you will need one for freshwater fishing.

HIKING &   Run by the Army Corps of Engineers, the **Herring Run Visitor Center** (✉ *U.*
WALKING   *S. 6, Bournedale* ☎ *508/759–4431, 508/759–5991 tides, weather, and special events*), on a bank of the canal with an excellent view, has picnic tables (close to noisy U.S. 6), access to the canal bike path, a herring run through which the fish travel on their spawning run in May, and short self-guided walking trails through the woodland. The visitor center is on the mainland side of the canal, between the bridges.

On the Cape side of the canal, the Army Corps of Engineers manages the **Tidal Flats Recreation Area** (✉ *Shore Rd.* ☎ *508/759–4431*), a small but peaceful canal-side park near the Cape railroad bridge. It's a pleasant site for picnicking or fishing, with a great view of the canal's ship traffic. There's also access to the canal bike path. In the late afternoon, between 5 and 7, you can watch the bridge lower to allow a service train to cross the canal; these times are approximate and can vary widely because of traffic and bridge work. To reach the recreation area, cross the Bourne Bridge and follow Trowbridge Road to Shore Road.

ICE-SKATING   **John Gallo Ice Arena** (✉ *231 Sandwich Rd.* ☎ *508/759–8904*) is the place to go for ice-skating year-round (except May). Lessons are offered and skate rental is available; admission is $3.

Time to Fly

So you're heading south on Route 3 toward the Cape, about 8 mi from the Sagamore Bridge. You're still speeding along, and you're beginning to feel relaxed, even a little smug. And why not? After all, you've carefully planned your schedule, cleverly outsmarting tens of thousands of other vacationers with a similar destination. But then, a sickening sense of dread poisons your mood as you catch a glimpse of a red sea of brake lights blurred by a haze of engine exhaust. Suddenly, you're not going anywhere.

The Sagamore Bridge, completed in 1935, was built to accommodate approximately 35,000 motorists heading to Cape Cod each day during peak season. Before crossing the bridge, travelers would safely navigate a rotary, branching off perhaps to fill their gas tanks or have lunch. At least that was the plan. Today the rotary and bridge handle a daily load of nearly 90,000 cars, minivans, and SUVs, all overflowing with bicycles, kayaks, baggage, and impatience. The quaint rotary, with its pretty plantings and convenient pit stops, has become many a driver's personal hell.

The elimination of this much-despised rotary sits at the center of the massive Sagamore "flyover." Long awaited, hotly debated, and completed just in time for the 2007 summer season, the project has been the state's most ambitious transportation undertaking since Boston's perpetual Big Dig. Costing an estimated $58 million, the work directly connects Route 3 to the Sagamore Bridge, diverting local traffic through a series of underpasses. The goal is to benefit those who want an unhindered passage over the bridge as well as local residents who simply want to drive across town without getting mired in the rotary. Estimates predict savings of anywhere from 18 to 33 minutes, but you'll likely still experience slowdowns, outright traffic jams, and some level of aggravation. So you won't always be flying . . . but hopefully you'll be moving faster than before.

SHOPPING

Cape Cod Factory Outlet Mall (⊠ *Factory Outlet Rd., Exit 1 off Rte. 6* ☎ *508/888-8417* ⊕ *www.capecodoutletmall.com*) has more than 20 outlet stores, including CorningWare-Corelle-Revere, Carter's, Van Heusen, Izod, Bass, and Reebok.

Christmas Tree Shops (⊠ *Cranberry Hwy. [Rte. 6A], Exit 1 off Rte. 6* ☎ *508/888-7010* ⊕ *www.christmastreeshops.com*) sell dishware and a wide variety of other household goods at bargain prices. There are other locations in Falmouth, Hyannis, West Yarmouth, West Dennis, and Orleans.

SANDWICH

★ *3 mi east of Sagamore Bridge, 11 mi west of Barnstable.*

A well-preserved New England village, Sandwich wears its history proudly, despite having become increasingly suburban in character over the past few decades, and its population soaring to more than 20,000. The oldest town on Cape Cod, Sandwich was established in

1637 by some of the Plymouth Pilgrims and incorporated on March 6, 1638. Driving through town past the white-column town hall, the gristmill on Shawme Pond, the First Church of Christ with its spindle-like spire, and the 18th- and 19th-century homes that line the streets is like driving back in time—you may feel as if you should be holding a horse's reins rather than the steering wheel of a car. When you reach Main Street, park the car and get out for a stroll. Look at old houses on Main Street, stop at a museum or two, and work your way to the delightful Shawme Pond. Unlike other Cape towns, whose deepwater ports opened the doors to prosperity in the whaling days, Sandwich was an industrial town for much of the 19th century. The main industry was the production of vividly colored glass, called Sandwich glass, which is now sought by collectors. The Boston and Sandwich Glass Company's factory here produced the glass from 1825 until 1888, when competition with glassmakers in the Midwest—and finally a union strike—closed it. While you walk, look for etched Sandwich glass from the old factory on front doors. There probably aren't two identical glass panels in town.

The **Sandwich Glass Museum,** with its 9,000 square feet of exhibits, has information about the history of the company, including a diorama showing how the factory looked in its heyday, an "ingredient room" showcasing a wide spectrum of glass colors along with the minerals added to the sand to obtain them, and an outstanding collection of blown and pressed glass in many shapes and shimmering hues. Large glass lamps, vases, and pitchers are impressive, as are the hundreds of candlesticks and small saucers on display. Glassmaking demonstrations are held in summer. A few galleries contain relics of the town's early history (the museum is also the Sandwich Historical Society). The extensive, ornate gift shop sells some handsome reproductions, including some made by local and national artisans. The museum also sponsors several walking tours of the town in July and August. ☒ *129 Main St., Sandwich Center* ☎ *508/888–0251* ⊕ *www.sandwichglass-museum.org* ☜ *$4.75* ☉ *Apr.–Dec., daily 9:30–5; Feb. and Mar., Wed.–Sun. 9:30–4.*

☾ A lovely place for a stroll or a picnic is the park around **Shawme Pond** (☒ *Water and Grove Sts., Sandwich Center*), a favorite fishing site for children. The ducks and swans love to be fed, though posted signs warn you not to indulge them. Across the way—a perfect backdrop for this setting—stands the spired, white 1848 First Church of Christ, inspired by a design by British architect Christopher Wren.

Where Shawme Pond drains over its dam, a little wooden bridge leads over a watercourse to the waterwheel-powered **Dexter Gristmill,** built in 1654. In season the miller demonstrates the grinding process, talks about the mill's operation, and sells its ground corn. ☒ *Water and Grove Sts., Sandwich Center* ☎ *508/888–4910 Sandwich Town Hall* ☜ *$3; combination ticket with Hoxie House $4* ☉ *Late May and early Sept.–late Sept., Sat. 10–4:45; June–early Sept., Mon.–Sat. 10–4:45.*

2

NEED A
BREAK?

The delightful **Dunbar Tea Shop** (⊠ *1 Water St. [Rte. 130], Sandwich Center* ☎ *508/833–2485*) is in a former billiards room–carriage house, now converted into a country cottage with paneled walls and assorted antiques and kitschy doodads. Lunch (from a smoked-fish platter with salad to quiche or a salmon tart), English cream tea, and tasty sweets are served from 11 to 5 daily, July through October (until 4:30 the rest of the year). A gift shop sells British tea, specialty foods, and home-decorating items.

FodorsChoice
★

The **Thornton W. Burgess Museum** is dedicated to the Sandwich native whose tales of Peter Cottontail, Reddy Fox, and a host of other creatures of the Old Briar Patch have been part of children's bedtimes for decades. Thornton Burgess (1874–1965), an avid conservationist, made his characters behave true to their species to educate children as he entertained them. Storytelling sessions, often including the live animal that the Burgess story is about, take place regularly in July and August. In the Discovery Room, kids can use their imaginations in the prop-filled classroom. On display are some of Burgess's 170 books (although children are welcome here, the exhibits are of the don't-touch variety). The small gift shop carries puppets, Burgess books, and Pairpoint Crystal cup plates decorated with Burgess characters. ⊠ *4 Water St. (Rte. 130), Sandwich Center* ☎ *508/888–4668* ⊕ *www.thorntonburgess.org* ⊠ *Donations accepted* ☉ *May–Oct., Mon.–Sat. 10–4, Sun. 1–4.*

Overlooking Shawme Pond is the **Hoxie House,** a remarkable old saltbox virtually unaltered since it was built in 1675. Even though people lived in it until the 1950s, the house was never modernized with electricity or plumbing. Furnishings reflect daily life in the colonial period, with some pieces on loan from the Museum of Fine Arts in Boston. Highlights are diamond-shaped lead-glass windows and a collection of antique textile machines. ⊠ *18 Water St. (Rte. 130), Sandwich Center* ☎ *508/888–1173* ⊠ *$3; combination ticket with Dexter Gristmill $4* ☉ *Late May–mid-June, Sat. 10–5, Sun. 1–5; mid-June–mid-Oct., Mon.–Sat. 10–5, Sun. 1–5.*

The **Old Town Cemetery** (⊠ *Grove St., Sandwich Center*), on the opposite side of Shawme Pond from Hoxie House, is a classic, undulating New England graveyard. You can stop in for a peaceful moment and trace the genealogy of old Sandwich. On Thursday in July and August, you can hear tales during narrated walking tours about the cemetery's more illustrious inhabitants; call the Sandwich Glass Museum for additional information.

If you're interested in very old houses (by U.S. standards anyway), there are two worthy examples privately owned yet open for touring. The **Wing Fort House** was built in 1641 and can boast the distinction of being the "oldest house in New England owned and occupied continuously by the same family for over three centuries." The interior reveals changing tastes in decor and architecture over the centuries. ⊠ *69 Springhill Rd. (off Rte. 6A), East Sandwich* ☎ *508/833–1540* ⊕ *www.wingfamily.org* ⊠ *$2* ☉ *Mid-June–late Sept., Tues.–Sat. 10–4.*

Also hailing from the 17th century is the **Benjamin Nye Homestead and Museum,** once the home of one of the first grist mills in the country. Although the mill is long gone, the scenic views are still present, as are the many original details within the home's modest walls. ⊠*85 Old County Rd. (off Rte. 6A), East Sandwich* ☎*508/888–4213* ⊕*www. nyefamily.org* 🖙*$3* ⊘*Mid-June–mid-Oct., Tues.–Sat. noon –4:30.*

ⓒ **Heritage Museums and Gardens,** 100 beautifully landscaped acres over-
FodorśChoice looking the upper end of Shawme Pond, includes gardens and a café
★ as well as an impressive complex of museum buildings with specialty collections ranging from cars to toys. In 1967 pharmaceuticals magnate Josiah K. Lilly III purchased the estate and turned it into a nonprofit museum. A highlight is the Shaker Round Barn, which showcases classic and historic cars—including a 1930 yellow-and-green Duesenberg built for Gary Cooper, a 1919 Pierce-Arrow, a 1915 Milburn Light Electric, and a 1911 Stanley Steamer—as well as art exhibitions. The American History museum houses the Cape Cod Baseball League Hall of Fame as well as antique firearms, a collection of 2,000 hand-painted miniature soldiers, military uniforms, and Native American arts. The art museum has an extensive Currier & Ives collection, Americana (including a mechanical-bank collection), antique toys such as a 1920 Hubley Royal Circus, and a working 1912 Coney Island–style carousel that both adults and little ones can ride as often as they like. A shuttle bus—equipped with a wheelchair lift and space to stow baby strollers—transports visitors every few minutes from the car museum to other exhibit sites.

Paths crisscross the grounds, which include gardens planted with day-lilies, hostas, heather, herbs, and fruit trees. Rhododendron enthusiasts will recognize the name of onetime estate owner and hybridizer Charles O. Dexter; the rhododendrons are in full glory from mid-May through mid-June. Daylilies reach their peak from mid-July through early August. Families visiting with youngsters should ask at the ticket office for Family Funpacks with children's activities, or the Clue tours—scavenger-hunt games for exploring the grounds. In summer, concerts are held in the gardens, often on Wednesday or Saturday evening or Sunday afternoon. The center of the complex is about ¾ mi on foot from the in-town end of Shawme Pond. ⊠*67 Grove St.* ☎*508/888–3300* ⊕*www.heritagemuseumsandgardens.org* 🖙*$12* ⊘*Apr.–Nov., daily 10–5; Nov.–Mar., call for very limited hrs.*

At the **Cape Cod Canal Visitor Center,** run by the Army Corps of Engineers, exhibits and video presentations describe the canal's history, area wildflowers, and local "critters." Among the special ranger-led programs are beach and dune walks, as well as evening star watches. The visitor center is opposite the Coast Guard Station, near Joe's Fish Market. ⊠*Ed Moffitt Dr.* ☎*508/833–9678* 🖙*Free* ⊘*Mid-May–mid-Oct., call for hrs.*

For a view of the bay, you can walk to Town Neck Beach on the **Sandwich Boardwalk,** built over a salt marsh, creek, and low dunes. In 1991 Hurricane Bob and an October nor'easter destroyed the previous boardwalk. Individuals and businesses donated planks to rebuild it, which volunteers then installed. The donors' names, jokes (GET OFF OUR BOARD); thoughts (SIMPLIFY/THOREAU); and memorials to lovers, grandparents, and boats are inscribed on the planks. The long sweep of Cape Cod Bay stretches out around the beach at the end of the walk, where a platform provides fine views, especially at sunset. Stone jetties, dunes, waving grasses, and the entrance to the canal are in the foreground, and you can look out toward Sandy Neck, Wellfleet, and Provincetown or toward the white cliffs beyond Sagamore. The sandy strip on this mostly rocky beach is near the rugosa rose–patch dunes; the flowers have a delicious fragrance, and it's a good place for birding. The creeks running through the salt marsh make for great canoeing. From the town center it's about a mile to the boardwalk; cross Route 6A on Jarves Street and at its end turn left, then right, and continue to the boardwalk parking lot.

At the **Sandwich Fish Hatchery,** the oldest fish hatchery in the country, you can see more than 200,000 brook, brown, and rainbow trout at various stages of development; they are raised to stock the state's ponds. The mesh over the raceways keeps kingfishers and herons from snagging a free lunch. You can buy feed for 25¢ and watch the fish jump for it. ⊠*164 Rte. 6A* 🕾*508/888–0008* ◻*Free* ⊗*Daily 9–3.*

OFF THE BEATEN PATH

Green Briar Nature Center and Jam Kitchen. Is it the soothing pond-side location or its simple earthiness—who's to say? Whatever the reason, this center, owned and operated by the Thornton Burgess Society, is a solid symbol of the old Cape. You pass a wildflower garden on your way in, and the Smiling Pool sparkles out back. Birds flit about the grounds, and great smells waft from vintage stoves in the Jam Kitchen, where you can watch as jams and pickles are made according to Ida Putnam's recipes, used here since 1903 (sun-cooked fruit preserves are especially superb). Come weekdays mid-April through mid-December to see jam being made in the Jam Kitchen; you can even take a jam-making class some evenings or Saturday. The nature center has classes for adults and children, as well as walks, lectures, and a May herb festival, where herbs, wildflowers, and perennials are for sale. The Briar Patch Conservation Area behind the building has nature trails—take a walk and visit the real live animals that inspired Peter Cottontail, Grandfather Frog, and other beloved Thornton Burgess characters. ⊠*6 Discovery Hill Rd., off Rte. 6A, East Sandwich* 🕾*508/888–6870* ⊕*www.thorntonburgess.org* ◻*$2 suggested donation* ⊗*Apr.–Dec., Mon.–Sat. 10–4, Sun. 1–4; Jan.–Mar., Tues.–Sat. 10–4.*

WHERE TO STAY & EAT

$$–$$$ ✕**Hemisphere.** The most striking feature here is the supreme vista: via a generous array of windows, the sun sets over Cape Cod Bay while all manner of boats prepare to make their passage through the Cape Cod Canal. With both lunch and dinner, the menu covers vast ground with everything from fried seafood favorites to the more sophisticated; try the seared scallops with herbed gnocchi, adorned with grilled prosciutto, watercress, and roasted garlic. Savor items from the raw bar on the outdoor deck for a real seaside experience. ⊠*98 Town Neck Rd.* 🕾*508/888–6166* ◻*AE, MC, V* ⊗*Closed Jan.–Mar.*

$–$$$ ✕**Aqua Grille.** At this smart-casual and reasonably priced bistro by the
★   marina, offerings range from Cape basics (clam chowder, fried sea-
food, boiled lobsters) to more creative contemporary fare, such as nut-
crusted halibut with an orange beurre blanc. The excellent lobster salad
comprises a hearty serving of greens, tomatoes, avocados, baby green
beans, and big, meaty lobster chunks. Sandwiches (salmon burgers,
turkey wraps) are also available. ⊠*14 Gallo Rd.* ☎*508/888–8889*
⊕*www.aquagrille.com* ⊟*AE, DC, MC, V* ⊙*Closed Nov.–mid-Apr.*

$–$$ ✕**Bee-Hive Tavern.** This informal and friendly colonial-style tavern hasn't
been here since Revolutionary times (it opened in the early '90s), but
the cozy dark-wood booths and wide-board floors look the part. The
kitchen turns out solid American fare, such as burgers and sandwiches,
fried seafood, Yankee pot roast, ribs, and steaks. Dinner-size salads
are also available. Reservations aren't officially taken, but you can call
ahead to make the wait a little easier. ⊠*406 Rte. 6A, East Sandwich*
☎*508/833–1184* ⊟*MC, V.*

¢–$ ✕**Marshland Restaurant and Bakery.** Sandwich's version of down-home
is this homey coffee shop tucked into a parking lot. For breakfast try
an Italian omelet, a rich mix of Italian sausage, fresh vegetables, and
cheese. The lunch specials—a grilled chicken club sandwich, the Cobb
salad, a turkey Reuben, a daily quiche, and the like—are the best choices
midday, and for dinner the prime rib does not disappoint. ⊠*109 Rte.
6A* ☎*508/888–9824* ⊟*No credit cards* ⊙*No dinner Mon.*

¢–$ ✕**Seafood Sam's.** Fried seafood reigns supreme at Sam's, across from the
Coast Guard station and a stone's throw from the Cape Cod Canal.
Order from the counter, take a number, and sit in an airy dining room
where the munch of fried clams accompanies the sound of lobsters
cracking open. Sam's also has branches in Harwichport, Falmouth, and
South Yarmouth. ⊠*6 Coast Guard Rd.* ☎*508/888–4629* ⊕*www.sea-
foodsams.com* ⊟*D, MC, V* ⊙*Closed early Nov.–early Mar.*

$$–$$$$ ✕⊞**Belfry Inne & Bistro.** This delightful one-of-a-kind inn comprises a
Fodor'sChoice   1902 former church, an ornate wood-frame Victorian, and an 1830
★   Federal-style house clustered on a main campus. Room themes in each
building nod to their respective histories—the Painted Lady's charm-
ingly appointed rooms, for example, are named after former inhabit-
ants. The luxurious rooms in the Abbey, named for the six days of
creation, have whirlpool tubs and gas fireplaces, and are set along a
corridor overlooking the restaurant below. (If it's available, splurge on
the Tuesday room—the incredible stained-glass "compass" window will
take your breath away.) The Bistro ($$–$$$$) serves dazzling, globally
inspired dishes such as black grouper roasted with tamarind-yogurt
sauce in a striking setting—look up at the church's original arches and
stained glass as you dine. Next door in the Victorian building, the
Painted Lady restaurant ($–$$) serves innovative renditions of home-
style American favorites, including a delicious baked mac-and-cheese.
Pros: Great in-town location, rooms in the Abbey and the Victorian
are especially bright, beautiful, and spacious. **Cons:** Many rooms only
accessible via steep stairs, some rooms in the Federal-style house can
be smallish. ⊠*8 Jarves St., 02563* ☎*508/888–8550 or 800/844–4542*
🖴*508/888–3922* ⊕*www.belfryinn.com* ⋑*20 rooms* ⚐*In-room: no*

TV *(some)*, *Wi-Fi (some)*, *whirlpool tubs (some)*, *fireplaces (some)*, *massage. In-hotel: 2 restaurants, bar, no-smoking rooms, no elevator* $\equiv$*AE, D, DC, MC, V* †☉†*BP.*

$$-$$$$ ✕⊞ **Dan'l Webster Inn and Spa.** Built on the site of a 17th-century inn, the Dan'l Webster is a contemporary hotel within the heart of Sandwich's historic downtown. Rooms are decked out in high-end colonial-inspired cherrywood and mahogany furnishings in traditional colors. You might find a Sheraton reproduction armoire in one room, a pencil-post four-poster bed in another; some units have fireplaces, and most have balconies overlooking the nicely manicured gardens. The restaurant ($$–$$$$) is a longtime favorite. Upscale, modern continental dishes, such as roast rack of lamb stuffed with spinach and olives and served with a cabernet sauce, take their places beside veal Oscar, roast prime rib, and other classics. A casual tavern serves pizzas, burgers, and salads. The spa offers a full slate of massage, facial, and beauty treatments. **Pros:** Ideal in-town location, full-service hotel facilities in a tasteful setting. **Cons:** If you're looking for an authentic historic lodging experience with antique detailing and decor, you won't find it here; very popular with business travelers and bus tours. ✉*149 Main St., 02563* ☎*508/888–3622 or 800/444–3566* 🖷*508/888–5156* ⊕*www.danl-websterinn.com* 🛏*35 rooms, 13 suites* ⚒*In-room: Wi-Fi. In-hotel: 2 restaurants, room service, pool, spa* $\equiv$*AE, D, DC, MC, V.*

$$-$$$$ ✕⊞ **Isaiah Jones Homestead Bed & Breakfast.** Innkeepers Don and Kather-
★ ine Sanderson may be somewhat new to the lodging business, but with extensive backgrounds in the global tourism industry, both know how to give their guests extraordinary service in an equally stellar setting. The aged Victorian is all graceful lines and high ceilings, adorned with authentic period antiques and moody stained glass. Despite intricate wallcoverings, sweeping velvet drapes, and canopy beds, the spacious rooms are uncluttered and welcoming. Recline in the comfortable parlor with afternoon cordials or peruse the DVD library for an in-room movie. You'll want to rest up after the three-course breakfast that might include homemade crabmeat quiche. The two suites in the adjacent carriage house have a simpler, cottage style; coffee will be delivered in the morning before breakfast is served in the main house. **Pros:** Easy walk to town center, ultimate in Victorian elegance and design, beautiful grounds, a pampered experience. **Cons:** Most rooms only accessible via steep stairs, some rooms don't have the luxurious bathtubs. ✉*165 Main St., 02563* ☎*508/888–9115 or 800/526–1625* 🖷*508/888–9648* ⊕*www.isaiahjones.com* 🛏*5 rooms, 2 suites* ⚒*In-room: no phone, DVD, Wi-Fi, whirlpool tubs (some), fireplaces (some). In-hotel: bicycles, no children under 12, no-smoking rooms, no elevator* $\equiv$*AE, D, MC, V* †☉†*BP.*

$$ ⊞ **Inn at Sandwich Center.** Across from the Sandwich Glass Museum,
★ this 18th-century house with fine colonial and Victorian furnishings is listed on the National Register of Historic Places. In addition to such decorative flourishes as ornate nonworking fireplaces and Oriental rugs, rooms contain high-thread-count linens, robes, and Gilchrist & Soames bath amenities. A gazebo on a nearby hill houses a secluded spa where you can arrange to have a professional massage. A hearty

breakfast is served in the keeping room, which contains a fireplace and an antique table (older than the inn) that seats 10. Gracious hosts Jan and Charlie Preus know a lot about the region and have created a warm and inviting inn that's appealing whether you seek quiet seclusion or the opportunity to mingle with fellow guests. **Pros:** Easy access to town center, working fireplaces for cool nights, intimate and friendly inn. **Cons:** Most rooms accessible only via steep, narrow stairs, Deacon's Room is on the small side. ⊠*118 Tupper Rd., 02563* ☎*508/888–6958 or 800/249–6949* ⊟*508/888–2746* ⊕*www.innatsandwich.com* ⌿*5 rooms* ⮑*In-room: no phone, no TV (some), Wi-Fi. In-hotel: no kids under 12, no-smoking rooms, no elevator* ⊟*MC, V* ⊗*Closed Jan.– Mar.* ❖|*BP.*

$ ▦**Earl of Sandwich Motor Manor.** Single-story Tudor-style buildings form a "U" around a duck pond and wooded lawn set with lawn chairs. Rooms, attractively, if simply, furnished, are nicely sized with large windows and dark pine headboards and doors. Many rooms have canopy beds. A continental plan is offered from late May to October. **Pros:** Calming countryside setting with picnic areas, reasonable rates, good location for exploring the area, though not in-town. **Cons:** Bathrooms are a little outdated, rooms with two double beds are a bit overcrowded and dark. ⊠*378 Rte. 6A, East Sandwich 02537* ☎*508/888–1415 or 800/442–3275* ⊟*508/833–1039* ⊕*www.earlofsandwich.com* ⌿*24 rooms* ⮑*In-room: refrigerator, Wi-Fi. In-hotel: pool, no-smoking rooms, some pets allowed, no elevator* ⊟*AE, D, DC, MC, V* ❖|*CP* ⊗*Closed Jan.–Mar.*

$ ▦**Sandy Neck Motel.** Like the roadside country motels of old, this white-shingled motel with cheery blue shutters offers simple and convenient lodging for a reasonable price. Standard rooms have queen or two double beds, outfitted with white bedspreads and matching wicker furniture. The expansive grounds are dotted with barbecue grills, picnic tables, and Adirondack chairs, set back a bit off Route 6A. The efficiency is a good bet for families on a budget (or who just like to make their own meals) with a full size kitchen and two bedrooms. The entrance to Sandy Neck Beach is about 1 mi away; for those in search of the entertainment and vacation glitz of Hyannis, it's a mere 15-minute drive. **Pros:** Quiet setting with picnic areas, reasonable rates, close to beach. **Cons:** Not for those looking for an in-town location. ⊠*669 Rte. 6A, East Sandwich 02537* ☎*508/362–3992 or 800/564–3992* ⊕*www.sandyneck.com* ⌿*11 rooms, 1 efficiency* ⮑*In-room: refrigerator, Wi-Fi. In-hotel: no-smoking rooms, no elevator* ⊟*AE, MC, V* ⊗*Closed Nov.–Apr.*

¢ ⚠**Shawme-Crowell State Forest.** Less than a mile from the Cape Cod Canal, this 742-acre state forest is a good base for local biking and hiking, and campers get free day use of Scusset Beach. Open-air campfires are allowed at the wooded tent and RV (no hookups) campsites. Heated bathroom and shower facilities are a blessing on chilly mornings. The campground is generally open year-round, but if you're planning a winter trip, call to confirm before visiting. ⊠*Rte. 130* ☎*508/888–0351, 877/422–6762 reservations* ⊕*www.reserveamerica.com* ⌿*285 sites* ⊟*MC, V.*

NIGHTLIFE & THE ARTS

THE ARTS **Heritage Museums and Gardens** (⊠ *67 Grove St.* ☎ *508/888–3300*) sponsors jazz and other concerts in its gardens from June to mid-September; bring chairs or blankets. Most concerts are free with admission to the complex. **Town-band concerts** (⊠ *Bandstand, Henry T. Wing Elementary School, Rte. 130 and Beale Ave., Sandwich Center* ☎ *508/888–5144*) are held Thursday evening from July through late August starting at 7:30.

NIGHTLIFE **Bobby Byrne's Pub** (⊠ *65 Rte. 6A* ☎ *508/888–6088*), with other locations in Hyannis and Mashpee, is a comfortable pub, with a jukebox, and good light and full menus.

British Beer Company (⊠ *46 Rte. 6A* ☎ *508/833–9590* ⊕ *www.british-beer.com*), with other locations in Cedarville, Falmouth, and Plymouth, has a traditional British "public house" atmosphere with a great menu that includes fish, ribs, and pizza. Sunday afternoons feature live, traditional Irish music; a variety of bands play Thursday through Saturday nights.

SPORTS & THE OUTDOORS

BEACHES **East Sandwich Beach,** on North Shore Road, lies behind the grass-covered dunes beyond a row of gray-shingle beach cottages. It's a long stretch of sand, but nearby parking is very limited (and restricted to residents between 8 AM and 4 PM in season). From Route 6A follow Ploughed Neck Road to North Shore Road.

Town Neck Beach, off Town Neck Road, is a long, dune-backed bay beach with a mix of sand and pebbles. You need a resident parking sticker to leave your car in the large parking area between 8 AM and 4 PM in season. There are restrooms and a snack bar.

GOLF **Sandwich Hollows Golf Club** (⊠ *1 Round Hill Rd., East Sandwich* ☎ *508/888–3384* ⊕ *www.sandwichhollows.com*) has an 18-hole, par-71 course that's open to the public.

Holly Ridge Golf Club (⊠ *121 Country Club Rd., Sandwich* ☎ *508/428–5577* ⊕ *www.hollyridgegolf.com*) has an 18-hole , par-54 course (you can opt to play just 9 holes) that's good for all levels of golfers.

SHOPPING

★ The **Brown Jug** (⊠ *155 Main St., Sandwich* ☎ *508/888–4669*) is a tantalizing gourmet-food shop in a cozy brown-shingle house in the center of Sandwich—the perfect place to pick up delicious picnic supplies. You'll find cheeses, chocolate, and all sorts of hard-to-find imported foods; you can also order tasty sandwiches to go.

The **Giving Tree** (⊠ *550 Rte. 6A, East Sandwich* ☎ *508/888–5446 or 888/246–3551* ⊕ *www.givingtreegallery.com*), an art gallery and sculpture garden, sells contemporary crafts, jewelry, metal sculpture, and prints. The shop is open Memorial Day through Christmas.

Joe's Lobster Mart (⊠ *Cape Cod Canal* ☎ *508/888–2971*), opposite Seafood Sam's and the Coast Guard station, sells fresh-from-the-tank lobsters. Call ahead, and they'll boil your crustaceans to order—a great idea for an easy dinner at your cottage or hotel or for a picnic overlooking the canal. Joe's also sells many varieties of fresh fish.

Sandwich Auction House (✉ *15 Tupper Rd.* ☎ *508/888–1926* ⊕ *www. sandwichauction.com*), which auctions antiques, general merchandise, and Oriental rugs, is a great place to spend part of a Wednesday night (Saturday in the off-season); come after 2 PM to preview the items for sale. This local institution has weekly sales; in addition, specialty sales every six to eight weeks feature upscale antiques received during that period. Sales are also held for antique and modern rugs.

FodorśChoice
★

Titcomb's Bookshop (✉ *432 Rte. 6A, East Sandwich* ☎ *508/888–2331* ⊕ *www.titcombsbookshop.com*) stocks used, rare, and new books, including a large collection of Cape and nautical titles and Americana, as well as an extensive selection of children's books.

EN ROUTE

Route 6A heads east from Sandwich, passing through the oldest settlements on the Cape. Part of the Old King's Highway historic district, the route is protected from development. Classic inns and enticing antiques shops alternate with traditional gray-shingle homes on this tree-lined road, and the woods periodically give way to broad vistas across the marshes. In autumn the foliage along the way is bright; maples with their feet wet in ponds and marshes put on a good display. Along Route 6A just east of Sandwich Center, you can stop to watch cranberries being harvested in flooded bogs. If you're heading down-Cape and you're not in a hurry, this is a lovely route to take. And if you do wish to take the faster but less-interesting U.S. 6 as your primary route through the region, it's easy to hop off here and there and travel certain stretches of parallel Route 6A.

FALMOUTH

2 mi south of West Falmouth, 15 mi south of Bourne Bridge, 4 mi north of Woods Hole.

Falmouth, the Cape's second-largest town, was settled in 1660 by Congregationalists from Barnstable who had been ostracized by their church and deprived of voting privileges and other civil rights for sympathizing with the Quakers (then the victims of severe repression). The town was incorporated in 1686 and named for Falmouth, England. The Falmouth area, sprawling over 44 square mi, includes eight villages: Falmouth, North Falmouth, West Falmouth, Hatchville, Teaticket, East Falmouth, Waquoit, and Woods Hole.

Much of Falmouth today is suburban, with a mix of old and new developments and a large year-round population. Many residents commute to other towns on the Cape, to southeastern Massachusetts, and even to Boston. The town has a quaint village center, with a typically old New England village green and a shop-lined Main Street. South of town center, Falmouth faces Nantucket Sound and has several often-crowded beaches popular with families. To the east, the Falmouth Heights neighborhood mixes inns, B&Bs, and private homes, nestled close together on residential streets leading to the sea. Bustling Grand Avenue, the main drag in Falmouth Heights, hugs the shore and the beach. Parks and ponds dot the town; one of the nicest, Grews Pond in Goodwill Park, is north of the town center—it's a lovely site for a picnic on a summer afternoon.

Today attractive old homes, some built by sea captains, flank the **Village Green,** which is listed on the National Register of Historic Places. It served as a militia training field in the 18th century and a grazing ground for horses in the early 19th century. Also on the green is the 1856 **Congregational Church,** built on the timbers of its 1796 predecessor, with a bell made by Paul Revere. The bell's cheery inscription reads: THE LIVING TO THE CHURCH I CALL, AND TO THE GRAVE I SUMMON ALL.

The **Falmouth Museums on the Green** represent life in colonial Cape Cod. The 1790 **Julia Wood House** retains wonderful architectural details— a widow's walk, wide-board floors, lead-glass windows, and a colonial kitchen with wide hearth. Antique embroideries, baby shoes and clothes, toys and dolls, portraits, furniture, and the trappings of an authentically equipped doctor's office, all from the house's onetime owner, fill the premises. Out back, a re-creation of the Hallett Barn displays antique farm implements, a 19th-century horse-drawn sleigh, and other interesting items. Next door, the smaller **Conant House,** a 1794 half-Cape (an asymmetrical 1½-story building), holds military memorabilia, whaling items, scrimshaw, sailors' valentines, and a genealogical- and historical-research library. One collection includes books, portraits, and other items relating to Katharine Lee Bates, the native daughter who wrote "America the Beautiful." The Falmouth Historical Society also owns the 1812 white Cape house where Bates was born, off-site at 16 Main Street. The house is no longer open to the public, but a plaque out front commemorates Bates's birth in 1859.

Guides give tours of the museums, and a formal garden with a gazebo and flagstone paths is adjacent. You can take a break with "Tea in Julia's Garden," which offers tea sandwiches, scones, and other refreshments on Thursday from 1 to 3 in July and August. There are also historical trolley tours in season; call for prices and times. Free walking tours of the town are available Tuesday at 4 in July and August. ⊠ *Village Green, 55 Palmer Ave., Falmouth Center* ☎ *508/548–4857* ⊕ *www.falmouthhistoricalsociety.org* 🖃 *Museums $5; tea $12, including museum admission* ⊙ *Late June–Sept., Tues.–Fri. 10–4, Sat. 10–1.*

The privately owned **Charles D. and Margaret K. Spohr Gardens,** three planted acres on Oyster Pond, are a pretty, peaceful place. The springtime explosion of more than 700,000 daffodils gives way in turn to the tulips, azaleas, magnolias, flowering crab apples, rhododendrons, lilies, and climbing hydrangeas that inspire garden goers in summer. A collection of old millstones, bronze church bells, and ships' anchors decorates the landscape. ⊠ *45 Fells Rd., off Oyster Pond Rd.* ☎ *508/548–0623* ⊕ *www.spohrgardens.org* 🖃 *Free* ⊙ *Daily sunrise–sunset.*

☾ Video-game rooms and candlepin bowling make the **Leary Family Amusement Center** a great place to take the kids on a rainy day. ✉*23 Town Hall Sq., off Rte. 28, Falmouth Center* ☎*508/540–4877.*

The village of **Woods Hole**, which dangles at the Cape's southwestern tip, has a unique personality shaped by its substantial intellectual community. As a major departure point for ferries to Martha's Vineyard, it draws crowds of through-traffic in season. Well known as a center for international marine research, Woods Hole is home to several major scientific institutions. The National Marine Fisheries Service was here first, established in 1871 to study fish management and conservation. In 1888 the Marine Biological Laboratory (MBL), a center for research and education in marine biology, moved in across the street. Then in 1930 the Woods Hole Oceanographic Institution (WHOI) arrived, and the U.S. Geological Survey's Branch of Marine Geology followed in the 1960s.

Most of the year Woods Hole is a peaceful community of intellectuals quietly going about their work. In summer, however, the basically one-street village overflows with thousands of scientists and graduate students who come from around the globe either to participate in summer studies at MBL, WHOI, or the National Academy of Sciences conference center or to work on independent research projects. A handful of waterside cafés and shops along Water Street compete for the distinction of having the most bicycles stacked up at the door. Parking, limited to a relatively small number of metered spots on the street, can be nearly impossible. If you're coming from Falmouth to wander around Woods Hole, either ride your bicycle down the straight and flat Shining Sea Trail or take the Cape Cod Regional Transit Authority's WHOOSH trolley.

Scientific forces join together at the **Marine Biological Laboratory–Woods Hole Oceanographic Institution Library** (✉*7 Marine Biological Laboratory St., off Water St.* ☎*508/289–7423* ⊕*www.mbl.edu*), one of the best collections of biological, ecological, and oceanographic literature in the world. The library has access to more than 200 computer databases and subscribes to more than 5,000 scientific journals in 40 languages, with complete collections of most. During World War II the librarian made arrangements with a German subscription agency to have German periodicals sent to neutral Switzerland and stored until the end of the war. Thus the library's German collections are uninterrupted, whereas even those of many German institutions are incomplete. All journals are always accessible, as they cannot be checked out, and because the library is open 24 hours a day. The Rare Books Room contains photographs, monographs, and prints, as well as journal collections that date from 1665.

Unless you are a scientific researcher, the only way you can get to see the library is by taking the **Marine Biological Laboratory tour** (☎*508/289–7623*). The one-hour tours (mid-June through August, weekdays at 1 and 2), led by retired scientists, include an introductory slide show as well as stops at the library, the Marine Resources Center (where living sea creatures col-

2

lected each day are kept), and one of the many working research labs. It's a good idea to call for reservations and meeting instructions at least a week in advance.

The **Woods Hole Oceanographic Institution** is the largest independent, private oceanographic laboratory in the world. Several buildings in the village of Woods Hole house its shore-based facilities; others are on a 200-acre campus nearby. During World War II its research focused on underwater explosives, submarine detection, and the development of antifouling paint. Today its $93 million annual budget helps to operate many laboratories with state-of-the-art equipment. A graduate program is offered jointly with

> ### THINK TANK
>
> Woods Hole's incredible concentration of scientific minds is due in part to the variety and abundance of marine life in the area's unpolluted waters and the village's natural deepwater port. Researchers here can easily exchange ideas and information and attend stimulating daily lectures and discussions (many open to the public) given by important scientists. The pooling of resources among the various institutions makes for economies of scale that benefit each while allowing all access to highly sophisticated equipment.

MIT. WHOI's research vessels roam the world's waters; its staff led the successful U.S.–French search for the *Titanic* (found about 400 mi off Newfoundland) in 1985.

The Woods Hole Oceanographic Institution is open to the public only on guided tours, but you can learn about it at the small **WHOI Exhibit Center,** with videos and exhibits on the institution and its various projects, including its research vessels. **One-hour walking tours** (☎508/289–2252) of the institution and its piers are offered in July and August, weekdays at 10:30 and 1:30; tours begin at the WHOI Information Office at 93 Water Street and are free, but reservations are required. ⊠*15 School St.* ☎*508/289–2663* ⊕*www.whoi.edu* ✉*$2 suggested donation* ⊙*Call for hrs.*

⟲ The compact **National Marine Fisheries Service Aquarium** displays 16 tanks
Fodor's Choice of regional fish and shellfish in several rooms, cramped but nonetheless
★ crammed with stuff to see. Magnifying glasses, a dissecting scope, and mini-squeegees hanging from the frosty tanks (a favorite tool for kids passing through) help you examine marine life. Several hands-on pools hold banded lobsters, crabs, snails, starfish, and other creatures. The top attraction is two harbor seals, on view in the outdoor pool near the entrance in summer; you can watch their feedings weekdays at 11 and 4. ■TIP➔ The aquarium's status as a federal facility mandates a check of your driver's license or other valid ID at the door, so come prepared with credentials and expect to wait in line for a few minutes, particularly on rainy days. ⊠*Albatross and Water Sts.* ☎*508/495–2267, 508/495–2001 recorded information* ⊕*www.nefsc.nmfs.gov/nefsc/aquarium* ✉*Free* ⊙*June–Aug., Tues.–Sat. 11–4; call for hrs off-season.*

**NEED A
BREAK?**

Pie in the Sky (✉ *10 Water St.* ☎ *508/540–5475*), a small bakery with indoor and outdoor seating, sells cookies, pastries, and coffees, as well as sandwiches. The Oreo-cookie bars are truly decadent. It's a short walk from the ferry terminal, and a good bet for breakfast.

The **Woods Hole Historical Museum** (formerly known as the Bradley House Museum) is a three-building complex that houses paintings, a restored Woods Hole Spritsail boat, boat models, and a model of the town as it looked in the 1890s. One room is filled with elegant ladies' clothing from the late 1800s. The archives hold old ships' logs, postcards, newspaper articles, maps, diaries, and photographs; more than 200 tapes of oral history provided by local residents; and a 100-volume library on maritime history. Free guided walking tours of the village depart from the museum, which is across from the Martha's Vineyard ferry parking lot, Tuesday at 4 in July and August. ✉ *573 Woods Hole Rd.* ☎ *508/548–7270* ⊕ *www.woodsholemuseum.org* ✐ *Free* ☉ *Museum mid-June–mid-Oct., Tues.–Sat. 10–4; archives year-round, Tues. and Thurs. 10–2.*

The 1888 **Episcopal Church of the Messiah,** a stone church with a conical steeple and a small medicinal-herb garden in the shape of a Celtic cross, is a good place for quiet reflection. The garden, enclosed by a holly hedge, has a bench for meditation. Inscriptions on either side of the carved gate read ENTER IN HOPE and DEPART IN PEACE. ✉ *22 Church St.* ☎ *508/548–2145* ✐ *Free* ☉ *Daily sunrise–sunset.*

Impressive **Nobska Light** (✉ *Church St.* ⊕ *www.lighthouse.cc/nobska*) has spectacular views from its base of the nearby Elizabeth Islands and of Martha's Vineyard, across Vineyard Sound. The 42-foot cast-iron tower, lined with brick, was built in 1876 with a stationary light. It shines red to indicate dangerous waters or white for safe passage. Since the light was automated in 1985, the adjacent keeper's quarters have been the headquarters of the Coast Guard group commander—a fitting passing of the torch from one safeguarder of ships to another. The lighthouse is open to the public only sporadically for tours; check with the Falmouth Chamber of Commerce for details.

The bucolic villages to the east (well, bucolic once you leave Route 28 and its strip malls) have much to offer nature lovers. **East Falmouth** and **Waquoit** sit on narrow fingers of land that poke out toward Nantucket Sound, so water is never far away here and comes in the form of quiet inlets and marshy bays rather than the crashing surf of the open ocean. Residential neighborhoods, with both seasonal and year-round homes, often end in dirt lanes that lead to the water. Menauhant Beach, the nicest beach in these towns, sits on a thin sliver of land with the sound on one side and a grass-lined cove on the other. Inland, the land is more rural, with a number of farms (and farm stands) still operating.

Overseen by the Massachusetts Audubon Society, **Ashumet Holly and Wildlife Sanctuary** is true to its name and its original plantsman, Wilfred Wheeler, with its 1,000-plus holly trees and shrubs composed of 65 American, Asian, and European varieties. Like Heritage Museums and

Gardens in Sandwich, this 45-acre tract of woodland, shady groves, meadows, and hiking trails was purchased and donated by Josiah K. Lilly III to preserve local land. Grassy Pond is home to numerous turtles and frogs, and in summer 35 nesting pairs of barn swallows live in the open rafters of the barn. Maps for self-guided tours cost $1. Tours to nearby Cuttyhunk Island (on a 50-foot sailing vessel) leave Woods Hole every Sunday from mid-July to early October; trips run from 9 to 5 and cost $50. ✉286 Ashumet Rd., East Falmouth ☎508/362–1426 ⊕www.massaudubon.org ⬛$3 ⊙Trails daily sunrise–sunset.

☯ **Waquoit Bay National Estuarine Research Reserve** encompasses 2,500 acres of estuary and barrier beach around the bay, making it a good birding site. **South Cape Beach** is part of the reserve; you can lie out on the sand or join one of the interpretive walks. **Flat Pond Trail** runs through several different habitats, including fresh- and saltwater marshes. **Washburn Island** (☎877/422–6762 camping permit) is accessible by boat (your own) or by Saturday-morning tours (call to reserve); it offers 330 acres of pine barrens and trails, swimming, and 11 wilderness campsites (a permit is required). At the **reserve headquarters,** a 23-acre estate, an exhibit center includes displays about the bay's plants and animals, the Cape Cod watershed, and local Wampanoag culture. An interactive exhibit, outside on the lawn, allows you to trace the path of a raindrop; pick up a ball (the pseudo-raindrop) and follow its journey from cloud to land to river and on through the water cycle. In July and August the center has nature programs for children and families, as well as a Saturday-afternoon open house from 2 to 4 PM with family programs and a Tuesday-evening lecture-performance series (you can bring a picnic). ✉149 Rte. 28, 3 mi west of Mashpee rotary, Waquoit ☎508/457–0495 ⊕www.waquoitbayreserve.org ⊙Exhibit center late June–early Sept., Mon.–Sat. 10–4; late May–late June, weekdays 10–4.

Tony Andrews Farm and Produce Stand has pick-your-own strawberries (June), peas and beans (June and July), herbs (July and August), and tomatoes (August), as well as other produce on the stand. The farm schedules hayrides in fall, and a haunted house is set up in October. You can pick your own pumpkins in fall and choose your Christmas tree in December. ✉394 Old Meeting House Rd., East Falmouth ☎508/548–4717 ⊙June–Oct.; call for hrs and for information about special events.

☯ **Coonamessett Farm** operates a farm store where you can assemble your
★ own gift baskets or purchase produce and specialty foods, as well as a small café serving soups, salads, baked goods, and beverages. Members of the farm's Pick-Your-Own club ($15-per-year membership; non-Cape residents can buy a one-day membership for $5) can pick strawberries, lettuces, herbs, rhubarb, and other fruits and vegetables. Members can also tour the greenhouses and fields, learn about hydroponic-growing systems, and visit the animals (call ahead to arrange tours). The farm also rents canoes for use on the adjacent Coonamessett Pond. On Friday nights in summer, don't miss the wonderful organic vegetarian-buffet dinners with live music. ✉277 Hatchville Rd., East Falmouth ☎508/563–2560 ⊕www.coonamessettfarm.com ⊙Call for seasonal hrs.

Rows and rows of grapevines—8,000 in all—line the fields of Kristina and Antonio Lazzari's **Cape Cod Winery**. It now produces seven wines; the Nobska red won a bronze medal at an International Eastern Wine Competition. ⊠ *681 Sandwich Rd., East Falmouth* ☎ *508/457–5592* ⊕ *www.capecodwinery.com* ⊗ *July and Aug., tastings Thurs.–Sun. 11–4; late May, June, and Sept.–late Dec., tastings weekends 11–4.*

> **ROAD-NAME GAME**
>
> As you head east from Falmouth Center on Route 28, the street signs change names as you travel through different areas. The road is Main Street until you pass Falmouth Heights Road, when Route 28 becomes Davis Straits. Farther east it becomes Teaticket Highway, then East Falmouth Highway, and then Waquoit Highway.

WHERE TO STAY & EAT

¢–$

EAST FALMOUTH & WAQUOIT

✗ **McGann's of Falmouth Pub and Restaurant.** McGann's calls itself "a touch of Ireland on Cape Cod," and the McGann family should know—they also have a pub in the town of Doolin, County Galway, Ireland. The place has the slightly frayed grit of an Irish country tavern, and the filling if heavy bar food comes with an Irish twist: Irish-style fish-and-chips, or Gaelic chicken in an Irish whiskey-and-bacon sauce, for example. Though Guinness reigns, the bar has 20 beers on draft. There's live music Friday, Saturday, and Sunday; Thursday is karaoke night. ⊠ *734 Teaticket Hwy. (Rte. 28), East Falmouth* ☎ *508/540–6656* ⚠ *Reservations not accepted* ☐ *AE, D, MC, V.*

¢–$

✗ **Moonakis Café.** Breakfast gets high marks at this humble roadside diner. You'll find all the standards and then some—eggs, pancakes, fruit salad—all nicely done. The chunky hash browns are fried with just the right amount of onions, and if the omelet with roasted tomatoes, olives, and goat cheese is on the menu, it's an excellent choice. Also recommended (if you're not on a diet) are the decadent Belgian waffles buried under strawberries, bananas, and whipped cream. Specials are always offered and change frequently. ⊠ *460 Waquoit Hwy. (Rte. 28), Waquoit* ☎ *508/457–9630* ☐ *No credit cards* ⊗ *No dinner.*

$$–$$$

▦ **Cape Wind.** If you're traveling with children who need space to run, this gray-shingle motel on 5 acres is a dependable though modest option. The rooms face a broad green lawn that slopes down to the bay; it's a great place to launch your canoe or kayak. The rooms are decidedly basic, with standard motel furnishings that are being continually updated and refreshed. All have refrigerators and coffeemakers, and some have microwaves; others have kitchenettes. The spacious one-bedroom apartment has a private terrace, but its half-basement location makes the interior rather dark. The motel is in a quiet residential neighborhood. **Pros:** Beautiful grounds with water views, access to water, good bet for families. **Cons:** Lots of families often means not so quiet. ⊠ *34 Maravista Ext., Teaticket, East Falmouth 02536* ☎ *508/548–3400 or 800/267–3401* 🖷 *508/495–0316* ⊕ *www.capewind.com* ⇨ *31 rooms, 1 apartment* ♿ *In-room: kitchen (some), refrigerator, Wi-Fi. In-hotel: pool, water sports, some pets allowed, no-smoking rooms, no elevator* ☐ *D, MC, V.*

2

$$–$$$ **Green Harbor Waterfront Lodging.** Although the modest rooms here are clean and adequate, it's the friendly summer camp–like feel that makes this attractive compound great for families. There are old-fashioned lawn swings, a swimming pool, umbrella-topped picnic tables, and barbecue grills; but the main attraction is the waterfront. It's not open ocean here but a peaceful tree-lined inlet, with rowboats and pedal boats for guests' use. Some of the no-frills rooms in the 1960s-vintage motel have microwaves and small refrigerators; others have kitchenettes. A spacious three-bedroom cottage has three full baths, an eat-in kitchen, and a living room with a fireplace and two sofa beds. It's down a quiet lane off Route 28. **Pros:** Great for active families, right on the water, a good spot to launch a kayak. **Cons:** Noise and activity levels can be a bit much for those seeking quiet retreat (without kids), rooms could use some updating but are perfectly adequate. ⊠ *134 Acapesket Rd., East Falmouth 02536* ☎ *508/548–4747 or 800/548–5556* 🖷 *508/540–1652* ⊕ *www.gogreenharbor.com* ⟳ *34 rooms, 1 cottage* ⚿ *In-room: kitchen (some), refrigerator (some), Wi-Fi. In-hotel: pools, beachfront, water sports, laundry facilities, no-smoking rooms, some pets allowed (fee), no elevator* ☰ *AE, D, DC, MC, V* ☉ *Closed Nov.–Apr.*

FALMOUTH ✕ **La Cucina Sul Mare.** Northern Italian and Mediterranean cooking is
$$–$$$ the specialty at this classy, popular place. The staff is friendly and the
Fodor's Choice setting is both intimate and festive, if a bit crowded. Calamari, warm
★ green salad with goat cheese and cranberries, a classic lemon chicken sautéed with shallots and capers, and a variety of specials—including plenty of local fresh fish—adorn the menu. The *zuppa de pesce,* a medley of seafood sautéed in olive oil and garlic and finished in a white wine herb-and-tomato broth, is a specialty. Make sure to come hungry—the portions here are huge—and expect a long wait during prime hours in season. ⊠ *237 Main St. (Rte. 28)* ☎ *508/548–5600* ⚏ *No reservations* ☰ *AE, D, MC, V.*

$$–$$$ ✕ **RoöBar City Bistro.** Sibling to the Chatham and Hyannis restaurants
★ of the same name, the RoöBar brings a distinctly urban hipness to Falmouth. The bar is a popular watering hole, and the menu—scallop and smoked-bacon chowder, Asian duck confit pizza, Gorgonzola-crusted filet mignon—draws its inspiration from many cultures. There's also a terrific wine list. ⊠ *285 Main St. (Rte. 28), Falmouth Center* ☎ *508/548–8600* ⊕ *www.theroobar.com* ☰ *AE, MC, V* ☉ *No lunch.*

$–$$$ ✕ **Firefly Woodfire Grill and Bar.** Both the menu and the interior change seasonally here, but you can watch your food being prepared in the open kitchen year-round. Much of the food is cooked with the heat of a wood-flamed fire, either in the beachstone oven or on the grill for which the restaurant is named; try one of the pizzas, or any grilled meat or seafood dish, such as cedar-plank maple-glazed salmon with sweet-potato hash and panfried mushrooms. There's also a full bar with an extensive wine list and beer selection, in addition to colorful cocktails. Pop and folk bands perform here regularly. ⊠ *271 Main St. (Rte. 28)* ☎ *508/548–7953* ⊕ *www.fireflywoodfiregrill.com* ☰ *AE, D, MC, V.*

$–$$$ ✕ **Quarterdeck Restaurant.** Part bar, part restaurant—but all Cape Cod—this spot is across the street from Falmouth's town hall, so the lunch talk tends to focus on local politics. The stained glass is not authentic, but the huge whaling harpoons certainly are. Low ceilings and rough-hewn beams seem a good match for the menu, which includes hearty sandwiches such as Reubens and grilled chorizo at lunch and specials at night. The swordfish kebab, skewered with mushrooms, onions, and green peppers and served over jasmine rice, is especially good. ✉ *164 Main St. (Rte. 28), Falmouth Center* ☎ *508/548–9900* ⊟ *AE, D, DC, MC, V.*

¢–$ ✕ **Betsy's Diner.** A classic American treasure, Betsy's is a shiny, happy, busy place with a reassuring pink-neon sign urging you to EAT HEAVY. The generous dining room, gleaming counter, and stools and booths by the big windows are done in pretty pastel mauve-and-cream tones. Memorabilia and neon grace the walls. Pancakes, waffles, and omelets are served all day, and typical dinner options include meat loaf and mashed potatoes, knockwurst and sauerkraut, and charbroiled pork chops. ✉ *457 Main St. (Rte. 28), Falmouth Center* ☎ *508/540–0060* ⌖ *Reservations not accepted* ⊟ *AE, D, MC, V* ⊙ *No dinner Sun.*

¢–$ ✕ **The Clam Shack.** Fried clams top the menu at this basic seafood joint right on Falmouth Harbor. The clams are crisp and fresh; the meaty lobster roll and the fish-and-chips platter are good choices, too. Place your order at the counter and then take your tray to the picnic tables on the roof deck for the best views. More tables are on the dock in back, or you can squeeze into the tiny dining room. Just don't plan on a late night here—the Shack closes most evenings around 8. ✉ *227 Clinton Ave., Falmouth Harbor* ☎ *508/540–7758* ⊟ *No credit cards* ⊙ *Closed early Sept.–late May.*

¢ ✕ **Maryellen's Portuguese Bakery.** It's easy to drive right past this no-frills spot hidden behind a Dairy Queen. Take a seat at the counter or at one of the few tables, and then order up breakfast with a Portuguese twist. Try the savory Portuguese omelet, filled with spicy *linguica* (sausage), parsley, onions, and cheese, or the French toast made with Portuguese bread. The lunch menu starts with BLTs and burgers but quickly moves on to kale soup and *cacoilha* (marinated pork). ✉ *829 Main St. (Rte. 28), near Falmouth Heights Rd.* ☎ *508/540–9696* ⊟ *No credit cards* ⊙ *No dinner.*

$$–$$$$ ✕▣ **Holiday Inn.** This chain hotel is a dependable option for families. A tried-and-true comfort formula has been applied here: large rooms with contemporary furnishings, suites with king-size beds, and a large pool area surrounded by patio furniture and greenery. The Kansas City Steakhouse ($$–$$$$) restaurant serves breakfast and dinner year-round; you'll find Cape Cod specialties as well as huge quantities of beef—it's an unexpectedly good restaurant despite its setting inside a chain property. The hotel is adjacent to a pond and is close to Falmouth Center. **Pros:** Big name dependability, distractions for the kids, not far from town center. **Cons:** Lack of regional character, not for those seeking a Cape Cod experience. ✉ *291 Jones Rd., 02540* ☎ *508/540–2000 or 800/465–4329* ⎙ *508/548–2712* ⊕ *www.capecodhi.com* ⊲ *93 rooms, 5 suites* ⌂ *In-room: Wi-Fi. In-hotel: restaurant, room service, pool, gym* ⊟ *AE, D, DC, MC, V.*

$$–$$$ ✕▦ **Coonamessett Inn.** At this delightful old-Cape-style inn-restaurant that's a famous setting for weddings and special occasions, five buildings of one- and two-bedroom suites ring a landscaped lawn that leads to a scenic wooded pond. Rooms are casually decorated, with bleached wood or pine paneling and New England antiques or reproductions. A large collection of Cape artist Ralph Cahoon's work appears throughout the inn. In the main dining room ($$–$$$$), a few contemporary flourishes enhance the traditional menu; you can still find rack of lamb and baked-stuffed lobster, but you might also see cumin-scented scallops with Israeli couscous. Lighter but still excellent food is served in the cozy Eli's Lounge ($). **Pros:** Lush, gardened grounds in historic setting, high marks in romantic-dining setting. **Cons:** Weddings are a constant here—not the place to be if you want to avoid that scene. ✉*311 Gifford St., at Jones Rd., 02540* ☎*508/548–2300* 🖷*508/540–9831* 🌐*www.capecodrestaurants.org/coonamessett* ✎*28 suites, 1 cottage* ♨*In-hotel: restaurant, bar, no-smoking rooms, no elevator* ▤*AE, D, MC, V* ⦿*CP.*

$$$–$$$$ ▦ **Inn on the Sound.** At this understated but stylish inn, perched on a
★ bluff overlooking Vineyard Sound, the living room and most of the guest rooms face the water. Most have queen-size beds, and all contain unfussy contemporary furnishings such as natural oak tables, unbleached cottons, ample shelf space, and ceiling fans; four have private decks. Common areas include an art-laden living room with a boulder fireplace, oversize windows, and modern white couches; a bistrolike breakfast room; and a porch with more stunning water views. **Pros:** Grand water views and nearness to beach (towels and chairs provided), quiet, elegant setting. **Cons:** Not an in-town location, must drive to area restaurants and attractions. ✉*313 Grand Ave., Falmouth Heights 02540* ☎*508/457–9666 or 800/564–9668* 🖷*508/457–9631* 🌐*www.innonthesound.com* ✎*10 rooms* ♨*In-room: Wi-Fi. In-hotel: beachfront, no kids under 10, no-smoking rooms, no elevator* ▤*MC, V* ⦿*BP.*

$$–$$$$ ▦ **Palmer House Inn.** This turn-of-the-20th-century Queen Anne home stands on a tree-lined street, just a short stroll from Falmouth's Village Green. The Victorian interior of Falmouth's largest B&B is pretty if slightly over the top, with heavy period furniture, endless lace, and ornate stained-glass windows—many rooms have fireplaces. One good bet is the 3rd-floor Tower Room, which has a view across the treetops. The large rooms in the 1910 carriage house are airier, with more tailored appointments, and four newer rooms, all with whirlpool baths, are less ornate. There's a two-bedroom suite in a separate cottage (where young children are permitted). A candlelight breakfast is served, and afternoon refreshments are available. **Pros:** Ideal, walk to town location, elegant breakfast. **Cons:** With all the Victorian flourish, the smallish rooms can feel a bit overdone, most rooms (1 is ADA compliant) are accessed via steep stairs (especially 3rd-floor rooms). ✉*81 Palmer Ave., 02540* ☎*508/548–1230 or 800/472–2632* 🖷*508/540– 1878* 🌐*www.palmerhouseinn.com* ✎*16 rooms, 1 cottage* ♨*In-hotel: bicycles, no-smoking rooms, no elevator* ▤*AE, D, MC, V* ⦿*BP.*

$$–$$$ ⚅**Mostly Hall B&B.** With its deep, landscaped yard and wrought-iron
★ fence, this elegant inn with a wraparound porch resembles a private
estate. (The house got its name when a young guest is said to have
exclaimed, "Look! It's mostly hall!") The imposing 1849 Italianate
house has an upscale European style with painted wall murals in several bedrooms; the Tuscany Room's walls suggest an intimate Tuscan
garden. Three of the rooms are more traditionally decorated, with colonial antiques; all have canopy beds. Some rooms have the benefit of
fireplaces for cool nights. Breakfast is served in the formal parlor or
outside on the veranda. Although the inn is steps from the town center,
you can lounge in the gardens and feel a world away. **Pros:** Walk to
town center, ample, parklike grounds, grand home in the Victorian tradition. **Cons:** Rooms accessed via steep stairs, bathrooms are a bit small,
the bathroom for one room (discounted) is down a set of stairs. ✉27
Main St. (Rte. 28), 02540 ☎*508/548–3786* 📠*508/548–5778* ⊕*www.
mostlyhall.com* �🛏*6 rooms* ⚒*In-room: DVD, Wi-Fi. In-hotel: no kids
under 18, no-smoking rooms, no elevator* ⊟*AE, D, MC, V* ⦿*BP.*

$–$$$ ⚅**Admiralty Inn.** This large roadside motel outside Falmouth Center has
several types of rooms and suites, and its child-friendly facilities make
it a good bet for families. Standard rooms have two queen-size beds or
one queen-size- and one Murphy bed. King Jacuzzi rooms have king-
size beds and whirlpool tubs in the bedroom. Town-house suites have
cathedral ceilings with skylights, two baths (one with whirlpool), a loft
with a king-size bed, a living room with a sofa bed, and a queen- or
king-size bed. **Pros:** Good spot for exploring the Falmouth area and not
far to island ferry terminals, good for those traveling with kids. **Cons:**
Some rooms remain a bit stale and outdated, but the inn is constantly
refurbishing. ✉*51 Teaticket Hwy. (Rte. 28), East Falmouth 02536*
☎*508/548–4240 or 800/341–5700* 📠*508/457–0535* ⊕*www.thead-
miraltyinn.com* �🛏*70 rooms, 28 suites* ⚒*In-room: microwave (some),
refrigerator, VCR (some), Wi-Fi. In-hotel: pools (1 indoor)* ⊟*AE, D,
DC, MC, V* ⦿*CP.*

$$ ⚅**Capt. Tom Lawrence House.** A lawn shaded by old maple trees surrounds this pretty white house, which is steps from downtown yet set
back from the street enough to feel secluded. Built in 1861 for a whaling captain, the intimate B&B has romantic rooms with antique and
painted furniture, Laura Ashley or Ralph Lauren linens, French country wallpaper, and thick carpeting. An efficiency apartment is bright,
spacious, and suitable for families, with a fully equipped eat-in kitchen.
Breakfast and afternoon snacks are served near the fireplace in the common room. The owners are extremely friendly and helpful. **Pros:** Easy
walk to Village Green and town center, authentic historic lodging, great
breakfasts. **Cons:** Rooms accessed via steep, curving staircase, some
rooms may feel a little tight. ✉*75 Locust St., 02540* ☎*508/548–9178*
📠*508/457–1790* ⊕*www.captaintomlawrence.com* �🛏*6 rooms, 1 efficiency* ⚒*In-room: no phone, refrigerator, Wi-Fi. In-hotel: bicycles, no
kids under 7 (except in efficiency), no-smoking rooms, no elevators*
⊟*AE, MC, V* ⦿*BP* ☾*Closed Jan.*

$$ ⚅**The Inn at Siders Lane.** Housed in a contemporary Federalist reproduc-
tion building nearly indistinguishable from its authentic neighbors, this

2

elegant B&B blends traditional New England hospitality and 19th-century style with modern amenities. Just steps from downtown's bustle, the Inn feels private and intimate on its quiet corner by the Village Green. Upstairs, the two spacious guest rooms are tastefully appointed with graceful furnishings in pale neutral tones. Each has a queen bed, private bath, and cable TV; the house also has central air-conditioning. Hosts Jim and Maureen Trodden serve a superb hot breakfast, and you can join them again in the afternoon for tea and fresh-baked cookies. **Pros:** Easy walk to activities of town, intimate setting with few other guests, privacy. **Cons:** Rooms are accessible only by stairs, not for those who prefer many other guests to chat with. ⊠ *51 W. Main St., 02540* ☎ *508/495–4359* ⊕ *www.innatsiderslane.com* ↪ *2 rooms* ⚘ *In-hotel: no-smoking rooms, no elevator* ▤ *MC, V* ◉ *BP.*

NORTH & WEST FALMOUTH

$–$$$

★

✕ **Chapoquoit Grill.** Comfortable and bustling, this unassuming local favorite has an Italian slant, starting with creative pastas and wood-fired pizzas. The long list of daily specials might include wood-grilled duck with orange-molasses glaze or sirloin with a tamarind-mango glaze. A fireplace and coral-color walls make the front room intimate, and the larger rear dining room seems vaguely tropical (with a palm tree in the middle). Expect daunting waits for a table on summer weekends; come early or late. ⊠ *410 W. Falmouth Hwy. (Rte. 28A), West Falmouth* ☎ *508/540–7794* ⚘ *Reservations not accepted* ▤ *MC, V* ◷ *No lunch.*

$$$–$$$$

★

▨ **Chapoquoit Inn.** Four-poster beds, elegant bedcovers, and garden views fill the rooms at this cozy B&B in a 1739 former Quaker homestead surrounded by woodland and flower beds. Owners Kim and Tim McIntyre (she's a former marketing exec, he's a landscape designer) have furnished their inn with antiques and other family heirlooms. In the sunny breakfast room, which opens to the deck, you might find lemon pancakes or crème brûlée French toast. The sands of Chapoquoit Beach are a short 10-minute walk away. **Pros:** Walk to beach (beach chairs and towels available), nearby public tennis courts (innkeepers will provide tennis rackets), intimate and elegant lodging in historic property. **Cons:** Not an in-town location, but several amenities nearby. ⊠ *495 W. Falmouth Hwy. (Rte. 28A), West Falmouth 02574* ☎ *508/540–7232 or 800/842–8994* ⊕ *www.chapoquoit.com* ↪ *7 rooms* ⚘ *In-room: no phone, VCR (some), no TV (some). In-hotel: bicycles, Wi-Fi, no kids under 12, no-smoking rooms, no elevator* ▤ *AE, MC, V* ◉ *BP.*

$$$–$$$$

▨ **Sea Crest Resort.** Location and amenities are strong draws at this modern conference center and resort, whose eight buildings sprawl along one end of beautiful Old Silver Beach—guests enjoy some 700 feet of frontage right along the sand. Rooms, done in dark blues and pastels, are crisp and clean; many have ocean views, and some have gas-log fireplaces. A number of lodging packages are available. The poolside deli, Oscars, is a good bet for a quick burger or sandwich if you don't want to stray far from the beach; it's easily accessible to nonguests. The resort gets high marks for its kids' day camp. **Pros:** A kids' paradise, with pools, beach, and plenty of activities, a popular spot for business conventions, exceptional beachfront location, nightly entertainment in summer. **Cons:** A kids' paradise often translates to less than quiet surroundings, not for those seeking an intimate, uncrowded lodging spot. ⊠*350 Quaker Rd., North Falmouth 02556* ☎*508/540–9400 or 800/225–3110* 🖷*508/548–0556* ⊕*www.seacrest-resort.com* 🛏*258 rooms, 8 suites* ᝣ*In-room: refrigerator, Wi-Fi. In-hotel: 2 restaurants, room service, bar, tennis courts, beachfront, water sports, pools, gym, children's programs (ages 3–12; summer only)* ▭*AE, D, DC, MC, V.*

\$\$–\$\$\$ 🏠**Beach Rose Inn.** This rambling 1863 farmhouse sits on more than an acre of peaceful landscape, slightly off the beaten trail but within close distance of local amenities. The outdoor fire pit is a great place to spend the cooler evenings outside, or relax in the hot tub. The rooms—some in the main inn, some in the adjacent carriage house—are furnished with quilts, Cape Cod art, and a mix of antiques and reproductions. The Falmouth Suite has an airy, private sunporch. All rooms have private baths, some with whirlpool tubs. A separate, tiny two-bedroom cottage rents by the day and by the week. Ask about planned special events that might include wine tastings, author talks, and artist workshops. **Pros:** Idyllic, retreatlike setting, perfect for those who want some quiet indulgence. **Cons:** Not an in-town location, must drive to beaches, restaurants, and other attractions. ⊠*17 Chase Rd., off Rte. 28A, West Falmouth 02574* ☎*508/540–5706 or 800/498–5706* 🖷*508/540–4880* ⊕*www.thebeachroseinn.com* 🛏*7 rooms, 1 suite, 1 cottage* ᝣ*In-room: no phone, kitchen (some), refrigerator (some), no TV (some). In-hotel: massage, hot tub, some pets allowed, no kids under 12, no-smoking rooms, no elevator* ▭*MC, V* ⑩*BP.*

\$ 🏠**Ideal Spot Motel.** Neat as a pin, quiet, and a bit old-fashioned, this gray-shingle motel in the heart of quiet West Falmouth village has simple, good-size, family-friendly rooms. Efficiencies have a queen-size bed or two doubles, plus a kitchen and a sitting area with a sofa bed; the large motel rooms have refrigerators. There's no pool, but Chapoquoit Beach is a mile away. The lovely grounds are decked with well-manicured greenery. **Pros:** Great for families and those who like to cook some of their vacation meals, convenient and simple lodging, beach less than 2 mi away. **Cons:** Nothing fancy about the standard rooms, not an in-town location. ⊠*614 W. Falmouth Hwy. (Rte. 28A), at Old Dock Rd., Box 465, West Falmouth 02574* ☎*508/548–2257 or 800/269–6910* ⊕*www.idealspotmotel.com* 🛏*12 efficiencies, 2 rooms* ᝣ*In-room: kitchen (some), refrigerator. In-hotel: no-smoking rooms, no elevator* ▭*D, MC, V* ⊙*Closed Dec.–Mar.*

WOODS HOLE ✕**Landfall.** Request a window table overlooking the water at this clas-
\$\$–\$\$\$\$ sic Cape seafood spot, where lobster pots, buoys, and other nautical paraphernalia hang from the ceilings. Lobster, fried clams, and baked scrod lead off the menu of traditional seafood fare. Though the kids will need their restaurant manners, it's still family friendly, and the children's all-you-can-eat specials are a great value. ⊠*2 Luscombe Ave.* ☎*508/548–1758* ⊕*www.woodshole.com/landfall* ▭*AE, MC, V* ⊙*Closed Dec.–Mar.*

2

$$–$$$ ✗ **Captain Kidd Restaurant & Bar.** The stately bar, festive atmosphere, and a small number of cozy tables that cluster around a woodstove and overlook Eel Pond make this a year-round favorite for locals. Baked halibut, pan-seared scallops, lemon-herb roasted chicken, lamb medallions, and fried calamari are a few of the favorites, served in a pub-like atmosphere. In the bar area, a lighter and less-expensive menu is offered, including pizzas, pastas, fish-and-chips, and fried seafood platters. ✉ *77 Water St.* ☎ *508/548–8563* ⊕ *www.thecaptainkidd.com* ▭ *AE, MC, V.*

$–$$$ ✗ **Shuckers World Famous Raw Bar and Cafe.** Some of the harborside tables at this casual nautical-theme restaurant are so close to the dock that you almost feel as if you're sitting in the bobbing sailboats. The menu ranges from jerk chicken to pasta primavera to lobster ravioli, but it's best to stick with the grilled fish and other simple seafood dishes. The "world-famous" lobster boil—a boiled lobster, steamed clams and mussels, and an ear of corn—is justifiably popular. ✉ *91A Water St.* ☎ *508/540–3850* ⊕ *www.woodshole.com/shuckers* ▭ *AE, D, MC, V* ⊙ *Closed Nov.–Apr., and Mon.–Thurs. mid-May–late May and early Sept.–mid-Oct.*

$$ ⛫ **Sands of Time Motor Inn and Harbor House.** Essentially two lodgings in one, this property on a hill above Woods Hole village houses both a motel and a Victorian-era inn. In the family-friendly motor inn, the furnishings are standard motel-style; the best views, looking out to the water, are from the 2nd-floor rooms, some of which have private balconies. The Harbor House is more eclectic—a canopy bed here, a claw-foot tub there; some rooms have fireplaces or private patios. **Pros:** Can't beat the location for harbor views, short walk to both downtown and island ferry terminals. **Cons:** Not for those looking for intimate, historic lodging. ✉ *549 Woods Hole Rd., 02543* ☎ *508/548–6300 or 800/841–0114* ⊟ *508/457–0160* ⊕ *www.sand-softime.com* ⊲ *35 rooms* ᕀ *In-room: refrigerator (some), Wi-Fi. In-hotel: pool, no-smoking rooms, no elevator* ▭ *AE, D, DC, MC, V* ⊙ *Closed mid-Nov.–mid-Apr.* ⧍ *CP.*

$–$$ ⛫ **Woods Hole Passage.** A century-old carriage house and barn have
★   been converted into a romantic showcase. The large rose-hue common room radiates comfort with its lace curtains and overstuffed furniture. One guest room (the smallest) is in the main house; the others are in the restored barn, where the upstairs rooms have soaring ceilings. Gregarious and helpful owner Deb Pruitt sells Martha's Vineyard ferry tickets at cost so you can avoid lines at the dock. You can enjoy a delicious breakfast on the patio in the lovely yard; early risers can request "breakfast-in-a-bag" to take on the road. Kids are accepted, by prior arrangement. **Pros:** Beautiful gardens, artful lodging in historic structure, extremely helpful innkeeper. **Cons:** Not an in-town location; must drive to restaurants, attractions, rooms accessed via steep stairs. ✉ *186 Woods Hole Rd., 02540* ☎ *508/548–9575 or 800/790–8976* ⊟ *508/540–4771* ⊕ *www.woodsholepassage.com* ⊲ *5 rooms* ᕀ *In-room: no phone, no TV, Wi-Fi. In-hotel: bicycles, no-smoking rooms, no elevator* ▭ *AE, D, MC, V* ⧍ *BP.*

NIGHTLIFE & THE ARTS

THE ARTS   The **College Light Opera Company** (⊠*Highfield Theatre, off Depot Ave., Falmouth* ☎*508/548–0668* ⊕*www.collegelightopera.com*) presents nine musicals or operettas for one week each, the results of a summer program involving music and theater majors from colleges around the country. The company includes more than 30 singers and an 18-piece orchestra. Be forewarned: the quality can vary from show to show.

The **Cape Cod Theatre Project** (☎*508/457–4242* ⊕*www.capecodtheatreproject.org*) helps develop new American plays through a series of staged readings. Each summer the project presents three or four readings, which are followed by audience discussion with the playwright. Productions have included works by Gloucester Stage Company director Israel Horovitz and by Pulitzer Prize winners Lanford Wilson and Paula Vogel. Performances take place at **Falmouth Academy** (⊠*7 Highfield Dr., off Depot Ave., Falmouth*) and in the **Woods Hole Community Hall** (⊠*Water St., Woods Hole*).

Performing at the same venues as the College Light Opera Company, the **Falmouth Theatre Guild** (⊠*Highfield Theatre, off Depot Ave.* ☎*508/548–0400* ⊕*www.falmouththeatreguild.org*) is a first-rate community theater that presents four plays—a mix of musicals and dramas—from fall through spring.

Falmouth's summer **town-band concerts** (⊠*Scranton Ave.* ☎*508/548–8500 or 800/526–8532*) are held in Marina Park on Thursday evening starting at 8.

The **Woods Hole Folk Music Society** (⊠*Community Hall, 68 Water St.* ☎*508/540–0320* ⊕*www.arts-cape.com/whfolkmusic*) presents professional and local folk and blues in a smoke- and alcohol-free environment, with refreshments available during intermission. Concerts by nationally known performers take place the first and third Sunday of the month from October to April.

Woods Hole Theater Company (⊠*Community Hall, 68 Water St.* ☎*508/540–6525* ⊕*www.woodsholetheater.org*), the community's resident theater group since 1974, presents several productions each year, generally between late spring and early fall.

NIGHTLIFE   **Liam Maguire's** (⊠*281 Rte. 28, Falmouth Center* ☎*508/548–0285*) is a festive, authentic Irish pub with nightly Irish and other acoustic music and dependable pub fare.

Nimrod Inn (⊠*100 Dillingham Ave., Falmouth Center* ☎*508/540–4132*) presents jazz and contemporary music at least six nights a week year-round. The Nimrod is also a great spot for late-night dining.

Sea Crest Resort (⊠*350 Quaker Rd., North Falmouth* ☎*508/540–9400*) has a summer and holiday-weekend schedule of nightly entertainment on the outdoor terrace, including dancing to country, Top 40, reggae, and jazz bands and a big-band DJ.

SPORTS & THE OUTDOORS

BASEBALL The **Falmouth Commodores** (✉ *790 Rte. 28, Falmouth* ☎ *508/432–6909* ⊕ *www.falcommodores.org*) of the collegiate Cape Cod Baseball League play their home games at Guv Fuller Field from mid-June to mid-August.

BEACHES **Chapoquoit Beach** (✉ *Chapoquoit Rd., West Falmouth*), a narrow stretch of white sand, lines a peninsula that juts dramatically into the bay. Resident parking stickers are required at the beach lot in season, but the surrounding roads are popular with bicyclists. The beach has lifeguards and portable toilets.

Falmouth Heights Beach on Grand Avenue is an often-crowded arc of sand on Nantucket Sound, backed by a row of inns and B&Bs. The beach has lifeguards (in summer) and portable toilets. There's a small strip of metered parking on Grand Avenue between Walden Avenue and Crescent Park Avenue.

Grews Pond in Goodwill Park, a pretty tree-lined freshwater pond with a sandy beach and lifeguarded swimming area, is popular with local families. You'll find several sites for picnicking, along with restrooms and a volleyball net; there's also a playground nearby. You can enter the park from Route 28 just north of Jones Road or from Gifford Street opposite St. Joseph's Cemetery. Parking is free.

Megansett Beach (✉ *County Rd., North Falmouth*), hidden in a residential neighborhood, is a small, family-friendly location. Weathered gray-shingle homes line the cove, and boats moored at the adjacent yacht club bob in the bay. The beach has lifeguards and a portable toilet but no other services. Resident parking stickers are required at the beach lot in season.

Menauhant Beach, on Menauhant Road in East Falmouth, is a long, narrow stretch of sand with a pond in a quiet residential neighborhood. Its slightly more secluded location means it can be a bit less crowded than the beaches near Falmouth Center. The beach has lifeguards, restrooms, outdoor showers, and a small snack bar. Public parking is available; in season the fee is $10.

★ **Old Silver Beach** (✉ *Off Quaker Rd., North Falmouth*) is a long, beautiful crescent of soft white sand bordered by the Sea Crest Resort at one end. It's especially good for small children because a sandbar keeps it shallow at the southern end and creates tidal pools full of crabs and minnows. The beach has lifeguards, restrooms, showers, and a snack bar. There's a $20 fee for parking in summer.

Surf Drive Beach, a family-friendly sandy cove on Surf Drive, faces Nantucket Sound with views out toward the Vineyard. The beach has restrooms and showers as well as lifeguards. Public parking is available; in summer the daily parking fee is $10.

Wood Neck Beach (✉ *Wood Neck Rd., West Falmouth*), in the Sippewisset area, is a sandy bay-side beach backed by grass-covered dunes. At high tide the beach is very narrow, but sandbars and shallow tidal pools make this a good place for children when the tide is out. Resident parking stickers are required in season.

BICYCLING The **Shining Sea Trail** is an easy 3½-mi route between Locust Street, Falmouth, and the Woods Hole ferry parking lot. It follows the coast, providing views of Vineyard Sound and dipping into oak and pine woods; a detour onto Church Street takes you to Nobska Light. A brochure is available at the trailheads. If you're going to Martha's Vineyard with your bike, you can park your car in one of Falmouth's Steamship Authority lots and ride the Shining Sea Trail to the ferry. (The free shuttle buses between the Falmouth lots and the Woods Hole ferry docks also have bike carriers.) There are plans to eventually extend the trail another 8 mi or so up through West Falmouth.

Corner Cycle (⊠*115 Palmer Ave., Falmouth* ☎*508/540–4195*) rents bikes (including tandems and children's bikes) by the hour, day, or week. It also rents Burley trailers for carrying small children and does on-site repairs. The shop is two blocks from the Shining Sea Trail. **Holiday Cycles** (⊠*465 Grand Ave., Falmouth Heights* ☎*508/540–3549*) has surrey, tandem, and other unusual bikes.

FISHING Freshwater ponds are good for perch, pickerel, trout, and more; you can obtain the required license (along with rental gear) at tackle shops, such as **Eastman's Sport & Tackle** (⊠*150 Rte. 28, Falmouth* ☎*508/548–6900* ⊕*www.eastmanstackle.com*).

Patriot Party Boats (⊠*227 Clinton Ave., Falmouth Harbor* ☎*508/548–2626 or 800/734–0088* ⊕*www.patriotpartyboats.com*) has deep-sea fishing from party or charter boats. Advance bookings are recommended, particularly for weekend trips.

HORSEBACK RIDING **Haland Stables** (⊠*878 Rte. 28A, West Falmouth* ☎*508/540–2552*) offers lessons and trail rides by reservation Monday through Saturday.

ICE-SKATING Skaters take to the ice at the **Falmouth Ice Arena** (⊠*9 Skating La., off Palmer Ave.* ☎*508/548–7080* ⊕*www.falmouthicearena.com*) fall through spring. You can rent skates from the pro shop.

RUNNING To run in the world-class **SBLI Falmouth Road Race** (✉*Box 732, Falmouth02541* ☎*508/540–7000* ⊕*www.falmouthroadrace.com*) in mid-August, send a self-addressed, stamped envelope to request an entry form. The race typically closes to entrants in early spring. A crowd of 75,000-plus spectators lines the streets of the 7-mi course, which covers a combination of winding and hilly terrain, flat stretches, and stunning ocean scenery. There are 10,000 registered runners (the spring application window is quite small, and if you cannot run a mile in less than 12 minutes, you are asked not to enter), as well as about 2,000 unofficial ones, making this an immense event for such a small town.

TENNIS & RACQUETBALL The huge **Falmouth Sports Center** (⊠*33 Highfield Dr.* ☎*508/548–7433*) has three outdoor- and six indoor tennis courts and two racquetball-handball courts, as well as steam rooms and saunas, a full health club, and physical-therapist services. Day and short-term rates are available.

SHOPPING

★ **Bean & Cod** (✉ *140 Rte. 28, Falmouth Center* ☎ *508/548–8840 or 800/ 558–8840* ⊕ *www.beanandcod.com*), a specialty food shop, sells cheeses, breads, and picnic fixings, along with pastas, coffees and teas, and unusual condiments. The store also packs and ships gift baskets.

Eight Cousins Children's Books (✉ *189 Rte. 28, Falmouth Center* ☎ *508/548–5548*) is the place to find reading material for toddlers through young adults. In addition to comprehensive sections on oceans and marine life, Native American peoples, and other Cape topics, the well-stocked shop also carries audiotapes, CDs, and games.

Europa (✉ *628 Rte. 28, West Falmouth* ☎ *508/540–7814*) is a small boutique in a charming old house with a great selection of jewelry, accessories, and gift items at fair prices. A second room is devoted to lamps and lamp repair.

Handworks (✉ *68 Water St., Woods Hole* ☎ *508/540–5291*), tucked in the back of the Community Hall building next to the drawbridge, is a cooperative arts-and-crafts gallery showcasing the work of local artists.

Howlingbird (✉ *91 Palmer Ave., Falmouth Center* ☎ *508/540–3787*) stocks detailed hand-silk-screened marine-theme T-shirts and sweatshirts, plus hand-painted cards and silk-screened hats and handbags.

Maxwell & Co. (✉ *200 Rte. 28, Falmouth Center* ☎ *508/540–8752*) has traditional men's and women's clothing with flair from European and American designers, handmade French shoes and boots, and leather goods and accessories.

Rosie Cheeks (✉ *233 Rte. 28, Falmouth Center* ☎ *508/548–4572*), whose name was inspired by the owner's daughter, specializes in creative women's clothing and jewelry, with a particularly nice selection of hand-knit sweaters.

MASHPEE

7 mi east of East Falmouth, 10 mi south of Sandwich.

Mashpee is one of two Massachusetts towns with both municipally governed– and Native American–governed areas (the other town is Aquinnah, formerly known as Gay Head, on Martha's Vineyard). In 1660 the Reverend Richard Bourne, a missionary, gave a 16-square-mi parcel of land to the Wampanoags (consider the irony—an outsider "giving" Native people their own land). Known as the Mashpee Plantation and governed by two local sachems, it was the first Native American reservation in the United States. In 1870 Mashpee was founded as a town. In 1974 the Mashpee Wampanoag Tribal Council was formed to continue its government with a chief, a supreme sachem, a medicine man, and clan mothers. More than 600 residents are descended from the original Wampanoags, and some continue to observe their ancient traditions. Today, several residential-resort communities have developed in the Mashpee area; the largest, the Country Club of New Seabury, has one of the best golf courses on the Cape. There are no hotels or inns in

CLOSE UP

Powwow, Wampanoag Style

Dancers and drummers re-creating ancient rhythms, and vivid deer-skin costumes decorated with colorful beads and bold plumage are a far cry from the fried clams, shingled saltboxes, and antiques shops that typify Cape Cod, yet they represent the very essence of a culture that has made this area home for thousands of years. It was the Wampanoag tribe who peacefully greeted, assisted, and befriended the Pilgrims who came ashore in 1620. And while their presence is often overlooked amid the luxury resorts and golf courses that dominate the town of Mashpee, the tribe continues to embrace and celebrate their ancestors' way of life.

The Mashpee Wampanoag Powwow, held every year since 1924, is a lively showcase of the tribe's traditions.

Open to the public, the early July Powwow is a large gathering of local Wampanoags and numerous tribes from throughout the northeast; some even travel here from the western states. Tents and tables fill the tribal grounds, selling everything from native foods to jewelry and T-shirts. A series of intricately costumed dancing and drumming contests takes place during the three-day festival, along with one of the most dramatic events—the fireball ceremony. This ancient healing ritual involves Wampanoag males in what looks a little bit like soccer—except the ball is on fire.

The Mashpee Wampanoag tribal grounds are in Mashpee, off Great Neck Road. For more info, call the **Tribal Council** (☎ 508/477-0208).

Mashpee, although New Seabury does have some home and condo rentals. Mashpee, with its villagelike Mashpee Commons outdoor mall, has also become a popular shopping and dining destination. Yet away from the stores, the town retains a more rural character, with wooded roads, inland ponds, and reminders of the area's original settlers.

The **Old Indian Burial Ground,** near the meetinghouse on Meeting House Road, is an 18th-century cemetery with headstones typical of the period, intricately carved with scenes and symbols and inscribed with witty sayings.

In a cavernous former church building, the **Cape Cod Children's Museum** welcomes kids with interactive play, science exhibits, a 30-foot pirate play ship, a planetarium, and other playtime activities. The museum is best suited for preschoolers and children in the early elementary grades. ⊠ 577 Great Neck Rd. S ☎ 508/539-8788 ⊕ www.capecodchildrens-museum.org ☎ $6 ⊙ Mon.–Sat. 10–5, Sun. noon–5. Reduced hrs in winter; call before visiting.

Perfect for bird-watching, fishing, or canoeing, the **Mashpee River Woodlands** occupy 391 acres along the Mashpee River. More than 8 mi of trails meander through the marshlands and pine forests. Park on Quinaquisset Avenue, River Road, or Mashpee Neck Road (where there's a public landing for canoe access). Trail maps are available at the Mashpee Chamber of Commerce. The trails are open daily from dawn to dusk.

WHERE TO EAT

$$–$$$$
Fodor's Choice
★
✕ **Bleu.** Chef Frederic Feufeu, a native of the Loire Valley, brings the flavors of France to this urbane restaurant in the pseudo-quaint Mashpee Commons retail and entertainment village. From bistro classics to haute cuisine and sophisticated lunch sandwiches to decadent desserts, the flavors are astounding. Seasonal specialties include roasted filet mignon with poached foie gras, fingerling potatoes, candied shallots, and bordelaise sauce. Shrimp tempura with miso mustard sauce and Asian slaw is one of the tempting lighter and less-expensive dishes served in the natty bar. There's also a jazz brunch on Sunday, from Labor Day to Memorial Day. ⊠ *7 Market St., Mashpee Commons* ☎*508/539–7907* ▭*AE, D, MC, V.*

$–$$$
★
✕ **Siena.** A boisterous, high-ceilinged space at Mashpee Commons, this modern Italian restaurant warms the hearts of patrons with its genuinely friendly service and well-crafted Tuscan cuisine. You might start with the exceptional buffalo mozzarella salad before moving on to a wood-grilled veal chop with marsala sauce, or linguine with sautéed littleneck clams, white wine, garlic, and parsley. Several fine brick-oven pizzas are offered, too. Grand Marnier flourless chocolate cake makes for a magnificent ending. In warm weather, you can dine on the ample patio. ⊠*11A Steeple St., Mashpee Commons* ☎*508/477–5929 or 877/477–5929* ▭*AE, D, MC, V.*

¢–$$
✕ **Popponesset Inn.** The surroundings, more so than the lobster rolls, burgers, grilled swordfish, steaks, and other straightforward offerings, are exceptional here. The site is a gem, with old Cape Cod saltbox houses nearby, lovely Nantucket Sound in the background, and perfect light in the evening. The restaurant has a lounge called Poppy's and comprises several small dining rooms, some with skylights and others looking over the water through glass walls. Sit outside, either under the tent or at one of the umbrella tables. You can dance to a band on some weekends. ⊠*95 Shore Dr., The Country Club of New Seabury* ☎*508/477–1100* ▭*AE, DC, MC, V* ⊗*Closed mid-Oct.–late Apr. Closed Mon.–Thurs. Sept. and Oct. No lunch.*

¢–$$
✕ **The Raw Bar.** At this funky little seafood joint, you can pull up a bar stool and chow down on giant lobster rolls, littlenecks, cherrystones, oysters, steamers, and peel-your-own shrimp, all easily washed down with a local brew or a rum punch. Despite a few picnic tables out back, the scene here is more "bar" than "seafood shack." There's live music some nights, too. ⊠*Popponesset Market Pl.* ☎*508/539–4858* ▭*AE, MC, V* ⊗*Closed late Oct.–early Apr.*

NIGHTLIFE & THE ARTS

Bobby Byrne's Pub (⊠*Mashpee Commons, Rtes. 28 and 151* ☎*508/477–0600*) is a comfortable pub with an outdoor café, a jukebox, and reliable pub fare.

The 90-member **Cape Cod Symphony Orchestra** (☎*508/362–1111* ⊕*www. capesymphony.org*) comes to Mashpee in July for its annual Sounds of Summer Pops Concert (it also performs an August concert in Orleans). The performance takes place at the Mashpee Commons.

SPORTS & THE OUTDOORS

BEACHES **Attaquin Park Beach** (⊠ *End of Lake Ave. off Rte. 130, near Great Neck Rd.* N) is a pretty, sandy place, with a spectacular view of the interconnecting Mashpee and Wakeby ponds, the Cape's largest freshwater expanse. It's popular for swimming, fishing, and boating, but resident parking stickers are required in season.

South Cape Beach is a 2½-mi-long state and town beach on warm Nantucket and Vineyard sounds, accessible via Great Neck Road south from the Mashpee rotary. You can walk to get a bit of privacy on this beach, which is wide, sandy, and pebbly in parts, with low dunes and marshland. The only services are portable toilets, although lifeguards are on duty in season. A hiking trail loops through marsh areas and ponds, linking it to the Waquoit Bay National Estuarine Research Reserve. Resident parking stickers are required for the town-beach parking section, but anybody may park at the state-beach section for $7 per day late May through early September (it's free off-season).

GOLF **The Country Club at New Seabury** (⊠ *Shore Dr., New Seabury* ☎ *508/477–9111*) has a superior 18-hole, par-72 championship layout on the water as well as an 18-hole, par-70 course. Both are open to the public October through May, depending on availability; reservations two days in advance are recommended, and proper attire is required.

HIKING & The 4 mi of walking trails at 135-acre **Lowell Holly Reservation** (⊠ *S.*
WALKING *Sandwich Rd. off Rte. 130* ☎ *508/679–2115* ⊕ *www.thetrustees.org*), administered by the Trustees of Reservations, wind through American beeches, hollies, white pines, and rhododendrons on a peninsula between Mashpee and Wakeby ponds. The reservation has picnic tables and a little swimming beach. A small free parking area is open year-round, and an additional parking lot opens from late May to early September ($6).

In summer, the **Mashpee Conservation Commission** (☎ *508/539–1400 Ext. 540 for schedules*) has information about free naturalist-led guided walks of Mashpee's woods and conservation areas. Family nature walks, animal scavenger hunts, and "pond scoops" to explore aquatic life are a few of the activities offered for kids and their parents; sunrise walks on South Cape Beach and natural-history tours of the Lowell Holly Reservation are also on the program.

SHOPPING

Mashpee Commons (⊠ *Junction of Rtes. 28 and 151* ☎ *508/477–5400* ⊕ *www.mashpeecommons.com*) has about 80 mostly upscale stores, including restaurants, art galleries, and a mix of local boutiques and national chains, in an attractive village square. There's also a multi-screen movie theater and free outdoor entertainment in summer. Some of the more unique shops include **M. Brann & Co.** (☎ *508/477–0299*), a creative home-and-gift shop that carries everything from funky refrigerator magnets and unusual candlesticks to handcrafted glassware, one-of-a-kind lamps, mirrors, and furniture, with many works by New England artists; **Soft As A Grape** (☎ *508/477–5331*), an elegant but sporty men's and women's clothier with several branches around the Cape; and **Cape Cod Toys** (☎508/477–2221), crammed full of anything the children might possibly need, including beach toys, board games, and science projects.

Popponesset Marketplace (✉*Off Great Neck Rd. S, New Seabury* ✛*2½ mi south of Rte. 28 from Mashpee rotary* ☎*508/477–9111* ⊕*www. popponessetmarketplace.com*), open from late spring to early fall, has 20 shops (boutique clothing, home furnishings), eating places (a raw bar, pizza, ribs, Ben & Jerry's), miniature golf, and weekend entertainment (bands, fashion or puppet shows, sing-alongs).

THE UPPER CAPE ESSENTIALS

To research prices, get advice from other travelers, and book travel arrangements, visit ⊕*www.fodors.com.*

TRANSPORTATION

BY BOAT & FERRY
Year-round ferries to Martha's Vineyard leave from Woods Hole. Seasonal Vineyard ferries leave from Falmouth. *For details* ⇨*Boat & Ferry Travel in Essentials in the back of this book.*

BY BUS
Peter Pan Bonanza offers direct bus service to Bourne, Falmouth, and the Woods Hole steamship terminal from Boston's Logan Airport, downtown Boston, Providence (Rhode Island), Fall River, and New Bedford, as well as connecting service from New York, Connecticut, and Providence's T. F. Green Airport. Some of the buses from Boston also make stops in Wareham. Bonanza runs a service between Bourne, Falmouth, and Woods Hole year-round. Plymouth & Brockton Street Railway provides bus service to Provincetown from downtown Boston and Logan Airport, with stops en route. The Logan Direct airport express service bypasses downtown Boston and stops in Plymouth, Sagamore, Barnstable, and Hyannis.

The Cape Cod Regional Transit Authority's SeaLine, H2O Line, Barnstable Villager, and Hyannis Villager buses travel between the Upper and Lower Cape. Service is not frequent—buses depart once every hour or two, depending on the time of day—so check the schedule before you set out. To travel between Falmouth and Woods Hole, the WHOOSH trolley, also run by the Cape Cod Regional Transit Authority, is convenient. *For more information, see* ⇨*Bus Travel in Essentials in the back of this book.*

Bus Depots Bonanza Bus Terminals (✉*South Station Bus Terminal, 700 Atlantic Ave., Boston* ☎*617/720–4110* ✉*Depot Ave., Falmouth* ☎*508/548–7588* ✉*Steamship Authority Piers, Woods Hole* ☎*508/548–5011*). **Hyannis Transportation Center** (✉*215 Iyannough Rd., Hyannis* ☎*508/775–8504*). **Plymouth & Brockton Street Railway Terminals** (✉*South Station Bus Terminal, 700 Atlantic Ave., Boston* ☎*508/746–0378*).

Bus Lines Bonanza Bus Lines (☎888/751–8800 ⊕ www.bonanzabus.com). **Cape Cod Regional Transit Authority** (☎800/352–7155 ⊕ www.capecodtransit.org). **Plymouth & Brockton Street Railway** (☎508/746–0378 ⊕ www.p-b.com).

BY TAXI

Taxi Company All Village Taxi (✉ Falmouth ☎508/540–7200).

CONTACTS & RESOURCES

CONDO & HOUSE RENTALS

Donahue Real Estate lists both apartments and houses for rent in the Falmouth area. Real Estate Associates lists properties (some pricey) ranging from beach cottages to waterfront estates, with a focus on more expensive houses. It covers Falmouth, Bourne, and Mashpee.

Local Agents Donahue Real Estate (✉ Falmouth ☎508/548–5412 ⊕ www. falmouthhomes.com). **Real Estate Associates** (✉ Falmouth, Mashpee, Sandwich ☎508/540–1500 🖷508/563–6943 ⊕ www.realestateassc.com).

VISITOR INFORMATION

The year-round visitor information center on Route 25, in a rest area about 3 mi west of the Bourne Bridge, is open daily 9 to 5 (with extended hours 8 AM to 10 PM from late May to mid-October). The Cape Cod Canal Region, which includes Sandwich, Bourne, and Wareham, has information centers at the Sagamore rotary, at a train depot in Buzzards Bay, and on Route 130 in Sandwich (near U.S. 6 intersection).

Tourist Information Cape Cod Canal Region Chamber of Commerce (✉ 70 Main St., Buzzards Bay 02532 ☎508/759–6000 ⊕ www.capecodcanalchamber. org). **Falmouth Chamber of Commerce** (✉ 20 Academy La., Falmouth 02541 ☎508/548–8500 or 800/526–8532 ⊕ www.falmouthchamber.com). **Mashpee Chamber of Commerce** (✉ N. Market St., Mashpee Commons [Rte. 151], 02649 ☎508/477–0792, 800/423–6274 outside Massachusetts ⊕ www.mashpeechamber. com). **Sandwich Chamber of Commerce** (✉ Box 744, 02563 ☎508/833–9755 ⊕ www.sandwichchamber.com).

The Mid Cape

WORD OF MOUTH

"By staying in the Mid-Cape area, you can get anywhere in an hour or less."

—sherry

"My husband and I rode the Cape Cod Trail from the start in Dennis to the National Seashore nonstop—lots of fun, and I believe you could stop for ice cream and snacks every two miles if you wanted!"

—JoyInVirginia

"My personal favorite beach is Chapin in Dennis. It's on the Bay side, so the water is cooler, but refreshing on a hot day. The sandbars are gorgeous, especially during a sunset . . . ."

—klw25

Updated
by Laura V.
Scheel

MORE A COLLOQUIALISM THAN A proper name, the designation "Mid Cape" refers to central Cape Cod, the most heavily populated—and touristed—part of the peninsula. To the north lies tranquil Cape Cod Bay, laced with wide beaches, inlets, creeks, and marshes. The tides on the bay are dramatic—at dead low some beaches double in size as tidal flats stretch out for hundreds to thousands of feet. The calmer waters on the bay side make these beaches particularly suitable for kids, and when the tide is out, they can explore and play in the tidal pools left behind.

The main thoroughfare through the north side of the Mid Cape is Route 6A, a scenic section that dates from 1684, making it one of the first major roads constructed on Cape Cod. Alternately called Old King's Highway, Main Street, and Hallet Street, the road winds through the villages of West Barnstable, Barnstable, Cummaquid, Yarmouth Port, and Dennis, with north-side harbors and beaches just a short drive from village centers. A residential and commercial mix, Route 6A is lined with antique captains' mansions and farmhouses that are now private homes, bed-and-breakfasts, art galleries, restaurants, and antiques shops. Protected by a historical society, colors and architecture along the road are kept to the standards set by early settlers.

On the south side of the Mid Cape, sunbathers flock to the expansive beaches along Nantucket Sound. The main thoroughfare here is the busy and overdeveloped Route 28, which passes through Centerville, Osterville, Hyannis, West and South Yarmouth, and Dennisport. This stretch is particularly unpleasant and tawdry between West Yarmouth and Dennisport, where it's lined with strip motels, clam shacks, miniature-golf courses, ice-cream parlors, and tacky T-shirt outlets. A draw for families in its 1960s heyday, the area hasn't seen much renovation since. However, if you stray from the congestion of Route 28, the serenity of soft sand and quiet back roads awaits. It's hard to get too lost on the Cape—you can't go far off the main roads without hitting water—so poking around is worth the risk.

Between routes 6A and 28 is the "mid" of the Mid Cape, a mostly residential area with some historic sections, a few quiet freshwater ponds, and the commercial sections of Hyannis. Nearby are tony Osterville and Hyannis Port, a well-groomed enclave and site of the Kennedy compound.

EXPLORING THE MID CAPE

The Mid Cape includes the towns of Barnstable, Yarmouth, and Dennis, each divided into smaller townships and villages. The town of Barnstable, for example, consists of Barnstable Village, West Barnstable, Cotuit, Marstons Mills, Osterville, Centerville, and Hyannis, with the smaller quasi villages (distinguished by their separate postal codes) of Craigville, Cummaquid, Hyannis Port, West Hyannis Port, and Wianno. Yarmouth contains Yarmouth Port, along the north shore, and the mid- and south villages of West Yarmouth and South Yarmouth. The town of Dennis's villages are easy to remember: Dennis, West Dennis, South Dennis, East Dennis, and Dennisport. Route 6A winds along the north shore through tree-shaded scenic towns and village centers, and Route 28 dips south through some of the more overdeveloped parts of the Cape. Generally speaking, if you want to avoid malls, heavy traffic, and cheesy motels, stay away from Route 28 from Falmouth to Chatham.

> **TOP 5**
>
> ■ The gentle surf of Sandy Neck Beach, along the north side of Barnstable Harbor
>
> ■ Biking along the scenic 25-mi Cape Cod Rail Trail, which begins in South Dennis and ends in South Wellfleet
>
> ■ Summertime performances at the Cape Cod Melody Tent in Hyannis
>
> ■ Sightseeing, fishing, and clamming at Bass River
>
> ■ Shopping the boutiques, crafts shops, bookstores, antiques centers, candy shops, and galleries along Route 6A

ABOUT THE RESTAURANTS

The Mid Cape is chock-full of eateries, ranging from sedate, high-end haute cuisine houses such as Hyannis's Paddock, the Regatta of Cotuit, and Dennis's Red Pheasant to such family-friendly places as the Red Cottage in Dennis. Expect good fun and great eats at the area's dozens of clam shacks and other super-casual restaurants along Route 28 in Yarmouth and Dennis. If you simply want lots of choices, head to Barnstable and its villages, particularly Hyannis, where a stroll down Main Street will bring you to a dozen fine restaurants ranging from lunch joints to Thai, Italian, Cajun, and upscale American dining establishments.

ABOUT THE HOTELS

On the northern (bay) side, Route 6A from Barnstable to Dennis has dozens of B&Bs, many in the elegant former homes of sea captains. In contrast, Route 28 on the south side has row after row of lodgings, from tacky roadside motels to medium-range family hotels, with larger seaside resorts along the side roads on Nantucket Sound. Main Street, Hyannis, is lined with motels, and several inns and B&Bs perch on side streets leading to Hyannis Harbor and Lewis Bay.

WHAT IT COSTS					
	$$$$	$$$	$$	$	¢
RESTAURANTS	over $30	$22–$30	$16–$22	$10–$16	under $10
HOTELS	over $260	$200–$260	$140–$200	$90–$140	under $90

Restaurant prices are per person for a main course at dinner. Hotel prices are for a standard double room, excluding 6% sales tax (more in some counties) and 1%–4% tourist tax.

TIMING

In summer the Mid Cape bustles with tourists. But from Columbus Day weekend through April, the area is a peaceful collection of towns and villages, with beaches (no fees) for strolling, trails for walking and biking, and a wealth of shopping and entertainment. Although the year-round population has ballooned in the last decade, the off-season is still a laid-back and welcome time to catch the best of the Cape minus the crowds. Fall sees bursts of color in the easily accessed forests and marshes; winter brings a slower pace of life and a holiday spirit that locals love to celebrate with Christmas strolls featuring tours of shops, B&Bs, and old homes. Spring is also quiet, as the Mid Cape awakens to blooming trees, warmer days, reopened B&Bs, newly landscaped golf courses, and flower festivals. Boats come out of hibernation—Hyannis Whale Watcher Cruises, for instance, starts its program in May.

BARNSTABLE

Barnstable Village is 11 mi east of Sandwich, Hyannis is 11 mi east of Mashpee.

With nearly 50,000 year-round residents, Barnstable is the largest town on the Cape, extending from the bay to the sea and comprising several prominent villages, including Centerville, Cotuit, and Osterville. The community of Hyannis feels like its own distinct municipality, but is actually a village within Barnstable.

Barnstable is also the second-oldest town on the Cape—it was founded in 1639, two years after Sandwich. You can sense its history in **Barnstable Village,** on and near Main Street (Route 6A), a lovely area of large old homes dominated by the Barnstable County Superior Courthouse. In the Village Hall is the Barnstable Comedy Club, one of the oldest community theater groups in the country. Just north of the village are the marshes and beaches of Cape Cod Bay, including beautiful Sandy Neck Beach, as well as busy Barnstable Harbor. The Cape Cod Conservatory of Music and Arts and Cape Cod Community College are also in the vicinity.

The **Olde Colonial Courthouse,** built in 1772 as the colony's second courthouse, is the home of **Tales of Cape Cod** (⊠*3018 Rte. 6A, Barnstable* ☎*508/362–8927*). The historical society holds a weekly slide-illustrated lecture on Tuesday in July and August, plus special events in the shoulder seasons: in May there's a lecture during Maritime Week, and in June there's one during Heritage Week. In September, a "mystery" bus trip takes visitors to areas of historic interest. While you're here, take a peek across the street at the old-fashioned English gardens at St. Mary's Episcopal Church.

The **Sturgis Library,** established in 1863, is in a 1644 building listed on the National Register of Historic Places. Its holdings date from the 17th century and include hundreds of maps and land charts, the definitive collection of Cape Cod genealogical material, and an extensive maritime history collection. ⊠*3090 Main St. (Rte. 6A), Barnstable* ☎*508/ 362–6636* ⊕*www.sturgislibrary.org* ⊗*Mon., Wed., Thurs., and Fri. 10–5, Tues. 1–8, Sat. 10–4.*

Opened in 2005 and continually evolving and expanding is the **Coast Guard Heritage Museum,** housed in the old Trayser building. The struc-

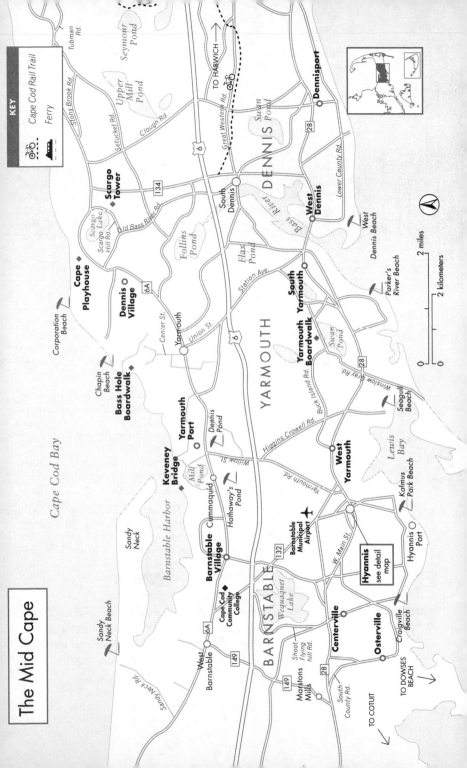

ture itself is on the National Register of Historic Places, and the museum is filled with all things related to this seafaring branch of the U.S. military. Artifacts and displays also highlight early lifesaving and lighthouse histories, and a small shop sells related books and items. Elsewhere on the grounds is the circa 1690 jail, with two cells bearing former inmates' graffiti. Call for the ongoing schedule of lectures and events. ⊠ *3353 Main St. (Rte. 6A), Barnstable* ☎ *508/362–8521* ≦ *$4* ⊙ *Mid-May–mid-Oct., Tues.–Sat. 10–3.*

If you're interested in Cape history, the **Nickerson Memorial Room** at **Cape Cod Community College** has the largest collection of Cape Cod information, including books, records, ships' logs, oral-history tapes, photographs, and films. It also has materials on the neighboring islands of Martha's Vineyard and Nantucket. ⊠ *2240 Iyanough Rd., off Rte. 132, West Barnstable* ☎ *508/362–2131 Ext. 4445* ⊕ *www.capecod. mass.edu* ⊙ *Mon., Wed., and Fri. 8:30–4:30.*

About 7 mi southwest of Barnstable Village, **Centerville** was once a busy seafaring village, its history evident in the 50 or so shipbuilders' and sea captains' houses along its quiet, tree-shaded streets. Offering the pleasures of sheltered ocean beaches on Nantucket Sound, such as **Craigville Beach,** and of freshwater swimming in Lake Wequaquet, it has been a popular vacation area since the mid-19th century. Shoot Flying Hill Road, named by Native Americans, is the highest point of land on the Cape, with panoramic views of Plymouth and Provincetown to the north and Falmouth and Hyannis to the south.

In a 19th-century house, the **Centerville Historical Society Museum** has furnished period rooms, Sandwich glass, miniature carvings of birds by Anthony Elmer Crowell, models of ships, marine artifacts, military uniforms and artifacts, antique tools, perfume bottles (dating from 1760 to 1920), historic costumes and quilts, and a research library. Each summer there are special costume exhibits or other shows. ⊠ *513 Main St., Centerville* ☎ *508/775–0331* ⊕ *www.centervillehistoricalmuseum. org* ≦ *$4* ⊙ *June–Oct., Wed.–Sat. noon–5.*

The **1856 Country Store** (⊠ *555 Main St., Centerville* ☎ *508/775–1856 or 888/750–1856* ⊕ *www.1856countrystore.com*) still sells penny candy, except that these days each candy costs at least 25 pennies. The store also carries newspapers, coffee, crafts, jams, and all kinds of gadgets and toys. You can sip your coffee—and take a political stance—by choosing a wooden bench out front, one is marked DEMOCRAT, and the other REPUBLICAN.

NEED A BREAK? Sample a variety of creamy homemade flavors at **Four Seas Ice Cream** (⊠ *360 S. Main St., Centerville* ☎ *508/775–1394*), a tradition for generations of summer visitors. The kitchen also turns out short-order lunch and dinner fare. It's open from late May to mid-September until 10:30 PM.

The **Centerville Library** (⊠ *585 Main St., Centerville* ☎ *508/790–6220* ⊕ *www.centervillelibrary.org*) has a 42-volume noncirculating set of transcripts of the Nuremberg Trials. The library is open Monday and

Wednesday 10 to 5; Tuesday and Thursday 10 to 7; Friday 10 to 3; and Saturday 10 to 2; it's closed on Sunday.

From Centerville, head west about 7 mi to reach **Cotuit**, a charming little community formed around seven homesteads belonging to the family of 18th-century trader Winslow Crocker. Much of the town lies along and just south of Route 28, west of Osterville and east of Mashpee, and its center is not much more than a crossroads with a post office, an old-time coffee shop, a pizza parlor, and a general store, which all seem unchanged since the 1940s. Large waterfront estates line sections of Main Street and Ocean View Drive, where small coves hide the uncrowded Loop Beach and Ropes Beach. It's best to get to the beaches by bike, since traffic is light and beach parking is for residents only.

The **Cahoon Museum of American Art** is in one of the old Crocker family buildings, a 1775 Georgian colonial farmhouse that was once a tavern and an overnight way station for travelers on the Hyannis–Sandwich stagecoach line. Displays include selections from the permanent collection of American primitive paintings by Ralph and Martha Cahoon, along with other 19th- and early-20th-century artists. Special exhibitions, classes, talks, and demonstrations are held throughout the summer. ⊠ *4676 Falmouth Rd. (Rte. 28), Cotuit* ☎ *508/428–7581* ⊕ *www. cahoonmuseum.org* ⊠ *$4* ⊙ *Feb.–Dec., Tues.–Sat. 10–4.*

The first motor-driven fire-fighting apparatus on Cape Cod, a 1916 Model T chemical-fire engine, is in the **Santuit-Cotuit Historical Society Museum,** behind the **Samuel Dottridge Homestead,** which itself dates from the early 1800s. ⊠ *1148 Main St., Cotuit* ☎ *508/428–0461* ⊠ *Free* ⊙ *Mid-June–mid-Oct., Thurs.–Sun. 2:30–5.*

Cotuit Library (⊠ *871 Main St., Cotuit* ☎ *508/428–8141* ⊕ *www.library. cotuit.ma.us*) has a noncirculating set of luxurious leather-bound classics. Library hours are 1:30 to 5:30 and 7 to 8:30 Monday; 9:30 to 5:30 Tuesday and Friday; 1:30 to 5:30 Wednesday; 9:30 to 5:30 and 7 to 8:30 Thursday; and 10 to 4 Saturday. The library is closed Sunday.

A wealthy Barnstable enclave 5 mi east of Cotuit, **Osterville** is lined with elegant waterfront houses, some of which are large "cottages" built in the 19th century when the area became popular with the monied set. You'll find that most beaches in the village, including the impressive **Dowses Beach,** are restricted to residents-only parking. Despite its haute homes, the village of Osterville retains the small-town charm that permeates the Cape; its Main Street and Wianno Avenue area has a collection of trendy boutiques and jewelry shops mixed with a library, a post office, and country stores. The village's festivals of Daff O'ville Day (late April) and Christmas Stroll (mid-December) are heavily attended.

The **Osterville Historical Society Museum,** in an 1824 sea captain's house, has antiques, dolls, and exhibits on Osterville's history. Two wooden-boat museums—each showcasing various sailing vessels—and the late-18th- century Cammett House are also on the property. ⊠ *155 W. Bay Rd., Osterville* ☎ *508/428–5861* ⊠ *$5* ⊙ *June–Sept., Thurs.–Sun. 1:30–4:30.*

NEED A BREAK?
Gone Chocolate (✉*858 Main St.* ☎*508/420–0202*) will tempt you with old-fashioned chocolate-pecan turtles, saltwater taffy, ice cream, and other confections.

❶–❹ Hyannis was named for the Native American Sachem Iyanno, who sold the area for $20 and two pairs of pants. Perhaps he would have sold it for far more had there been any indication that Hyannis would become known as the "home port of Cape Cod" or that the Kennedys would pitch so many tents here. Hyannis is effectively the transportation center of the Cape: it's near the airport, and ferries depart here for Nantucket and (in season) Martha's Vineyard. The busy roads feeding into the town are lined with the same big-box stores you'd find anywhere.

A bustling year-round hub of activity, Hyannis has the Cape's largest concentration of businesses, shops, malls, hotels and motels, restaurants, and entertainment venues. Main Street is lined with used-book and gift shops, jewelers, clothing stores, summer-wear and T-shirt shops, and ice-cream and candy stores. The street can have a somewhat forlorn, down-at-the-heels feeling, as the malls outside downtown have taken their toll on business, but there are plenty of good fun and fancy eateries here.

Perhaps best known for its association with the Kennedy clan, the Hyannis area was also a vacation site for President Ulysses S. Grant in 1874 and later for President Grover Cleveland. Today Hyannis is making an effort to preserve its historical connection with the sea. By 1840 more than 200 shipmasters had established homes in the Hyannis–Hyannis Port area. Aselton Park (at the intersection of South and Ocean streets) and the Village Green on Main Street are the sites of events celebrating this history, and Aselton Park marks the starting point of the scenic Walkway to the Sea, which extends to the dock area.

Three parallel streets run through the heart of town. Busy, shop-filled Main Street runs one-way from east to west; South Street runs from west to east; and North Street is open to two-way traffic. The airport rotary connects with heavily trafficked routes 132 and 28 and with U.S. 6. Off Ocean Street and Sea Street lie several excellent beaches, including Kalmus Park Beach, renowned for its stiff winds and hordes of windsurfers, and the smaller Veterans Park Beach, next to the Kennedy Memorial.

❶ In Main Street's Old Town Hall, the **John F. Kennedy Hyannis Museum** explores JFK's Cape years (1934–63) through enlarged and annotated photographs culled from the archives of the JFK Library near Boston, as well as a seven-minute video narrated by Walter Cronkite. The gift shop sells mugs, T-shirts, and presidential memorabilia. ✉*397 Main St., Downtown Hyannis* ☎*508/790–3077* ⊕*www.jfkhyannismuseum.org* ☞*$5* ⊙*Memorial Day–Oct., Mon.–Sat. 9–5, Sun. noon–5; Nov.–early Dec. and mid-Feb.–mid-Apr., Thurs.–Sat. 10–4, Sun. noon–4. Closed Jan.*

❷ The **St. Francis Xavier Church** (✉*347 South St., Downtown Hyannis* ☎*508/771–7200* ⊕*www.sfxp.org*) is where Rose Kennedy and her

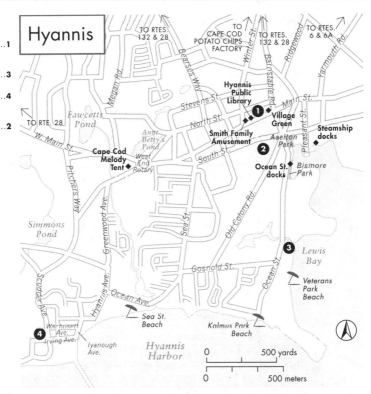

family worshipped during their summers on the Cape; the pew that John F. Kennedy used regularly is marked with a plaque.

NEED A BREAK?

In an unlikely spot amid several industrial buildings near the airport, **Pain D'Avignon** (✉ *192 Airport Rd.* ☎ *508/778-8588* ⊕ *www.paindavignon. com*) is nevertheless worth seeking out, especially if you're planning a picnic (although you can dine here at one of the few stainless-steel tables and chairs on a small patio). This quirky old-world-style bakery produces fine artisan breads that end up at some of the finest restaurants and gourmet shops in Boston. Drop in for delectable raisin-pecan or calamata-olive breads, cranberry bagels, chocolate-chip cookies, panini sandwiches, and fine gourmet supplies, such as cheeses, oils, and sauces.

❸ Beyond the bustling docks where waterfront restaurants draw crowds and ferries, harbor-tour boats, and deep-sea fishing vessels come and go, the quiet esplanade by the **John F. Kennedy Memorial** (✉ *Off Ocean St. south of Channel Point, Hyannis Harbor*) overlooks boat-filled Lewis Bay. JFK loved to sail these waters, and in 1966 the people of Barnstable erected a plaque and fountain pool here in his memory. Adjacent to the memorial is **Veterans Park,** with a beach, a tree-shaded picnic and barbecue area, and a playground.

Bismore Park (⊠ *Off Ocean St., Hyannis Harbor*) is part of a continuing and avid effort to revitalize downtown Hyannis and encourage folks to linger here and explore. In the summer season the green is populated with modest wood sheds—"shanties"—which artisans and artists rent and use as small workshops and stores.

❹ Hyannis Port became a hot spot for Americans during the Kennedy presidency, when the **Kennedy Compound** became the summer White House. The days of hordes of Secret Service agents and swarms of tourists trampling down the bushes are gone, and the area is once again a community of quietly posh estates—though the Kennedy mystique is such that tourists still seek it out. The best way to get a glimpse of the compound is from the water on one of the many harbor tours or cruises.

Joseph P. and Rose Kennedy bought their house here—the largest one, closest to the water—in 1929 as a healthful place to summer with their soon-to-be-nine kids. (Son Ted bought the house before his mother's death in 1995.) Sons Jack and Bobby bought neighboring houses in the 1950s. Jack's is the one at the corner of Scudder and Irving, with the 6-foot-high stockade fence on two sides. Bobby's is next to it, with a white fieldstone chimney. Ted bought a home on Squaw Island, a private island connected to the area by a causeway at the end of Scudder Avenue. It now belongs to his ex-wife, Joan. Eunice (Kennedy) and Sargent Shriver have a house near Squaw Island, on Atlantic Avenue.

The compound is relatively self-sufficient in terms of entertainment: Rose Kennedy's former abode (with 14 rooms and 9 baths) has a movie theater, a private beach, a boat dock, a swimming pool, a tennis court, and a sports field that was the scene of the famous Kennedy touch-football matches. Maria Shriver, Caroline Kennedy Schlossberg, and other family members have had their wedding receptions here. In the summer of 1999 family members waited at the compound, with local and international media lining the streets, for confirmation of John F. Kennedy Jr.'s death in a plane crash off Martha's Vineyard. He and his wife, Carolyn Bessette Kennedy, were flying her sister, Lauren Bessette, to the Vineyard before continuing on to a cousin's wedding in Hyannis; all three were killed.

OFF THE BEATEN PATH

Cape Cod Potato Chips Factory. There's a standing invitation on the back of the bag: come for a free tour of the factory and get free samples of the crunchy all-natural chips hand-cooked in kettles in small batches. ⊠*Independence Dr. (opposite Cape Cod Mall) to Breed's Hill Rd., off Rte. 132* ☎*508/775–3358* ⊕*www.capecodchips.com* ☉ *Weekdays 9–5.*

Hyannis Public Library (⊠*401 Main St., Downtown Hyannis* ☎*508/775–2280*) has a case full of books on JFK. Summer library hours are 11 to 5 Monday, Thursday, and Friday, and 11 to 8 Tuesday and Wednesday. The library is closed weekends in summer (Sunday and Monday in winter).

☉ Perfect for a rainy day, **Smith Family Amusement** is replete with bowling lanes, video-game rooms, and that old seaside favorite, Skee-ball. ⊠*441 Main St., Downtown Hyannis* ☎*508/775–3411* ☉*Daily; hrs vary.*

CLOSE UP

The New Face of Hyannis

More than one million people travel to Hyannis each year—but many are merely passing *through* the town on their way to its ferry docks and boats to the outlying islands. For decades, townsfolk wished that these travelers would spend a little bit of time—and money—in Hyannis, but there wasn't much to entice them to stay.

But today, changes are afoot. In a move to become more family-friendly, sophisticated, and appealing, Hyannis has been revitalizing its downtown and waterfront areas. One pleasant improvement is the "Walkway to the Sea," completed in 2006. This wave-patterned brick path winds from Main Street at the Village Green all the way down to Bismore Park at Hyannis Harbor. Along the way are colorful art installations of lobster buoys, com-

plete with educational information about the fishing industry. The Village Green itself is now host to a weekly Farmers' Market, free movie showings, and band concerts in the summer.

As part of the "Harbor Your Arts" initiative, a series of wood "shanties" now populate Aselton Park along the Walkway to the Sea. Juried artists and artisans rent the sheds as both work space and selling arenas for their products. A seasonal stage, where free musical and theatrical performances are held in summer, opened in 2006.

The entire downtown corridor is abuzz with building restorations, improvements, expansions, creative landscaping, new sidewalks, and spruced-up storefronts. You may just want to linger before catching your ferry.

3

WHERE TO STAY & EAT

BARNSTABLE
$$–$$$
✕ **Dolphin Restaurant.** For the scoop on local politics, eavesdrop at the Dolphin. A popular spot among local political figures, for decades this has been the place in town where opinions clash and deals are cut. The dark, inviting interior has a colonial feel. Lunch favorites include the shrimp-and-crab melt, rib-eye steak, and fish-and-chips. Dinner consists of a straightforward, well-prepared roster of traditional steaks, chops, and seafood grills and sautés. The small but welcoming bar is a good spot to chow down if you're dining solo. ⊠ *3250 Main St. (Rte. 6A)* ☎ *508/362–6610* ☐ *AE, DC, MC, V* ✪ *No lunch Sun.*

$–$$$
✕ **Barnstable Tavern & Grille.** This handsome old building right in the village center, across from the courthouse and Barnstable Comedy Club, holds both a formal restaurant and a more relaxed tavern. Fresh seafood dishes and the Tavern Keeper's Special (a medley of seafood in a casserole) are local favorites. Lighter lunch fare includes burgers, salads, and sandwiches. Look for live music on the patio Friday night. ⊠ *3176 Main St. (Rte. 6A)* ☎ *508/362–2355* ☐ *AE, MC, V.*

¢–$
★
✕ **Osterville Fish Too.** This combination seafood market and lunch place sits right on Barnstable Harbor at Millway Marina, giving it access to the freshest seafood around. It's tiny, with a fistful of outside picnic tables on a wooden deck and limited parking, but the fried clams and fish sandwiches are worth the inevitable wait. Arrive hungry and try the fat onion rings or the prodigious seafood platters (piled high with sole, shrimp, scallops, and clams). ⊠ *275 Mill Way* ☎ *508/362–2295* ☐ *MC, V* ✪ *Closed Oct.–Mar.*

¢ ✕**Whistleberries.** Most people settle for takeout from this tiny sandwich shop, but the lucky few who manage to grab one of the three counter spots or two tables are in for an olfactory treat. Breakfast options include fresh muffins; "scrambled" eggs (they're actually steamed by the cappuccino machine); bagels; or burrito sandwiches stuffed with cheese, bacon, veggies, rice, beans, and sour cream. For lunch, try a wrap—there are many tempting choices, from barbecued chicken to Mediterranean—red pepper, hummus, tabbouleh, tomato, onion, and feta cheese folded up in a spinach tortilla. ⊠*3261 Main St. (Rte. 6A)* ☎*508/362–6717* ▱*No credit cards* ☉*Closed Sun. No dinner.*

$$–$$$ 🏨**Acworth Inn.** This 1860 house 1 mi east of Barnstable Village has four large rooms and a spacious two-room suite. Rooms are decorated with soft pastels, lacy designer linens, and tasteful hand-painted furniture. The suite, with modern furnishings, also has a fireplace, whirlpool tub, TV–VCR, and refrigerator. Breakfast is family-style and includes granola, fresh muffins or homemade coffee cake, fruit, yogurt, and an entrée that might use herbs from the inn's gardens. Although the inn is not designed for small children, you can inquire about bringing older kids. **Pros:** Comfortable, intimate setting, good spot for exploring nearby towns along historic Route 6A, can arrange in-room spa treatments. **Cons:** Some rooms have tiny stall showers, rooms accessed via steep stairs. ⊠*4352 Main St. (Rte. 6A)* ✉*Box 256, Cummaquid 02637* ☎*508/362–3330 or 800/362–6363* 🖷*508/375–0304* ⊕*www. acworthinn.com* ⇄*4 rooms, 1 suite* ⚒*In-room: no phone, refrigerator (some), DVD (some), no TV (some), Wi-Fi. In-hotel: no kids under 12, no-smoking rooms, no elevator* ▱*AE, D, MC, V* ❛⊙❜*BP.*

$$–$$$ 🏨**Ashley Manor.** Set behind hedges and a wide lawn, this B&B is a short walk from the village center. The 1699 inn has preserved its antique wide-board floors and has open-hearth fireplaces (one with a beehive oven) in the living room, the dining room, and the keeping room. The rooms are toasty, too—all but one have working fireplaces, and the suites have whirlpool tubs. Antique and country furnishings, Oriental rugs, and glimmers of brass and crystal create an elegant feel. Breakfast is served on the backyard terrace or in the formal dining room. **Pros:** Less than 1 mi to restaurants and shops of Barnstable Village, spacious, authentically decorated rooms, working fireplaces for cooler nights, in-room spa treatments available. **Cons:** Rooms are on 2nd floor, accessed via very steep stairs. ⊠*3660 Main St. (Rte. 6A), Box 856, 02630* ☎*508/362–8044 or 888/535–2246* ⊕*www. ashleymanor.net* ⇄*2 rooms, 4 suites* ⚒*In-room: DVD, Wi-Fi. In-hotel: tennis court, no kids under 14, no-smoking rooms, no elevator* ▱*AE, D, MC, V* ❛⊙❜*BP.*

$$–$$$
Fodor'sChoice
★
🏨**Honeysuckle Hill.** Innkeepers Freddy and Ruth Riley provide plenty of little touches here: a guest fridge stocked with beverages (including wine and beer), beach chairs with umbrellas (perfect for nearby Sandy Neck Beach), and an always-full cookie jar. Additional indulgences include the self-serve liquor and cordial trays in the parlor. Guests are often seen carrying their evening cocktails to the gazebo for a game of cards. The airy, country-style guest rooms in this 1810 Queen Anne–style cottage have lots of white wicker, featherbeds, checked curtains,

and pastel-painted floors. The spacious 2nd-floor Wisteria Room overlooking the lush yard is a particularly comfortable retreat, and the screened-in porch is a peaceful place to sip early-morning coffee. **Pros:** Gracious and generous innkeepers, lush gardens on the grounds, tasteful, large rooms, very short drive to Sandy Neck Beach. **Cons:** Most rooms are accessed via steep stairs. ⊠*591 Main St. (Rte. 6A), West Barnstable 02668* ☎*508/362–8418 or 866/444–5522* ⊟*508/362–8386* ⊕*www.honeysucklehill.com* ⤴*4 rooms, 1 suite* ⚙*In-room: no phone, VCR (some). In-hotel: bicycles, hot tub, no kids under 12, no-smoking rooms, no elevator* ▤*AE, MC, V* ⦿*BP.*

$–$$$ 🖼**Lamb and Lion Inn.** Lamb and Lion occupies a 1740 farmhouse and barn, as well as several additions, with rooms and suites gathered around a courtyard and large swimming pool. Inside, some rooms are summery, with blue-and-white-stripe wallpaper and wicker chairs, while others are more staid, furnished with antiques and dark woods. The Innkeeper's Pride Suite has a fireplace and Jacuzzi tub that opens to a private deck; the rustic Barn-Stable, in the original barn, has three sleeping lofts that can accommodate six. Amenities include pickups and drop-offs from local ferries and the Barnstable Municipal Airport. **Pros:** Convenient location for area exploring, island ferry drop-offs a real bonus. **Cons:** Not for those looking or an in-town location or the antique-home experience. ⊠*2504 Main St. (Rte. 6A), Box 511, Barnstable 02630* ☎*508/362–6823 or 800/909–6923* ⊟*508/362–0227* ⊕*www.lambandlion.com* ⤴*4 rooms, 6 suites* ⚙*In-room: DVD, kitchen (some). In-hotel: pool, airport shuttle, some pets allowed (fee), no elevator* ▤*MC, V* ⦿*CP.*

$$ 🖼**Beechwood Inn.** Debbie and Ken Traugot's yellow-and-pale-green
★ 1853 Queen Anne house has gingerbread trim and is wrapped by a wide porch with wicker furniture and a glider swing. Named for the property's two magnificent and aged beech trees (one grand weeping, the other copper), the inn emphasizes its Victorian splendor. Although the parlor is pure mahogany-and-red-velvet Victorian, guest rooms (all with queen- or king-size beds) have antiques in lighter Victorian styles; several have fireplaces, and one has a bay view. Bathrooms have pedestal sinks and antique lighting fixtures. Breakfast is served in the dining room, which has a pressed-tin ceiling, a fireplace, and lace-covered tables. Afternoon tea and homemade snacks are also available. **Pros:** Exquisite lodging in historic Victorian, spacious rooms, choose from seven different beaches within a 5-mi radius. **Cons:** Most rooms accessed via narrow, curved stairs. ⊠*2839 Main St. (Rte. 6A), 02630* ☎*508/362–6618 or 800/609–6618* ⊟*508/362–0298* ⊕*www.beechwoodinn.com* ⤴*6 rooms* ⚙*In-room: no phone, refrigerator. In-hotel: bicycles, no kids under 12, no-smoking rooms, no elevator* ▤*AE, D, MC, V* ⦿*BP.*

$$ 🖼**The Highpointe Inn.** Debbie and Rich Howard's intimate haven is nes-
Fodor's Choice tled high on a hill overlooking dunes, the Great Salt Marsh, and the
★ Bay at Sandy Neck. Although it's just minutes from historic Route 6A, the light and airy B&B transports you to a dreamlike getaway, offering casual luxury at its best. Each of the inn's three rooms inspire serenity with comforting colors, decor, and magical views. Breakfast offers a

choice of five hot entrées and may include Rich's famed French toast and Debbie's homemade goodies. **Pros:** Immaculate and sophisticated lodging, can arrange for in-room spa services, serene and private setting. **Cons:** Not for those looking for a busy, in-town location or lodging in an antique home. ⊠ *70 High St.* ⌂ *Box 346, West Barnstable 02668* ☎ *508/362–4441 or 888/362–4441* 🖷 *508/362–4401* ⊕ *www.thehighpointeinn.com* ⇆ *3 rooms* ⚇ *In-room: no phone, DVD, refrigerator, Wi-Fi. In-hotel: gym, no kids under 12, no-smoking rooms, no elevator* ☐ *AE, D, MC, V* ⧖ *BP.*

CENTERVILLE, COTUIT & OSTERVILLE
$$$–$$$$

✕ **Five Bays Bistro.** With its stylish feel and creative menu, this contemporary bistro wouldn't be out of place in Boston or Manhattan. Dishes such as Asian spring rolls or tuna with wasabi sauce draw inspiration from the East, whereas others—perhaps a linguine, duck, and artichoke appetizer or an entrée of seared halibut with shallot risotto—have a more Mediterranean flavor. If you wear black, you won't clash with the eclectic artwork on the bright yellow walls. ⊠ *825 Main St., Osterville* ☎ *508/420–5559* ⊕ *www.fivebaysbistro.com* ☐ *AE, D, MC, V* ⊙ *No lunch.*

$$$–$$$$
Fodor's Choice
★

✕ **Regatta of Cotuit.** It's worth driving out of your way to this refined restaurant in a handsomely restored cinnamon-hued stagecoach inn filled with wood, brass, and Oriental rugs. Chef Heather Allen turns out wonderfully inventive versions of classic regional American fare, such as foie gras and scallops with a port-wine reduction and tropical-fruit chutney. The signature premium fillet of buffalo tenderloin is prepared differently each night, with seasonal starches and vegetables. The cozy taproom has its own bar menu, including globally influenced tapas (Cambodian spring rolls, Spanish-style duck empanadas) and colorful cocktails (prickly pear margaritas, apple martinis). ⊠ *4631 Falmouth Rd. (Rte. 28), Cotuit* ☎ *508/428–5715* ⊕ *www.regattaofcotuit.com* ⚇ *Reservations essential* ☐ *AE, MC, V.*

$–$$

✕ **Wimpy's.** No, this is not a fast-food hamburger joint—it's a Cape standby with an extensive menu that favors Italian food and fried fish, from chicken piccata to a seafood platter. Wimpy's loyal clientele fills a big family dining room, a sunny atrium, and a dark traditional tavern that has cozy booths and a fine old bar. Opt for the more inventive specials, such as tortilla-crusted salmon topped in a caper sauce, or try a simple prime rib (when available). You can get takeout here, too. ⊠ *752 Main St., Osterville* ☎ *508/428–6300, 508/428–3474 takeout* ☐ *AE, DC, MC, V.*

¢–$
★

✕ **Sweet Tomatoes.** Don't be put off by the prosaic setting of this small pizza place (it's in a shopping center behind Wimpy's). Sweet Tomatoes serves absolutely tantalizing pizza made with whole-wheat dough, plus a slew of calzones, panini sandwiches, grinders, and wraps, all with fresh, creative ingredients. Top picks among the pies include the Dirty Bomb, with shaved steak, portobello mushrooms, onions, peppers, mozzarella, and red sauce; and the tangy white three-cheese with mozzarella, ricotta, asiago, and garlic (try ordering it with anchovies for a little extra kick). The Mediterranean salad makes for a delicious starter. ⊠ *770 Main St., Osterville* ☎ *508/420–1717* ☐ *MC, V.*

$$ 🖭 **Centerville Corners Motor Lodge.** One of the few mid-Cape motels that's not on a traffic-choked, crassly developed road, this attractive redbrick and shingled motor lodge is in the heart of peaceful Centerville Village, facing the wonderful Four Seas Ice Cream parlor. Although the rooms are dull and the furnishings are dated, you can't beat the location. Golf packages are available. **Pros:** Good location; about ½ mi to Craigville Beach, affordable, off-season golf packages. **Cons:** Outdated decor, most rooms have a view of the parking lot. ⊠ *1338 Craigville Beach Rd., Centerville* 🖃 *Box 507, 02632* 🕾 *508/775–7223 or 800/242–1137* 🖷 *508/775–4147* ⊕ *www.centervillecorners.com* ⇥ *48 rooms* 🖒 *In-room: kitchen (some), Wi-Fi. In-hotel: pool, no-smoking rooms, some pets allowed (fee), no elevator* ⊟ *AE, D, MC, V* ☉ *Closed Nov.–Apr.* ⧍*CP.*

$$ 🖭 **Josiah Sampson House.** Guest rooms in this stunning 1793 Federal-style home near Cotuit's tranquil (and diminutive) village center have canopy beds, needlepoint rugs, antiques, and air-conditioning. Hannah's Room, the most spacious, has a queen-size four-poster bed and built-in window seats. The Sampson Room has an extra-large bathroom and a view of the backyard and handsome grounds. Tennis privileges ($8 for 1½ hours) are available at the Kings Grant Racquet Club next door. **Pros:** Very quiet and pastoral setting yet near Route 28, proximity to area beaches and Cape Cod Baseball League games. **Cons:** Not an in-town location, though a good base to explore area, one room's bathroom is a short walk down the hall. ⊠ *40 Old Kings Rd., off Main St., Cotuit* 🕾 *508/428–8383* ⊕ *www.josiahsampson.com* ⇥ *6 rooms* 🖒 *In-room: no phone, no TV. In-hotel: bicycles, no kids under 12, no-smoking rooms, no elevator* ⊟ *AE, MC, V* ⧍*BP.*

HYANNIS
$$–$$$$
★ ✕ **The Paddock.** The Paddock is synonymous with tried-and-true formal dining on the Cape. Sumptuous upholstery in the main dining room and old-style wicker on the breezy summer porch create authentic Victorian ambience. The menu is traditional yet subtly innovative, and fresh ingredients are combined in novel ways: baked thyme-and-cranberry encrusted sole with a citrus beurre blanc, for example. The steak au poivre, with several varieties of crushed peppercorns, is masterful; the fire-roasted salmon comes with black-bean chili and mango salsa. ⊠ *20 Scudder Ave., West End* 🕾 *508/775–7677* ⊕ *www.paddockcapecod.com* ⊟ *AE, DC, MC, V* ☉ *Closed mid-Nov.–Mar.*

$$–$$$$
★ ✕ **Roadhouse Café.** Candlelight flickers off the white-linen tablecloths and dark-wood wainscoting at the Roadhouse Café, a smart choice for a night out. Popular dishes include the roasted pepper-and-goat cheese appetizer and shrimp and basil pesto over linguine. In the more casual bistro and the mahogany bar, you can order from a separate menu, which includes thin-crust pizza as well as burgers and lighter fare. Listen to excellent straight-ahead jazz on Monday night year-round in the bistro. There's a piano bar the rest of the week from early July to early September and on Friday and Saturday in the off-season. ⊠ *488 South St., Downtown Hyannis* 🕾 *508/775–2386* ⊕ *www.roadhousecafe.com* ⧍ *Reservations essential* ⊟ *AE, D, MC, V* ☉ *No lunch.*

$$$
★ ✕ **Hannah Fusion Bar & Bistro.** Known and loved for its hip city atmosphere, intriguing and stylish drinks—ever had a saki martini?—and

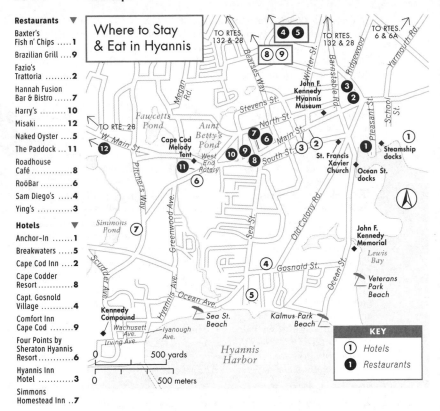

Where to Stay & Eat in Hyannis

artful blend of Far East and American flavors, this funky spot has staked a mightly claim on Main Street. There's an ample bar menu (half-price appetizers daily from 5 to 7) that tempts with everything from grilled-cheese pizza to edamame. For dinner, favorites include the Mongolian coffee-encrusted pork tenderloin or, for seafood lovers, the Thai seafood bouillabaisse, a combination of shrimp, scallops, calamari, fish, and mussels served over homemade pasta. A lively bar crowd lingers long after the kitchen closes. ⊠*615 Main St., Downtown Hyannis* ☎*508/778–5565* ⊕*www.hannahsbistro.com* ☰*AE, DC, MC, V* ⊘*No lunch.*

$$–$$$ ✕**Naked Oyster.** The big draw at this dapper restaurant with dark-
Fodor'sChoice wood-paneled walls and soft lighting is the extensive list of weekly
★ changing specials, which truly show off the kitchen's estimable talents. You'll always find several raw and "dressed" oyster dishes (such as barbecue oysters on the half shell with blue cheese, caramelized onions, and bacon) plus a nice range of salads and appetizers. Among the main dishes, consider the superb sliced duck breast with a port-wine and Rainier cherry sauce, or the sautéed shrimp in a piquant Thai peanut-cashew sauce over noodles. The oyster stew is also out of this world.

3

✉ *20 Independence Dr., off Rte. 132* ☎ *508/778–6500* 🍴*AE, D, DC, MC, V* ⊗ *No lunch weekends.*

$–$$$ ✗**Misaki.** Tucked away on quiet West Main Street, frantically popular Misaki serves authentic Japanese food in an intimate space with tables arranged closely together. The menu has a diverse array of traditional Japanese dishes, such as vegetable tempura, yaki soba, and chicken or beef teriyaki, but the sushi and sashimi—prepared by an experienced master sushi chef—are the real stars here. Try the tuna rolls, which are delectably soft and silky. Two traditional Japanese "sitting booths" are available by reservation. ✉ *379 W. Main St.* ☎ *508/771–3771* 🍴*AE, MC, V.*

$–$$$ ✗**RoöBar.** A bit of Manhattan on Main Street, RoöBar has a dark, sophisticated feel, with good music, low light, and a hip bar scene. A wood-fired oven produces "hand-spun to order" pizzas, such as Thai chicken with coconut-curry sauce. Other world-beat choices include shrimp and scallops with sweet-and-spicy Meyer lemon and crème fraîche sauce and cinnamon-raisin croutons. The owner is a member of the late actor Christopher Reeve's family, and a portion of all profits goes to the Christopher Reeve Foundation for Spinal Cord Research. ✉ *586 Main St., Downtown Hyannis* ☎ *508/778–6515* ⊕ *www.theroobar.com* 🍴*AE, MC, V* ⊗ *Closed Mon. in off-season. No lunch.*

¢–$$$ ✗**Baxter's Fish 'n' Chips.** Since fried seafood is a Cape staple, you may want to pay homage to one of the best Fry-o-lators around. Right on Hyannis Harbor, it's been a favorite of boaters and bathers alike since 1955. Generous portions of fried clams are delicious and cooked hot to order. The picnic tables outside, some set up on an old floating ferry, allow you to catch some rays while enjoying lobster, fish-and-chips, or something from the raw bar. If the weather's not on your side, there's indoor seating overlooking the harbor. A passageway off the dining room leads to Baxter's Boat House Club, a slightly more upscale space that has the same menu. ✉ *Pleasant St., Hyannis Harbor* ☎ *508/775–4490* ⊕ *www.baxterscapecod.com* ⌖*Reservations not accepted* 🍴*AE, DC, MC, V* ⊗ *Closed mid-Oct.–Apr. and weekdays early Sept.–mid-Oct.*

¢–$$$ ✗**Harry's.** This lovably divey-looking place serves up sizable portions of Cajun and creole dishes with great spices. The menu includes a number of meal-size sandwiches and burgers as well as blackened local fish that's done to perfection. The jambalaya will make you wonder if there's a bayou nearby. It's also a prime location for music: you can hear blues, zydeco, and folk music nightly year-round. ✉ *700 Main St., West End* ☎ *508/778–4188* ⊕ *www.harrysbluesbar.com* ⌖*Reservations not accepted* 🍴*AE, DC, MC, V.*

$–$$ ✗**Fazio's Trattoria.** Set in an old Italian-bakery building, swank but ★ affordable Fazio's looks like the trattoria it is, with wood floors, high ceilings, and a deli case full of fresh pasta, breads, and cheeses. There's also an espresso and cappuccino bar. Chef Tom Fazio's menu leans on fresh ingredients and herbed pastas, such as basil fettuccine with shrimp, lemon, and plum tomatoes. All ravioli, pastas, and breads are homemade, and the brick-oven pizzas are delicious. Take home some fresh cannoli for dessert. ⊠ *294 Main St., Downtown Hyannis* ☎ *508/775–9400* ⊕ *www.fazio.net* ▭ *AE, MC, V* ⊘ *No lunch.*

$–$$ ✗**Sam Diego's.** The bar has a busy social scene, and the menu has satisfying—if predictable—Tex-Mex burritos, enchiladas, and fajitas. Crispy deep-fried ice cream served in a giant goblet is a house favorite; the margaritas, which come in several flavors, are another crowd-pleaser. The prop-shop furnishings may be a little cheesy—sombreros, Aztec birds, and the like—but the place is fun, friendly, and popular with families. Weekday lunch options include an all-you-can-eat chili and taco bar, and dinner is served nightly until midnight. ⊠ *950 Iyanough Rd. (Rte. 132)* ☎ *508/771–8816* ⊕ *www.samdiegos.com* ▭ *AE, D, MC, V.*

¢–$$ ✗**Brazilian Grill.** The Cape has a large Brazilian population, and you
Fodor's Choice   can find many of these residents, plus plenty of satisfied visitors, at
★   this all-you-can-eat *churrascaria* (Brazilian barbecue). Waiters circulate through the dining room offering more than a dozen grilled meats—beef, pork, chicken, sausage, even quail—on long swordlike skewers. You can help yourself to a buffet of salads and side dishes, including *farofa* (a couscouslike dish made of manioc [also known as cassava or yuca]), plantains, rice, and beans. The atmosphere is often loud and jovial. For dessert, the homemade flan is the best anywhere. Dine on the redbrick patio in warm weather. ⊠ *680 Main St., West End* ☎ *508/771–0109* ▭ *AE, D, DC, MC, V.*

¢–$$ ✗**Ying's.** The huge menu at this little pan-Asian place presents Thai, Korean, and Japanese cuisines. Ying's sushi and sashimi combos are artful, and its many curried Thai seafood, noodle, and fried-rice dishes range from spicy to, well, really spicy. For something different, try the Korean *bibimbap* (vegetables, beef, and egg on rice with hot sauce). Tables are set up by the windows, and there's a sushi bar and a small lounge area with a selection of Asian beers. Try the sweet and thick Thai iced tea—you won't need dessert (but if you do, the fried ice cream is a treat). For more American-style food (as well as some Asian specialties) and nightly entertainment, check out Ying's other restaurant, the **Blue Anchor Cafe,** at 453 Main Street. ⊠ *59 Center St., East End* ☎ *508/790–2432* ▭ *AE, MC, V.*

$$–$$$$ ▥**Capt. Gosnold Village.** An easy walk from Kalmus Beach and town,
★   this peaceful, low-key colony of motel rooms and pink-shutter cottages is ideal for families. Kids can ride their bikes around the quiet street, and the pool is fenced in and watched over by a lifeguard. In some rooms, walls are attractively paneled with painted pine; floors are carpeted, and simple furnishings are colonial or modern. All cottages have decks and gas grills and receive maid service. Choose from efficiency units or one- to three-bedroom cottages. The cottages aren't air-conditioned, but you can rent an air-conditioning unit. **Pros:** A good bet for families, short walk to nearby beach. **Cons:** Not quite an in-town location, no water views. ⊠ *230 Gosnold St., 02601* ☎ *508/775–9111* ⊕ *www.captaingosnold.com* ⇆ *23 units* ⬡ *In-room: no a/c, kitchen (some). In-hotel: pool, playground, no elevator* ▭ *MC, V* ⊘ *Closed Nov.–mid-Apr.*

$$–$$$$ ⊡Four Points by Sheraton Hyannis Resort. As chains go, it's hard to beat this low-slung compound, with its beautiful grounds, extensive services, and superior resort facilities, including a popular golf course open to the public and a top-notch spa. The lobby is elegant; the rooms, if unremarkable in decor, feature private balconies or patios and particularly comfortable mattresses. Far from traffic and close to downtown and the water, Four Points has the best locale of any Hyannis chain property. **Pros:** Ideal for those who prefer the amenities of dependable chain hotels, easy access to bustle of downtown. **Cons:** Not for those seeking a regional lodging experience. ⊠*35 Scudder Ave., West End rotary, 02601* ☎*508/775–7775 or 800/325–3535* 🖷*508/778–6039* ⊕*www. sheraton.com* ⊲*224 rooms* ♿*In-room: VCR, dial-up. In-hotel: restaurant, room service, bar, golf course, tennis courts, pools, gym, spa* ▤*AE, D, DC, MC, V.*

$$–$$$ ⊡Anchor-In. Most rooms at this pale-green motel on the north end of Hyannis Harbor have harbor views and small balconies overlooking the water. Its simple street-side appearance belies its spacious accommodations and extensive grounds. Recent and continual upgrades to the rooms have enhanced the quality factor with down comforters, terry robes, triple sheets, king-size beds, and flat-screen televisions. Some rooms have refrigerators, and the larger deluxe and executive rooms have wraparound porches. Lisa and Skip Simpson deliver the warm, personal service of a small B&B. Ferries to Nantucket and Martha's Vineyard are just around the corner. **Pros:** Easy walk to downtown activity, island ferry terminals, and several waterfront restaurants, great harbor views from many rooms. **Cons:** 2nd-floor rooms accessed via stairways. ⊠*1 South St., 02601* ☎*508/775–0357* 🖷*508/775–1313* ⊕*www.anchorin.com* ⊲*43 rooms* ♿*In-room: refrigerator (some), DVD (some), Wi-Fi. In-hotel: pool, no elevator* ▤*AE, D, MC, V* ⊚|*CP.*

$$–$$$ ⊡Cape Codder Resort. Don't let the kids spy the indoor wave pool here—a fantasy of waves, waterfalls, and waterslides—or you'll never get out to see anything else on the Cape. Although it's sct on an unattractive stretch of Route 132, this sprawling, family-friendly compound has quite a few amenities, including an excellent spa. Rooms range from basic to more elaborate—the Cape Codder rooms are more upscale than the standard "deluxe" ones. The best rooms face the inner courtyard, overlooking the lawn or the "beach" (a stretch of sand that's used for seasonal clambakes). The suites are huge; several have spiral staircases that lead up to a sleeping loft. Note that the hotel is sometimes packed with conventioneers and that there's no conventional pool for swimming, apart from the kid-oriented wave pool. **Pros:** Good for those seeking a larger resort with many amenities for kids and adults, close to downtown, restaurants, and shopping. **Cons:** Not the place for peaceful poolside contemplation, not for those looking for a regional lodging experience. ⊠*1225 Iyanough Rd. (Rte. 132), 02601* ☎*508/771–3000 or 888/297–2200* 🖷*508/771–6564* ⊕*www. capecodderresort.com* ⊲*252 rooms, 8 suites* ♿*In-room: Wi-Fi. In-hotel: 2 restaurants, room service, bar, gym, playground, tennis court, spa* ▤*AE, D, DC, MC, V.*

$$–$$$ 🏨 **Simmons Homestead Inn.** At this 1820 former sea captain's estate, each room in the main house or the detached barn is named for an animal and decorated (somewhat excessively) accordingly. This offbeat and casual inn has rooms with antique, wicker, or canopied four-poster beds topped with brightly colored quilts; some have fireplaces, and some, such as the large, cheery Bird Room, have private decks. You can borrow 10-speed mountain bikes, and Simmons Pond is a short jaunt on the property's trail. Gregarious innkeeper Bill Putman encourages you to return each evening for a wine-and-socializing hour. He'll also be happy to show you his collection of nearly 60 vintage cars or his roughly 500 vintages of single-malt Scotch. About three dozen friendly cats roam about the property. **Pros:** Good place for people with pets, ample grounds and pond on the property, socializing among guests greatly encouraged with happy hours, great car collection. **Cons:** If you're not a cat lover, stay clear. ✉*288 Scudder Ave., Box 578, Hyannis Port 02647* ☎*508/778–4999 or 800/637–1649* 🖷*508/790–1342* ⊕*www.simmonshomesteadinn.com* ⬚*12 rooms, 2 suites* ♿*In-room: no a/c, no phone, no TV. In-hotel: bicycles, no-smoking rooms, some pets allowed (fee), no elevator* ⊟*AE, D, MC, V* ⦿|*BP.*

$$ 🏨 **Breakwaters.** These privately owned, weathered gray-shingle cottages rent by the week in summer (or nightly in spring and fall). It's a relaxed place, set on a quiet dead-end lane. Cottages are divided into one-, two-, and three-bedroom units and offer all the comforts of home. Each unit has one or two full baths; a kitchen with microwave, coffeemaker, refrigerator, toaster, and stove; TV and phone (local calls are free); and a deck or patio with a grill and picnic table. Most units have water views. An in-ground heated pool is less than 200 feet from the lifeguarded town beach on Nantucket Sound. Excluding Sunday, there is daily maid service. **Pros:** Excellent waterfront location, ideal for families and groups traveling together. **Cons:** Hard to reserve unless you're staying for a week; not the place for a quiet, private getaway (unless it's spring or fall). ✉*432 Sea St., Box 118, 02601* ☎🖷*508/775–6831* ⊕*www.thebreakwaters.com* ⬚*19 cottages* ♿*In-room: no a/c, kitchen. In-hotel: pool, beachfront, no-smoking rooms, no elevator* ⊟*No credit cards* ⊙*Closed mid-Oct.–Apr.*

$$ 🏨 **Comfort Inn Cape Cod.** All the rooms at this mid-range chain motel have white-oak-veneer furnishings and include one king-size or two double beds, a table and chairs or a desk and chair, and a wardrobe. Some king rooms have sofa beds. The quietest rooms are on the top floor, facing the pond and woods; all have free HBO and Nintendo, and pets are allowed. Although the location is fairly convenient to U.S. 6, the Comfort Inn is a few miles north of downtown Hyannis up traffic-choked Route 132—it is quiet and set well back from the road, though. **Pros:** Good package deals for travelers looking for deals; not far from downtown shopping, restaurants, and activities; good for travelers who like the large chain-hotel experience. **Cons:** Set along busy, heavily trafficked road; no views or peaceful settings. ✉*1470 Rte. 132, 02601* ☎*508/771–4804, 800/228–5150 reservations* 🖷*508/790–2336* ⊕*www.comfortinn-hyannis.com* ⬚*103 rooms, 1 suite* ♿*In-room:*

Ethernet. In-hotel: pool, gym, no-smoking rooms, some pets allowed ⊟*AE, D, DC, MC, V* ⏺*CP.*

$–$$ ⏺**Hyannis Inn Motel.** The main building of this second-oldest motel in Hyannis, a modest two-story spread, served as press headquarters during JFK's presidential campaign. Today, it's right in the heart of the downtown shopping and retail action. The main building's immaculate rooms have double, queen-size, or king-size beds; some have whirlpool tubs. Other deluxe rooms in a separate wing out back—are larger, sunnier, and quieter (they don't face Main Street) and have queen- or king-size beds, sleeper sofas, walk-in closets, and refrigerators. The restaurant serves breakfast only. **Pros:** Great for those who want to leave their cars and be right in the thick of downtown, spacious rooms (those in the separate wing are especially suited for families), nice outside sun decks for relaxing. **Cons:** Not a beachfront spot or one with water views, not for those who are seeking a more peaceful, countryside setting. ✉*473 Main St., 02601* ☎*508/775–0255 or 800/922–8993* 🖨*508/771–0456* ⊕*www.hyannisinn.com* 🛏*77 rooms* ⚐*In-room: refrigerator (some), dial-up. In-hotel: restaurant, bar, pool, no elevator* ⊟*AE, D, MC, V* ☉*Closed early Nov.–Feb.*

¢–$$ ⏺**Cape Cod Inn.** This centrally located inn on downtown Main Street is within walking distance of all of Hyannis's major sights. The no-frills rooms have large double beds; most, unfortunately, have views of a drab parking lot. The inn is attached to the Duck Inn Pub, a popular local hangout where breakfast is served. **Pros:** Right in the midst of downtown action, good spot for families (there's even a bowling alley next door), very reasonable rates. **Cons:** Not the place for a serene getaway, less than ideal views. ✉*447 Main St., 02601* ☎*508/775–3000* 🖨*508/771–1457* ⊕*www.capecodinnhyannis.com* 🛏*37 rooms, 3 suites* ⚐*In-room: Wi-Fi. In-hotel: restaurant, bar, pool, no elevator* ⊟*AE, D, MC, V* ⏺*CP.*

NIGHTLIFE & THE ARTS

THE ARTS The **Boston Pops Esplanade Orchestra** (☎*508/362–0066* ⊕*www.arts-foundationcapecod.org*) wows the crowd with its annual Pops by the Sea concert, held in August at the Hyannis Village Green. Each year a celebrity guest conductor strikes up the band for a few selected numbers; past baton bouncers have included Olympia Dukakis, Joan Kennedy, Mike Wallace, Art Buchwald, Maya Angelou, and Sebastian Junger.

In 1950 actress Gertrude Lawrence and her husband, producer-manager Richard Aldrich, opened the **Cape Cod Melody Tent** (✉*21 W. Main St., at West End rotary, Hyannis* ☎*508/775–5630, 800/347–0808 for tickets* ⊕*www.melodytent.com*) to showcase Broadway musicals and concerts. Today it's the Cape's top venue for pop concerts and comedy shows; performers who have played here, in the round, include the Indigo Girls; Lyle Lovett; Tony Bennett; Bill Cosby; and Crosby, Stills & Nash. The Tent also holds an 11 AM Wednesday children's theater series in July and August.

The 90-member **Cape Cod Symphony Orchestra,** under former D'Oyly Carte Opera conductor Royston Nash, gives regular classical and children's concerts with guest artists September through May. Performances are held at the Barnstable Performing Arts Center at **Barnstable High School** (⊠*744 W. Main St., Hyannis* ☎*508/362–1111* ⊕*www. capesymphony.org*).

Opera New England of Cape Cod (☎*508/398–1068* ⊕*www.capecodopera.org*) hosts two or three performances a year, in spring and fall, by the National Lyric Opera Company.

In July and August **town-band concerts** (☎*508/362–5230 or 877/492–6647*) are held on Wednesday evening at 7:30 on the Town Green on Main Street, Hyannis.

NIGHTLIFE   Hyannis is Barnstable's nightlife hub, with more than a dozen popular bars and taverns, most of them along Main Street in the heart of downtown. Elsewhere in this otherwise lightly developed town, bars and clubs are few and far between.

The **Barnstable Comedy Club** (⊠*Village Hall, Rte. 6A, Barnstable* ☎*508/362–6333* ⊕*www.barnstablecomedyclub.com*), the Cape's oldest amateur theater group (it was founded in the 1920s), gives much-praised musical and dramatic performances throughout the year. Folks who appeared here before they made it big include Geena Davis, Frances McDormand, and Kurt Vonnegut, a past president of the BCC.

The **British Beer Company** (⊠*412 Main St., Hyannis* ☎*508/771–1776* ⊕*www.britishbeer.com*) has a hearty selection of beers, from stouts to pilsners; most nights there's also live entertainment—usually local rock bands. The BBC also has branches on the Cape in Sandwich and Falmouth.

Bud's Country Lounge (⊠*3 Bearses Way, at Rte. 132, Hyannis* ☎*508/771–2505*) has pool tables and live music, dancing, and karaoke year-round.

Club 477/Mallory Dock (⊠*477 Yarmouth Rd., Hyannis* ☎*508/771–7511*), in the old Hyannis train station, is the Cape's only gay club outside Provincetown. There's a piano bar on the lower level and a dance bar on the upper floor with music almost as hot as the crowd.

The **Comedy Lounge** (⊠*Radisson Hotel Hyannis, Rte. 28, Hyannis* ☎*508/771–1700*), despite its location in a ubiquitous chain hotel, pulls in top comedy acts from throughout the Northeast. Shows are held Thursday through Saturday in summer; weekends only otherwise.

★   **Harry's Blues Bar** (⊠*700 Main St., Hyannis* ☎*508/778–4188* ⊕*www. harrysbluesbar.com*) is hopping nearly every night year-round, drawing blues lovers of all ages. Expect to see 21-year-olds and 70-year-olds dancing up a sweat side by side. Owner Laddie Durham fills the creole joint with crowd-pleasing bands and top-notch hospitality. In summer, crowds spill over from inside onto the two decks.

The **Island Merchant** (⊠*10 Ocean St., Hyannis* ☎*508/771–1337*) showcases a fine range of acoustic, blues, jazz, and rock—even spoken-word performers. The high-octane java keeps the joint jumpin'.

Pufferbellies (✉ *183 Rte. 28, Hyannis* ☎ *508/790–4300 or 800/233–4301*), in an old railroad roundhouse by the Hyannis tracks, is the Mid Cape's largest dance club, with several dance floors of swing, country line dancing, and DJ tunes, as well as eats, Internet terminals, and even volleyball courts.

★ After dinner, **RoöBar** (✉ *586 Main St., Hyannis* ☎ *508/778–6515* ⊕ *www.theroobar.com*) turns up the music and morphs into *the* place to see and be seen on Cape Cod. The Manhattan-esque haunt draws large crowds of attractive twenty- and thirtysomethings; expect to see lines of people out the door in summer. Personable bartenders and staff boost the already lively atmosphere.

SPORTS & THE OUTDOORS

BASEBALL The **Cotuit Kettleers** of the collegiate Cape Cod Baseball League play home games at **Lowell Park** (✉ *Lowell St., 2 mi south of Rte. 28, Cotuit* ☎ *508/428–3358* ⊕ *www.kettleers.org*) from mid-June to mid-August.

The **Hyannis Mets** (☎ *508/420–0962* ⊕ *www.hyannismets.org*) of the collegiate Cape Cod Baseball League play home games at **McKeon Field** (✉ *High School Rd., Downtown Hyannis*) from mid-June to mid-August.

BEACHES ■**TIP**➔ Daily parking fees at Barnstable beaches are $15 in season.

Hovering above Barnstable Harbor and the 4,000-acre Great Salt Marsh, **Sandy Neck Beach** stretches some 6 mi across a peninsula that ends at Sandy Neck Light. The beach is one of the Cape's most beautiful—dunes, sand, and sea spread endlessly east, west, and north. The marsh used to be harvested for salt hay; now it's a haven for birds, which are out and about in the greatest numbers in morning and evening, during low tide, and during spring and fall migrations. The lighthouse, standing a few feet from the eroding shoreline at the tip of the neck, has been out of commission since 1952. It was built in 1857 to replace an 1827 light, and it used to run on acetylene gas. It's now privately owned and no longer accessible from the beach. If you like to hike, ask at the ranger station for a trail brochure. The main beach at Sandy Neck has lifeguards, a snack bar, restrooms, and showers. As you travel east along Route 6A from Sandwich, Sandy Neck Road is just *before* the Barnstable line, although the beach itself is in West Barnstable. ✉ *Sandy Neck Rd., West Barnstable* ☉ *Daily 8 AM–9 PM, but staffed only until 5 PM.*

Hathaway's Pond (✉ *Off Phinney's La., Barnstable*) is a freshwater pond with a beach, restrooms, and a lifeguard (in season).

Craigville Beach, on Craigville Beach Road in Centerville, is a long, wide strand that is extremely popular with the collegiate crowd. The beach has lifeguards, showers, and restrooms, and there's food nearby.

Kalmus Park Beach, at the south end of Ocean Street in Hyannis, is a fine, wide sandy beach with an area set aside for windsurfers and a sheltered area that's good for kids. It has a snack bar, restrooms, showers, and lifeguards.

Also in Hyannis, **Veterans Park**, next to the John F. Kennedy Memorial on Ocean Street, has a small beach that's especially good for kids; it's sheltered from waves and fairly shallow. There are picnic tables, barbecue facilities, showers, and restrooms.

BICYCLING **Cascade Motor Lodge** (⊠ *201 Main St., Downtown Hyannis* ☎ *508/775–9717*), near the bus and train station, rents three-speed and mountain bikes by the half day, full day, and week.

BOATING **Eastern Mountain Sports** (⊠ *1513 Rte. 132, Hyannis* ☎ *508/362–8690*) rents kayaks, a variety of bicycles, and camping gear.

The catboat *Eventide* (⊠ *Ocean St. Dock, Hyannis* ☎ *508/775–0222 or 800/308–1837* ⊕ *www.catboat.com*) sails in Hyannis Harbor and out into Nantucket Sound on several one- and two-hour cruises; options include a nature tour and a sunset cruise.

Hy-Line (⊠ *Ocean St. Dock, Hyannis* ☎ *508/790–0696* ⊕ *www.hy-linecruises.com*) offers cruises on reproductions of old-time Maine coastal steamers. The one-hour tours of Hyannis Harbor and Lewis Bay include a view of the Kennedy compound and other points of interest.

FISHING **Aquarius Charters Inc.** (⊠ *Barnstable Harbor* ☎ *508/362–9617* ⊕ *www.aquariussportfishing.com*) supplies all gear on its 35-foot boat and offers four-, six-, and eight-hour trips for up to six people to catch bass, blues, tuna, and shark. Reservations are recommended.

Hy-Line (⊠ *Ocean St. Dock, Hyannis* ☎ *508/790–0696* ⊕ *www.hy-linecruises.com*) leads fishing trips on a walk-on basis in spring and fall, but reservations are mandatory in summer.

GOLF **Four Points by Sheraton Hyannis Resort** (⊠ *35 Scudder Ave., Hyannis* ☎ *508/775–7775*) has a beautifully landscaped, challenging 18-hole, par-3 course called Twin Brooks; it's open to nonguests. You may bump into some famous faces; many performers from the Cape Cod Melody Tent tee off here while they're in town.

HEALTH & **Barnstable Fitness Center** (⊠ *55 Attucks La., Independence Park, off*
FITNESS CLUBS *Rte. 132, Hyannis* ☎ *508/771–7734*) has an indoor pool, two aerobics rooms, cardiovascular and free-weight equipment, and a full schedule of fitness, yoga, and pilates classes. Day passes and short-term memberships are available.

Hyannis Athletic Club (⊠ *Sheraton Hyannis Hotel, Scudder La., West End rotary, Hyannis* ☎ *508/862–2535*) has two outdoor tennis courts, a fitness club, and indoor and outdoor pools. Day- and short-term memberships are available.

HORSEBACK **Holly Hill Farm** (⊠ *240 Flint St., Marstons Mills* ☎ *508/428–2621*
RIDING ⊕ *www.hollyhillstable.com*) offers horseback-riding instruction and a day camp but no trail rides.

ICE-SKATING The **Joseph P. Kennedy Jr. Memorial Skating Rink** (✉*141 Bassett La., Hyannis* ☎*508/790–6345*), named for the late Kennedy scion and war hero, offers skating October through March, with special times reserved for teenagers, youngsters, and families; skate rentals are available.

WHALE-WATCHING On **Hyannis Whale Watcher Cruises** out of Barnstable Harbor, a naturalist narrator comments on whale sightings and the natural history of Cape Cod Bay. Trips last about four hours, and there are concessions on board. In July and August you can cruise at sunset, too. Reservations are recommended. ✉*Millway Marina, off Phinney's La., Barnstable* ☎*508/362–6088 or 888/942–5392* ⊕*www.whales.net* ✑*$35* ⊙*May–Oct.*

SHOPPING

Main Street in downtown Hyannis has gradually been gentrified in recent years and has become one of the top shopping destinations on the Cape, buzzing with several art galleries and antiques shops, numerous clothiers, and a slew of other, mostly independent, boutiques and gift emporia. You'll also find quite a few restaurants along this walkable stretch, including several cafés that are nice for a cup of coffee or a light snack.

Cape Cod Mall (✉*Between Rtes. 132 and 28, Hyannis* ☎*508/771–0200* ⊕*www.capecodmall.com*), the Cape's largest, has 120 mid- to upper-end mostly chain shops, including department stores such as Macy's and Sears; smaller anchor stores such as Marshalls, Barnes & Noble, and Best Buy; and a 12-screen movie complex.

Christmas Tree Shops (✉*655 Iyanough Rd. [Rte. 132], Hyannis* ☎*508/778–5521* ⊕*www.christmastreeshops.com*), a Cape mainstay, are a bargain shoppers' haven. Take home Cape souvenirs at a great discount along with just about anything you might need—or not need—to decorate your home. The Hyannis store is the largest on the Cape.

Maps of Antiquity (✉*1022 Main St. [Rte. 6A], West Barnstable* ☎*508/362–7169*) sells original and reproduction maps of Cape Cod, New England, and other parts of the world. Some date to the 1700s.

★ **Oak & Ivory** (✉*1112 Main St., Osterville* ☎*508/428–9425* ⊕*www.oakandivory.com*) specializes in Nantucket lightship baskets made on the premises, as well as gold miniature baskets and scrimshaw. China, gold jewelry, and other gifts round out the selection.

The handsome flagship **Puritan of Cape Cod** (✉*408 Main St., Hyannis* ☎*508/775–2400*) store carries upscale clothing brands, from North Face to Eileen Fisher and Ralph Lauren; they also sell outdoor gear. Service is great here, and they also have several other stores around the Cape.

The **Sow's Ear Antique Company** (⊠*4698 Falmouth Rd. [Rte. 28], Cotuit* ☎*508/428–4931*), in a late 1600s house next to the Cahoon Museum, specializes in folk art—dolls, ship models, wood carvings, antique quilts, and paintings.

West Barnstable Tables (⊠*2454 Meetinghouse Way [Rte. 149], West Barnstable* ☎*508/362–2676*) has exquisite handcrafted tables, chairs, chests, and other furniture made from the finest woods.

The decor changes seasonally at **Whippletree** (⊠*660 Main St. [Rte. 6A], West Barnstable* ☎*508/362–3320* ⊕*www.thewhippletree.com*), a 1779 barn where Christmas decorations and country gift items hang from the rafters year-round. Goods include German nutcrackers, from Prussian soldiers to Casanovas.

For stunning arts and crafts imported from Africa, check out **Zizini** (⊠*382 Main St., Hyannis* ☎*508/790–2109*), which carries colorful ceramic and bead necklaces, handwoven pocketbooks, carved wooden masks, and abstract soapstone carvings. The store operates on a fair-trade policy, helping to support artisans who create the goods.

YARMOUTH

Yarmouth Port is 3 mi east of Barnstable Village, West Yarmouth is 2 mi east of Hyannis.

Once known as Mattacheese, or "the planting lands," Yarmouth was settled in 1639 by farmers from the Plymouth Bay Colony. The town's northernmost village of **Yarmouth Port** wasn't established as a distinct village until 1829. By then the Cape had begun a thriving maritime industry, and men turned to the sea to make their fortunes. Many impressive sea captains' houses—some now B&Bs and museums—still line enchanting Route 6A and nearby side streets, and Yarmouth Port has some real old-time stores in town. A mile's drive north of Route 6A is the small but lovely Gray's Beach, where a boardwalk at Bass Hole stretches hundreds of feet over the wide marsh and the Callery-Darling conservation land trails loop through forest and marshland.

Ⓒ Visit the **Edward Gorey House Museum** to explore the eccentric illustrations and offbeat humor of the late acclaimed artist. The regularly changing exhibitions, arranged in the downstairs rooms of Gorey's former home, include drawings of his oddball characters and reveal the mysterious psyche of the sometimes dark but always playful illustrator. Kids enjoy the section of the house with interactive exhibits that promote Gorey's lifelong dedication to animal welfare. ⊠*8 Strawberry La., Yarmouth Port* ☎*508/362–3909* ⊕*www.edwardgoreyhouse.org* ☞*$5* ⊙*Mid-Apr. to mid-Dec., Thurs.–Sat. 11–4, Sun. noon–4; July and Aug., Wed.– Sat. 11–4, Sun. noon–4; call to confirm off-season hours; closed mid-Dec.–Mid. Apr.*

★ For a peek into the past, make a stop at **Hallet's,** a country drugstore preserved as it was in 1889 when it was opened by Thacher Hallet, the present owner's grandfather. Hallet served not only as druggist but also as postmaster and justice of the peace. Sit at a swivel stool at the all-marble soda fountain and order their secret-recipe ice-cream soda and, in season, an inexpensive breakfast or lunch. ⊠*139 Main St. (Rte. 6A), Yarmouth Port* 🕾*508/362–3362* ⊘*Apr.–mid-Nov.; call for hrs.*

Above Hallet's Store, the **Thacher Taylor Hallet Museum** displays photographs and memorabilia of Yarmouth Port and the Hallet family. ⊠*139 Main St. (Rte. 6A), Yarmouth Port* 🕾*508/362–3362* ⊠*Donations accepted for museum* ⊘*Apr.–mid-Nov.; call for hrs.*

WORD OF MOUTH

"Yarmouth Port is great. Go to Hallett's on 6A for breakfast or ice cream. The Dennis beaches along 6A are among the best on the Cape (West Dennis, Corporation, Cold Storage). You are pretty centrally located, so you have a lot of restaurant choices depending on your price range and interests."

–xxx123

The 1886 **Village Pump** (⊠*220 Rte. 6A, Yarmouth Port*), a black wrought-iron mechanism long used for drawing household water, is topped by a lantern and surrounded by ironwork with cutouts of birds and animals. In front is a stone trough that was used for watering horses. It's across from the Parnassus Book Service.

The 1696 **Old Yarmouth Inn** (⊠*Rte. 6A, near Summer St., Yarmouth Port* 🕾*508/362–9962*), near the village pump, is the Cape's oldest inn and a onetime stagecoach stop.

The **Botanical Trails of the Historical Society of Old Yarmouth,** behind the **post office** (⊠*231 Main St., Yarmouth Port*), consists of 50 acres of oak and pine woods and a pond, accented by blueberries, lady's slippers, Indian pipes, rhododendrons, and hollies. Stone markers and arrows point out the 2 mi of trails; you'll find trail maps in the gatehouse mailbox. Just beyond the historical society's trails, you can find **Kelley Chapel,** built in 1873 by a father for his daughter, who was grieving over the death of her child. An iron woodstove and a pump organ dominate the simple interior. ⊠*Off Rte. 6A* ⊠*$1 suggested donation* ⊘*Gatehouse July and Aug., daily 1–4. Trails during daylight hrs year-round.*

The 1780 **Winslow Crocker House** is an elegantly symmetrical two-story Georgian with 12-over-12 small-pane windows and rich paneling in every room. Crocker was a well-to-do trader and land speculator; after his death, his two sons built a wall dividing the house in half. The structure was moved here from West Barnstable in 1936 by Mary Thacher, who donated it—along with her collection of 17th- to 19th-century furniture, pewter, hooked rugs, and ceramics—to Historic New England (formerly the Society for the Preservation of New England Antiquities), which operates it as a museum. ⊠*250 Main St. (Rte. 6A), Yarmouth Port* 🕾*617/227–3956* ⊕*www.historicnewengland.org* ⊠*$5* ⊘*June–mid-Oct., 1st and 3rd Sat. of month, tours at 11, noon, 1, 2, 3, and 4.*

Built in 1840 onto an existing 1740 house for a sea captain in the China trade, the **Captain Bangs Hallet House** is a white Greek-revival building with a hitching post out front and a weeping beech in back. The house and its contents typify a 19th-century sea captain's home, with pieces of pewter, china, nautical equipment, antique toys, and clothing on display. The kitchen has the original 1740 brick beehive oven and butter churns. ✉*11 Strawberry La., off Rte. 6A, Yarmouth Port* 🕾*508/362–3021* 🖅*$3* 🕙*June–mid-Oct., Thurs.–Sun. 1–4, tours at 1, 2, and 3.*

Purchased in 1640 and established as a prosperous farm in the late 1700s, the **Taylor-Bray Farm** (✉*Bray Farm Rd., Yarmouth Port* 🕾*508/385–9407* 🌐*www.taylorbrayfarm.org*) is listed on the National Register of Historic Places. Now a working farm for educational purposes, it hosts special events, such as an annual sheep shearing and a craft fair. The public is welcome to take advantage of the farm's picnic tables, walking trails, and great views of the tidal marsh year-round from dawn to dusk. Call for more information.

For a scenic loop with little traffic, turn north off Route 6A in Yarmouth Port onto Church Street or Thacher Street, then left onto Thacher Shore Road. In fall this route is especially beautiful, with impressive stands of blazing-red burning bush. Wooded segments alternate with open views of the marsh. Keep bearing right, and at the WATER STREET sign, the dirt road on the right will bring you to a wide-open view of marshland as it meets the bay. Don't drive in too far, or you may get stuck. As you come out, a right turn will take you to **Keveney Bridge,** a one-lane wooden bridge over marshy Mill Pond, and back to Route 6A.

🕲 One of Yarmouth Port's most beautiful areas is Bass Hole, which
★ stretches from Homer's Dock Road to the salt marsh. **Bass Hole Boardwalk** (✉*Trail entrance on Center St. near Gray's Beach parking lot*) extends over a marshy creek; amid the salt marshes, vegetated wetlands, and upland woods meander the 2½-mi **Callery-Darling nature trails.** Gray's Beach is a little crescent of sand with still water good for kids—but don't go beyond the roped-in swimming area, the only section where the current isn't strong. At the end of the boardwalk, benches provide a place to relax and look out over abundant marsh life and, across the creek, the beautiful, sandy shores of Dennis's Chapin Beach. At low tide you can walk out on the flats for almost a mile. It's a far cry from the 18th century, when a harbor here was the site of a schooner shipyard.

About 4 mi south of Yarmouth Port and directly east of Hyannis, you'll find **West Yarmouth.** The commercial hub (and the major road through the community) is, for better or worse, Route 28—the part of the Cape people love to hate. As you pass through the area—probably very slowly in summer traffic—it's one motel, strip mall, nightclub, and miniature-golf course after another. In 1989, as *Cape Cod Life* magazine put it, "the town [began] to plant 350 trees in hopes that eventually the trees' leaves, like the fig leaf of Biblical lore, [would] cover the shame of unkempt overdevelopment." Regardless of the glut of tacky tourist traps, there are some interesting sights in the little villages along the way. So take Route 28 if you want to intersperse amusements with your sightseeing, because you really can amuse yourself to no end here. If you want to avoid this road entirely, a sensible option is to take speedy U.S. 6 to the exit nearest what you want to visit and then cut south across the interior. If you must travel the Route 28 area, take Buck Island Road, which runs north of and parallel to much of the busy route in West and South Yarmouth.

Yelverton Crowe settled the village of West Yarmouth in 1643 after acquiring the land from a Native American sachem. The deal they struck was that Crowe could have as much land as he could traverse in an hour in exchange for an "ox-chain, a copper kettle . . . and a few trinkets." The first settlers were farmers; when Central Wharf near Mill Creek was built in the 1830s, the town turned to more commercial ventures as it became headquarters for the growing packet service that ferried passengers from the Cape to Boston.

Listed on the National Register of Historic Places, the 1710 **Baxter Grist Mill,** by the shore of Mill Pond, is the only mill on Cape Cod powered by an inside water turbine; the others use either wind or paddle wheels. The mill was converted to the indoor metal turbine in 1860 due to the pond's low water level and the damage done to the wooden paddle wheel by winter freezes. The original metal turbine is displayed on the grounds, and a reproduction powers the restored mill. A videotape tells the mill's history. There are no scheduled hours or tours, but feel free to walk around the grounds. ⊠*Rte. 28, across from Baxter Ave., West Yarmouth* ☎*508/362–3021* ⊕*www.hsoy.org/ historic/baxtermill.htm.*

A unique and lovely walking trail, the **Yarmouth Boardwalk** (⊠*Off Meadowbrook La., West Yarmouth*), stretches through swamp and marsh and leads to the edge of pretty Swan Pond, which is ringed with woods. To get here, take Winslow Gray Road northeast from Route 28, turn right on Meadowbrook Lane, and take it to the end.

ↄ An entertaining, educational, and occasionally hokey stop for kids, **ZooQuarium** has sea-lion shows, a petting zoo with native wildlife, a touch-friendly tidal pool, wandering peacocks, aquariums, and educational programs, plus pony rides in summer. The Children's Discovery Center presents changing exhibits such as *What's the Buzz on Bees* and *What's for Lunch* (for which kids can prepare meals for animals). ⊠*674 Main St. (Rte. 28), West Yarmouth* ☎*508/775–8883* ⊕*www. zooquariumcapecod.net* ⊠*$10* ☽ *Mid-Feb.–June and Sept.–late Nov., daily 9:30–4; June–Aug., daily 9:30–5.*

NEED A BREAK?

Jerry's Seafood and Dairy Freeze (⊠ *654 Main St. [Rte. 28], West Yarmouth* ☎*508/775–9752*), open year-round, serves fried clams and onion rings, along with thick frappes (milk shakes), frozen yogurt, and soft-serve ice cream at good prices.

A few miles east of West Yarmouth, you'll reach its similarly exuberant sister village, **South Yarmouth.** Here you can find charter boats, a river cruise, and boat and kayak rentals, plus seafood restaurants and markets. Like West Yarmouth, South Yarmouth has a stretch of blight and overdevelopment on Route 28, but it also has some nice beaches that are good for families. For a good indication of what the town looked like in the late 19th century, take a drive down Pleasant Street and the Main Street section south of Route 28 to view old homes in the Federal and Greek-revival styles. This section along Bass River was once home to the village's elite businessmen, bankers, and sea merchants.

LAY OF THE LAND

Locals sometimes refer to South Yarmouth as Bass River, after the river that separates the village from West Dennis.

Adding to the pastoral aura of the area is the **Judah Baker Windmill**; the grounds here are pretty and peaceful. For a closer look, the windmill is open Tuesday and Thursday during summer.

South Yarmouth was once known as Quaker Village for the large numbers of Quakers who settled the area in the 1770s after a smallpox epidemic wiped out the local Native American population. The 1809 **Quaker Meeting House** is still open for services. Two separate entrance doors and the partition down the center were meant to divide the sexes. The adjacent cemetery has simple markers with no epitaphs, an expression of the Friends' belief that all are equal in God's eyes. Behind the cemetery is a circa-1830 one-room Quaker schoolhouse. ⊠ *58 N. Main St., South Yarmouth* ☎ *508/398–3773* ⊙ *Services Sun. at 10.*

☺ **Pirate's Cove** is the most elaborate of the Cape's many miniature-golf
★ setups, with a hill, a waterfall, a stream, and the 18-hole Blackbeard's Challenge course. ⊠ *728 Main St. (Rte. 28), South Yarmouth* ☎ *508/394–6200* ⊙ *July and Aug., daily 9 AM–11 PM; late Apr.–June, Sept., and Oct., most days 10–8, but call.*

☺ For rainy-day fun, **Ryan Family Amusements** offers video-game rooms, Skee-Ball, and bowling. There's a snack bar that serves pizza, sandwiches, and beer and wine. ⊠ *1067 Main St. (Rte. 28), South Yarmouth* ☎ *508/394–5644* ⊙ *Daily; hrs vary.*

WHERE TO STAY & EAT

SOUTH
YARMOUTH
$$–$$$$
★

✕**902 Main.** This unassuming spot sits on a prosaic stretch of Route 28, but you won't find any of the main drag's hustle and trendy commercialism in here. Acclaimed chef Gilbert Pepin and his wife, Kolleen, want you to slow down and savor the rituals and flavors of good food and good wine. The menu changes every six weeks or so but might feature wild Orleans mussels in a broth of fennel, saffron, and tomatoes, and roast rack of lamb with truffle-mashed potatoes, asparagus, spinach, and a port-wine reduction. The refined, elegant space is staffed by highly professional servers. ⊠ *902 Main St. (Rte. 28)* ☎ *508/398–9902* ⊕ *www.902main.com* ⊟ *AE, D, MC, V* ⊙ *Closed Mon. No lunch.*

$$–$$$

✕**The Skipper.** This classic Cape restaurant has been around since 1936. Sit downstairs in the nautical-theme main room or upstairs on the outside deck, which has terrific views of nearby Nantucket Sound. The kitchen turns out an appealing mix of fish and shellfish dishes, plus a handful of Italian specialties and landlubber options (such as Yankee pot roast and prime rib au jus). Try the seared chili-garlic scallops or the Thai coconut shrimp-and-chicken over rice. ⊠ *152 S. Shore*

Dr. ☎*508/394–7406* ⚑*Reservations not accepted* ▤*AE, D, MC, V* ⊘*Closed Nov.–mid-Apr.*

¢–$$ ✘**Ardeo.** Despite its unpromising location in a shopping plaza, this smart-casual Mediterranean bistro has built a local following for its pizzas, pastas, salads, panini sandwiches, and Middle Eastern fare. Some may find the food more Americanized than authentic, but it's tasty nonetheless. There's something for everyone here—you could bring the kids, or your grandparents, or a group of pals, and it's a good choice for vegetarians, too. As testament to its popularity, additional locations have sprouted on Hyannis's Main Street and in Yarmouth. ✉*23 V Whites Path, Union Station Plaza, South Yarmouth* ☎*508/760–1500* ⊕*www.ardeocapecod.com* ▤*AE, D, MC, V.*

$$–$$$$ 🏨**Capt. Farris House.** Steps from the Bass River Bridge and a short spin
Fodor'sChoice away from congested Route 28 sits this imposing 1845 Greek-revival
★ home. Thoughtful amenities abound, from the plush bath robes, beach supplies, fresh flowers in each room, and a selection of complimentary cordials. The large rooms and suites have either antique or canopied beds, plush comforters, fancy drapes, and deep tile baths (all but one with a whirlpool tub). Some have fireplaces and sundecks. Breakfast is served in the formal dining room or the greenhouse-style interior courtyard and might include quiche with pumpkin-pecan scones or thick French toast. Baked goods and coffee are available after hours. **Pros:** Exquisite aged inn with beautiful grounds, ideal location for exploring Mid Cape area, close to area restaurants and attractions. **Cons:** Many rooms on 2nd floor (no elevator), not an in-town or on-beach location. ✉*308 Old Main St., 02664* ☎*508/760–2818 or 800/350–9477* 🖷*508/398–1262* ⊕*www.captainfarris.com* ⤶*6 rooms, 4 suites* ⌂*In-room: VCR, Wi-Fi. In-hotel: no kids under 12, no-smoking rooms, no elevator* ▤*AE, D, MC, V* ⏀*BP* ⊘*Closed Jan.*

$$–$$$$ 🏨**Ocean Mist.** This three-story, motel-style resort sits on its own private (if tiny) beach on Nantucket Sound. The rooms have generic modern furnishings, cable TV, and either wet bars (with sink and refrigerator) or fully stocked kitchenettes. The duplex loft suites are a step above, with cathedral ceilings, sitting areas with pullout sofas, skylights, and one or two private balconies. **Pros:** Great beachfront location, a good bet for those with children, rooms are well equipped. **Cons:** Not for those looking for quiet, oceanside retreat. ✉*97 S. Shore Dr., 02664* ☎*508/398–2633 or 800/248–6478* 🖷*508/760–3151* ⊕*www.capecodoceanresorts.com* ⤶*32 rooms, 31 suites* ⌂*In-room: kitchen (some), refrigerator. In-hotel: pool, beachfront, laundry facilities, no-smoking rooms, no elevator* ▤*AE, D, MC, V* ⊘*Closed Dec.–mid-Feb.*

$$–$$$$ 🏨**Seaside Cottages.** Right on Nantucket Sound, this 5-acre village of Cape-style cottages (studios and one- or two-bedroom units) has a view of scalloped beaches in both directions. Seaside was built in the 1940s, and the furnishings vary from cottage to cottage, since each is individually owned. All have kitchens or kitchenettes, and many have wood-burning fireplaces. The oceanfront cottages, right off a strip of grass set with lounge and Adirondack chairs, have the best views. Cottages in the adjacent pine grove are generally very pleasant, too. Rentals are by the week in summer; cottages can be rented by the night in late spring

and fall. **Pros:** Great beachfront location, linens and towels provided, spacious grounds. **Cons:** Cottages are very close together, not for those seeking ultimate privacy, very popular with families with small children, nightly reservations hard to come by. ⊠*135 S. Shore Dr., 02664* ☎*508/398–2533* ⊟*508/398–2523* ⊕*www.seasidecapecod.com* 🛏*42 cottages* ♨*In-room: no a/c, no phone, kitchen (some). In-hotel: beachfront, Wi-Fi, no elevator* ⊟*MC, V* ⊘*Closed mid-Oct.–Apr.*

$–$$ ⊞ **All Seasons Motor Inn.** This well-cared-for motor lodge in downtown South Yarmouth ranks above the others in town because of its great staff, a lovely outdoor pool with attractive grounds and patio furniture, and large guest rooms with clean and updated fixtures and furnishings—many have balconies or patios overlooking the pool and courtyard. Plus, it's right by the Cape Cod Creamery ice-cream shop. The dining room serves lunch by the pool during the summer season. **Pros:** Easy access to all the activities and amenities of busy Route 28, reasonable prices for well-equipped rooms, two pools. **Cons:** Not for a quiet romantic getaway (very popular with families with small children), no water views, not beachfront. ⊠*1199 Main St. (Rte. 28), South Yarmouth 02664* ☎*508/394–7600 or 800/527–0359* ⊟*508/398–7160* ⊕*www.allseasons.com* 🛏*114 rooms* ♨*In-room: refrigerator, DVD. In-hotel: pools, game room, gym, hot tub, sauna, no-smoking rooms, no elevator* ⊟*AE, D, MC, V* ⦿*CP.*

WEST YARMOUTH

$–$$$$ ✕ **Yarmouth House Restaurant.** This festive, family-owned, green-shingle restaurant has built a devoted local following over the years. The menu has classic Italian dishes such as chicken Parmesan and veal Marsala, as well as traditional grilled steaks and plenty of fresh seafood dishes. Try the filet mignon à la Neptune (topped with lobster meat and hollandaise sauce), and accompany your meal with a selection from their long list of beers, wines, and specialty cocktails. Early-bird specials, Sunday specials, and a kids' menu are available. ⊠*335 Main St. (Rte. 28)* ☎*508/771–5454* ⊕*www.yarmouthhouse.com* ⊟*AE, D, MC, V.*

¢ ✕ **Keltic Kitchen.** If you like to start your day with a substantial meal,
★ stop in at this friendly café for a traditional Irish breakfast—eggs, sausage, rashers (bacon), black-and-white pudding, home fries or beans, tomato, and brown bread or scones. The potato pancakes with sour cream and scallions are also tasty, as are the more "American" options, including French toast and omelets. At midday, you can still get breakfast, or choose from an assortment of sandwiches that might include corned beef or burgers. Just don't come by too late—the kitchen closes around 2 PM. ⊠*415 Main St. (Rte. 28)* ☎*508/771–4835* ⊟*No credit cards* ⊘*No dinner.*

$–$$$ ⊞ **Bayside Resort.** A bit more upscale than most of the properties along
★ Route 28, but still with extremely reasonable rates, the Bayside overlooks pristine salt marshes and, beyond them, Lewis Bay. Although it's not right on the water, there is a small beach and a large outdoor pool with a café (there's also an indoor pool). Rooms have contemporary light-wood furnishings, and several have cathedral ceilings, whirlpool tubs, and views toward the bay. Many members of the staff have worked here for years, which helps to explain the resort's family-friendly vibe. The Bayside Resort also offers a number of package

deals related to everything from golf to day trips to Martha's Vineyard and Nantucket. **Pros:** Ideal for families with children (organized kids' programs available), close to attractions of busy Route 28, reasonable rates, some water views, lots of specialized package deals. **Cons:** Beach is more like a sandy tanning area; no swimming, not for those seeking quiet and intimate surroundings. ⊠ *225 Main St. (Rte. 28), 02673* ☏ *508/775–5669 or 800/243–1114* 🖷 *508/775–8862* ⊕ *www.baysideresort.com* ⬐ *128 rooms* ♿ *In-room: refrigerators, Wi-Fi. In-hotel: pub, bar, pools, gym, beachfront, no elevator* ⊟ *AE, D, MC, V* ⫶⊙⫶*CP.*

$–$$$ ⫶⊡⫶**Cape Point Hotel.** Families flock to this sensibly priced miniresort, taking advantage of the many amenities, large rooms, patient and friendly staff, and the fact that kids are nearly always certain to find plenty of other playmates here, especially in summer. Rooms contain simple but updated modern furniture. The poolside Cabana Grill serves lunch in July and August (it's open until 4:30). Once you've stayed here once, you're eligible to receive the Cape Point's unbelievably low-priced off-season specials. The hotel puts together some great golf packages with a number of local clubs, and the same owners run the Mariner Motor Lodge *(⇨below)* and the even more affordable Town 'N Country Motor Lodge. **Pros:** Great for families with kids, reasonable and attractive golf package deals, close to all area attractions and restaurants. **Cons:** Not for those looking for a quiet retreat, no beachfront or water views. ⊠ *476 Main St. [Rte. 28], West Yarmouth 02673* ☏ *508/778–1500 or 800/323–9505* 🖷 *508/778–5516* ⊕ *www.capepointhotel. com* ⬐ *116 rooms* ♿ *In-room: DVD, Wi-Fi. In-hotel: restaurant, bar, pools, gym* ⊟ *AE, D, MC, V.*

$$ ⫶⊡⫶**Inn at Lewis Bay.** Affordable and beautiful, this 1920s Dutch Colonial
★   overlooks Lewis Bay, a short walk from the beach. Janet Vaughn, who owns the inn with her husband, David, is an avid quilter; her works top the antique or canopy beds and adorn the walls in the country-style rooms. Each room has a name and a theme; Whale Watch, with its distinctive navys and maroons, is one of two rooms with water views. Bountiful breakfasts are served in the dining room or on the spacious front porch, which is also a pleasant place for afternoon tea and home-baked cookies. It's in a quiet residential neighborhood south of the Route 28 fray. **Pros:** Only one block to beach, friendly and appealing B&B feel, peaceful surroundings. **Cons:** Some rooms up a set of stairs, not an in-town location. ⊠ *57 Maine Ave., 02673* ☏ *508/771–3433 or 800/962–6679* 🖷 *508/790–1186* ⊕ *www.innatlewisbay.com* ⬐ *6 rooms* ♿ *In-room: no phone, no TV (some), Wi-Fi. In-hotel: no kids under 12, no-smoking rooms, no elevator* ⊟ *AE, MC, V* ⫶⊙⫶*BP.*

$ ⫶⊡⫶**Mariner Motor Lodge.** Although crowded Route 28 is more commercial than serene, it's also home to several value-packed hotels. The Mariner is a good family lodging and a bargain. Although the rooms are standard-issue motel—think basic furnishings such as floral bedcovers and carpets that can take a direct hit from a spilled soft drink—the outdoor pool is heated and large, and a heated indoor pool, with an oversize whirlpool hot tub, is great for rainy days. Also on-site are a miniature-golf course and vending machines for snacks. Kids stay free, and weekday rates are reduced. **Pros:** Ideal for those traveling with children, great golf packages, reasonable rates, close to attractions and restaurants. **Cons:** Not for a quiet retreat, no beachfront or water views. ⊠*573 Main St. (Rte. 28), 02673* ☎*508/771–7887 or 800/445–4050* 🖷*508/771–2811* ⊕*www.mariner-capecod.com* ⤴*100 rooms* ᝪ*In-room: safe, refrigerator. In-hotel: restaurant, pools, no-smoking rooms, Wi-Fi, no elevator* ⊟*AE, D, MC, V.*

YARMOUTH PORT
$$–$$$$
★

✕ **Abbicci.** Set inside a dapper yellow 1755 house nestled beneath tower-ing shade trees, Abbicci is an airy, smartly decorated space with a hand-some black-slate bar. One of the first to bring northern Italian cooking to Cape Cod, chef-owner Marietta Hickey has remained true to tradi-tion, offering fish and elegant pastas during summer and heartier dishes in the winter months. She prepares rich and full-tasting fare; one of the most pleasing is roast rack and grilled leg of lamb with a Cabernet mint demi-glace. There's also a creative tapas menu, making this a great choice for grazing and sipping wine, too. ⊠*43 Main St. (Rte. 6A)* ☎*508/362–3501* ⊕*www.abbicci.com* ⊟*AE, D, DC, MC, V.*

$$–$$$$

✕ **Old Yarmouth Inn Restaurant & Tavern.** Established in 1696, this inn—the oldest on Cape Cod—now primarily functions as a restaurant (rooms are available in season). It comprises a main dining room, which is bright and airy, and two smaller and more intimate ones, plus the wood-paneled Tavern, which has a full bar and serves more casual fare. Fresh ingredients are a priority, so the menu changes seasonally; the wide range of meat, poultry, seafood, and pasta dishes infused with clever combinations of familiar flavors offers something for just about everyone. The Sunday brunch is popular. ⊠*223 Main St. (Rte. 6A)* ☎*508/362–9962* ⊕*www.oldyarmouthinn.com* ⊟*AE, D, MC, V* ⊗*Closed Mon., Jan.–May.*

$–$$$
Fodor'sChoice
★

✕ **Inaho.** Yuji Watanabe, chef-owner of the Cape's best Japanese restau-rant, makes early-morning journeys to Boston's fish markets to shop for the freshest local catch. His selection of sushi and sashimi is vast and artful, and vegetable and seafood tempura come out of the kitchen fluffy and light. If you're a teriyaki lover, you can't do any better than the chicken's beautiful blend of sweet and sour. One remarkable ele-ment of the restaurant is its artful lighting: small pinpoint lights on the food accentuate the presentation in a dramatic way. The serene and simple Japanese garden out back has a traditional koi pond. ⊠*157 Main St. (Rte. 6A)* ☎*508/362–5522* ⊟*MC, V.*

$$–$$$

▥ **The Inn at Cape Cod.** A stately Greek-revival building with imposing col-umns, the inn has one of the most dramatic facades of any house on the Cape; it sits near the Botanical Trails and has its own fine gardens, patios, and tree-shaded lawns. On the 1st floor, the Joshua Sears Room, with a mahogany king-size four-poster bed and antique furnishings, is a tradi-tional Victorian chamber. Upstairs, the romantic Village Suite, with an Italian armoire and cherrywood writing desk, opens to the front porch; the frilly Victorian Room has its own fireplace. Some smaller rooms, par-ticularly the basic Guest Room, are pint-size. **Pros:** Elegant and intimate historic lodging, close to attractions of scenic Route 6A. **Cons:** Some rooms a bit small, no water views or direct beach access, some rooms accessed via steep stairs. ⊠*4 Summer St., 02675* ☎*508/375–0590 or 800/850–7301* 🖷*508/362–9520* ⊕*www.innatcapecod.com* ⤴*7 rooms, 2 suites* ᝪ*In-*

room: DVD, VCR, Wi-Fi. In-hotel: no-smoking rooms, no elevator ☰AE, *D, DC, MC, V* ⦿BP.

$$–$$$ 🖵 **Liberty Hill Inn.** Smartly but traditionally furnished common areas—
Fodor's Choice including the high-ceiling parlor, the formal dining room, and the wrap-
★ around porch—are a major draw to this dignified 1825 Greek-revival
house. Guest rooms in both the main building and the carriage house
are filled with a mix of old-world romantic charm and modern amenities; each is uniquely decorated, and some have whirlpool tubs and
fireplaces for those chilly evenings. Breakfast might include blueberry
French toast or a frittata, and afternoon tea is also available. For those
traveling with children under five, please make advanced arrangements
with the innkeepers. **Pros:** Elegant, historic, and tasteful surroundings,
beautiful grounds, romantic and intimate setting. **Cons:** Some rooms
accessed only via some steep stairs, some bathrooms have only small
shower stalls, not a waterfront location. ⊠*77 Main St. (Rte. 6A),
02675* ☎*508/362–3976 or 800/821–3977* 🖷*508/362–6485* ⊕*www.
libertyhillinn.com* ♥*8 rooms, 1 suite* ⚹*In-room: Wi-Fi. In-hotel: no-
smoking rooms, no elevator* ☰AE, D, MC, V ⦿BP.

NIGHTLIFE & THE ARTS

Cape Cod Irish Village (⊠*512 Main St. (Rte. 28), West Yarmouth*
☎*508/771–0100*) has dancing to two- or three-piece bands performing
traditional and popular Irish music year-round. The crowd is mostly
couples and people over 35.

Oliver's (⊠*6 Bray Farm Rd., off Rte. 6A, Yarmouth Port* ☎*508/362–
6062*) has live music in a variety of genres in its tavern on weekends
year-round.

West Yarmouth's summertime **town-band concerts** are held on Monday
in July and August at 7 PM at **Mattacheese Middle School** (⊠*Off Higgins
Crowell Rd., West Yarmouth* ☎*508/778–1008*).

SPORTS & THE OUTDOORS

BASEBALL   The **Yarmouth-Dennis Red Sox** of the collegiate Cape Cod Baseball
League play home games at **Red Wilson Field** (⊠*Station Ave., South
Yarmouth* ☎*508/394–9387* ⊕*www.ydredsox.org*) from mid-June to
mid-August.

BEACHES   Parking at Yarmouth beaches for nonresidents is $12 on weekdays and
$15 on weekends Memorial Day through Labor Day.

Dennis Pond (⊠*Off Summer St., Yarmouth Port*) is a freshwater pond
with a sandy beach, restrooms, and a seasonal snack bar. In season, a
resident parking sticker is required.

The **Flax Pond** (⊠*N. Main St. between High Bank and Great Western Rds., South Yarmouth*) recreation area has freshwater swimming,
a lifeguard, and ducks, but no sand beach, just pine needle–covered
ground. There's a pine-shaded picnic area with grills, as well as tennis
and basketball courts and plenty of parking.

Parker's River Beach (⊠*South Shore Dr., South Yarmouth*), a flat stretch
of sand on warm Nantucket Sound, is perfect for families. It has a

lifeguard, a concession stand, a gazebo and picnic area, a playground, outdoor showers, and restrooms.

Seagull Beach (⊠*Seagull Rd. off South Sea Ave., West Yarmouth*), a long, wide beach along Nantucket Sound, has restrooms and a seasonal concession stand.

BIKE RENTAL **Bike Zone Inc.** (⊠*1124 Rte. 28, South Yarmouth* ☎*508/398–5550*) rents and sells bicycles; it's also a good local resource for all things related to cycling on the Cape.

BOATING **Great Marsh Kayak Tours** (⊠*Rte. 28, West Yarmouth* ⚓*Next to ZooQuarium* ☎*508/775–6447 or 866/395–2925* ⊕*www.greatmarshkayaktours. com*) offers a range of great excursions along the water, from fly-fishing trips to sunset jaunts—you can also customize your own itinerary.

FISHING **Truman's** (⊠*608 Rte. 28, West Yarmouth* ☎*508/771–3470*) can supply you with a required freshwater license and rental gear.

GOLF **Blue Rock Golf Course** (⊠*Off Great Western Rd., South Yarmouth* ☎*508/398–9295*) is a highly regarded, easy-to-walk 18-hole, par-3, 3,000-yard public course crossed by a pond. The pro shop rents clubs; reservations are mandatory in season.

HEALTH & **Mid Cape Racquet Club** (⊠*193 White's Path, South Yarmouth* ☎*508/* FITNESS CLUBS *394–3511* ⊕*www.midcaperacquet.com*) has one racquetball, one squash, and nine indoor tennis courts; indoor basketball; a sauna, steam room, and whirlpools; massage services; and a free-weight and cardiovascular room—plus day care. It also offers spinning, kickboxing, and body pump classes. Daily rates are available.

SOCCER The **Cape Cod Crusaders,** of the D-3 League, play action-packed home matches at the Alan Carlsen Field at **Dennis-Yarmouth Regional High School** (⊠*Station Ave., South Yarmouth* ☎*508/394–1171* ⊕*www. capecodcrusaders.com*) from May to mid-August.

SHOPPING

Cummaquid Fine Arts (⊠*4275 Main St. [Rte. 6A], Cummaquid* ☎*508/ 362–2593*) has works by contemporary resident Cape Cod artists, all beautifully displayed in an old home.

Parnassus Book Service (⊠*220 Rte. 6A, Yarmouth Port* ☎*508/362– 6420*), occupying a three-story 1840 former general store, has a huge selection of old and new books—Cape Cod, maritime, Americana, antiquarian, and others—and is a great place to browse. Its bookstall, outside on the building's side, is open 24 hours a day and works on the honor system—tally up your purchases and leave the money in the mail slot. Parnassus also carries Robert Bateman's nature prints.

Peach Tree Designs (⊠*173 Rte. 6A, Yarmouth Port* ☎*508/362–8317*) carries home furnishings and decorative accessories; some are from local craftspeople, all are beautifully made.

DENNIS

Dennis Village is 4 mi east of Yarmouth Port, West Dennis is 1 mi east of South Yarmouth.

Like Yarmouth, Dennis has a split personality. The town's southern villages, such as Dennis Port and West Dennis, tend to be heavily developed and commercialized and are more popular with families, whereas the northern section, anchored by historic **Dennis Village,** is peaceful and dignified, with countless old homes and inns lining Route 6A.

The backstreets of Dennis Village still retain the colonial charm of its seafaring days. The town, which was incorporated in 1793, was named for the Reverend Josiah Dennis. There were 379 sea captains living here when fishing, salt making, and shipbuilding were the main industries, and the elegant houses they constructed—now museums and B&Bs—still line the streets. In 1816, resident Henry Hall discovered that adding sand to his cranberry fields' soil improved the size of his harvest and the quality of the fruit. The following decades saw cranberry farming and tourism become the Cape's main commercial enterprises. Dennis has a number of conservation areas and nature trails and numerous freshwater ponds for swimming. The village center has antiques shops, general stores, a post office, and ice-cream shops. There's also a village green with a bandstand, the site of occasional summer concerts.

The **Josiah Dennis Manse,** a saltbox house with add-ons, was built in 1736 for the Reverend Josiah Dennis. Inside, the home reflects life in the Reverend Dennis's day. A child's room includes antique furniture and toys, the keeping room has a fireplace and cooking utensils, and the attic exhibits spinning and weaving equipment. Throughout you'll see china, pewter, and portraits of sea captains. The Maritime Wing has ship models, paintings, and nautical artifacts. On the grounds is a 1770 one-room schoolhouse, furnished with wood-and-wrought-iron desks and chairs. ⊠ *77 Nobscussett Rd., at Whig St., Dennis Village* 🖀 *508/385–2232* ✉ *Donations accepted* ☉ *Late June–Sept., Tues. 10–noon, Thurs. 2–4.*

On a clear day, you'll have unbeatable views of Scargo Lake, Dennis Village's scattered houses below, Cape Cod Bay, and distant Provincetown from the top of **Scargo Tower.** A wooden tower built on this site in 1874 was one of the Cape's first tourist attractions; visitors would pay 5¢ to climb to the top for the views. That tower burned down, and the present all-stone 30-foot tower was built in 1901 to replace it. Winding stairs bring you to the top; don't forget to read the unsightly, but amusing, graffiti on the way up. Expect crowds at sunrise and sunset. ⊠ *Scargo Hill Rd., off Rte. 6A or Old Bass River Rd., Dennis Village* 🖀 *Free* ☉ *Daily sunrise–sunset.*

NEED A BREAK? Dip into homemade ice cream and frozen yogurt at the **Ice Cream Smuggler** (⌂ *716 Rte. 6A, Dennis Village* ☎ *508/385–5307*), across the street from the town green and cemetery. The ginger ice cream is a specialty, but order the triple hot-fudge sundae for the ultimate decadence.

Fodor'sChoice ★ For Broadway-style dramas, comedies, and musicals, as well as kids' plays, you can attend a production at the **Cape Playhouse,** the oldest professional summer theater in the country. In 1927 Raymond Moore, who had been working with a theatrical troupe in Provincetown, bought an 1838 former Unitarian meetinghouse and converted it into a theater. The original pews still serve as seats. The opening performance was *The Guardsman,* starring Basil Rathbone; other stars who performed here in the early days—some in their professional stage debuts—include Bette Davis (who first worked here as an usher), Gregory Peck, Lana Turner, Ginger Rogers, Humphrey Bogart, Tallulah Bankhead, and Henry Fonda, who appeared with his then-unknown 20-year-old daughter, Jane. Cape resident Shirley Booth was such an admirer of the playhouse that she donated her Oscar (for *Come Back Little Sheba*) and her Emmy (for *Hazel*) to the theater; both are on display in the lobby during the season. Behind-the-scene tours are also given in season; call for a schedule. The playhouse offers children's theater on Friday morning during July and August. Also on the 26-acre property, now known as the Cape Playhouse Center for the Arts, are a restaurant, the **Cape Cod Museum of Art,** and the **Cape Cinema,** whose exterior was designed in the style of the Congregational church in Centerville. Inside, a 6,400-square-foot mural of heavenly skies—designed by Massachusetts artist Rockwell Kent, who also designed the gold-sunburst curtain—covers the ceiling. ⌂*820 Rte. 6A, Dennis Village* ☎*508/385–3911 or 877/385–3911* ⊕*www.capeplayhouse.com* ⊙ *Call for tour schedule.*

NEED A BREAK? Indulge in sumptuous baked goods at **Buckie's Biscotti** (⌂ *780 Main St. [Rte. 6A], Dennis Village* ☎ *508/385–4700*), just behind the Dennis Post Office near the Cape Playhouse. Have a slice of pie—try the Italian home-style ricotta or the key lime, arguably the Cape's best—or another tasty treat, then wash it all down with a cappuccino or latte.

The **Cape Cod Museum of Art** has a permanent collection of more than 850 works by Cape-associated artists. Important pieces include a portrait of a fisherman's wife by Charles Hawthorne, the father of the Provincetown art colony; a 1924 portrait of a Portuguese fisherman's daughter by William Paxton, one of the first artists to summer in Provincetown; a collection of wood-block prints by Varujan Boghosian, a member of Provincetown's Long Point Gallery cooperative; an oil sketch by Karl Knaths, who painted in Provincetown from 1919 until his death in 1971; and works by abstract expressionist Hans Hoffman and many of his students. The museum also plays host to interesting temporary exhibitions, film festivals, lectures, art classes, and trips. The outdoor sculpture garden has an eclectic collection on display; it's a pleasant place to take a short stroll. Admission is by donation on

Thursday. ✉ *60 Hope La., on grounds of Cape Playhouse, off Rte. 6A, Dennis Village* ☎ *508/385–4477* ⊕ *www.ccmoa.org* ☜ *$8* ☉ *Mon.– Sat. 10–5, Sun. noon–5* ☉ *Closed Mon. mid-Oct–late May.*

In another one of those tricks of Cape geography, the village of **West Dennis** is actually south of South Dennis, on the east side of the Bass River. Dennisport is farther east, near the Harwich town line. If you're driving between West Dennis and Harwich, Lower County Road, with occasional glimpses of the sea between the cottages and beachfront hotels, is a more scenic alternative to overdeveloped Route 28.

The Mid Cape's last southern village is **Dennisport,** a prime summer-resort area, with gray-shingle cottages, summer houses and condominiums, and lots of white-picket fences covered with rambling roses. The Union Wharf Packing Company operated here in the 1850s, and sail makers and ship chandlers lined the shore. Sunbathers now pack the sands where sea clams once laid primary claim.

NEED A BREAK? Set in a rustic mid-19th-century barn decorated with a working nickelodeon, the **Sundae School Ice Cream Parlor** (✉ *387 Lower County Rd., Dennisport* ☎ *508/394–9122*), open mid-April through mid-October, serves great homemade ice cream, frozen yogurt, real whipped cream, and old-fashioned sarsaparilla and cream soda from an antique marble soda fountain.

WHERE TO STAY & EAT

DENNISPORT
$$–$$$$
Fodor's Choice
★

✕ **Ocean House.** Overlooking Nantucket Sound, this noisy but superb restaurant has views to match the spectacular food and service. For dinner, try apple mustard–glazed Atlantic salmon with creamy cheddar grits, followed by caramelized sugar–encrusted vanilla-bean crème brûlée. Chef Anthony Silvestri changes the menu seasonally. There are plenty of decadent options to chose from. Half-plates are available for many entrées, ideal for smaller appetites or sharing. ✉ *End of Depot St., Dennisport* ☎ *508/394–0700* ☐ *AE, D, MC, V* ☉ *Closed Mon. (and Tues. in spring and fall); no lunch. Closed Jan. and Feb.*

$–$$$

✕ **Swan River Seafood Restaurant.** From the right table you can have a beautiful view of the Swan River marsh and Nantucket Sound beyond at this informal little eatery, which turns out great fresh fish in both traditional and creative preparations. Besides the usual fried and simmered choices, try mako shark au poivre or scrod San Sebastian, simmered in garlic broth with littleneck clams. There's also a take-out window. ✉ *5 Lower County Rd.* ☎ *508/394–4466* ☐ *AE, MC, V* ☉ *Closed mid-Sept.–late May. No lunch weekdays late May–mid-June.*

$–$$

✕ **Clancy's.** A local landmark on the bucolic Swan River, Clancy's is popular—the parking lot is often jammed by 5 PM, so expect a substantial wait during peak hours in season. This is an enormous operation, with long family tables, round tables, booths, a deck overlooking the river, and two bars. On the seemingly endless menu are several variations of nachos, salads, and chili. Clancy's likes to be creative with the names of its dishes, so you can find items such as steak Lucifer (sirloin topped with lobster, asparagus, and béarnaise sauce) and a Sunday-brunch menu with the likes of crab, steak, or eggs Benny. ✉ *8 Upper*

County Rd. ☎508/394–6661 ♨Reservations not accepted ☰AE, DC, MC, V.

$$–$$$$ ⌷**The Corsair and Cross Rip.** These motels, built side by side, offer clean and crisp rooms, many with captivating beach views. Rooms in the main motel buildings range from smaller "value" units with one queen bed to pricier deluxe accommodations with kitchenettes and sitting areas, plus a few spacious condo-style suites. Three large three- and four-bedroom vacation houses are also available for rent; they can sleep up to 12 and are fully equipped with luxurious amenities. Decor in the motel buildings is more basic, but between the oceanfront location (there are three private beaches) and the extensive facilities, you probably won't be spending much time in your room. There are also laundry facilities on-site. Suites and houses require a one-week minimum stay in season. **Pros:** Right on the beach, plenty of activities and three pools to choose from, great for families. **Cons:** Not for those seeking a quiet retreat (big family destination). ⊠*33 and 41 Chase Ave., 02639* ☎*508/398–2279 or 800/889–8037* ⊕*www.corsaircrossrip. com* ⌖*37 rooms, 6 suites* ⌂*In-room: kitchen (some), refrigerator, Wi-Fi. In-hotel: beachfront, pools, laundry facilities, no-smoking rooms, no elevator* ☰*AE, D, MC, V* ⊙*Closed late Oct.–Mar.*

$$ ⌷**English Garden Bed & Breakfast.** Anita and Joe Sangiolo—she's a former actress and he's a retired engineer—have turned their comfortable 1922 home into an equally comfortable B&B. The eight rooms are done in a cheerful country style, with quilts, four-poster or iron beds, and pine armoires; four rooms have ocean views. The adjacent carriage house has two modern suites, each with a bedroom, separate living area with gas fireplace, in-room laundry and kitchenette—these are available on a weekly basis. Beach chairs and towels are provided (the house is a block from the sand), and Joe has put together a meticulously detailed notebook of things to do. Film buffs take note: one of the two guest parlors has a TV–VCR and a collection of classic movies. **Pros:** Walk to beach, quiet area, gracious, helpful innkeepers, many ocean-view rooms. **Cons:** Not an in-town location, rooms on 2nd and 3rd floors via stairs. ⊠*32 Inman Rd., 02639* ☎*508/398–2915 or 888/788–1908* ♨*508/398–2852* ⊕*www.anenglishgardenbb.com* ⌖*9 rooms, 2 suites* ⌂*In-room: kitchen (some). In-hotel: Wi-Fi, no kids under 10 (except in suites), no-smoking rooms, no elevator* ☰*D, MC, V* ⊙*Closed Nov.–mid-Apr.* ⍔*BP.*

$–$$ ⌷**The Garlands.** Old Wharf Road in Dennisport is lined with strip motels and cottage colonies, but few places provide comfort and views to match this bi-level motel-style complex. There are 20 units in all; 18 are two-bedroom suites. Each unit has a fully equipped kitchen, private sundeck or patio, and daily maid service. The oceanfront VIP suites, simply named A and B (two bedrooms) and C and D (one bedroom), are the best picks here—the nearly floor-to-ceiling windows offer unobstructed water views; at high tide you're almost in the surf. **Pros:** Ideal beachfront location, fully equipped units for convenience. **Cons:** Not an in-town location, no credit cards. ⊠*117 Old Wharf Rd., Box 506, 02639* ☎*508/398–6987* ⊕*www.thegarlandscapecod.com* ⌖*20 suites*

⚿*In-room: no a/c, kitchen. In-hotel: beachfront, no children under 5, no elevator* ⊟*No credit cards* ⊘*Closed mid-Oct.–mid-Apr.*

DENNIS VILLAGE
$$–$$$$
Fodor'sChoice
★

✗**Red Pheasant.** This is one of the Cape's best cozy country restaurants, with a consistently good kitchen where creative American food is prepared with elaborate sauces and herb combinations. For instance, organic chicken is served with an intense preserved-lemon and fresh thyme sauce, and exquisitely grilled veal chops come with a dense red wine-and-portobello mushroom sauce. In fall, look for the specialty game dishes, including venison and quail. Try to reserve a table in the more intimate Garden Room. The expansive wine list is excellent. A nice Sunday brunch is served from mid-October to June. ⊠*905 Main St. (Rte. 6A)* ⚏*Box 486, Dennis, MA 02638* ☏*508/385-2133* ⊕*www.redpheasantinn.com* ⚘*Reservations essential* ⊟*AE, D, MC, V* ⊘*No lunch.*

$$–$$$$

✗**Scargo Café.** With the Cape Playhouse right across the street, this upscale contemporary American restaurant is a favorite before- and after-show haunt. There's plenty of seafood on the eclectic menu, such as the "Seafood Romance" with clams, scallops, and shrimp, but carnivores will also take delight, with such dishes as ginger duckling, rack of lamb, and twin filet mignons. Lighter meals include scallops harpooned on a skewer and tucked in bacon, and an Asian-style fish sandwich served with seaweed salad. An added plus: the kitchen stays open until 11 PM in summer. ⊠*799 Main St. (Rte. 6A)* ☏*508/385-8200* ⊕*www.scargocafe.com* ⊟*AE, D, MC, V.*

$$–$$$
★

✗**Gina's by the Sea.** Some places are less than the sum of their parts; Gina's is more. This funky old building is tucked into a sand dune, so that the aroma of fine northern Italian cooking blends with a fresh breeze off the bay. The dining room is tasteful, cozy, and especially wonderful in fall when the fireplace is blazing. Blackboard specials could include angel-hair pasta or linguine with clams. If you don't want a long wait, come early or late. An enthusiastic staff rounds out the experience. ⊠*134 Taunton Ave.* ☏*508/385-3213* ⚘*Reservations not accepted* ⊟*AE, MC, V* ⊘*Closed Dec.–Mar. and Mon.–Wed.*

$–$$
Fodor'sChoice
★

✗**Cap'n Frosty's.** A great stop after the beach, this is where locals go to get their fried seafood. This modest joint has a regular menu that includes ice cream, a small specials board, and a counter where you order and take a number written on a french-fries box. The staff is young and hard working, pumping out fresh fried clams and fish-and-chips on paper plates. All frying is done in 100% canola oil, and rice pilaf is offered as a substitute for fries. There's seating inside as well as outside on a shady brick patio. ⊠*219 Main St. (Rte. 6A)* ☏*508/385-8548* ⚘*Reservations not accepted* ⊟*MC, V* ⊘*Closed early Sept.–Mar.*

¢–$

✗**Grumpy's Restaurant.** This airy diner consistently packs its tables and counter space year-round, and for good reason. From baked goods to waffles and eggs done any way you like them, Grumpy's jump-starts your day with generous portions for breakfast and lunch. Get here early to avoid a line that often curls out the door. ⊠*1408 Main St. (Rte. 6A)* ☏*508/385-2911* ⚘*Reservations not accepted* ⊟*MC, V* ⊘*No dinner.*

¢   ✗**Red Cottage Restaurant.** Up Old Bass River Road ½ mi north of the
Fodor\$Choice   town hall, the Red Cottage is indeed a red cottage and serves breakfast
★   and lunch year-round. Locals pack this place even in the off-season,
and you can expect a wait in the summer. The cottage is a no-frills,
friendly place with food that runs the gamut from decadent stuffed
French toast specials to a list of health-conscious offerings with egg
whites, "lite" cheese, and turkey bacon. The grill is in plain view; if you
want to watch your meal being cooked, the swivel stools at the counter
have the best angle. Bottomless cups of coffee are served in an interesting collection of mismatched mugs. The breakfasts are better than the
lunches, but both are no-nonsense and just plain reliably good. ⊠*36
Old Bass River Rd.* ☎*508/394–2923* ⌀*Reservations not accepted*
⊟*No credit cards* ☾*No dinner.*

\$\$–\$\$\$ ▦**Scargo Manor.** This 1895 sea captain's home has a prime location
on Scargo Lake, with a private beach and dock. Inside, innkeepers
Larry and Debbie Bain display a collection of art and antiques amid
the Victorian furnishings. There's plenty of room to spread out on the
big screened porch, in the sitting room or more formal living room, or
in the cozy 3rd-floor reading room. If you want a lake view, choose the
cozy all-blue Hydrangea Room, with a pineapple-top four-poster bed
and a skylight overhead. For more space, the Captain Howe's Suite
has a king-size canopy bed, plus a separate sitting room with a working fireplace that's bigger than the guest rooms at many other B&Bs.
Kids 5 and up are welcome. **Pros:** Great freshwater lakefront location
for swimming and boating, many rooms have water views, historic
lodging. **Cons:** Rooms are accessed via steep stairs, some rooms have
small shower stalls. ⊠*909 Main St. (Rte. 6A), 02638* ☎*508/385–5534
or 800/595–0034* ⊟*508/385–9791* ⊕*www.scargomanor.com* ⇆*4
rooms, 2 suites* ⌂*In-room: no phone, Wi-Fi. In-hotel: beachfront,
bicycles, no-smoking rooms, no elevator* ⊟*D, MC, V* ⦿*BP.*

\$–\$\$\$ ▦**Isaiah Hall B&B Inn.** Lilacs and pink roses trail along the white-picket
Fodor\$Choice   fence outside this 1857 Greek-revival farmhouse on a quiet residential
★   road near the bay. Innkeepers Jerry and Judy Neal set the scene for a
romantic getaway with guest rooms that have country antiques, flo-
ral-print wallpapers, and homey touches, such as quilts and Priscilla
curtains. In the attached carriage house, rooms have three walls sten-
ciled white and one paneled with knotty pine, and some have small
balconies overlooking a wooded lawn with gardens, grape arbors, and
berry bushes. The carriage-house suite has a king-size bed, a separate
sitting area with a pullout couch, and a refrigerator. Common areas
such as the dining room are elegant. Make-it-yourself popcorn, tea,
coffee, and soft drinks are always available. **Pros:** Beautiful grounds in
very quiet, historic setting, not far from area beaches and attractions.
Cons: Many rooms accessed via very steep steps, some rooms are on
the small side. ⊠*152 Whig St., Box 1007, 02638* ☎*508/385–9928
or 800/736–0160* ⊟*508/385–5879* ⊕*www.isaiahhallinn.com* ⇆*10
rooms, 2 suites* ⌂*In-room: VCR, Wi-Fi (some). In-hotel: no kids under
7, no-smoking rooms, no elevator* ⊟*AE, D, MC, V* ⦿*CP.*

WEST DENNIS   ✗**Kream 'N Kone.** The Kream 'N Kone has been going strong since
¢–\$\$ 1953: order up some fried clams and a shake or a soda, get a number,

wait five minutes, and sit down to some of the best fast food anywhere. Fried food will overflow your paper plate onto a plastic tray, but it's so good that what you thought you'd never be able to finish somehow vanishes. The onion rings in particular are a knockout. At times the prices seem surprisingly high, but the quality and quantity of what you get are well worth the splurge. ⊠*Corner of Rtes. 134 and 28* ☎*508/394–0808* ⊟*MC, V* ☾*Closed Nov.–Jan.*

$$$–$$$$ ⌨**Lighthouse Inn.** On a small private beach adjacent to West Dennis Beach, this venerable Cape resort has been in family hands since 1938. The main inn was built around a still-operational 1855 lighthouse. Along a landscaped lawn are 23 individual one- to three-bedroom cottages made entirely of shingles and five larger buildings with multiple guest rooms. Cottages have decks, fireplaces, two double (or one double and one king-size) beds, and sitting areas (but no kitchens). In the main inn are five guest rooms, a living room, a library, and a waterfront restaurant serving New England fare. In summer, supervised kids' activities give parents some private time. **Pros:** Good beachfront location, tons of activities for those traveling with children. **Cons:** Not for those seeking quiet, intimate lodging (lots of kids about). ⊠*1 Lighthouse Rd., Box 128, 02670* ☎*508/398–2244* 🖶*508/398–5658* ⊕*www. lighthouseinn.com* ⇋*40 rooms, 23 cottages* ⌖*In-room: refrigerator, Wi-Fi. In-hotel: restaurant, room service, bar, tennis court, miniature golf, pool, beachfront, children's programs (ages 3–12), playground, no elevator* ⊟*MC, V* ☾*Closed mid-Oct.–mid-May* ⌑*BP, MAP.*

$–$$$ ⌨**Shady Hollow Inn.** Dedicated vegetarians, owners Ann Hart and David Dennis found B&B travel a challenge, so they opened their own veggie-friendly inn in tranquil South Dennis, well off the beaten path. Their breakfasts, which might include omelets, dairy-free baked goods, or a tofu quiche, are designed to appeal to anyone, from foodies to strict vegans. By prior arrangement, they can also prepare vegetarian dinners. Furnishings in their comfortable home are Mission-style; the guest rooms have quilt-topped beds, and the largest—the airy 1st-floor Westwind—has a striking painted mantel. **Pros:** Located central in area historic district, intimate and peaceful lodging in comfortable setting. **Cons:** Some rooms accessed via stairs, not an in-town or beachfront location. ⊠*370 Main St., South Dennis 02660* ☎*508/394–7474* ⊕*www.shadyhollowinn.com* ⇋*4 rooms, 3 with bath* ⌖*In-room: no phone, VCR. In-hotel: bicycles, no kids under 10, no-smoking rooms, no elevator* ⊟*MC, V* ⌑*BP.*

NIGHTLIFE & THE ARTS

The **Cape Playhouse** (⊠*820 Main St. (Rte. 6A), Dennis Village* ☎*508/ 385–3911 or 877/385–3911* ⊕*www.capeplayhouse.com*), an 1838 former Unitarian meetinghouse, is the oldest professional summer theater in the country. Top stars appear here each summer, and the playhouse also mounts kids' shows on Friday morning in July and August. On the grounds of the Cape Playhouse is the artsy **Cape Cinema** (☎*508/385–2503* ⊕*www.capecinema.com*), which shows foreign and first-run films throughout the summer.

Improper Bostonian (⊠*Rte. 28, Dennisport* ☎*508/394–7416*), open only in summer, has a mix of live music and DJ-spun dance tunes several nights a week and attracts a young crowd.

Lost Dog Pub (⊠*1374 Rte. 134, Dennis Village* ☎*508/385–6177*) offers basic pub eats and a relaxed social atmosphere; it's a popular place for locals and visitors to grab a beer after a long day.

Reel Art (⊠*60 Hope La., Dennis Village* ☎*508/385–4477*), at the Cape Museum of Fine Arts, shows avant-garde, classic, art, and independent films on weekends September through April. Call for a schedule.

The **Sand Bar** (⊠*Lighthouse Rd., West Dennis* ☎*508/398–7586*) presents the boogie-woogie piano playing of local legend Rock King, who's been tickling the ivories—and people's funny bones—since the 1960s. The club is closed from mid-October to mid-May.

In season, you can dance to a DJ and live bands at **Sundancer's** (⊠*116 Main St. [Rte. 28], West Dennis* ☎*508/394–1600*). It's closed December and January.

SPORTS & THE OUTDOORS

BEACHES   Parking at all Dennis beaches is $15 a day in season for nonresidents.

Chapin Beach (⊠*Chapin Beach Rd., Dennis Village*) is a lovely dune-backed bay beach with long tidal flats—you can walk really far out at low tide. It has no lifeguards or services.

Corporation Beach (⊠*Corporation Rd., Dennis Village*) has lifeguards, showers, restrooms, and a food stand. Once a packet landing owned by a corporation of the townsfolk, the beautiful crescent of white sand backed by low dunes now serves a decidedly noncorporate purpose as a public beach.

Mayflower Beach (⊠*Dunes Rd. off Bayview Rd., Dennis Village*) reveals hundreds of feet of tidal flats at low tide. The beach has restrooms, showers, lifeguards, and a food stand.

For freshwater swimming, **Scargo Lake** (⊠*Access off Rte. 6A or Scargo Hill Rd., Dennis Village*) has two beaches with restrooms, playgrounds, and a picnic area. The sandy-bottom lake is shallow along the shore, which is good for kids. It's surrounded by woods and is stocked for fishing.

The **West Dennis Beach** (⊠*Lighthouse Rd. off Lower County Rd., West Dennis*) is one of the best on the south shore. A breakwater was started here in 1837 in an effort to protect the mouth of Bass River, but was abandoned when a sandbar formed on the shore side. It's a long, wide, and popular sandy beach, stretching for 1½ mi, with marshland and the Bass River across from it. Popular with windsurfers, the beach also has bathhouses, lifeguards, a playground, concessions, and parking for 1,000 cars.

BICYCLING   You can pick up the 25-mi Cape Cod Rail Trail at several points along its path. In fact, riding the entire trail in one day doesn't do justice to its sights and side trips (though it certainly can be done). Many cyclists,

Riding the Rail

In the late 1800s visitors to Cape Cod could take the train from Boston all the way to Provincetown. But with the construction of the Sagamore and Bourne bridges in the mid-1930s, the age of the automobile truly arrived on the Cape. Today, although passenger trains no longer serve Cape Cod, the former train paths provide another more leisurely way to explore the Cape—by bicycle.

The Cape's premier bike path, the Cape Cod Rail Trail, was constructed in 1978 and extended in the mid-1990s—it now offers a scenic ride from South Dennis to South Wellfleet. Following the paved right-of-way of the old Penn Central Railroad, it's 25 mi long, passing salt marshes, cranberry bogs, ponds, and Nickerson State Park, which has its own path.

Some serious bikers whiz along at top speed, but that's not the only way to travel. Along the way there are plenty of tempting places to veer off to spend an hour or two on the beach, to stop for lunch or ice cream, or just to smell the pine trees and imagine what the Cape looked like years ago. The terrain is easy to moderate in difficulty and is generally quite flat, so it's great for youngsters.

The trail starts at a parking lot off busy Route 134 south of U.S. 6, near Theophilus Smith Road in South Dennis; it ends at the post office in South Wellfleet. The Dennis Chamber of Commerce will give you a free rail trail map with distance markings to various points along the trail. The map also notes the location of parking lots en route if you want to cover only a segment: in Harwich (across from Pleasant Lake Store on Pleasant Lake Avenue), Brewster (at Nickerson State Park), and Eastham (at the Salt Pond Visitor Center). Several bike shops near the trail in Dennis, Brewster, and Eastham can also provide information as well rentals.

Experienced rail-trailers suggest breaking the trail in segments, perhaps starting in the middle near Nickerson State Park and looping to one end and back. If you want to return to your starting point by public transportation, the easiest way is to start in Dennis, ride to Orleans, and catch the bike-rack-equipped H20 Line bus back to Dennis; contact the Cape Cod Regional Transit Authority for a schedule and route information.

Remember that wheels yield to heels, so cyclists should give walkers the right-of-way. Pass slower traffic on the left, and call out a warning before you pass. Kids under 13 must wear helmets. The trail can get crowded at times; if you prefer solitude (or cooler temperatures), set out earlier in the morning or later in the afternoon.

Busy bike trails share the same fate as roads: maintenance projects and expansion. A 3-mi spur leads from the rail trail through Harwich to the Chatham line, and a new extension continues on into Chatham center. Plans to extend the trail westward into Yarmouth are also in the works. **Nickerson State Park** (☎ 508/896–3491) maintains the rail trail; to view a map of the route before you leave home, go to their Web site.

—*By Carolyn Heller*

especially those with small kids, prefer the piecemeal method because they can relax and enjoy the sights—and not turn their legs into jelly.

The ride in Dennis starts as a flat, straight spin through a small pine forest—a good warm-up exercise. Your first road crossing is at busy Great Western Road, one of the town's major thoroughfares, after which you'll pass Sand Pond and Flax Pond in Harwich. The Dennis part of the trail is short, but it's worth starting here for the ample parking at the trail's entrance and for the several bike-rental places that set up shop on Route 134.

A guidebook published by the Dennis Chamber of Commerce includes bike tours and maps. You can rent bikes from a number of places along the Cape Cod Rail Trail. **Barbara's Bike Shop** (✉ *430 Rte. 134, Dennis Village* ☎ *508/760–4723*) is at the Rail Trail entrance.

BOATING   **Cape Cod Waterways** (✉ *16 Rte. 28, Dennisport* ☎ *508/398–0080*) rents canoes, kayaks, and electric paddleboats for leisurely travel on the Swan River.

FISHING   Sesuit Harbor, on the bay side of Dennis off Route 6A, is busy with fishing and pleasure boats; several are available for fishing charters. The *Bluefish* (✉ *Sesuit Harbor* ✐ *Box 113, Dennis Village 02638* ☎ *508/385–7265* ⊕ *www.sunsol.com/bluefish*) makes four-, six-, and eight-hour fishing excursions. The *LAD-NAV* (✉ *Sesuit Harbor* ✐ *Box 2002, East Dennis 02641* ☎ *508/385–8150* ⊕ *www.lad-nav.com*) takes as many as six anglers per trip on a 36-foot fishing vessel.

ICE-SKATING   You can ice-skate at the **Tony Kent Arena** (✉ *8 Gages Way, South Dennis* ☎ *508/760–2400*) fall though spring and on Saturday in summer. Keep your eyes peeled: this is where Nancy Kerrigan and Paul Wylie train. Rental skates are available.

JOGGING   **Lifecourse** (✉ *Bob Crowell Rd. and Old Bass River Rd., South Dennis*) is a 1½-mi jogging trail through the woods, with 20 exercise stations along the way. It's part of a recreation area that includes basketball and handball courts, ball fields, a playground, and a picnic area.

SHOPPING

Antiques Center of Cape Cod (✉ *243 Main St. [Rte. 6A], Dennis Village* ☎ *508/385–6400*) is a large and busy market populated by more than 160 dealers offering furniture, artwork, jewelry, china, clocks, books, antique dolls, and other collectibles.

Armchair Bookstore (✉ *619 Main St. [Rte. 6A], Dennis Village* ☎ *508/385–0900*) carries a large selection of new releases, plus numerous books about Cape lore, history, and sights. Also on hand are cards and knickknacks and a kids' section with books, games, and toys.

Cape Cod Shoe Mart (✉ *271 Main St. [Rte. 28], Dennisport* ☎ *508/398–6000*) has such brand names as Capezio, Dexter, Clark, Esprit, Nike, Reebok, L. A. Gear, and Rockport.

Emily's Beach Barn (⊠ *708 Main St. [Rte. 6A], Dennis Village* ☎ *508/385–8328*) has fashionable women's beachwear, from bathing suits and wraps to sun hats and summer dresses and tops.

★ **Robert C. Eldred Co.** (⊠ *1483 Rte. 6A, East Dennis* ☎ *508/385–3116* ⊕ *www.eldreds.com*) holds more than two-dozen auctions per year, dealing in Americana; estate jewelry; top-quality antiques; marine, Asian, American, and European art; tools; and dolls. Its "general antiques and accessories" auctions put less-expensive wares on the block.

Ross Coppelman, Goldsmith (⊠ *1439 Rte. 6A, East Dennis* ☎ *508/385–7900* ⊕ *www.rosscoppelman.com*) sells original jewelry in high-karat gold, semiprecious gemstones, and other materials (customized wedding bands are a specialty). The pieces are designed by Coppelman, a self-taught goldsmith who has been honing his craft for over 30 years. Be sure to take a peek into the tiny workshop as you enter the showroom.

Fodor'sChoice **Scargo Pottery** (⊠ *30 Dr. Lord's Rd. S, off Rte. 6A, Dennis Village* ★ ☎ *508/385–3894* ⊕ *www.scargopottery.com*) is in a pine forest, where potter Harry Holl's unusual wares—such as his signature castle birdhouses—sit on tree stumps and hang from branches. Inside are the workshop and kiln, plus work by Holl's four daughters. With luck you can catch a potter at the wheel; viewing is, in fact, encouraged.

THE MID CAPE ESSENTIALS

To research prices, get advice from other travelers, and book travel arrangements, visit ⊕ *www.fodors.com.*

TRANSPORTATION

BY BOAT & FERRY

Ferries to Nantucket and Martha's Vineyard leave from Hyannis year-round. *For details, see* ⇨ *Boat & Ferry Travel in Essentials in the back of this book.*

BY BUS

Hyannis is the Cape's transit hub, and is served by a number of bus routes, including the local Hyannis Villager and the Barnstable Villager lines. Buses also link Hyannis with Orleans, Woods Hole, Provincetown, Plymouth, downtown Boston, and Logan airport, as well as various towns on each route. *For more information, see* ⇨ *Bus Travel in Essentials in the back of this book.*

Bus Depots Hyannis Transportation Center (⊠ *215 Iyanough Rd., Hyannis* ☎ *508/775-8504* ⊕ *www.capecodtransit.org*). **Plymouth & Brockton Street Railway Terminals** (⊠ *South Station Bus Terminal, 700 Atlantic Ave., Boston* ☎ *508/746-0378*).

BY TAXI

There are taxi stands at the Hyannis airport, the Hyannis bus station, and the Capetown Mall, across the street from the Cape Cod Mall. In Hyannis, call Checker Taxi for pickups. Dick's Taxi will pick you up and has a stand at the airport. John's Taxi & Limousine picks up in Dennis and Harwich only but will take passengers all over the Cape. Town Taxi is found at several locations around Hyannis, including Capetown Mall, the bus station, and on W. Main Street.

Taxi Companies Checker Taxi (☎ *508/771–8294*). **Dick's Taxi** (☎ *508/428–4918*). **John's Taxi & Limousine** (☎ *508/394–3209*). **Town Taxi** (☎ *508/771–5555 or 888/771–8696*).

CONTACTS & RESOURCES

CONDO & HOUSE RENTALS

Century 21, Sam Ingram Real Estate handles rentals throughout the Mid Cape region. Great Vacations Inc. specializes in locating vacation rentals in Brewster, Dennis, and Orleans. Peter McDowell Associates offers a wide selection of properties for rent by the week, month, or season; the company also rents larger homes for family reunions and other gatherings. Most places are in Dennis. Waterfront Rentals covers Bourne to Truro, listing everything from condos to estates.

Local Agents Century 21, Sam Ingram Real Estate (✉ *938 Rte. 6A, Yarmouth Port 02675* ☎ *508/362–1191 or 800/676–3340* 🖷 *508/362–7889* ⊕ *www. century21samingram.com*). **Great Vacations Inc.** (✉ *2660 Rte. 6A, Brewster 02631* ☎ *508/896–2090*). **Peter McDowell Associates** (✉ *585 Main St. [Rte. 6A], Dennis 02638* ☎ *508/385–9114 or 888/385–9114* ✉ *11 Main St. [Rte. 28], Dennisport 02639* ☎ *508/394–5400 or 800/870–5401* ⊕ *www.capecodproperties.com*). **Waterfront Rentals** (✉ *20 Pilgrim Rd., West Yarmouth 02673* ☎ *508/778–1818* 🖷 *508/771–3563* ⊕ *www.waterfrontrentalsinc.com*).

TOURS

Cape Cod Soaring Adventures offers glider flights and lessons out of Marstons Mills.

Information Cape Cod Soaring Adventures (☎ *508/420–4201* ⊕ *www.cape-codsoaring.com*).

VISITOR INFORMATION

The Cape Cod Chamber of Commerce is open year-round, Monday through Saturday 9 to 5 and Sunday 10 to 4.

Tourist Information Cape Cod Chamber of Commerce (✉ *Junction of U.S. 6 and 132* 🕮 *Box 790, Hyannis 02601* ☎ *508/862–0700 or 888/332–2732* ⊕ *www. capecodchamber.org*). **Dennis Chamber of Commerce** (✉ *242 Swan River Rd., West Dennis* 🕮 *Box 275, South Dennis 02660* ☎ *508/398–3568 or 800/243–9920* ⊕ *www.dennischamber.com*). **Hyannis Chamber of Commerce** (✉ *1481 Rte. 132* 🕮 *Box 100, Hyannis 02601* ☎ *508/775–2201 or 877/492–6647* ⊕ *www.hyannis. com*). **Yarmouth Chamber of Commerce** (✉ *424 Rte. 28, West Yarmouth 02673* 🕮 *Box 479, South Yarmouth 02664* ☎ *508/778–1008 or 800/732–1008* ⊕ *www. yarmouthcapecod.com Information center* ✉ *U.S. 6 heading east between exits 6 and 7* ☎ *508/362–9796*).

The Lower Cape

WORD OF MOUTH

"As I drove back to my condo, starving, I spotted the Brewster Inn and Chowder House from the road . . . I had some of the best mahi mahi I ever ate that night! I literally had to drag myself out of there before I slipped into a culinary coma."

—T.M.

"Be sure to check out a Bay beach at low tide. If you've never seen Cape Cod Bay at low tide, you're in for a surprising treat . . . you'll be able to walk out for a mile of so!"

—ccrosner

Updated
by Laura V.
Scheel

SPECKLED WITH STILL-ACTIVE CRANBERRY BOGS, sturdy trees, and pastures, the Lower Cape exudes a peaceful residential aura. You won't find roadways cluttered with minigolf complexes, trampolines, or bumper boats here. And although an influx of year-round residents has transformed much of the Upper Cape into a commuter's haven, the Lower Cape still has a quiet sense of history and simple purpose.

Rich in history and Cape flavor, Brewster and Harwich stand opposite each other in the area just shy of the Cape's elbow. Harwich, farther inland, has antique homes, rambling old burial grounds, and a modest town center with shops, restaurants, museums, churches, and public parks. Brewster is similarly historical; examples of Victorian, Greek-revival, and colonial architecture abound, most meticulously preserved. Many homes have been converted to welcoming guesthouses and bed-and-breakfasts, whereas others are privately owned.

The traditional, elegant town of Chatham perches dramatically at the end of the peninsular elbow. It's here that the Atlantic begins to wet the shores of the Cape, sometimes with frightening strength. Chatham has shown its vulnerability to the forces of nature over the years, as little by little the town's shores have succumbed to the insatiable sea.

North of Chatham is Orleans, supply center of the Lower and Outer Capes, replete with large grocery chains and shopping plazas. The famed Nauset Beach is here, its dune-backed shores crammed with sun-seeking revelers in summer. Orleans also has a rich history—you just have to leave the maze of industry to find it. Continuing north, you can reach Eastham, a town often overlooked because of its position on busy U.S. 6. It too is perfectly charming, if you know where to look.

The Lower Cape is blessed with large tracts of open space, set aside for conservation. South of Chatham, the Monomoy National Wildlife Refuge is a twin-island bird sanctuary. Here dozens of species of birds are free to feed, nest, and expand their numbers without human meddling. Recreation seekers should head straight to Nickerson State Park in Brewster to frolic in freshwater ponds or enjoy a serene bike ride under the shade of stately white pine, oak, and maple trees. In Eastham, where the Cape Cod National Seashore officially begins, the Salt Pond Visitor Center has a wealth of area information, educational programs, and guided tours.

EXPLORING THE LOWER CAPE

The towns of Harwich, Chatham, Brewster, Orleans, and Eastham make up the Lower Cape. Of these, only Brewster and Orleans touch Route 6A. Harwich, Chatham, and Orleans span Route 28—but don't fear. Although it's known for traffic, Route 28's congestion eases as the road winds toward the Lower Cape. Eastham sits along U.S. 6, which is the fastest way to get to all the towns—but if you're concerned about the journey as well as the destination, it's worthwhile to amble along Route 28 or 6A. Along the way, picturesque harbors, scenic side roads, and the towns' main streets, antiques stores, romantic inns, and colonial homes dot the landscape. Follow Route 28 into Chatham and make your way to the Chatham Lighthouse for breathtaking views of Nantucket Sound.

ABOUT THE RESTAURANTS

Each town has its own batch of treasured and traditional restaurants, and all will be crowded in summer. A significant number of restaurants close their doors once the crowds thin in October—including the beloved fried-seafood shacks—but plenty remain open throughout the year. Fresh seafood is a major staple.

If you are celebrating a milestone or hoping to delight someone special, Brewster's Chillingsworth impresses with French-country elegance. The Chatham Bars Inn recalls an era of gentle tranquility. If you're undecided, a stroll down Chatham's Main Street will tempt your palate. The restaurants in Orleans, Brewster, Harwich, and Eastham are spread out through the towns, but top restaurants such as the Brewster Fish House are worth finding.

Most Cape towns—including Chatham, Orleans, Eastham, Brewster, and Harwich—have banished smoking from restaurants and bars; smokers can retreat for a break outdoors.

TOP 5
■ Shelling Cape Cod Bay's beaches at low tide
■ Walking the forested trails of Nickerson State Park in Brewster
■ Browsing the art galleries on Chatham's Main Street
■ Listening to music and poetry at Eastham's First Encounter Coffee House
■ Devouring the lobster roll at Brax Landing in Harwich Port

ABOUT THE HOTELS

Money made in early maritime fortunes helped build exquisite homes, many of which are now unique and lovely inns. Chatham is blessed with dozens of these aged beauties, most with all the modern conveniences. B&Bs and intimate guesthouses are the primary lodging choices, but even larger hotels such as Chatham Bars Inn and the Chatham Wayside Inn capture the charm of Old Cape Cod. Expect fewer hotel and motel options on this part of the Cape. However, there are a few roadside or waterfront hotels outside the town centers. These complexes, which usually welcome families with small children, can be a bit softer on the wallet.

Brewster is essentially a B&B kind of town, offering lodging in former sea captains' homes. Harwich and Orleans have a mixture of both family-friendly hotel complexes and lovingly restored inns. Eastham has quite a few large-scale hotels along U.S. 6, including a Sheraton. Don't expect to find bargains here during the high season.

Other options include camping or weekly cottage rentals—all towns have the Cape's trademark cottage colonies. Note that in summer these must be secured well in advance, usually through a local real-estate agent.

TIMING

Although the crowds of summer are testament to the appeal of the Lower Cape and its spectacular beaches, outdoor pursuits, crafts and art shows, concerts, and special events, the region is becoming a popular year-round destination. Because of its ocean-side climate, spring and fall are simply lesser shades of full-blown summer. Seasonal businesses reopen in late May and early June, but lodging rates remain less pricey than during the high season, and the agonies of summertime traffic, long waits at restaurants, and parking restrictions at area beaches can be avoided. September, October, and even November are the same. The waters usually remain warm enough to swim well into October, and many shops attempt to rid their stocks of merchandise by having generous sales.

You won't get the expected splendors of New England foliage on the Lower Cape, because the landscape changes are subtle. Swaying salt-marsh grasses turn golden, cranberry bogs explode into ruby-red quilts, and the ocean relaxes into a deep, deep blue. The light becomes softer and its patterns more dramatic on both land and sea. In the towns of Harwich, Brewster, and Orleans, where the soil is substantial enough to support mighty oaks and maples, the colors of autumn do peer through. A drive along Route 6A under the canopy of changing leaves is just as breathtaking as a summer jaunt past blooming gardens.

WHAT IT COSTS				
$$$$	$$$	$$	$	¢
RESTAURANTS over $30	$22–$30	$16–$22	$10–$16	under $10
HOTELS over $260	$200–$260	$140–$200	$90–$140	under $90

Restaurant prices are per person for a main course at dinner. Hotel prices are for a standard double room in high season, excluding 6% state tax, local taxes, and gratuities. Some inns add a 15% service charge.

BREWSTER

6 mi north of Chatham, 5 mi west of Orleans, 20 mi east of Sandwich.

Brewster calls itself the Sea Captains' Town, honoring its rich heritage as a seafaring community. Historic Route 6A, the Old King's Highway, winds through its center. This road, the old stagecoach route, was once nearly the only one at this end of the Cape, and residents and legislators alike are determined to keep it well preserved. Homes and businesses must adhere to historic detail: there are no neon signs, no strip malls—only the gentle facades of a graceful era.

Named for Plymouth leader William Brewster, the area was settled in 1659 but was not incorporated as a separate town until 1803. In the early 1800s, Brewster was the terminus of a packet cargo service from Boston. In 1849 Henry David Thoreau wrote that "this town has more

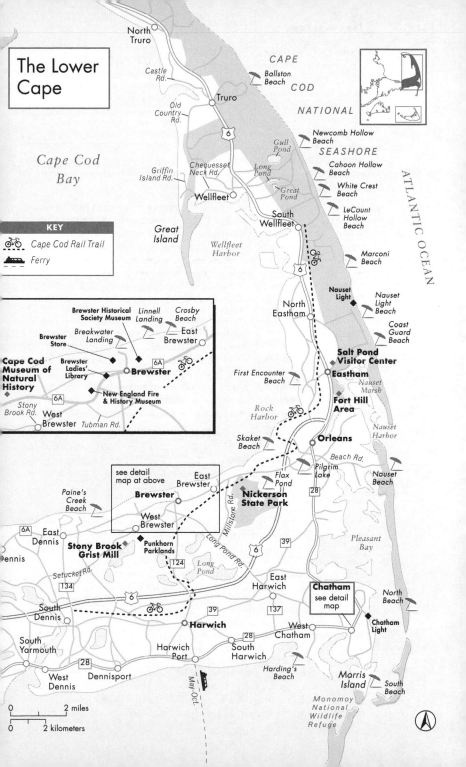

The Lower Cape

KEY
🚲 Cape Cod Rail Trail
⛴ Ferry

Cape Cod Bay

Cape Cod Bay

North Truro

Castle Rd.

Ballston Beach

CAPE

COD

NATIONAL

SEASHORE

Old Country Rd.

Truro

6

Newcomb Hollow Beach

Gull Pond

Cahoon Hollow Beach

Griffin Island Rd.

Chequesset Neck Rd.

Long Pond

White Crest Beach

Wellfleet

Great Pond

LeCount Hollow Beach

Great Island

South Wellfleet

6

Wellfleet Harbor

Marconi Beach

ATLANTIC OCEAN

North Eastham

Nauset Light

Nauset Light Beach

First Encounter Beach

Coast Guard Beach

Salt Pond Visitor Center

Eastham

Nauset Marsh

Rock Harbor

Fort Hill Area

Nauset Harbor

Skaket Beach

Orleans

Beach Rd.

Pilgrim Lake

Nauset Beach

Flax Pond

28

Brewster detail map

Brewster Historical Society Museum

Linnell Landing

Crosby Beach

Breakwater Landing

East Brewster

Brewster Store

Cape Cod Museum of Natural History

6A

Brewster Ladies' Library

Brewster

Stony Brook Rd.

6A

New England Fire & History Museum

West Brewster

Tubman Rd.

see detail map at above

East Brewster

Brewster

Paine's Creek Beach

West Brewster

Nickerson State Park

6A

East Dennis

Dennis

Stony Brook Grist Mill

Punkhorn Parklands

124

Long Pond

East Harwich

Pleasant Bay

Setucket Rd.

134

6

Chatham
see detail map

North Beach

South Dennis

39

39

137

West Chatham

Chatham Light

South Yarmouth

Harwich

28

Harwich Port

South Harwich

Morris Island

South Beach

West Dennis

28

Dennisport

May-Oct.

Harding's Beach

Monomoy National Wildlife Refuge

0   2 miles
0   2 kilometers

mates and masters of vessels than any other town in the country." Many mansions built for sea captains remain, and quite a few have been turned into handsome B&Bs (though in recent years, more than a few of these have reverted to private homes). In the 18th and 19th centuries, the bay side of Brewster

LAY OF THE LAND

In Brewster, Route 6A is also known as Main Street.

was the site of a major salt-making industry. Of the 450 saltworks operating on the Cape in the 1830s, more than 60 were here.

Brewster's location on Cape Cod Bay makes it a perfect place to learn about the region's ecology. The Cape Cod Museum of Natural History is here, and the area is rich in conservation lands, state parks, forests, freshwater ponds, and brackish marshes. When the tide is low in Cape Cod Bay, you can stroll the beaches and explore tidal pools up to 2 mi from the shore on the Brewster flats. When it's high tide, the water is relatively warm and very calm for swimming. Both Nickerson State Park and the Punkhorn Parklands have thousands of acres through which to wander.

Windmills used to be prominent in Cape Cod towns; the Brewster area once had four. The 1795 **Higgins Farm Windmill** (⊠ *Off Rte. 6A, just west of the Cape Cod Museum of Natural History, West Brewster* ⊙ *Mid-June–mid-Oct., Thurs.–Sat. 1–4*)—an octagonal-type mill shingled in weathered pine with a roof like an upturned boat—was moved here in 1974 and has been restored. The millstones are original. At night the mill is often spotlighted, which makes for quite a sight.

On the grounds of the Higgins Farm Windmill in Drummer Boy Park, the one-room **Harris-Black House** dates to 1795. Today, the restored building is partially furnished and is dominated by a brick hearth and original woodwork. ⊠ *Off Rte. 6A, just west of Cape Cod Museum of Natural History, West Brewster* ☎ *508/896–9521* 🖥 *Free* ⊙ *July–Sept., Thurs.–Sat. 1–4*.

A short drive from Route 6A is the **Stony Brook Grist Mill**, a restored, operating 19th-century fulling mill (a mill that shrinks and thickens cloth), now also a museum. The old mill's waterwheel slowly turns in a small, tree-lined brook. Inside, exhibits include old mill equipment and looms; you can watch cornmeal being stone-ground and get a lesson in weaving on a 100-year-old loom. Out back, across wooden bridges, a bench has a view of the pond and of the sluices leading into the mill area.

Early each spring, in April and early May, Stony Brook's **Herring Run** boils with alewives (herring) making their way to spawning waters; it's an amazing sight. The fish swim in from Cape Cod Bay up Paine's Creek to Stony Brook and the ponds beyond it. The herring run, a rushing stream across the street from the mill, consists of ladders that help the fish climb the rocky waters. Seagulls swarm in and pluck herring from the run into midair. Sadly, disturbingly low numbers of returning herring have prompted the state to issue a three-year moratorium on fish harvests at the run. Starting with the spring of 2006, no herring can be taken from the stream, ending a long-standing tradition in hopes of increasing fish stocks. Farther down the path to the stream, there's an ivy-covered stone wishing well and a wooden bridge with a bench. ⊠ *Stony Brook Rd., West Brewster* ⊹ *Off Rte. 6A* ☎ *No phone* ⊕ *www.brewsterhistoricalsociety.org* ⊠ *Donations accepted* ۞ *May–Aug., Thurs.–Sat. 2–5.*

For nature enthusiasts, a visit to the **Cape Cod Museum of Natural History** is a must; it's just a short drive west from the heart of Brewster along Route 6A. The spacious museum and pristine grounds include guided field walks, a shop, a natural-history library, lectures, classes, nature and marine exhibits such as a working beehive, and a pond- and sea-life room with live specimens. Walking trails wind through 80 acres of forest, marshland, and ponds, all rich in birds and other wildlife. The exhibit hall upstairs has a wall display of aerial photographs documenting the process by which the famous Chatham sandbar was split in two. The museum also has guided canoe and kayak trips from May through September and several cruises that explore Cape waterways. Onboard naturalists point out the wildlife and relay historical information about each habitat. Call for tour times and fees, and sign up as early as you can. The museum has wildlife movies and slide lectures in the auditorium on Wednesday at 7:30, from early July through August. There are children's and family activities in summer, including full- and half-day workshops and one- and two-week day camps consisting of art and nature classes for preschoolers through ninth graders. ⊠ *869 Main St. (Rte. 6A), West Brewster* ☎ *508/896–3867, 800/479–3867 in Massachusetts* ⊕ *www.ccmnh.org* ⊠ *$8* ۞ *Oct.–Apr., Wed.–Sun. 11–3; Apr. and May, Wed.–Sun. 10–4; June–Sept., daily 10–4.*

The **Brewster Ladies' Library** (⊠ *1822 Main St. (Rte. 6A)* ☎ *508/896–3913* ⊕ *www.brewsterladieslibrary.org*) is in both a restored Victorian building and a more recent addition. The library is host to a full schedule of regular events for all ages, including book discussion groups, lectures, readings, and craft programs for children.

At the junction of Route 124, the **Brewster Store** (⊠ *1935 Main St. [Rte. 6A]* ☎ *508/896–3744* ⊕ *www.brewsterstore.com*) is a local landmark. Built in 1852 as a church, it's a typical New England general store with such essentials as the daily papers, penny candy, and benches out front for conversation. Out back, the Brewster Scoop serves ice cream mid-June through early September. Upstairs, the old front of the store has been re-created, and memorabilia from antique toys to World War II bond posters are displayed. Downstairs there's a working antique nickelodeon.

NEED A BREAK?

If you need a quick break, **Hopkins House Gift and Bakery** (⊠ *2727 Main St. [Rte. 6A], East Brewster* ☎ *508/896–9337*) is the perfect pit stop. Wash down a chewy hermit cookie, baked with molasses and raisins, with some strong, hot coffee. A home-furnishings shop attached to the bakery might tempt you to stretch your legs a while longer.

Known as the Church of the Sea Captains, the handsome **First Parish Church** (✉ *1969 Main St. [Rte. 6A]* ☎ *508/896–5577*), with Gothic windows and a capped bell tower, is full of pews marked with the names of famous Brewster seamen. Out back is an old graveyard where militiamen, clergy, farmers, and sea

> **DID YOU KNOW?**
>
> Horatio Alger, author of rags-to-riches stories such as *Ragged Dick*, served as minister of Brewster's First Parish Church from 1864–66.

captains rest side by side. The church is the site of a summer musical program, which includes the ever-popular Tanglewood marionette show, Tuesday through Thursday mornings at 9:30.

The **Brewster Historical Society Museum,** in an 1830s house, has a sea captain's room with paintings and artifacts, an 1890 barbershop, a child's room with antique toys and clothing, a room of women's period gowns and accessories, and other exhibits on local history and architecture. Out back, a ¼-mi nature trail over dunes leads to the bay. ✉ *3371 Rte. 6A, East Brewster* ☎ *508/896–9521* ⊕ *www.brewster-historicalsociety.org* ⊠ *Free* ☉ *June and Sept., weekends 1–4; July and Aug., Tues.–Fri. 1–4.*

For a lovely hike or run through the local wilds, try the **Punkhorn Parklands,** with freshwater kettle-hole ponds and 45 mi of scenic trails meandering through 800 acres of meadows, marshes, and pine forests. ✉ *End of Run Hill Rd., off Stony Brook Rd., West Brewster.*

☼ **Nickerson State Park**'s 1,961 acres were once part of a vast estate belonging to Roland C. Nickerson, son of Samuel Nickerson, a Chatham native who became a multimillionaire and founder of the First National Bank of Chicago. Today the land is open to the public for recreation. Roland and his wife, Addie, lavishly entertained such visitors as President Grover Cleveland at their private beach and hunting lodge in English country-house style, with coachmen dressed in tails and top hats and a bugler announcing carriages entering the front gates. Like a village unto itself, the estate gardens provided much of the household's food, supplemented by game from its woods and fish from its ponds. It also had its own electric plant and a 9-hole golf course by the water. The enormous mansion Samuel built for his son in 1886 burned to the ground 20 years later, and Roland died two weeks after the event. The grand stone mansion built to replace it in 1908 is now part of the Ocean Edge resort. In 1934 Addie donated the land for the state park in memory of Roland and their son, who died during the 1918 flu epidemic.

The park consists of acres of oak, pitch pine, hemlock, and spruce forest speckled with seven freshwater kettle ponds formed by glacial action. Some ponds are stocked with trout for fishing. You can swim in the ponds, canoe, sail, motorboat, bike along 8 mi of paved trails that have access to the Cape Cod Rail Trail, picnic, and cross-country ski in winter. Bird-watchers seek out the thrushes, wrens, warblers, woodpeckers, finches, larks, Canada geese, cormorants, great blue herons, hawks, owls, ospreys, and other species that frequent the park. Occasionally, red foxes and white-tailed deer are spotted in the woods. Both tent and RV camping are extremely popular here, and nature programs are offered in season. A map of the park is available on-site. ✉*3488 Rte. 6A, East Brewster* ☎*508/896–3491* ⊕*www.mass.gov/dcr* ✉*Free* ⊗*Daily dawn–dusk.*

NEED A BREAK?

Box Lunch (✉*302 Underpass Rd. near Cape Cod Rail Trail crossing South Brewster* ☎*508/896–1234*), famous for its "rollwiches," has a few branches on the Cape. This location has the same tasty selection of breakfast and lunch roll-ups, perfect for grabbing a bite while you're on the Cape Cod Rail Trail or just touring around. In summer Box Lunch stays open until 9 PM; it closes at 4 PM when the weather turns cooler.

4

WHERE TO STAY & EAT

$$$$ ★ ✗**Bramble Inn.** Inside an inviting 1860s white house in Brewster's historical village center, this romantic property presents well-crafted, globally inspired contemporary fare in five dining rooms with floral wallpaper or wood-paneled walls, hung with gilt-framed mirrors and watercolor and oil paintings (much of the artwork is for sale). During the warmer months, dine on a patio amid fragrant flower beds. The four-course prix-fixe menu changes often and has included such memorable treats as black-bean blini topped with smoked salmon and salmon caviar, and grilled lamb stacked over pinto bean puree and a Guadalajaran-inspired rose-petal mole sauce. Sunday through Thursday you can also order à la carte from a lighter bistro menu, which is served in the bar as well as on one of the garden patios. There are also a few attractive overnight rooms. ✉*2019 Main St. (Rte. 6A), East Brewster* ☎*508/896–7644* ⊕*www.brambleinn.com* ▤*AE, D, MC, V* ⊗*Closed Jan.–Mar. No lunch.*

$$$$ Fodor'sChoice ★ ✗**Chillingsworth.** One of the crown jewels of Cape restaurants, Chillingsworth combines formal presentation with an excellent French menu and a diverse wine cellar to create a memorable dining experience. Super-rich risotto, roast lobster, and grilled Angus sirloin are favorites. Dinner in the main dining rooms is prix fixe and includes seven courses—appetizer, soup, salad, sorbet, entrée, "amusements," and dessert, plus coffee or tea. Less expensive à la carte options for lunch, dinner, and Sunday brunch are served in the more casual, patio-style Bistro. There are also a few guest rooms here for overnighting. ✉*2449 Main St. (Rte. 6A), East Brewster* ☎*508/896–3640* ⊕*www.chillingsworth.com* ▤*AE, DC, MC, V* ⊗*Closed Thanksgiving –mid-May.*

$$–$$$$ Fodor'sChoice ★ ✗**Brewster Fish House.** Humble on the outside yet vibrant and flavorful within, the Fish House has carved a niche for itself: Cape Cod standards such as classic scrod and New England boiled dinner share billing with both traditional and more inspired preparations of duck, rack of lamb, Cornish hen, and tenderloin of beef. Locals are known to drive from all points of the Cape to this lovably rickety restaurant for the super-fresh fish. The wine list includes a flavorful selection of by-the-glass offerings. ✉*2208 Main St. (Rte. 6A), Brewster* ☎*508/896–7867* ⊗*Reservations not accepted* ▤*MC, V.*

$–$$ ✕**Brewster Inn and Chowder House.** The consistently excellent food at this long-standing Cape institution continues to live up to its great reputation among locals. Home cooking in the traditional New England style is the rule; you'll find no fancy or fussy fusion recipes here—just comfort food. Look for simple but tasty meat and seafood standards, and don't miss the rich and full-bodied New England clam chowder. The service is friendly, the prices are kind, and you won't leave hungry. The restaurant serves lunch and dinner daily year-round. ⊠*1993 Main St. (Rte. 6A)* ☎*508/896–7771* ⊟*MC, V.*

¢–$$ ✕**JT's Seafood.** Fresh and ample portions of fried seafood take center stage at this casual joint, which is very popular with families. Pick from several seafood platters, or gnaw on baby back ribs or burgers if you need a break from the fruits of the sea. Several items, including corn dogs, grilled cheese (lunch only), and peanut butter and jelly, are good kid-friendly choices. Place your order at the counter and sit inside or out. Leave your mark by sticking a pin in your town's name on the big map by the order counter. Takeout is also available. ⊠*2689 Main St. (Rte. 6A)* ☎*508/896–3355* ⌂*Reservations not accepted* ⊟*MC, V* ⊗*Closed mid-Oct.–mid-Apr.*

¢–$ ✕**Laurino's Tavern.** There's something timeless about this noisy pizza joint and American eatery with warm wood paneling, generous booth-style seating, and red-and-white-checkered tablecloths, plus a big patio and a playground for kids. Meatball grinders, steak-and-cheese sandwiches, and specialty pizzas are mainstays. Try a buffalo-chicken pizza, topped with wing sauce and cheddar cheese, with a blue cheese dipping sauce. Lasagna, shrimp scampi, and mussels marinara are popular choices. The long, friendly bar is a great place to sit with a buddy over a beer and a big plate of Macho Nachos. In summer live music serenades the late-night crowd. ⊠*3668 Main St. (Rte. 6A), East Brewster* ☎*508/896–6135* ⌂*Reservations not accepted* ⊟*AE, MC, V.*

$$$–$$$$ ⊞**Ocean Edge.** One of the Cape's few full-service resorts, Ocean Edge
★ is a luxury beachfront community where accommodations range from hotel rooms in the conference center to one- to three-bedroom condominiums in the woods and two- to three-bedroom beachfront villas. Condominiums have full kitchens and washer-dryers; some units have fireplaces, and many have ocean views. All rooms and condos have balconies or patios. There's also a championship 18-hole golf course and tennis courts. Clambakes, concerts, and tournaments take place throughout the summer. **Pros:** Great for golfers, many rooms on Cape Cod Bay side with beach access and water views, full-service resort. **Cons:** Not for those looking for intimate lodging experience. ⊠*2907 Main St. (Rte. 6A), 02631* ☎*508/896–9000 or 800/343–6074* ⊟*508/896–9123* ⊕*www.oceanedge.com* ⊅*292 condominium units, 90 rooms* ⌂*In-room: Wi-Fi. In-hotel: 4 restaurants, room service, bar, tennis courts, pools, gym, beachfront, bicycles, concierge, children's programs (ages 4–17), laundry facilities* ⊟*AE, D, DC, MC, V.*

$$–$$$$ ⊞**Brewster By The Sea Inn &Spa.** Weather permitting, a three-course breakfast is served on the patio overlooking a swimming pool and 2 acres of landscaped gardens at this restored, beautifully decorated 1846 farmhouse on historic Route 6A. A fireplace is the focal point in one guest room, and another has a king-size canopy bed and sliders that open onto a private deck. Three more guest rooms, furnished with authentic and reproduction antiques, fireplaces, and hot tubs, are in an adjacent carriage house. Afternoon tea is included. Some off-season weekends are centered around cooking workshops and murder-mystery sleuths; ask about spa and/or dinner packages. **Pros:** Intimate lodging, ideal for those who want to fully relax away from busy distractions. **Cons:** Not an in-town or beachside location, not for those traveling with children. ⊠*716 Main St. (Rte. 6A), 02631* ☎*508/896–3910 or 800/892–3910* 📠*508/896–4232* ⊕*www.brewsterbythesea.com* ✑*6 rooms, 2 suites* ⚘*In-room: Wi-Fi. In-hotel: pool, spa, no kids under 16, no-smoking rooms, no elevator* ▤*AE, D, MC, V* ⎥*BP.*

$$ **Isaiah Clark House.** This former 18th-century sea captain's residence, just west of the town proper, retains its wide-plank flooring and low, sloping ceilings and has a varied selection of antiques. The original inhabitants have left their mark all over the house, from the scrawled signature of 13-year-old son Jeremiah in a closet to the framed historic documents and photographs on the walls to the namesake of each of the rooms (all Clark family women). Most rooms have queen-size four-poster or canopy beds, braided rugs, and fireplaces. The extensive gardens yield some of the fruit used in the homemade pies, muffins, and breads that are served at breakfast. **Pros:** Beautifully maintained, historic lodging, outdoor shower available for post-beach refresher, beaches and town center just a few minutes away. **Cons:** Due to the home's advanced age, some rooms are on the smaller side and are accessed via steep stairs. ⊠*1187 Main St. (Rte. 6A), 02631* ☎*508/896–2223 or 800/822–4001* ⊕*www.isaiahclark.com* ✑*7 rooms* ⚘*In-room: no phone, Wi-Fi. In-hotel: no kids under 10, no-smoking rooms, no elevator* ▤*AE, MC, V* ⎥*BP.*

$-$$ **Candleberry Inn.** This 1790s Georgian mansion sits along a peaceful stretch of scenic Main Street and was once the home of writer Horatio Alger. The sun-filled rooms are unfussy but elegant, with Oriental rugs, wide-plank floors, original woodwork, and tall windows with the original wavy glass. Several have working fireplaces, and two particularly cozy units—the Seabreeze and Treetops rooms—have pitched ceilings and access to a deck overlooking the leafy grounds and fragrant gardens. The Seacroft Suite has French doors leading to a large sitting area. Gracious innkeepers Stuart and Charlotte Fyfe serve a delicious full breakfast out by the garden in summer and in a cozy dining room during the cooler months. **Pros:** In the heart of historic Brewster village, authentic historic lodging, spacious gardens and grounds. **Cons:** Many rooms accessed via steep stairs, some rooms are on the smaller size due to the home's age. ⊠*1882 Main St. (Rte. 6A), 02631* ☎*508/896–3300 or 800/573–4769* 📠*508/896–4016* ⊕*www.candleberryinn.com* ✑*7 rooms, 1 suite* ⚘*In-hotel: no kids under 10, no-smoking rooms, no elevator* ▤*AE, D, DC, MC, V* ⎥*BP.*

¢–$$ **Old Sea Pines Inn.** With its white-column portico and wraparound
Fodor's Choice veranda overlooking a broad lawn, Old Sea Pines, which housed a young
★ ladies' boarding school in the early 1900s, resembles a vintage summer estate. Climb the sweeping staircase to guest rooms decorated with

4

reproduction wallpaper, antiques, and framed old photographs. Some are quite large; others have fireplaces. One of the more popular rooms has a sitting area in an enclosed sunporch. Rooms in a newer building are simple, with bright white modern baths and cast-iron queen-size beds. Some rooms have shared bathrooms. The inn also holds a Sunday night Broadway musical dinner revue from mid-June through mid-September. **Pros:** Not far from town center, beautiful grounds, reasonable rates in historic setting. **Cons:** Some rooms have shared baths, many rooms accessed steep stairway on upper floors. ⊠ *2553 Main St. (Rte. 6A), Box 1070, 02631* ☎ *508/896–6114* 🖷 *508/632–0084* ⊕ *www. oldseapineinn.com* 🛏 *24 rooms, 19 with bath, 5 suites* ⅃ *In-room: no phone, no TV (some), Wi-Fi. In-hotel: dining room, no kids under 8 (except for family suites), no-smoking rooms, no elevator* ⊟ *AE, D, MC, V* ⊗ *Closed Jan.–Mar.* ⦶⦶ *BP.*

¢   🌲 **Nickerson State Park.** Shaded by a canopy of white pine, hemlock, and spruce, Nickerson State Park is a nature-lover's haven. Encompassing close to 2,000 acres of wooded landscape teeming with wildlife, the park is the Cape's largest and most popular camping site. While away a summer afternoon trout fishing, walking, biking on 8 mi of paved trails (which connect to the Cape Cod Rail Trail), canoeing, sailing, motorboating, or bird-watching; there are four ponds for swimming, plus ocean beaches nearby. RVs must be self-contained. Maps and schedules of park programs are available at the park entrance. Campground reservations are accepted six months in advance, mid-April through mid-October, and sites are available on a walk-in basis only the rest of the year. There's a $9.50 fee per reservation; note that camping fees are slightly lower for in-state residents. ⅃ *Flush toilets, dump station, drinking water, showers, fire grates, grills, picnic tables, public telephone, general store, play area, ranger station, swimming (ponds)* 🛏 *420 sites, some yurts* ⊠ *3488 Rte. 6A, 02631* ☎ *508/896–3491, 877/422–6762 reservations* 🖷 *508/896–3103* ⊕ *www.mass.gov/dcr* ⊟ *No credit cards.*

NIGHTLIFE & THE ARTS

The **Cape Cod Repertory Theatre Co.** (⊠ *3379 Rte. 6A, West Brewster* ☎ *508/896–1888* ⊕ *www.caperep.org*) performs several impressive productions, from original works to classics, in its indoor Arts and Crafts–style theater way back in the woods. The season runs from May to November. Mesmerizing entertainment for children, in the form of lively outdoor (and often interactive) theater, is provided here, too. Performances of fairy tales, music, and folk tales are given on Tuesday and Friday mornings at 10 in June, July, and August. The theater is just west of Nickerson State Park.

Sunday evenings by the bay are filled with the sounds of the **town-band concerts** (⊠ *Rte. 6A, West Brewster*), held in the gazebo on the grounds of Drummer Boy Park. The park is about ½ mi west of the Cape Cod Museum of Natural History, on the western side of Brewster. Families with little ones will delight in the park's playground with its ornate wood facilities.

The **Woodshed** (✉*1993 Main St. [Rte. 6A]* ☎*508/896–7771*), the rustic bar at the Brewster Inn, is a good place to soak up local color and listen to pop duos or bands that perform nightly. It's open from May through October.

SPORTS & THE OUTDOORS

BASEBALL   The **Brewster Whitecaps** (☎*508/385–5073* ⊕*www.brewsterwhitecaps. com*) of the collegiate Cape Cod Baseball League play home games at **Stony Brook School** (✉*Underpass Rd., Brewster*) from mid-June to mid-August.

BEACHES   **Flax Pond** (✉*3488 Main St. [Rte. 6A], East Brewster* ☎*508/896–3491*) in Nickerson State Park, surrounded by pines, has picnic areas, a bathhouse, and water-sports rentals.

Brewster's bay beaches all have access to the flats that at low tide make for very interesting tidal-pool exploration. Eponymous roads to each beach branch off Route 6A; there's limited parking. All of the bay beaches require a daily, weekly, or seasonal parking pass (which for nonresidents cost $15, $40, and $125, respectively); these can be purchased at the town hall (☎*508/896–4511*). **Breakwater Landing** is one of the most popular beaches in town and has an ample parking area. **Linnell Landing** has a smaller lot and tends to fill up quickly. A favorite among the toddler crowd and the sunset seekers, **Paine's Creek** also lacks a large lot, but if you get there early enough, you can find a spot. Harder to find down a dead-end street but worth it, **Robbin's Hill** is known for its intriguing tidal pools. Farther east off Route 6A is **Crosby Beach,** ideal for beach walkers—you can trek straightway to Orleans if you so desire.

BICYCLING   The **Cape Cod Rail Trail** has many access points in Brewster, among them Long Pond Road, Underpass Road, and Nickerson State Park.

Brewster Bike (✉*442 Underpass Rd.* ☎*508/896–8149*) carries a large selection of bikes for rent.

The **Rail Trail Bike and Kayak** (✉*302 Underpass Rd.* ☎*508/896–8200*) rents bikes, including children's bikes, and in-line skates. Parking is free, and there's a picnic area with easy access to the Rail Trail.

FISHING   Many of Brewster's freshwater ponds are good for catching perch, pickerel, and other fish; five ponds are well stocked with trout. Especially good for fishing is Cliff Pond in Nickerson State Park. You'll need a **fishing license,** available from the town hall. ✉*2198 Main St. (Rte. 6A), East Brewster* ☎*508/896–4506.*

GOLF   The **Captain's Golf Course** (✉*1000 Freeman's Way, east of Rte. 6* ☎*508/896–1716 or 877/843–9081*) is an excellent public facility with 2 fine 18-hole courses—*Golf Digest* has named it one of the leading public courses in the nation.

Ocean Edge Golf Course (✉*Villages Dr., off Rte. 6A, East Brewster* ☎*508/896–5911*), an 18-hole, par-72 course winding around five ponds, has Scottish-style pot bunkers and challenging terrain. Three-day residential and commuter golf schools are offered in spring and early summer.

HORSEBACK RIDING
Woodsong Farm (✉ *121 Lund Farm Way, South Brewster* ☎ *508/896–5800* ⊕ *www.woodsongfarm.com*) has instruction and day programs, but no rentals or trail rides; it also has a horsemanship day-camp program for kids 5 to 18.

TENNIS
The **Ocean Edge** (✉ *2907 Main St. [Rte. 6A], East Brewster* ☎ *508/896–9000*) resort has five clay and six Plexipave courts. It offers lessons and round-robins and hosts a tennis school, with weekend packages and video analysis.

Run by the town and open to the public at no charge are four **public tennis courts,** all just behind the fire and police stations on 1673 Route 6A. Two basketball courts are also available for public use.

WATER SPORTS
Cape Cod Sea Camps (✉ *Box 1880, Brewster 02631* ☎ *508/896–3451*) teaches team sports, archery, art, drama, sailing, and water sports to kids ages 4 to 17.

Jack's Boat Rentals (✉ *Flax Pond, Nickerson State Park, Rte. 6A, East Brewster* ☎ *508/896–8556*) rents canoes, kayaks, Seacycles, Sunfish, pedal boats, and sailboards; guide-led kayak tours are also offered.

SHOPPING

B. D. Hutchinson (✉ *1274 Long Pond Rd., South Brewster* ☎ *508/896–6395*), a watch and clock maker, sells antique and collectible watches, clocks, and music boxes.

★ **Brewster Book Store** (✉ *2648 Main St. [Rte. 6A], East Brewster* ☎ *508/896–6543 or 800/823–6543*) prides itself on being a special Cape bookstore. It's filled to the rafters with all manner of books by local and international authors and has an extensive fiction selection and kids section. A full schedule of author signings and children's story times continues year-round.

Countryside Antiques (✉ *2052 Main St. [Rte. 6A], Brewster* ☎ *508/240–0525*) specializes in European and Asian antique furniture, home-accent pieces, china, and silver.

HandCraft House (✉ *3996 Rte. 6A, East Brewster* ☎ *508/240–1412 or 888/826–4393*) has "handmade in the USA" art for the home and garden, wood sculptures, handblown glass, stoneware, watercolors, and jewelry.

Kemp Pottery (✉ *258 Main St. [Rte. 6A], West Brewster* ☎ *508/385–5782*) has functional and decorative stoneware and porcelain, fountains, garden sculpture, pottery sinks, and stained glass.

Kings Way Books and Antiques (✉ *774 Main St. [Rte. 6A], West Brewster* ☎ *508/896–3639*) sells out-of-print and rare books—they have a large medieval section—plus small antiques, china, glass, silver, coins, and linens.

Lemon Tree Village (✉1069 Main St. [Rte. 6A]) is a cheery complex filled with many unusual stores. You can find garden statuary, top-of-the-line cooking implements, locally made arts and crafts, pottery, birding supplies, clothing, gifts, jewelry, and toys. There's even a café next door if all that shopping makes you hungry.

Open from April through October, the **Satucket Farm Stand** (✉76 Harwich Rd. [Rte. 124], off Rte. 6A ☎508/896–5540) is a real old-fashioned farm stand and bakery. Most produce is grown on the premises, and you can fill your basket with home-baked scones and breads, fruit pies, produce, herbs, and flowers.

The **Spectrum** (✉369 Main St. [Rte. 6A], West Brewster ☎508/385–3322) carries a great selection of imaginative American arts and crafts, including pottery, stained glass, and art glass.

★ **Sydenstricker Galleries** (✉490 Main St. [Rte. 6A], West Brewster ☎508/385–3272) stocks glassware handcrafted by a unique process, which you can watch while you're in the shop.

4

HARWICH

6 mi south of Brewster, 5 mi east of Dennis.

Originally known as Setucket, Harwich separated from Brewster in 1694 and was renamed for the famous English seaport. Like other townships on the Cape, Harwich is actually a cluster of several small villages, including Harwich Port. Historically, the villages of Harwich were marked by their generous number of churches and the styles of worship they practiced—small villages often sprang up around these centers of faith.

Harwich and Harwich Port are the commercial centers, and although the two have very different natures, both have graceful old architecture and rich histories. Harwich Port is the more bustling of the two: brimming with shops, calm-water beaches, restaurants, and hotel complexes, it packs all manner of entertainment and frivolity along its roadways. Harwich is more relaxed; its commerce is more centered, and its outlying areas are graced with greenery, large shade trees, and historic homesteads. The Harwich Historical Society has a strong presence here, maintaining exhibits and artifacts significant to the town's past.

The Cape's famous cranberry industry took off in Harwich in 1844, when Alvin Cahoon was its principal grower. Today you'll still find cranberry bogs throughout Harwich, and each September the town holds a **Cranberry Festival** to celebrate the importance of this indigenous berry; the festival is usually scheduled during the week after Labor Day.

Three naturally sheltered harbors on Nantucket Sound make the town, like its English namesake, popular with boaters. You'll find dozens of elegant sailboats and elaborate yachts in Harwich's harbors, plus plenty of charter-fishing boats. Each year in August the town pays celebratory homage to its large boating population with a grand regatta, Sails Around the Cape.

Beaches are plentiful in Harwich, and nearly all rest on the warm and mild waters of Nantucket Sound. Freshwater ponds, ideal for swimming as well as small-scale canoeing and kayaking, also speckle the area. Several conservation areas have miles of secluded walking trails, many alongside vivid cranberry bogs.

Once the home of a private-school offering the first high school–level curriculum in Harwich, the pillared 1844 Greek-revival building of the **Brooks Academy Museum** now houses the museum of the **Harwich Historical Society**. In addition to a large photo-history collection and exhibits on artist Charles Cahoon (grandson of cranberry grower Alvin), the sociotechnological history of cranberry culture, and shoe making, the museum has antique clothing and textiles, china and glass, fans, and toys. There's also an extensive genealogical collection for researchers. On the grounds is a powder house used to store gunpowder during the Revolutionary War, as well as a restored 1872 outhouse that could spur your appreciation for indoor plumbing. ⊠ *80 Parallel St.* ☎ *508/432–8089* ☞ *Donations accepted* ☉ *Late June–Sept., Wed.– Sat. 1–4; Oct., Thurs. and Fri. 1–4.*

☾ **Brooks Park** on Main Street (Route 28) is a good place to stretch your legs; it has a playground, picnic tables, a ball field, tennis courts, and a bandstand where summer concerts are held.

☾ For children who have spent too much time in the car watching you drive, a spin behind the wheel of one of 20 top-of-the-line go-karts at **Bud's Go-Karts** may be just the thing. ⊠ *9 Sisson Rd., off Rte. 28, Harwich Port* ☎ *508/432–4964* ☉ *June–early Sept., Mon.–Sat. 9 AM–11 PM, Sun. 10 AM–11 PM.*

☾ **Grand Slam Entertainment** has softball- and baseball-batting cages and pitching machines, including one with fastballs up to 80 mph and a Wiffle-ball machine for younger kids, plus a bumper-boat pool and a video-arcade room. ⊠ *322 Main St. (Rte. 28), Harwich Port* ☎ *508/430– 1155* ⊕ *www.grandslamentertainment.com* ☉ *Apr., May, and Sept.–mid-Oct., Mon.–Sat. 11–7, Sun. 11–9; June–Aug., daily 9 AM–10 PM.*

☾ The **Trampoline Center** has 12 trampolines set up at ground level over pits for safety. ⊠ *296 Main St. (Rte. 28), West Harwich* ☎ *508/432–8717* ☉ *Apr.–mid-June, weekends, hrs vary widely, call ahead; mid-June–early Sept., daily 9 AM–11 PM.*

WHERE TO STAY & EAT

$$$–$$$$ ✕ **Cape Sea Grille.** Sitting primly inside a dashing Gothic Victorian house
★ on a side street off hectic Route 28, this gem with distant sea views cultivates a refined ambience with fresh flowers, white linens, and vibrant wall murals. Specialties from the ever-changing menu include crispy duck confit with Swiss chard, roasted beets, and a red-wine glaze; and grilled Atlantic salmon wrapped in prosciutto with melon, cucumbers, toasted Israeli couscous, and a wild-blackberry vinaigrette. Chef-owner Douglas Ramler (formerly of Boston's noted Hamersley's Bistro) relies

on the freshest ingredients. ⊠*31 Sea St., Harwich Port* ☎*508/432–4745* ⊟*AE, D, MC, V* ⊗*Closed Dec.–early Apr. No lunch.*

$$$–$$$$　✕**L'Alouette.** Owners Alan and Gretchen Champney serve authentic French food in this unassuming gray-shingle house with a loyal following among foodies in the know. Look for traditional and contemporary selections such as butter-poached lobster with a saffron-vanilla sauce, Moroccan braised lamb with preserved lemon and mint, and sun-dried-tomato-crusted halibut with a lemon, roasted garlic, and sage sauce and wilted spinach. Desserts here are a particular delight, especially the light and not-too-sweet tarte tatin. There's also a superb wine list. ⊠*787 Main St. (Rte. 28), Harwich Port* ☎*508/430–0405* ⊟*AE, DC, MC, V* ⊗*No lunch.*

$$–$$$　✕**Buca's Tuscan Roadhouse.** This romantic roadhouse near the Chatham
★　border, with a vintage Ford station wagon parked out front, has crisp red-and-white-checked tablecloths and a vibe that might just transport you to Italy—and if it doesn't, the food will. From *zuppe* to aged pecorino, Gorgonzola, and ricotta salad with figs to veal with red wine, balsamic butter, sun-dried cherries, and roasted tomatoes, this is mouthwatering Italian fare taken far beyond traditional home cooking. ⊠*4 Depot Rd., Harwich* ☎*508/432–6900* ⊕*www.bucasroadhouse. com* ⊟*MC, V* ⊗*No lunch.*

$$–$$$　✕**The Port.** An urbane and homey storefront café in downtown Har-
★　wich Port, the kitchen focuses on fairly traditional American fare, especially seafood, but with some inventive interpretations. You might, for instance, sample pan-seared shrimp with baby spinach and red and yellow tomatoes with a white wine–truffle sauce and angel-hair pasta, or grilled pork with Jamaican jerk spices alongside lemongrass-steamed rice and veggies. The Thai-style lobster-crab cake with wasabi sour cream makes for a nice starter. The menu is long and ambitious, and there's also an extensive, well-chosen wine list. ⊠*541 Main St. (Rte. 28)* ☎*508/430–5410* ⊟*AE, MC, V* ⚐*Reservations only for parties of 5 or more* ⊗*Closed Dec.–Apr. No lunch.*

$$　✕**Brax Landing.** In this local stalwart perched alongside busy Saquatucket Harbor, you can get a menu tip-off as you pass by tanks full of steamers and lobsters in the corridor leading to the dining room. The restaurant sprawls around a big bar that serves specialty drinks such as the Banzai (frozen piña colada with a float of dark rum). The swordfish with pineapple-mango salsa and the herb-crusted Chatham scrod are favorites, both served simply and well. And if you've been after the ultimate lobster roll—and never thought you could get full on one—sample the one at Brax Landing, bursting with the meat of a 1¼-pound lobster. There's also a notable children's menu, and Sunday brunch is an institution. ⊠*705 Main St. (Rte. 28 at Saquatucket Harbor), Harwich Port* ☎*508/432–5515* ⚐*Reservations not accepted* ⊟*AE, DC, MC, V* ⊗*Restaurant closed Jan. and Feb.; bar open year-round.*

¢–$$　✕**400 East.** This big, dark restaurant buzzing with conversation is in a nondescript shopping plaza. The menu includes teriyaki chicken, prime rib, lobster ravioli, burgers, and baked scrod, but also has excellent pizza, with toppings such as wild mushrooms, blue cheese, and chicken sausage. Eating at the busy, U-shape bar is a good alternative to waiting for a table. The 400 has a cousin restaurant (also called the 400) down-town on Main Street. ⊠*1421 Orleans Rd. (Rte. 39)* ☎*508/432–1800* ▤*AE, D, MC, V.*

¢–$ ✕**Ay! Caramba Café.** This unassuming, no-frills café in downtown Har-
★   wich is a great place to fill up on authentic Mexican fare—not easy to find in these parts—without cleaning out your wallet. Choose from tasty quesadillas, burritos, tostadas, and tacos, or go for one of the large combination plates, complete with rice and either refried beans or vegetables. More ambitious offerings include a nicely seasoned chicken mole, and Yucatán-style tuna steak with roasted pepper and pineapple salsa. The drinking crowd is young and boisterous here, and there's an extensive tequila menu—enthusiasts can even join the restaurant's Tequila Club. In warm weather, grab a seat on the outdoor patio. ⊠*703 Main St., Harwich* ☎*508/432–9800* ⊕*www.aycarambacafe. com* ▤*MC, V* ☉*Closed Sun. Nov.–Mar.*

$$$$ ✕▥**Wequassett Inn Resort & Golf Club.** Twenty Cape-style cottages and an
Fodor'sChoice   attractive hotel make up this traditionally elegant resort by the sea. Set
★   on 22 acres of shaded landscape partially surrounded by Pleasant Bay, the Wequassett is an informally upscale resort. An attentive staff, eve-ning entertainment, fun in the sun, and golf at the exclusive Cape Cod National Golf Club are just a few of the benefits you can count on at Wequassett. Chef Bill Brodsky's creative globally inspired cuisine graces the menus of the three restaurants—the star being the sophisticated 28 Atlantic ($$$–$$$$), which is one of the top destination restaurants on the Cape, serving such stellar creations as yellowfin and salmon tar-tare, and caramelized skate wing with beet-daikon-horseradish salad and watercress jus. The Pool Bar & Grill serves cocktails, beverages, snacks, and light lunch fare poolside. After a day at the beach or on the links, retire to your spacious room and relax amid fresh pine furniture, floral bedcovers or handmade quilts, and overflowing window boxes. Or, sip a cocktail on the lawn outside your private cottage-style room overlooking Pleasant Bay. **Pros:** Full-service resort in idyllic, waterfront setting, activities and programs for all ages, babysitting services on-site, elegant surroundings. **Cons:** Rates are very steep, not an in-town location. ⊠*2173 Orleans Rd. (Rte. 28), 02633* ⌂*2173 Orleans Rd., Rte. 28, East Harwich 02645* ☎*508/432–5400 or 800/225–7125* ⎙*508/432–5032* ⊕*www.wequassett.com* ⬦*102 rooms, 2 suites* ⌂*In-hotel: 3 restaurants, room service, bar, tennis courts, pool, gym, water sports, children's programs, no elevator* ▤*AE, D, DC, MC, V* ☉*Closed Nov.–Mar.* ◉*FAP.*

$$$–$$$$ ▥**Alyce's Dunscroft by-the-Sea.** This charming, luxurious beach house
★   sits a half block from Nantucket Sound and within walking distance of several restaurants, yet it's on a peaceful street away from the crowds. The rooms, named after a diverse selection of famous couples (Scarlet and Rhett, Sonny and Cher), have many romantic amenities, including king- and queen-size lace-canopy and four-poster beds, whirlpool tubs, cotton robes, and some working fireplaces. The cottage suite has a liv-ing room with a fireplace, kitchenette, and a Jacuzzi. In the common gathering room, you'll find a baby grand piano and extensive library. Alyce's full breakfasts are fantastic (she makes killer French toast).

Pros: Walk to beach, elegant and romantic lodging in a quiet setting, grand breakfasts. **Cons:** Some rooms accessed via steep stairs, no water views. ✉24 Pilgrim Rd., Harwich Port 02646 ☎508/432–0810 or 800/432–4345 ⊕www.dunscroftbythesea.com ↩8 rooms, 1 cottage ⅍In-room: kitchen (some), Wi-Fi. In-hotel: no kids under 16, no elevator ⊟AE, MC, V ⦿BP.

$$$–$$$$ ✠**Winstead Inn and Beach Resort.** Comprising two distinct properties,
★ the Winstead Inn and Beach Resort offer a two-for-one Cape Cod experience. Harking back to an earlier era, the airy, attractive Beach Resort sits on a private beach overlooking Nantucket Sound. You can gaze at the sweep of coast and surrounding grasslands while enjoying a generous continental breakfast from rockers and umbrella tables on the deck and wraparound porches. At the other end of the spectrum, the Winstead Inn sits along a quiet street on the edge of downtown. Greenery surrounds this Gothic Victorian house, and many of the rooms have a view of the outdoor pool. Guests at either property can use the amenities and facilities at both locations. **Pros:** One property sits right on the sand of private beach and most rooms have water views, pool privileges at sister property, spacious, elegant rooms. **Cons:** Many rooms located up steep stairs, not for those on a budget. ✉114 Parallel St., 02645 ✉4 Braddock La., Harwich Port 02646 ☎508/432–4444 or 800/870–4405 ⊕www.winsteadinn.com ↩18 rooms, 4 suites ⅍In-room: Wi-Fi. In-hotel: pool, no-smoking rooms, no elevator ⊟AE, MC, V ⦿CP.

$–$$$ ✠**Lion's Head Inn.** Actually a bit closer to Dennisport than to Harwich and Harwich Port, this well-maintained early-19th-century sea captain's home sits along a quiet street in a peaceful neighborhood a little less than a mile north of the sea. Innkeepers Marilyn and Tom Hull run this low-key, reasonably priced B&B and also rent out a pair of one-bedroom cottages with full kitchens and living rooms with double futons (so each can sleep a total of four); the cottages are available weekly in summer and for shorter stays the rest of the year. Rooms are modestly but tastefully appointed, with country quilts and a smattering of antiques. A big plus here is the large outdoor pool and attractive patio. **Pros:** Set back off busy Route 28 yet not far from area attractions, good location for exploring Dennis and Harwich areas, large outdoor pool. **Cons:** Many rooms accessed via steep stairs, room decor could use a little freshening, though comfortable, not an in-town or beachfront location. ✉186 Belmont Rd., West Harwich 02671 ☎508/432–7766 or 800/321–3155 ⊕www.capecodinns.com ↩5 rooms, 1 suite, 2 cottages ⅍In-room: kitchen (some), no TV (some). In-hotel: pool, no elevator ⊟D, MC, V ⦿CP.

NIGHTLIFE & THE ARTS

THE ARTS The **First Congregational Church** (✉Main St. at corner of Rtes. 39 and 124, Harwich ☎508/432–1053) closes its day of worship with Sunday-evening Candlelight Concerts at 7:30 from July through September.

Harwich Junior Theatre (✉105 Division St., West Harwich ☎508/432–2002 ⊕www.hjtcapecod.org) gives theater classes for kids year-round and presents 12 family-oriented productions.

Town-band concerts (☎508/432–1600) in Harwich take place in summer on Tuesday evening at 7:30 in Brooks Park.

NIGHTLIFE   The **Hot Stove Saloon** (✉551 Main St. [Rte. 28], Harwich Port ☎508/432–9911) is a convivial spot for tasty pub fare and a wide selection of beers and cocktails. The baseball-theme tavern also airs sporting events on TV.

Irish Pub (✉126 Main St. [Rte. 28], West Harwich ☎508/432–8808) has dancing to bands—playing Irish, American, and dance music—as well as sing-alongs, pool, darts, sports TV, and pub food in the bar.

Jake Rooney's Pub (✉119 Brooks Rd., off Rte. 28, Harwich Port ☎508/430–1100) is a comfortable watering hole. Keno and live entertainment five nights a week make it a fun place to hang out with friends.

Wequassett Inn Resort & Golf Club (✉173 Orleans Rd. [Rte. 28], Pleasant Bay ☎508/432–5400) has a jazz duo or piano music nightly in its lounge in July and August (jacket requested).

SPORTS & THE OUTDOORS

BASEBALL   The **Harwich Mariners** (✉Harwich High School, Oak St. ☎508/432–2000 ⊕www.harwichmariners.org) of the collegiate Cape Cod Baseball League play home games at Whitehouse Field on Oak Street from mid-June through mid-August.

BEACHES   Harwich has 21 beaches, more than any other Cape town. Most of the ocean beaches are on Nantucket Sound, where the water is a bit calmer and warmer. Freshwater pond beaches are also abundant. Nonresident beach parking stickers, sold at the **Harwich Community Center** (✉100 Oak St. ☎508/432–7638), cost $55 for one week, and $125 for the season, which runs from June through Labor Day. Ask for the free map of the town's beaches when you get your sticker.

BICYCLING   The **Bike Depot** (✉500 Depot St. ☎508/430–4375) has rentals, including some antique bikes. It's in North Harwich, right off the bike trail.

BOATING   Whether you're in the mood to sail under the moonlight, hire a private charter, or learn to navigate yourself, **Cape Sail** (✉337 Saquatucket Harbor, off Rte. 28, Harwich Port ☎508/896–2730) can accommodate any whim.

Sturgis Boat Works (✉337 Main St., Rte. 28, Harwich Port ☎508/432–5996) rents Sunfish, kayaks, and other small sailboats by the day or week.

Nauti Jane's (✉Off Rte. 28 at Wequassett Inn, East Harwich ☎508/430–6893) has Day Sailers, power boats, or peaceful kayaks for rent.

FISHING   Fishing trips are operated on a walk-on basis from spring through fall on the *Golden Eagle* (✉Wychmere Harbor, Harwich Port ☎508/432–5611).

The *Yankee* (✉Saquatucket Harbor, Harwich Port ☎508/432–2520) invites passengers in search of fluke, scup, sea bass, and tautog aboard its 65-foot party boat. Two trips depart daily Monday through Saturday in season; there's also one on Sunday. Reservations are recommended.

GOLF **Cranberry Valley Golf Course** (✉ *183 Oak St.* ☎ *508/430–5234* ⊕ *www. cranberrygolfcourse.com*) has a championship layout of 18 well-groomed holes surrounded by cranberry bogs.

Harwich Port Golf Club (✉ *South and Forest Sts., Harwich Port* ☎ *508/432–0250*) has a 9-hole course that's great for beginners.

SHOPPING

Cape Cod Braided Rug Co. (✉ *537 Rte. 28, Harwich Port* ☎ *508/432–3133*) makes braided rugs in all colors, styles, and sizes.

★ **Cape Cod Lavender Farm** (✉ *Corner of Rte. 124 and Weston Woods Rd., off U.S. 6, Exit 10, Harwich* ☎ *508/432–8397*) consists of some 14,000 lavender plants, making it one of the largest such farms on the East Coast. Apart from the plants themselves, the farm makes and sells soaps and bath salts, candles, potpourri, marmalade, lemonade, and many other lavender-infused goods and gifts. Keep your eyes peeled for their sign (on the right) as you're driving south on Route 124—it's easy to miss.

Cedar Spring Herb Farm (✉ *159 Long Pond Dr., Harwich* ☎ *508/430–4372* ⊕ *www.cedarspringherbfarm.com*) spreads out over 7 acres of walking trails, picnic areas, and fragrant, lush herb gardens. The emphasis here is health, both of the spiritual and physical sort; all herb products for sale are made from organic plants, and there is a full schedule of lectures, classes, and ceremonial healings and events. The farm is open from May to November.

820 Main Gallery (✉ *820 Main St. [Rte. 28], Harwich Port* ☎ *508/430–7622*) sells original works in oil, acrylics, watercolors, and photography, as well as limited-edition prints by established local artists. The gallery specializes in regional land- and seascapes.

The **Potted Geranium** (✉ *188 Main St. [Rte. 28], West Harwich* ☎ *508/432–1114*) stocks country-inspired home-related gifts, including colorful wind flags, handcrafted items, and wind chimes.

CHATHAM

❶–❻ *5 mi east of Harwich, 8 mi south of Orleans.*

Low-key, well-heeled Chatham feels like a sliver of Nantucket that's floated over to the Cape. It's neatly groomed and blue-blooded yet artsy, prim but eccentric, straight-arrow but with loads of personality. Originally populated by Native Americans, Chatham came into the hands of white settlers from Plymouth in 1656, when William Nickerson traded a boat for the 17 square mi of land that make up the town. In 1712 the area separated from Eastham and was incorporated as a town; the surnames of the Pilgrims who first settled here still dominate the census list. Although Chatham was originally a farming community, the sea finally lured townspeople to turn to fishing for their livelihood, and the industry has held strong to this day.

At the bent elbow of the Cape, with water nearly surrounding it, Chatham has all the charm of a quietly posh seaside resort, with plenty of shops but none of the crass commercialism that plagues some other towns on the Cape. And it's charming: the town has gray-shingle houses with tidy awnings and cheerful flower gardens, an attractive Main Street with crafts and antiques stores alongside dapper cafés, and a five-and-dime. It's a traditional town (said to have more registered Republican voters than any other town on Cape Cod), where elegant summer cottages share the view with stately homes rich in Yankee architectural detail. In fact, this tiny town by the sea is where you'll find some of the finest examples of bow-roof houses in the country. Chatham's nowhere near as kitschy as Provincetown, but it's not overly quaint, either—it's casual and fun, in a refined New England way.

Because of its location at the elbow, Chatham is not a town you just pass through—it's a destination in itself. During summer months, the town bursts into bloom as hydrangeas blossom in shades of cobalt blue, indigo, and deep violet. And although it can get crowded in high season—and even on weekends during shoulder seasons—Chatham remains a true New England village.

❶ Authentic all the way, the **Railroad Museum** is in a restored 1887 depot. Exhibits include a walk-through 1910 New York Central caboose, old photographs, equipment, thousands of train models, and a diorama of the 1915 Chatham rail yards. ⊠*153 Depot Rd., West Chatham* 🕾*No phone* ⊕*www.chathamrailroadmuseum.com* ⌂*Free* ⊙*Mid-June–mid-Sept., Tues.–Sat. 10–4.*

The **Play-a-round,** a multilevel wooden playground of turrets, twisting tubular slides, and jungle gyms, was designed with the input of local children and built by volunteers. There's a section for people with disabilities and a fenced-in area for small children. ⊠*Depot Rd., across from Railroad Museum, West Chatham.*

On **Queen Anne Road** around Oyster Pond, half-Cape houses, open fields, and rolling pastures reveal the area's colonial and agricultural history.

❷ ★ Built by sea captain Joseph C. Atwood in 1752 and occupied by his descendants until it was sold to the Chatham Historical Society in 1926, the **Atwood House Museum** has a gambrel roof, variable-width floor planks, fireplaces, an old kitchen with a wide hearth and a beehive oven, and some antique dolls and toys. The New Gallery displays portraits of local sea captains. The Joseph C. Lincoln Room has the manuscripts, first editions, and mementos of the Chatham writer, and there is an antique tool room in the basement. The 1974 Durand Wing has collections of seashells from around the world and threaded Sand-

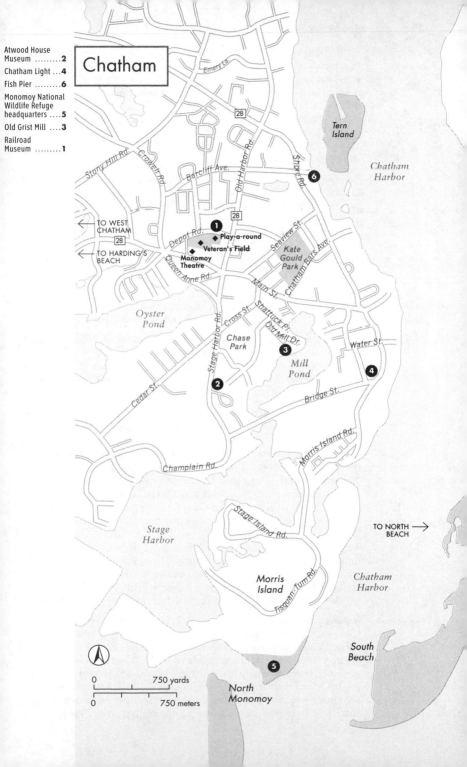

Chatham

Emery La.

28

Story Hill Rd.

Crowell Rd.

Barcliff Ave.

Orr Harbor Rd.

Shore Rd.

6

Tern
Island

Chatham
Harbor

28

← TO WEST
CHATHAM

28

Depot Rd.

1 ◆ Play-a-round
◆ Veteran's Field
◆ Monomoy
Theatre

Seaview St.

Kate
Gould
Park

Chatham Bars Ave.

← TO HARDING'S
BEACH

Queen Anne Rd.

Main St.

Oyster
Pond

Stage Harbor Rd.

Cross St.

Shattuck Pl.

Old Mill Dr.

Chase
Park

3

Mill
Pond

Water St.

4

Cedar St.

2

Bridge St.

Champlain Rd.

Morris Island Rd.

Stage Island Rd.

Stage
Harbor

TO NORTH →
BEACH

Morris
Island

Tisquan-Tum Rd.

Chatham
Harbor

South
Beach

5

0   750 yards

0   750 meters

North
Monomoy

wich glass, as well as Parian-ware figures, unglazed porcelain vases, figurines, and busts. In a remodeled freight shed are the stunning and provocative murals (1932–45) by Alice Stallknecht Wight portraying religious scenes in Chatham settings. On the grounds are an herb garden, the old turret and lens from the Chatham Light, and a simple camp house rescued from eroding North Beach. ⊠ *347 Stage Harbor Rd., West Chatham* ☎ *508/945–2493* ⊕ *www.chathamhistoricalsociety.org* ⊠ *$5* ⊙ *Mid-June–mid-Oct., Tues.–Sat. 1–4 (opens at 10 AM on rainy days); July and Aug., Tues.–Sat. 10–4.*

❸ The **Old Grist Mill,** one of a number of windmills still on the Cape, was built in 1797 by Colonel Benjamin Godfrey for the purpose of grinding corn. How practical the mill actually was is a matter of debate: for it to work properly, a wind speed of at least 20 mph was necessary, but winds more than 25 mph required the miller to reef the sails or to quit grinding altogether. The mill was moved to its present location from Miller Hill in 1956 and extensively renovated. ⊠ *Old Mill Dr. near Mill Pond* ⊠ *Free* ⊙ *July and Aug., weekdays 10–3.*

Mill Pond is a lovely place to stop for a picnic. There's fishing from the bridge, and you'll often see bullrakers at work, plying the pond's muddy bottom with 20-foot rakes in search of shellfish.

Stage Harbor, sheltered by Morris Island, is where Samuel de Champlain anchored in 1606. The street on its north side is, not surprisingly, called Champlain Road. A skirmish here between Europeans and Native Americans marked the first bloodshed in New England between Native people and colonial settlers.

❹ The famous view from **Chatham Light** (⊠ *Main St. near Bridge St.,*
★ *West Chatham*)—of the harbor, the offshore sandbars, and the ocean beyond—justifies the crowds that gather to share it. The lighthouse is especially dramatic on a foggy night, as the beacon's light pierces the mist. Coin-operated telescopes allow a close look at the famous "Chatham Break," the result of a fierce 1987 nor'easter that blasted a channel through a barrier beach just off the coast; it's now known as North and South beaches. The Cape Cod Museum of Natural History in Brewster has a display of photos documenting the process of erosion leading up to and following the break. The U.S. Coast Guard auxiliary, which supervises the lighthouse, offers tours April through September on most Wednesdays of each month. The lighthouse is also open by appointment and on three special occasions during the year: Seafest, an annual tribute to the maritime industry held in mid-October; mid-May's Cape Cod Maritime Week; and June's Cape Heritage Week.

Fodor's Choice **Monomoy National Wildlife Refuge** is a 2,500-acre preserve including the
★ Monomoy Islands, a fragile 9-mi-long barrier-beach area south of Chatham. Monomoy's North and South islands were created when a storm divided the former Monomoy Island in 1978. Monomoy was itself separated from the mainland in a 1958 storm. A haven for bird-watchers, the island is an important stop along the North Atlantic Flyway for migratory waterfowl and shorebirds—peak migration times are May and late July. It also provides nesting and resting grounds for 285 spe-

cies, including gulls—great black-backed, herring, and laughing—and several tern species. White-tailed deer also live on the islands, and harbor and gray seals frequent the shores in winter. The only structure on the islands is the **South Monomoy Lighthouse**, built in 1849.

Monomoy is a quiet, peaceful place of sand and beach grass, tidal flats, dunes, marshes, freshwater ponds, thickets of bayberry and beach plum, and a few pines. Because the refuge harbors several endangered species, activities are limited. Certain areas are fenced off to protect nesting areas of terns and the threatened piping plover. Several groups conduct tours of the islands, including the Massachusetts Audubon Society in South Wellfleet and the Cape Cod Museum of Natural History in Brewster, many with a focus on bird-watching. Most of these tours cost about $20 to $35 per person, depending on the length of the tour and the itinerary. In season, the *Rip Ryder* (☎508/945–5450 ⊕*www.monomoyislandferry.com*) will take you over from Chatham for bird- or seal-watching tours; private charters are also available. Another excellent option is **Monomoy Island Excursions** (☎*508/430–7772*), which offers seal and seabird tours and boat trips out around Monomoy Island, leaving from Saquatucket Harbor on a 43-foot high-speed catamaran. **Outermost Adventures** (☎*508/945–5858* ⊕*www.outermostharbor.com*) also provides water taxi services out to Monomoy Island and offers fishing, birding, and seal-watching cruises.

⑤ The **Monomoy National Wildlife Refuge headquarters** (✉*Off Morris Island Rd., Morris Island* ☎*508/945–0594* ⊕*http://monomoy.fws.gov*), on the misleadingly named Morris Island (it's connected to the mainland), has a visitor center and bookstore, open daily 8 to 4, where you can pick up pamphlets on Monomoy and the birds, wildlife, and flora and fauna found there. A ¾-mi interpretive walking trail around Morris Island, closed at high tide, gives a good view of the refuge and the surrounding waters. The area itself is open daily for exploring from dawn to dusk. Nature's prowess is evident and perpetual in this fragile spot: in November of 2006, a fierce storm recrafted the waterways, actually linking, by land, the tip of nearby South Beach to South Monomoy Island. This natural land bridge has enabled hikers to walk the distance—something that hasn't been possible for nearly half a century. The powerful union of wind and sea will most likely change the face of the islands yet again.

⑥ The **Fish Pier** (✉*Shore Rd. and Barcliff Ave., North Chatham*) bustles with activity when Chatham's fishing fleet returns, sometime between noon and 2 PM daily, depending on the tide. The unloading of the boats is a big local event, drawing crowds who watch it all from an observation deck. From their fishing grounds 3 to 100 mi offshore, fishermen bring in haddock, cod, flounder, lobster, halibut, and pollack, which are packed in ice and shipped to New York and Boston or sold at the fish market here. You might also see sand sharks being unloaded. Typically they are sent, either fresh or frozen, to French and German markets. Also here is *The Provider,* a monument to the town's fishing industry, showing a hand pulling a fish-filled net from the sea.

The **Eldredge Public Library** (✉ *564 Main St.* ☎ *508/945–5170*) has a special genealogy department as well as story times for kids, book-discussion groups, and special programs and lectures.

Known for their artful contemporary treatment of blown glass, Jim Holmes and Deborah Doane of the **Chatham Glass Company** create everything from candleholders to unique vases in a vast spectrum of colors. You can watch them perform the fascinating process of glassblowing here. ✉ *758 Main St.* ☎ *508/945–5547* ⊕ *www.chathamglass.com* ☉ *Late May–early Sept., Mon.–Sat. 10–5; early Sept.–late May, daily 10–5.*

> ## ROUGH NEIGHBORHOOD
>
> Chatham's position on the confluence of Nantucket Sound and the Atlantic Ocean makes the town especially vulnerable to the destructive wrath of stormy seas. Many a home and beachfront have been lost to the tumultuous waters. But like any stalwart New England character, Chatham will continue to hold on to its fortunes, its past, and its future.

NEED A BREAK?

If you're looking for a fat and fancy sandwich, a morning bagel, or an afternoon cappuccino pick-me-up, stop in at the **Chatham Village Cafe** (✉ *400 Main St.* ☎ *508/945–2525*). Eat inside at one of the few tables for some good street-side people-watching, or head over to the Village Green for an impromptu picnic. Head to **Buffy's** (✉ *456 Main St.* ☎ *508/945–5990*) for Chatham's finest (and only homemade) ice cream. You can nosh on your cone at one of the tables set along the lawn outside, beneath a prodigious apple tree. Don't overlook the fresh-squeezed lime rickies and tangy smoothies. **Carmine's** (✉ *595 Main St.* ☎ *508/945–5300*) serves some of the best New York–style pizza (by the slice or the pie) outside New York. There are just a handful of tables inside this storefront eatery in the heart of downtown, which is also an excellent source for grinders and mouthwatering gelato.

WHERE TO STAY & EAT

$$–$$$ ✕ **Campari's Bistro.** It's just a short drive north of downtown, toward Pleasant Bay, to reach this reliable spot known for good regional Italian fare. The softly lighted dining room has large and comfy booths and wood paneling, and you can also dine in the casual tavern, which is more appropriate for families. Nice starters include lemon-poached shrimp wrapped in prosciutto, and crab cakes with creole mustard aioli. Seafood Florentine and veal-and-spinach-stuffed cannelloni rank among the better entrées, but the wood-fired thin-crust pizzas steal the show here. ✉ *323 Orleans Rd. (Rte. 28), North Chatham* ☎ *508/945–9123* ⊕ *www.camparis.com* ☰ *AE, D, DC, MC, V* ☉ *No lunch.*

$$–$$$ ✕ **Christian's.** French and New England influences are found at this landmark restaurant, although local opinions vary on the quality of the food. The menu includes grilled prime meats and fresh Cape Cod seafood, such as pepper-grilled swordfish over lobster-whipped potatoes. The mahogany-panel bar and upstairs sunroom serve a lighter menu

that remains strong on seafood. As attractive as the formal downstairs may be, the upstairs is more of a happening scene, with live piano music most evenings. ⊠443 Main St. ☏508/945–3362 ⊟DC, MC, V ⊗Closed weekdays Jan.–Mar. No lunch.

$$–$$$
Fodor's Choice
★
✕**Pisces.** An intimate dining room inside a simple yellow house not far from the Harwich border, Pisces, as its name suggests, serves coastal-inspired fare—if it swims in local waters, you can probably sample it here. A rich chowder of lobster, butternut squash, and corn is a terrific way to start your meal. Move on to Mediterranean-style fisherman's stew in saffron-lobster broth, or roasted cod with a simple but flavorful dressing of tomatoes, capers, lemon, and olive oil. Complement your dinner with a selection from the extensive wine list, which offers more than 20 vintages by the glass. ⊠2653 Main St., South Chatham ⓓ2653 Main St., Rte. 28, South Chatham02659 ☏508/432–4600 ⊟MC, V ⊗Closed Dec.–Mar. No lunch.

$$–$$$
★
✕**Vining's Bistro.** An exceptionally inventive menu and a determination not to rest on its laurels make this restaurant a standout. The wood grill infuses many dishes with a distinctive flavor heightened further by the chef's use of zesty rubs and spices from all over the globe. The Thai-style crab cakes come with a sharp chili-cucumber vinaigrette, and pan-roasted sea scallops are served with smoked bacon, mixed mushrooms, and caramelized red-onion confit. The restaurant is upstairs at the Gallery Building, and many windows look out on the art below. Though the atmosphere is casual, this is not a family place; there is a deliberate lack of high chairs, booster seats, and kiddie-meal options. ⊠595 Main St. ☏508/945–5033 ⚑Reservations not accepted ⊟AE, MC, V ⊗Closed Jan.–mid-Apr.

$–$$$
★
✕**Impudent Oyster.** A cozy, festive locals' tavern with an unfailingly cheerful staff and superb but reasonably priced seafood, this always-packed restaurant sits inside a dapper house just off Main Street. It's a great place for a romantic meal or dinner with friends or kids, and the menu offers light burgers and sandwiches as well as more substantial fare. Mussels with white-wine sauce is a consistent favorite. The dining room is split-level, with a bar in back on the lower level. There's not a ton of seating, so reserve early on weekends. ⊠15 Chatham Bars Ave. ☏508/945–3545 ⊟AE, MC, V.

$–$$$
✕**Marley's.** You'll find traditional New England fare—often served with a decidedly international flair—at Marley's, one of the best family restaurants in the area. Scallops prepared with pineapple, rum, and brown sugar and topped with a coconut-macaroon crust are a favorite. Crab cakes and Cajun blackened salmon served with poached shrimp and crabmeat are house specialties. Steak, prime rib, chicken potpie, lobster, and steamers round out the menu, which also includes several vegetarian dishes. ⊠1077 Main St., West Chatham ☏508/945–1700 ⊟AE, MC, V ⊗No lunch.

$$
✕**Chatham Squire.** If you order anything local here from the long list of tried-and-true American standbys, you won't go wrong. The fish is as fresh and good as you get on Cape Cod, and the kitchen continues to innovate while still remaining true to its Cape roots. The calamari is always tender, the New England smoked fish plate delicious, and the

clam chowder is a must. Expect a long wait in season, in which case you can visit the bar and pick up on the local gossip. ✉ *487 Main St.* ☎ *508/945–0945* ⊕ *www.thesquire.com* ⚹ *Reservations not accepted* ⊟ *AE, D, MC, V.*

$$$–$$$$ ✕☷ **Queen Anne Inn.** Built in 1840 as a wedding present for the daughter
★ of a famous clipper-ship captain, the Queen Anne first opened as an inn in 1874. Some of the large guest rooms have working fireplaces, balconies, and hot tubs. The lavish studio rooms in the Victorian cottage are particularly dashing and convey more of a colonial Caribbean flair. Lingering and lounging are encouraged—around the large heated outdoor pool, at the tables on the veranda, in front of the fireplace in the sitting room, or in the plush parlor. The place has a wonderful, cozy feel in winter, making it a great year-round option, though the restaurant is closed in winter. Run by locally renowned chef Toby Hill, the Eldredge Room ($$$–$$$$; closed Jan.–Apr., no lunch) turns out sublime regional American fare, including an updated fish-and-chips consisting of truffle-crusted flounder, frites, truffle tartar sauce, and malt vinaigrette, and crispy honey-Dijon venison "lollipops" with a chocolate-zinfandel dipping sauce. There's also an extensive American caviar menu. **Pros:** Spacious and thoughtfully decorated rooms in historic setting, well-suited for relaxing with hot tubs and fireplaces. **Cons:** It's a generous walk to the town center, rooms accessed via steep stairs. ✉ *70 Queen Anne Rd., 02633* ☎ *508/945–0394 or 800/545–4667* 🖷 *508/945–4884* ⊕ *www.queenanneinn.com* 📹 *33 rooms* ⚹ *In-room: Wi-Fi. In-hotel: restaurant, bar, tennis courts, pool, no-smoking rooms, no elevator* ⊟ *AE, D, MC, V* ⊘ *Closed Jan. and Mar. (open Feb.).*

$$$$ ☷ **Chatham Bars Inn.** Overlooking Pleasant Bay from atop a windswept bluff, Chatham Bars Inn is a grande-dame hotel that has long been one of the Cape's most coveted retreats. The ground-floor lobby gives way to the formal restaurant on one side and a porch-fronted lounge on the other. Elegant guest rooms in the resort's main inn and cottages are filled with hand-painted furnishings by local artists and colorful fabrics depicting sunny seaside scenes. Adding to the well-heeled flavor of the inn is an additional massive spa complex, complete with a 4,000-square-foot hydrotherapy pool. If you'd like to be as close as possible to this pampering palace, you can stay in one of the lavishly appointed suites within the new space. **Pros:** Many rooms look out to serene ocean waters, well-appointed rooms in a full-service resort, plenty of activities for all ages. **Cons:** Not an in-town location, not for those looking for smaller, more intimate lodging establishments, rates are fairly steep. ✉ *297 Shore Rd., 02633* ☎ *508/945–0096 or 800/527–4884* 🖷 *508/945–5491* ⊕ *www.chathambarsinn.com* 📹 *149 rooms, 68 suites* ⚹ *In-room: DVD, Wi-Fi. In-hotel: 4 restaurants, bar, tennis courts, pools, gym, spa, beachfront, children's programs (ages 4–14)* ⊟ *AE, D, MC, V.*

$$$–$$$$ ☷ **Captain's House Inn.** A Victorian tile ceiling, wide-board floors, and
★ elaborate moldings and wainscoting are just part of what makes Jill and James Meyer's inn one of the Cape's most popular. Each room has its own personality; some are quite large, and all have fireplaces. The Hiram Harding Room, in the bow-roof Captain's Cottage, has 200-

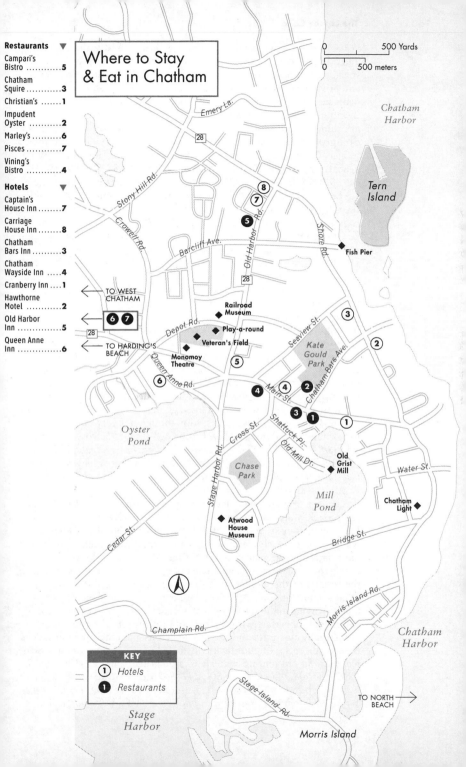

Where to Stay & Eat in Chatham

500 Yards
500 meters

Chatham Harbor

Tern Island

Emery La.

28

Stony Hill Rd.

Crowell Rd.

Barcliff Ave.

Old Harbor Rd.

Shore Rd.

Fish Pier

28

TO WEST CHATHAM

Depot Rd.

Railroad Museum

Play-a-round

Veteran's Field

Seaview St.

Kate Gould Park

Chatham Bars Ave.

28

TO HARDING'S BEACH

Queen Anne Rd.

Monomoy Theatre

Main St.

Cross St.

Shattuck Pl.

Old Mill Dr.

Oyster Pond

Chase Park

Old Grist Mill

Water St.

Mill Pond

Chatham Light

Atwood House Museum

Bridge St.

Stage Harbor Rd.

Cedar St.

Champlain Rd.

Morris Island Rd.

Chatham Harbor

Stage Island Rd.

TO NORTH BEACH

Stage Harbor

Morris Island

KEY

① Hotels

❶ Restaurants

year-old hand-hewn ceiling beams, a wall of raised walnut paneling, and a large, central working fireplace. Suites in the former stables are spacious and have hot tubs, fireplaces, TV–DVDs, mini-refrigerators, and private patios or balconies. A young staff of British hospitality students serves an over-the-top full breakfast each morning and high tea in the afternoon. The herb and flower gardens and neatly trimmed lawns are stunning. **Pros:** Elegant lodging in authentic historic setting, beautiful grounds ideal for croquet (accoutrements provided), pampered service. **Cons:** Many rooms accessed via steep stairs, not an in-town or beachfront location. ✉*369 Old Harbor Rd., 02633* ☎*508/945–0127 or 800/315–0728* 🖷*508/945–0866* ⊕*www.captainshouseinn.com* ⬫*12 rooms, 4 suites* ⌂*In-room: refrigerator (some), DVD, Wi-Fi. In-hotel: pool, gym, laundry service, no kids under 10, no-smoking rooms, no elevator* ▭*AE, D, MC, V* ¶⊙∣*BP.*

$$$–$$$$ 🖭**Carriage House Inn.** Innkeepers Paula and Tim Miller have brought
★   a sense of fresh, beach-resort elegance to this aged inn just outside of Chatham's town center. Rooms throughout the inn are a blend of contemporary with a distinct Cape Cod feel; walls are painted in soothing hues of cream, soft blues, and greens and each is blessedly uncluttered with unnecessary frills. The former stables contain three larger and more secluded rooms with high-pitched ceilings, fireplaces, and French or sliding-glass doors leading to private outdoor areas. Paula brings her extensive spa experience to the mix; guests can indulge in an array of luxury treatments in the privacy of one's room. Each morning a delicious full breakfast begins the day, which might include Tim's special blueberry baked French toast. The beach is a mile away. **Pros:** Beautifully appointed, spacious rooms, added decadence of in-house spa services, ample and well-maintained grounds, romantic and intimate setting. **Cons:** Near a busy intersection though not very loud, long walk to town, no water views or beachfront. ✉*407 Old Harbor Rd., 02633* ☎*508/945–4688 or 800/355–8868* ⊕*www.thecarriagehouseinn.com* ⬫*6 rooms* ⌂*In-room: DVD, Wi-Fi (some). In-hotel: bicycles, spa services, no kids under 12, Wi-Fi, no-smoking rooms, no elevator* ▭*AE, D, MC, V* ¶⊙∣*BP.*

$$$–$$$$ 🖭**Chatham Wayside Inn.** Once a stop on a turn-of-the-20th-century stagecoach route, this venerable inn is still an oasis for weary travelers. Everything is crisp and colorful here, from the floral comforters and wallpapers to freshly painted walls and bright carpeting. Some rooms have balconies, fireplaces, and hot tubs. With a great location smack-dab in the center of town, you may not have to leave your room to hear the sounds of the weekly town-band concerts. The restaurant serves reliable contemporary American fare and a very good Sunday brunch. Guests staying in the spring and fall seasons can enjoy a complimentary continental breakfast with their room rate. **Pros:** Right in the center of town, many amenities and services, spacious and efficient rooms. **Cons:** Not for those seeking authentic historic lodging—more of an upscale feel than an old inn, no water views or beachfront. ✉*512 Main St., 02633* ☎*508/945–5550 or 800/242–8426* 🖷*508/945–3407* ⊕*www. waysideinn.com* ⬫*56 rooms* ⌂*In-room: VCR (some), DVD (some), Wi-Fi. In-hotel: gym, restaurant, pool* ▭*D, MC, V* ⊗*Closed Jan.*

$$$–$$$$ ⊞**Cranberry Inn.** This grand 1830s inn is a short walk east of the commercial span of Main Street, near the heart of downtown—but it has a protected marsh in its backyard. Billed as the oldest continuously operating lodging establishment in Chatham, the inn is filled with antique and reproduction furniture, plus handmade quilts, braided rugs, and other homey touches. The 18 rooms and suites come in a wide variety of shapes and sizes, some of them accommodating as many as six guests. Several rooms have fireplaces, wet bars, and private balconies. Breakfast, which is also available to the public by reservation, is served in a lovely dining room that also provides the setting for an informal afternoon tea with delicious sweets and treats. An intimate pub with a wood-burning fireplace has a full liquor license and is open to the public. On hot days you can cool off on the great big north-facing veranda overlooking Main Street. **Pros:** Fine location and an easy walk to town center, spacious rooms, many with fireplaces for chilly nights, gym privileges at local club (fee). **Cons:** No water views or beachfront, not for those traveling with young children. ⊠ *359 Main St., 02633* ☎ *508/945–9232 or 800/332–4667* 📠 *508/945–3769* ⊕ *www.cranberryinn.com* 🛏 *15 rooms, 3 suites* ⏃ *In-room: Wi-Fi. In-hotel: pub, bar, no kids under 12, no-smoking rooms, no elevator* ⊟ *AE, D, MC, V* �TΟΙ*BP.*

$$$–$$$$ ⊞**Old Harbor Inn.** Congenial, thoughtful hosts Ray and Judith Braz run this cheery B&B set inside a handsome 1930s colonial-revival house a few steps from Main Street and downtown shopping. You'll receive plenty of extras and treats, from in-room snack baskets and extensive complimentary bath products to hair dryers and fluffy robes. Most rooms feel distinctly Victorian in flavor—the cozy yet spacious Port Fortune room has exposed beams, pitched ceilings, white wicker furniture, and Laura Ashley linens. If it's luxury you're after, book the Stage Harbor Suite, which has a two-person Jacuzzi and separate shower. Relax out back on the deck or in the verdant, shaded garden. **Pros:** Quick walk to center of town, well-appointed rooms with plenty of amenities. **Cons:** Not a beachfront location. ⊠ *22 Old Harbor Rd., 02633* ☎ *508/945–4434 or 800/942–4434* ⊕ *www.chathamoldharborinn.com* 🛏 *7 rooms, 1 suite* ⏃ *In-room: no phone, refrigerator, VCR. In-hotel: gym, Wi-Fi, no-smoking rooms, no elevator* ⊟ *MC, V* �ΤΟΙ*BP.*

$$–$$$ ⊞**Hawthorne Motel.** Beyond the Hawthorne Motel's modest roadside appearance extends a private beach overlooking Pleasant Bay, the Atlantic, and Chatham Harbor. Nearly all the rooms have stunning water views. Choose from spotless, no-nonsense, simply decorated motel rooms or kitchenette efficiency units with small refrigerators, two heating plates, and a countertop-sink work area. There's also a two-bedroom cottage (rented by the week in season) with full kitchen and a separate living–dining room, plus amenities such as a VCR and an outdoor grill. The center of town is just a short walk away. Long-distance calls within the Lower 48 states are free, and the lobby has a computer with high-speed Internet access, fresh-brewed coffee, and complimentary morning newspapers. **Pros:** Supreme waterfront location (most rooms have direct views), easy access to nearby attractions and activities, pretty reasonable for the area. **Cons:** Rooms are pretty standard motel fare though clean and comfortable, a 10- to 15-minute walk to town center. ⌧*196 Shore Rd., 02633* ☎*508/945–0372* ⊕*www. thehawthorne.com* ⤶*16 rooms, 10 efficiencies, 1 cottage* ♿*In-room: kitchen (some), refrigerator, Wi-Fi. In-hotel: public Internet, no-smoking rooms, no elevator* ☰*MC, V* ☻*Closed mid-Oct.–mid-May.*

NIGHTLIFE & THE ARTS

THE ARTS   **Chatham Drama Guild** (⌧*134 Crowell Rd.* ☎*508/945–0510* ⊕*www. chathamdramaguild.com*) stages productions year-round, including musicals, comedies, and dramas.

The **Creative Arts Center** (⌧*154 Crowell Rd.* ☎*508/945–3583* ⊕*www. capecodcreativearts.org*) thrives year-round with classes, changing gallery exhibitions, demonstrations, lectures, and other activities.

In July and August the **Guild of Chatham Painters** presents an outdoor art gallery on Thursday and Friday from 9:30 to 5 on the Main Street School's lawn. ⌧*Main St.*

The **Monomoy Theatre** (⌧*776 Main St.* ☎*508/945–1589* ⊕*www. monomoytheatre.org*) stages summer productions—thrillers, musicals, classics, and modern drama—by the Ohio University Players.

Chatham's summer **town-band concerts** (⌧*Kate Gould Park, Main St.* ☎*508/945–5199*) begin at 8 PM on Friday and draw up to 6,000 people. As many as 500 fox-trot on the roped-off dance floor, and there are special dances for children and sing-alongs for all.

NIGHTLIFE   **Chatham Squire** (⌧*487 Main St.* ☎*508/945–0945*), with four bars—including a raw bar—is a rollicking year-round local hangout, drawing a young crowd to the bar side and a mixed crowd of locals to the restaurant.

After great success in Hyannis and Falmouth, the owners of the **RoöBar** (⌧*907 Main St.* ☎*508/945–9988* ⊕*www.theroobar.com*) opened a third location in Chatham, transforming what was once a Friendly's into an elegant bar and bistro. Patrons enjoy an extensive wine list, great mixed drinks, and varied entertainment—usually rock music—on the weekends.

SPORTS & THE OUTDOORS

BASEBALL   The **Cape Cod Baseball League,** begun in 1885, is an invitational league of college players that counts Carlton Fisk, Ron Darling, Mo Vaughn, Nomar Garciaparra, and the late Thurman Munson as alumni. Considered the country's best summer league, it's scouted by every major-league team. The 10 teams of the Cape Cod Baseball League play a 44-game season from mid-June to mid-August; games held at all 10 fields are free. The **Chatham A's** (⌧*Veterans' Field, Main and Depot Sts. by rotary* ☎*508/996–5004* ⊕*www.chathamas.com*) games are great entertainment.

Baseball clinics (⌧*Veterans' Field, Main and Depot Sts. by rotary* ☎*508/432–6909*)—for kids 6 through 8, 9 through 12, and 13 through 17—are offered in one-week sessions by the Chatham A's in

4

summer. The other nine town teams in the Cape league also conduct clinics (☎508/996–5004 information).

BEACHES **Outermost Harbor Marine** (⊠*Morris Island Rd., Morris Island* ☎*508/ 945–2030*) runs shuttles to South Beach; rides cost $15 round-trip for adults (including parking).

Harding's Beach (⊠*Harding's Beach Rd., off Barn Hill Rd., West Chatham*), west of Chatham center, is open to the public and charges daily parking fees to nonresidents in season. Lifeguards are stationed here in summer. This beach can get crowded, so plan to arrive early or late. Nonresident parking fees at Chatham beaches are $15 daily, $60 weekly, and $125 seasonally.

BICYCLING All manner of bikes are available for rent at **Chatham Cycle** (⊠*193 Depot Rd.* ☎*508/945–8981*).

Monomoy Sail & Cycle (⊠*275 Orleans Rd., North Chatham* ☎*508/945– 0811*) rents bicycles as well as sailboards.

BOATING **Monomoy Sail & Cycle** (⊠*275 Orleans Rd., North Chatham* ☎*508/945– 0811*) rents sailboards and Sunfish.

Rip Ryder (☎*508/945–5450*) boat tours offers naturalist-led trips that leave from the Monomoy National Wildlife Refuge area to view birds and seals and explore the rich and ever-changing habitat of the North and South Monomoy Island areas.

Nauti Jane's (⊠ *Ridgevale Beach at Ridgevale Rd., Chatham* ☎*508/432– 4339*) has Day Sailers and peaceful kayaks for rent.

GOLF **Chatham Seaside Links** (⊠*Seaview St., West Chatham* ☎*508/945–4774*), a 9-hole course, is good for beginners.

SURFING The Lower and Outer Cape beaches, including North Beach in Chatham, are the best on the peninsula for surfing, which is tops when there's a storm offshore. Chatham does not have any surf shops, but you'll find them in nearby Orleans.

TENNIS **Chatham Bars Inn** (⊠*297 Shore Rd.* ☎*508/945–0096 Ext. 1155*) offers three waterfront all-weather tennis courts, which are open to the public by reservation for $15 an hour. You can also take lessons and visit the pro shop.

The town maintains two public tennis parks, one on Depot Road next to the Railroad Museum at No. 153 and the other at the middle school on Crowell Road.

SHOPPING

Main Street is a busy shopping area with a diverse range of merchandise, from the pocketbook friendly to the pricier and more upscale. Here you'll find galleries, crafts, clothing stores, bookstores, and a few good antiques shops.

★ **Chatham Jam and Jelly Shop** (⊠*10 Vineyard Ave., at Rte. 28, West Chatham* ☎*508/945–3052 or 877/526–7467*) sells delicious concoctions like rose-petal jelly, apple-lavender chutney, and beach-plum jam, as

CLOSE UP

The Cape Cod Baseball League

At the Baseball Hall of Fame in Cooperstown, New York, you can find a poster announcing a showdown between archrivals Sandwich and Barnstable. The date? July 4, 1885. In the 120-plus years since that day, the Cape's ball-playing tradition has continued unabated. To see a game on the Cape today is to come into contact with baseball's roots—you'll remember why you love the sport.

As they have since the 1950s, top-ranked college baseball players from around the country descend on the Cape when school lets out, just in time to begin the season in mid-June. Each player joins one of the league's 10 teams, each based in a different town: the Bourne Braves, Wareham Gatemen, Falmouth Commodores, Cotuit Kettleers, Hyannis Mets, Dennis-Yarmouth Red Sox, Harwich Mariners, Brewster Whitecaps, Chatham Athletics (A's), and the Orleans Cardinals.

Players lodge with local families and work day jobs cutting lawns, painting houses, or giving baseball clinics in town parks. In the evening, though, their lives are given over to baseball.

The Cape League's motto is "Where the Stars of Tomorrow Shine Tonight." By latest count, one of every eight active major-league ballplayers spent a summer in the Cape League on the way up. You could build an all-star roster with names such as Nomar Garciaparra, Frank Thomas, Jeff Bagwell, Todd Helton, and Barry Zito.

To enshrine these heroes past, the Cape League inducted the first members into its Hall of Fame at the Heritage Museums & Gardens in Sandwich in January 2001. Among the 12 players honored were Thurman Munson, Mike Flanagan, Jeff Reardon, Mo Vaughn, and Frank Thomas.

Yet as good as the baseball is—you'll often see major-league scouts at a game—another great reason to come out to the ballpark is . . . the ballpark. Chatham's Veterans Field is the Cape's Monster Park at Candlestick Point: much like the San Francisco park, fog tends to engulf the games here. Orleans's Eldredge Park is a local favorite—immaculate, cozy, and comfortable. Some parks have bleachers; in others, it's up to you to bring your own chair or blanket and stretch out behind a dugout or baseline. Children are free to roam and can even try for foul balls—which they are, however, asked to return because, after all, balls don't grow on trees. When hunger hits, the ice-cream truck and hot-dog stand are never far away.

Games start at either 5 or 7, depending on whether the field has lights; occasionally there are afternoon games. Each team plays 44 games in a season, so finding one is rarely a problem (⊕ www.capecodbaseball. org has information). And, best of all, they're always free. The Cape's baseball scene is so American, the ambience so relaxed and refreshing, it's tempting to invoke the old Field of Dreams analogy. But the league needs no Hollywood comparison. This is the real thing.

—Seth Rolbein

well as all the old standbys. All preserves are made on-site in small batches, and about 75 of the 120-plus varieties are available for sampling (which is encouraged).

Clambake Celebrations (✉ *1223 C Main St.* ☎ *508/945–7771 or 877/792–7771*) prepares full clambakes, including lobsters, clams, mussels, corn, potatoes, onions, and sausage, for you to take out; it'll even lend you a charcoal grill. The company also delivers via air year-round if necessary. The food is layered in seaweed in a pot and ready to steam.

The **Crooked Fence** (✉ *593 Main St.* ☎ *508/945–4622*), tucked inconspicuously behind Dunkin' Donuts, stocks eclectic, well-chosen home furnishings and gifts, such as cast-iron planters, Nantucket baskets, wind chimes, imported Tuscan tableware, and models of vintage planes and boats.

The **East Wind Silver Co.** (✉ *878 Main St.* ☎ *508/945–8935*) specializes in artful silver jewelry but also sells watercolor paintings, pottery, fountains, and Tiffany-style lighting.

Marion's Pie Shop (✉ *2022 Main St. [Rte. 28], West Chatham* ☎ *508/432–9439*) sells homemade and home-style fruit breads, pastries, prepared foods such as lasagna, Boston baked beans, chowder base, and, of course, pies, both savory and sweet.

S. Wilder & Co. (✉ *309 Orleans Rd. [Rte. 28], North Chatham* ☎ *877/794–5337*), also known as Cape Cod Lanterns, displays old-style colonial crafts. Handcrafted brass and copper lanterns are made here.

Tale of the Cod (✉ *450 Main St., Chatham* ☎ *508/945–0347*) has a wide selection of Chatham-related gifts for the home or individual, including painted furniture; specialty dolls; Chatham-themed rugs, throws, and glass.

Yankee Ingenuity (✉ *525 Main St.* ☎ *508/945–1288*) stocks a varied selection of unique jewelry and lamps and a wide assortment of unusual, beautiful trinkets at reasonable (especially for Chatham) prices.

Yellow Umbrella Books (✉ *501 Main St.* ☎ *508/945–0144*) has an excellent selection of new books, many about Cape Cod, as well as used books.

EN ROUTE

North of Chatham and on the way to Orleans, you'll encounter perhaps the most beautiful stretch of Route 28, the road that's so blighted by overdevelopment in Harwich, Dennis, and Yarmouth. Along here, the narrow road twists and turns alongside the western shoreline of rippling **Pleasant Bay.** Turn east onto any number of peaceful country roads, and you'll end up near the water and within view of Nauset Spit and Pleasant Bay's several islands. This is excellent biking and jogging territory—but keep in mind that Route 28 is fairly narrow along this span, with a tiny shoulder, so keep your eye out for oncoming traffic.

ORLEANS

8 mi north of Chatham, 35 mi east of Sagamore Bridge.

Named for Louis-Philippe de Bourbon, *duc d'Orléans* (duke of Orléans), who reputedly visited the area during his exile from France in the 1790s, Orleans was incorporated as a town in 1797. Historically, it has the distinction of being the only place in the continental United States to have received enemy fire during either world war. In July 1918 a German submarine fired on commercial barges off the coast. Four were sunk, and one shell is reported to have fallen on American soil.

Today Orleans is part quiet seaside village and part bustling center with strip malls. The commercial hub of the region, Orleans is one of the more steadily populated areas, year-round, of the Lower Cape. Yet the town retains a fervent commitment to preserving its past, and residents, in support of local mom-and-pop shops, maintain an active refusal policy of many big-time corporations.

Orleans has a long heritage in fishing and seafaring, and many beautifully preserved homes remain from the colonial era. Many are found in the small village of East Orleans, home of the town's Historical Society and Museum. In other areas of town, such as down by Rock Harbor, more modestly grand homes stand near the water's edge.

As you head north, this is the first Cape town to touch both Cape Cod Bay and the Atlantic Ocean. Nauset Beach, on the Atlantic, is enormously popular. Backed by towering dunes dotted with sea grass and colorful *rosa Rugosa,* this beach could be the starting point for a long but beautiful trek clear to the very tip of the Cape. Skaket Beach, just south of Rock Harbor, is the main bay-side beach and affords both scenic views and calm, warm waters for swimming.

A walk along Rock Harbor Road, a winding street lined with gray-shingle Cape houses, white-picket fences, and neat gardens, leads to the bay-side **Rock Harbor,** site of a War of 1812 skirmish in which the Orleans militia kept a British warship from docking. In the 19th century Orleans had an active saltworks, and a flourishing packet service between Rock Harbor and Boston developed. Today the former packet landing is the base of charter-fishing and party boats in season, as well as of a small commercial fishing fleet whose catch hits the counters at the fish market and small restaurant here. Sunsets over the harbor are spectacular. Don't be surprised to see a line of trees (real, though not thriving) marking the narrow boat channel out to the bay. New markers are installed each season.

The Community of Jesus, a religious community whose members come from a variety of Christian traditions, owns a large chunk of the Rock Harbor area. Their dramatic cathedral, the **Church of the Transfiguration,** showcases the work of local and international artisans, and reflects the community's dedication to the arts. Inside there's an organ with thousands of pipes, authentic frescoes depicting Biblical scenes, colorful stained-glass windows, and gorgeous, intricate mosaic work mixing religious themes with images of local flora and fauna. ⊠*Rock Harbor Rd. across from Rock Harbor* ☎*508/255–1054, 508/255–6204 tours* ⊕*www.communityofjesus.org* ☜*Free, donations accepted* ⊘*Tours Tues., Fri., and Sat. at 3, Thurs.–Tues. at sunset; services are open to public.*

NEED A BREAK?

The **Cottage St. Bakery** (⊠*5 Cottage St.* ☎*508/255–2821*) prepares delicious artisanal breads, pastries, cakes, and sweets, as well as healthful breakfast and lunch fare, from homemade granola to hefty sandwiches.

The 1890 **French Cable Station Museum** was the stateside landing point for the 3,000-mi-long transatlantic cable that originated in Brittany. Another cable laid between Orleans and New York City completed the France–New York link, and many important messages were communicated through the station. During World War I, when it was an essential connection between army headquarters in Washington and the American Expeditionary Force in France, the station was under guard by the marines. By 1959 telephone service had rendered the station obsolete, and it closed—but the equipment is still in place. ⊠*41 S. Orleans Rd., Orleans* ☎*508/240–1735* ☜*Donations accepted* ⊘*June, Fri.–Sun. 1–4; July–early Sept., Mon.–Sat. 1–4.*

The **Jonathan Young Windmill,** a pretty if somewhat incongruous sight on the busy highway, is a landmark from the days of salt making in Orleans, when it would pump saltwater into shallow vaults for evaporation. A program explaining the history and operation of the mill demonstrates the old millstone and grinding process. ⊠*Rte. 6A and Town Cove, Orleans* ⊘*July and Aug., daily 11–4; June and Sept., weekends 11–4.*

NEED A BREAK?

Grab a baked treat, chocolates of all varieties, and any number of coffee concoctions at the **Chocolate Sparrow** (⊠*5 Old Colony Way* ☎*508/240–2230*), located right by the Cape Cod Rail Trail. The adjacent Ice Cream at the Sparrow serves tasty hard and soft ice cream.

The **Academy of Performing Arts** (⊠*5 Giddiah Hill Rd.* ☎*508/255–5510 or 508/255–1963* ⊕*www.apacape.org*) offers two-week sessions of theater, music, and dance classes to kids ages 8 to 12, with a show at the end of each session. It also schedules year-round classes for ages four to adult in dance, music, and drama. The academy's theater is at 120 Main Street.

Snow Library (⊠*Main St. and Rte. 28* ☎*508/240–3760*) has been in operation since around 1876; today there are kids' story hours and numerous lecture programs.

WHERE TO STAY & EAT

$$–$$$$ ✕**Abba.** Abba serves inspired pan-Mediterranean cuisine in an elegant
★ and intimate setting. Chef and co-owner Erez Pinhas skillfully combines Middle Eastern, Asian, and Southern European flavors in such

CLOSE UP

Rotary 101

The English cheerfully call them "roundabouts," and while that light-hearted moniker might sound like it describes a fun (albeit slightly nauseating) carnival ride, rotaries are serious business. Uninitiated drivers are often so confused upon entering one that they either ignore all rules of the road or freeze up completely. Both reactions will likely cause horns to blare and the fists and fingers of your fellow motorists to come out in full force. But it doesn't have to be this way. Follow a few simple rules, and you'll be swinging around traffic circles like a local. The most important thing to remember is that drivers who are already in the rotary have

the right of way: those entering must yield to the traffic in the rotary. This means that if you're approaching the rotary, you must wait until there is enough space for you to enter—you can't just hit the gas and hope for the best. Because if you do, you probably just caused a fellow motorist to commit another cardinal sin: stopping while in the rotary. Either that, or he just hit you. Using a rotary is actually a very simple concept. Now that you know the rules, you may even grow to appreciate their exquisite logic (at the very least, you'll see fewer unfriendly hand gestures).

–Laura V. Scheel

dishes as scallops with fettuccine and asparagus in a curry cream sauce, and grilled filet mignon with Jerusalem artichokes, asparagus, pearl onions, and a morel-mushroom sauce. Cushy pillows on the banquettes and soft candlelight flickering from Moroccan glass votives add a touch of opulence. Reservations suggested. ⊠ *Old Colony Way and West Rd.* ☎ *508/255-8144* ⊕ *www.abbarestaurant.com* ⊟ *AE, D, MC, V* ⊙ *Closed Mon. No lunch.*

\$\$–\$\$\$\$ ✕ **Captain Linnell House.** Sea captain Eben Linnell built this stunning
★   mansion in the 1850s, basing its design on a neoclassical villa he'd once visited in the South of France. Linnell's masterpiece now contains one of the Cape's most esteemed formal restaurants, a longtime favorite for celebrating special occasions. A competent and polite staff serves continental cuisine, which is consistently superb. The kitchen tends to stick with tried-and-true classics, such as herb-and-mustard-crusted rack of lamb with a pinot-noir reduction, and grilled Black Angus steak au poivre with a zinfandel-peppercorn sauce. Considering the fine ingredients and opulent surroundings, it's an excellent value. ⊠ *137 Skaket Beach Rd.* ☎ *508/255-3400* ⊟ *AE, MC, V* ⊙ *No lunch.*

\$\$–\$\$\$\$ ✕ **Nauset Beach Club.** Locals have long favored this upscale but casual
★   trattoria on the road leading out to Nauset Beach. The kitchen produces seasonally inspired regional Italian food with an emphasis on locally harvested seafood and produce. Choose from a fixed-price option (offered daily at two early seatings; the earliest one is a bargain, starting at just \$19 for three courses Sunday through Thursday) or the à la carte menu for such favorites as grilled lemon- and cracked-pepper sirloin with truffle oil and baby arugula, and pistachio-crusted rack of lamb with caramelized fennel. The off-season warms up with wood oven–fired dishes; in fall and winter, truffles appear artfully in various

presentations. ⊠*222 Main St., East Orleans* ☎*508/255–8547* ⊟*AE, D, DC, MC, V* ⊘*No lunch.*

$$–$$$ ✕**Academy Ocean Grill.** Owner and chef Christian Schultz, who originally opened Christian's in Chatham, has earned plenty of kudos on the Lower Cape for his artful and inventive globally influenced cooking, and his present establishment lives up to his sterling reputation. Academy Ocean Grill occupies a stately shingle house surrounded by profusive gardens—in warm weather, you can dine on the patio amid the flowers and greenery. Top dishes include chunky crab cakes, monkfish pan-seared with Thai curry, and traditional veal saltimbocca. An exceptional wine list rounds out the offerings. ⊠*2 Academy Pl., off Rte. 28* ☎*508/240–1585* ⊟*AE, D, MC, V* ⊘*Closed mid-Jan.–mid-Apr.*

4

$$–$$$ ✕**The Beacon Room.** Adorned with crisp linens, frilly curtains, and wood furnishings, this homey cottage bistro serves up a nice mix of seafood and meats enhanced with sophisticated and inventive flavors. Start with the Gorgonzola, sun-dried cranberry, and walnut salad, then move on to sesame-crusted salmon with cilantro oil or pecan-crusted venison with a sauce of red zinfandel and pan drippings. In warmer months, dinner on the garden patio is particularly urbane. An ambitious wine list complements the fine selection. No reservations, although there is a call-ahead waiting list for busy summer nights. ⊠*23 West Rd.* ☎*508/255–2211* ♻*Reservations not accepted* ⊟ *MC, V.*

$$–$$$ ✕**Mahoney's Atlantic Bar and Grill.** Chef Ted Mahoney cooked for years at
★ one of Provincetown's busiest restaurants before opening this always-hopping downtown spot that serves commendable dinner fare and draws big crowds for cocktails and appetizers. The menu emphasizes grilled vegetables and polenta, drunken shellfish steamed in ale, and tuna sashimi. The bar is long and comfortable, and on many evenings you can sip your martini or California wine to live music. ⊠*28 Main St.* ☎*508/255–5505* ⊟*AE, MC, V.*

$–$$$ ✕**Saltwater Grille.** Although it has seen many transformations over the last few years, this spot may have finally found its niche. The former Binnacle Tavern has been eliminated, though its spirit lives on in the menu, where old favorites like delicious pizzas with some inventive toppings (apples, linguica sausage, pine nuts, Brie), generous burgers, specialty sandwiches, and an extensive menu of designer martinis can be had. Inside, it's a bit like eating in your favorite bright beach house. You'll find grilled meats and seafood aplenty here, as well as a good selection of pastas and salads. ⊠*20 S. Orleans Rd. (Rte. 28)* ☎*508/255–5149* ⊟*AE, MC, V* ♻*Reservations not accepted* ⊘*No lunch.*

¢–$$ ✕**Land Ho!** Tried-and-true tavern fare is the rule at Orleans' flagship
★ local restaurant. The scene is usually fun and boisterous; dozens of homemade wooden signs hang from the rafters above the red-checked tablecloths. The burgers and the sea-clam pie are both excellent, and the blackboard specials change daily. This is a good place for a rainy-day lunch. On weekend nights, it livens up even more with the music of local bands. ⊠*38 Cove Rd. (Rte. 6A)* ☎*508/255–5165* ♻*Reservations not accepted* ⊟*AE, MC, V.*

¢–$ ✕ **Sir Cricket's Fish and Chips.** For a beautifully turned-out fish sandwich, pull into this tiny local favorite, a hole-in-the-wall attached to Nauset Fish & Lobster Pool. Built mainly for takeout, this no-frills fish joint does have three or four tiny tables and a soda machine. Try the fresh oyster roll or go for a full fisherman's platter. As you eat, check out the chair seats—each is an exquisitely rendered mini-mural of Orleans history or a personality painted by legendary local artist Dan Joy. ✉ *39 Cranberry Hwy. (Rte. 6A)* ☎ *508/255–4453* ⚓ *Reservations not accepted* ⊟ *No credit cards.*

$$–$$$$ ✕ ⊡ **Orleans Inn.** This 1875 sea captain's mansion nearly met with the
FodorʼsChoice   wrecking ball before Ed Maas and his family took over the place in the
★   late '90s; today the Maas clan continues to run this bustling inn and restaurant with warmth and enthusiasm. The imposing, turreted structure has two distinct faces: one turned toward a busy intersection and a large shopping plaza, whereas the other looks longingly over tranquil Town Cove. Rooms here are simply but charmingly appointed with classic wood furniture and floral quilts on the beds; the larger waterfront suites have sitting areas and great views of the harbor. Common areas include a kitchenette with a microwave and toaster oven and a sitting room in the basement with a large TV and videos. The restaurant ($–$$$), which uses some creative ingredients in its traditional standbys, serves up large portions of fish-and-chips, grilled sirloin, and grilled salmon with orange-honey glaze. There's also an excellent Sunday brunch. Remarkably, the inn has no cancellation fee: you must pay in full for your stay at the time of booking, but even if you cancel the day of arrival, you'll receive a full refund. Local and long-distance phone calls are complimentary, too. **Pros:** Great waterfront location, outdoor dining overlooking the cove (about the only place in town), gracious hosts, many amenities. **Cons:** Some rooms face busy intersection rather than the water, rooms accessed via steep stairs. ✉ *3 Old County Rd., 02653* ✉ *Box 188, Orleans 02653* ☎ *508/255–2222 or 800/863–3039* 🖶 *508/255–6722* ⊕ *www.orleansinn.com* ◀ *8 rooms, 3 suites* & *In-room: VCR/DVD, fireplaces, refrigerator, Wi-Fi. In-hotel: restaurant, bar, no-smoking rooms, no elevator* ⊟ *AE, MC, V* ⧆ *BP.*

$$$–$$$$ ⊡ **A Little Inn on Pleasant Bay.** Run by sisters Sandra Zeller and Pamela
★   Adam and Sandra's husband, Bernd Zeller—all of whom have extensive corporate and hospitality backgrounds—this gorgeously decorated inn occupies a 1798 building set on a bluff beside a cranberry bog, across Route 28 from the bay for which it's named. The main house has four rooms, and two adjoining nearby buildings contain another five rooms. Many of the accommodations look clear out to the bay, and others face the lush gardens. The Mercury room has French doors leading out to a private garden patio, and the spacious Wianno room is warmed by a fireplace and has a lovely sitting area. The roomy, modern bathrooms are among the nicest of any hotel on the Cape. The breakfast buffet includes a dazzling variety of fresh fruits, baked goods, smoked fish, cold cuts, fine cheeses, yogurts, cereals, and other treats. It's more substantial than many full breakfasts, and you can enjoy it while sitting on the pretty patio, admiring Pleasant Bay in the distance. **Pros:** Peaceful, pastoral setting with great water views; abundant buf-

fet breakfast; spacious, well-appointed rooms. **Cons:** Not an in-town location; must drive a distance to either Orleans or Chatham. ⊠*654 S. Orleans Rd., Box 190, South Orleans 02662* ☎*508/255–0780 or 888/332–3351* ⊕*www.alittleinnonpleasantbay.com* ⤺*9 rooms* ⌂*In-room: no phone, no TV, Wi-Fi. In-hotel: no kids under 10, no-smoking rooms, no elevator* ⊟*AE, MC, V* ⏁*CP* ⊘*Closed Nov.–Apr.*

$$–$$$ ⚏**Cove Motel.** Consisting of two main buildings overlooking Orleans
★   Town Cove, this tidy but prosaic year-round motel has large rooms, most with decks or patios overlooking the water. Furnishings are undistinguished but updated and pleasant, and rooms have tasteful, neutral color schemes. Some units have fireplaces and kitchens, and two-room suites can comfortably accommodate four guests. An attractive picnic area overlooks the heated pool. You can't beat the location, and in summer you'll receive a complimentary boat tour around Town Cove. **Pros:** Many water-view rooms, right on Town Cove, easy walk throughout town. **Cons:** Sits right on semi-busy road, not for those looking for authentic historic lodging. ⊠*13 S. Orleans Rd. (Rte. 28), Box 279, 02653* ☎*508/255–1203 or 800/343–2233* ⊕*www.thecoveorleans. com* ⤺*37 rooms, 10 suites* ⌂*In-room: kitchen (some), refrigerator, DVD. In-hotel: pool, Wi-Fi, no elevator* ⊟*AE, D, MC, V.*

$–$$ ⚏**Nauset House Inn.** You could easily spend a day trying out all the places to relax here. There's a parlor with comfortable chairs and a large fireplace, an orchard set with picnic tables, and a lush conservatory with a weeping cherry tree in its center. Rooms in both the main building and the adjacent Carriage House have stenciled walls, quilts, and unusual antique pieces, as well as hand-painted furniture, stained glass, and prints done by one of the owners. The beach is ½ mi away (they'll set you up with beach chairs and towels), and the attractions of town are close—but not too close. Those rooms with a shared bath all cost $95 or less. **Pros:** Authentic historic lodging in peaceful setting, ideal for relaxing and getting away from distractions, can walk to excellent ocean beach. **Cons:** Many rooms must share a bath (though discounted), some rooms accessed via steep stairways. ⊠*143 Beach Rd., Box 774, East Orleans 02643* ☎*508/255–2195* ⊕*www.nausethouse-inn.com* ⤺*14 rooms, 8 with bath* ⌂*In-room: no phones, no TV, no a/c, Wi-Fi (some). In-hotel: Wi-Fi, no children under 12, no-smoking rooms, no elevator* ⊟*D, MC, V* ⊘*Closed Nov.–Mar.* ⏁*BP.*

$–$$ ⚏**Skaket Beach Motel.** Rooms in this convenient-to-everything inland motel overlooking a busy intersection are well sized; a handful of suites have kitchens and two or three bedrooms. Outdoor facilities include horseshoes, a heated pool, and grills. **Pros:** Tasty homemade blueberry muffins in the morning, central location for exploring the area, good for those traveling with children (pool, lawn games). **Cons:** Faces very busy intersection, pool area can be loud with nearby traffic. ⊠*203 Cranberry Hwy. (Rte. 6A), 02653* ☎*508/255–1020 or 800/835–0298* 🖷*508/255–6487* ⊕*www.skaketbeachmotel.com* ⤺*40 rooms, 6 suites* ⌂*In-room: kitchen (some), refrigerator, Wi-Fi (some). In-hotel: pool, laundry, Wi-Fi, no elevator* ⊟*MC, V* ⊘*Closed late Nov.–Mar.* ⏁*CP.*

NIGHTLIFE & THE ARTS

The **Academy Playhouse** (⊠*120 Main St.* ☎*508/255–1963*), one of the oldest community theaters on the Cape, stages 12 or 13 productions year-round, including original works.

The **Stages Theatre Company** (☎*508/255–3999* ⊕*www.gdaf.org*) puts on music and theater events several times a year. The group is affiliated with the Community of Jesus; performances are held on the Community's grounds at Rock Harbor.

The **Cape & Islands Chamber Music Festival** (☎*508/945–8060* ⊕*www. capecodchambermusic.org*) presents three weeks of top-caliber performances, including a jazz night, at various locations in August.

Land Ho! (⊠*38 Cove Rd. [Rte. 6A]* ☎*508/255–5165*) has live local bands frequently and throughout the year.

Coast (⊠*Rte. 6A and Rte. 28* ☎*508/240–1112*) features live performances by local bands representing a wide range of tastes, from rock to folk and blues, Wednesday through Saturday evenings.

Mahoney's Atlantic Bar and Grill (⊠*28 Main St.* ☎*508/255–5505*) regularly has live jazz and blues in the bar area; call for times.

Free ocean-side concerts are held in the gazebo at **Nauset Beach** each Monday evening from 7 to 9 in July and August. The resident fried-clam shack stays open until 10.

SPORTS & THE OUTDOORS

BASEBALL The **Orleans Cardinals** (☎*508/255–0793* ⊕*www.orleanscardinals. com*) of the collegiate Cape Cod Baseball League play home games at **Eldredge Park** (⊠*Rte. 28*) from mid-June to mid-August.

BEACHES The town-managed **Nauset Beach** (⊠*Beach Rd., Nauset Heights* ☎*508/240–3780*)—not to be confused with Nauset Light Beach on the National Seashore—is a 10-mi sweep of sandy ocean beach with low dunes and large waves good for bodysurfing or board surfing. The beach has lifeguards, restrooms, showers, and a food concession. Despite its size, the massive parking lot often fills up when the sun is strong; arrive quite early or in the late afternoon if you want to claim a spot. The beach is open to off-road vehicles with a special permit. Daily parking fees are $15; a one-week pass costs $50, and a season pass is $110. Entrance is free with a resident sticker. For more information, call the parks department.

Freshwater seekers can access **Pilgrim Lake** (⊠*Pilgrim Lake Rd. off Monument Rd. and Rte. 28, South Orleans*), which has the same parking and sticker fees as Nauset Beach.

■ **NEED A BREAK?** For a quick fix for your sweet tooth or something more substantial like a cup of homemade soup, grilled panini or other great sandwiches, head to **Cape Cup** (⊠*54 Main St.* ☎*508/255–1989*). It's also a great spot for a hot blast of espresso when you need a jolt or a breakfast treat.

Skaket Beach (⊠*Skaket Beach Rd., Namskaket* ☎*508/240–3775*) on Cape Cod Bay is a sandy stretch with calm, warm water good for children. It's a good place to watch motorboats, fishing charters, and sailboats as they leave the channel at Rock Harbor or take in the spectacular evening sunsets. There are restrooms, lifeguards, and a snack bar. Daily parking fees are the same as at Nauset Beach.

BOATING   **Arey's Pond Boat Yard** (⊠*43 Arey's La., off Rte. 28, South Orleans* ☎*508/ 255–0994*) has a sailing school with individual and group lessons.

☾   What kid doesn't want to put on an eye-patch and sail the seven seas? Make your little buccaneer's fantasy a reality on a trip with **Pirate Adventures** (⊠*Behind Goose Hummock, off Rte. 6A, Orleans* ☎*508/255– 8811*) on the *Sea Gypsy*. You'll fire cannons, get your face painted, hear tall tales, and, of course, find buried treasures. Six trips depart daily and ply the waters of Town Cove from mid-June through Labor Day.

FISHING   Many of Orleans's freshwater ponds offer good fishing for perch, pickerel, trout, and more. The required fishing license, along with rental gear, is available at the **Goose Hummock Shop** (⊠*15 Rte. 6A* ☎*508/255– 0455*), which also rents kayaks and gives kayaking lessons and tours.

Rock Harbor Charter Boat Service (⊠*Rock Harbor* ☎*508/255–9757, 800/287–1771 in Massachusetts*) goes for bass and blues in the bay from spring through fall. Walk-ons and charters are both available.

HEALTH &   **Willy's Gym** (⊠*21 Old Colony Way* ☎*508/255–6826* ⊕*www.willys-*
FITNESS CLUBS   *gym.com*) is one of the Cape's top fitness facilities, with state-of-the-art cardio and weight-training equipment and studios for yoga, pilates, martial arts, aerobics, and dance classes. Daily, weekly, and monthly passes are available. The on-site Kembali Spa offers a wide range of massage and treatment options. This 27,000-square-foot location is the original Willy's; the one in Eastham is even larger.

SPAS   **Heaven Scent You** (⊠*13 Cove Rd.* ☎*508/240–2508*) offers massage, spa services, and beauty treatments—everything you need for some relaxation and rejuvenation.

After an extensive renovation of an aged Victorian in 2006, the formerly hidden day spa **Welstar** (⊠*42 S. Orleans Rd.* ☎*508/240–1422 or 800/893–6008* ⊕*www.dayspacapecod.com*) now has a prominent location on busy Route 28 in the center of Orleans. Decadent specialty treatments include crystal balancing (for refocusing the body's energy), seaweed contouring masks, warm stone massages, facials, manicures, pedicures, and many more esoteric treats.

SPORTING   **Nauset Sports** (⊠*Jeremiah Sq., Rte. 6A at rotary* ☎*508/255–4742*)
GOODS–   rents surf-, body, skim-, and wake boards; kayaks; wet suits; in-line
RENTALS   skates; and tennis rackets.

For bike rentals just across the way from the Cape Cod Rail Trail, head to **Orleans Cycle** (⊠*26 Main St.* ☎*508/255–9115*).

SURFING The Lower and Outer Cape beaches, including Nauset Beach in Orleans, are the best spots for surfing, especially when there's a storm offshore. For a surf report—water temperature, weather, surf, tanning factor—call ☎508/240–2229.

Pump House Surf Co. (✉9 Rte. 6A ☎508/240–2226) rents wet suits and surfboards, and sells boards and gear.

SHOPPING
Baseball Shop (✉26 Main St. ☎508/240–1063) sells licensed products relating to baseball and other sports—new and collectible cards (and nonsports cards) as well as hats, clothing, and videos.

Bird Watcher's General Store (✉36 Rte. 6A ☎508/255–6974 or 800/562–1512) stocks nearly everything avian but the birds themselves: feeders, paintings, houses, books, binoculars, calls, bird-theme apparel, and more.

Karol Richardson (✉47 Main St. ☎508/255–3944) sells fine contemporary clothing, plus silk wraps and scarves, hats, shoes, handbags, and handcrafted jewelry. You'll usually pay more for the quality goods here, but bargains can be found at the shop's off-season warehouse sales.

Kemp Pottery (✉9 Cranberry Hwy. [Rte. 6A] ☎508/255–5853) displays functional and decorative stoneware and porcelain, fountains, garden sculpture, sinks, and stained glass.

Oceana (✉1 Main St. Sq. ☎508/240–1414) has a beautiful selection of nautical-theme home accents, gifts, and jewelry, as well as colorful hooked rugs made by Cape artist Claire Murray.

The **Orleans Farmers' Market** (✉Old Colony Way across from Capt'n Elmers ☎508/255–0951) is the place to go for local delicacies such as fresh produce, flowers, and homemade goodies. It's open 8 AM to noon Saturday mornings throughout the summer. Be forewarned—early birds get the best selection, and things tend to disappear quickly.

Village Farm Market (✉199 Main St., East Orleans ☎508/255–1949) sells local produce, fresh sandwiches and roll-ups, salads (salad bar or prepared varieties), homemade soup, ice cream, fresh-baked breads, and other supplies for a great picnic. A wide assortment of flowers, both dried and fresh, are sold, adding great color to the beautiful, beamed old-style barn.

ART & CRAFTS The **Addison Art Gallery** (✉43 S. Orleans Rd. [Rte. 28] ☎508/255–
GALLERIES 6200), in four rooms of a brick-red Cape house, represents more than two dozen regional artists. Peruse the collection of contemporary works, many of which were inspired by life on Cape Cod. The sculpture garden in the side yard is a perfect complement to the tasteful gallery. Receptions, where you can often meet the week's featured artist, are held year-round from 5 to 7 on Saturday night.

Gallery 31 (✉31 Main St. ☎508/247–9469) is a partnership of nearly one dozen local artists, representing a wide range of mediums and styles.

Left Bank Gallery (✉8 Cove Rd. ☎508/247–9172) carries an eclectic mix of handcrafted jewelry, fine art by both local and national artists, hand-painted furniture, pottery, and handmade clothing.

On Tuesday and Sunday in July and August, **Nauset Painters** (Tues. ✉Depot Sq. at Old Colony Way Sun. ✉Sandwich Cooperative Bank, 51 Main St.) presents outdoor juried art shows.

The **Orleans Art Association** (✉137 Main St.) holds outdoor art shows from 10 to 5 each Thursday and Friday in July and August on the grounds of the American Legion Hall.

At various times in June, July, and August, the **Orleans Professional Arts and Crafts Association** (✉Rte. 28) sponsors a giant outdoor show on the grounds of the Nauset Middle School featuring the works of more than 100 artists and craftspeople. For specific dates and times check the free town guide published by the Chamber of Commerce.

The **Rowley Gallery & Doug Johnson Gallery** (✉76 Rte. 6A ☎508/240–7827 and 508/255–3690) includes an unusual mix of contemporary art and tribal artifacts.

★ **Tree's Place** (✉Rte. 6A at Rte. 28 ☎508/255–1330 or 888/255–1330), one of the Cape's best and most original shops, has a collection of handcrafted kaleidoscopes, as well as art glass, hand-painted porcelain and pottery, handblown stemware, jewelry, imported ceramic tiles, and fine art. Tree's displays the work of New England artists, including Robert Vickery, Don Stone, and Elizabeth Mumford (whose popular folk art is bordered in mottos and poetic phrases). Champagne openings are held on Saturday night in summer.

EASTHAM

3 mi north of Orleans, 6 mi south of Wellfleet.

Often overlooked on the speedy drive up toward Provincetown on U.S. 6, Eastham is a town full of hidden treasures. Unlike other towns on the Cape, it has no official town center or Main Street; the highway bisects Eastham, and the town is spread out on both Cape Cod Bay and the Atlantic. Amid the gas stations, convenience stores, restaurants, and large motel complexes, Eastham's wealth of natural beauty takes a little exploring to find.

One such gem is the National Seashore, which officially begins here and comprises thousands of acres of wooded areas, salt marshes, and wild, open-ocean beaches. The Salt Pond Visitor Center just off U.S. 6 is one of Cape Cod National Seashore's main centers, host to numerous nature and history programs and lectures; it also maintains a paved bike path. Nearby is the much-beloved Nauset Light, the red-

and-white-stripe lighthouse saved from imminent destruction when it was moved from its perilous perch atop eroding cliffs. The Fort Hill area is another pretty spot, with lots of walking trails and a stately old mansion called the Penniman House.

It was here in 1620 that an exploring band of *Mayflower* passengers met the Nauset tribe on a bay-side beach, which they then named First Encounter Beach. The meeting was peaceful, but the Pilgrims moved on to Plymouth anyway. Nearly a quarter century later, they returned to settle the area, which they originally called by its Native American name, Nawsett. Eastham was incorporated as a town on June 7, 1651.

Like many other Cape towns, Eastham started as a farming community and later turned to the sea and to salt making for its livelihood; at one time there were more than 50 saltworks in town. A less typical industry that once flourished here was asparagus growing; from the late 1800s through the 1920s, Eastham was known as the asparagus capital of the United States. The runner-up crop, Eastham turnips, are still the pride of many a harvest table.

★   The road to the Cape Cod National Seashore's **Fort Hill Area** (⊠ *Fort Hill Rd., off U.S. 6*) winds past the **Captain Edward Penniman House,** ending at a parking area with a lovely view of old farmland traced with stone fences that rolls gently down to **Nauset Marsh** and a red-maple swamp. Appreciated by bird-watchers and nature photographers, the 1-mi **Red Maple Swamp Trail** begins outside the Penniman House and winds through the area, branching into two separate paths, one of which eventually turns into a boardwalk that meanders through wetlands. The other path leads directly to Skiff Hill, an overlook with benches and informative plaques that quote Samuel de Champlain's account of the area from when he moored off Nauset Marsh in 1605. Also on Skiff Hill is Indian Rock, a large boulder moved to the hill from the marsh below. Once used by the local Nauset tribe as a sharpening stone, the rock is cut with deep grooves and smoothed in circles where ax heads were whetted.

The French Second Empire–style **Captain Edward Penniman House** was built in 1868 for a whaling captain. The impressive exterior is notable for its mansard roof; its cupola, which once commanded a dramatic view of bay and sea; and its whale-jawbone entrance gate. The interior is open for guided tours or for browsing through changing exhibits. Call ahead to find out when tours are available. ⊠ *Fort Hill Rd., Fort Hill Area* ☎ *508/255–3421* ☎ *Free* ☉ *Weekdays 1–4.*

The park at Samoset Road has as its centerpiece the **Eastham Windmill,** the oldest windmill on Cape Cod. A smock mill built in Plymouth in the early 1680s, it was moved to this site in 1793 and is the only Cape windmill still on the site where it was used commercially. The mill was restored by local shipwreck historian William Quinn and friends. The park often comes alive with town festivals and concerts, and occasionally demonstrations are given on the inner workings of the mill. Each September, just after Labor Day, Eastham celebrates its history and the change of the season with the annual Windmill Weekend, an event with a full roster of activities for all ages. ⊠ *U.S. 6 at Samoset Rd.* 🖃 *Free* ⊗ *Late June–early Sept., Mon.–Sat. 10–5, Sun. 1–5.*

Frozen in time, the 1741 **Swift-Daley House** was once the home of Gustavus Swift, founder of the Swift meatpacking company. Inside the full Cape with bow roof you can find beautiful pumpkin-pine woodwork and wide-board floors, a ship's-cabin staircase that, like the bow roof, was built by ships' carpenters, and fireplaces in every downstairs room. The colonial-era furnishings include an old cannonball rope bed, tools, a melodeon (similar to an accordion), and a ceremonial quilt decorated with beads and coins. Among the antique clothing is a stunning 1850 wedding dress. Out back is a tool museum. ⊠ *U.S. 6, next to Eastham post office* 🕾 *No phone* ⊕ *www.easthamhistorical.org* 🖃 *Free; donations accepted* ⊗ *July and Aug., weekdays 10–1; Sept., Sat. 10–1.*

A great spot for watching sunsets over the bay, **First Encounter Beach** (⊠ *End of Samoset Rd. off U.S. 6*) is rich in history. Near the parking lot, a bronze marker commemorates the first encounter between local Native Americans and passengers from the *Mayflower,* led by Captain Myles Standish, who explored the entire area for five weeks in November and December 1620 before moving on to Plymouth. The remains of a navy target ship retired after 25 years of battering now rest on a sandbar about 1 mi out.

☾ The Cape's most expansive national treasure, the **Cape Cod National Seashore** was established in 1961 under the administration of President John F. Kennedy, for whom Cape Cod was home and haven. The 27,000-acre seashore, extending from Chatham to Provincetown, encompasses and protects 30 mi of superb ocean beaches; great rolling dunes; swamps, marshes, and wetlands; pitch-pine and scrub-oak forest; all kinds of wildlife; and a number of historic structures. Self-guided nature trails, as well as biking and horse trails, lace through these landscapes. Hiking trails lead to a red-maple swamp, **Nauset Marsh,** and to **Salt Pond,** in which breeding shellfish are suspended from floating "nurseries"; their offspring will later be used to seed the flats. Also in the seashore is the Buttonbush Trail, a nature path for people with vision impairments. A hike or bike ride to Coast Guard Beach leads to a turnout looking out over marsh and sea. A section of the cliff here was washed away in 1990, revealing the remains of a prehistoric dwelling.

Salt Pond Visitor Center is the first visitor center of the Cape Cod National Seashore that you encounter as you travel down-Cape toward the tip (the other, the **Province Lands Visitor Center,** is in Provincetown). The Salt Pond Visitor Center offers guided walks, tours, boat trips, demonstrations, and lectures from mid-April through Thanksgiving, as well as evening beach walks, campfire talks, and other programs in summer. The center includes a museum with displays on whaling and the old saltworks, as well as early Cape Cod artifacts including scrimshaw, the journal that Mrs. Penniman kept while on a whaling voyage with her husband, and some of the Pennimans' possessions, such as their tea service and the captain's top hat. A good bookstore and an air-conditioned auditorium showing films on geology, sea rescues, whaling, Henry David Thoreau, and Guglielmo Marconi are also here. Something's going on most summer evenings at the outdoor amphitheater, from slide-show talks to military-band concerts. ⊠*Doane Rd. off U.S. 6* ☎*508/255–3421* ⊕*www.nps.gov/caco* ⊠*Free* ⊙*Daily 9–4:30 (hrs extended slightly in summer).*

Roads and bicycle trails lead to **Coast Guard and Nauset Light beaches** (⊠*Off Ocean View Dr.*), which begin an unbroken 30-mi stretch of barrier beach extending to Provincetown—the "Cape Cod Beach" of Thoreau's 1865 classic, *Cape Cod.* You can still walk its length, as Thoreau did, though the Atlantic continues to claim more of the Cape's eastern shore every year. The site of the famous beach cottage of Henry Beston's 1928 book, *The Outermost House,* is to the south, near the end of Nauset spit. Designated as a literary landmark in 1964, the cottage was, alas, destroyed in the Great Blizzard of February 1978.

Moved 350 feet back from its perch at cliff's edge in 1996, the much-photographed red-and-white **Nauset Light** (⊠*Ocean View Dr. and Cable Rd.* ☎*508/240–2612* ⊕*www.nausetlight.org*) still tops the bluff where the Three Sisters Lighthouses once stood; the Sisters themselves can be seen in a little landlocked park surrounded by trees, reached by paved walkways off Nauset Light Beach's parking lot. How the lighthouses got there is a long story. In 1838 three brick lighthouses were built 150 feet apart on the bluffs in Eastham overlooking a particularly dangerous area of shoals (shifting underwater sandbars). In 1892, after the eroding cliff dropped the towers into the ocean, they were replaced with three wooden towers. In 1918 two were moved away, as was the third in 1923. Eventually the National Park Service acquired the Three Sisters and brought them together in the inland park, where they would be safe, rather than returning them to the eroding coast. The Fresnel lens from the last working lighthouse is on display at the **Salt Pond Visitor Center.** Lectures on and guided walks to the lighthouses are conducted throughout the season.

WHERE TO STAY & EAT

$–$$$ ✕**Arnold's Lobster & Clam Bar.** You can't miss this hot spot on the side of Route 6: look for the riot of colorful flowers lining the road and the patient folks waiting in long lines in the parking lot. That crowd is testament to the freshness and flavors that come out of this busy kitchen for lunch, dinner, and takeout, putting forth everything from grilled burgers to 3-pound lobsters. There's ice cream for after dinner (or while you wait) and an artfully designed miniature golf course to keep the kids happy. They're situated next to the bike trail. ⊠*3580 State Hwy. (U.S. 6), Eastham* ☎*508/255–2575* ▬*No credit cards* ⊙*Closed Nov.–Apr.*

$–$$ ✕**Fairway Restaurant and Pizzeria.** The friendly family-run Fairway specializes in Italian comfort food and pizzas. Attached to the Hole in One Donut Shop (very popular among locals), the Fairway puts a jar of crayons on every paper-covered table and sells its own brand of root beer. Entrées come with salad and homemade rolls. Try the eggplant Parmesan, fettuccine and meatballs, or a well-stuffed calzone. You can order from the extensive breakfast menu from 6:30 to 11:30 AM. ⊠4295 U.S. 6 ☎508/255–3893 ⚐*Reservations not accepted* ⊘*No lunch* ⊟*AE, D, DC, MC, V.*

¢–$$ ✕**The Friendly Fisherman.** Not just another roadside lobster shack with buoys and nets for decoration, this place is serious about its fresh seafood. It's both a great place to pick up ingredients to cook at home—there's a fish and produce market on-site—and a good bet for dining out on such favorites as fish-and-chips, fried scallops, and lobster. The market also sells homemade pies, breads, soups, stews, and pasta. ⊠*U. S. 6, North Eastham* ☎*508/255–6770 or 508/255–3009* ⊟*AE, MC, V* ⊘*Closed Nov.–Apr.*

$$$–$$$$ 🏠**Fort Hill Bed and Breakfast.** Gordon and Jean Avery run this enchanting
Fodor's Choice B&B in an 1864 Greek-revival farmhouse nestled in the tranquil Fort
★ Hill area. The location is perfect—minutes off busy Route 6, but steps away from quiet, secluded trails that wind through cedar forests, fields crisscrossed by old stone fences, and a red-maple swamp. Two cozy suites in the main house, tastefully decorated with period pieces and antiques, share a living room with fireplace. The crown jewel, however, is the light and airy Nantucket Cottage, modeled after a Truro barn. It's so homey—with stone floors, a gas fireplace, a classic white-and-blue Cape Cod bedroom loft, and a private garden—that you'll want to move in. Breakfasts are superb, with offerings like oven-poached pears in sweet cream, and buttermilk-currant scones; the cheesy-chive egg soufflé is a masterpiece. **Pros:** Serene, pastoral setting, close to nature trails and superb views of National Seashore, private and elegant lodging. **Cons:** No water views or beachfront, not an in-town location. ⊠*75 Fort Hill Rd., 02642* ☎*508/240–2870* ⊕*www.forthillbedandbreakfast.com* ⚐*2 suites, 1 cottage* ⚲*In-room: no phones, kitchen (some), refrigerator, DVD (some), VCR (some), Wi-Fi. In-hotel: no elevator* ⊟*No credit cards* ⊙*BP.*

$$$–$$$$ 🏠**Whalewalk Inn & Spa.** This 1830 whaling master's home is on
Fodor's Choice 3-landscaped acres. Wide-board pine floors, fireplaces, and 19th-cen-
★ tury country antiques provide historical appeal. Rooms in the main inn have four-poster twin, double, or queen-size beds; floral fabrics; and antique or reproduction furniture. Suites with fully equipped kitchens are in the converted barn and guesthouse. A secluded saltbox cottage has a fireplace, kitchen, and private patio. Deluxe rooms in the carriage house have fireplaces, hot tubs, and air-conditioning. The property also has an opulent state-of-the-art spa, complete with a small resistance pool and fitness center. Above the spa is the inn's most sumptuous suite, with vaulted ceilings, fireplace, entertainment center, and two-person hot tub. Breakfast is served in the cheerful sunroom or on the garden patio. **Pros:** Beautiful grounds, elegantly appointed rooms with added benefit of decadent spa treatments. **Cons:** No water views or beachfront, not an in-town location. ⊠*220 Bridge Rd., 02642* ☎*508/255–0617 or 800/440–1281* ⊕*www.whalewalkinn.com* ⚐*11 rooms, 5 suites* ⚲*In-room: kitchen (some), refrigerator (some), DVD (some) VCR (some), Wi-Fi. In-hotel: pool, gym, spa, no-smoking rooms, no elevator* ⊟*AE, D, MC, V* ⊙*BP.*

$$–$$$$ ⊡ **Four Points Sheraton.** This reliable if ordinary midrange chain hotel is at the entrance to the National Seashore. Rooms have views of the tropical indoor pool (with lush plants, pirate-theme bar, and resident live parrot), the parking lot, or the woods. Outside rooms are a little bigger and brighter and have mini-refrigerators. **Pros:** Good location for exploring outer Cape area, great for those with kids (pools), full service hotel. **Cons:** No water views or beachfront, standard chain-hotel fare rather than unique lodging. ⊠*3800 U.S. 6, 02642* ☎*508/255–5000 or 800/533–3986* 🖷*508/240–1870* ⊕*www.capecodfourpoints. com* ➱*107 rooms, 2 suites* ⚒*In-room: refrigerator, Wi-Fi. In-hotel: restaurant, room service, bar, tennis courts, pools, gym, no elevator* ⊟*AE, D, DC, MC, V.*

$$–$$$$ ⊡ **Inn at the Oaks.** If it weren't for this three-story inn's vivid-yellow paint job, it would be lost among the trees, even though it's right along U.S. 6. Both the Cape Cod Rail Trail and the Salt Pond Visitor Center are just across the road. Victorian touches at this 19th-century refuge include graceful high ceilings and intricate interior wood molding. Each room has antiques, brass beds, and soft down comforters, plus a few modern amenities such as DVD players; some have claw-foot tubs, which are great to slide into after a day at the beach. **Pros:** Very close to both Cape Cod Rail Trail and National Seashore, good bet for those traveling with kids who want to experience nonhotel lodging, can book on-site massage services. **Cons:** Right off busy U.S. 6, not for those looking for quiet (away from kids) getaway. ⊠*3085 County Rd. (U.S. 6), 02642* ☎*508/255–1886* 🖷*508/240–0345* ⊕*www.innattheoaks.com* ➱*10 rooms, 4 suites* ⚒*In-room: DVD, Wi-Fi. In-hotel: some pets allowed (fee), hot tub, no elevator* ⊟*AE, D, MC, V* ⎟◯⎟*BP.*

$$–$$$$ ⊡ **Penny House Inn & Spa.** Tucked behind a wave of privet hedge,
 ★   this rambling gray-shingle inn's spacious rooms are furnished with antiques, collectibles, and wicker. The luxurious accommodations are cozy rather than stuffy; many are romantic, with whirlpool tubs, fireplaces, or both. Some rooms are larger, with sitting areas; suites have separate bedrooms and sitting rooms and can sleep up to five. Take a dip in the saltwater pool, or indulge in a massage, facial, or mud wrap in the on-site spa room. Common areas include a Great Room with lots of windows and a selection of videos, a combination sunroom-library, and a garden patio with umbrella tables. A full homemade breakfast starts the day, and afternoon tea is available. **Pros:** Rooms are private and secluded; ideal for a romantic getaway, full range of luxury spa services to choose from, not far from National Seashore and area beaches. **Cons:** Sits just off busy U.S. 6 (though set back a little), no water views or beachfront. ⊠*4885 County Rd. (U.S. 6), 02642* ☎*508/255–6632 or 800/554–1751* 🖷*508/255–4893* ⊕*www.pennyhouseinn.com* ➱*10 rooms, 3 suites* ⚒*In-room: refrigerator (some), VCR (some) DVD (some), Wi-Fi. In-hotel: pool, spa, no children under 8, no-smoking rooms, no elevator* ⊟*AE, D, MC, V* ⎟◯⎟*BP.*

$–$$ ⊡ **Ocean Park Inn.** Rooms at this property, run by the same owners as the adjacent Four Points Sheraton, are clean, simple, and straightforward. There are larger family units available—one with a fireplace— but most rooms are for double occupancy, with full- or queen-size beds.

You are welcome to use the amenities, including the pools and tennis courts, of the Four Points Sheraton. **Pros:** Lots of special packages make for some good deals, good bet for those traveling with kids, shares amenities with larger hotel next door, close to bike trail and area beaches. **Cons:** No water views or beachfront, just off busy Route 6. ⊠ *3900 U.S. 6, 02642* ☎ *508/255–1132 or 800/862–5550* 🖷 *508/255–5250* ⊕ *www.capecodopi.com* ➷ *54 rooms, 1 suite* ♿ *In-room: refrigerator. In-hotel: laundry facilities, no elevator* ☰ *AE, D, DC, MC, V* ☉ *Closed Nov.–Mar.*

$ 🏨 **Cove Bluffs Motel.** This old-fashioned haven for nature lovers and families is nestled among the trees and within walking distance of Orleans Town Cove and several nature trails. Settle into a standard motel room or choose a more self-sufficient getaway in studio or two-bedroom housekeeping units with stoves, refrigerators, and microwaves. Grounds include basketball courts, shuffleboard, swing sets, a playhouse, a sandbox, grills, and swinging hammocks in the shade. **Pros:** Peaceful setting near Town Cove, ideal for those traveling with children, reasonable rates, good base for exploring area. **Cons:** Not an in-town location, not for those looking for authentic historic lodging. ⊠ *25 Seaview Rd. (U.S. 6), Box 297, 02642* ☎ *508/240–1616* ⊕ *www.capecod-orleans.com/covebluffs* ➷ *5 rooms, 8 housekeeping units* ♿ *In-hotel: pool, laundry facilities, no-smoking rooms, no elevator* ☰ *MC, V* ☉ *Closed Nov.–Mar.*

¢ 🏨 **Hostelling International–Mid Cape.** On 3 wooded acres near the Cape Cod Rail Trail and a 15-minute walk from the bay, this hostel has cabins that sleep six to eight each; two can be used as family cabins. It has a common area and a kitchen, and there are a number of guest programs. **Pros:** Perfect for those on limited budget, no-frills, family-style lodging, quiet location near bike trail and bay beaches, a step above camping. **Cons:** Sharing lodging, bathrooms, and kitchens in dorm-style setting, not for those looking for privacy or luxury. ⊠ *75 Goody Hallet Dr., 02642* ☎ *508/255–2785* ⊕ *www.usahostels.org* ➷ *8 cabins* ♿ *In-room: no a/c, kitchen, no TV, no elevator* ☰ *MC, V* ☉ *Closed mid-Sept.–mid-May.*

⛺ **Atlantic Oaks Campground.** This campground in a pine and oak forest is less than 1 mi north of the Salt Pond Visitor Center and minutes from Cape Cod National Seashore. Primarily an RV camp (year-round hookups are available), it offers limited tenting as well. You can rent bikes, and there's direct access to the Cape Cod Rail Trail. Reservations are essential during peak season. ♿ *Flush toilets, full hookups, drinking water, guest laundry, showers, fire grates, grills, picnic tables, electricity, public telephone, general store, play area, swimming (pond and ocean)* ➷ *99 RV sites, 12 tent sites* ⊠ *3700 U.S. 6, 02642* ☎ *508/255–1437 or 800/332–2267* 🖷 *508/247–8216* ⊕ *www.atlanticoaks.com* ☰ *D, MC, V* ☉ *Closed Nov.–Apr.*

NIGHTLIFE & THE ARTS

The **Cape Cod National Seashore** (☎ *508/255–3421 information*) sponsors summer-evening programs, such as slide shows, sunset beach walks, concerts by local groups or military bands, and campfire sing-alongs.

The **Eastham Painters Guild** holds outdoor art shows every Thursday, Friday, and holiday weekends from 9 to 5, July through October, at the Schoolhouse Museum. ⊠*Next to Salt Pond Visitor Center, off U.S. 6.*

First Encounter Coffee House (⊠*Chapel in the Pines, Samoset Rd.* ☎*508/255–5438*) presents a mixture of professional and local folk and blues in a smoke-and-alcohol-free environment, with refreshments available during intermission. National acts are booked for the second and fourth Saturday. It's closed May and December.

Sea Dog Restaurant & Saloon (⊠*4100 U.S. 6* ☎*508/255–2650*) serves pub food and drinks in a lively atmosphere. Live acoustic music is played year-round on varying nights; call for a schedule. It's closed Monday.

SPORTS & THE OUTDOORS

BEACHES On the bay side of the Outer Cape, **First Encounter Beach** (⊠*End of Samoset Rd. off U.S. 6*) is open to the public and charges daily parking fees of $15 to nonresidents in season (weekly and season passes are also available; call the town hall at ☎508/240–5972). Parking fees or passes also apply to several other bay beaches and ponds, both saltwater and freshwater.

★ **Coast Guard Beach** (⊠*Off Ocean View Dr.*), part of the National Seashore, is a long beach backed by low grass and heathland. A handsome former Coast Guard station is also here, though it's not open to the public. The beach has no parking lot of its own, so park at the Salt Pond Visitor Center or at the lot up Doane Road from the center and take the free shuttle to the beach. At high tide the size of the beach shrinks considerably, so watch your blanket. There are showers here, and lifeguards are posted between June and August. A daily charge of $15 for cars or a season pass (by far the best bargain) for $45 grants admission to all six National Seashore swimming beaches.

Fodor'sChoice **Nauset Light Beach** (⊠*Off Ocean View Dr.*), adjacent to Coast Guard
★ Beach, continues the National Seashore landscape of long, sandy beach backed by tall dunes, grass, and heathland. It has showers and lifeguards in summer, but as with other National Seashore beaches, there's no food concession. Nauset charges $15 daily per car; a $45 season pass admits you here and to the other five National Seashore swimming beaches.

BICYCLING The **Idle Times Bike Shop** (⊠*4550 U.S. 6 and Brackett Rd.* ☎*508/255–8281*) provides bikes of all sizes and types and is right near the Cape Cod Rail Trail.

The **Little Capistrano Bike Shop** (⊠*Salt Pond Rd. across from Salt Pond Visitor Center* ☎*508/255–6515*) has plenty of bikes and trailers available for rent and is between the Cape Cod Rail Trail and the National Seashore Bike Trail.

Nauset Trail, maintained by the Cape Cod National Seashore, stretches 1½ mi from Salt Pond Visitor Center through groves of apple and locust trees to Coast Guard Beach.

HEALTH & **Willy's Gym** (✉️*4730 U.S. 6, North Eastham* ☎️*508/255–6370*
FITNESS CLUBS ☎️*508/255–6826*) is the astounding 100,000-square-foot branch of
the original Willy's in Orleans. Kids will love Play World, a massive
indoor playground. Other facilities include an Olympic-size, SaltSys-
tem indoor pool, a rock-climbing wall, an indoor NBA basketball
court, and indoor- and outdoor-tennis courts, along with a vast selection of exercise machines and studio classes. After your workout, relax
in the hot tub, steam room, or sauna—or book a massage or skin-care
treatment at Kembali Spa. You can also peruse the pro shop, or perhaps
grab a bite at the Tiger restaurant … and if you run out of things to
do, there's even free Wi-Fi access on-site. Willy's also hosts free movie
nights and other arts and community programs, which are open to the
public. You can buy a day, week, or month pass.

SURFING Eastham's ocean beaches are great for surfing and trying out a new
sport that's gaining in popularity: kiteboarding. Basically a combination of surfing and windboarding, kiteboarding is a speedy sport that
will definitely get your blood pumping.

Little Overhead Surf & Kiteboard (✉️*4900 U.S. 6* ☎️*508/240–1455* ⊕*www.
littleoverhead.com*) has a full stock of surfboards and kiteboards, as
well as all the necessary accoutrements; they even provide instruction.

THE LOWER CAPE ESSENTIALS

*To research prices, get advice from other travelers, and book travel
arrangements, visit ⊕www.fodors.com.*

TRANSPORTATION

BY BOAT & FERRY

In season, the ferry from Harwich to Nantucket is a less hectic alternative to the Hyannis crowd. *For details, ⇨ Boat & Ferry Travel in
Essentials in the back of this book.*

BY BUS

A bus connecting Hyannis and Orleans serves the Lower Cape region.
For details, ⇨ Bus Travel in Essentials in the back of this book.

BY TAXI

John's Taxi & Limousine picks up only in Dennis and Harwich but will
take you anywhere on the Cape.

Taxi Companies Eldredge Taxi (✉️*Chatham* ☎️*508/945-0068*). **John's Taxi &
Limousine** (☎️*508/394-3209*).

CONTACTS & RESOURCES

CONDO & HOUSE RENTALS

Commonwealth Associates can assist in finding vacation rentals in the
Harwiches, including waterfront properties. Great Locations Inc. specializes in vacation rentals in Brewster, Dennis, and Orleans.

Local Agents **Commonwealth Associates** (✉ *Harwich Port* ☎ *508/432–2618* ⊕ *www.commonwealthrealestate.com*). **Great Locations Inc.** (✉ *Brewster* ☎ *508/896–2090 or 800/626–9984* ⊕ *www.greatlocationsre.com*).

VISITOR INFORMATION

Some local chambers of commerce are open only in season. The Brewster Chamber of Commerce is in the Brewster town offices building. The office includes a visitor center and the offices of the Brewster Chamber of Commerce and Board of Trade United.

Tourist Information **Brewster Chamber of Commerce** (✉ *2198 Main St. [Rte. 6A], Box 1241, 02631* ☎ *508/896–3500* ⊕ *www.brewstercapecod.org*). **Chatham Chamber of Commerce** (✇ *Box 793, 02633* ☎ *508/945–5199 or 800/715–5567* ⊕ *www.chathamcapecod.org Seasonal visitor center* ✉ *Rtes. 28 and 137, South Chatham Information booth* ✉ *533 Main St., Chatham*). **Eastham Chamber of Commerce** (✉ *U.S. 6 at Fort Hill Rd., Box 1329, 02642* ☎ *508/240–7211* ⊕ *www. easthamchamber.com*). **Harwich Chamber of Commerce** (☎ *508/432–1600 or 800/442–7942* ⊕ *www.harwichcc.com Seasonal visitor center* ✉ *One Schoolhouse Rd. and Rte. 28, Harwich Port*). **Orleans Chamber of Commerce** (✇ *Box 153, 02653 Information booth* ✉ *44 Main St.* ☎ *508/255–1386 or 800/856–1386* ⊕ *www.capecod-orleans.com*).

The Outer Cape

WORD OF MOUTH

"You can't go wrong with any of the beaches on the Cape Cod National Seashore."

—Boss Ton

"I like Provincetown because the ocean is as much a part of the downtown as are the smells of garlic and wood fires."

—outofblue

By Andrew
Collins

TECHNICALLY PART OF THE LOWER Cape, the Outer Cape is nonetheless its own entity, forming the wrist and fist of Cape Cod. There's a sense of abandon here, in the hedonistic summertime frenzy of Provincetown and out on the windswept landscape of dunes and marshes. As you drive down here, the land flattens out, vegetation gets sparser and more coniferous, and the sea feels closer as the land narrows. Much of the region is undeveloped, protected by the Cape Cod National Seashore. Long, straight, dune-backed beaches appear to go on forever; inland, trails wind through wind-stunted forests of scrub pine, beech, and oak. Wellfleet is a quiet town, with art galleries, upscale shops, and a calm—but active—harbor. With an expanse of high dunes, estuaries, salt marshes, pine forests, rivers, and winding back roads, Truro is the least-populated, least-developed town on the entire Cape.

The promise of solitude has long drawn artists and writers out here. Provincetown has two faces—a quiet little fishing village in winter and a magnet for throngs of pleasure seekers (including a substantial gay and lesbian community) in summer, who come for the rugged beaches, photogenic streets lined with historic homes, zany nightlife, shops selling everything from antiques to zoot suits, and the galleries, readings, and art classes that carry on Provincetown's rich history as an art colony.

EXPLORING THE OUTER CAPE

Making your way around narrow Outer Cape, you really have one key option for getting around: driving along U.S. 6. There are some less congested but slower and indirect roads between the area's two least-developed communities, Wellfleet and Truro. In Wellfleet, many businesses and attractions are strung along U.S. 6, but there's also a compact downtown with art galleries, cafés, and boutiques that's ideal for strolling. Truro has just the tiniest commercial district and its few attractions are best reached by car, as they're somewhat far apart. In Provincetown, on the other hand, a car—especially in summer—can actually be a hindrance. This is a walkable town with two main thoroughfares, Commercial and Bradford streets. You could easily spend a full day or two just walking around downtown and checking out the dozens and dozens of shops, galleries, and restaurants. Provincetown also has some excellent beaches, which are a short drive or bike ride from downtown.

ABOUT THE RESTAURANTS

Dining on the Outer Cape means everything from humble fried-clam shacks to candlelit elegance. Many restaurants have withstood the tests of time and fashion and have developed loyal followings that keep their doors open year after year. Menus frequently highlight local seafood. Wellfleet's restaurants, while not inexpensive, cater as much to families as to adult sophisticates and typically have menus offering a wide range of items, from less-expensive burgers and fried-seafood platters to creatively prepared steaks and fish grills. Truro has just a handful of restaurants spread out along the byways. Provincetown opens a world of great variation to the eager diner. There are a number of snazzy, hip restaurants in town, all aglow with candles, crystal, and fine linens, but you'll find an equal number of lively and boisterous cafés. Many have outdoor seating, providing good views of the town's constant action. Smoking is banned inside all of the town's bars and restaurants.

In the height of the summer season, you may have to wait awhile for a table—even if you have a reservation. To make matters worse, in the past few years Cape Cod has been experiencing a labor shortage; good help is at a premium, and this has caused some restaurants to shorten their season or reduce their hours.

> **TOP 5**
>
> ■ Walking the ocean beaches on the Cape Cod National Seashore
>
> ■ Browsing Wellfleet's art galleries
>
> ■ Saying you saw Marconi Station
>
> ■ Strolling Commercial Street in Provincetown
>
> ■ Dune buggying Province Lands with Art's Dune Tours

ABOUT THE HOTELS

Lodging options on the Outer Cape are diverse. Wellfleet has several cozy inns and bed-and-breakfasts in the center of town, with a few larger motels on busy U.S. 6. Despite the strict building codes, there are a surprising number of large (though not imposing) hotel complexes and cottage colonies spread out along Cape Cod Bay in North Truro. These places may be crowded, but they're also right on the sand, with commanding views of sunsets and the Provincetown skyline.

Provincetown's lodging scene has changed dramatically in recent years, as a number of old guesthouses and inns have been sold and converted to private homes. Those that remain have mostly transformed themselves from modest, affordable lodgings to sophisticated—and quite pricey—fine inns. With the shrinkage in available rooms, it's become even harder to find a room during the summer months. Minimum stays of at least three nights are often the norm during the peak season and holiday times, and sometimes there's a week minimum in July and August. That being said, more and more Provincetown properties have begun staying open for most or even all of the year—if you don't feel a need to visit during the busiest time of year, consider the quieter, yet still wonderfully atmospheric, off months. May, June, September, and October are especially nice, as most of the town's restaurants and shops are still open then, but hotel rates are lower and rooms easier to find.

WHAT IT COSTS					
	$$$$	$$$	$$	$	¢
RESTAURANTS	over $30	$22–$30	$16–$22	$10–$16	under $10
HOTELS	over $260	$200–$260	$140–$200	$90–$140	under $90

Restaurant prices are per person for a main course at dinner. Hotel prices are for a standard double room, excluding 6% sales tax (more in some counties) and 1%–4% tourist tax.

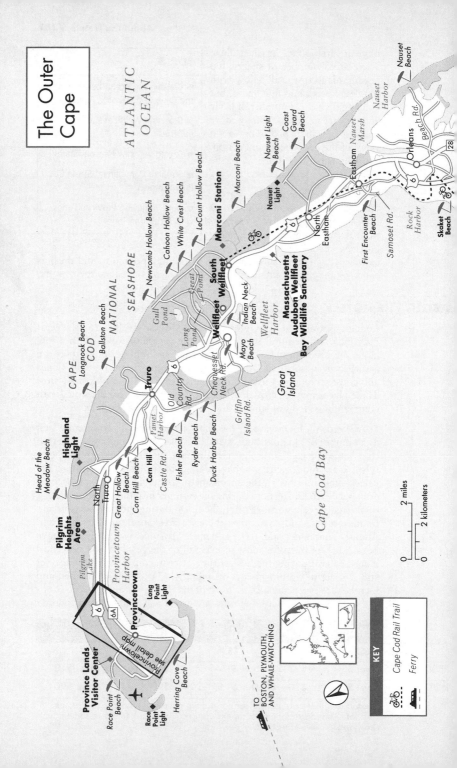

The Outer Cape

ATLANTIC OCEAN

CAPE COD NATIONAL SEASHORE

Cape Cod Bay

Province Lands Visitor Center
Race Point Beach
Race Point Light
Herring Cove Beach
Provincetown
Long Point Light
Provincetown Harbor
Provincetown see detail map
6
6A
Pilgrim Heights Area
Pilgrim Lake
Head of the Meadow Beach
Highland Light
North Truro
Great Hollow Beach
Corn Hill Beach
Corn Hill
Castle Rd.
Longnook Beach
Ballston Beach
Fisher Beach
Ryder Beach
Truro
6
Old Country Rd.
Pamet Harbor
Duck Harbor Beach
Griffin Island Rd.
Chequesset Neck Rd.
Great Island
Gull Pond
Long Pond
Great Pond
Newcomb Hollow Beach
Cahoon Hollow Beach
White Crest Beach
LeCount Hollow Beach
South Wellfleet
Wellfleet
Mayo Beach
Indian Neck Beach
Wellfleet Harbor
Massachusetts Audubon Wellfleet Bay Wildlife Sanctuary
Marconi Station
Marconi Beach
Nauset Light
Nauset Light Beach
Coast Guard Beach
6
North Eastham
First Encounter Beach
Samoset Rd.
Eastham
Nauset Marsh
Nauset Harbor
Nauset Beach
Beach Rd.
Orleans
6
28
Rock Harbor
Skaket Beach

TO BOSTON, PLYMOUTH, AND WHALE-WATCHING

0   2 miles
0   2 kilometers

KEY
🚲   Cape Cod Rail Trail
      Ferry

TIMING

Prime time on the Outer Cape—when everything is open—is from Memorial Day to around Columbus Day; July and August are by far the most crowded times. The shoulder seasons of late May and June, and after Labor Day, have become more and more popular with childless travelers who aren't locked into a school schedule. Rates are lower during these times, and restaurants and shops are still open. If the weather has been generous, swimming is still a pleasant possibility.

Wellfleet pretty much seals itself up after Columbus Day; most galleries and restaurants close, leaving just a handful of year-round businesses. But you'll have the entire outside world to explore, now free of thousands of others trying to do the same thing. Ocean climates keep winters milder than on the mainland. It's quiet—beautifully so—and distractions and pleasures take on a more basic flavor.

Provincetown clears out as well, but not as fully as Wellfleet. Various theme weekends throughout the year have boosted tourism in the off-season, and there are always readings, films, and places to eat. The off-season is truly a time to discover the essence of the place, see its changing natural beauty, and experience a more restful and relaxed pace.

WELLFLEET & SOUTH WELLFLEET

6 mi north of Eastham, 13 mi southeast of Provincetown.

Still famous for its world-renowned and succulent namesake oysters and, with Truro, for having been a colonial whaling and cod-fishing port, Wellfleet is today a tranquil community; many artists and writers call it home. Less than 2 mi wide, it's one of the most attractively developed Cape resort towns, with a number of fine restaurants, historic houses, art galleries, and a good old Main Street in the village proper. The South Wellfleet section of town extends to the North Eastham border and has a wonderful Audubon sanctuary and a drive-in theater that doubles on weekends as a flea market. There's no village center here, just a handful of motels, restaurants, and businesses along busy U.S. 6.

The downtown center of Wellfleet is quite compact, so it's actually best to leave your car in one of the public parking areas and take off on foot. Historic buildings that once housed oyster and fish-drying shacks or stately residences now contain upscale art galleries, designer-clothing stores, and restaurants. Wellfleet's small-town nature still somehow accommodates the demands of a major tourist industry; the year-round population of around 2,800 residents explodes to more than 18,000 people in July and August.

Tourism isn't the only industry, though. Fishing boats still head out from the harbor daily in search of scallops, cod, and other fish. Shellfishing accounts for a major portion of the town's economy. Whaling played a role in the 18th and 19th centuries; a raucous whaling tavern once thrived out on the now-sunken Billingsgate Island. Dozens of world-traveling sea captains found their way to Wellfleet as well, the effect evident in many of the grand old houses that line the narrow streets of town. The Wellfleet Historical Society is a fine stop for those who wish to see the town as it was in its early days. Natural splendor, as well as history and sophisticated artistic culture, accounts for Wellfleet's popularity. The beaches are spectacular, with their towering sand dunes, bracing surf, and miles of unfettered expanse. Seemingly endless wooded paths in the domain of the National Seashore make for terrific walking and hiking trails, and the sheltered waters of the tidal Herring River and Wellfleet Harbor are a favorite destination for canoeists, kayakers, windsurfers, and sailors.

★ **Marconi Station,** on the Atlantic side of the Cape's forearm, is the site of the first transatlantic wireless station erected on the U.S. mainland. Italian radio and wireless-telegraphy pioneer Guglielmo Marconi sent the first American wireless message from here to Europe—"most cordial greetings and good wishes" from President Theodore Roosevelt to King Edward VII of England—on January 18, 1903. The station broadcasted news for 15 years. An outdoor shelter contains a model of the original station, of which only fragments remain as a result of cliff erosion; parts of the tower bases are sometimes visible on the beach below, where they fell. The Cape Cod National Seashore's administrative headquarters is here, and though it is not an official visitor center, it can provide information at times when the centers are closed. Inside there's a mock-up of the spark-gap transmitter Marconi used. Off the parking lot, a 1½-mi trail and boardwalk lead through the **Atlantic White Cedar Swamp,** one of the most beautiful trails on the seashore; free maps and guides are available at the trailhead. **Marconi Beach,** south of the station on Marconi Beach Road, is another of the National Seashore's ocean beaches. ⊠*Marconi Site Rd., South Wellfleet* ☎*508/349–3785* ⊕*www.nps.gov/caco* ✉*Free* ⊙*Daily 8–4:30.*

For a **scenic loop** through a classic Cape landscape near Wellfleet's Atlantic beaches—with scrub and pines on the left, heathland meeting cliffs and ocean below on the right—take LeCount Hollow Road just north of the Marconi Station turnoff. All the beaches on this strip rest at the bottom of a tall grass-covered dune, which lends dramatic character to this outermost shore. The first of the four, **LeCount Hollow,** is restricted to residents or temporary residents in season, as is the last, **Newcomb Hollow,** with a scalloped shoreline of golden sand. In between, **White Crest** and **Cahoon Hollow** are town-managed public beaches. Cahoon has a hot restaurant and dancing spot, the Beachcomber. Backtrack to Cahoon Hollow Road and turn west for the southernmost entrance to the town of Wellfleet proper, across U.S. 6.

NEED A BREAK?

The Blue Willow (⊠*South Wellfleet Post Office Sq., 1426 U.S. 6* ☎*508/349–0900*) is tiny, but the food is grand, transcending what you'd find in other take-out places. Treats like crab cakes, crispy duck, tarragon chicken salad, and pasta dishes are made on the premises. For breakfast, there are daily frittata and quiche specials, as well as muffins, scones, and pastries. Outside is a mini–farmers' market with fresh vegetables and flowers. Right at the Cape Cod Rail Trail, it's a good spot to grab a snack or pick up the complete makings of a beach picnic or fine dinner. It's across from the chamber of commerce information booth and open daily year-round.

Wellfleet's **First Congregational Church** (⊠*200 Main St., Downtown Wellfleet* ☎*508/349–6877*), a courtly 1850 Greek-revival building, is said to have the only town clock in the world that strikes on ship's bells. The church's interior is lovely, with pale blue walls, a brass chandelier hanging from an enormous gilt ceiling rosette, subtly colored stained-glass windows, and

WORD OF MOUTH

"If you're here on a weekend, drive along Ocean View Drive in Wellfleet, and at White Crest Beach, on the Atlantic, you will see kite surfers riding the waves, as well as the wind riders catching the thermal winds off the dunes."

—capecodshanty

pews curved to form an amphitheater facing the altar and the 738-pipe Hook and Hastings tracker-action organ, dating from 1873. To the right is a Tiffany-style window depicting a clipper ship. Concerts are given in July and August on Sunday at 8 PM.

For a glimpse into Wellfleet's past, the diminutive **Wellfleet Historical Society Museum** exhibits furniture, paintings, shipwreck salvage, needlework, navigation equipment, early photographs, Native American artifacts, and clothing. Short guided walks around the center of town are given Tuesday and Friday mornings at 10:15 in July and August for $3. ⊠*266 Main St., Downtown Wellfleet* ☎*508/349–9157* ⊕*www. wellfleethistoricalsociety.com* ⊠*Free* ⊙*Late June–early Sept., Wed., Thurs., and Sat. 1–4, Tues. and Fri. 10–4.*

The **Wellfleet Public Library** (⊠*55 W. Main St., Downtown Wellfleet* ☎*508/349–0310* ⊕*www.wellfleetlibrary.org*) reflects the literary life of Wellfleet with readings, lectures, and exhibits by noted writers and artists in the community, and the collection of books for adults and children is impressive. Also available are videos, books on tape, and Internet access. Among the writers who have spent time here are Mary McCarthy, Edmund Wilson, Annie Dillard, and Marge Piercy.

Main Street is a good place to start if you're in the mood for shopping.

Commercial Street has all the flavor of the fishing town that Wellfleet remains; galleries and shops occupy small weathered-shingle houses.

A good stroll around town would take in Commercial and Main streets, ending perhaps at **Uncle Tim's Bridge** (⊠*Off E. Commercial St., Downtown Wellfleet*). The short walk across this arching landmark—with its beautiful, much-photographed view over marshland and a tidal creek—leads to a small wooded island.

NEED A BREAK?

Box Lunch (⊠*50 Briar La.* ☎*508/349–2178* ⊕*www.boxlunch.com*) is a popular Cape franchise that you may have seen elsewhere, but this is the original location. It serves up hot and cold roll-up sandwiches, a style it claims to have invented and perfected. A wide variety of fillings are available for breakfast, lunch, or early dinner. This tiny place gets ferociously busy in the summer season—call your order in ahead of time if you can.

Commercial Street leads to the **Wellfleet Pier** (☎ *508/349–9818 for a fishing permit*), busy with fishing boats, sailboats, yachts, charters, and party boats. At the twice-daily low tides, you can dig on the tidal flats for oysters, clams, and quahogs.

Chequessett Neck Road makes for a pretty 2½-mi drive from the harbor to the bay past Sunset Hill—a great place to catch one. At the end, on the left, is a parking lot and wooded picnic area from which nature trails lead off to **Great Island** (✉ *Off Chequessett Neck Rd., west of Downtown Wellfleet*), perfect for beachcombers and solitude seekers. The "island" is actually a peninsula connected by a sand spit built by tidal action. More than 7 mi of trails wind along the inner marshes and the water—these are the most difficult paths on the seashore because they're mostly in soft sand. In the 17th century, a tavern and shore whaling lookout towers stood here; residents pastured animals and engaged in oystering and cranberry harvesting. By 1800 the hardwood forest that had covered the island had been cut down for use in the building of ships and homes. The pitch pines and other growth you see here (and all over the Cape) today were introduced in the 1830s to keep the soil from washing into the sea. Cape Cod National Seashore offers occasional guided hikes on Great Island and, from February through April, seal walks. To the right of the Great Island lot, a road leads to **Griffin Island,** which has its own walking trail.

☾
Fodor's Choice
★

A trip to the Outer Cape isn't complete without a visit to the **Massachusetts Audubon Wellfleet Bay Wildlife Sanctuary,** an 1,100-acre haven for more than 250 species of birds attracted by the varied habitats found here. The jewel of the Massachusetts Audubon Society, the sanctuary is a superb place for walking, birding, and watching the sun set over the salt marsh and bay. The **Esther Underwood Johnson Nature Center** contains two 700-gallon aquariums that offer an up-close look at marine life common to the Cape's tidal flats and marshlands. Other rotating exhibits illustrate different facets of the area's ecology and natural history. From the center you can hike five short nature trails, including a fascinating Boardwalk Trail that leads over a salt marsh to a small beach—or you can wander through the Butterfly Garden. Note that as of this writing the center was closed for repairs and reconstruction, and there's no timetable in place as to when it will reopen—check first before going. The center's interpretive programs are still in place, however, and the sanctuary remains open for hiking.

The Audubon Society is host to naturalist-led wildlife tours around the Cape, including trips to the Monomoy Islands, year-round. There are bay cruises; bird, wildlife, and insect walks; hikes; snorkeling; winter seal cruises; and birding, canoe, and kayak trips. The sanctuary also has camps for children in July and August and weeklong field schools for adults. Phone reservations are required for some programs. ✉ *291 U.S. 6* ☎ *508/349–2615* ⊕ *www.wellfleetbay.org* 🖃 *$5* ☉ *Trails daily 8 AM–dusk; nature center late May–mid-Oct., daily 8:30–5; mid-Oct.–late May, Tues.–Sun. 8:30–5.*

WHERE TO STAY & EAT

$–$$$ ✕**Bookstore and Restaurant.** This quirky place, with great views of Wellfleet Harbor and Great Island, serves consistently tasty—if predictable—fare. It's attached to a funky vintage bookstore close to the town docks, and there's ample outdoor seating. The kitchen serves American classics, from grilled filet mignon and vegetable penne primavera to fresh seafood (the shellfish comes right from Wellfleet Harbor), including a first-rate oyster stew. There's live music Thursday to Sunday in summer, and the adjoining Bombshelter sports bar is a diverting spot to watch a game on TV. ✉ *50 Kendrick Ave., across from Mayo Beach* ☎ *508/349–3154* ⊕ *www.wellfleetoyster.com* ▤ *AE, D, MC, V* ⊗ *Closed mid-Dec.–mid-Feb.*

$–$$$ ✕**Finely JP's.** Chef John Pontius consistently turns out wonderful, affordable food full of the best Mediterranean and local influences and ingredients at his beloved restaurant along U.S. 6. The unassuming roadhouse restaurant was redesigned and enlarged in 2006—it's now a handsome, Arts and Crafts–inspired structure. Appetizers are especially good, among them oysters *Bienville* (baked in a white wine–cream sauce topped with Parmesan cheese and bread crumbs), and jerk-spiced duck salad with a raspberry vinaigrette. The Wellfleet paella draws rave reviews and a steady handful of locals, but the chef is not afraid to cook down-home barbecue pork ribs, either. Off-season hours vary, so call ahead—and be sure not to confuse this place with PJ's, down the road. ✉ *554 U.S. 6, South Wellfleet* ☎ *508/349–7500* ⌂ *Reservations not accepted* ▤ *D, MC, V* ⊗ *Closed some nights during off-season. No lunch.*

Fodor'sChoice
★

$–$$$ ✕**Lighthouse Restaurant.** A line snakes out the door of this simple wood-frame house on summer mornings for classic bacon-and-egg breakfasts and tasty blueberry pancakes. Try a plate of steamers and a beer for lunch and perhaps chowder, cod fritters, lemon-butter scallops, and another beer for dinner—but keep in mind that it's as much about the value and the people-watching here as the food itself. Mexican fare, margaritas, and Dos Equis beer are served on Thursday. There's a large deck, and downstairs you can order coffees, gelato, and lighter fare from the Lighthouse To-Go-Shoppe. ✉ *Main St., Downtown Wellfleet* ☎ *508/349–3681* ⊕ *www.mainstreetlighthouse.com* ⌂ *Reservations not accepted* ▤ *D, MC, V.*

$–$$$ ✕**Marconi Beach Restaurant.** The nondescript interior of this cavernous restaurant in South Wellfleet may not inspire you, but once you pull up and smell the enticing aroma of barbecue from the smoker in back, it's hard to resist the temptation to step inside for a meal. Drop in for a lighter dish, such as a pulled-pork sandwich or a few littlenecks and oysters from the raw bar, or savor a more substantial meal, perhaps a platter of smoked barbecue ribs, a grilled Porterhouse steak, or fish-and-chips. It's all pretty tasty, but the barbecue stands out—you could order most of the other items on the menu at any nearby steak and seafood joint. ✉ *545 U.S. 6* ☎ *508/349–6025* ⊕ *www.marconibeachrestaurant.net* ▤ *AE, D, MC, V* ⊗ *Closed mid-Oct.–early Apr.*

$–$$$ ✕**PJ's Family Restaurant.** There's always a good-size but fast-moving line here, waiting for a heap of steamers or a creamy soft-serve cone. At

5

PJ's you place your order and take a number. Food is served in utilitarian style: Styrofoam soup bowls, paper plates, plastic forks. The lobster-and-corn chowder doesn't have much lobster in it, so stick to the traditional clam chowder. Fried calamari and clam or oyster plates are generous and fresh. Try the dense, spicy stuffed clams and a pile of crispy onion rings. ⊠ *U.S. 6 near Downtown Wellfleet exit* ☎ *508/349–2126* ⚇ *Reservations not accepted* ▤ *MC, V* ⊘ *Closed Nov.–mid-Apr.*

$–$$$　✕ **Van Rensselaer's.** This cavernous, casual family seafood restaurant across from Marconi Station—not too far from the Eastham town line—stands out for its nice mix of traditional standbys (baked-stuffed lobster, prime rib) and more creative offerings. You might start with coconut tempura shrimp with an orange-ginger sauce or steamed littleneck clams with lemongrass-ginger-soy butter. Favorite main dishes include potato-crusted salmon with lobster-butter, and cranberry-orange duck with sweet-potato puree. Lighter and more affordable fare is available from a bistro menu. The restaurant also serves breakfast as well as an excellent Sunday brunch, where you might try smoked salmon Benedict. The same family has run the place since 1968. ⊠ *U.S. 6* ☎ *508/349–2127* ⊕ *www.vanrensselaers.com* ▤ *AE, D, DC, MC, V* ⊘ *Closed Nov.–mid-Apr. No lunch.*

$–$$$　✕ **Wicked Oyster.** In a rambling, gray clapboard house just off U.S. 6
Fodor's Choice　on the main road into Wellfleet village, the Wicked Oyster serves up
★　the most innovative fare in Wellfleet. Try the rosemary-and-scallion-crusted half rack of lamb over roasted-shallot-and-garlic potato salad, or the local mussels in tomato broth with smoky bacon, cilantro, jalapeño, and lime. Oyster stew and the Harry's Bar open-face burger (with caramelized onions, fresh mozzarella, and Worcestershire mayonnaise) are among the top lunch dishes. Breakfast is a favorite here—try the smoked salmon Benedict. There's also an outstanding wine list. Live music is offered many nights. Note that a new chef took over in 2007. ⊠ *50 Main St., Wellfleet* ☎ *508/349–3455* ▤ *AE, D, MC, V* ⊘ *No dinner Wed.*

$–$$　✕ **Moby Dick's.** A meal at this good-natured, rough-hewn fish shack with a hyper-nautical theme is an absolute Cape Cod tradition for some people. There's a giant blackboard menu (order up front, and food is brought to you); a big, breezy screened-in porch in which to eat; and red-checkered tablecloths. Go for the Nantucket Bucket—a pound of whole-belly Monomoy steamers, a pound of native mussels, and corn on the cob served in a bucket. Also consider the rich and creamy lobster bisque or the complete lobster-in-the-rough dinner. Bring your own libations, and if you need to kill time, stop inside Moby's Cargo, the bustling gift shop next door. ⊠ *U.S. 6 near Truro border* ☎ *508/349–9795* ⊕ *www.mobydicksrestaurant.com* ⚇ *Reservations not accepted* ▤ *AE, MC, V* ⊘ *Closed mid-Oct.–Apr.* ⛾ *BYOB.*

$–$$　✕ **Winslow's Tavern.** Known as Aesop's Table until new owners took
★　over in 2005 and completely renovated the interior, this 1805 Federal-style captain's house contains five dining rooms; try for a table on the porch overlooking the center of town. The kitchen specializes in bistro-inspired seafood, mostly with American and Italian preparations.

Bacon-wrapped scallops with mango chutney, garlic-and-butter-grilled lobster with sweet-corn relish, and panfried ham-stuffed trout with roast baby tomatoes rank among the better dishes. Head to the cozy lounge upstairs (it's open until 1 AM) for a drink—it's filled with plush sofas. The same owners run the popular Moby Dick's seafood restaurant. ✉*316 Main St., Downtown Wellfleet* ☎*508/349–6450* ⊕*www.winslowstavern.com* ▤*AE, DC, MC, V* ☻*Closed mid-Oct.–mid-May.*

¢–$$ ✕**Mac's Seafood.** Right at Wellfleet Harbor, this ambitious little spot has
★ some of the freshest seafood around. There's not a whole lot of seating here—some inside and some outside on picnic tables—but when you've got a succulent mouthful of raw oyster or fried scallop, who cares? You can always sit along the pier and soak up the great water views while you chow down. This place serves a vast variety of seafood, plus sushi, Mexican fare (grilled-scallop burritos), linguica sausage sandwiches, and raw-bar items. There's also a selection of smoked fish, pâtés, lobster, and fish you can take home to grill yourself. Mac's also has two take-out seafood markets (open year-round) in downtown Wellfleet and Truro, and in spring 2006, they added **Mac's Shack** (91 Commercial St., 508/349–6333), a funky sit-down BYOB restaurant in a rambling mid-19th-century barn overlooking Duck Creek, with a lobster boat on the roof. ✉*Wellfleet Town Pier, Wellfleet Harbor* ☎*508/349–0404* ⊕*www.macsseafood.com* ▤*MC, V* ☻*Closed mid-Oct.–late May.*

¢–$ ✕**Flying Fish.** Set inside a handsome little Cape-style house with wood floors and a simple dining room, this downtown café serves a wide range of foods—spinach-feta pizzas, Greek salads, curried-chicken-salad sandwiches, hummus platters, ice cream, smoothies, and a full range of coffees and pastries. It's perfect for a full sit-down meal or a quick bite on the go. Don't forget to check out the selection of fresh-baked pastries. ✉*28 Briar La.* ☎*508/349–7292* ▤*MC, V* ☻*Closed Oct.–Apr.*

$$$–$$$$ ▥**Surf Side Cottages.** Scattered on either side of Ocean View Drive,
★ accommodations here range from units in a piney grove to well-equipped ocean-side cottages; all accommodate two or more guests (six can stay in the largest units). The cottages are a one-minute walk from the Maguire's Landing town beach (LeCount Hollow), a beautiful wide strand of sand, dunes, and surf. Though most of the exteriors are retro-cool Floridian, with pastel shingles and flat roofs, cottage interiors are Cape-style, including knotty-pine paneling. All units have phones, wood-burning fireplaces, screened porches, kitchens, and grills. Some have roof decks with an ocean view and outdoor showers. Ocean-side cottages have dishwashers. **Pros:** You're steps from the ocean, ideal for longer holidays and cooking in your own unit, an architecturally interesting compound. **Cons:** Some of the decor and interiors in units could stand some updating, not within walking distance of shops or restaurants. ✉*Ocean View Dr.* ⌂*Box 937, South Wellfleet 02663* ☎*508/349–3959* ☐*508/349–3959* ⊕*www.surfsidevacation.com* ➦*19 cottages* ⌂*In-room: kitchen, no a/c, no TVs. In-hotel: no elevator, some pets allowed (fee)* ⌁*1- to 2-wk minimum in summer* ▤*No credit cards* ☻*Closed Nov.–Mar.*

$$–$$$ 🏠**Aunt Sukie's Bayside Bed & Breakfast.** Hosts Sue and Dan Hamar treat
★ you like you're actual guests in their home, a part-contemporary, part-
antique inn with three rooms and multiple decks. It's set on the marsh
grass fronting Wellfleet Harbor and Cape Cod Bay, along a quiet residential stretch of road near Power's Landing. The birds, the water, and
the stunning bay views will probably be enough to keep you content
in the shade of trees with a pair of binoculars. Rooms are welcoming, with flowered quilts and private decks, and the two upstairs beds
grant vistas of the water without a lift of the head. The room in the
antique portion of the home has a gas fireplace, a brick patio, and a
grand claw-foot tub. The owners also have a full house for rent about
a mile away; it comfortably accommodates two couples or a family of
four and is rented weekly from May through October. **Pros:** Property
looks out at Cape Cod Bay, rooms are private and quiet, ample decks
and pretty grounds. **Cons:** It's intimate (just two rooms), a little too
far to walk to dining and shopping. ⊠*525 Chequessett Neck Rd.,
02667* ☎*508/349–2804 or 800/420–9999* ⊕*www.auntsukies.com*
⤴*2 rooms, 1 suite* ♿*In-room: refrigerator, no TV, Wi-Fi. In-hotel:
no elevator, beachfront, no kids under 10, no-smoking rooms* ⊟*MC,
V* ⊘*Closed Nov.–mid-June* ⦿*CP.*

$$ 🏠**Blue Gateways.** This inn—a home built in 1712—combines the sim-
ple comforts of colonial times with a modern sense of leisure. The
original three-sided fireplace still reigns on the ground floor, which has
wide-plank pine floors and generous beams. Upstairs are three ample
guest rooms with quilts, antiques, hooked rugs, and private bathrooms.
Gardens, fish-filled ponds, and private sitting areas are just outside.
Common areas include a chess table, plenty of reading materials, a
sunporch with cable TV and a VCR, and a small kitchen area with a
microwave and refrigerator. It's a short walk from downtown Well-
fleet's galleries and restaurants. **Pros:** Steps from dining and shopping,
house exudes historical charm, beautiful gardens to relax in. **Cons:** A
short walk to harbor and drive to ocean, quaintly old-fashioned aes-
thetic isn't for everyone. ⊠*252 Main St., 02667* ☎*508/349–7530*
⊕*www.bluegateways.com* ⤴*3 rooms* ♿*In-room: no phone, no TV.
In-hotel: no elevator, no kids under 12* ⊟*AE, D, MC, V* ⊘*Closed
early Sept.–late May* ⦿*CP.*

$$ 🏠**Stone Lion Inn.** B&Bs are meant to feel a bit like homes away from
Fodor'sChoice home—places to feel welcome, at ease, and taken care of. All of these
★ requirements are met at the Stone Lion Inn, a gracious mansard roof
Victorian just outside the town center and a short walk away from
both the harbor and the village. Rooms have queen beds, ceiling fans
to encourage the breezes, hardwood floors, and a mix of antiques and
contemporary pieces that balance the house's 19th-century heritage
with today's decorating sensibilities. Relax amid the gardens, in the
outdoor shower, or in the pretty common room. New Yorkers may
recognize the subtle Brooklyn theme—nostalgic, yet happily devoid of
frenzy. **Pros:** Short walk from harbor and shopping, stylish yet unpre-
tentious decor, friendly and helpful owners **Cons:** Need a car to get to
ocean, not appropriate for younger kids. ⊠*130 Commercial St., 02667*
☎*508/349–9565* ⊕*www.stonelioncapecod.com* ⤴*3 rooms, 1 apart-*

ment, 1 cottage ☆ In-room: some kitchenettes, refrigerators, no phone (some), no TV (some), Wi-Fi. In-hotel: no elevator, no kids under 10 ⊟*MC, V* ⦿|*BP.*

$$ ⊞**Wellfleet Motel & Lodge.** A mile from Marconi Beach, opposite the Audubon sanctuary, this clean and tasteful (although somewhat pricey) highway-side complex sits on 12 wooded acres. Rooms in the single-story motel aren't fancy but are renovated regularly; those in the two-story lodge are bright and spacious, with king- or queen-size beds and balconies or patios. The property offers direct access to the Cape Cod Rail Trail, and barbecue grills are available in a garden picnic area. **Pros:** Short drive or bike ride from beach, right on Cape Cod Bike Trail, many units with balcony or patio. **Cons:** Right on busy road, need a car to reach Wellfleet's charming downtown, motel-style rooms. ✉*146 U.S. 6* ⌂*Box 606, South Wellfleet 02663* ☎*508/349–3535 or 800/852–2900* ☒*508/349–1192* ⊕*www.wellfleetmotel.com* ⟳*57 rooms, 8 suites* ☆ *In-room: Wi-Fi. In-hotel: restaurant, bar, pools, no elevator* ⊟*AE, DC, MC, V* ⊘*Closed Dec.–Mar.*

$–$$ ⊞**Even'tide.** Long a summer favorite, this motel is set back off the main road, surrounded by 5 acres of trees and lawns; it's close to the Cape Cod Rail Trail. A central attraction is the 60-foot indoor pool (although Wellfleet's beaches are also close by). Rooms have simple modern furnishings; choose from doubles, two-room family suites, and efficiencies with kitchens. Cottages speckled about the property are available for stays of a week or longer. The staff is friendly and enthusiastic. **Pros:** Short drive or bike ride from beach, right by Cape Cod Rail Trail, two-room suites are a bargain for families. **Cons:** Right on busy road, need a car to reach Wellfleet's charming downtown, motel-style rooms. ✉*650 U.S. 6, South Wellfleet 02663* ☎*508/349–3410 or 800/368–0007* ☒*508/349–7804* ⊕*www.eventidemotel.com* ⟳*31 units, 10 cottages* ☆ *In-room: kitchen (some), refrigerators, dial-up. In-hotel: pool, no elevator, laundry facilities, public Wi-Fi* ⌛*1- or 2-wk minimum for cottages in summer* ⊟*MC, V* ⊘*Closed Nov. and Dec.*

$–$$ ⊞**Southfleet Motor Inn.** Geared toward active families, this carefully maintained motor inn is directly across from the entrance to the National Seashore at Marconi Station for easy access to ocean beaches. Bring your bikes to cruise the 25-mi Cape Cod Rail Trail. Rooms, which have utilitarian furnishings and an assortment of beds, can sleep up to five people. The pools and game room (with a Ping-Pong table) keep the kids busy and happy. **Pros:** Short drive or bike ride from beach, lots of on-site diversions for kids, reasonable rates. **Cons:** Right on busy road, need a car to reach Wellfleet's charming downtown, motel-style rooms. ✉*U.S. 6, across from Marconi Station, 02667* ☎*508/349–3580 or 800/334–3715* ⊕*www.southfleetmotorinn.com* ⟳*30 rooms* ☆ *In-room: refrigerator, Wi-Fi. In-hotel: 2 restaurants, bar, pools, bicycles, no elevator, laundry facilities* ⊟*AE, MC, V* ⊘*Closed mid-Oct.–late-Apr.*

¢–$ ⊞**Holden Inn.** If you're watching your budget and can deal with modest basics and rather drab furnishings, try this no-frills old-timey place on a tree-shaded street just outside the town center but within walking distance of several galleries and restaurants. Rooms are simply decorated

5

with Grandma's house–type wallpapers, ruffled sheer or country-style curtains, and antiques such as brass-and-white-iron or spindle beds or marble-top tables. Private baths with old porcelain sinks are available in the adjacent 1840 and 1890 buildings. The lodge has shared baths, an outdoor shower, and a large screened-in porch with a lovely view of the bay and Great Island, far below. The main house has a common room and a screened front porch with rockers and a bay view through the trees. **Pros:** Rock-bottom prices, walking distance to harbor and village shopping, pretty, tree-shaded grounds. **Cons:** Rooms are bare-bones and very old-fashioned feeling, many units share a bath. ⊠*140 Commercial St., Box 816, Wellfleet 02667* ☎*508/349–3450* ⊕*www. theholdeninn.com* ⇆*26 rooms, 10 with bath* ⚬*In-room: no phone, no TV. In-hotel: no elevator* ▭*No credit cards* ☉*Closed Nov.–Apr.*

¢–$ 📠**Inn at Duck Creeke.** Set on 5 wooded acres by a duck pond, a creek, and a salt marsh, this old inn consists of a circa-1815 main building and three other houses from the same era. Rooms in the main inn (except rustic 3rd-floor rooms) and in the Saltworks house have a simple charm but could use some upgrading. Typical furnishings include claw-foot tubs, country antiques, lace curtains, chenille spreads, and rag rugs on hardwood floors. The two-room Carriage House is cabinlike, with rough barn-board and plaster walls. There's full-service dining at Sweet Seasons or pub dining with entertainment at the Tavern Room. **Pros:** Very low rates, walking distance to downtown, good restaurant and pub on-site. **Cons:** some units share a bath, long walk to harbor or ocean. ⊠*70 Main St., Box 364, Wellfleet 02667* ☎*508/349–9333* ⊕*www.innatduckcreeke.com* ⇆*26 rooms, 17 with bath* ⚬*In-room: no a/c (some), no phone, no TV. In-hotel: 2 restaurants, no elevator* ▭*AE, MC, V* ☉*Closed Nov.–late Apr.* ▮⚬*CP.*

NIGHTLIFE & THE ARTS

THE ARTS During July and August the **First Congregational Church** (⊠*200 Main St., Downtown Wellfleet* ☎*508/349–6877*) trades the serenity of worship for Sunday evening concerts. The music begins at 8 PM and could include opera, blues, jazz, or chamber music.

The drive-in movie is alive and well on Cape Cod at the **Wellfleet Drive-In Theater** (⊠*51 U.S. 6, South Wellfleet* ☎*508/349–7176* ⊕*www.wellfleetcinemas.com*), which is right by the Eastham town line. Films start at dusk nightly in season (May through September), and there's also a standard indoor cinema with four screens, a miniature-golf course, and a dairy bar and grill.

Art galleries are open for cocktail receptions to celebrate show openings on Saturday evening in July and August during the **Wellfleet Gallery Crawl.** You can walk from gallery to gallery, meeting the featured artists and checking out their works.

★   The well-regarded **Wellfleet Harbor Actors Theater (WHAT)** (⊠*Kendrick St. past E. Commercial St., near Wellfleet Harbor* ☎*508/349–6835 or 866/252–9428* ⊕*www.what.org*) opened a first-rate 200-seat theater, the Julie Harris Stage, in June 2007. It complements the company's original 90-seat Harbor Stage, which is now used seasonally for more experimental works as well as serving as a venue for playwrights to produce new pieces. In the new theater, WHAT continues its tradition, since 1985, of showing provocative, often edgy, world premieres of American plays, satires, farces, and black comedies in its mid-May to late-November season.

Beachcomber (✉*1120 Calloon Hollow Rd., off Ocean View Dr.* ☎*508/349–6055*) is big with the college crowd. It's right on the beach, with national touring acts most nights, weekend happy hours with live reggae, and dancing nightly in summer. You can order appetizers, salads, burgers, seafood, and barbecue indoors or at tables by the beachfront bar. There's also a raw bar. Beachcomber is closed October through April.

A number of organizations sponsor outdoor activities at night, including the **Massachusetts Audubon Wellfleet Bay Wildlife Sanctuary**'s night hikes and lecture series.

In the venerable Inn at Duck Creeke, the **Tavern Room** (✉*70 Main St., U.S. 6 exit to Downtown Wellfleet* ☎*508/349–7369*), set in an 1800s building with a beam ceiling, a fireplace, and a bar covered in nautical charts, has live entertainment—anything from jazz and pop to country and Latin ensembles. Munchies are served alongside a menu of traditional and Latin/Caribbean-inspired dishes.

Kick up your heels and grab a twirling partner for a long-standing Wellfleet tradition, the **Wednesday Night Square Dance.** Down at the town pier in July and August, the music and live calling by master caller Irvin "Toots" Tousignant begins at 7 and lasts as long as *you* can.

SPORTS & THE OUTDOORS
The state-of-the-art Skateboard Park down at **Baker's Field** (✉*Kendrick Ave. just past Wellfleet Town Pier, near Wellfleet Harbor*) was professionally designed for tricks and safety; it's manned by local teens.

BEACHES **Public Beaches.** Extensive storm-induced erosion has made the cliffs to most of Wellfleet's ocean beaches quite steep—so be prepared for a taxing trek up and down the dune slope.

Cahoon Hollow Beach (✉*Ocean View Dr.*) has lifeguards, restrooms, and a restaurant and music club on the sand. This beach tends to attract younger and slightly rowdier crowds; it's a big Sunday-afternoon party place. There are daily parking fees of $15 for nonresidents in season only; parking is free for those with beach stickers.

Fodor'sChoice **Marconi Beach** (✉*Off U.S. 6*), part of the Cape Cod National Sea-★ shore, charges $15 for daily parking or $45 for a season pass that provides access to all six National Seashore swimming beaches. There are lifeguards, restrooms, and outdoor showers from late June through early September, which is the only period when admission fees are collected.

Mayo Beach (✉*Commercial St., adjacent to Wellfleet Pier*) is free, but swimming here is pleasant only around high tide—once the water recedes, it's all mud and sharp shells. You can park for free at the small lot by Great Island on the bay.

White Crest Beach (⊠ *Ocean View Dr.*) is a prime surfer hangout where the dudes often spend more time waiting for waves than actually riding them. Lifeguards are on duty daily 9 AM to 5 PM from July through Labor Day weekend. If you're up to the challenge, join one of the spontaneous volleyball games that frequently pop up. There are daily parking fees of $15 for nonresidents in season only; parking is free for those with beach stickers.

Restricted Beaches. Resident or temporary resident parking stickers are required for access to Wellfleet beaches in season only, from the last week of June through Labor Day. To get a three-day ($30), weekly ($60), or season ($200) pass, visit the Beach Sticker Booth on the town pier with your car registration in hand and a proof-of-stay form, available from rental agencies and hotels. For the rest of the year anyone can visit the beaches for free. Note that people arriving on foot or by bicycle can visit the beaches at any time; the sticker is for parking only. These parking restrictions apply to all beaches listed below.

For information about restricted beaches, call the **Wellfleet Chamber of Commerce** (☎ *508/349–2510*).

☺ **Duck Harbor Beach** (⊠ *End of Chequessett Neck Rd.*) seems like it's nearly at the end of the world. Its shores are on the warm waters of Cape Cod Bay, and there's plenty of room to wander and find your own private space. You can look out to Provincetown across the bay, but the finest view by far is the nightly sunset.

Indian Neck Beach (⊠ *Pilgrim Spring Rd. off U.S. 6*) is on the bay side, fronting Wellfleet Harbor, and is thus affected by the tides. Low tide reveals plenty of beach but less water—you'll have to walk way out before your hips get wet. It's a good spot to watch the comings and goings of fishing boats from Wellfleet Pier. With its shallow and calm waters, warmer temperatures, and ample opportunity for treasure hunting at low tide, it's also a great beach for families.

★ **LeCount Hollow Beach** (⊠ *Ocean View Dr.*) is the beach closest to U.S. 6 in South Wellfleet, along the meandering Ocean View Drive. The dunes are steep here, so be prepared to carry all beach belongings down (and up) the sandy slope.

Newcomb Hollow Beach (⊠ *Ocean View Dr.*) is the northernmost beach on the Wellfleet strip, closest to Truro. If you keep your eyes on the horizon, it's not at all uncommon to see the distant spout of a passing whale. This beach is also a popular nighttime fishing spot.

The **Wellfleet Ponds,** nestled in the woods between U.S. 6 and the ocean, were formed by glaciers and are fed by underground springs. Mild temperatures and clear, clean waters make swimming here pleasant for the whole family, a refreshing change from the bracing salty surf of the Atlantic. The ponds are also perfect for canoeing, sailing, or kayaking (boats are available from Jack's Boat Rentals). A Wellfleet beach sticker is required to visit these fragile ecosystems in season (the sticker is only for cars, though—anyone can walk or ride a bike over to the ponds). Motorized boats are not allowed.

BICYCLING   The Cape Cod Rail Trail ends at the South Wellfleet post office. Other scenic routes for bicyclists include winding, tree-lined Old County Road, just outside Wellfleet center at the end of West Main Street. Ambitious riders can bike all the way to Truro on this often bumpy road, but be sure to watch for vehicular traffic around the tight curves. Ocean View Drive, on the ocean side, winds through miles of wooded areas; there are several ponds along the route that are perfect for taking a quick dip. The Wellfleet Chamber of Commerce publishes a pamphlet, "Bicycling in Wellfleet," with an annotated map.

Idle Times Bike Shop, Inc. (✉ *U.S. 6, just west of Cahoon Hollow Rd.* ☎ *508/349–9161* ⊕ *www.idletimesbikes.com*) opens Memorial Day and rents bikes, trailer bikes (a tandem bike with a backseat for children who are big enough to pedal), and trailer attachments for the littler passengers. The shop also handles repairs and sells parts and assorted accessories. Depending on the crowds and weather, it usually remains open until Columbus Day, but there's a branch in Eastham open year-round.

BOATING   **Jack's Boat Rental** (✉ *Gull Pond, south of U.S. 6* ☎ *508/349–9808 or 508/221–8226* ⊕ *www.jacksboatrental.com*) has canoes, kayaks, Sunfish, pedal boats, surfboards, Boogie boards, and sailboards. Guided kayak tours are also available.

Wellfleet Marine Corp. (✉ *Wellfleet Town Pier, Wellfleet Harbor* ☎ *508/349–2233*) rents sailboats and motorboats in various sizes by the hour or the day.

FISHING   You can climb aboard the charter boat *Jac's Mate* (✉ *Wellfleet Town Pier, Wellfleet Harbor* ☎ *508/255–2978* ⊕ *http://users.rcn.com/jacsmate*) for fishing expeditions in search of bass and blues.

The *Naviator* (✉ *Wellfleet Town Pier, Wellfleet Harbor* ☎ *508/349–6003* ⊕ *www.naviator.com*) operates fishing trips on a walk-on basis from spring through fall. Rods, reels, and bait are included.

GOLF & TENNIS   Wellfleet maintains several tennis courts at **Baker's Field** near the town pier. Call the **Recreation Department** (☎ *508/349–0330*) for fees and reservations.

Chequessett Yacht Country Club (✉ *680 Chequessett Neck Rd., west of Downtown Wellfleet* ☎ *508/349–3704* ⊕ *www.cycc.net*) is a semiprivate club (public use on space-available basis) with a 9-hole golf course (there are two sets of tees, so you can play 18 holes by repeating the layout) and 5 hard-surface tennis courts by the bay. Lessons are available.

Oliver's (✉ *U.S. 6, west of Downtown Wellfleet exit* ☎ *508/349–3330*), which has one Truflex and seven clay courts, offers tennis lessons and arranges matches.

SURFING   Atlantic-coast **Marconi** and **White Crest** beaches are the best for surfing. Surfboard rentals can be arranged at Jack's Boat Rental.

SHOPPING

ART GALLERIES   **Andre Pottery** (✉ *5 Commercial St., Downtown Wellfleet* ☎ *508/349–2299* ⊕ *www.andrepottery.com*) specializes in handmade bowls, vases, and pitchers, mostly in greens, blues, and grays, the shades of the sea and shore.

Blue Heron Gallery (✉ *20 Bank St., Downtown Wellfleet* ☎ *508/349–6724* ⊕ *www.blueheronfineart.com*) is one of the Cape's best galleries, with contemporary works—including Cape scenes, jewelry, sculpture, and pottery—by regional and nationally recognized artists, among them Steve Allrich and Del Filardi.

★ **Brophy's Fine Art** (✉ *313 Main St., Downtown Wellfleet* ☎ *508/349–6479* ⊕ *www.brophysfineart.com*), one of the few year-round shops in Wellfleet, carries a nice selection of pottery, jewelry, and landscape paintings by several prominent New England artists as well as the beautiful stained-glass works of owner Thomas Brophy.

Cove Gallery (✉ *15 Commercial St., Downtown Wellfleet* ☎ *508/349–2530* ⊕ *www.covegallery.com*) displays the works of John Grillo, Tomie dePaola, and Leonard Baskin, among others. The gallery hosts Saturday-night artist receptions in July and August.

★ **Kendall Art Gallery** (✉ *40 Main St., Downtown Wellfleet* ☎ *508/349–2482* ⊕ *www.kendallartgallery.com*) carries eclectic modern works, including Harry Marinsky's bronzes in the sculpture garden, photography by Walter Baron and Alan Hoelzle, watercolors by Walter Dorrell, and contemporary art by several prominent Chinese artists. Receptions are held on Saturday evenings.

Left-Bank Gallery (✉ *25 Commercial St.* ☎ *508/349–9451* ✉ *3 W. Main St., Downtown Wellfleet* ☎ *508/349–7939* ⊕ *www.leftbankgallery. com*) has two branches here and another in Orleans. The larger one, on Commercial Street, displays the larger works of local and national artists and sells fine crafts in the back room facing Duck Creek. The other gallery has fine handcrafted jewelry, silk and chenille scarves, hats, and small works of original art and photography.

Nicholas Harrison Gallery (✉ *275 Main St., Downtown Wellfleet* ☎ *508/349–7799* ⊕ *www.thenicholasharrisongallery.com*) has made a name for itself in the area of lovely and unusual American crafts, including beautiful lamps, resin-and-silver jewelry, and hand-painted cabinets. Owners Mark and Laura Evangelista are also accomplished potters, and you'll see their vibrant ceramic works here as well.

SPECIALTY   **Abiyoyo** (✉ *286 Main St., Downtown Wellfleet* ☎ *508/349–3422*) has
STORES   a full line of Wellfleet T-shirts and sweatshirts, along with shoes, children's clothing, and bath and beauty products.

Chocolate Sparrow (✉ *326 Main St., Downtown Wellfleet* ☎ *508/349–1333*) makes nine types of fudge, luscious hand-dipped chocolates, and a wide array of decadent baked goods and sweets. This is a seasonal branch of the well-known shop that began in Eastham and also has a location in Orleans; it's open May through early September.

Eccentricity (⊠*361 Main St., Downtown Wellfleet* ☎*508/349–3634*) keeps the corner of Main and Briar offbeat. One of the most interesting stores on the Cape, it sells gorgeous kimonos, ethnic-inspired cotton clothing, African carved-wood sculptures, barbershop paintings, odd Mexican items, and trinkets. The owners also run Off Center, a similarly lively shop across the street.

★ **Herridge Books** (⊠*11 E. Main St., between U.S. 6 and town center, Downtown Wellfleet* ☎*508/349–1323*) is the perfect store for a town that has been host to so many writers. Its dignified literary fiction, art and architecture, literary biography and letters, mystery, Americana, sports, and other sections are full of used books in very nice condition. Herridge also carries new editions on the Cape and its history.

Jules Besch Stationers (⊠*15 Bank St., Downtown Wellfleet* ☎*508/349–1231*) has extraordinary cards, fine stationery, journals, papers, and pens. Proprietor Michael Tuck's warm and welcoming nature is as beautiful as his products are; he also offers full calligraphy services.

Karol Richardson (⊠*11 W. Main St., Downtown Wellfleet* ☎*508/349–6378* ⊕*www.karolrichardson.com*) fashions women's wear in luxurious fabrics and sells interesting shoes, hats, and jewelry.

Kite Gallery (⊠*75 Commercial St., Downtown Wellfleet* ☎*508/349–7387*) overlooks a salt marsh and stocks kites and all kinds of colorful beach toys, windsocks, flags, and garden goodies.

Pickle and Puppy (⊠*355 Main St., Downtown Wellfleet* ☎*508/349–0606*) has a bit of everything: housewares, T-shirts, fanciful foodstuffs, ceramics, and luxury bath and beauty-parlor items, plus a selection of unusual children's toys, games, and puzzles.

Secret Garden (⊠*Main St., Downtown Wellfleet* ☎*508/349–1444*) doesn't waste any precious space—the walls are covered from floor to ceiling with whimsical folk-art pieces, handbags, clothing, and decorative accessories. They also have good buys on sterling silver jewelry.

Wellfleet Marketplace (⊠*295 Main St., Downtown Wellfleet* ☎*508/349–3156*) is *the* place to pick up gourmet foods in town. Besides a branch of Mac's Seafood, you'll also find great deli treats, organic produce, and other tasty foods.

FLEA MARKET The giant **Wellfleet Flea Market** (⊠*51 U.S. 6, South Wellfleet* ☎*508/349–Fodor'sChoice 0541*) sets up shop in the parking lot of the Wellfleet Drive-In Theater
★ mid-April through June and September and October, weekends and Monday holidays 8 to 4; July and August, Monday holidays, Wednesday and Thursday, and weekends 8 to 4. You'll find antiques, sweat socks, old advertising posters, books, Beanie Babies, Guatemalan sweaters, plants, trinkets, and plenty more among the 300 vendors. On Monday and Tuesday in July and August the vendors make way for large arts-and-crafts shows. A snack bar and playground keep fatigue at bay.

**EN
ROUTE**

If you're in the mood for a quiet, lovely ride winding through what the Cape might have looked like before Europeans arrived, follow **Old County Road** from Wellfleet to Truro on the bay side. It's bumpy and beautiful, with a stream or two along the way. So cycle on it, or drive slowly, or just stop and walk to take in the nature around you.

TRURO

2 mi north of Wellfleet, 7 mi southeast of Provincetown.

Settled in 1697, Truro has had several names. It was originally called Pamet after the local Native Americans, but in 1705 the name was changed to Dangerfield in response to all the sailing mishaps off its shores. "Truroe" was the final choice, named for a Cornish town that homesick settlers thought it resembled; the final 'e' was eventually dropped. The town relied on the sea for its income—whaling, shipbuilding, and cod fishing were the main industries.

Today Truro is a town of high dunes, estuaries, and rivers fringed by grasses, rolling moors, and houses sheltered in tiny valleys. It's a popular retreat for artists, writers, politicos, and numerous vacationing psychoanalysts. Edward Hopper summered here from 1930 to 1967, finding the Cape light ideal for his austere brand of realism. One of the largest towns on the Cape in terms of land area—almost 43 square mi—it's also the smallest in population, with about 1,400 year-round residents. Truro is also the Cape's narrowest town, and from a high perch you can see the Atlantic Ocean on one side and Cape Cod Bay on the other.

If you thought neighboring Wellfleet's downtown was small, wait until you see—or don't see—Truro's. It consists of a post office, a town hall, and a shop or two—you'll know it by the sign that says DOWNTOWN TRURO at a little plaza entrance. Truro also has a library, a firehouse, and a police station, but that's about all. The North Truro section contains most of the town's restaurants and accommodations, most either along U.S. 6 or fronting the bay along Route 6A (Shore Road), just south of the Provincetown border. Many who live or vacation in Truro choose it for its easygoing, quiet personality and lack of development—and it's close proximity to the excitement and commerce of Provincetown.

☺ For a few hours of exploring, take the children to **Pamet Harbor** (✉ *Depot Rd.*). At low tide you can walk out on the flats and discover the creatures of the salt marsh. A nearby plaque identifies plants and animals and describes the area's ecological importance.

On **Corn Hill** (✉ *Off Corn Hill Rd.*), near the beach area of the same name, a tablet commemorates the finding of a buried cache of corn by Myles Standish and the *Mayflower* crew. They took it to Plymouth and used it as seed, returning later to pay the Native Americans for what they'd taken.

Truro's Edward Hopper

The Outer Cape has inspired thousands of acclaimed artists, but perhaps none is more closely associated with its serene yet romantic landscape than Edward Hopper, the esteemed realist painter who lived in Truro for most of the last four decades of his life. Quiet Truro, with its peaceful, sandy lanes, suited the introspective Hopper perfectly.

Hopper, born in Nyack, New York, in 1882, enjoyed little commercial or critical success before middle age. Early in his career, he worked as a commercial illustrator to support himself while living in New York City's Greenwich Village. At age 43 he married Josephine Nivison. It was during the 1920s, after his marriage, that Hopper achieved marked success as both an oil painter and watercolorist and became known for his starkly realistic scenes, often depicting public places filled with people, such as his most iconic work, *Nighthawks.*

Edward and Josephine first summered in Truro in 1930, and a few years later they designed their own Truro home. Much of Hopper's work conveyed the emptiness and alienation of big-city life, and although his Cape paintings were similar in their simplicity, they nevertheless offered a slightly more hopeful vision, if for no other reason than their tendency to focus more on the region's sensuous luminosity than strictly on lonely or bored people.

Most famously, his Truro work captured the undulating auburn hills along Pamet Road in *Corn Hill Truro Cape Cod.* Other notable paintings that portray the Outer Cape include *Cape Cod Evening* (1939), *Route 6 Eastham* (1941), *Martha McKeen of Wellfleet* (1944), and *Cape Cod Morning* (1950).

–by Andrew Collins

The **Truro Center for the Arts at Castle Hill,** in a converted 19th-century barn, has summer arts-and-crafts workshops for children, as well as courses and single classes in art, crafts, photography, and writing for adults. Teachers have included notable New York- and Provincetown-based artists. ⊠*10 Meetinghouse Rd.* ☎*508/349–7511* ⊕*www.castlehill.org.*

NEED A BREAK?

Jams (⊠**14 Truro Center Rd., off U.S. 6 in Truro Center** ☎**508/349–1616)** **has fixings for a great picnic lunch: sandwiches, fresh produce, a bottle of wine or Evian, or a sweet treat. Unless you like getting your knees knocked, don't bother sitting at the bench outside—besides, the best part of the Cape awaits just outside the door.**

Built at the turn of the 20th century as a summer hotel, the **Highland House Museum,** operated by the Truro Historical Society, has 17th-century firearms, mementos of shipwrecks, early fishing and whaling gear, ship models, a pirate's chest, and scrimshaw. One room exhibits wood carvings, paintings, blown glass, and ship models by Courtney Allen, artist and founder of Truro's historical society. The museum also holds local art and artifact shows each year. ⊠*6 Lighthouse Rd., off S. Highland Rd., North Truro* ☎*508/487–3397* ⊕*www.trurohistori-*

cal.org ✇$4; $6 for combo admission with Highland Light ⊙ Late May–Sept., Mon.–Sat. 10–4:30, Sun. 1–4:30.

Truly a breathtaking sight, **Highland Light,** also called Cape Cod Light, is the Cape's oldest lighthouse. It was the last to become automated, in 1986. The first light on this site, powered by 24 whale-oil lamps, began warning ships of Truro's treacherous sandbars in 1798—the dreaded Peaked Hills Bars alone, to the north, claimed hundreds of ships. The current light, a white-painted 66-foot tower built in 1857, is powered by two 1,000-watt bulbs reflected by a huge Fresnel lens; its beacon is visible for more than 20 mi.

One of four active lighthouses on the Outer Cape, Highland Light has the distinction of being listed in the National Register of Historic Places. Henry David Thoreau used it as a stopover in his travels across the Cape's backside (as the Atlantic side of the Outer Cape is called). Erosion threatened to cut this lighthouse from the 117-foot cliff on which it stood and drop it into the sea; thanks to a concerted effort by local residents and lighthouse lovers, the necessary funds were raised, and the lighthouse was moved back 450 feet to safety (while remaining surrounded by the Highland Links golf course). Twenty-five-minute tours of the lighthouse are given daily in summer. Children must be at least 51 inches tall to climb the tower. ✉ *Off S. Highland Rd.* ☎ *508/487–3397* ⊕ *www.trurohistorical.org* ✇$4; $6 for combo admission with Highland House Museum ⊙ Mid-May– mid-Oct., daily 10–5:30.

The gardens of **A Touch of Heaven** are beautiful—and, unlike most gardens, are meant to be picked. The lawns are set with benches and birdbaths, and the flowers are so abundant that you won't feel guilty about gathering a bunch to take home. ✉ *Pond Village Heights, North Truro* ☎ *No phone* ✇ *Free* ⊙ *Daily dawn–dusk.*

Worth a stop as much for its verdant grounds and tranquil setting inside a rambling 1830s farmhouse as for its enjoyable (and increasingly respectable) wines, **Truro Vineyards of Cape Cod Winery** produces a number of excellent wines. New owners bought the winery in spring 2007 and have plans to step up production a bit, and experiment with some new vintages. At the moment, the vineyard makes a commendable Cabernet Franc, Chardonnay, sauvignon blanc, vignole, and several others. They also make a red table wine that's flavored with cranberries and known for its unusual bottle, shaped like a lighthouse (along with two other "lighthouse" varieties)—it's a fun souvenir. ✉ *Rte. 6A, North Truro* ☎ *508/487–6200* ⊕ *www.trurovineyardsofcapecod.com* ⊙ *Apr., Fri.–Sat. 11–5, Sun. noon–5; May–late Nov., Mon.–Sat. 11–5, Sun. noon–5* ✇ *Free.*

At the **Pilgrim Heights Area** (✉ *Off U.S. 6*) of the Cape Cod National Seashore, a short trail leads to the spring where members of a Pilgrim exploring party stopped to refill their casks, tasting their first New England water in the process. Walking through this still-wild area of oak, pitch pine, bayberry, blueberry, beach plum, and azalea gives you a taste of what it was like for these voyagers in search of a new home.

"Being thus passed the vast ocean ..." William Bradford wrote in *Of Plimoth Plantation,* "they had no friends to welcome them, no inns to entertain them or refresh their weather-beaten bodies; no houses, or much less towns to repair to, to seek for succour."

From an overlook you can see the bluffs of High Head, where glaciers pushed a mass of earth before melting and receding. Another path leads to a swamp, and a bike trail leads to Head of the Meadow Beach, often a less crowded alternative to others in the area.

WHERE TO STAY & EAT

$–$$$$ ✕ **Whitman House.** What began as a modest pancake house has been transformed by the Rice family into a vast—if touristy—restaurant, but pewter plates, candlelight, and rustic wood accents make the place feel comfortably tavernlike. Predictable seafood, steaks, and surf-and-turf combos (consider the crabmeat casserole with petite filet mignon) keep the menu uncomplicated, and the portions ample. Lunch and lighter dinner fare are served daily in the Bass Tavern. If you have to wait for a table, browse in the adjacent Amish quilt shop. ✉ *Off U.S. 6* ☎ *508/487–1740* ⊕ *www.whitmanhouse.com* ▤ *AE, D, DC, MC, V* ⊘ *Closed Jan.–Mar.*

$$–$$$ ✕ **Terra Luna.** An insider's favorite for fresh and inventive bistro fare
★ with an Italian slant, Terra Luna has an intimate art-filled dining room with lace curtains, beam ceilings, and simple wooden tables. The food is stylish, with sophisticated sauces for both fish and meat dishes. The littleneck clams with sausage, fennel, garlic, and tomatoes is a house favorite, and seared duck breast with a port-wine reduction, braised red cabbage, and French lentils is an excellent alternative to the usual fish. For dessert, don't miss the unusual blackberry polenta custard. ✉ *104 Shore Rd. (Rte. 6A), North Truro* ☎ *508/487–1019* ▤ *AE, MC, V* ⊘ *Closed late Oct.–mid-May. No lunch.*

$–$$$ ✕ **Adrian's.** Adrian Cyr's restaurant crowns a high bluff overlooking Pilgrim Lake and all of Provincetown; his cooking also hits great heights. Cayenne-crusted salmon with maple-mustard sauce is just one of the well-prepared dishes here. Tuscan salad is also a hit, with tomatoes, olives, fresh basil, plenty of garlic, and balsamic vinegar. Pizzas, too, are standouts, especially one made with cornmeal dough and topped with shrimp and artichokes. The outdoor deck overflows at the popular breakfasts and brunches, served every day in season and weekends in spring and fall—try the cranberry pancakes with orange butter. ✉ *Outer Reach Hotel, 535 U.S. 6, North Truro 02652* ☎ *508/487–4360* ⊕ *www.adriansrestaurant.com* ▤ *AE, MC, V* ⊘ *Closed mid-Oct.–late May and Mon.–Wed. spring and fall. No lunch.*

$–$$$ ⊞ **Horizons Beach Resort.** You'll discover a wide range of accommodations at this nicely cared for compound fronting a stunning 500-foot stretch of beach, including spacious waterfront efficiencies, dune-facing studios (some of them set inside a distinctive pagoda inspired building), and private bungalows with separate sitting areas, kitchenettes, and—in some cases—fireplaces. Rates vary greatly according to view and proximity to the water, but you're also relatively close to the beach as well as the resort's swimming pool. A professional, thoughtful staff, spotless rooms, and casual, contemporary furnishings make this a highly popular getaway among the several properties on North Truro's Route 6A. **Pros:** Rooms are near or even face the beach and harbor, nice variety of accommodation styles and configurations, beautifully maintained. **Cons:** A long walk to Provincetown dining and shopping, pricey if you want a water view unit, no Wi-Fi. ⊠ *190 Rte. 6A* ⌂ *Box 146, North Truro 02652* ☎ *508/487–0042 or 800/782–0742* ⊕ *www. horizonsbeach.com* ⇨ *44 rooms, 3 bungalows* ⚲ *In-room: kitchen (some), refrigerator, VCR, dial-up. In-hotel: pool, beachfront, no elevator* ⊟ *MC, V* ⊘ *Closed mid-Oct.–mid-May.*

$$
Fodor'sChoice
★

Crow's Nest Resort. Amid the mostly run-of-the-mill motels and cottage compounds along Route 6A in North Truro, this beautifully refurbished all-suites beachfront property stands head and shoulders above the rest. It's been around since the mid-1960s, but the rooms are refreshingly contemporary with tile and oak floors, modern kitchen appliances, light-wood furniture, and country quilts. Ground-floor units front an attractive wooden deck overlooking the bay, and upstairs units have private balconies with similar views. You can choose from studio, two-bedroom, and three-bedroom units, and all have full kitchens, fireplaces, Jacuzzi tubs, and washers and dryers, making them perfect for longer stays. The resort also rents three attractive beachfront bungalows, called Crown's Nest Cottages, about a half-mile away. Given the prime location, friendly service, and top-notch facilities and furnishings, this is one of the Outer Cape's best values for families and friends traveling together. **Pros:** Furnishings are tasteful and contemporary, rooms have fantastic water views, all units have decks or balconies. **Cons:** A long walk to Provincetown dining and shopping, no pool, along a busy strip of motels and cottages. ⊠ *496 Rte. 6A, Box 177, 02652* ☎ *508/487–9031 or 800/499–9799* ⊕ *www.caperesort.com* ⇨ *21 suites* ⚲ *In-room: kitchen, DVD, Ethernet. In-hotel: beachfront, no elevator* ⊟ *AE, MC, V* ⊘ *Closed late Nov.–early Apr.*

$–$$ **Cape View Motel.** The true appeal of this tan-clapboard roadside motel is its noble perch on a westward bluff, looking out over Cape Cod Bay sunsets and the distant lights of Provincetown. Deluxe rooms have private balconies, as well as fully equipped kitchenettes and a king bed or two doubles. The style inside can't compete with the vistas outside, but the rooms are clean, simple, reasonably priced, and a 10-minute drive to Provincetown. Free coffee and doughnuts are provided in the morning. **Pros:** Inexpensive rooms, nice harbor views from the bluff-top location, some units have kitchenettes. **Cons:** Simple but prosaic room decor, few restaurants or shops within walking distance, feels a bit dated. ⊠ *Junction of U.S. 6 and Rte. 6A, Box 114, 02652* ☎ *508/487–0363 or 800/224–3232* ⊕ *www.capeviewmotel.com* ⇨ *32 rooms* ⚲ *In-room: kitchen (some), refrigerator, dial-up. In-hotel: pool, beachfront, no elevator* ⊟ *AE, MC, V* ⊘ *Closed mid-Oct.–mid-Apr.*

$–$$ **Sea Gull Motel.** This motel's location, right on the beach and close to the Provincetown border, is its real draw. It's been family run for decades, so you may feel like you're spending time in someone's summerhouse. Most rooms have splendid water views; lodging is in standard motel rooms, motel studios, and beach apartments—the latter two are rented weekly, but you can rent rooms by the night. **Pros:** Reasonable rates, beachfront location, very family-friendly. **Cons:** Rooms aren't especially fancy, a long walk to Provincetown dining and shopping, along a busy strip of motels and cottages. ⊠ *Rte. 6A* ⌂ *Box 126, North Truro 02652* ☎ *508/487–9070* ⊕ *www.capecodtravel.com/ seagullmotel* ⇆ *26 rooms* ♿ *In-room: kitchen (some), refrigerator, dial-up. In-hotel: beachfront, no elevator* ⊟ *AE, D, MC, V* ☯ *Closed mid-Oct.–mid-May.*

$–$$ **Top Mast Resort.** This North Truro beach motel complex, which sits
★ on 52 acres across U.S. 6 from Cape Cod National Seashore, had seen better days before its owners purchased two adjacent buildings and began an extensive refurbishment and expansion, completed in early 2007. Improvements include new kitchen appliances and cabinets, tile flooring and new carpeting, and attractive furnishings. The resort also has added a new office, a restaurant serving traditional American fare, a pool, tennis courts, and a playground, and a gym and indoor pool and Jacuzzi are planned for 2008. Most rooms are along the beach, but there are also some significantly less-expensive units in a building across the road, facing the swimming pool and landscaped gardens. Two cottages are available on a weekly basis. **Pros:** Underwent a huge renovation in 2006, right on the harbor with great views, lots of on-site diversions for kids. **Cons:** A long walk to Provincetown dining and shopping, along a busy strip of motels and cottages, a rather large compound: not ideal if you're seeking intimacy and seclusion. ⊠ *209 Rte. 6A* ⌂ *Box 44, North Truro 02652* ☎ *508/487–1189 or 800/917–0024* ⊕ *www.topmastresort.com* ⇆ *72 rooms, 2 cottages* ♿ *In-room: kitchen (some), refrigerator, Ethernet. In-hotel: restaurant, tennis courts, pool, beachfront, public Wi-Fi, no elevator* ⊟ *MC, V* ☯ *Closed late Oct.–early May.*

¢ **Hostelling International–Truro.** In a former Coast Guard station right
★ on the dunes, this handsome, well-placed, and nicely maintained hostel has kitchen facilities, a common area, and naturalist-led programs—not to mention panoramic views of the ocean and dunes. It's also right by the ½-mi-long Cranberry Bog Trail, which takes you by a refurbished cranberry bog and an old bog house. The dorm rooms are single-sex, and there are no curfews or lockouts—just come and go as you like. Guided kayak tours are available. **Pros:** Cheapest rooms on Outer Cape, mostly dorm-style with several people per room, you share common bathrooms. **Cons:** Fantastic beachside location, no curfew or lockout times, guided kayak tours and naturalist walks provide plenty of diversions. ⊠ *N. Pamet Rd., Box 402, Truro 02666* ☎ *508/349–3889 or 888/901–2086* ⊕ *www.capecodhostels.org* ⇆ *42 beds, 2 private rooms* ⊟ *MC, V* ☯ *Closed early Sept.–late-June.*

SPORTS & THE OUTDOORS

BEACHES Parking at a number of Truro's **town beaches** is reserved for residents and renters in season, although anyone can walk or bicycle in. Ask at the **town hall** (☎ *508/349–3635*) about a obtaining seasonal sticker.

Corn Hill Beach (⊠ *Corn Hill Rd.*), on the bay, has beautiful views of Provincetown. The waters are generally calm and warm, typical of bay beaches. There are restrooms on-site. Parking requires a Truro beach sticker or a $15 daily fee.

Truro has several other accessible beaches stretched along Cape Cod Bay. All are beautiful and ideal for long, lazy days of watching boats go by and taking in views of Provincetown in the distance.

Cold Storage Beach (✉ *Pond Rd. off Rte. 6A [Shore Rd.]*) is just as popular with anglers looking for passing blues and stripers as it is with sunseekers and swimmers. A Truro beach sticker is required for parking.

Just off one of Truro's backcountry roads, **Fisher Road Beach** (✉ *Fisher Rd.*) has a smaller parking area, so it's usually quiet. A Truro beach sticker is required for parking.

To get to **Great Hollow Beach** (✉ *Great Hollow Rd. off U.S. 6*) you must be ready to scale some moderate stairs from the parking lot to the sands below. A Truro beach sticker is required for parking.

Ryder Beach (✉ *Ryder Beach Rd. off Old County Rd.*) rests just below a rise in the small dunes. A Truro beach sticker is required for parking.

On the ocean side, three spectacular beaches are marked by massive dunes and bracing surf.

Ballston Beach (✉ *Pamet Rd.*) lies at the end of the winding, residential Pamet Road, backed by the golden hills that artist Edward Hopper made famous in his Truro paintings. Parking is reserved for residents and renters in season, although anyone can walk or bicycle in.

★
Fodor'sChoice
★
Coast Guard Beach (✉ *Coast Guard Rd.*) sits just down the road from Highland Light. Parking is for residents and renters with stickers only, although anyone can walk or bicycle in to enjoy this pristine swath of golden sand that stretches for miles in either direction and sees relatively few crowds—even in the heart of summer. Keep in mind that the parking area is small and tends to fill quickly.

Head of the Meadow Beach (✉ *Head of the Meadow Rd. off U.S. 6*) in North Truro, part of the Cape Cod National Seashore, is often less crowded than other beaches in the area. There are basic restroom facilities available in summer and no showers. The daily parking fee is $15 in season (late June–early Sept.); you can also purchase a season pass ($45) that is good for all National Seashore locations.

A not-so-secret favorite of nude sunbathers, **Longnook Beach** (✉ *Long Nook Rd.*) shares the senses of wildness and isolation synonymous with Truro's outer reaches. Truro beach stickers are required for parking.

The **Head of the Meadow Trail** provides 2 mi of easy cycling between dunes and salt marshes from High Head Road, off Route 6A in North Truro, to the Head of the Meadow Beach parking lot.

BICYCLING
★
Cape Outback Adventures (☎ *508/349–1617 or 800/864–0070* ⊕ *www.capeoutback.com*) has friendly instruction and guided tours for kayakers, mountain bikers, and beginning surfers. Times and location are arranged by phone, and owner Richard Miller and his staff provide

equipment. Kayak trips explore areas in both Wellfleet and Truro, and off-road mountain-biking excursions take place in the vast wooded areas within the National Seashore. Surfing instruction is available by the hour. These trips are designed for all ages and skill levels.

GOLF ★ The **Highland Golf Links** (⊠ *Lighthouse Rd., North Truro* ☎ *508/487– 9201* ⊕ *www.truro-ma.gov/golf.html*), a 9-hole, par-36 course on a cliff overlooking the Atlantic and Highland Light, is unique for its resemblance to Scottish links.

SURFING **Longnook Beach** (⊠ *End of Long Nook Rd., off U.S. 6*) is good for surfing.

SHOPPING

Atlantic Spice Co. (⊠ *U.S. 6 at Rte. 6A, North Truro* ☎ *508/487–6100 or 800/316–7965* ⊕ *www.atlanticspice.com*) has spices, teas, and pot-pourris, as well as herbs, dried flowers, soaps, sauces, and kitchenware items.

Whitman House Quilt Shop (⊠ *County Rd. just off U.S. 6, North Truro* ☎ *508/487–3204* ⊕ *www.whitmanhousequilts.com*) sells Amish quilts and other country items.

PROVINCETOWN

❶ – ⓫ *7 mi northwest of Truro, 27 mi north of Orleans, 62 mi from Saga-more Bridge.*

The Cape's smallest town in area and its second smallest in year-round population, Provincetown is a place of liberating creativity, startling originality, and substantial diversity. Like so much of Cape Cod, it's also a town that's become progressively—and rather dramatically—more upscale and sophisticated in recent years. A number of the casual—if cheesy—T-shirt and souvenir shops that once lined the town's main drag, Commercial Street, have given way to first-rate art galleries and upscale boutiques. Many of the town's funky B&Bs and inns, which once felt more like glorified boarding houses than proper accommodations, have been sold as private homes or transformed into fabulous, upscale hideaways with fine antiques, flat-screen TVs and DVD players, and cushy amenities.

With the change has come at least a mild concern that Provincetown may become too upscale and cosmopolitan for its own good—but so far there's little evidence that this lovably eccentric, individualistic place will ever become any less freespirited. A strong sense of community spirit and civic pride remains. In the busy downtown, Portuguese-American fishermen mix with painters, poets, writers, whale-watching families, cruise-ship passengers on brief stopovers, and gay and lesbian residents and visitors. In summer Commercial Street is packed with sightseers and shoppers hunting for treasures in the overwhelming number of galleries and crafts shops. At night raucous music and people spill out of bars, drag shows, and sing-along lounges galore. It's a fun, crazy place, with the extra dimension of the fishing fleet unloading their catch at MacMillan Wharf, in the center of the action.

The town's 8 square mi are also rich in history. The fist at the very tip of the Cape, Provincetown has shores that curve protectively around a natural harbor, perfect for sailors from any epoch to anchor. Historical records suggest that Thorvald, brother of Viking Leif Erikson, came ashore here in AD 1004 to repair the keel of his boat and consequently named the area Kjalarness, or Cape of the Keel. Bartholomew Gosnold came to Provincetown in 1602 and named the area Cape Cod after the abundant codfish he found in the local waters.

The Pilgrims remain Provincetown's most famous visitors. On Monday, November 21, 1620, the *Mayflower* dropped anchor in Provincetown Harbor after a difficult 63-day voyage from England. While in the harbor the passengers signed the Mayflower Compact, the first document to declare a democratic form of government in America. One of the first things the ever-practical Pilgrims did was come ashore to wash their clothes, thus beginning the ages-old New England tradition of Monday wash day. They lingered for five weeks before moving on to Plymouth. Plaques and parks throughout town commemorate the landing.

Incorporated as a town in 1727, Provincetown was for many decades a bustling seaport, with fishing and whaling as its major industries. In the late 19th century, groups of Portuguese fishermen and whalers began to settle here, lending their expertise and culture to an already cosmopolitan town. Fishing is still an important source of income for many Provincetown locals, but now the town ranks among the world's leading whale-watching—rather than whale-hunting—outposts.

Artists began coming here in the late 1890s to take advantage of the unusual Cape Cod light—in fact, Provincetown is the nation's oldest continuous art colony. Poets, writers, and actors have also been part of the art scene. Eugene O'Neill's first plays were written and produced here, and the Fine Arts Work Center continues to have in its ranks some of the most important writers working today.

During the early 1900s, Provincetown became known as Greenwich Village North. Artists from New York and Europe discovered the town's unspoiled beauty, special light, lively community, and colorful Portuguese flavor. By 1916, with five art schools flourishing here, painters' easels were nearly as common as shells on the beach. This bohemian community, along with the availability of inexpensive summer lodgings, attracted young rebels and writers as well, including John Reed (*Ten Days That Shook the World*) and Mary Heaton Vorse (*Footnote to Folly*), who in 1915 began the Cape's first significant theater group, the Provincetown Players. The young, then unknown Eugene O'Neill joined them in 1916, when his *Bound East for Cardiff* premiered in a tiny wharf-side East End fish house. After 1916 the Players moved on to New York. Their theater, at present-day 571 Commercial Street, is long gone, but a model of it and the old Lewis Wharf on which it stood is on display at the Pilgrim Monument museum.

Provincetown

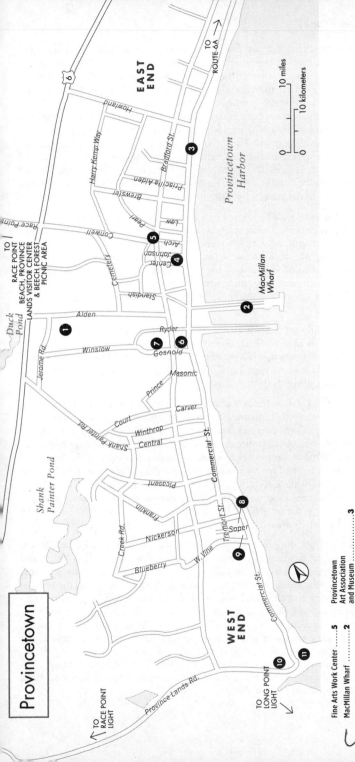

Near the Provincetown border, **massive dunes** actually meet the road in places, turning U.S. 6 into a sand-swept highway. Scattered among the dunes are primitive cottages called dune shacks, built from flotsam and other found materials, that have provided atmospheric as well as cheap lodgings to a number of famous artists and writers over the years—among them poet Harry Kemp, Eugene O'Neill, e. e. cummings, Jack Kerouac, and Norman Mailer. The few surviving shacks are privately leased from the Cape Cod National Seashore, whose proposal to demolish the shacks was halted by their inclusion on the National Register of Historic Places in 1988. The dunes are fragile and should not be walked on, but paths lead through them to the ocean. You can see some of the shacks by van on Art's Dune Tours.

The **Province Lands** begin at High Head in Truro and stretch to the tip of Provincetown. The area is scattered with ponds, cranberry bogs, and scrub; unfortunately, this terrain provides optimal conditions for the deer tick, which can cause Lyme disease, so use extra caution. More than 7 mi of bike and walking trails lace through forests of stunted pines, beech, and oak and across desertlike expanses of rolling dunes. Protected against development, the Province Lands are the "wilds" of the Cape.

A beautiful spot to stop for lunch before biking to the beach, the **Beech Forest picnic area** (⊠ *Race Point Rd., east of U.S. 6*) in the National Seashore borders a small pond covered with water lilies. The adjacent bike trails lead to Herring Cove and Race Point beaches, which are both part of the National Seashore.

Inside the **Province Lands Visitor Center** in the Cape Cod National Seashore, you'll find literature and nature-related gifts, frequent short films on local geology, and exhibits on the life of the dunes and the shore. You can also pick up information on guided walks, birding trips, lectures, bonfires, and other current programs throughout the seashore, as well as on the Province Lands' own beaches, Race Point and Herring Cove, and walking, biking, and horse trails. Don't miss the wonderful 360-degree view of the dunes and the surrounding ocean from the observation deck. ⊠ *Race Point Rd., east of U.S. 6* ☎ *508/487–1256* ⊕ *www.nps.gov/caco* ⊠ *Free* ⊙ *Early May–late Oct., daily 9–5.*

Not far from the present Coast Guard station is the **Old Harbor Station,** a U.S. Life Saving Service building rescued from an eroding beach and towed here by barge from Chatham in 1977. It's reached by a boardwalk across the sand, and plaques along the way tell about the lifesaving service and the whales seen offshore. Inside are displays of such equipment as Lyle guns, which shot rescue lines out to ships in distress when seas were too violent to launch a surfboat, and breeches buoys, in which passengers were hauled across those lines to safety. There are reenactments of this old-fashioned lifesaving procedure at 6:30 on Thursday night in summer. ⊠ *Race Point Beach, end of Race Point Rd.* ☎ *No phone* ⊠ *Donations accepted; Thurs. night $3* ⊙ *July and Aug., daily 3–5 (also 6–8 on Thurs.).*

★ Provincetown's main downtown thoroughfare, **Commercial Street,** is 3 mi from end to end. In season, driving from one end to the other could take forever, so wear comfortable shoes and get ready to walk (although going on foot will take awhile, too, due to the crowds). You'll see signs for parking lots as you head into town. Take a casual stroll and check out the many architectural styles (Greek revival, Victorian, Second Empire, and Gothic, to name a few) used in the design of the impressive houses for wealthy sea captains and merchants. Be on the lookout for blue plaques fastened to housefronts explaining their historical significance—practically the entire town has been designated part of the Provincetown Historic District. The Historical Society puts out a series of walking-tour pamphlets—available for about $1 each at many shops in town as well as at the chamber of commerce visitor center—with maps and information on the history of many buildings and the (more or less) famous folk who have occupied them. You may also want to pick up a free Provincetown gallery guide.

5

The center of town is where the crowds and most of the touristy shops are. The quiet East End is mostly residential, with an increasing number of nationally renowned galleries; the similarly quiet West End has a number of small inns with neat lawns and elaborate gardens.

NEED A BREAK? The **Aquarium Shops Food Court** (✉ *205–209 Commercial St.*) contains a handful of excellent little fast-food spots. Grab outstanding Mexican fare at **Big Daddy's Burritos;** Asian snacks at **Fortune Cookie;** and silky smooth Italian ice cream, hot cocoa, and smoothies at **I Dream of Gelato.** The **Provincetown Fudge Factory** (✉ *210 Commercial St., Downtown Center* ☎ *508/487-2850* ⊕ *www.ptownfudge.com*), across from the post office, makes silky peanut-butter cups, chocolates, saltwater taffy, yard-long licorice whips, custom-flavor frozen yogurt, and the creamiest fudge on the Cape—and will ship sweet goodies to you, too.

❶ The first thing you'll see in Provincetown is the **Pilgrim Monument.** This
★ grandiose edifice, which seems somewhat out of proportion to the rest of the low-rise town, commemorates the Pilgrims' first landing in the New World and their signing of the Mayflower Compact (the first colonial-American rules of self-governance) before they set off from Provincetown Harbor to explore the mainland. Climb the 116 steps and 60 short ramps of the 252-foot-high tower for a panoramic view—dunes on one side, harbor on the other, and the entire bay side of Cape Cod beyond. On an exceptionally clear day you can see the Boston skyline. At the tower's base is a museum of Lower Cape and Provincetown history, with exhibits on whaling, shipwrecks, and scrimshaw; a diorama of the *Mayflower;* and another of a glass factory.

The tower was erected of granite shipped from Maine, according to a design modeled on a tower in Siena, Italy. President Theodore Roosevelt laid the cornerstone in 1907, and President Howard Taft attended the 1910 dedication. On Thanksgiving Eve, in a ceremony that includes a museum tour and open house, 5,000 white and gold lights that drape the tower are illuminated—a display that can be seen from as far away as the Cape Cod Canal. They are lighted nightly into the New Year. ⊠*High Pole Hill Rd.* ☎*508/487–1310* ⊕*www.pilgrim-monument. org* ✉*$7* ⊙*Early Apr.–June and Sept.–Oct., daily 9–4:15; July and Aug., daily 9–6:15; Nov., weekends 9–4:15.*

② **MacMillan Wharf,** with its large municipal parking facility, is a sensible place to start a tour of town. It's one of five remaining wharves of the original 54 that once jutted into the bay. The wharf serves as the base for P-town whale-watch boats, fishing charters, high-speed ferries, and party boats. The **Chamber of Commerce** is also here, with all kinds of information and events schedules. Kiosks at the wharf have restroom and parking-lot locations, bus schedules, and other information for visitors.

The former Provincetown Marina building, on MacMillan Wharf, holds the **Expedition** *Whydah* **Sea Lab and Learning Center,** a home for artifacts recovered from the pirate ship *Whydah,* which sank off the coast of Wellfleet in 1717. The *Whydah* is the only pirate shipwreck ever authenticated anywhere in the world, and the museum, though tiny, is entertaining and educational, with one display on the restoration and conservation processes and another on the untold story of the 18th-century pirating life. The curators hope to eventually collect all the recovered pieces; some are on loan to other museums across the country. ⊠*16 MacMillan Wharf, Downtown Center* ☎*508/487–8899 or 800/949–3241* ⊕*www.whydah.com* ✉*$8* ⊙*June–early Sept., daily 10–8; Apr., May, and early Sept.–Oct., daily 10–5; Nov. and Dec., weekends 10–4.*

③ Founded in 1914 to collect and show the works of artists with Provincetown connections, the **Provincetown Art Association and Museum** *(PAAM)* has a 1,650-piece permanent collection, displayed in changing exhibits that mix up-and-comers with established 20th-century figures, including Milton Avery, Philip Evergood, William Gropper, Charles Hawthorne, Robert Motherwell, Claes Oldenburg, Man Ray, John Singer Sargent, Andy Warhol, and Agnes Weinrich. Some of the work hung in the four bright galleries is for sale. The museum store carries books of local interest, including works by or about area artists and authors, as well as posters, crafts, cards, and gift items. PAAM-sponsored year-round courses (one day and longer) offer the opportunity to study under such talents as Hilda Neily, Franny Golden, and Doug Ritter. A stunning, contemporary wing was added in 2005, greatly expanding the exhibit space. ⊠*460 Commercial St., East End* ☎*508/487–1750* ⊕*www.paam.org* ✉*$3 donation suggested* ⊙*Late May–early July and Sept., daily noon–5, also Fri. and Sat. 8* PM*–10* PM*; early July and Aug., daily noon–5 and 8* PM*–10* PM*; Oct.–May, Thurs.–Sun. noon–5.*

FodorśChoice ★

④ In 2005, the **Provincetown Public Library** moved into the beautifully ★ restored and redesigned Center Methodist Church, a towering 1860 beauty in the East End whose steeple you can see from the harbor and much of town. On rainy days, this is a wonderful place to read, work, or check your e-mail on one of the several public computers. You can also check out *The Rose Dorothea,* a half-scale replica of an early

1900s fishing schooner that was built by some 15 Provincetown fishermen and woodworkers as a tribute to the town's rich nautical heritage. The 62-foot-long boat has ingeniously been built into the library's 2nd floor. Architecturally, this is one of the town's most striking and distinctive buildings, but it's also a great cultural resource, hosting children's storytelling on Wednesday and Saturday mornings, educational workshops, and other community events. There's also a children's room with computers, books, and educational resources. As of this writing, the building's lower level is under construction—when it opens in summer 2008, it will house a gallery space showing rotating local exhibits. ✉*356 Commercial St., East End* ☎*508/487-7094* ⊕*www.ptownlib. com* ✑*Free* ⊙*Mon. and Fri. 10–5, Tues. and Thurs. noon–8, Wed. 10–8, Sat. 10–2, Sun. 1–5.*

NEED A BREAK?

Wired Puppy (✉ *379 Commercial St., East End* ☎ *508/487-0017*) is a slick but comfy Internet café with hardwood floors and mod seating. They serve outstanding organic coffees and teas—the knowledgeable staff can help you choose just the right beverage—plus a nice variety of cookies, brownies, and treats. There's free Wi-Fi if you bring your own laptop, or you can borrow a laptop here.

Nearby, the **Purple Feather Dessert Cafe** (✉ *334 Commercial St., East End* ☎ *508/487-9100*) comes in handy when you're craving superb handmade chocolates, decadent cakes, and house-made gelato and sorbets.

5 To see or hear the work of up-and-coming artists, visit the gallery or attend a reading at the **Fine Arts Work Center** *(FAWC).* A nonprofit organization founded in 1968, the FAWC sponsors 10 writers and 10 artists from October through May each year, providing them with a place to live and work, a stipend, and access to artists and teachers. A summer program has open-enrollment workshops in both writing and the visual arts. The buildings in the complex around the center, which it owns, were formerly part of Day's Lumber Yard Studios, built above a lumberyard by a patron of the arts to provide poor artists with cheap accommodations. Robert Motherwell, Hans Hoffmann, and Helen Frankenthaler have been among the studios' roster of residents over the years. ✉*24 Pearl St., East End* ☎*508/487-9960* ⊕*www.fawc. org* ✑*Free, $5 for events and readings* ⊙*Weekdays 9–5, events are usually held in evening.*

6 The **town hall** was used by the Provincetown Art Association as its first exhibit space. Paintings donated to the town over the years—including Provincetown scenes by Charles Hawthorne and WPA–era murals by Ross Moffett—are still displayed here. ✉*260 Commercial St., Downtown Center* ☎*508/487-7000* ⊙*Weekdays 8–5.*

7 In a little park behind the town hall is the **Mayflower Compact Plaque** (✉*Bradford St., Downtown Center*), carved in bas-relief by sculptor Cyrus Dalin and depicting the historic signing.

8 An **octagonal house** (⊠ *74 Commercial St., West End*) built in 1850 is an interesting piece of Provincetown architecture in the West End. The house is not open to the public.

9 The oldest building in town, dating from 1746, is the small Cape-style **Seth Nickerson House** (⊠ *72 Commercial St., West End*), which is still a private home. It was built by a ship's carpenter, with massive pegged, hand-hewn oak beams and wide-board floors. Modern renovations have somewhat obscured the glimpse into centuries past that it once possessed, but it's still impressive.

> **GHOST SHIP**
>
> During the American Revolution, Provincetown Harbor was controlled by the British, who used it as a port from which to sail to Boston and launch attacks on colonial and French vessels. In November 1778, the 64-gun British frigate *Somerset* ran aground and was wrecked off Provincetown's Race Point. Every 60 years or so, the shifting sands uncover its remains.

10 The bronze **Pilgrim Plaque** (⊠ *West end of Commercial St., Downtown Center*), set into a boulder at the center of a little park, commemorates the first footfall of the Pilgrims onto Cape soil—Provincetown's humble equivalent to Plymouth Rock.

11 In the **Provincetown Inn** (⊠ *1 Commercial St., West End* ☎ *508/487–9500*) you can see a series of 19 murals, painted in the 1930s from old postcards, depicting life in the 19th-century town. The inn still operates as a hotel; the murals are in the lobby and hallways.

WHERE TO STAY & EAT

$$$–$$$$
★ ✕ **Bistro at Crowne Pointe.** Opened in 2005 in the snazzy Crowne Pointe Inn, this intimate, casually handsome space occupies the parlor and sunroom of a grand sea-captain's mansion. The kitchen serves finely crafted, healthful, modern American food, such as wasabi-dusted seared tuna with a sesame-sake-soy dipping sauce, followed by seared lamb medallions with a feta-mint pesto rub and a ragout of roasted tomatoes, artichoke hearts, and asparagus. A lighter menu offers veggie burgers, lobster rolls, and similarly casual fare for a fraction of the price. ⊠ *82 Bradford St.* ☎ *508/487–6767* ⊕ *www.crownepointe.com* ⌂ *Reservations essential* ▤ *AE, D, MC, V.*

$$$–$$$$
★ ✕ **Cafe Edwige.** A longtime East End restaurant set rather discreetly up a flight of stairs, Cafe Edwige consists of an intimate dining room with varnished-wood floors and dim lighting, and a casual side patio with tile tables and billowing drapes. Start things off at the bar with one of their signature white-ginger cosmos, and perhaps the tuna-avocado tartare appetizer with sweet-chili vinaigrette and wasabi cream, which has long been a staple here. Popular entrées from the contemporary menu include the Brazilian seafood *moqueca* (halibut, shrimp, scallops, coconut milk, and palm oil simmered with basmati rice); and the grilled New Zealand rack of lamb with a feta-risotto-spinach cake, haricot vert, and a lamb demi-glace. For breakfast, consider the omelet with Portobello mushrooms and Brie. ⊠ *333 Commercial St.*

☎508/487–4020 ▭MC, V ⊘Closed Oct.–Apr., Mon.–Thurs. May–mid-June, and Wed.

$$$–$$$$ ✗**Front Street.** Front Street is very good and quite romantic, if not as
★ revered by locals as it used to be (in part because several noteworthy
competitors have opened in recent years). Here classic Italian cooking
is linked to offerings from Greece, southern France, and even North
Africa. There's a nightly char-grilled fish special: match salmon, halibut,
or tuna with a Latin, Berber, or Cajun spice rub; lemon-caper butter;
or a ginger-soy-wasabi glaze. Other stellar dishes include sage-and-butternut risotto with crisped baby spinach, and truffled wild-mushroom
bisque. The wine list is also a winner. Finish things off with coffee-toffee pie. ⊠230 Commercial St. ☎508/487–9715 ⊕www.frontstreetrestaurant.com ⌖Reservations essential ▭AE, D, MC, V ⊘Closed
Jan.–mid-May and Mon. and Tues. No lunch.

$$$–$$$$ ✗**Red Inn.** Inside the striking red house on P'town's West End that's
also an enchanting B&B, the Red Inn is perhaps even better known
as one of the Outer Cape's most romantic dining destinations—the
views are simply stunning. The remarkable setting aside, the inventive contemporary fare as well as the service can be hit-or-miss, especially given the lofty prices. You might start off with the Kobe beef
mini burgers seared rare with rémoulade sauce, before moving on to
chili-rubbed pork chops with a tomatillo salsa. Breakfast and lunch
are also served. ⊠15 Commercial St. ☎508/487–7334 ⊕www.theredinn.com ▭AE, MC, V.

$$–$$$$ ✗**Ciro & Sal's.** Tucked inside a cozy house down an alley behind Commercial Street, this longtime local favorite offers a low-key, romantic
alternative to some of the town's busier restaurants. The most memorable tables are inside a cozy brick wine cellar; the rest fill a pair of
art-filled dining rooms; one is warmed by a huge fireplace. You can
also relax with a cocktail on the garden patio. The restaurant is justly
known for its fresh pastas and bountiful antipasto selections. Favorite
entrées include calamari sautéed with anchovies, lemon, garlic, and
cream; and chicken livers sautéed with prosciutto, Marsala wine, and
sage. Hours vary during the off-season—call ahead. ⊠4 Kiley Ct.
☎508/487–6444 ⊕www.ciroandsals.com ▭AE, D, MC, V ⊘Closed
Jan. and Wed. No lunch.

$$–$$$$ ✗**Devon's.** This unassuming, tiny white cottage—with a dining room
Fodor's Choice that seats just 42 lucky patrons—serves up some of the best food in
★ town. Specialties from the oft-changing menu include pan-seared halibut with caramelized orange glaze, black rice, and sautéed beet greens;
and free-range seared duck with a Syrah reduction, red-onion marmalade, and couscous primavera. Another plus is their great little wine
list. Be sure to save some room for knockout dessert selections like
blackberry mousse over ginger-lemon polenta cake with wildberry
coulis. Devon's also serves up a terrific breakfast each day until 1 PM,
where you might sample truffle cheese-and-baby spinach omelets with
rosemary homefries. Hours are limited in May and October; it's best
to phone ahead. ⊠401½ Commercial St. ☎508/487–4773 ⊕www.
devons.org ⌖Reservations essential ▭MC, V ⊘Closed Wed. and
Nov.–Apr.

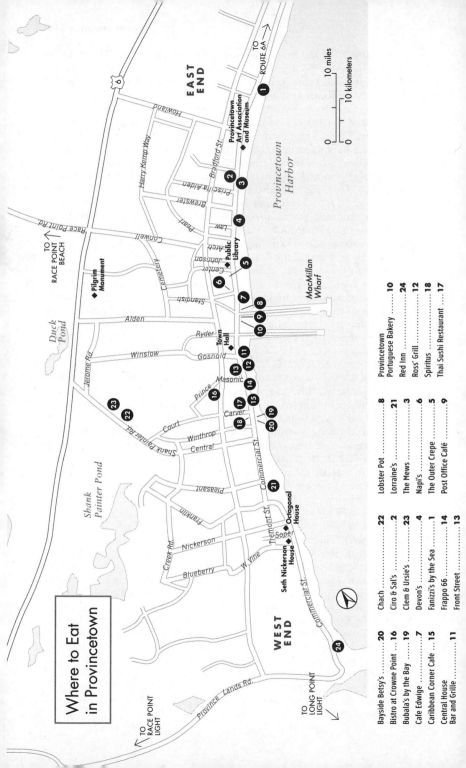

Where to Eat in Provincetown

EAST END

WEST END

TO ROUTE 6A

TO RACE POINT BEACH

TO RACE POINT LIGHT

TO LONG POINT LIGHT

Provincetown Harbor

Shank Painter Pond

Duck Pond

Race Point Rd
Shank Painter Rd
Jerome Rd
Cemetery
Conwell
Pearl
Law
Arch
Johnson
Center
Standish
Alden
Winslow
Gosnold
Prince
Masonic
Court
Winthrop
Central
Carver
Pleasant
Franklin
Nickerson
Blueberry
W. Vine
Creek Rd
Tremont St.
Soper
Commercial St.
Ryder
Bradford St.
Priscilla Alden
Brewster
Harry Kemp Way
Howland
Province Lands Rd.

Pilgrim Monument
Provincetown Art Association and Museum
Public Library
Town Hall
MacMillan Wharf
Octagonal House
Seth Nickerson House

10 miles
10 kilometers

Bayside Betsy's	**20**
Bistro at Crowne Point	**16**
Bubala's by the Bay	**19**
Cafe Edwige	**7**
Caribbean Corner Cafe	**15**
Central House Bar and Grille	**11**
Chach	**22**
Ciro & Sal's	**2**
Clem & Ursie's	**23**
Devon's	**4**
Fanizzi's by the Sea	**1**
Frappo 66	**14**
Front Street	**13**
Lobster Pot	**8**
Lorraine's	**21**
The Mews	**3**
Napi's	**6**
The Outer Crepe	**5**
Post Office Café	**9**
Provincetown	**10**
Portuguese Bakery	**24**
Red Inn	**12**
Ross' Grill	**18**
Spiritus	**17**

$$–$$$
★
✕Lorraine's. In a cozy cottage toward the West End, Lorraine's has an intimate feel, but the nouvelle Latin American–inspired menu is as good as ever. An appetizer of blackened seafood tostadas with black bean-and-corn relish packs a punch, and the tender, slow-cooked pork carnitas are a revelation. Also wonderful is a mesquite-grilled rack of lamb with roasted-garlic chipotle demi-glace. The bar draws a loyal, lively crowd and is famous for its long list of premium tequilas. A tantalizing brunch is served in summer—consider the chorizo with scrambled eggs, tortillas, and beans. ✉*133 Commercial St.* ☎*508/487–6074* ⏺*www. lorrainesrestaurant.com* ▤*MC, V* ⏲*Closed Mon.–Wed. Nov.–Mar. No lunch.*

$$–$$$
Fodor'sChoice
★
✕The Mews. This perennial favorite with magnificent harbor views focuses on seafood and grilled meats with a cross-cultural flair. Some popular entrées include roasted vegetable and polenta lasagna with a tomato-olive sauce; and Vietnamese shaking beef wok sautéed with scallions and red onions and a lime–black pepper dipping sauce. A piano bar upstairs serves lunch (weekdays in summer) and dinner from a light, less-expensive café menu (burgers, lobster dumplings in miso). The view of the bay from the bar is nearly perfect, and the gentle lighting makes this a romantic spot to have a drink. Brunch is also served daily in season. The restaurant claims its vodka bar is New England's largest, with some 230 varieties. ✉*429 Commercial St.* ☎*508/487–1500* ⏺*www.mews.com* ▤*AE, D, DC, MC, V* ⏲*Closed Jan. No lunch weekdays off-season or Sat. mid-Oct.–late May.*

$$–$$$
✕Napi's. A steady favorite for its lively ambience and dependable Mediterranean fare, Napi's presents a long and varied menu. The food and the interior share a penchant for unusual, striking juxtapositions—a classical sculpture in front of an abstract canvas, for instance. On the gustatory front, look for sharp combinations such as Thai chicken and shrimp, cod amandine, and steak tenderloin topped with Brie. Asparagus ravioli is just one of several very nice vegetarian dishes. ✉*7 Freeman St.* ☎*508/487–1145 or 800/571–6274* ⏺*www.napis-restaurant. com* ▤*AE, D, DC, MC, V* ⏲*No lunch May–Sept.*

$$–$$$
★
✕Ross' Grill. Likening itself to a French bistro with American tastes, the kitchen here is modest but busy, preparing everything from scratch, including its signature hand-cut, double-dipped french fries. Local fish and shellfish dominate the menu; a favorite is the sautéed local sea scallops with leeks, garlic, and pear tomatoes over linguine. Portions are generous—you'll get eight meaty racks of baby New Zealand lamb—and prices are reasonable. Choose from 75 wines by the glass. The location is grand: up on the 2nd floor of the Whaler's Wharf complex, views of Provincetown Harbor are unlimited. It's a popular place, so expect a wait. ✉*237 Commercial St.* ☎*508/487–8878* ⏺*Reservations not accepted* ▤*AE, MC, V* ⏲*Closed Tues. and Wed. Jan.–mid-Apr.*

$–$$$
✕Bayside Betsy's. Named for the feisty chef and co-owner, this campy, infectiously fun bar-and-grill serves a mix of homespun American favorites and slightly more contemporary dishes, such as lobster tortellini, seafood wontons with orange-horseradish sauce, and classic steamed mussels in white wine with garlic, shallots, and tomatoes. Nightly specials often reflect the luck of local fishermen. You might try pan-seared

scallops with chorizo tossed with fettuccine. You can expect reliable food for breakfast (try the banana-walnut pancakes), lunch, and dinner year-round, but the real draws are the colorful people-watching, good-natured attitude, and nice views of Provincetown Harbor. ⊠*177 Commercial St.* ☎*508/487–6566* ⊕*www.baysidebetsys.com* ☰*AE, D, MC, V* ⊘*Closed Mon.–Wed. Nov.–May.*

$–$$$ ✕**Bubala's by the Bay.** Look for the bright yellow building adorned on top with campy carved birds. The kitchen rarely stops, serving breakfast, lunch, and dinner; it's known for seafood bought directly off local boats, although the food here is less impressive than the views and the festive setting, with outdoor seats overlooking Commercial Street and indoor seating facing the bay. Lobster salad, seafood cassoulet with white beans and chorizo, and grilled venison rack with currant, sage, and shiitake demi-glace are reliable options. The wine list is priced practically at retail, and the U-shape bar picks up into the evening. It's one of the few Commercial Street restaurants with off-street parking. ⊠*183 Commercial St.* ☎*508/487–0773* ⊕*www.bubalas.com* ☰*AE, D, MC, V* ⊘*Closed late Oct.–late Apr.*

$–$$$ ✕**Fanizzi's by the Sea.** A dependable, year-round East Ender that sits
★ directly over the bay and offers fine water views, Fanizzi's presents a varied menu strong on well-prepared comfort food (including a memorable chicken potpie and juicy burgers), but often with a few creative twists. The baked cod is served with a tangy coating of almonds and mustard, and the hearty roasted half chicken is glazed with fresh garlic, lemon juice, rosemary, and thyme. You can order burgers and substantive dinner salads, including a fine salmon Caesar. The dining room, lined with large windows, is softly lighted and casual. Sunday brunch is a favorite with locals. ⊠*539 Commercial St.* ☎*508/487–1964* ⊕*www.fanizzisrestaurant.com* ☰*AE, D, DC, MC, V.*

$–$$$ ✕**Lobster Pot.** Provincetown's Lobster Pot is fit to do battle with all the lobster shanties anywhere (and everywhere) else on the Cape—it's often jammed with tourists, but that's truly a reflection of the generally high quality. The hardworking kitchen turns out classic New England cooking: lobsters, generous and filling seafood platters (try the seafood Pico with a half lobster, shrimp, littlenecks, mussels, calamari, and fish over pasta with tomatoes, rose wine, onions, and garlic), and some of the best chowder around. The Asian bouillabaisse is another favorite. The upstairs deck overlooks the comings and goings of the harbor and is a great spot for lunch. There's also a take-out lobster market and bakery on the premises. You'll have to wait in line, but you'll be in the center of town—an ideal place for people-watching. ⊠*321 Commercial St.* ☎*508/487–0842* ⊕*www.ptownlobsterpot.com* ⚠*Reservations not accepted* ☰*AE, D, DC, MC, V* ⊘*Closed Jan.*

$–$$$ ✕**Post Office Cafe.** A dapper yet casual bistro beneath Provincetown's favorite cabaret bar, the Post Office serves food most nights until 1 AM, making it one of the area's best options for late-night snacking. The kitchen turns out a mix of substantial but straightforward American entrées, such as scallops Alfredo, along with lighter pub favorites. Sandwiches are a specialty; consider the grilled yellowfin tuna and greens on focaccia, or the grilled portobello mushroom with artichokes, sundried tomatoes, roasted red peppers, feta cheese, and mixed greens on a pita. The place becomes increasingly festive—even a little raucous—the later it gets. ⊠*303 Commercial St.* ☎*508/487–3892* ▤*AE, D, MC, V.*

¢–$$$ ✕**Clem & Ursie's.** It's worth the short drive or long walk from downtown
Fodor's Choice to sample the tantalizing seafood prepared at this colorful café, grocery
★ market, cocktail bar, and bakery. The mammoth menu touches on just about every kind of food from the ocean: tuna steaks, crab claws, squid stew, Japanese baby octopus salad, hot lobster rolls, lobster scampi. The Buffalo shrimp are addictive, and be sure to try the Portuguese clam pie. A nice range of nonfishy items is offered, too, from pulled-pork barbecue to bacon cheeseburgers—plus great desserts like pistachio cake and stuffed ice-cream sandwiches dipped in chocolate. You order and pay at the counter and grab a seat inside the decidedly casual dining room; they bring your chow out to you. The market has the best selection of cheeses in town plus countless seafood items, oils and vinegars, and gourmet goods. ⊠*85 Shank Painter Rd.* ☎*508/487–2333* ⊕*www.clemandursies.com* ▤*MC, V* ☉*Closed mid-Nov.–mid-Apr.*

$$ ✕**Central House Bar and Grille.** The dining component at the action-packed Crown & Anchor gay resort, Central House serves commendable contemporary American fare, such as pomegranate-honey-glazed chicken with grilled pineapple relish; and pan-roasted scallops with grits, buttered baby carrots, and snap-pea salad. Several lighter options are offered, too, including three kinds of mac-and-cheese. For breakfast, you might try the lobster Benedict or French toast topped with Vermont syrup, sweet butter, and powdered sugar. Apart from the good food, this is one of the best venues in town for socializing and observing the assorted merry-makers who frequent the resort's many bars. ⊠*247 Commercial St.* ☎*508/487–1430* ⊕*www.onlyatthecrown.com* ▤*AE, D, MC, V* ☉*Closed Wed. and Thurs. off-season.*

¢–$$ ✕**Thai Sushi Restaurant.** Bringing a much-needed dose of Asian cooking to the Outer Cape, this cozy eatery inside the shaggy Gifford House Inn serves reasonably authentic, well-seasoned fare. You might start with a salad of spicy minced chicken with fresh ginger, lime, and roasted peanuts, or the fried crab rolls. Excellent main dishes include sweet-and-sour squid with stir-fried pineapple and veggies, basil fried rice with tofu and vegetables, salmon pad thai, and boneless duck with tamarind sauce. ⊠*9 Carver St.* ☎*508/487–0889* ▤*MC, V.*

¢–$ ✕**Caribbean Corner Cafe.** A simply, family-run spot in the heart of the Commercial Street retail and dining action, this cheerful café produces a staggering variety of Caribbean as well as Latin American treats. Prices are reasonable, the service wonderfully friendly, and the crowd a good mix of visitors and locals. The kitchen uses mostly natural and organic ingredients—start with *bollitos* (steamed cornmeal rolls with a homemade tomato-pepper-herb sauce) or a Venezuelan salad topped with fresh tuna. Popular mains include boneless pork stew with a rich and a slightly spicy Caribbean sauce and plantains, or curried chicken. The *quesillo* rum flan makes for a great ending. ⊠*206–208 Commercial St.* ☎*508/487–2023* ⊕*www.caluvesu.com* ▤*MC, V.*

¢–$ ✕**Chach.** A cute, airy, and contemporary clapboard restaurant out on Shank Painter Road toward the beach, Chach is a big hit with locals.

5

It's a sweet little place serving creative omelets (try one with green chili, cheddar, and sour cream), vanilla custard French toast with Vermont maple syrup, fried chicken salad with buttermilk dressing, and falafel sandwiches with cucumber-mint sauce. Fresh ingredients and artful presentation make this a winner. Closing time is 3 PM. ⊠*73 Shank Painter Rd.* ☎*508/487–1530* ▭*MC, V* ⊘*No dinner.*

¢–$ ✕**Frappo 66.** Adjoining the Provincetown Art House Theatre and The-
★ atre Cinema Café, this eatery presents fresh and imaginative contemporary American fare in a low-cost, no-hassle setting—you can explore the prepared foods on display at the counter or order à la carte from a menu, mixing and matching main courses and sides as you wish, and then choose your own seat in the sunny dining room or on the patio overlooking Commercial Street (or order to go). Service is quick, and prices are low. The menu changes daily but might feature pork vindaloo, tomato-and-mint couscous, tuna-avocado tartar, fried oysters over baby spinach, sweet-pea-falafel sandwiches, warm flourless chocolate torte—the menu is seemingly endless. ⊠*214 Commercial St.* ☎*508/487–9066* ▭*MC, V.*

¢–$ ✕**Provincetown Portuguese Bakery.** This town standby makes fresh Portuguese breads and pastries and serves breakfast and lunch all day from March to October. Although it may be difficult to choose among the sweet splendor, favorite pastries include *malassadas,* a sweet fried dough, lemon custard, and the more unusual *trutas,* with rich, sweet potato filling. It's open until 11 PM in summer. ⊠*299 Commercial St.* ☎*508/487–1803* ▭*No credit cards* ⊘*Closed Nov.–Feb. No dinner.*

¢ ✕**The Outer Crepe.** In the same cute spot that held the much-loved Tofu-A-Go-Go, this festive, playfully named creperie has fast earned kudos for its delicious and affordable savory and sweet creations, which are served from 9 to 8 daily. Morning highlights include the fried-egg and cheddar breakfast sandwiches. Later you might consider the Frenchie crepe (with black-forest ham, Gruyère, and Dijon mustard), or the sweet Strawlala crepe, packed with fresh strawberries and rich Nutella spread. There's a casual dining area upstairs and more seating out on a front deck with great views of passersby along Commercial Street. ⊠*336 Commercial St.* ☎*508/487–6237* ▭*No credit cards.*

¢ ✕**Spiritus.** The local bars close at 1 AM, at which point this pizza joint–coffee stand becomes the town's epicenter. It's the ultimate place to see and be seen, pizza slice in hand and witty banter at the ready. In the morning, the same counter serves restorative coffee and croissants as well as Häagen-Dazs ice cream. ⊠*190 Commercial St.* ☎*508/487–2808* ⊕*www.spirituspizza.com* ▭*No credit cards* ⊘*Closed Nov.–Apr.*

$$$–$$$$ ▦**Benchmark Inn & Central.** Made up of two separate buildings on a quiet, narrow street just a block from downtown, this is an inn of simple, refined luxury. Rooms are painted in soothing neutral tones, floors are bare wood, and fresh flowers are placed atop every stainless-steel wet bar; the bathrooms have marble tile and hair dryers. Most rooms have private entrances and fireplaces; some have skylights and private balconies with rooftop and water views. When you're ready to turn in, indulge in the nightly turndown service. There are also three very large and cushy penthouse suites. The management is environmentally con-

scious, using mostly "green" products and practices. **Pros:** Large and in some cases huge rooms, immaculate and luxurious, an environmentally conscious property. **Cons:** Among the highest rates in town, water views are limited or nonexistent from many rooms, significant minimum-stay requirements in summer. ✉ *6 and 8 Dyer St., 02657* ☎ *508/487–7440 or 888/487–7440* 🖷 *508/487–3446* ⊕ *www.benchmarkinn.com* 🛏*11 rooms, 3 suites* ♿ *In-room: refrigerator, DVD, Wi-Fi. In-hotel: pool, concierge, no elevator, laundry service, airport shuttle,* ▭ *AE, MC, V* ⊘ *Closed Jan.–late Feb.*

$$$–$$$$

Fodor's Choice

★

🏨 **Brass Key.** One of the Cape's most luxurious small resorts, this meticulously kept year-round getaway comprises a beautifully restored main house—originally an 1828 sea captain's home—and several other carefully groomed buildings and cottages. Rooms mix antiques with such modern amenities as Bose stereos and TV–VCRs (loaner laptops and iPod docks are also available). Deluxe rooms come with gas fireplaces and whirlpool baths or French doors opening onto wrought-iron balconies. A widow's-walk sundeck has a panoramic view of Cape Cod Bay. Complimentary cocktails are served in the courtyard; in winter, wine is served before a roaring fire in the common room. As is true of many of Provincetown's smaller hotels, the Brass Key draws a largely gay clientele, especially in summer, but the owners and staff make everyone feel welcome and pampered. **Pros:** Ultraposh rooms, beautiful and secluded grounds, pool on-site. **Cons:** Among the highest rates in town, rooms close to Bradford Street can get a bit of noise, significant minimum-stay requirements in summer. ✉ *67 Bradford St., 02657* ☎ *508/487–9005 or 800/842–9858* 🖷 *508/487–9020* ⊕ *www.brasskey.com* 🛏*42 rooms* ♿ *In-room: safe, VCR, Wi-Fi. In-hotel: pool, no elevator, no kids under 16* ▭ *AE, D, MC, V* ⦿*CP.*

$$$–$$$$

🏨 **Crown & Anchor.** If you're looking to eat, sleep, and live amid the pulsing entertainment center of Provincetown, this is the place. Upstairs from the daily clamor of drag shows and discos are 18 rooms handsomely adorned with Oriental rugs and deep cranberry hues. Deluxe rooms have two-person whirlpool tubs, fireplaces, and private balconies facing Provincetown Harbor; all rooms have the choice of a king or two full-size beds. In addition, two rooms are fully ADA compliant. One drawback, however, is that you can hear the din and vibration of music and conversation downstairs in the bars and discos until about midnight or 1 AM on many evenings. Complimentary continental breakfast is served, but why not take advantage of the choice room service and simply stay in bed? There's a dependable restaurant, Central House, as well. A highly professional staff with a great attitude holds everything together. **Pros:** Many bars and dining options on-site, in heart of central P'town retail and entertainment district, some rooms have harbor views. **Cons:** Noise from bars and clubs carries to many rooms, not a good choice if you have kids, contemporary vibe lacks historic quaintness of some older properties. ✉ *247 Commercial St., 02657* ☎ *508/487–1430* 🖷 *508/487–3237* ⊕ *www.onlyatthecrown. com* 🛏*18 rooms* ♿ *In-room: refrigerator, Wi-Fi. In-hotel: restaurants, bars, pool, beachfront, no elevator* ▭ *AE, D, MC, V* ⦿*CP.*

5

$$$–$$$$ 🏨**Crowne Pointe Historic Inn and Spa.** Created meticulously from six dif-
Fodor's Choice ferent buildings, this inn has not left a single detail unattended. Own-
★ ers Tom Walter and David Sanford skillfully mix luxury and comfort.
Period furniture and antiques fill the common areas and rooms; a
queen-size bed is the smallest you'll find, dressed in 300-thread-count
linens, with treats on the pillow for nightly turndown service. Many
rooms have fireplaces: in one room, you can view the flames from your
bed or the whirlpool tub. Penthouse suites have two floors of living
space with a full kitchen, and many rooms have private balconies with
water or town views. The grounds are accented with brick pathways,
flowers, and trees. Start the day with a full, hot breakfast, then graze on
freshly baked treats and wine and cheese in the afternoon—there's also
an excellent restaurant, the Bistro at Crowne Pointe. In the handsome,
full-service Shui Spa, you might opt for such soothing treatments as
Shiatsu massage, craniosacral therapy, or the honey-almond body pol-
ish. **Pros:** Great on-site amenities such as spa and restaurant, posh and
luxurious room decor, professional and well-trained staff. **Cons:** Among
the highest rates in town, significant minimum-stay requirements in
summer, contemporary vibe lacks historic quaintness of some older
properties. ⊠*82 Bradford St., 02657* 🕾*508/487–6767 or 877/276–
9631* 🖷*508/487–5554* ⊕*www.crownepointe.com* 🛏*37 rooms, 3
suites* 🔧*In-room: kitchen (some), refrigerator, DVD, Ethernet, Wi-
Fi (some). In-hotel: pool, spa, concierge, no elevator, laundry service,
public Wi-Fi, airport shuttle* ⊟*AE, D, MC, V* �🍽*BP.*

$$$–$$$$ 🏨**Red Inn.** A rambling red 1915 house that once was host to Franklin
and Eleanor Roosevelt, this small, luxurious inn has been completely
refurbished after several years of neglect. Most of the airy rooms afford
bay views, and all are fitted with big plush beds with high-thread-
count linens, goose-down comforters, and pillow-top mattresses. Other
luxe amenities include radio–CD players, phones with voice mail, and
high-speed Internet. The Cape Light Room contains a decorative fire-
place with an ornate hand-painted fresco, and the secluded Chauffer's
Cottage has a living room with a soaring vaulted ceiling and a sun-
deck with far-reaching water views. The restaurant offers some of the
best bay views in town. **Pros:** Charmed and peaceful West End set-
ting, closer to national seashore than most P'town accommodations,
ultra-posh rooms. **Cons:** Among the highest rates in town, far West End
location is a long walk from most dining and nightlife, not geared to
children. ⊠*15 Commercial St., 02657* 🕾*508/487–7334 or 866/473–
3466* 🖷*508/487–5115* ⊕*www.theredinn.com* 🛏*4 rooms, 2 suites, 2
cottages* 🔧*In-room: refrigerator, VCR, Ethernet. In-hotel: restaurant,
room service, no elevator, parking (no fee), no kids under 18* ⊟*AE,
MC, V* ⍟*CP.*

$$–$$$$ 🏨**Anchor Inn.** Run by the same talented team that operates the West
★ End's Red Inn, this regal, turreted beach house in the heart of Province-
town enjoys a wonderful location just steps from bars, shops, and restaurants as well as unobstructed water views from most rooms (rooms
without water views cost a fraction of the price). White-picket porches
and balconies envelope the inn's dapper shingle exterior. You won't find
frill and excess here—the airy rooms are done in a palette of whites and

Where to Stay in Provincetown

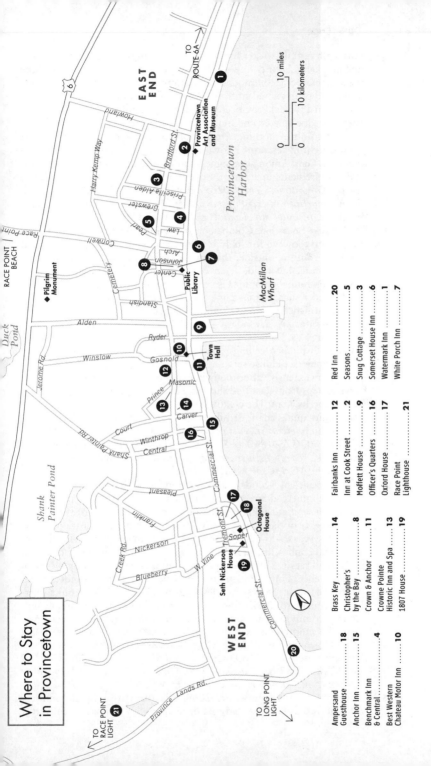

Ampersand Guesthouse 18
Anchor Inn 15
Benchmark Inn & Central 4
Best Western Chateau Motor Inn 10
Brass Key 14
Christopher's by the Bay 8
Crown & Anchor 11
Crowne Pointe Historic Inn and Spa 13
1807 House 19
Fairbanks Inn 12
Inn at Cook Street 2
Moffett House 9
Officer's Quarters 16
Oxford House 17
Race Point Lighthouse 21
Red Inn 20
Seasons 5
Snug Cottage 3
Somerset House Inn 6
Watermark Inn 1
White Porch Inn 7

tans, with tasteful wicker furniture and, in many cases, four-poster beds and fireplaces. Four cottage units have private entrances, and the three most romantic accommodations occupy the turret. With a spacious lobby and professional staff, the Anchor feels more like a small luxury hotel than a typical Provincetown guesthouse, but an air of informality keeps the vibe relaxed and fun. There's a substantial continental-breakfast buffet in the morning. **Pros:** Unobstructed water views from most rooms, right in center of P'town action, rooms have sleek and luxurious style. **Cons:** Among the highest rates in town, significant minimum-stay requirements in summer, busy location. ⊠ *175 Commercial St., west of Downtown Center, 02657* ☎ *508/487–0432 or 800/858–2657* ⊕ *www.anchorinnbeachhouse.com* ⚲ *25 rooms* ⬧ *In-room: refrigerator, VCR. In-hotel: no elevator* ⊟ *MC, V* ⦿ *CP.*

$$–$$$$ ⊞ **Somerset House Inn.** Competent and helpful owners run this cheer-
★ ful property known for its hip, whimsical decor and superb personal service. From the outside, the inn looks like a classic 1830s Provincetown house, but inside it's a cozy den of mod sofas and cool colors. A communal computer is equipped with high-speed wireless, and you'll find reams of magazines throughout the common areas. The sleekly furnished rooms are compact but charming. Some have eclectic themes—safari, Asia, modern—and all have updated amenities, such as flat-screen TVs, DVD players, and L'Occitaine toiletries. The 3rd-floor units, with pitched ceilings, are especially romantic; some have fireplaces. Somerset House serves one of the better breakfasts in town and also has an extensive afternoon wine-and-cheese social. **Pros:** Top-notch service, steps from East End shopping and dining, lots of on-site amenities and perks. **Cons:** The creative room themes may not suit every taste, some units quite small, 3rd-floor rooms require some stair-climbing. ⊠ *378 Commercial St., east of Downtown Center, 02657* ☎ *508/487– 0383 or 800/575–1850* ⊟ *508/487–4237* ⊕ *www.somersethouseinn. com* ⚲ *12 rooms* ⬧ *In-room: refrigerator, DVD, Wi-Fi. In-hotel: no elevator* ⊟ *AE, MC, V* ⦿ *BP.*

$$–$$$$ ⊞ **Watermark Inn.** A modern all-suites inn facing the bay at the very east end of Commercial Street, the Watermark has enormous accommodations with separate living–dining rooms, making it a favorite for longer stays (weekly or daily rates are available in summer; rates are daily the rest of the year). Although these airy suites with tall windows feel more like rental condos than hotel rooms, they do come with fine linens and daily maid service. It's a very private setup, and guests enjoy plenty of independence. Four suites on the top level have private sundecks and panoramic water views; two less-expensive ground-floor units overlook a courtyard. **Pros:** Close to East End shopping and dining, spacious accommodations are nice for longer stays, great water views. **Cons:** Feels more like a condo than a hotel, far East End location is a 10- to 15-minute walk from many businesses, least expensive rooms have no water view. ⊠ *603 Commercial St., 02657* ☎ *508/487–0165* ⊟ *508/487–2383* ⊕ *www.watermark-inn.com* ⚲ *10 suites* ⬧ *In-room: kitchen (some). In-hotel: no elevator* ⊟ *MC, V.*

$$$ ⊞ **Inn at Cook Street.** In winter 2006, this attractive East End inn just
★ off Bradford Street was sold to a developer who planned to convert it

into condos, but Connecticut transplants Lisa Feistel and Doreen Birdsell quickly stepped in, snapped it up, and turned it back into a terrific place to stay. The enthusiastic innkeepers have done an admirable job decorating the 1836 Greek revival where author Michael Cunningham penned *Home at the End of the World* one winter. The sophisticated rooms have high-thread-count linens, flat-screen TVs, and well-placed reading lights; two have decks, three have fireplaces, and three have private entrances. Continental breakfast includes organic cappuccino, herbal teas, fruit and breads, and a hot entrée such as pancakes or omelets. Guests can relax in a hammock out back amid the fragrant gardens or walk a block to the galleries along Commercial Street. **Pros:** Top-notch staff and service, steps from East End shopping and dining, elegant yet unfussy furnishings. **Cons:** Rooms close to Bradford Street can get a bit of noise, a bit of a walk from West End businesses, no water views. ⊠*7 Cook St., 02657* 🕾*508/487–3894 or 888/266–5655* ⊕*www.innatcookstreet.com* ⇨*5 rooms, 2 suites, 2 cottages* ⚷*In-room: kitchen (some), refrigerator, DVD, Wi-Fi. In-hotel: no elevator, no kids under 16* ▤*MC, V* ℟*BP.*

$$–$$$ 🏨**1807 House.** This weathered, craggy old house that dates to 1783
★ (it was moved to this spot in 1807, hence the name) doesn't look like much more than a cottage from the quiet stretch of Commercial Street it faces, but behind the facade you'll find a beautifully kept inn with cozy, low-ceilinged rooms. Several tastefully furnished and very private apartments and studios are in back. The dramatic Red Room, overlooking Provincetown Bay, contains a hulking four-poster mahogany bed, and the Artist's Studio, perhaps the most romantic unit, occupies a 2nd-floor perch with a balcony affording water views; French doors lead into this light-flooded room with a high cathedral ceiling. This is one of the West End's little treasures—and a good value to boot. **Pros:** Charming West End location, feels secluded and private, elegantly furnished. **Cons:** Long walk from East End businesses, sleepy vibe not ideal for social butterflies, kitchens only in some units. ⊠*54 Commercial St., West End, 02657* 🕾*508/487–2173 or 888/522–1807* ⊕*www.1807house.com* ⇨*3 rooms, 1 suite, 4 apartments* ⚷*In-room: kitchen (some), refrigerator, VCR, Wi-Fi. In-hotel: no elevator* ▤*AE, MC, V* ℟*CP.*

$$–$$$ 🏨**Officer's Quarters.** Built in 1887 for a sea captain, this stately, white, mansard-roof Victorian is only a short walk from the center of town and is across the street from Provincetown Bay. The owners have done a wonderful job adding their own touches while maintaining this B&B's outstanding reputation. Room 3, done in vibrant reds, has a four-poster bed, a gas fireplace, and private access to the garden. Most rooms have water views; some have private decks. **Pros:** Handsome 1880s sea captain's home, some pets allowed, great central location. **Cons:** Right in center of action, rather intimate with just 6 rooms so not ideal if you're seeking anonymity, significant minimum-stay requirements in summer. ⊠*164 Commercial St., 02657* 🕾*508/487–1850 or 800/400–2278* ⊕*www.officersquarters.org* ⇨*6 rooms* ⚷*In-room: refrigerator, DVD (some), Wi-Fi. In-hotel: no elevator, some pets allowed (fee)* ▤*AE, D, MC, V* ℟*CP.*

5

$$–$$$ ⚑ **Oxford House.** Run by the former owners of the outstanding Beacon-
★ light Guesthouse, the Oxford sits in the heart of the West End along
a quiet lane and is decorated in the spirit of a British country house.
Rooms come with linen robes, CD player/radios, phones with voice
mail, and beds that have 480-thread-count linens and fluffy duvets—
rooms on the ground floor have wood-burning fireplaces. You can save
a bundle by booking either the Merton or Hertford rooms, which share
a bath; the Worcester Room has its own private entrance. The evening
wine hour is a great time to mingle with fellow guests. All phone calls
within the continental United States are free. **Pros:** Highly professional
and friendly service, peaceful and charming West End setting, beautifully furnished. **Cons:** Some rooms share a bath, it's a relatively long
walk to East End businesses, quiet locale may not work if you want
to be in center of action. ⊠ *8 Cottage St., 02657* ☎ *508/487–9103
or 888/456–9103* ⊕ *www.oxfordguesthouse.com* ⇔ *5 rooms, 3 with
bath, 1 suite* ⬧ *In-room: refrigerator, VCR, Wi-Fi. In-hotel: no elevator*
⊟ *AE, D, MC, V* ⦿ *CP.*

$$–$$$ ⚑ **White Porch Inn.** Innkeepers Tom Bantle and Tom Shirk took what
★ had been a decrepit, almost dodgy, old-school Provincetown guest
house and have transformed it into a sterling, light-filled B&B. Seven
of the nine rooms, all of which are named for Cape Cod lighthouses,
have gas fireplaces, and three have Jacuzzi tubs. White, tan, and chocolate color schemes, bead-board walls, and pedestal sinks in the bathrooms (some of these have radiant-floor heating) impart a crisp, clean
modern-beach-house flare; large closets and drawers built in to the
bottoms of custom-made beds are welcome amenities. Opt for one of
the carriage-house rooms for more seclusion—you can always mingle
with your fellow guests and gracious hosts on the inn's eponymous
white porch while enjoying selections from the bounteous breakfast
buffet. **Pros:** Brand-new and immaculate, steps from East End shopping
and dining, enthusiastic and friendly staff. **Cons:** Most rooms without
much of a water view, somewhat long walk to West End shopping and
businesses, limited grounds. ⊠ *7 Johnson St., 02657* ☎ *508/364–2549
or 866/922–0333* ⊕ *www.whiteporchinn.com* ⇔ *9 rooms* ⬧ *In-room:
refrigerator (some), DVD, Wi-Fi. In-hotel: no elevator, airport shuttle*
⊟ *MC, V* ⦿ *CP.*

$–$$$ ⚑ **Best Western Chateau Motor Inn.** This inn may be part of a chain, but
the personal attention of owners Charlotte and Bill Gordon, whose
family has run the place for decades, shows in the landscaped grounds
and in the well-maintained modern rooms with wall-to-wall carpeting
and tile baths. Atop a hill with expansive views of marsh, dunes, and
sea, the motel is a longish walk to the center of town but relatively close
to beaches. There's talk of the hotel eventually closing, but it's expected
to remain open through at least 2008. **Pros:** A big enough place to suit
those seeking anonymity, closer to national seashore beaches than most
P'town lodgings, lovely grounds. **Cons:** Has that cookie-cutter chain
feel, a bit of a walk from most dining and shops. ⊠ *105 Bradford St.
Ext., Box 558, 02657* ☎ *508/487–1286 or 800/528–1234* ☎ *508/487–
3557* ⊕ *www.bestwestern.com/chateaumotorinn* ⇔ *54 rooms* ⬧ *In-*

room: refrigerator. In-hotel: pool, public Internet, no elevator ⊟*AE,*
D, DC, MC, V ☉*Closed Nov.–Apr.* ⑩*CP.*

$–$$$ 🏨**Fairbanks Inn.** This meticulously restored colonial inn a block from
Commercial Street includes the 1776 main house and auxiliary build-
ings. Guest rooms have four-poster or canopy beds, Oriental rugs on
wide-board floors, and antique furnishings; some have fireplaces or
kitchens. Many original touches remain here, from the 18th-century
wallpaper to artifacts from the inn's first residents. The baths are on
the small side, but they help preserve the colonial integrity of the home.
The garden and the wicker-filled sunporch are good places for after-
noon cocktails or breakfast—which you can also enjoy inside before
the warm glow of the fireplace on cold days. **Pros:** Central location steps
from shops and restaurants, nice variety of room sizes and configura-
tions, rich with historic character. **Cons:** Rooms close to Bradford Street
can get a bit of noise. ⊠*90 Bradford St., 02657* ☎*508/487–0386
or 800/324–7265* ⊕*www.fairbanksinn.com* ⏎*13 rooms, 1 efficiency*
⟐*In-room: kitchen (some), refrigerators (some), VCR, Wi-Fi. In-hotel:
parking (no fee), no elevator* ⊟*AE, MC, V* ⑩*CP.*

$$ 🏨**Race Point Lighthouse.** One of the most unusual lodging opportunities
on the Cape, the restored 1840 keeper's house at the stunning Race
Point Lighthouse has three sparsley furnished guest rooms with lace
curtains, braided rugs, and simple wooden chests and tables—pillows
and blankets are provided, but you'll need to bring your own linens,
towels, drinking water, and food. The house does have solar-powered
electricity and central heating. You don't stay here because it's cushy,
but rather to enjoy the seclusion and romance of staying at an authentic, working lighthouse with a pristine beach just outside the window.
Opportunities to see whales, dolphins, and migratory birds abound,
both from the grounds and from the house itself. A gift shop on premises sells shrimshaw, sweatshirts, ballcaps, and other keepsakes. The
maximum stay is four nights. If you're not able to spend the night,
keep in mind that the lighthouse itself is open for tours a few Saturdays
per month from mid-May through mid-October. **Pros:** One of the most
distinctive lodging experiences on Cape Cod, truly secluded setting,
might just see a whale or dolphin swimming outside your window.
Cons: Very limited amenities, books up fast, extremely isolated. ⊠*Off
Race Point Rd. at Cape Cod National Seashore* ⏏*Box 570, North
Truro 02652* ☎*508/487–9930* ⊕*www.racepointlighthouse.net* ⏎*3
rooms* ⟐*In-room: no phone, refrigerator, no TV* ⊟*No credit cards*
☉*Closed mid-Oct.–Apr.*

$$ 🏨**Seasons.** This petite 1860s cream-color Victorian with a Dutch-style
gambrel roof is an outstanding value. Owners John Mirthes and Rick
Reynolds run a relaxed ship, freely offering guests advice on local res-
taurants and lending out chairs, towels, and cooler bags for the beach.
Rick is a professional chef and prepares exceptional breakfasts replete
with filling hot entrées, such as pumpkin pancakes with maple-poached
pears, which can render lunch unnecessary. Rooms contain mostly clas-
sic Victorian pieces, wallpapers, and fabrics—it's a little old-fashioned,
especially compared with all the flashier and more social guesthouses
in town, and that's a big reason many guests here come back year

after year. Save a hello for sweet old Buddy, the house cat. **Pros:** Excellent value, friendly and first-rate staff, easy walk to numerous shops and restaurants. **Cons:** Rooms close to Bradford Street can get a bit of noise, a tad frilly. ⊠*160 Bradford St., east of Downtown Center, 02657* ☎*508/487–2283 or 800/563–0113* ⊕*www.provincetownseasons.com* ⤶*5 rooms* ⚲*In-room: no phone, refrigerator (some), DVD, Wi-Fi. In-hotel: no elevator* ☰*MC, V* ⍾*BP.*

$$ ⊡**Snug Cottage.** Noted for its extensive floral gardens and enviable perch atop one of the larger bluffs in town, this convivial Arts and Crafts–style inn dates to 1825 and is decked in smashing English country antiques and fabrics. The oversize accommodations have distinctly British names (Victoria Suite, Royal Scott); most are full suites with sitting areas, and many have wood-burning fireplaces and private outdoor entrances. The Churchill Suite has 10 big windows overlooking the flowers and bushes outside, and the York Suite has a partial view of Cape Cod Bay. All rooms have phones with voice mail and high-speed Internet, plus clock radios with CD players. Nightly turndown service and plush robes in each room lend a touch of elegance. **Pros:** Steps from East End dining and shopping, stunning grounds and gardens, most units are extremely spacious. **Cons:** Rooms close to Bradford Street can get a bit of noise, a bit of a walk from West End businesses, the top suites don't come cheaply. ⊠*178 Bradford St., east of Downtown Center, 02657* ☎*508/487–1616 or 800/432–2334* 🖷*508/487–5123* ⊕*www.snugcottage.com* ⤶*3 rooms, 5 suites* ⚲*In-room: kitchen (some), DVD, Wi-Fi. In-hotel: no elevator, no-smoking rooms* ☰*AE, D, MC, V* ⍾*BP.*

$–$$ ⊡**Ampersand Guesthouse.** Helpful, low-key owners Robert Vetrick and Ken Janson (the latter an architect) run this peaceful West End inn that feels far from the din of Commercial Street but is actually just a short walk away. This natty mid-19th-century Greek-revival guesthouse contains nine eclectically furnished rooms, many with high-pitched ceilings, fireplaces, and tall windows—furnishings tend toward simple, understated, and elegant. For more seclusion, book the studio apartment in the neighboring carriage house, which also has a kitchen. Guests relax in the leafy yard with pretty gardens, or out on the sundeck on the 2nd floor, with views of the harbor a couple of blocks away. Robert bakes fresh muffins each morning as part of the continental breakfast, which is served before a fireplace on cooler days. **Pros:** Peaceful and charming West End location, stylish and well-chosen decor, great value. **Cons:** Have to walk a bit to reach East End businesses, some rooms smallish. ⊠*6 Cottage St., West End, 02657* ☎*508/487–0959* ⊕*www.ampersandguesthouse.com* ⤶*9 rooms, 1 apartment* ⚲*In-room: kitchen (some), refrigerator (some), VCR. In-hotel: no elevator* ☰*AE, MC, V* ⍾*CP.*

$–$$
Fodor'sChoice
★
⊡**Christopher's by the Bay.** The rooms in this elegant but reasonably priced art-inspired inn are named after the greats—Rembrandt, Picasso, Monet, Van Gogh—and are warmly appointed with brass beds and rich fabrics. Several of these tall-windowed rooms have partial views of the bay, and all receive plenty of light. The building is a graceful old Victorian surrounded by carefully maintained gardens

and brick patios. Rooms on the upper floors are compact and share bathrooms, but they're also very low priced. Set back from the bustle, it's just a quick walk from the center of town. Helpful owners Jim Rizzo and Dave McGlothlin often throw guest barbecues on Sunday. **Pros:** Excellent value, steps from East End shopping and dining, service is extremely friendly and professional. **Cons:** Least expensive rooms share a bath, some units are very cozy, 3rd-floor rooms are a climb. ⊠ *8 Johnson St., east of Downtown Center, 02657* ☎☎ *508/487–9263* ☎ *877/487–9263* ⊕ *www.christophersbythebay.com* ⌁ *10 rooms, 5 with bath* ⌂ *In-room: Wi-Fi, refrigerator, VCR. In-hotel: no elevator, some pets allowed (fee)* ⊟ *AE, MC, V* ⏧ *BP.*

¢–$ 🛏 **Moffett House.** This simple, affordable, handsomely refurbished Cape-style B&B lies down a charming, narrow alley that runs between Commercial and Bradford streets. There are 10 cheerfully furnished rooms, most of them with shared baths (some of these have unbelievably low rates), and all have top-notch linens and country quilts, and 20-inch flat-screen TVs; some rooms have pitched ceilings with rustic beams. Guests are free to use the common kitchen, a computer in the lobby, and may also borrow the inn's Trek mountain bikes at no charge. It's a friendly option that's ideal for budget travelers. **Pros:** Great value, right in center of business district yet set back from street, free mountain bikes. **Cons:** Most rooms have shared bath, minimal grounds, no optimal views. ⊠ *296A Commercial St., 02657* ☎ *508/487–6615 or 800/990–8865* ⊕ *www.moffetthouse.com* ⌁ *10 rooms, 3 with bath* ⌂ *In-room: refrigerator, DVD, Wi-Fi. In-hotel: bicycles, no elevator* ⊟ *MC, V* ⏧ *CP.*

NIGHTLIFE & THE ARTS

THE ARTS **Provincetown Inn** (⊠ *1 Commercial St., West End* ☎ *508/487–9500* ⊕ *www.ptownfringe.org*) hosts several unusual theater productions in summer; look for shows performed by C.A.P.E. Inc. Theatre and those offered during the Provincetown Fringe Festival in August. The inn also hosts nights of live music.

The annual **Provincetown International Film Festival** (☎ *508/487–3456* ⊕ *www.ptownfilmfest.com*) has become so popular that most of the screenings sell out. Aside from a full schedule of independent films, there are guest appearances by such notables as director John Waters, Lily Tomlin, and Christine Vachon. The festival hits town in mid-June.

Established in 2005 as a merger of the Provincetown Repertory Theatre and the Provincetown Theatre Company, the **New Provincetown Players** (⊠ *Provincetown Theatre, 238 Bradford St., Downtown Center* ☎ *508/487–9793 or 800/791–7487* ⊕ *www.newprovincetownplayers. org*) hosts a wide variety of performances throughout the year, especially during the summer high season, including classic and modern drama as well as works by local authors.

Whalers' Wharf (⊠ *237–241 Commercial St., Downtown Center*) resembles an old European marketplace, with a brick pathway that leads straight to the beach and a rotunda theater alive with street performers and entertainment. The 1st floor of the building holds shops; upstairs are artists' stu-

Provincetown: America's Gay Summer Playground

America's original gay resort, Provincetown developed as an artists' colony at the turn of the 20th century. In 1899, a young artist and entrepreneur named Charles Hawthorne founded the Cape Cod School of Art. Within 20 years, a half dozen art schools opened, the Provincetown Art Association staged its first exhibitions, and the Provincetown Players, a small band of modernist theater folk, began to produce plays on a small wharf in the town's East End.

After a year in Provincetown the players moved to New York City's Greenwich Village, where gay culture was already thriving. This kinship helped spur Provincetown's early flourishing as a gay community. Tourism became a significant revenue source, and local homes began letting rooms to the hundreds of writers, painters, and other creative spirits drawn to the town's thriving arts community.

Over the next few decades, many innovative writers and artists spent time in Provincetown, including several openly gay luminaries such as Truman Capote and Tennessee Williams. The town became identified increasingly for its willingness to flout convention, and it was by the 1960s a haven for anyone whose artistic leaning, political platform, or sexual persuasion was subject to persecution elsewhere in America. This hotbed of counterculture naturally nurtured one of the country's most significant gay communities.

Today Provincetown is as appealing to artists as it is to gay and lesbian—as well as straight—tourists. The awareness brought by the AIDS crisis and, most recently, Massachusetts's becoming the first state to legalize same-sex marriage has turned the town into the most visibly gay vacation community in America.

—by Andrew Collins

dios and a museum dedicated to the town's history. At the **Provincetown Art House Theatre** (☎*508/487–9222* ⊕*www.ptownarthouse.com*) moviegoers can view the latest in independent films, classics, and movies you won't find in the usual megaplex. The building, which was completely renovated just prior to the 2007 season, comprises two stages, improved seating, a terrific restaurant (Frappo 66), and a wall with changing art exhibits. Presentations by the local Theatre Go Round (www.theatregoround.com), including campy cabaret shows and generally humorous plays, are held here also.

NIGHTLIFE   **Atlantic House** (✉*4 Masonic Pl., Downtown Center* ☎*508/487–3821*),
★ the grandfather of the gay nightlife scene, is the only gay bar open year-round. It has several lounge areas and an outdoor patio.

Boatslip Beach Club (✉*161 Commercial St., Downtown Center, toward West End* ☎*508/487–1669*) holds a gay and lesbian late-afternoon tea dance daily in summer and on weekends in spring and fall on the outdoor pool deck. The club has indoor and outdoor dance floors. There's ballroom dancing here, in addition to two-stepping Thursday through Sunday nights. There was talk of converting the Boatslip into condos in 2006, but as of this writing an agreement was tentatively in place to keep it operating as is.

The **Cape Cod National Seashore** schedules summer evening programs, such as slide shows, sunset beach walks, concerts (local groups, military bands), and sing-alongs, at its **Province Lands Visitor Center** (✉*Race Point Rd., east of U.S. 6* ☎*508/487–1256*); sunset campfire talks are also held on the beaches in Provincetown.

Club Euro (✉*258 Commercial St., Downtown Center* ☎*508/487–2505*) has weekend concerts by big names in world music, including African music, Jamaican reggae, Chicago blues, and Louisiana zydeco. The venue, a handsomely restored 1843 Congregational church that later housed a movie theater, is an eerie ocean dreamscape with sea-green walls with a half-submerged, three-dimensional mermaid spouting fish, and a black ceiling high above. Pool tables and a late-night menu are available.

★ The gay-oriented **Crown & Anchor Complex** (✉*247 Commercial St., Downtown Center* ☎*508/487–1430*) has plenty of action—perhaps the most in town—with Wave video bar, the Vault leather bar, several stages, and a giant disco called Paramount. Seven nightly shows in summer range from cabaret to comedy.

Governor Bradford Restaurant (✉*312 Commercial St., Downtown Center* ☎*508/487–9618*) is perhaps better known as a sometimes-rowdy pool and dance hall. In the afternoon you can play chess or backgammon at the tables by the window. After 8 PM, the place revs up with live music or a DJ spinning everything from hip-hop to disco.

Pied Bar (✉*193A Commercial St., Downtown Center, toward West End* ☎*508/487–1527*) draws hordes of gay men to its post–tea dance gathering at 6:30 every evening in July and August and weekends during the shoulder seasons. Later in the evening, the crowd is mostly (though not exclusively) women. The club has a deck overlooking the harbor, a small dance floor with a good sound system, and two bars.

The **Post Office Cabaret** (✉*303 Commercial St., Downtown Center* ☎*508/487–3892*) has long been a dishy and lively spot for piano cabaret. The upstairs lounge draws some of the top talents in the region, and downstairs an excellent restaurant serves dependable American bistro fare until 1 AM most nights.

The **Squealing Pig** (✉*335 Commercial St., Downtown Center, toward East End* ☎*508/487–5804*) has DJs presenting rock, hip-hop, reggae, and house; they also show late-night movies on Monday. There's never a cover charge, and the kitchen turns out super-tasty bar chow, from burgers to fish-and-chips.

Vixen (✉*336 Commercial St., Downtown Center* ☎*508/487–6424*), a lively women's club, gets packed with dancers. On most nights, before the dance crowd sets in, there are both national and local women entertainers. Look for live music and comedy. There are also a couple of pool tables in the front room.

SPORTS & THE OUTDOORS

BEACHES The entire stretch of Commercial Street is backed by the waters of Provincetown Harbor, and most hotels have private beaches. Farther into town there are plenty of places to settle on the sand and take a refreshing dip—just be mindful of the busy boat traffic.

Herring Cove Beach is relatively calm and warm for a National Seashore beach, but it's not as pretty as some because its parking lot isn't hidden behind dunes. However, the lot to the right of the bathhouse is a great place to watch the sunset. There's a hot-dog stand, as well as showers and restrooms. Lifeguards are on duty in season. From late June through early September, parking costs $15 per day, or $45 for a yearly pass to all National Seashore beaches.

For a day of fairly private beachcombing and great views, you can walk across the stone jetty at low tide to **Long Point,** a sand spit south of town with two lighthouses and two Civil War bunkers—called Fort Useless and Fort Ridiculous because they were hardly needed. It's a 2-mi walk across soft sand—beware of poison ivy and deer ticks if you stray from the path—or hire a boat at **Flyer's** (☎ *508/487–0898 or 800/750–0898 ⊕ www.flyersboats.com*) to drop you off and pick you up; the cost is $8 one-way, $12 round-trip.

Fodor'sChoice **Race Point Beach** (⊠ *Race Point Rd., east of U.S. 6*), one of the Cape
★ Cod National Seashore beaches in Provincetown, has a wide swath of sand stretching far off into the distance around the point and Coast Guard station. Behind the beach is pure duneland, and bike trails lead off the parking lot. Because of its position on a point facing north, the beach gets sun all day long (east coast beaches get fullest sun early in the day). Parking is available, there are showers and restrooms, and lifeguards are stationed in season. From late June through early September, parking costs $15 per day, or $45 for a yearly pass good at all National Seashore beaches.

BICYCLING **Arnold's** (⊠ *329 Commercial St., Downtown Center* ☎ *508/487–0844*) rents all types of bikes, including children's.

The **Beech Forest bike trail** (⊠ *Off Race Point Rd., east of U.S. 6*) in the National Seashore offers an especially nice ride through a shady forest to Bennett Pond.

Gale Force Bikes (⊠ *144 Bradford St. Ext.* ☎ *508/487–4849 ⊕ www. galeforcebikes.com*) stocks a wide variety of bikes for sale and for rent; it's also a good source for parts and repairs.

The **Province Lands Trail** is a 5¼-mi loop off the Beech Forest parking lot on Race Point Road, with spurs to Herring Cove and Race Point beaches and to Bennett Pond. The paths wind up and down hills amid dunes, marshes, woods, and ponds, affording spectacular views. More than 7 mi of bike trails lace through the dunes, cranberry bogs, and scrub pine of the National Seashore, with many access points, including Herring Cove and Race Point.

P'town Bikes (⊠*42 Bradford St., east of Downtown Center* ☎*508/487–8735* ⊕*www.ptownbikes.com*) has Trek and Mongoose mountain bikes at good rates, and you can reserve online. The shop also provides free locks and maps.

BOATING & KAYAKING

Bay Lady II **Excursion Schooner** (⊠*MacMillan Wharf, Downtown Center* ☎*508/487–9308* ⊕*www.sailcapecod.com*), a beautiful 73-foot sailing vessel, heads out for two-hour cruises three times daily. You're welcome to bring your own spirits and snacks for this scenic and peaceful sail.

Flyer's Boat Rental (⊠*131A Commercial St., West End* ☎*508/487–0898 or 800/750–0898* ⊕*www.flyersboats.com*) has kayaks, surfbikes, Sunfish, Hobies, Force 5s, Lightnings, powerboats, and rowboats. Flyer's will also shuttle you to Long Point.

Venture Athletics Kayak Shop (⊠*237 Commercial St., Unit 13A, Downtown Center* ☎*508/487–9442* ⊕*www.ventureathletics.com*) rents kayaks and equipment and offers guided kayak tours. The company also operates the nearby **Venture Athletics Outdoor Shop** (⊠*306 Commercial St., Downtown Center* ☎*508/487–2395*), which sells all kinds of sporting gear and clothing.

FISHING

You can go after fluke, bluefish, and striped bass on a walk-on basis from spring through fall with **Cee Jay Fishing Parties** (⊠*MacMillan Wharf, Downtown Center* ☎*508/487–4330*).

PARASAILING

Provincetown Parasail (⊠*MacMillan Wharf* ☎*508/487–UFLY* ⊕*www.provincetownparasailing.com*) offer high-flying parasailing adventures, which take you some 300 feet above town and Cape Cod Bay.

SPAS

Jonathan Williams Salon & Spa (⊠*139A Bradford St.* ☎*508/487–0422* ⊕*www.jonathanwilliamssalonandspa.com*) offers a wide range of spa treatments, including skin treatments, hair care, pedicures, and aromatherapy. At the posh Crowne Pointe Historic Inn, the intimate and fabulous **Shui Spa** (⊠*82 Bradford St.* ☎*508/487–6767* ⊕*www.crownepointe.com*) pampers guests with everything from hot stone massage to sweet-sugar body scrubs to grape wine-peel facials.

TENNIS

Herring Cove Tennis Club (⊠*21 Bradford St. Ext., east of Downtown Center* ☎*508/487–9512* ⊕*www.herringcovetennis.com*) has five clay courts and offers lessons.

Provincetown Tennis Club (⊠*288 Bradford St. Ext., east of Downtown Center* ☎*508/487–9574*) has five clay and two hard courts open to nonmembers; you can also take lessons with the resident tennis pro.

TOURS
Fodor's Choice
★

Art's Dune Tours (⊠*Commercial and Standish Sts., Downtown Center* ☎*508/487–1950* ⊕*www.artsdunetours.com*) has been taking eager passengers into the dunes of Province Lands since 1946. Bumpy but controlled rides transport you through sometimes sandy vistas peppered with beach grass and along shoreline patrolled by seagulls and sandpipers. Tours are filled with lively tales, including the fascinating history of the exclusive (and reclusive) dune shacks (18 still stand today). These one-hour tours are offered several times daily; especially intriguing are the sunset and moonlight tours. Rides coupled with clambakes or barbecues are popular; call for availability and pricing.

Harbor Tours on the *Viking Princess* (⊠*MacMillan Wharf, Downtown Center* ☎*508/487–7323* ⊕*www.capecodecotours.com*) are given in mornings throughout the summer. These narrated excursions tell stories of shipwrecks and pirate raids and pass by Civil War forts and the Long Point Lighthouse. There are also sunset cruises, "critter cruises" with onboard naturalists, and kids-oriented "pirate fun cruises."

★ **P-town Pedicab** (☎*508/487–0660* ⊕*www.ptownpedicabs.com*) provides highly enjoyable town tours in vehicles you won't find in too many places around the country. A guide pedals you and up to two more guests around town in an open-air three-wheel chariotlike cab, pointing out local sights and offering an unusual perspective on this already unusual town. The company also offers customized gallery-hopping, ghost–graveyard, shopping, and history tours. It's a memorable way to see the area.

Provincetown Trolley (☎*508/487–9483* ⊕*www.provincetowntrolley. com*) offers 40-minute narrated tours of Provincetown, which leave from outside town hall every 30 minutes daily 10 to 4, and every hour daily 5 to 7 PM. The ride takes you through downtown, out to the Provincetown Monument, and by the beaches; the fare is $8.

WHALE-
WATCHING
One of the joys of Cape Cod is spotting whales swimming in and around the feeding grounds at Stellwagen Bank, about 6 mi off the tip of Provincetown. On a sunny day the boat ride out into open ocean is part of the pleasure, but the thrill, of course, is in seeing these great creatures. You might spot minke whales; humpbacks (who put on the best show when they breach); finbacks; or perhaps the most endangered great whale species, the right whale. Dolphins are a welcome sight as well; they play in the boat's bow waves. Many people also come aboard for birding, especially during spring and fall migration. You can see gannets, shearwaters, and storm petrels, among many others. Several boats take you out to sea (and bring you back) with morning, afternoon, or sunset trips lasting from three to four hours. All boats have food service, but remember to take sunscreen and a sweater or jacket—the breeze makes it chilly. Some boats stock seasickness pills, but if you're susceptible, come prepared.

The municipal parking area by the harbor in Provincetown fills up by noon in summer; consider taking a morning boat to avoid crowds and the hottest sun. Although April may be cold, it's one of the better months for spotting whales, who at that time have just migrated north after mating and are very hungry. Good food is, after all, what brings the whales to this part of the Atlantic.

Dolphin Fleet tours are accompanied by scientists from the Center for Coastal Studies in Provincetown, who provide commentary while collecting data on the whale population they've been monitoring for years. They know many of the whales by name and will tell you about their habits and histories. Reservations are required. ⊠*Ticket office: Cham-*

CLOSE UP

Dune Shacks

Provincetown's rich artistic legacy continues to manifest itself in the dozens of galleries along Commercial Street and through countless resident writers and painters. But out along the seashore, along a 3-mi stretch of sand extending from about Race Point to High Head (in Truro), you can see a more unusual remnant of the town's artistic past—the dune shacks.

These small, austere structures were built by the Life Saving Service in the 19th century to house seamen. Sometime around the 1920s, long after the dune shacks ceased housing life-saving personnel, many of the community's creative or eccentric spirits began using them as retreats and hideaways. Probably the most famous of these was playwright Eugene O'Neill, who purchased one and spent many summers there with his wife, Agnes Boulton. O'Neill penned *Anna Christie* (1920) and *The Hairy Ape* (1921) while living in his shack, and in doing so gave the whole collection of dune shacks something of an arty cachet.

Other Provincetown artists soon followed O'Neill, including the self-proclaimed "poet of the dunes," Harry Kemp, who wrote many a verse about the seashore's stark, desolate splendor. Author Hazel Hawthorne-Werner wrote *The Salt House,* a memoir tracing her time amid the dunes, in 1929. It's said that this book helped get the shacks, along with the entire dunes district, onto the National Register of Historic Places, helping to preserve them for years to come. In later years, Jack Kerouac, e.e. cummings, Norman Mailer, and Jackson Pollack also lived in these primitive structures.

The dune shacks haven't been modernized much—none has electricity, running water, or toilets. You stay in them for a chance to be with nature and perhaps commune with the spirits of artists who have gone before you. The dune shacks are now all set along the part of the Cape Cod National Seashore that is known as the Province Lands. The park owns most of the Provincetown dune shacks, though a few are managed by nonprofit groups aimed at preserving them and their legacy. Some of these organizations, such as the Peaked Hills Bars Trust and the Provincetown Community Compact, allow visitors to stay in the dune shacks through a variety of arrangements. Both groups run an artist-in-residence program—artists can apply for short stays in some of the shacks during the summer season. Only a handful of applicants are admitted each year.

If you're not an artist, you can enter a lottery for the opportunity to lease one of the shacks for a week in spring or fall. If you're interested in applying to spend time in a dune shack or you'd like to join one of the nonprofit organizations that sponsors them, contact **Dune Shacks** (✉ *Box 1705, Provincetown 02657* ☎ *508/487—3635*).

If you're simply interested in exploring the terrain and seeing the shacks, you can either book a tour with **Art's Dune Tours** (☎ *508/487–1950 or 800/894–1951* ⊕ *www.artsdunetours. com*), or park behind the Cape Inn, on Snail Road just off U.S. 6, where a 3-mi trail winds through the dunes and past many of the dune shacks.

—*by Andrew Collins*

5

ber of Commerce building at MacMillan Wharf, Downtown Center ☎508/240–3636 or 800/826–9300 ⊕*www.whalewatch.com* ✉*$33* ⊙*Tours mid-Apr.–Oct.*

The *Portuguese Princess sails with a naturalist on board to narrate. The snack bar sells Portuguese specialties. Tickets* ✉*70 Shank Painter Rd., ticket office, east of Downtown Center* ✉*Whale Watchers General Store, 309 Commercial St., Downtown Center* ☎*508/487–2651* or 800/442–3188 ⊕*www.princesswhalewatch.com* ✉*$33* ⊙*Tours mid-May–Oct.*

SHOPPING

ART GALLERIES   **Albert Merola Gallery** (✉*424 Commercial St., Downtown Center,*
★   *toward East End* ☎*508/487–4424* ⊕*www.albertmerolagallery.com*) focuses on 20th-century and contemporary master prints and Picasso ceramics. The gallery showcases artists from in and around Provincetown, Boston, and New York, including James Balla, Richard Baker, and iconic gay filmmaker and arbiter of bad taste, John Waters.

Berta Walker Gallery (✉*208 Bradford St., east of Downtown Center, toward East End* ☎*508/487–6411* ⊕*www.bertawalker.com*) specializes in Provincetown-affiliated artists, including Selina Trieff and Nancy Whorf, and such Provincetown legends as Ross Moffett, Charles Hawthorne, Hans Hofmann, and Karl Knaths.

Charles-Baltivik Gallery (✉*432 Commercial St., east of Downtown Center, toward East End* ☎*508/487–3611* ⊕*www.cbgallery.net*) features several leading contemporary artists and has a small sculpture garden.

The **DNA Gallery** (✉*288 Bradford St., east of Downtown Center, toward East End* ☎*508/487–7700* ⊕*www.dnagallery.com*) represents artists working in various media, including many emerging talents.

Ernden Fine Art Gallery (✉*397 Commercial St., Downtown Center, toward East End* ☎*508/487–6700* ⊕*www.erndengallery.com*) is one of the more recent additions to the emerging local art scene, showing works by an impressive range of both newer and established painters and photographers.

★   **Gallery Voyeur** (✉*444 Commercial St., east of Downtown Center, toward East End* ☎*508/487–3678* ⊕*www.voy-art.com*) shows artist-owner Johniene Papandreas' provocative, larger-than-life portraits, which are inspired by classical and Romantic artists of the past.

Hilda Neily Art Gallery (✉*432 Commercial St., Downtown Center, toward East End* ☎*508/487–6300* ⊕*www.hildaneilygallery.com*) is named for its featured artist, who was once a student of impressionist painter Henry Hensche.

Fodor'sChoice   **Julie Heller Gallery** (✉*2 Gosnold St., Downtown Center* ☎*508/487–*
★   *2169* ⊕*www.juliehellergallery.com*) has contemporary artists as well as some Provincetown icons. The gallery has works from the Sol Wilson and Milton Avery estates, as well as from such greats as Robert Motherwell, Agnes Weinrich, and Blanche Lazzell.

Rice/Polak Gallery (✉430 Commercial St., Downtown Center, toward East End ☎508/487–1052 ⊕www.ricepolakgallery.com) stocks a remarkably comprehensive and eclectic variety of contemporary works, from paintings and pastels to photography and sculpture.

★ The **Schoolhouse Galleries** (✉494 Commercial St., Downtown Center, toward East End ☎508/487–4800 ⊕www.theschoolhousegalleries. com), in an 1844 former school, shows the works of more than 25 local and national artists and photographers.

Simie Maryles Gallery (✉435 Commercial St., Downtown Center, toward East End ☎508/487–7878 ⊕www.simiemaryles.com) represents about 15 contemporary artists, most of whom work in traditional styles. Oil paintings, glasswork, ceramics, and metal sculpture are among the strong suits here.

The **William-Scott Gallery** (✉439 Commercial St., Downtown Center, toward East End ☎508/487–4040 ⊕www.williamscottgallery.com) primarily shows contemporary works such as John Dowd's reflective, realistic Cape 'scapes.

SPECIALTY
STORES
Farland Provisions (✉150 Bradford St., Downtown Center ☎508/487–0045) proffers all kinds of fine foods and snacks, including excellent deli sandwiches.

Forbidden Fruit (✉173 Commercial St., Downtown Center, toward West End ☎508/487–9800) is a one-stop shop for all irreverent and offbeat gifts, from strange costumes to erotic trinkets to Gothic tchotchkes.

ID (✉220A Commercial St., Downtown Center, toward West End ☎508/487–1154) stocks a wonderful array of Mexican pottery, cool clocks, offbeat jewelry, and retro-hip greeting cards and stationery.

Impulse (✉188 Commercial St., Downtown Center, toward West End ☎508/487–1154) has contemporary American crafts, including jewelry and an extraordinary kaleidoscope collection. The Autograph Gallery exhibits framed photographs, letters, and documents signed by celebrities.

Kidstuff (✉371 Commercial St., Downtown Center, toward East End ☎508/487–0714) carries unusual, colorful children's wear.

Lady'Z Vintage Clothing (✉389 Commercial St., Downtown Center, toward East End ☎508/487–2251) offers racks of sexy, campy, bold, and offbeat secondhand fashions. It's a favorite of drag queens, who especially favor the costume jewelry and boas, but there are all kinds of cool threads here.

Little Gorgeous Things (✉359 Commercial St., Downtown Center, toward East End ☎508/487–6171) has just the curious little tchotchke, collectible, vintage furnishing, painting, or objet d'art to complete your summer house. It carries the creations of more than 100 local craftspeople and artists.

Marc Jacobs (⊠184 *Commercial St., Downtown Center, toward West End* ☎508/487–0723), the world-class designer, opened a Provincetown location in 2007. Drop in to peruse the fashion-forward threads.

★ **Marine Specialties, Inc.** (⊠235 *Commercial St., Downtown Center* ☎508/487–1730) is full of treasures, knickknacks, and clothing. Here you can purchase some very reasonably priced casual- and military-style clothing, as well as seashells, marine supplies, stained-glass lamps, candles, rubber sharks (you get the idea), and prints of old advertisements.

Moda Fina (⊠349 *Commercial St., Downtown Center* ☎508/487–6632) displays an eclectic selection of women's fashions, shoes, and jewelry—everything from flowing linen or silk eveningwear to funky and casual pieces. Unique Mexican crafts are also for sale.

Now Voyager Bookstore (⊠357 *Commercial St., Downtown Center* ☎508/487–0848) is a first-rate independent bookstore with an emphasis on lesbian and gay titles; the store hosts prominent authors throughout the year (especially in summer) and has a small art gallery.

Peter's Royal Navy (⊠120 *Commercial St., Downtown Center, toward West End* ☎508/487–7141), with its whimsical window displays, appeals to fans of all things British with a great selection of linens, authentic Royal Navy flatware, Bay Rhum toiletries, antique model ships, and fine nautical memorabilia.

Provincetown Antique Market (⊠131 *Commercial St., Downtown Center, toward West End* ☎508/487–1115) has one of the town's better selections of vintage lighting, jewelry, Bakelite, costumes, toys, textiles, and furnishings.

Remembrances of Things Past (⊠376 *Commercial St., Downtown Center, toward East End* ☎508/487–9443) deals with articles from the 1920s to the 1960s, including Bakelite and other jewelry, telephones, neon items, ephemera, and autographed celebrity photographs.

Silk & Feathers (⊠377 *Commercial St., Downtown Center, toward East End* ☎508/487–2057) carries an assortment of fine lingerie, women's clothing, and jewelry.

Tim's Used Books (⊠242 *Commercial St., Downtown Center* ☎508/487–0005) is packed with volumes of volumes—rooms of used-but-in-good-shape books, including some rare and out-of-print texts.

★ **Utilities** (⊠393 *Commercial St., Downtown Center, toward East End* ☎508/487–6800) supplies customers with some of the coolest kitchen and bathroom gadgetry and decorative pieces around.

Wa (⊠184 *Commercial St., Downtown Center, toward West End* ☎508/487–6355) is an oasis of peace and Zen-like tranquillity. Unusual- and Japanese-inspired items include fountains, home-accent pieces, and framed (and sometimes frightening) tropical insects.

West End Antiques (⊠146 *Commercial St., Downtown Center, toward West End* ☎508/487–6723) sells everything from $4 postcards to a

$3,000 model ship. Handmade dolls and high-quality glassware—Steuben, Orrefors, and Hawkes—are also available.

THE OUTER CAPE ESSENTIALS

To research prices, get advice from other travelers, and book travel arrangements, visit www.fodors.com.

TRANSPORTATION

BY BOAT & FERRY

In season, ferries run from Provincetown to Boston and Plymouth. *For more information, see ⇨ Boat & Ferry Travel in Essentials in the back of this book.*

BY BUS

Plymouth & Brockton Street Railway provides bus service to Provincetown from downtown Boston or Logan Airport, with stops en route. *For more information, see ⇨ Bus Travel in Essentials in the back of this book.*

The Shuttle, run by the Cape Cod Regional Transit Authority, provides a much-needed transportation boost. The route begins at Horton's Camping Resort in Truro and continues to Provincetown along Route 6A; it stops wherever a passenger or roadside flagger dictates. Once in Provincetown, the shuttle continues up Bradford Street, with alternating trips to Herring Cove Beach and Pilgrim Park as well as summertime service up to Provincetown Airport and Race Point Beach. It runs every 30 minutes and is outfitted to carry bicycles. The service is popular and reasonably priced ($1 for a single fare, $3 for a day pass), and the only trouble seems to be finding parking on the Truro end (plans are in the works to find alternative parking areas). The shuttle runs throughout the day from late May until mid-October, with more limited service during the off-season.

There are no bus stations or depots, per se, in the Outer Cape, though there are designated stops within each town: in Provincetown, in front of the Chamber of Commerce office on Commercial Street; in Truro, at Dutra's Market–Route 6A (Shore Road); in North Truro, at Depot Road, near the Truro Post Office and Jams store; in Wellfleet, at D& D market on U.S. 6 and in Wellfleet Village; and in South Wellfleet on Main Street in front of Town Hall.

Bus Lines Plymouth & Brockton Street Railway (☎508/746–0378 ⊕www. p-b.com). **Shuttle** (☎800/352–7155 ⊕ www.capecodtransit.org).

BY TAXI

The companies below provide cab service throughout the Outer Cape. Mercedes Cab Co. offers local and long-distance service in vintage Mercedes sedans.

Taxi Companies Cape Cab (✉Provincetown ☎508/487–2222). **Jody's Taxi** (✉Provincetown ☎508/487–0265). **Mercedes Cab** (✉Provincetown ☎508/487–3333). **Queen Cab** (✉Provincetown ☎508/487–5500).

CONTACTS & RESOURCES

VISITOR INFORMATION

The Provincetown Chamber of Commerce is open from March until New Year's Day and has the only staffed visitor center in town, just off Commercial Street near MacMillan Wharf. The Provincetown Business Guild specializes in gay tourism and is open year-round to offer answers over the phone or send out its directory—but it has no visitor center. The Truro Chamber of Commerce and Wellfleet Chamber are open from mid-May through mid-October.

Tourist Information **Provincetown** (✉ *307 Commercial St., Box 1017, 02657* ☎ *508/487–3424* ⊕ *www.ptownchamber.com*). **Provincetown Business Guild (gay and lesbian)** (✉ *3 Freman St., No. 2, Box 421–94, 02657* ☎ *508/487–2313 or 800/637–8696* ⊕ *www.ptown.org*). **Truro** (✉ *U.S. 6 at Head of the Meadow Rd. ⌂ Box 26, North Truro 02652* ☎ *508/487–1288* ⊕ *www.trurochamberofcommerce. com*). **Wellfleet** (⌂ *Box 571, 02667* ☎ *508/349–2510* ✉ *Information center off U.S. 6 in South Wellfleet* ⊕ *www.wellfleetchamber.com*).

Martha's Vineyard

WORD OF MOUTH

"In Aquinnah, we took numerous photographs of the beautiful cliffs and striking brick lighthouse. The cliffs had colorful strata in the afternoon light. What a gorgeous place!"

—volcam

"I prefer Martha's Vineyard for its more varied terrain and views, beautiful beaches, rolling hills, and indescribable Aquinnah clay cliffs. You can see it all from a tour bus on a day trip"

—Kingajh

By Andrew
Collins

FAR LESS DEVELOPED THAN CAPE COD—thanks to a few local conservation organizations—yet more cosmopolitan than neighboring Nantucket, Martha's Vineyard is an island with a double life. From Memorial Day through Labor Day the quieter, some might say real, Vineyard quickens into a vibrant, star-studded place. Edgartown floods with people who come to wander narrow streets flanked with elegant boutiques, stately whaling captains' homes, and charming inns. The busy main port, Vineyard Haven, welcomes day-trippers fresh off ferries and private yachts to browse in its own array of shops. Oak Bluffs, where pizza and ice-cream emporiums reign supreme, attracts diverse crowds with its boardwalk-town air and nightspots that cater to high-spirited, carefree youth.

Summer regulars have included a host of celebrities over the years, among them William Styron, Art Buchwald, Walter Cronkite, Beverly Sills, Patricia Neal, Spike Lee, and Diane Sawyer. Former president Clinton and his wife, Senator Hillary Clinton, are frequent visitors. Concerts, theater, dance performances, and lecture series draw top talent to the island; a county agricultural fair, weekly farmers' markets, and miles of walking trails provide earthier pleasures.

Most people know the Vineyard's summer persona, but in many ways its other self has even more appeal, for the off-season island is a place of peace and simple beauty. Drivers traversing country lanes through the agricultural center of the island find time to linger over pastoral and ocean vistas, without being pushed along by a throng of other cars, bicycles, and mopeds. In nature reserves, the voices of summer are gone, leaving only the sounds of birdsong and the crackle of leaves underfoot. Private beaches open to the public, and the water sparkles under crisp, blue skies.

Locals are at their convivial best off-season. After the craziness of their short moneymaking months, they reestablish contact with friends and take up pastimes temporarily crowded out by work. The result for visitors—besides the extra dose of friendliness—is that cultural, educational, and recreational events continue year-round.

ABOUT THE RESTAURANTS

From fried fish at roadside stands to boiled lobster and foie gras at fancy French restaurants and a growing array of international influences—Thai, Brazilian, Japanese, Mexican, to name just a few—the Vineyard serves an amazing variety of culinary choices.

The majority of eating establishments, both take-out and sit-down, are concentrated in the three Down-Island towns of Vineyard Haven, Oak Bluffs, and Edgartown. As you travel Up-Island—to West Tisbury, Chilmark, and Aquinnah—choices dwindle, especially when it comes to sit-down dinners. Sadly, Vineyard diners—all-American institutions where you can get an honest, no-frills meal at reasonable prices—are a dying breed. Luckily, you can pick up sandwiches, pastries, and other to-go specialties at a number of places around the island, and with good planning you can eat well on a modest budget and splurge for an elegant dinner.

Most restaurants are open on weekends starting in late spring, and by Memorial Day weekend most are serving daily. Although the season seems to stretch longer each year, most restaurants remain open full time through Columbus Day weekend, then only weekends through Thanksgiving (a small handful of die-hard restaurants remain open year-round). Dress, even for the upscale spots, is casual; a man in a sport jacket is a rare sight. Reservations are highly recommended in the summer months.

TOP 5

■ A ride on the enduring Flying Horses Carousel

■ An outdoor candlelit meal at the Sweet Life Café

■ The views at Aquinnah Cliffs

■ Grazing at the West Tisbury Farmers' Market

■ The fishing at Wasque Point on Chappaquiddick

ABOUT THE HOTELS

The variety of lodging options on Martha's Vineyard ranges from historic whaling captains' mansions filled with antiques to sprawling modern oceanfront hotels to cozy cottages in the woods. When choosing your accommodations, keep in mind that each town has a different personality: Oak Bluffs tends to cater to a younger, active, nightlife-oriented crowd; Edgartown is more subdued and dignified. Chilmark has beautiful beaches and miles of conservation lands, but not much of a downtown shopping area. Vineyard Haven provides a nice balance of downtown bustle and rustic charm. Bear in mind that many of the island's bed-and-breakfasts, set in vintage homes filled with art and antiques, have age restrictions—call ahead if you're traveling with a family. And remember that in July and August, the height of the summer season, minimum stays of as many as four nights may be required. If you're planning to visit for a week or more, consider renting a house. *For more lodging information, including rental properties and B&Bs, (⇨ Accommodations in Essentials at the back of this book.)*

WHAT IT COSTS					
	$$$$	$$$	$$	$	¢
RESTAURANTS	over $30	$22–$30	$16–$22	$10–$16	under $10
HOTELS	over $260	$200–$260	$140–$200	$90–$140	under $90

Restaurant prices are per person for a main course at dinner. Hotel prices are for a standard double room, excluding 6% sales tax (more in some counties) and 1%–4% tourist tax.

You should make reservations for summer stays as far in advance as possible; late winter is not too early. Rates in season are very high but can fall by as much as 50% in the off-season. The Martha's Vineyard Chamber of Commerce (⇨ *Visitor Information in Martha's Vineyard Essentials at the end of this chapter*) maintains a listing of availability in the peak tourist season, from mid-June to mid-September.

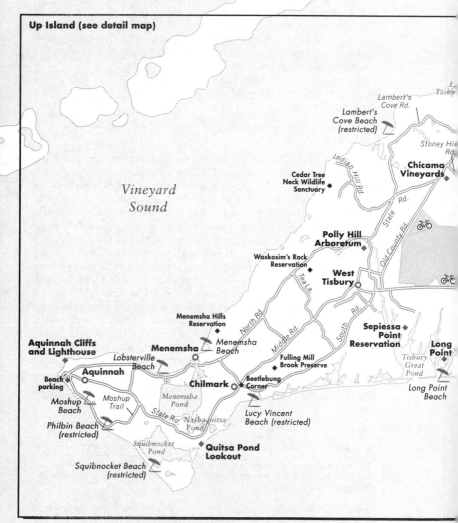

Martha's Vineyard

Up Island (see detail map)

Lambert's
Cove Rd.

L.
Tashn

Lambert's
Cove Beach
(restricted)

Stoney Hi
Rd.

**Chicama
Vineyards**

Cedar Tree
Neck Wildlife
Sanctuary

*Vineyard
Sound*

Indian Hill Rd.

State Rd.

Old County Rd.

**Polly Hill
Arboretum**

Waskosim's Rock
Reservation

**West
Tisbury**

Tea La.

Menemsha Hills
Reservation

North Rd.

Middle Rd.

South Rd.

**Sepiessa
Point
Reservation**

**Long
Point**

Menemsha

*Menemsha
Beach*

Fulling Mill
Brook Preserve

*Tisbury
Great
Pond*

**Aquinnah Cliffs
and Lighthouse**

*Lobsterville
Beach*

Chilmark

**Beetlebung
Corner**

*Long Point
Beach*

Beach
parking

Aquinnah

*Menemsha
Pond*

Moshup Trail

Lucy Vincent
Beach (restricted)

*Moshup
Beach*

State Rd.

*Nashaquitsa
Pond*

*Philbin Beach
(restricted)*

*Squibnocket
Pond*

**Quitsa Pond
Lookout**

*Squibnocket Beach
(restricted)*

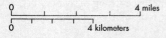

0   4 miles

0   4 kilometers

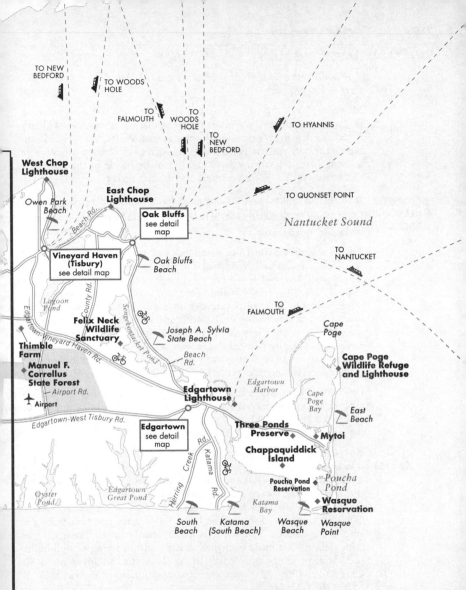

TO NEW
BEDFORD

TO WOODS
HOLE

TO
FALMOUTH

TO
WOODS
HOLE

TO
NEW
BEDFORD

TO HYANNIS

**West Chop
Lighthouse**

*Owen Park
Beach*

**East Chop
Lighthouse**

Oak Bluffs
see detail
map

TO QUONSET POINT

Nantucket Sound

Beach Rd.

**Vineyard Haven
(Tisbury)**
see detail map

*Oak Bluffs
Beach*

County Rd.

*Lagoon
Pond*

TO
NANTUCKET

**Felix Neck
Wildlife
Sanctuary**

Sengekontacket Pond

*Joseph A. Sylvia
State Beach*

TO
FALMOUTH

*Cape
Poge*

**Thimble
Farm**

Edgartown-Vineyard Haven Rd.

*Beach
Rd.*

**Cape Poge
Wildlife Refuge
and Lighthouse**

**Manuel F.
Correllus
State Forest**

Airport Rd.

*Edgartown
Harbor*

*Cape
Poge
Bay*

Airport

**Edgartown
Lighthouse**

*East
Beach*

Edgartown-West Tisbury Rd.

Edgartown
see detail
map

**Three Ponds
Preserve**

Mytoi

Herring Creek Rd.

Katama Rd.

**Chappaquiddick
Island**

*Oyster
Pond*

*Edgartown
Great Pond*

**Poucha Pond
Reservation**

*Poucha
Pond*

**Wasque
Reservation**

*Katama
Bay*

*South
Beach*

*Katama
(South Beach)*

*Wasque
Beach*

*Wasque
Point*

ATLANTIC OCEAN

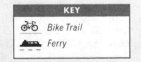

VINEYARD HAVEN (TISBURY)

7 mi southeast of Woods Hole, 3½ mi west of Oak Bluffs, 8 mi northwest of Edgartown.

Most people call this town Vineyard Haven because of the name of the port where ferries arrive, but its official name is Tisbury. Not as hightoned as Edgartown or as honky-tonk as Oak Bluffs, Vineyard Haven blends the past and the present with a touch of the bohemian. Visitors arriving here step off the ferry right into the bustle of the harbor, a block from the shops and restaurants of Main Street.

NEED A BREAK?

The delicious breads, pastries, and quick-lunch items at **Black Dog Bakery** (⊠ *11 Water St.* ☎ *508/693–4786*) are simply not to be missed—it's a popular stop for good reason.

The stately, neoclassic 1844 **Association Hall** houses the town hall and the Katharine Cornell Memorial Theatre, created in part with funds that Cornell (1898–1974)—one of America's foremost stage actresses in the 1920s, '30s, and '40s and a longtime summer resident—donated in her will. The walls of the theater on the 2nd floor are painted with murals depicting whaling expeditions and a Native American gathering, and the ceiling resembles a blue sky with seagulls overhead. Island artist Stan Murphy painted the murals on the occasion of the town's tercentenary in 1971. The theater occasionally holds performances of plays, concerts, and dances. ⊠ *51 Spring St.* ☎ *508/696–4200.*

One of two lighthouses that mark the opening to the harbor, the 52-foot white-and-black **West Chop Lighthouse** was built of brick in 1838 to replace an 1817 wood building. It's been moved back from the edge of the eroding bluff twice. ⊠ *W. Chop Rd. (Main St.).*

WHERE TO STAY & EAT

$$$–$$$$ ✕ **Le Grenier.** Owner-chef Jean Dupon has been serving classic French food since the late 1970s above the M. V. Bagel Authority at the upper end of Vineyard Haven's downtown. All this time, he's been consistently loyal to the French standards: frogs' legs, sweetbreads, lobster flambéed with calvados, chicken livers Provençale, and tournedos are among the entrées. The decor is hardly stuffy in the French tradition; rather, it's almost backyard casual, with a string of lightbulbs and souvenir wine-bottle corks lining the walls. ⊠ *Upper Main St.* ☎ *508/693–4906* ⊕ *www.legrenierrestaurant.com* ▤ *AE, MC, V* ⚱*BYOB* ☉ *No lunch.*

$$–$$$$ ✕ **Black Dog Tavern.** This island landmark—which is more popular with tourists than locals—lies just steps from the ferry terminal in Vineyard Haven. In July and August, the wait for breakfast (with an expansive omelet assortment) can be as much as an hour from 8 AM on. Why? Partly because the ambience inside—roaring fireplace, dark-wood walls, maritime memorabilia, and a grand view of the water—makes everyone feel so at home. The menu is heavy on local fish, chowders, and chops. Lighter fare is available until 7 PM in the Black Dog Bakery Cafe. ⊠ *20 Beach St. Ext.* ☎ *508/693–9223* ⌁ *Reservations not accepted* ▤ *AE, D, MC, V* ⚱*BYOB.*

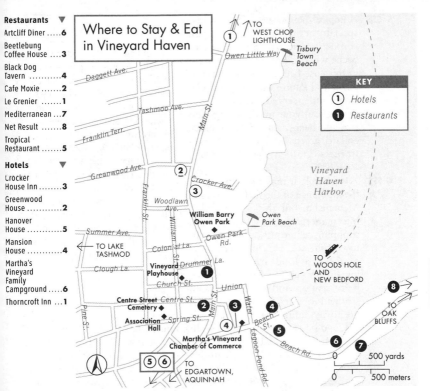

Restaurants ▼
Artcliff Diner **6**
Beetlebung Coffee House **3**
Black Dog Tavern **4**
Cafe Moxie **2**
Le Grenier **1**
Mediterranean ...**7**
Net Result **8**
Tropical Restaurant **5**

Hotels ▼
Crocker House Inn **3**
Greenwood House **2**
Hanover House **5**
Mansion House **4**
Martha's Vineyard Family Campground **6**
Thorncroft Inn ...**1**

Where to Stay & Eat in Vineyard Haven

KEY
① Hotels
❶ Restaurants

$–$$$$ ✕**Mediterranean.** Opened in 2004 by well-regarded talented chefs and restaurateurs Leslie and Douglas Hewson, this sunny, informal eatery overlooking the harbor has become a favorite with locals for reliable, freshly prepared pan-Mediterranean food—ingredients and recipes reflect Moroccan, Spanish, French, and Italian influences. You might start with the savory artichoke Française sautéed in garlic, herbs, and lemon-butter. Excellent main dishes include oven-roasted salt cod with crabmeat, and grilled sliced lamb with a rosemary reduction and a goat cheese–and–tomato tart. Pastry chef Leslie has earned a loyal following with her flaky baklava topped with lemon ice cream. ⊠*52 Beach Rd.* ☎*508/693–1617 or 888/693–1617* ▭*AE, D, MC, V* ⌂*BYOB* ⊘*No lunch Sun.*

$$–$$$ ✕**Cafe Moxie.** Open year-round, this classy restaurant has a handsome wooden bar (though it's a dry town) and local artists' work on the walls. Chef Austin Racine's mussels, steamed in garlic and ginger and served over noodles, are a favorite. For something fancier, try a duck breast wrapped in Swiss chard over a white-bean-and-duck ragout, or herbed gnocchi with garlic, leeks, roasted tomato, and chèvre. Hours tend to vary at a whim, so call first. ⊠*Main St. at Centre St.* ☎*508/693–1484* ▭*D, MC, V* ⌂*BYOB* ⊘*Closed Mon. No dinner Tues. and Oct.–Apr.*

$–$$$ ✕ **Tropical Restaurant.** The house specialty at this roadside restaurant is *rodizio,* a Brazilian style of barbecue where slow-roasted meats—in this case beef, chicken, sausage, pork, and lamb—are carved tableside and served continuously throughout your meal. Along with rice and beans, side dishes include collard greens and yucca. ✉ *Five Corners* ☎508/696–0715 ☐*MC, V* BYOB.

> **BYOB**
>
> Part of how the Vineyard maintains its charm—and part of what makes it somewhat frustrating as well—is that alcoholic beverages have, until recently, been sold in retail stores and in restaurants in only two towns: Edgartown and Oak Bluffs. As of 2008, Vineyard Haven and Aquinnah will be allowed to sell alcohol in restaurants. At restaurants in the so-called "dry" towns of West Tisbury and Chilmark, you can BYOB, but expect to be charged up to $8 for corkage fees (this includes the opening of the bottle and the provision of glasses).

¢–$$$ ✕ **Net Result.** It may not have quite
★ the ambience of the fish markets in Menemsha, but this simple takeout market and restaurant in a shopping center just outside downtown Vineyard Haven serves some of the best food around, including superb sublime lobster bisque, hefty scallop and oyster platters, steamed lobsters, grilled swordfish sandwiches, and crab salad. There are always additional daily specials that reflect what's been caught that day, and Net Result also has a sushi counter: the Martha's Vineyard roll is a favorite, packed with tuna, salmon, yellowtail, and avocado and wrapped in seaweed. You can dine at picnic tables outside and view Vineyard Haven's harbor across the busy road. ✉ *Tisbury Marketplace, 79 Beach Rd.* ☎508/693–6071 ⊕*www.mvseafood.com* ☐*MC, V.*

¢–$ ✕ **ArtCliff Diner.** This vintage diner has been a year-round breakfast and lunch meeting place for locals since 1943. Owner–chef Gina Stanley, who was on call to make desserts for Blair House when she lived in Washington, D.C., serves anything but ordinary diner fare. She whips up pecan pancakes with real rum raisins for breakfast, and crepes with chèvre, arugula, or almost anything you ask for at lunch. A small porch was added in 2007. ✉*39 Beach Rd.* ☎*508/693–1224* ☐*No credit cards* ☉*Closed Wed. No dinner.*

¢ ✕ **Beetlebung Coffee House.** This cozy coffeehouse is within easy walking distance of the ferry terminal and downtown shops and restaurants. A hip crowd convenes here for the great sandwiches (try the Taos panini, with flame-roasted New Mexico green chilies, turkey, and cheddar), designer-coffee drinks, and delicious desserts. The breakfast "eggwich," with Black Forest ham, poached egg, and Vermont cheddar, is a treat. There's an attractive side patio that's perfect on a warm afternoon. ✉*32 Beach St.* ☎*508/696–7122* ☐*MC, V.*

$$$$ ▥ **Crocker House Inn.** This 1924 farmhouse-style inn is tucked into a
★ quiet lane off Main Street, minutes from the ferries and Owen Park Beach. The rooms are decorated casually with understated flair—pastel-painted walls, softly upholstered wing-back chairs, and whitewicker nightstands. Each contains a small, wall-mounted "honor bar,"

with a disposable camera, suntan lotion, and other useful sundries. Three rooms have soothing whirlpool tubs, and two have fireplaces. No. 6, with a small porch and a private entrance, has the best view of the harbor. Breakfast is served at a large farmer's table inside the small common room and kitchen area. Jeff and Jynell Kristal are the young, friendly owners, and Jynell also creates whimsically painted glassware, which is available for sale. **Pros:** Great owners, short walk from town, easygoing vibe. **Cons:** You pay a premium for this location, decor is more casual than posh, books up quickly in summer. ⊠ *12 Crocker Ave., Box 1658, 02568* ☎ *508/693–1151 or 800/772–0206* ⊕ *www.crockerhouseinn.com* 🛏 *8 rooms* ₰ *In-room: Wi-Fi. In-hotel: no elevator, no kids under 12* ☰ *MC, V* ⦿ *CP.*

$$$$ 🏨 **Mansion House.** There has been a hostelry on this Main Street site just above Vineyard Haven Harbor since 1794; today's Mansion House opened in 2003, following a major fire to its predecessor. Apart from the cheerful, summery rooms—some with balconies, gas fireplaces, and soaking tubs—the cupola deck provides a pleasant spot for a respite. It affords sweeping views of the harbor, the town, and the lagoon that stretches between Vineyard Haven and Oak Bluffs. Afternoon cookies and lemonade are served there or you can BYOB. The hotel's Zephrus Restaurant serves reliable American fare and is also a nice spot for cocktails. **Pros:** Restaurant and spa on-site, steps from Vineyard Haven shopping and ferry, light-filled rooms. **Cons:** No grounds to speak of, center-of-it-all locale can be a little noisy, not historic. ⊠ *9 Main St., Box 428, 02568* ☎ *509/693–2200 or 800/332–4112* ⊕ *www.mvmansionhouse.com* 🛏 *32 rooms, 11 suites* ₰ *In-room: refrigerator, Wi-Fi. In-hotel: restaurant, room service, pool, gym, spa* ☰ *AE, D, MC, V* ⦿ *CP.*

$$$$ 🏨 **Thorncroft Inn.** On 2½ wooded acres about 1 mi from the ferry, this inn's main building, a 1918 Craftsman bungalow, combines fine colonial and richly carved Renaissance-revival antiques with tasteful reproductions to create a somewhat formal environment. Most rooms have working fireplaces and canopy beds; three rooms have two-person whirlpool baths, and two have private hot-tub spas. Rooms in the carriage house, set apart from the main house via a breezeway, are more secluded. **Pros:** Short walk from town, antiques galore, carriage-house rooms have lots of privacy. **Cons:** A bit formal and fussy, antiques galore, some rooms are very small given the steep rates. ⊠ *460 Main St., Box 1022, 02568* ☎ *508/693–3333 or 800/332–1236* 🖷 *508/693–5419* ⊕ *www.thorncroft.com* 🛏 *14 rooms, 1 cottage* ₰ *In-room: refrigerator (some), VCR, Ethernet. In-hotel: restaurant, no kids under 13* ☰ *AE, D, DC, MC, V* ⦿ *BP.*

$$–$$$ 🏨 **Greenwood House.** A low-key B&B on a quiet lane around the corner from Vineyard Haven's public library, the Greenwood House is one of the better values in town. Affable innkeepers Kathy Stinson and Larry Gomez own this homey, three-story Arts and Crafts–style cottage with classic shingle siding and a shaded yard. The rooms are decorated with a mix of antiques and contemporary pieces, including brass and four-poster beds, island artwork, and functional but attractive nightstands and bureaus. It's a 10- to 15-minute walk from the ferry and even closer

6

to many shops and restaurants. **Pros:** Easy walk to shops and dining, good value, personal service. **Cons:** Some rooms a bit small, no room phones. ⊠*40 Greenwood Ave., Box 2734, 02568* ☎*508/693–6150 or 866/693–6150* ⊕*www.greenwoodhouse.com* ☞*4 rooms* ⟁*In-room: refrigerator, dial-up. In-hotel: no elevator* ⊟*AE, MC, V* ⦿*BP.*

$$–$$$ ⊞ **Hanover House.** Set on ½ acre of landscaped lawn on a busy road—but within walking distance of the ferry—this three-property, children-friendly inn consists of a classic, home-style B&B, a country inn, and a carriage house. Rooms are decorated with a combination of antiques and reproduction furniture, mostly in the Victorian style, and each has individual flair: in one, an antique sewing machine serves as the TV stand. The three carriage-house suites have private decks or patios, two have kitchenettes, and one has a gas fireplace. **Pros:** Good value, 10-minute walk to shops and dining, kitchenettes in some units. **Cons:** Off busy road, no water or beach views from most units, stall showers in a couple of units. ⊠*28 Edgartown Rd., Box 2108, 02568* ☎*508/693–1066 or 800/696–8633* ⊕*www.hanoverhouseinn.com* ☞*12 rooms, 3 suites* ⟁*In-room: kitchen (some), Wi-Fi. In-hotel: no elevator* ⊟*AE, D, MC, V* ⊗*Closed Dec.–Mar.* ⦿*BP.*

¢   ⟁ **Martha's Vineyard Family Campground.** Wooded sites, a ball field,
★   a camp store, bicycle rentals, and electrical and water hookups are among the facilities at this 20-acre campsite a few miles from Vineyard Haven. A step up from tents are 21 rustic one- or two-room cabins, which come with electricity, refrigerators, gas grills, and combinations of double and bunk beds (but bring your own bedding). The campground also has hookups for trailers. This is the only campsite on the island, so book early; discounts are available for extended stays. No dogs or motorcycles are allowed. **Pros:** Great value, secluded setting, has some private cabins. **Cons:** No dogs allowed, 1½-mi walk from town, books up fast. ⊠*569 Edgartown Rd., Box 1557, 02568* ☎*508/693–3772* 🖳*508/693–5767* ⊕*www.campmvfc.com* ☞*130 tent sites, 50 RV sites, 21 cabins* ⟁*Refrigerator (some), bicycles, laundry facilities, play area* ⊟*D, MC, V* ⊗*Closed mid-Oct.–mid-May.*

NIGHTLIFE & THE ARTS

The **Vineyard Playhouse** (⊠*24 Church St.* ☎*508/696–6300* ⊕*www. vineyardplayhouse.org*) has a year-round schedule of professional productions. From mid-June through early September, a troupe performs drama, classics, and comedies on the air-conditioned main stage; summer Shakespeare and other productions take place at the natural amphitheater at Tashmoo Overlook on State Road in Vineyard Haven—bring insect repellent and a blanket or lawn chair. Children's programs and a summer camp are also scheduled, and local art exhibitions are held throughout the year. The theater is wheelchair-accessible and provides hearing devices.

SPORTS & THE OUTDOORS

Lake Tashmoo Town Beach (⊠*End of Herring Creek Rd.*) provides swimmers with access to the warm, relatively shallow, brackish lake—or cooler, gentler Vineyard Sound. **Owen Park Beach** (⊠*Off Main St.*), a small, sandy harbor beach, is just steps away from the ferry terminal in Vineyard Haven, making it a great spot to catch some last rays before heading home. **Tisbury Town Beach** (✉ *End of Owen Little Way off Main St.*) is a public beach next to the Vineyard Haven Yacht Club.

SHOPPING

All Things Oriental (✉ *123 Beach Rd.* ☎ *508/693–8375*) sells new and antique jewelry, porcelains, paintings, furniture, and more, all with an Asian theme.

★ **Belushi Pisano Gallery** (✉ *18 State Rd.* ☎ *508/696–8988*), operated by Victor Pisano and Judith Belushi Pisano, is an extension of the Second Chance Foundation, a nonprofit organization that aims to assist artists on Martha's Vineyard during times of financial duress; proceeds from the gallery's sales fund the foundation. It's a handsome space carrying works in all types of media by more than 20 of the island's top artists. There's also a small coffeehouse.

Bowl & Board (✉ *35 Main St.* ☎ *508/693–9441*) is summer-home central. It carries everything you need to cozy up in a summer rental.

Bramhall & Dunn (✉ *19 Main St.* ☎ *508/693–6437*) carries crafts, linens, hand-knit sweaters, and fine antique country-pine furniture.

Bunch of Grapes Bookstore (✉ *44 Main St.* ☎ *508/693–2291*) sells new books and sponsors book signings.

Midnight Farm (✉ *18 Water-Cromwell La.* ☎ *508/693–1997*), co-owned by Carly Simon and Tamara Weiss, stocks furniture, clothes, shoes, jewelry, linens, dinnerware, books, soaps, candles, garden supplies, snack foods, and, of course, Carly's books and CDs.

Fodor's Choice **Rainy Day** (✉ *66 Main St.* ☎ *508/693–1830*), as the name suggests, carries gifts and amusements that are perfect for one of the island's gloomy rainy days, when you just need a warm, dry diversion. You'll find toys, crafts, cards, soaps, and more.

Tisbury Antiques & Interiors (✉ *339 State Rd.* ☎ *508/693–8333*) carries a vast selection of 18th- and 19th-century English, French, and Italian antiques, plus fine lighting fixtures, Cornishware, estate jewelry, and vintage books and postcards.

★ Nationally renowned for their distinctive, hand-sculpted metal weathervanes, **Tuck and Holand** (✉ *275 State Rd.* ☎ *508/693–3914 or 888/693–3914*) has a studio gallery a 10-minute walk from downtown. Here you can examine Anthony Holand and Travis Tuck's otherworldly creations, including copper Martha's Vineyard wall maps, school-of-bluefish chandeliers, and the signature custom weathervanes.

Wind's Up! (✉ *199 Beach Rd.* ☎ *508/693–4340*) sells swimwear, windsurfing and sailing equipment, Boogie boards, and other outdoor gear.

OAK BLUFFS

3½ mi east of Vineyard Haven.

Circuit Avenue is the bustling center of the Oak Bluffs action, with most of the town's shops, bars, and restaurants. Colorful gingerbread-trimmed guesthouses and food and souvenir joints enliven Oak Bluffs Harbor, once the setting for several grand hotels (the 1879 Wesley Hotel on Lake Avenue is the last remaining one). This small town is more high spirited than haute, more fun than refined.

The **East Chop Lighthouse** was built out of cast iron in 1876 to replace an 1828 tower (used as part of a semaphore system of visual signaling between the island and Boston) that burned down. The 40-foot structure stands high atop a 79-foot bluff with spectacular views of Nantucket Sound. ⊠*E. Chop Dr.* ☎*508/627–4441* ☑*$3* ☉*Late June–mid-Sept., Sun. 1 hr before sunset–1 hr after sunset.*

NEED A BREAK?

The **Coop de Ville** (⊠ *Dockside Marketplace, Oak Bluffs Harbor* ☎ *508/693–3420*) teems with people eager to sample simple fried seafood and raw-bar delectables (the oysters are fantastic). Eat out on the patio deck overlooking the water to enjoy the view. It's open May to mid-October.

☾ A National Historic Landmark, the **Flying Horses Carousel** is the nation's oldest continuously operating carousel. Handcrafted in 1876 (the horses have real horse hair and glass eyes), the ride gives children a taste of entertainment from a TV-free era. ⊠*Oak Bluffs Ave.* ☎*508/693–9481* ☑*Rides $1.50, book of 8 tickets $10* ☉*Late May–early Sept., daily 10–10; Easter–late May, weekends 10–5; early Sept.–mid-Oct., weekdays 11–4:30, weekends 10–5.*

★ Don't miss **Oak Bluffs Campground,** a 34-acre warren of streets tightly packed with more than 300 Carpenter Gothic Victorian cottages with wedding-cake trim, gaily painted in pastels. As you wander through this fairy-tale setting, imagine it on a balmy summer evening, lighted by the warm glow of hundreds of Japanese paper lanterns hung from every cottage porch. This describes the scene on Illumination Night at the end of the Camp Meeting season—which is attended these days by some fourth- and fifth-generation cottagers. Attendees mark the occasion as they have for more than a century, with lights, song, and open houses for families and friends. Note that because of overwhelming crowds of onlookers in seasons past, the date is not announced until the week before. Ninety-minute tours are conducted Tuesday and Thursday, July and August, at 10 AM. ⊠*Off Circuit Ave.* ☎*508/693–0525* ⊕*www.mvcma.org/* ☑*Tour $10.*

WHERE TO STAY & EAT

$$$$
Fodor$Choice
★

✕**Sweet Life Café.** Housed in a charming Victorian house, this island favorite's warm tones, low lighting, and handsome antique furniture will make you feel like you've entered someone's home—but the cooking is more sophisticated than home-style. Dishes on the menu are prepared in inventive ways; duck breast is roasted with a lavender-rosemary-honey glaze, and the gazpacho is a white version with

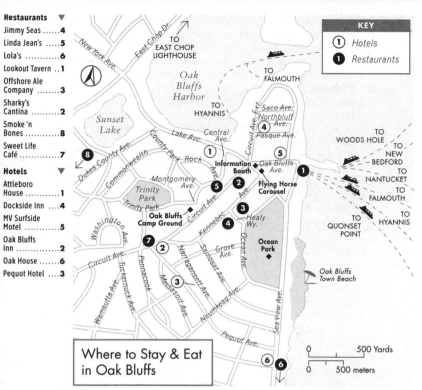

Where to Stay & Eat in Oak Bluffs

steamed clams, sliced red grapes, and smoked-paprika oil. The desserts are superb; try the warm chocolate fondant (a sort of soufflé) with toasted-almond ice cream. There's outdoor dining by candlelight in a shrub-enclosed garden, with heaters for cold nights. The same owners run **Slice of Life** (⊠ *50 Circuit Ave.* ☎ *508/693–3838*), a more casual, less-expensive bakery and café nearby. ⊠ *Upper Circuit Ave. at far end of town* ☎ *508/696–0200* ⌕ *Reservations essential* ☰ *AE, D, MC, V* ☽ *Closed Jan.–Mar.*

$$–$$$$ ✗**Jimmy Seas.** The irresistible fragrance of sautéed garlic wafting out these doors beckons lovers of the "stinking rose." Most dishes come in the pan they're cooked in and are among the biggest portions you'll find on the island. Classic red-sauce Italian dishes include *vongole* (whole littleneck clams) marinara and linguine puttanesca. A brightly colored porch and painted ceilings add to the place's charm, although service can be a little uneven. ⊠ *32 Kennebec Ave.* ☎ *508/696–8550* ⌕ *Reservations not accepted* ☰ *MC, V.*

$$–$$$$ ✗**Lola's.** This festive spot draws a party crowd. On one side, a spirited bar hosts live music; an enclosed patio for dining and a large separate dining room are on another side. Ribs as well as Southern and Louisiana standards such as crawfish étouffée and grilled swordfish with key lime–dill sauce fill the long menu; Sunday mornings are reserved for an all-you-can-eat buffet brunch, often with live gospel or jazz. This is

more of a scene than a relaxing dining spot. However, the bar is big and welcoming, and the wall mural is full of familiar local faces. Lighter, less-expensive fare, such as chicken jambalaya and fried catfish, is available from the pub menu. ⊠*Beach Rd., about 1 mi from Oak Bluffs* ☎*508/693–5007* ⊕*www.lolassouthernseafood.com* ⊟*DC, MC, V.*

$–$$$$ ✗**Offshore Ale Company.** The island's first and only microbrewery restaurant has become quite popular. There are private wooden booths, dark wood throughout, a dartboard in the corner, and live music throughout the year (Wednesday-night Irish-music jams are a hoot). Take your own peanuts from a barrel by the door and drop the shells on the floor; then order from a menu that includes steaks and burgers, chicken, pasta, gumbo, and fish. However, to truly appreciate the beer, try it with one of the wood-fired brick-oven pizzas. ⊠*30 Kennebec Ave.* ☎*508/693–2626* ⊕*www.offshoreale.com* ⚄*Reservations not accepted* ⊗*No lunch Mon. and Tues. Oct.–May* ⊟*AE, MC, V.*

$–$$$ ✗**Smoke 'n Bones.** This is the island's only rib joint, with its own smoker out back and a cord of hickory, apple, oak, and mesquite wood stacked up around the lot. Treats from the smoker include Asian-style dry-rubbed ribs and North Carolina–style pulled pork. The homemade onion rings are addictive. The place has a cookie-cutter, prefab feeling, with all the appropriate touches—neon flames around the kitchen and marble bones for doorknobs. If you're a true rib aficionado, this may not satisfy you, but on the Vineyard it's an offbeat treat. ⊠*20 Oakland Ave.* ☎*508/696–7427* ⊕*www.smokenbonesmv.com* ⚄*Reservations not accepted* ⊗*Closed Jan.–Mar.* ⊟*MC, V.*

¢–$$ ✗**Lookout Tavern.** There are two things about this easygoing Oak Bluffs seafood joint that make it stand out. First, its rustic dining room affords direct views of the sea and incoming ferry boats—it's truly the perfect "lookout" if you love watching boats ply the island's waters. Second, it serves usual seafood platters plus first-rate sushi, from the salmon and tuna rolls to more unusual treats, like the Inkwell Roll, with barbecued eel, cucumber, avocado, crabmeat, and seaweed salad. Highlights from the traditional menu include the grilled Cuban sandwich, the snow-crab dinner, fish-and-chips, or the fried scallop plate. ⊠*8 Seaview Ave. Ext.* ☎*508/696–9844* ⊟*AE, D, DC, MC, V.*

¢–$$ ✗**Sharky's Cantina.** This small storefront restaurant opened in 2006 to
★ rave reviews. Sharky's serves tasty—somewhat creative—Mexican and Southwestern fare and great drinks, and you may wait awhile to get a table. But once you're in, savor spicy tortilla soup, lobster quesadillas, steak burritos, chicken mole, and Gaucho-style skirt steak. There's an extensive margarita list (they're strong here), and for dessert try apple-pie empanadas drizzled with caramel sauce. Limited items from the menu are served until around midnight during the summer season. ⊠*31 Circuit Ave.* ☎*508/693–7501* ⊕*www.sharkyscantina.com* ⚄*Reservations not accepted* ⊟*AE, MC, V.*

¢–$ ✗**Linda Jean's.** This is a classic local hangout, a diner that serves food
★ the way a diner should: with hearty helpings and inexpensive prices. Want breakfast at 6 AM? No problem. Want breakfast at 11:30 AM? No problem. Tired of the gourmet world and want comfortable booths, friendly waitresses, and few frills? No problem. The only problem: you

may have to wait—even at 6 AM. ⊠*34 Circuit Ave.* ☎*508/693–4093* ⌖*Reservations not accepted* ▭*No credit cards.*

$$$–$$$$ ⊡**Oak Bluffs Inn.** A tan octagonal viewing tower dominates this rosy-hue Victorian B&B with a veranda on Oak Bluffs' main street, a short stroll from the beach. Victorian and country pieces fill the high-ceilinged rooms, all of which have private baths and gauzy white curtains; one has a four-poster bed. One very large room in the carriage house can accommodate three adults or two adults and two kids. **Pros:** Steps from shops and restaurants, handsome building, well-chosen antiques. **Cons:** In the thick of the commercial district, a tad frilly, location can be a little noisy. ⊠*64 Circuit Ave., at Pequot Ave., Box 2546, 02557* ☎*508/693–7171 or 800/955–6235* ⌖*508/693–8787* ⊕*www.oakbluffsinn.com* ⌑*9 rooms* ⌖*In-hotel: no elevator* ▭*AE, MC, V* ⊙*Closed Nov.–early Apr.* ⦿*CP.*

$$$–$$$$ ⊡**Oak House.** The wraparound veranda of this courtly pastel-painted
★ 1872 Victorian looks across a busy street to the beach and out across Nantucket Sound. Several rooms have private terraces or balconies; if you're bothered by noise, ask for a room in back. Ceilings, wall paneling, wainscoting, and furnishings are all in richly painted or polished oak, and all this well-preserved wood creates an appropriate setting for the choice antique furniture and nautical-theme accessories. An elegant afternoon tea with cakes and cookies is served in a glassed-in sunporch. **Pros:** Stunning decor, romantic and adult-oriented, some rooms have water views. **Cons:** Some rooms get street noise, old-fashioned vibe might turn off minimalists, busy location. ⊠*79 Seaview Ave., Box 299, 02557* ☎*508/693–4187 or 866/693–5805* ⊕*www.vineyardinns.com* ⌑*8 rooms, 2 suites* ⌖*In-hotel: no kids under 10, no elevator* ▭*AE, D, MC, V* ⊙*Closed mid-Oct.–mid-May* ⦿*CP.*

$$–$$$ ⊡**Dockside Inn.** This gingerbread Victorian-style inn built in the late '80s, decked with broad porches, sits right by the dock, steps from the ferry landing and downtown shops, restaurants, and bars. Kids are welcome, and they'll have plenty to do in town and at nearby beaches. Some rooms open onto building-length balconies. **Pros:** Close to everything, very kid-friendly, big porches. **Cons:** Front of inn right on street, busy location, lots of kids in summer. ⊠*9 Circuit Ave., Box 1206, 02557* ☎*508/693–2966 or 800/245–5979* ⊕*www.vineyardinns.com* ⌑*17 rooms, 5 suites, 2 apartments* ⌖*In-room: kitchen (some), VCR, Wi-Fi. In-hotel: no elevator* ▭*AE, MC, V* ⊙*Closed late Oct.–mid-May* ⦿*CP.*

$$–$$$ ⊡**Martha's Vineyard Surfside Motel.** These two buildings stand right in the thick of things, steps from restaurants and nightlife, so it tends to get noisy in summer. Rooms are spacious and bright (especially corner units), smartly decorated with carpets, stylish wallpaper, tile floors, and fairly standard but attractive chain-style furnishings that include a table and chairs. Deluxe rooms have water views. Four suites have whirlpool baths, and two are wheelchair-accessible. The staff is helpful and courteous. **Pros:** Affordable by MV standards, large rooms, close to dining and shopping. **Cons:** Busy location, more functional than romantic, lots of kids. ⊠*70 Oak Bluffs Ave., Box 2507, 02557* ☎*508/693–2500 or 800/537–3007* ⌖*508/693–7343* ⊕*www.mvsurfside.com* ⌑*34*

rooms, 4 suites ⅍ In-room: refrigerator, Ethernet. In-hotel: restaurant, no elevator, some pets allowed (fee) ☰AE, D, MC, V.

$$–$$$ ▥ **Pequot Hotel.** The bustle of downtown Oak Bluffs is a pleasant five-minute walk past Carpenter Gothic houses from this casual cedar-shingle inn on a tree-lined street. The furniture is quirky but comfortable; the old wing has the most atmosphere. In the main section of the building, the 1st floor has a wide porch with rocking chairs—perfect for enjoying coffee or tea with the cookies that are set out in the afternoon—and a small breakfast room where you help yourself to bagels, muffins, and cereal in the morning. The hotel is one block from the beaches that line Oak Bluffs–Edgartown Road. **Pros:** Steps from shops and dining, reasonable rates, charmingly offbeat. **Cons:** Dated decor, no room phones, some rooms are small. ✉19 Pequot Ave., 02557 ☎508/693–5087 or 800/947–8704 ⎙508/696–9413 ⊕www. pequothotel.com ⟿29 rooms, 1 3-bedroom apartment ⅍ In-room: no phone, Wi-Fi. In-hotel: no elevator ☰AE, D, MC, V ⊗Closed mid-Oct.–Apr. ⎆CP.

$ ▥ **Attleboro House.** This guesthouse, part of the Methodist Association Camp Grounds, is across the street from busy Oak Bluffs Harbor. The big 1874 gingerbread Victorian, an inn since its construction, has wraparound verandas on two floors and small, simple rooms with powder-blue walls, lacy white curtains, and a few antiques. Some rooms have sinks. Singles have three-quarter beds, and every room is provided linen exchange (but no chambermaid service) during a stay. The five shared baths are rustic and old but clean. **Pros:** Super affordable, steps from restaurants and shops, sinks in some rooms. **Cons:** Shared bathrooms, zero frills, no Web site. ✉42 Lake Ave., Box 1564, 02557 ☎508/693–4346 ⟿11 rooms with shared bath ⅍ In-room: no TV. In-hotel: no elevator ☰AE, D, MC, V ⊗Closed Oct.–May ⎆CP.

NIGHTLIFE & THE ARTS

Dark and crowded, the **Island House** (✉11 Circuit Ave. ☎508/693–4516) hosts a mixture of rock, blues, and reggae for younger crowds whose ears crave volume.

The **Lampost** (✉6 Circuit Ave. ☎508/696–9352) is a good, old-fashioned neighborhood bar with a DJ and dancing. In addition to events such as an '80s night, a Brazilian night, and a Hawaiian night, there are also swing nights. The bar attracts a young crowd.

Lola's (✉Beach Rd. ☎508/693–5007), a popular restaurant, has a lively bar that hosts local musicians. There's a great pub menu year-round, and you can also get regular restaurant cuisine at the bar.

The island's only family brewpub, **Offshore Ale** (✉Kennebec Ave. ☎508/693–2626) hosts live Latin, folk, and blues year-round and serves its own beer and ales and a terrific pub menu. Cozy up to the fireplace with a pint on cool nights.

The **Ritz Café** (✉4 Circuit Ave. ☎508/693–9851) is a popular year-round bar with a pool table that's removed in the summer to make way for dancing. There's an eclectic mix of live performances, including rock, blues, and reggae, from Monday through Saturday in summer and on weekends in the off-season.

SPORTS & THE OUTDOORS

BEACH **Joseph A. Sylvia State Beach** (⊠*Between Oak Bluffs and Edgartown, off Beach Rd.*) is a 6-mi-long sandy beach with a view of Cape Cod across Nantucket Sound. Food vendors and calm, warm waters make this a popular spot for families.

FISHING **Dick's Bait & Tackle** (⊠*New York Ave.* ☎*508/693–7669*) rents gear, sells accessories and bait, and keeps a current copy of the fishing regulations.

GOLF **Farm Neck Golf Club** (⊠*County Rd.* ☎*508/693–3057*), a scmiprivatc club on marsh-rimmed Sengekontacket Pond, has a driving range and 18 holes in a championship layout. Reservations are required 48 hours in advance.

KAYAKING Carolyn "Chick" Dowd runs great kayaking tours and offers expert instruction through her company **Island Spirit Sea-Kayak Adventures** (☎*508/693–9727* ⊕*www.islandsspirit.com*). Tours range from day trips around Cape Pogue to evening sunset and full-moon paddles.

SHOPPING

Book Den East (⊠*71 New York Ave.* ☎*508/693–3946*) stocks 20,000 out-of-print, antiquarian, and paperback books.

B*tru (⊠*40 Circuit Ave.* ☎*508/693–5222*) sells wonderfully stylish, offbeat, funky clothing and accessories.

If you're looking for out-of-the-ordinary, **Craftworks** (⊠*42 Circuit Ave.* ☎*508/693–7463*) carries outrageous painted furniture, ceramic figures, folk art, and home accessories—all handmade by American artists.

Laughing Bear (⊠*33 Circuit Ave.* ☎*508/693–9342*) carries women's clothing made of Balinese or Indian batiks plus jewelry and accessories from around the world.

The **Secret Garden** (⊠*41 Circuit Ave.* ☎*508/693–4759*), set in a yellow gingerbread cottage, has a complete line of Shelia collectibles— miniature wooden versions of Camp Ground houses and other island landmarks.

ART GALLERIES **Cousen Rose Gallery** (⊠*71 Circuit Ave.* ☎*508/693–6656*) displays works by many island artists, including Myrna Morris, John Breckenridge, Marietta Cleasby, Deborah Colter, Lynn Hoefs, Ray Prosser, and Renee Balter. During the summer months, be sure to inquire about children's art classes.

Dragonfly Gallery (⊠*Dukes County and Vineyard Aves.* ☎*508/693–8877*) changes shows weekly and holds artist receptions—featuring jazz pianist John Alaimo—every other Saturday during the summer from 4 to 7 PM. Check the local papers for a schedule of artists.

6

EDGARTOWN

6 mi southeast of Oak Bluffs.

★ Stop at a complex of buildings and lawn exhibits that constitutes the **Martha's Vineyard Historical Society** to orient yourself historically before making your way around town. The opening hours and admission listed below apply to all the buildings and exhibits—including the Thomas Cooke House, the Francis Foster Museum, the Capt. Francis Pease House, and the Carriage Shed—and the Huntington Reference Library of Vineyard History, which contains archives of oral history, letters, and law documents. The museum sells an excellent Edgartown walking-tour booklet full of anecdotes and the history of the people who have lived in the town's houses over the past three centuries; you can purchase the booklet at the entrance gatehouse in summer or at the library in winter. ⊠ *Cooke and School Sts.* ☎ *508/627–4441* ⊕ *www. marthasvineyardhistory.org* ☜ *$7* ⊙ *Mid-Mar.–mid-June and early Oct.–late Dec., Wed.–Fri. 1–4, Sat. 10–4; mid-June–early Oct., Tues.– Sat. 10–5; early Jan.–mid-Mar., Sat. 10–4.*

Once a well-to-do whaling center, Edgartown remains the Vineyard's toniest town and has preserved parts of its elegant past. Sea captains' houses from the 18th and 19th centuries, ensconced in well-manicured gardens and lawns, line the streets.

The island's oldest dwelling is the 1672 **Vincent House Museum.** A tour of this weathered-shingle farmhouse takes you along a time line that starts with the sparse furnishings of the 1600s and ends in a Federal-style parlor of the 1800s. ⊠ *Main St.* ☎ *508/627–4440* ⊕ *www.mvpreservation. org/tours.html* ☜ *Museum $5* ⊙ *May–mid-Oct., Mon.–Sat. 10:30–3.*

The **Edgartown Lighthouse,** surrounded by a public beach, provides a great view (but seaweedy bathing). The white cast-iron tower was floated by barge from Ipswich, Massachusetts, in 1938. ⊠ *Off N. Water St.*

NEED A BREAK? If you need a pick-me-up, pop into **Espresso Love** (⊠ *3 S. Water St.* ☎ *508/627–9211*) for a cappuccino and a homemade raspberry scone or blueberry muffin. If you prefer something cold, the staff also makes fruit smoothies. Light lunch fare is served: bagel sandwiches, soups, and delicious pastries and cookies—all homemade, of course. It's by the Edgartown bus station.

♺ The 350-acre **Felix Neck Wildlife Sanctuary,** a Massachusetts Audubon
★ Society preserve 3 mi outside Edgartown toward Oak Bluffs and Vineyard Haven, has 2 mi of hiking trails traversing marshland, fields, woods, seashore, and waterfowl and reptile ponds. Naturalist-led events include sunset hikes, stargazing, snake or bird walks, and canoeing. ⊠ *Off Edgartown–Vineyard Haven Rd.* ☎ *508/627–4850* ☜ *$4* ⊙ *Center June–Aug., Mon.–Sat. 8–4, Sun. 10–3; Sept.–May, Tues.–Sat. 8–4, Sun. noon–4. Trails daily sunrise–7* PM.

WHERE TO STAY & EAT

$$$$ ✕**Atria.** One of the island's more urbane venues, Atria feels like a big-★ city bistro and cocktail lounge, with a swank dining room, glam crowd, and artful food presentations. Chef Christian Thornton uses eclectic, globally influenced ingredients to come up with such entrées as cracklin' pork shank with collard greens and sour cream–mustard sauce; and grilled lamb T-bones with Tuscan-style white beans, roasted tomatoes, grilled artichokes, and a red-wine reduction. Top starters include steak tartar with crisp shallots, capers, truffle oil, and aged balsamic vinegar; and braised-veal-cheek ravioli with stuffed squash blossoms, shaved Parmesan, and truffle oil. The chocolate-molten cake with cappuccino ice cream is a great finish. There's jazz certain evenings. ✉ *137 Main St.* ☎ *508/627–5850* ⊕ *www.atriamv.com* ⊟ *AE, MC, V.*

$$$–$$$$ ✕**Alchemy Bistro and Bar.** According to the menu, the dictionary meaning of *alchemy* is "a magic power having as its asserted aim the discovery of a panacea and the preparation of the elixir of longevity"—lofty goals for a French-style bistro. This high-class version has elegant gray wainscoting, classic paper-covered white tablecloths, old wooden floors, and an opening cut into the ceiling to reveal the 2nd-floor tables. The only things missing are the patina of age, experience, cigarette smoke—and French working folk's prices—but you can expect quality and imagination. One example is the fried cornmeal-dusted soft-shell crab with lemon risotto, sweet peas, and artichokes. The alcohol list, long and complete, includes cognacs, grappas, and beers. ✉ *71 Main St.* ☎ *508/627–9999* ⊟ *AE, MC, V.*

$$$–$$$$ ✕**Detente.** A dark, intimate wine bar and restaurant with hardwood **Fodor's**Choice floors and rich banquette seating, Detente serves more than a dozen ★ wines by the glass as well as numerous half-bottles. Even if you're not much of an oenophile, it's worth a trip just for the innovative food, much of it from local farms and seafood purveyors. Try the complex starter of ahi-tuna tartare with toasted pine nuts, vanilla-pear puree, ginger, and arugula salad, followed by such choice entrées as roasted roasted venison loin with thyme spaetzle, sautéed Swiss chard, blue cheese, roasted figs, and a port reduction; or lemon-honey–basted halibut with potato au gratin, truffled leek puree, roasted artichokes, and oven-dried tomatoes. ✉ *Nevin Sq., off Water St.* ☎ *508/627–8810* ⊕ *www.detentewinebar.com* ⊟ *AE, MC, V* ⊘ *Closed Tues. and Jan.–mid-Apr. No lunch.*

$$$–$$$$ ✕**Lure.** The airy restaurant at Winnetu Oceanside Resort draws plenty **Fodor's**Choice of discerning diners, including plenty of nonhotel guests, to sample ★ some of the most exquisite and creatively prepared seafood on the island. It's the only dining room with a south-facing water view, and it's a stunning one at that. The staff here is young, eager to please, and friendly, and chef Mark Goldberg, previously of Boston's famed Mistral restaurant, knows his way around a kitchen. You won't find a better lobster dish on the island than Lure's tender butter-poached version topped with roasted corn and fava beans and served alongside buttery cornbread. Locally caught fluke with littleneck clams, leeks, smoked bacon, and a rich chowder broth is another star. Finish off with the molten Valhrona chocolate cake with vanilla ice cream and

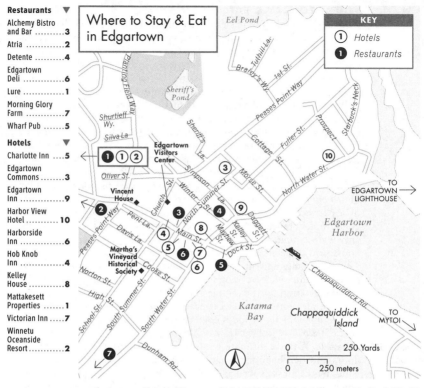

raspberry coulis. ⊠*Katama Rd.* ☎*508/627–3663* ⊟*AE, D, MC, V* ⊘*No lunch.*

$–$$$ ✕**Wharf Pub.** The name may sound generic, and the menu tends toward the predictable—shrimp scampi, prime rib, burgers, and steaks—but this lively bar and grill in the heart of Edgartown earns kudos for its well-prepared food, inviting dining room and pair of bars, and easy-going vibe. Standouts include the grilled flank steak with fries and a horseradish cream sauce, and the Cobb salad with ham and chicken. You can tune in to a game on the TV or mingle with locals. It's nothing fancy, but this year-round mainstay is consistently reliable and a great bet for singles, groups of friends, and—especially during the day—families. ⊠*Lower Main St.* ☎*508/627–9966* ⊟*AE, D, MC, V.*

¢–$ ✕**Morning Glory Farm.** Fresh farm greens in the salads and vegetables in
★ the soups; homemade pies, cookies, and cakes; and a picnic table and grass to enjoy them on make this an ideal place for a simple country lunch. ⊠*W. Tisbury Rd.* ☎*508/627–9003* ⊟*No credit cards.*

¢ ✕**Edgartown Deli.** A no-frills place with a down-home, happy feeling, this deli has walls and a glass counter plastered with specials written on multicolored paper. Brightly lighted booths fill one side of the room, and customers line up at the counter for orders to go. Breakfast specials, served from 8 until 10:45, include egg, cheese, and *linguiça* (garlicky Portuguese sausage) on a roll. Lunch sandwiches include corned beef and Swiss, roast beef, turkey, pastrami, or steak and cheese. ⊠*52 Main St.* ☎*508/627–4789* ⚠*Reservations not accepted* ⊟*No credit cards* ⊘*Closed Nov.–Apr. No dinner.*

$$$$ 🏨**Charlotte Inn.** From the moment you walk up to the dark-wood
Fodor'sChoice Scottish barrister's check-in desk at this regal 1864 inn, you'll be sur-
★ rounded by the trappings and customs of a bygone era. Guests' names are handwritten into the register by the dignified and attentive staff. Beautiful antique furnishings, objets d'art, and paintings fill the property—the book you pick up in your room might be an 18th-century edition of Voltaire, and your bed could be a hand-carved four-poster. All rooms have hair dryers and robes; rooms in the carriage house have fireplaces and French doors that open into the brick courtyard as well as private patios. The elegant atmosphere that pervades the property extends to the inn's swank restaurant, the Catch. **Pros:** Over-the-top lavish, quiet yet convenient location, beautifully landscaped. **Cons:** Restaurant has changed over a lot lately, can feel overly formal, intimidating if you don't adore museum-quality antiques. ⊠*27 S. Summer St., 02539* ☎*508/627–4751 or 800/735–2478* 📠*508/627–4652* ⊕*www. relaischateaux.com* ⇆*21 rooms, 2 suites* ⚲*In-room: Ethernet. In-hotel: restaurant, no elevator, no kids under 14* ⊟*AE, MC, V* ⦿⧵*CP.*

$$$$ 🏨**Harbor View Hotel.** The centerpiece of this historic hotel that under-
★ went a massive overhaul completed in 2007 is a gray-shingle, 1891 Victorian building with wraparound veranda and a gazebo. Accommodations are also in a complex of nearby buildings in a residential neighborhood. The contemporary town houses have cathedral ceilings, decks, kitchens, and large living areas with sofa beds. Rooms in other buildings are laid out like upscale motor-lodge units but have the same fine decor and plush in-room amenties, from CD clock radios to L'Occitane bath products. A beach, good for walking, stretches ¾ mi from the hotel's dock, and the sheltered bay is a great place for kids to swim. Packages and theme weekends are available. The hotel is also home to the Coach House restaurant, a worthy spot for a full meal that also has an excellent, lighter bar menu. Plans for 2008 include a top-notch full-service spa. **Pros:** Great harbor views, not far from restaurants, recently renovated. **Cons:** Close to but a few blocks from commercial district, less intimate than B&Bs, steep rates. ⊠*131 N. Water St., Box 7, 02539* ☎*508/627–7000 or 800/225–6005* 📠*508/742– 1042* ⊕*www.harbor-view.com* ⇆*102 rooms, 22 suites* ⚲*In-room: kitchen (some), refrigerator, Wi-Fi. In-hotel: 2 restaurants, room service, tennis courts, pool, gym, spa, concierge, laundry service* ⊟*AE, DC, MC, V.*

$$$$ 🏨**Hob Knob Inn.** This 19th-century Gothic-revival inn blends the amenities and service of a luxury hotel with the ambience and charm of a small B&B. A short walk from the harbor, it's on the main road into town—but far enough out to avoid crowds. Rooms are gracious and quite large by island standards; the upper floors have dormer windows. Art and antiques help capture the island's rural, seaside charm, and many rooms overlook the spectacular gardens. The inn also runs fishing trips and charters on its 27-foot Boston Whaler. Full breakfast and lavish afternoon tea are included. **Pros:** Spacious rooms, afternoon tea included, easy walk to harbor yet slightly removed from crowds. **Cons:** Steep rates, service can sometimes feel a bit impersonal, near but not overlooking harbor. ⊠ *128 Main St., 02539* ☎ *508/627–9510 or 800/696–2723* 🖷 *508/627–4560* ⊕ *www.hobknob.com* ⮐ *17 rooms, 1 suite* ♿ *In-room: Wi-Fi. In-hotel: gym, bicycles, no elevator, no kids under 10* ⊟ *AE, MC, V* ⫟*BP.*

$$$$ 🖵 **Kelley House.** In the center of town, this sister property of the Harbor View combines services and amenities with a country-inn feel. A new owner for both properties has instituted a number of major improvements to the decor and facilities in 2007. The 1742 white clapboard main house and the adjacent Garden House are surrounded by pink roses. Large suites in the Chappaquiddick House and the two spacious town houses in the Wheel House have porches (most with harbor views) and living rooms. The Newes from America, a dark and cozy spot with original hand-hewn timbers and ballast-brick walls, serves typical pub victuals and microbrewed beers on tap. **Pros:** Lots of historic charm, pretty gardens, some harbor views. **Cons:** On street with lots of pedestrian traffic, pricey, frequent wedding locale. ⊠ *23 Kelley St., Box 37, 02539* ☎ *508/627–7900 or 800/225–6005* 🖷 *508/627–8142* ⊕ *www.kelley-house.com* ⮐ *52 rooms, 8 suites, 2 town-house units* ♿ *In-room: kitchen (some), Ethernet. In-hotel: restaurant, bar, tennis courts, pool, laundry service* ⊟ *AE, DC, MC, V* ⊘ *Closed mid-Oct.–Apr.* ⫟*CP.*

$$$$ 🖵 **Mattakesett Properties.** This attractive resort complex, which is part of the nearby Winnetu Oceanside Resort, sits close to South Beach. Mattakesett differs from the Winnetu in that all of its units are owner-furnished town houses and condominiums with three to four bedrooms; guests at either property can use the amenities at both. All homes have fireplaces and decks. The children's programs are extensive, and the pool and barbecue grills make this a favorite for families. Bookings at Mattakesett are taken on a per-week basis only. A vintage fire truck and livery are used to shuttle you around the area. **Pros:** Access to Winnetu facilities, pretty good value for large families. **Cons:** Some units more nicely decorated than others, a longish walk from town, lots of kids in summer. ⊠ *Katama Rd., RFD 270, 02539* ☎ *508/627–4747 or 978/443–1733* ⊕ *www.winnetu.com/mattakesett.htm* ⮐ *92 units* ♿ *In-room: kitchen, Ethernet (some), Wi-Fi (some). In-hotel: tennis courts, pool, gym, children's programs (ages 3–12), laundry facilities, no elevator* ⊟ *AE, MC, V* ⊘ *Mattakesett closed Nov.–Apr.*

$$$$
Fodor's Choice
★
🖵 **Winnetu Oceanside Resort.** A departure from most properties on the island, the contemporary Winnetu—styled after the grand multistory resorts of the gilded age—both encourages families and provides a contemporary seaside-resort experience for couples. This all-suites property has units that can sleep up to 11 guests. All have kitchens and decks or patios with views. Room decor is stylish and modern but casual enough so that kids feel right at home. The resort arranges bicycling and kayaking trips, lighthouse tours, and other island activities. The General Store carries snacks, and the superb Lure restaurant, the only one on the island with a south-facing water view, prepares tasty box lunches for the beach. (It's open to the public and specializes

in gourmet fish fare.) The staff will stock your kitchen in advance of your arrival on request and can arrange a wide range of island tours and activities, from bike trips to yoga classes. Clambakes are held on the grounds on Wednesday evening. In summer, all stays must be a minimum of three nights. **Pros:** Outstanding staff, tons of activities, fantastic restaurant. **Cons:** Pricey, a longish walk from town, lots of kids in summer. ✉ *Katama Rd., RFD 270, 02539* ☎ *508/627–4747 or 978/443–1733* ⊕ *www.winnetu.com* ⤶ *22 suites* ⅋ *In-room: kitchen, VCR, some Ethernet, some Wi-Fi. In-hotel: restaurant, tennis courts, pools, gym, concierge, children's programs (ages 3–12), laundry facilities* ⊟ *MC, V* ☾ *Closed Dec.–mid-Apr.*

$$$–$$$$

★

🔝 **Victorian Inn.** White with the classic black shutters of the town's historic homes and fronted by ornate columns, this appropriately named inn sits a block from the downtown harbor; it was built as the home of 19th-century whaling captain Lafayette Rowley. Today the inn's three floors are done in dark woods and bold floral wallpapers, with rugs over wood floors. Several rooms hold handmade reproduction four-poster beds. Breakfast, served in season in the brick-patio garden, includes creative muffins and breads. **Pros:** Staff is top-notch, super romantic, close to restaurants. **Cons:** You better love high-style Victoriana, not geared toward families, lots of pedestrian traffic. ✉ *24 S. Water St., 02539* ☎ *508/627–4784* ⊕ *www.thevic.com* ⤶ *14 rooms* ⅋ *In-room: Wi-Fi. In-hotel: no elevator, no kids under 8* ⊟ *MC, V* ☉| *BP.*

$$–$$$$

🔝 **Harborside Inn.** Edgartown's only true waterfront accommodation, with boat docks at the end of its nicely landscaped lawn, this large inn provides a central town location, harbor-view decks, and plenty of amenities. Seven two- and three-story buildings sprawl around formal rose beds, brick walkways, a brick patio, and a heated pool. Rooms have colonial-style but modern furnishings, brass beds and lamps, and textured wallpapers. Some units have terraces facing Edgartown Harbor. **Pros:** Steps from restaurants and shops, immaculate rooms, lovely gardens. **Cons:** In center of Edgartown action and crowds, it's run as condo-timeshare, lots of kids in summer. ✉ *3 S. Water St., Box 67, 02539* ☎ *508/627–4321 or 800/627–4009* 🖶 *508/627–7566* ⊕ *www. theharborsideinn.com* ⤶ *87 rooms, 3 suites* ⅋ *In-room: refrigerator, Ethernet. In-hotel: pool* ⊟ *AE, MC, V* ☾ *Closed mid-Nov.–mid-Apr.*

$–$$$$

🔝 **Edgartown Inn.** The inside of the former home of whaling captain Thomas Worth still evokes its late 18th century origins. In fact, its cozy parlor and antique-filled rooms look as if the captain still lives here. The inn was also the spot where Nathaniel Hawthorne wrote much of his *Twice Told Tales* during a stay. Many an Edgartonian joins inn guests in the paneled dining room or back garden for breakfast in summertime. **Pros:** Great value, main inn building is rich in history, close to Edgartown shopping and dining. **Cons:** No Internet access, doesn't accept credit cards, least-expensive rooms have shared baths. ✉ *56 N. Water St., 02539* ☎ *508/627–4794* 🖶 *508/627–9420* ⊕ *www.edgartowninn. com* ⤶ *20 rooms, 4 with shared bath* ⊟ *No credit cards.*

$$–$$$

🔝 **Edgartown Commons.** This condominium complex of seven buildings, which includes an old house and motel rooms set around a busy pool, is just a couple of blocks from town. Studios and one- or two-bedroom

6

condos all have full kitchens, and some are very spacious. Each has been decorated by its individual owner, so the decor varies—some have an older look, others are new and bright. Definitely family-oriented, the place is abuzz with kids; rooms away from the pool are quieter. **Pros:** Nice big pool, full kitchens in units, great for families. **Cons:** Decor varies according to each unit's owner, lacks historical character, lots of kids. ⊠*20 Pease's Point Way, Box 1293, 02539* ☎*508/627–4671 or 800/439–4671* 🖶*508/627–4271* ⊕*www.edgartowncommons.com* ⇩*35 units* ⭘*In-room: no phone, kitchen (some), some Wi-Fi. In-hotel: pool, laundry facilities, no elevator, public Wi-Fi* ⊟*AE, MC, V* ☉*Closed mid-Oct.–Apr.*

NIGHTLIFE & THE ARTS

NIGHTLIFE The **Atria Bar** (⊠*137 Main St.* ☎*508/627–5850*) is off the beaten path, but it's a quiet, comfortable place to escape the summer crowds. Enjoy one of the clever drinks, including the Aunt Katherine Manhattan (Maker's Mark and sweet vermouth, served neat), and the Espresso Martini (Stoli vanilla vodka, Kahlúa, Tia Maria, and a shot of fresh espresso).

Outerland (⊠*Martha's Vineyard Airport, Edgartown–W. Tisbury Rd.* ☎*508/693–1137*) books big-name acts such as Medeski, Martin and Wood, Ben Lee, Kate Taylor, and the Derek Trucks Band play.

The Wharf (⊠*Lower Main St.* ☎*508/627–9966*) is a great spot for tasty food and a terrific place for cocktails, people-watching, and listening to live rock and pop music.

SPORTS & THE OUTDOORS

Bend-in-the-Road Beach (⊠*Beach Rd.*), the town's public beach, is backed by low, grassy dunes and wild roses. **Little Beach** (⊠*End of Fuller St.*) is a lesser-known beach that looks like a crooked pinkie pointing into Eel Pond; it's a great place for bird-watching (be careful of the fenced-off piping plover breeding grounds in the dunes).

Big Eye Charters (☎*508/627–3649*) leads fishing charters from Edgartown Harbor. **Coop's Bait and Tackle** (⊠*147 W. Tisbury Rd.* ☎*508/627–3909*) sells accessories and bait, rents fishing gear, and books fishing charters.

SHOPPING

Claudia (⊠*35 Winter St.* ☎*508/627–8306*) brings you back to another era with its clever windows, antique display cases, and fabulous French fragrances. You'll find designer, vintage-looking, and fine gold and silver jewelry in a variety of price ranges.

David Le Breton, the owner of **Edgartown Books** (⊠*44 Main St.* ☎*508/627–8463*), is a true bibliophile. He carries a large selection of current and island-related titles and will be happy to make a summer reading recommendation.

The **Edgartown Scrimshaw Gallery** (⊠*43 Main St.* ☎*508/627–9439*) showcases a large collection of scrimshaw, including some antique pieces.

Pick up fine tea accoutrements, chocolates, and gourmet items at **English Butler** (⊠ *22 Winter St.* ☎ *508/627–1013*), a dainty boutique that hosts cheeky tea parties (gossip is encouraged) on Wednesday night.

The **Old Sculpin Gallery** (⊠ *58 Dock St.* ☎ *508/627–4881*) is the Martha's Vineyard Art Association's headquarters.

CHAPPAQUIDDICK ISLAND

1 mi southeast of Edgartown.

A sparsely populated area with many nature preserves, Chappaquiddick Island makes for a pleasant day trip or bike ride on a sunny day. The "island" is actually connected to the Vineyard by a long sand spit that begins in South Beach in Katama. It's a spectacular 2¾-mi walk, or you can take the ferry ($10 for car and driver and $3 for each additional passenger), which departs about every five minutes from 7 AM to midnight daily, June to mid-October, and less frequently from 7 AM to 11:15 PM mid-October to May.

The Land Bank's 226-acre **Three Ponds Preserve** (⊠ *Off Chappaquiddick Rd.*) is a popular, scenic picnicking spot. Mown grasses surround a serpentine pond with an island in its center and a woodland backdrop behind—a truly lovely setting. Across the road are fields, woods, and another pond.

Fodor'sChoice The Trustees of Reservations' 14-acre **Mytoi** preserve is a serene, beautifully tended, Japanese-inspired garden with a creek-fed pool spanned ★ by a bridge and rimmed with Japanese maples, azaleas, bamboo, and irises. A boardwalk runs through part of the grounds, where you're apt to see box turtles and hear the sounds of songbirds. There are few more enchanting spots on the island. The garden was created in 1958 by a private citizen. Restroom facilities are available. ⊠ *Dike Rd., [1/5] mi from intersection with Chappaquiddick Rd.* ☎ *508/627–7689* ☎ *Free* ☉ *Daily sunrise–sunset.*

A conglomeration of habitats where you can swim, walk, fish, or just sit and enjoy the surroundings, the **Cape Poge Wildlife Refuge** (⊠ *East end of Dike Rd., 3 mi from Chappaquiddick ferry landing*), on the easternmost shore of Chappaquiddick Island, is more than 6 square mi of wilderness. Its dunes, woods, cedar thickets, moors, salt marshes, ponds, tidal flats, and barrier beach serve as an important migration stopover and nesting area for numerous sea- and shorebirds. The best way to get to the refuge is as part of a naturalist-led **jeep drive** (☎ *508/627–3599*).

★ The 200-acre **Wasque Reservation** (pronounced *wayce*-kwee) is mostly a vast beach. Closing off the south end of Katama Bay, this is where Chappaquiddick connects to the mainland Vineyard. You can fish, sunbathe, take the trail by Swan Pond, walk to the island's southeasternmost tip at Wasque Point, or dip into the surf—use caution, as the currents are strong. Wasque Beach is accessed by a flat boardwalk with benches overlooking the west end of Swan Pond. It's a pretty walk skirting the

6

pond, with ocean views on one side and poles for osprey nests on the other. Atop a bluff is a pine-shaded picnic grove with a spectacular, practically 180-degree panorama. ⊠ *At east end of Wasque Rd., 5 mi from Chappaquiddick ferry landing* ☎ *508/627–7260* ☎ *Cars $3, plus $3 per adult late May–mid-Sept.; free rest of yr* ⊙ *Property 24 hrs. Gatehouse late May–mid-Oct., daily 9–5.*

SPORTS & THE OUTDOORS

BEACHES   **East Beach,** one of the area's best beaches, is accessible by car from Dike Road. There is a $3 fee to enter the beach. **Wasque Beach,** at the Wasque Reservation, is an uncrowded ½-mi sandy beach with a parking lot and restrooms. The surf and currents are sometimes strong.

WEST TISBURY

8 mi west of Edgartown, 6½ mi south of Vineyard Haven.

West Tisbury retains its rural appeal and maintains its agricultural tradition at several active horse and produce farms. The town center looks very much like a small New England village, complete with a white-steepled church.

★   A rich and expansive collection of flora and serene walking trails are the attractions of the **Polly Hill Arboretum.** Horticulturist and part-time Vineyard resident Polly Hill, now in her nineties, has over the years tended some 2,000 species of plants and developed nearly 100 species herself on her old sheep farm in West Tisbury. On-site are azaleas, tree peonies, dogwoods, hollies, lilacs, magnolias, and more. Hill raised them from seeds without the use of a greenhouse, and her patience is the inspiration of the arboretum. Now run as a nonprofit center, the arboretum also runs guided tours, a lecture series, and a visitor center and gift shop. ⊠ *809 State Rd.* ☎ *508/693–9426* ⊕ *www.pollyhillarboretum.org* ☎ *$5* ⊙ *Grounds daily sunrise–sunset. Visitor center late May–mid-Oct., daily 9:30–4; guided tours by appointment.*

■ NEED A
BREAK?   Step back in time with a visit to **Alley's General Store** (⊠ *State Rd.* ☎ *508/693–0088*), the heart of town since 1858. Alley's sells a truly general variety of goods: everything from hammers to housewares and dill pickles to sweet muffins as well as great things you find only in a country store. There's even a post office inside. Behind the parking lot, Garcia's at Back Alley's serves tasty sandwiches and pastries to go year-round.

Long Point, a 632-acre Trustees of Reservations preserve with an open area of grassland and heath, provides a lovely walk with the promise of a refreshing swim at its end. The area is bounded on the east by freshwater Homer's Pond, on the west by saltwater Tisbury Great Pond, and on the south by fantastic, mile-long South Beach on the Atlantic Ocean. Long Cove Pond, a sandy freshwater swimming pond, is an ideal spot for bird-watchers. ⊠ *Mid-June–mid-Sept., turn left onto unmarked dirt road (Waldron's Bottom Rd., look for mailboxes) 3/10 mi west of airport on Edgartown–W. Tisbury Rd.; at end, follow signs to Long Point parking lot. Mid-Sept.–mid-June, follow unpaved Deep Bottom Rd.*

(1 mi west of airport) 2 mi to lot ☎*508/693–7392* ✉*Mid-June–mid-Sept., $10 per vehicle plus $3 per adult; free rest of yr* ⊙*Daily 9–6.*

A rather unique island undertaking, the **Chicama Vineyards** is the fruit of the Mathiesen family's labors. From 3 acres of trees and rocks, George—a broadcaster from San Francisco—his wife, Cathy, and their six children have built a fine vineyard. They started in 1971 with 18,000 vinifera vines, and today the winery produces nearly 100,000 bottles a year from Chardonnay, Cabernet, and other European grapes. Chenin blanc, Merlot, and a cranberry dessert wine are among their 10 or more tasty varieties. A shop selling their wine, along with herbed vinegars, mustards, jellies, and other foods prepared on the premises, is open year-round. ✉*Stoney Hill Rd.* ☎*508/693–0309* ⊕*www.chicamavineyards.com* ✉*Free tours and tastings* ⊙*Late May–mid-Oct., Mon.–Sat. 11–5, Sun. 1–5, tours at 2 and 4; call for off-season hrs and tastings.*

In season you can pick your own strawberries, raspberries, and flowers at **Thimble Farm**, where you can also buy preboxed fruit if you're not feeling quite so agrarian. The farm also sells cut flowers, melons, pumpkins, hydroponic tomatoes, and other produce. ✉*Stoney Hill Rd.* ☎*508/693–6396* ⊙*June–early Oct., Tues.–Sun. 10–5.*

★ At the center of the island, the **Manuel F. Correllus State Forest** is a 5,000-acre pine and scrub-oak forest crisscrossed with hiking trails and circled by a paved but rough bike trail (mopeds are prohibited). You'll also find a 2-mi nature trail, a 2-mi par fitness course, and horse trails. The West Tisbury side of the state forest joins with an equally large Edgartown parcel to virtually surround the airport. ✉*Headquarters on Barnes Rd. by airport* ☎*508/693–2540* ✉*Free* ⊙*Daily sunrise–sunset.*

A paradise for bird-watchers, **Sepiessa Point Reservation** consists of 164 acres on splendid Tisbury Great Pond, with expansive pond and ocean views, walking trails around coves and saltwater marshes, bird-watching, horse trails, swimming, and a boat launch. ✉*New La., which becomes Tiah's Cove Rd., off W. Tisbury Rd.* ☎*508/627–7141* ✉*Free* ⊙*Daily sunrise–sunset.*

WHERE TO STAY & EAT

$$$–$$$$
Fodor's Choice
★

×🏨 **Lambert's Cove Inn and Restaurant.** A narrow road winds through pine woods and beside creeper-covered stone walls to this posh, handsomely designed inn surrounded by gardens and old stone walls. In 2005, genial innkeepers Scott Jones and I. Kell Hicklin bought what had been a slightly fading 1790 farmhouse inn and gave it a clean, crisp makeover. The richly appointed rooms each have decorative schemes and antiques based on grand East Coast–resort towns, from Key West to Bar Harbor. Those in the outbuildings are airy and a bit more contemporary, some with decks and porches. Guests receive free passes to beautiful and private Lambert's Cove beach. Fireplaces and hardwood floors lend warmth to the stellar contemporary restaurant ($$$; reservations essential), where you might dine on crab cakes with caper aioli and shaved-fennel salad, or a main course of braised veal cheeks with sweet corn-English pea risotto and a Madeira wine reduction.

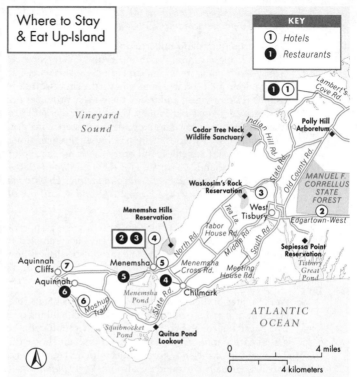

Pros: Smart and contemporary decor, fantastic restaurant, serene and verdant grounds. **Cons:** Need a car to explore island from here, not for budget travelers, total seclusion is a drawback if you love being in center of action. ⊠ *Off Lambert's Cove Rd.* ☌ *R.R. 1, Box 422, Vineyard Haven 02568* ☎ *508/693–2298* 🖶 *508/693–7890* ⊕ *www.lambertscoveinn.com* ⇆ *17 rooms* ⚐ *In-room: DVD, Ethernet. In-hotel: restaurant, tennis court, pool, no elevator* ⊟ *AE, MC, V* ⦿ *BP.*

¢ 🏠 **Martha's Vineyard International Hostel.** The only budget, roof-over-your-head alternative in season, this hostel is one of the country's best. The large, common kitchen is outfitted with multiple refrigerators and stoves (barbecue grills are available, too), the common room has a fireplace and plenty of books, and you'll catch wind of local events on the bulletin board. Morning chores are required in summer. The hostel runs summer programs on island history, as well as nature tours. It's near a bike path, and 2 mi from the airport and about 3 mi from the nearest beach. Buses stop out front. **Pros:** It's cheap, it's just off a bike path, it's a fun place to meet young and active backpackers. **Cons:** It's cheap, you need to rely on bus or bike to get to restaurants and towns, prepare to enjoy doing those morning chores during high season. ⊠ *Edgartown–W. Tisbury Rd., Box 158, 02575* ☎ *508/693–2665* ⊕ *www.usahostels.org* ⇆ *78 dorm-style beds* ⚐ *In-hotel: laundry facilities, no elevator* ⊟ *MC, V* ⊘ *Closed mid-Oct.–mid-Apr.*

SPORTS & THE OUTDOORS

Lambert's Cove Beach (⊠ *Lambert's Cove Rd.*), one of the island's prettiest, has fine sand and clear water. The Vineyard Sound Beach has calm waters; it's good for children.

SHOPPING

The **Granary Gallery at the Red Barn** (⊠ *Old County Rd.* ☎ *508/693–0455*) displays early-American furniture and exhibits artworks by island and international artists.

CHILMARK

5½ mi southwest of West Tisbury.

Chilmark is a rural village where ocean-view roads, rustic woodlands, and lack of crowds have drawn chic summer visitors and resulted in stratospheric real-estate prices. Laced with rough roads and winding stone fences that once separated fields and pastures, Chilmark reminds people of what the Vineyard was like in an earlier time, before the developers came.

6

NEED A BREAK?

The **Chilmark Store** (⊠ *7 State Rd.* ☎ *508/645–3655*) serves up pizza, burgers, salads, and deli sandwiches—it's a solid take-out lunch spot. If you've bicycled into town, the wooden rockers on the porch may be just the place to take a break—or find a picnic spot of your own nearby to enjoy a fish burger or a slice of the pizza of the day. It's open from May to mid-October.

WHERE TO STAY & EAT

$$$–$$$$ ✕**At the Cornerway.** Jamaican chef Deon Thomas brings cuisine rich in his home island's flavors to this American-style bistro. Adventurous diners can try braised goat shoulder with prunes and pearl onions; those with less-exotic tastes can choose from offerings like oven-crisped orange duck with a chambord drizzle, and roasted grouper curry with lime-mango chutney. Whichever pleases your palate, make sure to finish with either the coconut bread pudding or chocolate rum cake. If you want to hear what your dinner companions have to say, ask for a corner seat away from the atrium. The acoustics are terrible in this barnlike structure that once hosted square dances. ⊠ *Beetlebung Corner* ☎ *508/645–9300* ⊕ *www.atthecornerway.com* ▤ *AE, MC, V* ⌂▯*BYOB.*

$$$–$$$$ ✕▧**Inn at Blueberry Hill.** Exclusive and secluded, this cedar-shingle retreat on 56 acres of former farmland puts you in the heart of the rural Vineyard. The restaurant, Theo's ($$$–$$$$), is relaxed and elegant, with fresh, health-conscious food that is thoughtfully prepared. You might dine on maple-spiced duck breast with sweet-potato gnocchi, or seared sea scallops with a basil-grapefruit-tarragon beurre blanc. A continental breakfast is included in the room rate, and a box lunch is available for a picnic on the beach (the inn runs a guest shuttle to Lucy Vincent and Squibnocket beaches). Rooms are sparsely but tastefully decorated with simple island-made furniture; most have glass doors that open onto terraces or private decks. There is a large par-

lor-library with a fireplace. **Pros:** Lots of privacy, many rooms have terraces with views, terrific restaurant. **Cons:** Not a great choice for children, a long drive from town centers, Wi-Fi in common room but not individual guest rooms. ⊠ *74 North Rd., 02535* ☎ *508/645–3322 or 800/356–3322* ☐ *508/645–3799* ⊕ *www.blueberryinn.com* ➪ *25 rooms* ♿ *In-hotel: restaurant, tennis court, pool, gym, airport shuttle, public Wi-Fi, no kids under 12, no elevator* ▤ *AE, MC, V* ⊘ *Closed Nov.–Apr.* ⦿| *CP.*

SPORTS & THE OUTDOORS

★ A dirt road leads off South Road to beautiful **Lucy Vincent Beach,** which in summer is open only to Chilmark residents and those staying in town.

Squibnocket Beach (⊠ *Off South Rd.*), on the south shore, is a narrow stretch of boulder-strewn coastline that is part smooth rocks and pebbles, part fine sand. The area has good waves, and it's popular with surfers. During the season, this beach is restricted to residents and visitors with passes.

SHOPPING

★ **Chilmark Chocolates** (⊠ *State Rd.* ☎ *508/645–3013*) sells superior chocolates and what might just be the world's finest butter crunch, which you can sometimes watch being made in the back room.

★ **Martha's Vineyard Glassworks** (⊠ *683 State Rd.* ☎ *508/693–6026*) makes a great stop not just to browse the colorful, stunningly crafted contemporary glass pieces but also to watch the artists at work in the glassblowing studio.

MENEMSHA

★ *1½ mi northwest of Chilmark.*

Unspoiled by the "progress" of the past few decades, the working port of Menemsha is a jumble of weathered fishing shacks, fishing and pleasure boats, drying nets, and lobster pots. Several scenes from the movie *Jaws* were filmed here. The village is popular with cyclists who like to stop for ice cream or chowder.

WHERE TO STAY & EAT

$$$$ ✕ **Home Port.** A classic seafood-in-the-rough experience since the 1930s, this breezy seasonal island institution serves absolutely the freshest lobster around (including a hefty 3-pound lobster that'll set you back $60), plus steamers, scallops, smoked bluefish pâté and local fish. The fishing nets and other nautical paraphernalia hanging on the knotty-pine walls bring you back to a bygone era. Sailors from all around southern New England savor the chance to pull into Menemsha for a meal at this stalwart, where commoners often rub shoulders with celebs. You can also get your meal to go and enjoy it on the lawn or by the dock overlooking the harbor. ⊠ *At end of North Rd.* ☎ *508/645–2679* ⊕ *www.home-portmv.com* ⟵ *Reservations essential* ▤ *MC, V* ⦿| *BYOB* ⊘ *Closed mid-Oct.–mid-Apr. No lunch.*

Martha's Vineyard Trivia

The year-round population of the island is about 15,000. On any given day in summer, the population increases fivefold, to an estimated 75,000.

Some four decades after the island was charted in 1602, Bay Colony businessman Thomas Mayhew struck a deal with the Crown and purchased Martha's Vineyard, as well as Nantucket and the Elizabeth Islands, for @40.

Jeanne and Hugh Taylor, the latter the brother of recording star James Taylor, operate the Outermost Inn, by the lighthouse in Aquinnah.

Total shoreline: 126 mi. Total land area: 100 square mi.

Martha's Vineyard was formed more than 20,000 years ago as great sheets of ice, as thick as 2 mi, descended from the frigid northern climes into what is now New England, pushing great chunks of earth and rock before them. When the glaciers melted and receded, the island, as well as Nantucket and Cape Cod, remained in their wake.

When residents say they are going "Up-Island," they mean they're heading to the western areas of Aquinnah, Chilmark, Menemsha, and West Tisbury. The designation is based on nautical terminology, where heading west means going "up" in longitude. "Down-Island" refers to Vineyard Haven, Oak Bluffs, and Edgartown.

During the height of the 19th-century whaling era, It was considered good luck to have an Aquinnah Wampanoag on board. The Wampanoags were renowned as sailors and harpooners. Town residents voted to change the name of Gay Head to Aquinnah in 1997, and the official change was signed into law on May 7, 1998.

The North American continent's last heath hen, an eastern prairie chicken, died in a forest fire on Martha's Vineyard in 1932. A monument to it stands in the State Forest just off the West Tisbury–Edgartown Road.

West Tisbury resident, farmer, and sailor Joshua Slocum became the first man to sail solo around the world. He set out in 1895 in his 36-foot sloop and returned three years later. Ten years later he was lost at sea.

Despite the fact that Great Harbour was renamed Edgartown after the young son of the Duke of York, the unfortunate three-year-old died one month before the name became official.

6

¢–$$ ✕**Larsen's.** Basically a retail fish store, Larsen's has a raw take-out coun-
Fodor's Choice ter and will also boil lobsters for you. Dig into a plate of fresh little-
★ necks or cherrystones. Oysters are not a bad alternative. There's also seafood chowder and a variety of smoked fish and dips. Bring your own bottle of wine or beer, buy your dinner here, and then set up on the rocks, the docks, or the beach: there's no finer alfresco rustic dining on the island. Larsen's closes at 6 PM weekdays, 7 PM weekends. ✉*Dutcher's Dock* ☎*508/645–2680* ▭*MC, V* ⏚*BYOB* ☺*Closed mid-Oct.–mid-May.*

¢–$ ✕**The Bite.** Fried everything—clams, fish-and-chips, you name it—is on the menu at this simple, roadside shack, where two outdoor picnic tables are the only seating options. Small, medium, and large are the three options: all of them are perfect if you're craving that classic seaside fried lunch. But don't come on a rainy day, unless you want to get wet—the lines here can be long. To beat the crowds, try arriving between traditional mealtimes. The best advice, however, is be patient and don't arrive too hungry. The Bite is open 11 AM–3 PM in spring and fall and until 8:45 PM in summer. ✉ *29 Basin Rd.* ☎ *509/645–9239* 🌐 *www.thebitemenemsha.com* ▭ *No credit cards* ⏲ *Closed Oct.–late May.*

$$$–$$$$ ★ ✕🏨 **Beach Plum Inn.** This mansard-roof inn, bought by the nearby Menemsha Inn in 2005, is surrounded by 7 acres of lavish formal gardens and lush woodland; it sits on a bluff over Menemsha Harbor. The floral-theme rooms—five in the main house and six in cottages—have gorgeous furnishings, and some have whirlpool tubs; in the Daffodil room, bathed in shades of yellow and blue, you'll find a hand-painted queen bed and a romantic balcony. A vaulted, beamed ceiling rises over the bedroom of the secluded Morning Glory Cottage. As romantic settings go, it's hard to beat the restaurant ($$$$) here, with its knock-out harbor views, especially at sunset. For dinner, consider such memorable fare as pan-seared scallops with orange-mango-fennel salad, and the mixed grill of lamb chop with rhubarb compote, filet mignon, orange-infused duck, and chicken-apple sausage with truffle risotto. **Pros:** Gardens will blow you away, short walk to adorable fishing village of Menemsha, superb restaurant. **Cons:** A bit of a drive from any major towns, public Wi-Fi but none in rooms, pricey. ✉ *North Rd., 02552* ☎ *508/645–9454 or 877/645–7398* 🌐 *www.beachpluminn.com* *11 rooms* *In-room: refrigerator, dial-up. In-hotel: tennis court, gym, concierge, public Wi-Fi, no elevator* ▭ *AE, D, MC, V* ⏲ *Closed Nov.–Apr.* *BP.*

$$$–$$$$ 🏨 **Menemsha Inn and Cottages.** For 40 years the late *Life* photographer Alfred Eisenstaedt returned to his cottage on the hill here for the panoramic view of Vineyard Sound and Cuttyhunk beyond the trees below. These cottages, which are owned by the neighboring Beach Plum Inn, all have screened porches, fireplaces, and kitchens, tumble down a hillside behind the main house and vary in privacy and views. You can also stay in the 1989 inn building or the pleasant Carriage House. All rooms have private decks, most with sunset views. Suites include sitting areas, desks, and big tiled baths. A continental breakfast is served in a solarium-style breakfast room with a deck facing the ocean. Passes and shuttle transportation to both Squibnocket and Lucy Vincent Beaches are provided. **Pros:** Wonderfully secluded locale on 14 acres, short walk to adorable fishing village of Menemsha, sunset views from private decks. **Cons:** Not for the budget-minded, need a car to explore island from here, public Wi-Fi but none in rooms. ✉ *North Rd., Box 38, 02552* ☎ *508/645–2521* 🌐 *www.menemshainn.com* *15 rooms, 11 cottages, 1 2-bedroom house* *In-room: kitchen (some), refrigerator (some), VCR, dial-up. In-hotel: tennis court, gym, public Wi-Fi, no elevator* ▭ *MC, V* ⏲ *Closed Dec.–mid-Apr.* *CP.*

SPORTS & THE OUTDOORS

Menemsha Hills Reservation (✉ *North Rd. just north of Menemsha*) has 4 mi of some of the most challenging, steep, and breathtaking hiking trails on the island, including a stroll up to Martha's Vineyard's second-highest point and another ramble that descends down through the windswept valley to boulder-strewn Vineyard Sound Beach.

AQUINNAH

6½ mi west of Menemsha, 10 mi southwest of West Tisbury, 17 mi southwest of Vineyard Haven.

Aquinnah, called Gay Head until the town voted to change its name in 1997, is an official Native American township. The Wampanoag tribe is the guardian of the 420 acres that constitute the Aquinnah Native American Reservation. Aquinnah (pronounced a-*kwih*-nah) is Wampanoag for "land under the hill." The town is best known for the red-hued Aquinnah Cliffs.

Quitsa Pond Lookout (⊠ *State Rd.*) has a good view of the adjoining Menemsha and Nashaquitsa ponds, the woods, and the ocean beyond.

Fodor's Choice
★
A National Historic Landmark, the spectacular **Aquinnah Cliffs** are part of the Wampanoag reservation land. These dramatically striated walls of red clay are the island's major attraction, as evidenced by the tour bus–filled parking lot. Native American crafts and food shops line the short approach to the overlook, from which you can see the Elizabeth Islands to the northeast across Vineyard Sound and Noman's Land Island—part wildlife preserve, part military bombing-practice site—3 mi off the Vineyard's southern coast. ⊠ *State Rd.*

The brick **Aquinnah Lighthouse** is stationed precariously atop the rapidly eroding cliffs. It's open to the public on summer weekends at sunset, weather permitting. Across from the lighthouse parking area, you'll see the historic Vanderhoop Homestead (www.vanderhoophomestead. org), a handsome 1880s house that's currently being restored. Plans are to turn the house into community cultural center and museum on Aquinnah's rich history. ⊠ *Lighthouse Rd.* ☎ *508/645–2211* ☞ *$2.*

WHERE TO STAY & EAT

$$$–$$$$ ✕**The Aquinnah Restaurant.** At the far end of the row of fast-food take-out spots and souvenir shops at the Gay Head Cliffs is this restaurant owned and operated by members of the Vanderhoop and Madison families, native Wampanoags. The family took back the lease in 2000 after a four-year hiatus, and the restaurant has regained its reputation as a homey place to eat. For breakfast try the Tomahawk Special, two homemade fish cakes covered with salsa on top of poached eggs with melted cheddar cheese. The lunch menu includes sandwiches, burgers, and healthful-sounding salads. Dinner entrées include sautéed shrimp, scallops, and lobster with rotini in a chardonnay sauce, and striped bass in a mussel-and-saffron sauce. The home-baked pies (banana cream, pecan, or fruit) come wrapped in a moist and flaky crust. ⊠ *State Rd.* ☎ *508/645–3867* ☰ *MC, V* ☾ *Closed mid-Oct.–mid-Apr.*

$$$$ ✕🛏**Outermost Inn.** This rambling, sun-filled inn by the Aquinnah Cliffs
★ stands alone on acres of moorland, a 10-minute walk from the beach. The house is wrapped in windows revealing views of sea and sky in three directions, and there are great views of the Aquinnah Lighthouse

from the wide porch and patio. The inn is clean and contemporary, with white walls and polished light-wood floors. Each room has a phone, and one has a whirlpool tub. The restaurant, open to the public, serves dinner nightly in summer and is all prix fixe at $72 (reservations are essential, and it's BYOB). **Pros:** Spectacular setting high atop Gay Head Cliffs, daily trips available on the inn's catamaran, wonderful food. **Cons:** Outermost location is far bigger towns on island, steep rates, not suitable for young kids. ✉*Lighthouse Rd., R.R. 1, Box 171, 02535* ☎*508/645-3511* 🖷*508/645-3514* ⊕*www.outermostinn.com* ⬝*7 rooms* ⚭*In-room: no a/c, dial-up. In-hotel: restaurant, no elevator, no kids under 12* ▤*AE, D, MC, V* ⊘*Closed mid-Oct.–mid-May* ❘⊘❘*BP.*

$-$$ 🚪**Duck Inn.** The Duck Inn, originally an 18th-century home built by
★   Native American seafarer George Belain, sits on a bucolic 5-acre bluff overlooking the ocean, with the Aquinnah Lighthouse standing sentinel to the north. The eclectic, fun interior blends peach stucco walls, Native American rugs and wall hangings, and ducks. Three upstairs rooms come with balconies; a suite in the stone-wall lower level (cool in summer, warm in winter) has views of the rolling fields; and a small attached cabin (closed in winter) with separate bath is the least expensive room. The 1st-floor's common room, with a working 1928 Glenwood stove, piano, and fireplace, is the heart of the inn. Massage and facial therapies are available, and the healthful breakfast fare includes waffles with strawberries and omelets or chocolate crepes. This inn is very informal—kids and pets are welcome—and one night is free with a week's stay. **Pros:** A good value on this part of the island, totally secluded, ocean views. **Cons:** A longish drive from any large town, a very informal operation with no Web site, peaceful setting isn't ideal if you like lots of bustle. ✉*10 Duck Pond Way, off State Rd., Box 160, 02535* ☎*508/645-9018* 🖷*508/645-2790* ⬝*4 rooms, 1 suite* ⚭*In-hotel: some pets allowed* ▤*MC, V* ❘⊘❘*BP.*

MARTHA'S VINEYARD ESSENTIALS

To research prices, get advice from other travelers, and book travel arrangements, visit www.fodors.com.

TRANSPORTATION

BY AIR

⇨ *Air Travel in Essentials in the back of this book.*

BY BIKE

Martha's Vineyard offers superb terrain for biking—you can pick up a map that shows the island's many dedicated bike paths from the chamber of commerce. Several shops throughout the island rent bicycles, many of them close to the ferry terminals. Martha's Vineyard Strictly Bikes rents bike racks for your car.

Bike Rentals DeBettencourt's (✉*Circuit Ave. Exit, Oak Bluffs* ☎*508/693-0011*). **Edgartown Bicycles** (✉*Upper Main St., Edgartown* ☎*508/627-9008*). **Martha's Vineyard Strictly Bikes** (✉*24 Union St., Vineyard Haven* ☎*508/693-0782*).

BY BOAT & FERRY

⇨ *Boat & Ferry Travel in Smart Travel Trips in the back of this book.*

BY BUS

The big buses of the Martha's Vineyard Transit Authority (VTA) provide regular service to all six towns on the island, with frequent stops in peak season and very limited service in winter. The fare is $1 per town, including the town of departure. One-day ($6), three-day ($15), one-week ($25), and one-month ($40) passes are available at the Edgartown Visitors Center. The VTA also has two free in-town shuttle-bus routes, one in Edgartown and one in Vineyard Haven.

Bus Information Martha's Vineyard Transit Authority (*VIA* ☎ *508/693–9940* ⊕ *www.vineyardtransit.com*).

BY CAR

Traffic can be a challenge on Martha's Vineyard, especially in season, but driving can be worth the hassle if you really want to see the whole island and travel freely among towns. Bringing a car over on the ferry in summer, however, requires reservations far in advance, costs almost double what it does in the off-season, and necessitates standing in long lines—it's sometimes easier and more economical to rent a car once you're on the island, and then only for the days when you plan to explore. Where you stay and what you plan on seeing can greatly influence your transportation plans; discuss the different options for getting around Martha's Vineyard with your innkeeper or hotel staff as soon as you've booked a room.

Note that permits, fees, and certain equipment is needed for driving on Katama Beach and Wasque Reservation. Contact the chamber of commerce or park rangers for details.

You can book rentals on Martha's Vineyard through the Woods Hole ferry terminal free phone. The agencies listed below have rental desks at the airport. Cost is $80 to $170 per day for a sedan; renting a four-wheel-drive vehicle costs around $150 per day (seasonal prices fluctuate widely).

Martha's Vineyard Agencies AAA Island (☎ *508/627–6800 or 800/627–6333* ⊕ *www.mvautorental.com*). **Adventure Rentals** (✉ *Beach Rd., Vineyard Haven* ☎ *508/693–1959*).

BY TAXI

Taxis meet all scheduled ferries and flights, and there are taxi stands by the Flying Horses Carousel in Oak Bluffs, at the foot of Main Street in Edgartown, and by the steamship office in Vineyard Haven. Fares range from $6 within a town to $35 to $42 one-way from Vineyard Haven to Aquinnah.

Rates double between 1 AM and 7 AM. Note that limousine companies often provide service both on- and off-island.

Martha's Vineyard Taxi Companies **AdamCab** (☎ *508/627–4462 or 800/281–4462* ⊕ *www.adamcab.com*). **All Island Taxi** (☎ *508/693–2929 or 800/693–8294*). **Atlantic Cab** (☎ *508/693–7110 or 877/477–8294*).**Mario's** (☎ *508/693–8399*).

CONTACTS & RESOURCES

TOURS

Liz Villard's Vineyard History Tours leads walking tours of Edgartown's "history, architecture, ghosts, and gossip," including a stop at the Vincent House. Tours are run from April through December; call for times. Liz and her guides also lead similar tours of Oak Bluffs and Vineyard Haven. Walks last a little more than an hour.

Contacts **Vineyard History Tours** (☎ *508/627–8619*).

VISITOR INFORMATION

The Martha's Vineyard Chamber of Commerce is two blocks from the Vineyard Haven ferry. The chamber information booth by the Vineyard Haven steamship terminal is open late May to the last weekend in June, Friday through Sunday 8 to 8; July through early September, daily 8 to 8; and early September through mid-October, Friday through Sunday 8:30 to 5:30. The chamber itself is open weekdays 9 to 5. There are also town information kiosks on Circuit Avenue in Oak Bluffs and on Church Street in Edgartown.

Tourist Information **Martha's Vineyard Chamber of Commerce** (⊠ *Beach Rd.* ⅅ *Box 1698, Vineyard Haven 02568* ☎ *508/693–4486 or 800/505–4815* ⊕ *www.mvy.com*).

Nantucket

WORD OF MOUTH

"I keep going back to Nantucket for the natural beauty of its beaches, the sense of being far away from the mainland, and the smell of Rosa rugosa everywhere outside of town."

—MarieF

"It's not for everyone. The prices are out of control: gas, houses, rents, meals, goods and services, ferry tickets for your auto, etc., etc. But for many of us, it's the BEST."

—rhkkmk

By Sandy
MacDonald

FOR THE FIRST TIME SINCE its golden age as a world-renowned whaling capital in the early 1800s, the tiny island of Nantucket is decidedly on a roll. Modest shingled cottages that might have gone begging for a buyer a few decades ago now fetch an easy million-plus. The more than 800 pre-1840 structures that compose the core of Nantucket Town—a National Landmark Historic District—only rarely change hands, and then at exalted prices. As for the trophy houses—megamansions built in the hinterlands for rich arrivistes—they're consistently off the charts, setting new records only to break them.

Still, Nantucket's ascending chic isn't what attracts most people to the island in the first place, or keeps them coming back. Its allure has more to do with how, at the height of summer, a cooling fog will drift in across the multihued moors; or the way rambling wild roses, the gaudy pink Rosa rugosa, perfume a hidden path to the beach.

Essentially Nantucket is *all* beach—a boomerang-shape sand spit consisting of detritus left by a glacier that receded millennia ago. Off Cape Cod, some 26 mi out to sea, the island measures 3½ by 14 mi at its widest points, while encompassing—such are the miracles of inlets and bays—about 80 mi of sandy shoreline, all of it open, as a matter of local pride, to absolutely everyone.

The small commercial area of Nantucket Town is the center of island activity, just as it has been since the early 1700s. It's only a few square blocks of mostly historical buildings, lovingly restored inns, and boutiques and galleries leading up from the pretty harbor and waterfront, where the ferries dock. Beyond it, quiet residential roads fan out to points around the island; Siasconset (known locally as 'Sconset) lies 8 mi to the east, Surfside 3 mi to the south, and Madaket 6 mi west of town. Thus far, the outlying areas appear relatively rural; however, increasing "infill" threatens the tranquility.

Still, on a day when sun scintillates on sand and the thrumming waves hint at an eternal rhythm, it's hard to imagine that anything could ever go too terribly wrong here. As summer succeeds summer, children will continue to construct their fanciful if foredoomed sand castles and marvel over the odd treasures the tides drag in. Adults will gladly play along, if allowed, remembering their own seemingly endless days of summer and imagining more of the same for their children's children and so on and on. Perfection can be surprisingly simple, after all, and even if Nantucket's current cachet should fade, the island's timeless pleasures will endure.

ABOUT THE RESTAURANTS

For such a tiny island, Nantucket is rife with great restaurants—"world class" would not be an exaggeration. Of course, with New York–level sophistication come New York–level prices. And whereas the titans of industry who flock here for a bit of high-rent R&R might not blink at the prospect of a $40 or even $50 entrée, the rest of us must sometimes suppress a nervous gulp. Is it worth it? Again and again, in venues that vie for the title of most recherché, the answer is yes.

Reservations can be hard to come by in high season, or during popular weekends such as December's Christmas Stroll and the Daffodil Festival in April, so plan and make dinner reservations well ahead. You may still be able to squeeze into a popular establishment at the last minute if you're willing to eat unfashionably early or decadently late. In any month other than July or August, call ahead to check hours of operation.

> ## TOP 5
>
> ■ Endless roaming along Nantucket's shoreline
>
> ■ Unhilly bike paths that wind past moors, bogs, and forests
>
> ■ The observation deck at the Whaling Museum
>
> ■ Justifiably popular Surfside Beach
>
> ■ A boat ride on *The Endeavor*, Slip 101, Straight Wharf

ABOUT THE HOTELS

From small bed-and-breakfasts to the island's few surviving grand hotels, Nantucket knows the value of hospitality. A unique "product" plus good service—as busy as this little island gets—are the deciding factors that keep visitors coming back year after year. The majority of lodgings are in town, convenient to the shops and restaurants; the downside is that you may be subjected to street noise on summer evenings. Those seeking quiet might prefer the inns on the periphery of town, a 5- to 10-minute walk from Main Street. The most remote inns, in 'Sconset and Wauwinet, also tend to be among the most expensive. Families with children will probably want to consider the larger, less formal hotels, since many of the small, historic B&Bs are furnished with antiques.

Nantucket is notoriously expensive, so don't expect to find many bargains in terms of lodging, especially in summer. The best rates can be found in the off-season; however, the spring and fall shoulder seasons are also growing in popularity, and such special-event weekends as the Daffodil Festival in late April and Christmas Stroll in early December command peak-season rates. Most inns charge upward of $150 a night in summer, and many go higher. The only truly "budget" facility you'll find is the youth hostel, which is also the only option for roughing it, since camping is prohibited anywhere on-island.

WHAT IT COSTS					
	$$$$	$$$	$$	$	¢
RESTAURANTS	over $30	$22–$30	$16–$22	$10–$16	under $10
HOTELS	over $260	$200–$260	$140–$200	$90–$140	under $90

Restaurant prices are per person for a main course at dinner. Hotel prices are for a standard double room, excluding 6% sales tax (more in some counties) and 1%–4% tourist tax.

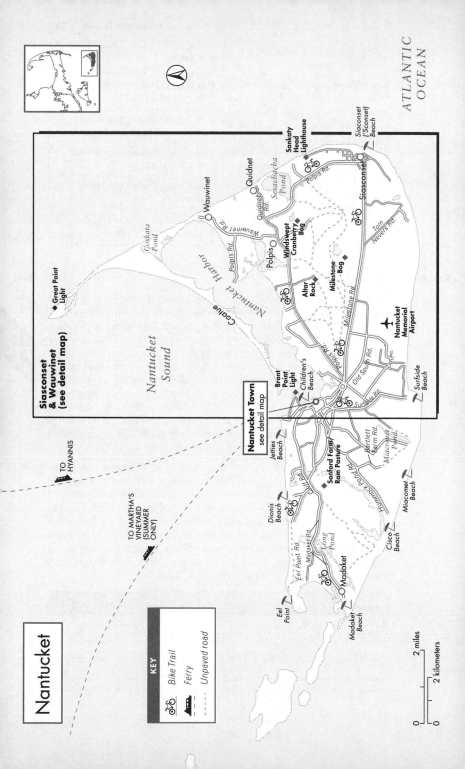

NANTUCKET TOWN

30 mi southeast of Hyannis, 107 mi southeast of Boston.

At the height of its prosperity in the early 19th century, the little town of Nantucket was the foremost whaling port in the world. Shipowners and sea captains built elegant mansions, which today remain remarkably unchanged, thanks to a very strict building code initiated in the 1950s. The entire town of Nantucket is now an official National Historic District encompassing more than 800 pre-1840 structures within 1 square mi.

Given its compact nature, Nantucket definitely merits consideration as a day trip—a prospect made easier by the introduction of fast ferries (the crossing now takes an hour) from Hyannis. Day-trippers usually take in the architecture and historical sites and browse the pricey boutiques. After dining at one of the many delightful restaurants, you can hop a ferry back—or, if you're not in a hurry, stay the night at one of the town's luxurious historic inns.

Nantucket Town has one of the country's finest historical districts, with beautiful 18th- and 19th-century architecture and a museum of whaling history.

FodorsChoice
★
The **Nantucket Historical Association (NHA)** (☎*508/228–1894* ⊕*www. nha.org*) maintains an assortment of venerable properties in town, including the gloriously expanded Whaling Museum. An $18 pass gets you into all of the association's sites.

① **African Meeting House.** When the island abolished slavery in 1773, Nantucket became a destination for free blacks and escaping slaves. The African Meeting House was built in the 1820s as a schoolhouse, and it functioned as such until 1846, when the island's schools were integrated. A complete restoration has returned the site to its authentic 1880s appearance. ⊠*29 York St.* ☎*508/228–9833* ⊕*www.afroammuseum. org* ⌹*Free* ☼*July and Aug., Tues.–Sat. 11–3, Sun. 1–3.*

⑮ **Brant Point Light.** This 26-foot-tall, white-painted beauty has views of the harbor and town. The point was once the site of the second-oldest lighthouse in the country (1746); the present, much-photographed light was built in 1902. ⊠*End of Easton St., across footbridge.*

⑬ **First Congregational Church.** The tower of this church provides the best
★ view of Nantucket—for those willing to climb its 92 steps. Rising 120 feet, the tower is capped by a weather vane depicting a whale catch. Peek in at the church's 1852 trompe l'oeil ceiling. ⊠*62 Centre St.* ☎*508/228–0950* ⊕*www.nantucketfcc.org* ⌹*Tower tour $2.50* ☼*Mid-June–mid-Oct., Mon.–Sat. 10–4: Daffodil and Memorial weekends, Fri. and Sat.; services Sun. 10 AM.*

⑦ **Hadwen House.** The pair of magnificent white porticoed Greek-revival mansions on upper Main Street—commonly referred to as the Two Greeks—were built in 1845 and 1846 by wealthy factory owner William Hadwen. No. 94, built as a wedding gift for his adopted niece, was modeled on the Athenian Tower of the Winds, with Corinthian capitals

7

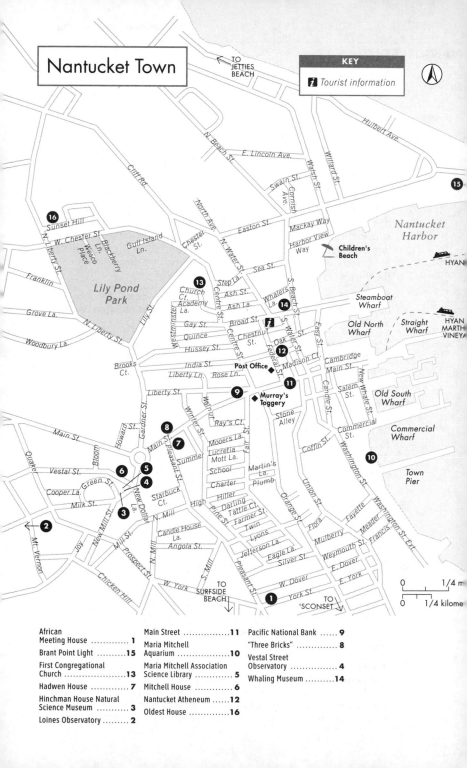

Nantucket Town

TO
JETTIES
BEACH

Hulbert Ave.

N. Beach St.

E. Lincoln Ave.

Walsh St.

Willard St.

Swain St.

Cornish Ave.

Mackay Way

15

Nantucket Harbor

HYAN

16 Sunset Hill

W. Chester St.

Liberty St.

Wesco Place

Blackberry Ln.

Gull Island Ln.

Chester St.

N. Water St.

N. Ave.

Easton St.

Sea St.

Harbor View Way

Children's Beach

Steamboat Wharf

Old North Wharf

Straight Wharf

HYANN MARTH VINEYA

Franklin

Grove La.

Woodbury La.

N. Liberty St.

Lily Pond Park

Lily St.

Westminster

Church Academy La.

Centre St.

Step La.

Ash St.

Ash La.

Whalers La.

S. Beach St.

13

14

Gay St.

Broad St.

ℹ️

Quince

Chestnut St.

Oak St.

S. Water St.

Easy St.

Hussey St.

Centre St.

Federal St.

12

Madison Ct.

Cambridge St.

Brooks Ct.

India St.

Post Office

Main St.

Candle St.

Salem St.

New Whale St.

Old South Wharf

Liberty Ln.

Rose Ln.

11

Liberty St.

9

Murray's Toggery

Stone Alley

Commercial St.

Commercial Wharf

Gardner St.

Walnut St.

Ray's Ct.

Coffin St.

Washington St.

Main St.

8

Winter St.

Mooers La.

Martin's La.

Howard St.

7

Summer St.

Lucretia Mott La.

Plumb

Union St.

Town Pier

Main St.

Pleasant St.

School

Charter

10

Bloom

Vestal St.

6

5

Hiller

Darling

Tattle Ct.

Flora

Quaker

Green St.

4

Starbuck Ct.

High

Pine St.

Farmer St.

Fayette

Cooper La.

Milk St.

3

N. Mill

Twin

Mulberry

Meader St.

Francis St. Ext.

2

Joy

New Mill St.

Mill St.

Candle House La.

Angola St.

Lyons

Jefferson La.

Eagle La.

Weymouth St.

Washington St.

Mt. Vernon

Prospect St.

N. Mill St.

S. Mill

W. York

Silver St.

E. Dover

E. York

Chicken Hill

TO SURFSIDE BEACH

Pleasant St.

W. Dover

1

York St.

TO 'SCONSET

0 .... 1/4 m

0 .... 1/4 kilome

on the entry columns, a domed-stair hall with statuary niches, and an oculus. The Hadwens' own domicile, at No. 96, is now a museum, and its contents reflect how the wealthy of the period lived. Inside, on a guided tour, you'll see such architectural details as the grand circular staircase, fine plasterwork, and carved Italian-marble mantels. ✉*96 Main St.* ☎*508/228–1894* ⊕*www.nha.org* ▦*NHA Combination Pass or Historic Sites Pass only* ⊙*Mid-May–mid-Oct., Mon.–Sat. 10–5, Sun. noon–5.*

⓫ **Main Street.** After the Great Fire of 1846 leveled all its wooden buildings, Main Street was widened to prevent future flames from hopping across the street. The cobblestone thoroughfare has a harmonious symmetry: the Pacific Club anchors its foot, and the Pacific National Bank, another redbrick building, squares off the head. The cobblestones were brought to the island as ballast in returning ships and laid to prevent the wheels of carts heavily laden with whale oil from sinking into the dirt. At the center of Lower Main is an old horse trough, today overflowing with flowers. From here the street gently rises; at the bank it narrows to its prefire width and leaves the commercial district for an area of mansions that escaped the blaze.

NEED A BREAK?
You can breakfast or lunch inexpensively at the lunch counter at **Nantucket Pharmacy** (✉*45 Main St.* ☎*508/228–0180*). "The Strip," a hodgepodge of fun fast-food eateries on Broad Street near Steamboat Wharf, is another good option for a quick meal. Besides fresh-squeezed juices, the **Juice Bar** (✉*12 Broad St.* ☎*508/228–5799*), open April through mid-October, serves homemade ice cream and frozen yogurt with waffle cones and toppings. Long lines signal that good things come to those who wait.

Maria Mitchell Association (MMA). Established in 1902 by Vassar students and astronomer Maria Mitchell's family, the association administers the **Mitchell House** (✉*1 Vestal St.* ☎*508/228–2896* ⊕*www.mmo.org* ▦*$5 or MMA pass*), the **Maria Mitchell Association Science Library** (✉*2 Vestal St.* ☎*508/228–9219* ⊕*www.mmo.org* ▦*Reserved for scholars, by appointment*), the **Hinchman House Natural Science Museum** (✉*7 Milk St.* ☎*508/228–0898* ⊕*www.mmo.org* ▦*$5 or MMA pass*), the **Maria Mitchell Aquarium** (✉*28 Washington St., near Commercial Wharf* ☎*508/228–5387* ⊕*www.mmo.org* ▦*$4 or MMA pass*), the **Vestal Street Observatory** (✉*3 Vestal St.* ☎*508/228–9273* ⊕*www.mmo.org* ▦*$5 or MMA pass*), and the **Loines Observatory** (✉*59 Milk St. Ext.* ☎*508/228–9273* ⊕*www.mmo.org* ▦*$10*). The MMA Museum Pass is a combination admission ticket to the Mitchell House, the Hinchman House, the Vestal Street Observatory, and the aquarium; it's $10 for adults and $6 for senior citizens and children ages 6 to 14. In summer, the association conducts inexpensive classes for adults and children on astronomy, natural science, and Nantucket history. ✉*4 Vestal St.* ☎*508/228–9198* ⊕*www.mmo.org.*

⓬ **Nantucket Atheneum.** Nantucket's town library is a great white Greek-revival building, with a windowless facade and fluted Ionic columns. Completed in 1847 to replace a structure lost to the 1846 fire, it's one of the oldest libraries in continuous service in the United States. Astronomer Maria Mitchell was its first librarian. Opening ceremonies included a dedication by Ralph Waldo Emerson, who—along with Daniel Webster, Henry David Thoreau, Frederick Douglass, Lucretia Mott, and John James Audubon—later delivered lectures in the library's 2nd-floor Great Hall. During the 19th century the hall was the center of island culture—a role it fulfills to this day. The adjoining Atheneum Park is a great place to relax for a while, and the spacious Weezie Library for Children hosts readings and activities—a welcome respite for a rainy day. ⊠*1 India St.* ☎*508/228–1110* ⊕*www.nantucketatheneum.org* ۞*Late May–early Sept., Mon., Wed., Fri., and Sat. 9:30–5, Tues. and Thurs. 9:30–8; early Sept.–late May, Tues. and Thurs. 9:30–8, Wed., Fri., and Sat. 9:30–5.*

⑯ Oldest House. History and architecture buffs should be sure to get a look at this hilltop house, also called the Jethro Coffin House, built in 1686 as a wedding gift for Jethro and Mary Gardner Coffin. The most striking feature of the saltbox is the massive central brick chimney with a brick-horseshoe adornment said to ward away witches. Other highlights are the enormous hearths and diamond-pane leaded-glass windows. Cutaway panels show 17th-century construction techniques. An NHA interpreter will tell you about the home's history and the interior's sparse furnishings, including an antique loom. ⊠*Sunset Hill (a 10- to 15-min walk along Centre St. from Main St.)* ☎*508/228–1894* ⊕*www.nha.org* ۞*NHA Combination Pass or Historic Sites Pass* ۞*Mid-May–mid-Oct., Mon.–Sat. 10–5, Sun. noon–5.*

⑨ Pacific National Bank. Like the Pacific Club (a social club that counts whalers' descendants among its members) it faces, the bank, dating to 1818 and still in use today, is a monument to the far-flung voyages of the Nantucket whaling ships it financed. Inside, above old-style teller cages, are 1954 murals of scenes from the whaling days. Note the **Meridian Stone** on the south side of the building and to the left—it's about 3 feet high and pointed on top. Placed here in the 1830s by astronomers Maria Mitchell and her father, William, it marks the town's precise meridian—an important point to early navigators. ⊠*61 Main St.*

⑧ "Three Bricks." Many of the mansions of the golden age of whaling
★ were built on Upper Main Street. These well-known identical redbrick homes, with columned Greek-revival porches at their front entrances, were built between 1836 and 1838 by whaling merchant Joseph Starbuck for his three sons. They are not open to the public. ⊠*93–97 Main St.*

⑭ Immersing you in Nantucket's whaling past with exhibits that include
☾ a fully rigged whaleboat and a skeleton of a 46-foot sperm whale, the
FodorsChoice **Whaling Museum**—a complex that includes a restored 1846 spermaceti candle factory—is a must-see. The museum received a $14 million
★ expansion and refurbishment in 2005. Items on view in the handsome galleries include harpoons and other whale-hunting implements; portraits of whaling captains and their wives (a few of whom went whaling

as well); the South Seas curiosities they brought home; a large collection of sailors' crafts, a full-size tryworks once used to process whale oil aboard ship; and the original 16-foot-high 1850 lens from Sankaty Head Lighthouse. The Children's Discovery Room provides interactive-learning opportunities. Be sure to climb—or take the elevator—up to the observation deck for a view of the harbor. ⊠13–15 Broad St. ☎508/228–1894 ☎$15 or NHA Combination Pass ☉Jan.–mid-Apr., Fri.–Sun. 11–4; mid-Apr.–mid-May and mid-Oct.–mid-Dec., Thurs.–Mon. 11–4; mid-May–mid-Oct., Mon.–Wed., Fri.–Sun. 10–5, Thurs. 10–8.

GREASY LUCK

Nantucket's preeminence as the world's whaling capital (at least until the early 1800s, when New Bedford's deeper harbor took the lead) resulted from a fluke, when, in 1712, Captain Christopher Hussey's crew speared a sperm whale. The whale's waxy spermaceti, it was found, could be used for candles in place of lantern oil, produced by the messy, endless task of cooking down whale blubber. The captains made out like bandits—their grand houses still stand as proof—but the trade went into a downward spiral with the discovery of petroleum in 1836.

WHERE TO EAT

$$$$ ✕**Company of the Cauldron.** In this
★ tiny dining room, a sconce-lighted haven of architectural salvage, chef-owner All Kovalencik issues only one menu per evening. Fans gladly forgo multiple choice when the chef's choice is invariably so dead-on. Rundowns of the weekly roster are available over the phone or online, and a typically tantalizing lineup might start with seared scallops with a grilled fennel bulb and citrus coulis, Cisco Stout–marinated beef filet with potato mille-feuille, and peanut butter pain perdu with Concord grape sherbet (a playful nod to PB&J). Given the close quarters, expect to come away not only sated but better acquainted with your near neighbors—and in love with Mary Keller's celestial harp. ⊠7 India St. ☎508/228–4016 ⊕www.companyofthecauldron.com ⚅Reservations essential ▤MC, V ☉Closed Jan.–Mar. No lunch.

$$$$ ✕**Òran Mór.** In 2004 chef-owner Christopher Freeman abandoned the
★ cushy confines of Topper's at the Wauwinet to strike out on his own at this tasteful little restaurant—a trio of butter-yellow rooms accessed via a copper-encased stairway. Initially, Freeman may have erred on the side of nouvelle-cuisine minginess (a Topper's carryover, perhaps), but now that he's firmly ensconced, the innate generosity of a born chef is beginning to emerge. The artistry was there all along and now shines in exuberant dishes such as cloud-light lemon-garlic gnocchi, Peking duck breast with baby bok choy and roast-plum chutney, and mascarpone cheesecake brûlée. Decades ago, this space was a New American trend-setter known as the Second Story: Freeman does its legacy proud. ⊠2 S. Beach St. ☎508/228–8655 ⊕www.oranmorbistro.com ▤AE, MC, V ☉No lunch.

$$$$ ✕**the pearl.** This ultracool space—a sophisticated upstairs cousin to the
★ Boarding House—is seriously chic, with a white onyx bar lighted in a Curaçao blue and, behind an aquarium divider, cushy white-leather

banquettes. These—plus the garden porch, where tasting dinners can be prearranged—are the power seats. However, everyone is well served by Seth Raynor's enthusiasm for the bold flavors of Asian cuisine, especially in its street-wise guise. You may have a tough time choosing between the lobster salad with fresh-shaved hearts of palm and the signature wok-fried lobster with lo-mein and grilled lime—so do yourself a favor and order both. Raynor also pulls off a stellar Japanese variation on steak fries (the latter come dusted with tasty choy shichimi). ⊠*12 Federal St.* ☎*508/228–9701* ⊕*www.boardinghouse-pearl.com* ▭*AE, MC, V* ☾*Closed Jan.–Apr. No lunch.*

$$$$ ✕**21 Federal.** An avatar of the New American culinary revolution since
★ 1985, 21 Federal retains its creative edge, thanks to the ever-avant menus of chef Russell Jaehnig. Nothing is too outré, mind you, in this handsome 1847 Greek-revival house with sconce-lighted, dove-gray interiors—except perhaps the boisterous young crowd (the bar scene is quite popular). The cuisine, however, has a spark to match the spirited clientele: try the seared sea scallops matched with mango, avocado puree, and ancho chilis, or tender Kobe beef cheek atop white-truffle polenta with caramelized fennel. Pastry chef Benjamin Woodbury has come up with the showiest—and tastiest—dessert on-island: coconut blanc mange "oysters" nestled in white-chocolate shells, with dollops of passion-fruit mignonette. ⊠*21 Federal St.* ☎*508/228–2121* ⊕*www.21federal.com* ▭*AE, MC, V* ☾*No lunch* ☾*Closed mid-Oct.– late Nov. and mid-Dec.–mid-May.*

$$$$ ✕**Water Street.** Two stylish young couples initiated this chic eatery with cinnamon walls and handsome leather highback chairs. The locally provisioned, all-organic cuisine calls on micro-diced taste explosions— wild blueberry preserves and sherry gastric spark the seared foie gras, and charred-tomato gazpacho underlies the fresh-caught local striped bass. The vanilla-laced Bartlett Farm corn soup, which packs a bonus chunk of crab tempura, is nonpareil, and the closing "Study in Chocolate" is deeply satisfying. ⊠*21 S. Water St.* ☎*508/228–0189* ⊕*www. waterstreetnantucket.com* ▭*D, MC, V* ☾*Closed Jan.–Mar.*

$$$–$$$$ ✕**American Seasons.** Picture a farmhouse gone sexy: That's the mood—
Fodor'sChoice wholesome yet seductive—at this candlelighted hideaway, where
★ inspired young chef Michael LaScola marshalls local bounty to concoct a culinary Trip-Tik that ranges across the countryside, from the Pacific Coast to New England, by way of the Wild West and Down South. From his signature foie gras–crème brûlée (served with a plum-ginger compote and parsnip fries) to roast-duck breast with cornbread pudding, and onward to blood-orange crème brûlée, expect spectacular pan-regional pyrotechnics. ⊠*80 Centre St.* ☎*508/228–7111* ▭*AE, MC, V* ☾*Closed Jan.–mid-Apr. No lunch.*

$$$–$$$$ ✕**Black-Eyed Susan's.** From a passing glance, you'd never peg this seem-
★ ingly humble storefront as one of Nantucket's chic eateries—but as the invariable lines attest, it is. The luncheonette setup is offset by improbably fancy glass chandeliers, and foodies lay claim to the stools to observe chef Jeff Worster's often pyromaniacal "open kitchen." The dinner menu, which changes every few weeks, ventures boldly around the world. The breakfasts (served until 1 PM) include such eye-open-

ers as hearty Pennsylvania dutch pancakes fortified with Jarlsberg cheese. ⊠*10 India St.* ☎*508/325–0308* ▤*No credit cards* ⌂*BYOB* ☽*Closed Nov.–Mar. No dinner Sun. No lunch.*

$$$–$$$$ ✕**The Boarding House.** Beyond the throngs of twentysomethings noisily mingling at the bar, you'll encounter a culinary oasis, a vaulted semi-subterranean space reminiscent of a private wine cellar, with leather banquettes circling antique-gold walls. Here, under the watchful eye of star chef–owner Seth Raynor, chef de cuisine Erin Zircher showcases her skill with Mediterranean market cuisine. Comfort is the universal watchword: it's implicit in the creamy Spanish-style almond soup bejeweled with roasted grapes and seared day scallops, and in the signature dessert, warm dark-chocolate chocolate-chip cookies (like mini-molten cakes) served with a pair of "mini malted milk shakes." Come summer, you can sample from the menu at the sidewalk café—provided you succeed in snagging a table. ⊠*12 Federal St.* ☎*508/228–9622* ⊕*www. boardinghouse-pearl.com* ▤*AE, MC, V* ☽*Closed Jan.–Mar.*

$$$–$$$$ ✕**Brant Point Grill.** With its beautiful broad lawn set harborside, the Brant Point Grill—in-house restaurant for the elegant White Elephant hotel—has ventured beyond its à la carte haute–steak house menu with some protein-heavy variations—such as Kobe-beef meatballs, and slow-cooked pork shank with lemon spaetzle—that can weigh in on the heavy side as summer fare. Always appealing, though, is the straightforward salmon grilled on a firecone set up right outside, and the spritely salads—e.g., mesclun with a grilled orange-cranberry vinaigrette—are reliably refreshing. Desserts like the Guinness ice-cream mud pie are sure-fire resolution-destroyers, as is the Sunday brunch, featuring a make-your-own Bloody Mary station. ⊠*50 Easton St.* ☎*508/325–1320 or 800/445–6574* ⊕*www.whiteelephanthotel.com* ▤*AE, D, DC, MC, V* ☽*Closed Jan.–Mar.*

$$$–$$$$ ✕**DeMarco.** Northern Italian cuisine debuted on-island at this cored-out clapboard house in 1980, slightly ahead of the wave. The delights endure: "badly cut" homemade pasta, for instance, in a sauce of wild mushrooms, prosciutto, and fresh sage, or luscious lobster cannelloni enrobed in a corn zabaglione. Braised lamb shank comes nestled in Parmesan-polenta custard, and the pannacotta gets a bit of added zip from a rhubarb compote. The prevailing aesthetic may be rustic, but the results read as rare delicacies in these parts. ⊠*9 India St.* ☎*508/228–1836* ⊕*www.demarcorestaurant.com* ▤*AE, D, MC, V* ☽*Closed Mid-Oct.–Apr. No lunch.*

$$$–$$$$ ✕**Fifty-Six Union.** You can tell there's a playful spirit at work here, just from the overdressed mannequin usually propped up at a hefty granite café table out front. Venture inside, though, and you'll find a city-sophisticated space, with a civilized grown-ups' bar. Inside or out (the lovely garden out back harbors a chef's table), Peter Jannelle's cuisine delivers global pizzazz. You'll want to make a habit of the truffle-asiago frites, not to mention the mussels in mild Thai curry broth, and the Javanese spicy fried rice. ⊠*56 Union St.* ☎*508/228–6135* ▤*AE, MC, V* ☽*No lunch.*

$$$–$$$$ ✕**Languedoc Bistro.** The only thing not exquisitely Gallic about this auberge-style restaurant, founded in 1975, is the portioning: Ameri-

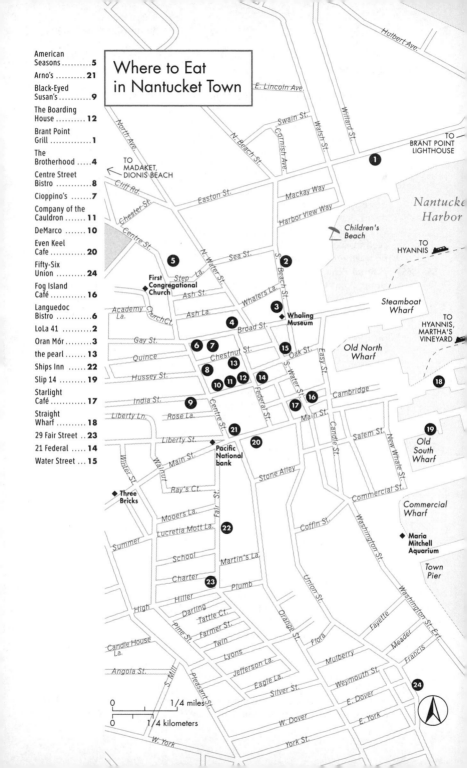

Where to Eat in Nantucket Town

can appetites will be satisfied—and then some—by the roasted rare Kobe rib eye, not to mention the oven-roasted lobster swimming in creamy polenta and festooned with parsnip "ribbons." Dining moods are divided into two modes: you can opt for the fairly formal upstairs rooms or the bistro-style conviviality of the cellar. In season, the patio is a lovely place to toy with a salad—or to tackle a decadent, over-generous dessert. ⊠ *24 Broad St.* ☎ *508/228–2552* ⊕ *www.lelanguedoc. com* ⊟ *AE, MC, V* ⊘ *Closed Jan.–mid-Apr.*

$$$–$$$$

Fodor's Choice

★

✕ **Straight Wharf.** This loftlike restaurant with harborside deck has enjoyed legendary status since the mid-'70s, when chef Marion Morash used to get a helping hand from culinary buddy Julia Child. The young couple who took over in 2006—Gabriel Frasca and Amanda Lydon—were fast-rising stars on the Boston restaurant scene, but their approach here is the antithesis of flashy. If anything, they have lent this venerable institution a more barefoot air, appropriate to the place and season—hurricane lamps lend a soft glow to well-spaced tables lined with butcher paper; dish towels serve as napkins. Intense champions of local produce and catches, Frasca and Lydon concoct stellar dishes like lobster-stuffed zucchini flowers with saffron–tomato vinaigrette, and line-caught swordfish in a vaguely Moroccan melange of golden raisins, pine nuts, and mint. Everything from cuisine to service entrances, and the price—for Nantucket—is right. If you'd like a preview, try the less costly café menu at the adjoining bar—provided you can get in. ⊠ *6 Harbor Sq., Straight Wharf* ☎ *508/228–4499* ⊟ *AE, MC, V* ⊘ *Closed mid-Oct.–mid-May.*

$$$–$$$$

✕ **29 Fair Street.** This 1709 abode spent the past half-century as a restaurant–slash–rooming house, and now that the owners of 'Sconset's Summer House are running the show, it's a lot cheerier: the wood-paneled interior has been spiffed with colorful silk pillows, and the menu has morphed into sunny Mediterranean staples. Fear not, fans of the beef Wellington and breakfast popovers for which the former Woodbox was long famed: they remain on the menu—alongside such welcome innovations such as lobster wrapped in *kataif* (angel-hair filo). The desserts are a Francophile's dream come true. ⊠ *29 Fair St.* ☎ *508/228–7800* ⊟ *AE, MC, V* ⊘ *Closed Mon. and Jan.–Apr. No lunch.*

$$–$$$$

✕ **LoLa 41.** A hopping bar scene—LoLa 41 became *the* place to hang the minute it opened in '06—somewhat impedes the culinary experience here, but an evolving menu means that chefs at this trendy Galley Beach offshoot come up with compelling new dishes every few weeks. Just one bite, and you'll be hooked on the calamari doused with ultraspicy Korean clay-pot-aged *kochujang* (a chili-bean paste), not to mention the "indulgent mac & cheese" made with four artisanal North California varieties. ⊠ *15 S. Beach St.* ☎ *508/325–4001* ⊟ *MC, V.*

$$–$$$$

✕ **Ships Inn.** Tucked beneath Captain Obed Starbuck's handsome 1831 mansion, this peach-tinted, candlelighted restaurant is a light and lovely haven where French cuisine meets a California sensibility and both cultures are the richer for it. If you want to eat healthy, you can—but why not sin a little and sup on warm cauliflower soup with Vermont cheddar, or grilled Chatham sea scallops served with black-truffle hollandaise? The grilled shrimp with Belgian endive (braised into sweet

7

submission) is a guilt-free option—easily undone as you preorder the soufflé du jour. ⊠*13 Fair St.* ☎*508/228–0040* ⊕*www.shipsinnnantucket.com* ⊟*AE, D, MC, V* ⊘*Closed late Oct.–mid-Apr. No lunch.*

$$$
★
✕**Centre Street Bistro.** Tiny—there are 20 seats indoors, and as many out—and perfect, this gem of a bistro is a find that devoted locals almost wish they could keep to themselves. Chef–owners Tim and Ruth Pitts's sizzling cuisine is a match for the persimmon-orange color scheme of this cozy hideaway lined with cushioned banquettes and splashed with exuberant flower paintings. Portions—whether of the sesame-crusted shrimp atop red-curry rice noodles, or the Angus-beef tenderloin with goat cheese and white-truffle oil—are so ample as to quell the heartiest of appetites. Desserts are as lavish (try the warm flourless chocolate cake wrapped in filo) as the prices are modest. ⊠*29 Centre St.* ☎*508/228–8470* ⊕*www.nantucketbistro.com* ⊟*MC, V.*

$$$
✕**Slip 14.** With its picturesque setting at the end of a shell-lined lane flanked by galleries, Slip 14 is an ideal spot to while away a summer night: portions are large, prices are fair—and all is well with the world. Skip the dull lobster cake, but feast on the refreshing likes of yellowfin-tuna ceviche with red grapes and jicama, and definitely succumb to any cobbler you encounter on the dessert list. ⊠*14 Old South Wharf* ☎*508/228–2033* ⊕*www.slip14.com* ⊟*AE, MC, V* ⊘*Closed Oct.–Apr.*

$$–$$$
✕**Arno's.** Arno's, which has a prime location right on Main Street, presents lush breakfasts (some featuring lobster), hearty lunches, and fairly ambitious dinners, all with generous portions. (Warning: the salads could constitute meals in themselves.) Molly Dee's nostalgic canvases adorn the brick walls, and a wine bar—offering 41 options by the glass or flight—invites adult schmoozing. Expect some envious looks—from inside and outside—if you get the prime spot in the storefront window. ⊠*41 Main St.* ☎*508/228–7001* ⊕*www.arnos.net* ⊟*AE, MC, V* ⊘*Closed mid-Jan.–Mar.*

$$–$$$
☺
✕**The Brotherhood.** No, it's not really an 1840s whaling bar—though the atmospheric basement, which dates all the way back to 1972, presents a more convincing front than the open, family-friendly upper floors added in 2005. Upstairs or down, inside or out, you can dive into the same juicy burgers—incontrovertibly the best on-island–and signature curly fries. As a boon for late-night celebrants, the kitchen stays open 'til midnight in season. ⊠*23 Broad St.* ☎*508/228–2551* ⊕*www.brotherhoodofthieves.com* ⊟*MC, V.*

$$–$$$
✕**Cioppino's.** Tracy Root's elegant house-restaurant has been popular since day one (in 1990). An appetizer of cool, deconstructed lobster with lemony hollandaise is the perfect answer to an overwarm evening, and awfully well priced. Beyond the signature dish—a San Franciscan seafood stew—the menu is ambitious, marrying classic technique and contemporary taste. Desserts—especially the tangy house-made key lime pie—have their own following. ⊠*20 Broad St.* ☎*508/228–4622* ⊕*www.cioppinos.com* ⊟*AE, D, DC, MC, V* ⊘*Closed Nov.–Apr.* ⊘*No lunch.*

$$–$$$
☺
✕**Even Keel Cafe.** This former ice-cream parlor, with its tin ceilings and pretty backyard patio, is no mere restaurant—it's the very heart

of town, especially off-season, when, as a public service, patrons are treated to two-for-one entrées (price-gouging is not in owner Marshall Thompson's vocabulary). It's the first place to head for a fancy coffee or a creative meal. The lobster risotto, studded with Bartlett Farm corn, holds its own against contenders at the fanciest restaurants in town, and the grilled salmon salad with pomegranate ginger vinaigrette makes for an ideal midday meal. ⊠*40 Main St.* ☏*508/228–1979* ⊕*www. evenkeelcafe.com* ⊟*AE, MC, V.*

$$–$$$ ✕**Starlight Café.** This tiny movie-theater anteroom and enclosed patio, spiffed up with cinematic artifacts, offers a casual menu—think mac 'n' cheese with lobster. It's ideal for a pre- or post-flick feed, and yes, you're allowed to take your drinks into the theater. Also, with a dinner reservation you can get a movie reservation—a great way to leapfrog the line. ⊠*1 N. Union St.* ☏*508/228–4479* ⊕*www.starlightnantucket.com* ⊟*AE, D, MC, V.*

$–$$ ✕**Fog Island Café.** Cherished year-round for its exceptional breakfasts, ☺ Fog Island is just as fine a spot for lunch—or, in season, a charitably priced dinner. The storefront space is cheerily decked out in a fresh country style (echoed in the friendly service), and chef-owners Mark and Anne Dawson—both Culinary Institute of America grads—seem determined to provide the best possible value to transients and natives alike. Consider starting the day with pesto scrambled eggs and ending it with sesame-crusted tuna with Thai noodles. ⊠*7 S. Water St.* ☏*508/228–1818* ⊕*www.fogisland.com* ⊟*MC, V.*

⇨ *Where to Stay & Eat Outside Nantucket Town map for these properties.*

NANTUCKET ✕**Galley Beach.** A beloved institution since 1958, this modest cottage
TOWN plunked right on the Cliffside Beach Club's swath of sand has managed
OUTSKIRTS to stay fresh and luxe thanks to three generations of congenial restau-
$$$$ rateurs. Chef W. Scott Osif, who has manned the stoves since 2003, is a self-professed minimalist. Though the menu may encompass all sorts of exotic ingredients (chayote squash, ponzu, Honshimeji mushrooms, and the like), the results tend to be tastefully subdued—like country-club cuisine, only with a rather elaborate pedigree. Some relatively straightforward dishes (like the unadulterated crab cake, and the caramelized sea scallops with uni-muscat sauce) are perfection; others may come across as too plain. Still, it's impossible to fault the setting. The deck, with its gay blue-and-white awning ringed with red geraniums, takes in a 180-degree beach view; it's perfectly oriented to capture what photographers call "the golden moment." ⊠*54 Jefferson Ave.* ☏*508/228–9641* ⊟*AE, MC, V* ☉*Closed mid-Oct.–mid-May.*

$$$–$$$$ ✕**The SeaGrille.** Though it may lack the flashy profile of other top island restaurants, this mid-island eatery deserves its popularity. The lobster bisque alone, even without the bonus of a dill-flecked pastry bonnet, warrants a following, as does the free-form seafood ravioli. Off-season, the dining room, with its murals of wharf and street scenes, is a peaceful haven. When summer arrives, so do the faithful hordes of crowds. ⊠*45 Sparks Ave.* ☏*508/325–5700* ⊕*www.theseagrille.com* ⊟*AE, MC, V.*

$$-$$$$ ✕**Sfoglia.** Culinary Institute of America grads Ron and Colleen Suhanosky appointed their celery-tinted trattoria with mismatched tables (including some enamel-top honeys from the '40s), chairs, crockery—even silverware. You'll feast on home-style Italian dishes such as gnocchi with pecorini romano, or chicken "al mattone" (cooked under a brick). Desserts—Colleen's province—include rustic seasonal tarts and seductive semifreddos. Sfoglia's New York branch on the Upper East Side has earned solid foodie kudos. ⊠*130 Pleasant St.* ☎*508/325–4500* ⊕*www.sfogliarestaurant.com* ▭*No credit cards* ☾*Closed Sun.*

$$$ ✕**Cinco.** With this eclectic tapas oasis, affable owner Michael Sturgis
Fodor'sChoice has made mid-island a true dining destination. The festive mood is irre-
★ sistible: it starts with the setting (a candlelighted patio leading to intimate rooms painted in dark, sexy colors) and culminates in a parade of thrilling "small plates" meant for sharing. Don't be surprised if you find yourself getting possessive over the grilled lamb chops sauced with lime "mojo," say, or the bay scallops tossed with pear brown butter—just order more for the table. Chef Jean-Luc Matecat tinkers with the menu daily, and keeps a bar menu going to 1 AM–ideal for those who like to observe a Spanish dinner hour. ⊠*5 Amelia Dr.* ☎*508/325–5151* ⊕*www.cinco5.com* ▭*AE, MC, V* ☾*Closed Jan.–Mar. No lunch.*

¢ ✕**The Downyflake.** Locals flock here for bountiful breakfasts—featuring much sought-after homemade doughnuts—and well-priced lunches, from codfish cakes to burgers. ⊠*18 Sparks Ave.* ☎*508/228–4533* ▭*No credit cards* ☾*Closed Jan.–Mar. No dinner.*

WHERE TO STAY

Nantucket has a low profile, so none of the inns or hotels listed has an elevator. Some of the more recently renovated inns do have rooms compliant with the Americans with Disabilities Act; inquire ahead. Also, none of the properties listed permit smoking: Nantucket learned its lesson with the Great Fire of 1846.

$$$$ ▣**The Beachside at Nantucket.** Nantucket has only one "motel" in the
☾ classic rooms-around-a-pool configuration, and it's a honey—not at all out of place amid its tony neighbors. Between the town and Jetties Beach (both are within a bracing 10-minute walk), the complex ascends to two stories; rooms—decor is of the cheery wicker-and-florals school—have little pool-view terraces separated by whitewashed latticework. Families naturally flock here, but business travelers are equally well served. **Pros:** Kids have company, near the beach, pretty rooms. **Cons:** Kids rule, sounds carry from the pool, location not actually beachside. ⊠*30 N. Beach St., 02554* ☎*508/228–2241 or 800/322–4433* ☎*508/228–8901* ⊕*www.thebeachside.com* ⇱*87 rooms, 3 suites* ⌂*In-room: refrigerator, Wi-Fi. In-hotel: pool, no-smoking room, some pets allowed* ▭*AE, D, DC, MC, V* ☾*Closed early Dec.–late Apr.* ☖*CP.*

$$$$ ▣**The Cottages at the Boat Basin.** These weathered-shingle cottages sit on
☾ South Wharf, amid the yachts—you could reserve a mooring and bring your own boat. Cottages range from studios to three bedrooms, and each has attractive modern decor with a nautical flavor: white walls,

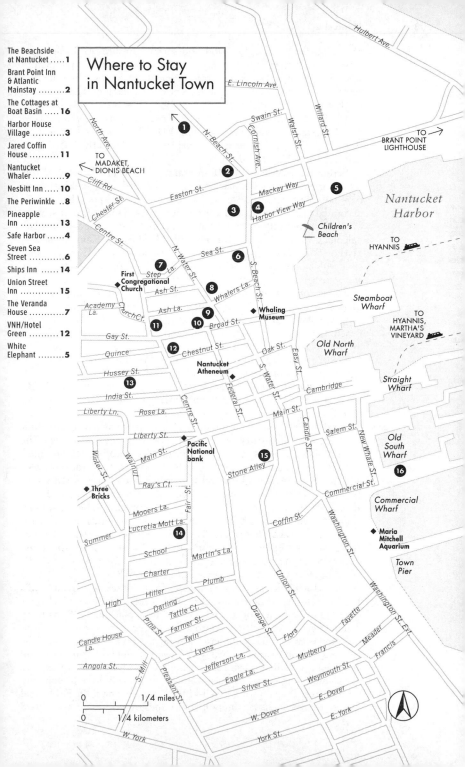

Where to Stay in Nantucket Town

Nantucket Harbor

E. Lincoln Ave.

Swain St.

Walsh St.

Willard St.

Hulbert Ave.

TO → BRANT POINT LIGHTHOUSE

N. Beach St.

Cornish Ave.

North Ave.

TO MADAKET, DIONIS BEACH ←

Cliff Rd.

Chester St.

Centre St.

Academy La.

Church Ct.

Gay St.

Quince

Hussey St.

India St.

Liberty Ln.

Rose La.

Liberty St.

Main St.

Walnut

Winter St.

Ray's Ct.

◆ Three Bricks

Mooers La.

Lucretia Mott La.

Summer

School

Charter

High

Hiller

Darling

Tattle Ct.

Pine St.

Farmer St.

Candle House La.

Angola St.

S. Mill

Twin

Lyons

Jefferson La.

Eagle La.

Silver St.

W. York

York St.

W. Dover

E. Dover

E. York

Easton St.

Mackay Way

Harbor View Way

Children's Beach

TO HYANNIS

N. Water St.

Sea St.

S. Beach St.

Step La.

First Congregational Church

Ash St.

Whalers La.

Ash La.

Broad St.

◆ Whaling Museum

Steamboat Wharf

TO HYANNIS, MARTHA'S VINEYARD

Chestnut St.

Oak St.

East St.

Old North Wharf

Nantucket Atheneum ◆

Federal St.

S. Water St.

Cambridge

Straight Wharf

Main St.

Centre St.

Fair St.

Pacific National bank ◆

Stone Alley

Candle St.

Salem St.

New Whale St.

Old South Wharf

Commercial St.

Commercial Wharf

Coffin St.

Washington St.

◆ Maria Mitchell Aquarium

Martin's La.

Union St.

Plumb

Flora

Mulberry

Fayette

Weymouth St.

Meader

Washington St. Ext.

Francis

Town Pier

Pleasant St.

0   1/4 miles

0   1/4 kilometers

navy-blue rugs, and light-wood floors and furniture. All have water views, though they're not always equal—some cottages have picture windows plus a little garden terrace. **Pros:** Right on the water, marina access, center of town. **Cons:** Tourist central, attendant noise, occasional fog horns. ⊠*New Whale St., Box 1139, 02554* ☎*508/325–1499 or 866/838–9253* ⎙*508/228–7639* ⊕*www.thecottagesnantucket.com* ⇆*23 cottages* ⌂*In-room: kitchen, DVD, Wi-Fi. In-hotel: concierge, some pets allowed, no-smoking rooms* ☰*AE, D, DC, MC, V* ⊘*Closed late Oct.–mid-May* ¶⊙¶*BP.*

$$$$ ⛫ **Harbor House Village.** An 1886 grand hotel forms the core of this
☖ family-oriented complex, where nicely landscaped brick walkways lead to a half-dozen town houses and an outdoor heated pool. Rooms are decorated in a pale-pine-and-wicker motif, in a summery color scheme of white, sunny yellow, and hydrangea blue; many come with private balconies. Owner Stephen Karp installed his favorite Chinese chefs in Harbor Wok, open in season. Babysitters are on call in season, and children's programs are offered from mid-June to Labor Day. Dogs get a special welcome at the "Woof Hotel," a dozen rooms dedicated to canine comfort—with dog beds, treats, and even a "Yappy Hour" for socializing. As of this writing, a spa was being developed for the property. **Pros:** Child- and pet-friendly, in town, close to Children's Beach. **Cons:** Geared more to families than romance, large scale can mean impersonal, some rooms near busy street. ⊠*S. Beach St., Box 1139, 02554* ☎*508/228–1500 or 866/325–9300* ⎙*508/228–7639* ⊕*www.harborhousevillage.com* ⇆*98 rooms* ⌂*In-room: Wi-Fi. In-hotel: restaurant, bar, pool concierge, children's programs (ages 3–13), ferry shuttle, some pets allowed, no-smoking rooms, no elevator* ☰*AE, D, DC, MC, V* ⊘*Closed late Oct.–late Apr.* ¶⊙¶*CP.*

$$$$ ⛫ **Jared Coffin House.** The largest house in town when it was built in 1845, this three-story brick manse is still plenty impressive. The antiques-filled parlors are a study in timeless good taste. The inn's umbrella extends to two other nearby buildings, the handsomest of which is the 1842 Greek-revival Harrison Gray House. Rooms vary greatly in terms of size and grandeur (the inn even has some very affordable singles). **Pros:** Elegant parlors, knowledgeable concierge, old-money aura. **Cons:** Lack of dining, some tiny rooms, street noise for those in front. ⊠*29 Broad St., Box 1580, 02554* ☎*508/228–2405 or 800/248–2405* ⊕*www.jaredcoffinhouse.com* ⇆*43 rooms* ⌂*In-room: no a/c (some), Wi-Fi. In-hotel: concierge, no-smoking rooms* ☰*AE, D, DC, MC, V* ⊘*Closed early Dec.–mid-May* ¶⊙¶*BP.*

$$$$ ⛫ **Nantucket Whaler.** Let's not mince words: the suites carved out of this
★ 1850 Greek-revival house are gorgeous. Neither Calliope Ligelis nor Randi Ott, the New Yorkers who rescued the place in 1999, had any design experience, but they approached the project as if preparing to welcome friends. Each suite has a private entrance and a kitchen. The spacious bedrooms are lavished with flowers, well-chosen antiques, and fine linens, including plush robes. Couples who have come to explore not so much the island as one another will scarcely have to come up for air. **Pros:** Pretty rooms, well-kitted out, romantic. **Cons:** No real reception area, lacks a common room, the usual in-town noise. ⊠*8*

N. Water St., Box 1337, 02554 ☎*508/228–6597 or 888/808–6597* 🖷*508/228–6291* ∰*www.nantucketwhaler.com* ⇆*12 suites* ♿*In-room: DVD, Wi-Fi. In-hotel: no kids under 11, no-smoking rooms, refrigerator* ⊟*AE, MC, V* ⊗*Closed Jan. and Feb.*

$$$$

Fodor's Choice

★

⊞ **Union Street Inn.** Ken Withrow worked in the hotel business, Deborah Withrow in high-end retail display, and guests get the best of both worlds. This 1770 house, a stone's throw from the bustle of Main Street, has been respectfully yet lavishly restored. Guests are treated to Frette linens, plump duvets, and lush robes (the better to lounge around in, my dear), as well as a full gourmet breakfast served on the tree-shaded garden patio. **Pros:** Pampering by pros, sensual pleasures, conducive to romance. **Cons:** No nearby beach, bustle of town, some small rooms (disclosed on Web site). ✉*7 Union St., 02554* ☎*508/228–9222 or 800/225–5116* 🖷*508/325–0848* ∰*www.unioninn.com* ⇆*12 rooms* ♿*In-room: Wi-Fi. In-hotel: no kids under 12, no-smoking rooms* ⊟*AE, MC, V* ¶⊚|BP.*

$$$$

⊞ **VNH–Vanessa Noel Hotel and Hotel Green.** Minimalist chic has waltzed in the door—in a sweet pair of kitty heels. Opened in 2002 by native New Yorker and island-summerer shoe designer Vanessa Noel, VNH is a living catalog of trendy decor: each of the eight rooms (some admittedly as small as shoeboxes) boasts Armani Casa bedside tables, Philippe Starck bathroom fixtures, Mascioni linens, and Bulgari toiletries. Though the concept might seem a bit at odds with the island aesthetic, you'd be hard pressed to name a hotel with these touches outside a metropolis. Organo-purists will want to check out Noel's 2006 addition a few doors down: the 10-room Hotel Green—distinguished by its grass windowboxes—has milk-painted walls, hemp shower curtains (the water is dechlorinated), and Ayurvedic body products. Rooms in the latter are slightly less pricy, as well as open to children. Both inns share an outdoor breakfast café and VNH harbors the seasonal Cafe V, a caviar bar serving light bites. **Pros:** Centrally located, trendy, glamour quotient. **Cons:** Street noise, size of rooms, preciousness factor. ✉*5 Chestnut St., at Centre St., 02554* ☎*508/228–5300* ∰*www.vanessanoelhotel.com* ⇆*18 rooms* ♿*In-hotel: bar, refrigerator, no kids* ⊟*AE, D, MC, V.*

$$$$

★

⊞ **The Veranda House.** A fixture since the early 1880s, the former Overlook, whose tiers of balconies take in a sweeping harbor vista, has been treated to a trendy "retro-chic" overhaul. The exterior may look unchanged, but the rooms got a makeover that introduced Frette linens, Simon Pearce lamps, Italian-tile rainfall showers, and the like. The buffet breakfasts are equally lush, featuring frittatas and stuffed French toast. **Pros:** Central but quiet location, harbor views, impeccable condition. **Cons:** Children's is the only close beach, decor a bit austere, pricy (though not for Nantucket). ✉*3 Step La., Box 1112, 02554* ☎*508/228–0695* ∰*www.theverandahouse.com* ⇆*17 rooms, 1 suite* ♿*In-room: DVD, Wi-Fi. In-hotel: concierge, no kids under 10* ⊟*AE, D, MC, V* ⊗*Closed early Dec. to mid-May* ¶⊚|BP.*

$$$$

⊞ **White Elephant.** The White Elephant, a 1920s behemoth right on Nantucket Harbor, seems determined to keep raising the bar in service and style. The complex—a main building plus a cluster of cottages with breezy country-chic decor—hugs the harbor, leaving just enough room for a sweep of emerald lawn and the veranda of the hotel's in-house restaurant, the Brant Point Grill, where jazz combos entertain in season. Prices are lofty but, for the echelon it attracts, not all that extreme. **Pros:** Right on harbor, elegant, built-in entertainment. **Cons:** Can be snooty, Children's the only nearby beach, expensive. ⊠*Easton St., Box 1139, 02554* ☎*508/228–2500 or 800/445–6574* 🖷*508/325–1195* ⊕*www. whiteelephanthotel.com* ⇩*21 rooms, 31 suites, 11 cottages* ⚐*In-room: safe, refrigerator, DVD, dial-up, Ethernet. In-hotel: restaurant, room service, bar, laundry service, concierge, ferry shuttle, no-smoking rooms* ⊟*AE, D, DC, MC, V* ☉*Closed Jan.–Mar.* ⦿*BP.*

$$$–$$$$ 🏨**Pineapple Inn.** No expense was spared in retrofitting this 1838 Greek-
    ★   revival captain's house for its new role as pamperer. It's decorated with impeccable taste, with down quilts and marble-finished baths. Breakfast is served in a formal dining room or beside the garden fountain. Whaling captains displayed a pineapple on their stoops upon completion of a successful journey, signaling the neighbors to come celebrate; here that spirit prevails daily—as it does at three sister properties (The Summer House–Fair Street; The Summer House–India Street, and the 29 Fair Street Inn), comprising 48 in-town rooms all told, operated under the auspices of the splendid Summer House out in 'Sconset. **Pros:** True Nantucket elegance, quiet location, cushy quarters. **Cons:** Some small rooms (Web site warns), no nearby beach, communal breakfast set-up (not everyone's cup of cappucino). ⊠*10 Hussey St., 02554* ☎*508/228–9992* 🖷*508/325–6051* ⊕*www.pineappleinn.com* ⇩*12 rooms* ⚐*In-room: Wi-Fi. In-hotel: no-smoking rooms* ⊟*AE, MC, V* ☉*Closed mid-Dec.–late Apr.* ⦿*CP.*

$$$–$$$$ 🏨**Seven Sea Street.** If this red-oak post-and-beam B&B looks awfully well preserved, that's because it was custom-built in 1987. Decked out in Early American style (decorative stenciling, fishnet-canopy beds, braided rugs), it offers the ambience of antiquity without all the creaky drawbacks. The Deluxe Suite, with its cathedral ceiling, full kitchen, gas fireplace, and harbor view, warrants a leisurely stay. Two satellite buildings up your odds of booking a room. **Pros:** Quiet side street, central location, handsome decor. **Cons:** Some rooms smallish, some darkish, Children's the only nearby beach. ⊠*7 Sea St., 02554* ☎*508/228–3577 or 800/651–9262* 🖷*508/228–3578* ⊕*www.sevenseastreetinn.com* ⇩*13 rooms, 2 suites* ⚐*In-room: refrigerator, VCR, Wi-Fi. In-hotel: some pets allowed, no kids under 5, no-smoking rooms* ⊟*AE, D, MC, V* ⦿*CP.*

$$–$$$$ 🏨**The Periwinkle.** Sara Shlosser-O'Reilly's B&B has spark—and a variety of rooms ranging from affordable singles to nice-size quarters with canopied king-size beds and harbor views. In one especially pretty setting, the blue-ribbon pattern of the wallpaper matches the cushions and canopy: it's like living in a nicely wrapped gift. **Pros:** Central location, pretty decor, heavenly baking aromas, garden for lounging. **Cons:** Usual town noises, Children's the only nearby beach, tiny breakfast room (opt for the garden). ⊠*7–9 N. Water St., Box 1816, 02554* ☎*508/228–9267 or 800/837–2921* 🖷*508/228–0245* ⊕*www.theperiwinkle.com*

Navigating the Rental Market

If you're going to be staying for a week or more, you might want to consider renting a cottage or house—an arrangement that gives you a chance to settle in and get a real taste of island living. Many visitors, especially those with children, find renting more relaxing than staying in a hotel or an inn. With your own kitchen, you'll save money by eating in; plus you can enjoy such homey summer pleasures as barbecues. Though decor can vary from chichi to weatherworn, most cottages come equipped with all you'll need to ensure a comfortable stay. Steer clear of a house without linens; it's a sign of bad things to come. The better houses come fully accoutered: not just with basics but with luxury touches like cable or satellite TV, a CD player, gourmet kitchen implements, beach chairs, and bikes.

Finding a great cottage or house can be tough, however, especially since so many are rented a year or more in advance by returning guests. The time to start your search is a summer ahead, though you can occasionally find a property as late as spring. A good way to shop is to stop in and visit Realtors when you happen to be in town. Be prepared for a bit of sticker shock, though. Prices are generally about twice what you'd have to pay on Cape Cod or even the Vineyard. In summer, very rustic (read shabby) rentals start at about $1,200 a week and can run to many times that ($3,500 and up) for multibedroom or waterfront properties.

Information Country Village Rentals (✉ 10 Straight Wharf ☎ 508/228—8840 or 800/599–7368 ⊕ www.cvrandr.com) knows its clientele, who like to flit to sweet spots like Stowe and St. Bart's. **Lucille Jordan Real Estate** (✉ 8 Federal St. ☎ 508/228–4449 ⊕ www.jordanre. com) has a broad rental inventory; check the photos lining the storefront windows. The **Maury People** (✉ 35–37 Main St. ☎ 508/228–1881 🖷 508/228–1481 ⊕ www.maurypeople.com), associated with Sotheby's, has more than 1,000 private homes in its rental inventory, including historic and beach homes; service is not only knowledgeable but personable. **Preferred Properties** (✉ 76 Easton St. ☎ 508/228–2320 or 800/338–7715 🖷 508/228–8464 ⊕ www.preferredpropertiesre.com) is a Christie's affiliate whose offerings range "from cottages in the sand to castles on the cliff."

🛏 *16 rooms, 1 cottage* ♿ *In-room: refrigerators, DVD (some), VCRs (some), Wi-Fi. In-hotel: no-smoking rooms* ▭*D, MC, V* ⦿*CP.*

$$$ 🏨 **Safe Harbor.** The name is apt: children *and* pets are welcome at this homey B&B with an enviable location mere steps from Children's Beach. Some of the rooms harboring American and Oriental antiques have water views; some have private decks. Everyone's welcome to sit on the wide front porch and enjoy the ocean breezes. **Pros:** Family-friendly, laid-back, well cared for. **Cons:** Noise can carry from Children's Beach, boat-launch traffic, occasional fog horns. ✉ *2 Harborview Way, 02554* 🖷 *508/228–3222 or 800/651–9262* ⦿ *www.beesknees.net/ safeharbor* 🛏 *5 rooms* ♿ *In-room: Wi-Fi. In-hotel: some pets allowed* ▭*AE, MC, V* ⦿*CP.*

$$–$$$ 🖼**Brant Point Inn & Atlantic Mainstay.** You can't beat the edge-of-town location (Jetties Beach is a mere five-minute walk), especially given the modest rates that prevail at this pair of handsome post-and-beam guesthouses. Innkeeper Thea Kaizer grew up in a Nantucket inn; her husband, Peter, leads fishing charters, and should you catch something, he'll expedite it to the restaurant of your choice. **Pros:** Friendly native owners, comfy/casual, near town and beaches. **Cons:** Lack of air-conditioning (though unneeded), over-casual for some tastes, on busy road. ⊠*6 N. Beach St., 02554* ☎*508/228–5442* 🖷*508/228–8498* ⊕*www. brantpointinn.com* ⇖*17 rooms, 2 suites* ⌂*In-room: no a/c, refrigerator* ▤*AE, MC, V* ⏐⌷⏐*CP.*

$$–$$$ 🖼**Ships Inn.** This 1831 home exudes history: it was built for whal-
★   ing captain Obed Starbuck on the site of the birthplace of abolitionist Lucretia Mott. Guest rooms, named for the ships Starbuck commanded, are furnished with period antiques and pretty wall coverings. The basement has a restaurant of the same name (delighted murmurings waft up); it generates a wonderful continental breakfast and afternoon tea. **Pros:** Large rooms, handsome decor, fine in-house restaurant. **Cons:** Front rooms face street, exuberant exiting diners, uphill from ferries. ⊠*13 Fair St., 02554* ☎*508/228–0040 or 888/872–4052* ⊕*www.ship-sinnnantucket.com* ⇖*13 rooms, 11 with bath* ⌂*In-room: refrigerator. In-hotel: restaurant, no kids under 8, no-smoking rooms* ▤*AE, D, MC, V* ⊙*Closed Jan.–Apr.* ⏐⌷⏐*CP.*

$–$$ 🖼**Nesbitt Inn.** The last real deal left in town, this homey Victorian has been in the same family since 1914. Fourth-generation proprietors Joanne and Steve Marcoux are so nice, and the rates so reasonable, you're willing to overlook the shared baths and gently worn furnishings. Here you'll find the authentic, pre-glitz Nantucket. **Pros:** Friendly native owners, no pretense, the true Nantucket. **Cons:** Noisy street, small rooms, shabby (but clean). ⊠*21 Broad St., Box 1019, 02554* ☎*508/228–0156* 🖷*508/228–2446* ⇖*12 rooms share 3 baths, 1 room with private bath, 2 cottages* ⌂*In-hotel: no-smoking rooms* ▤*MC, V* ⏐⌷⏐*CP.*

NANTUCKET ⇨ *Where to Stay & Eat Outside Nantucket Town map for these*
TOWN *properties.*
OUTSKIRTS

$$$$ 🖼**Cliffside Beach Club.** Which way to the beach? You're on it: this snaz-
☾   zily updated 1920s beach club stakes its claim with a flotilla of colorful
★   umbrellas—somewhat miffing natives, who consider sand rights anathema. Local politics aside, this is one prime chunk of gentle bay beach, and the complex makes the most of its site, with a gorgeous cathedral-ceiling lobby decorated with hanging quilts and rooms of every size and shape enhanced by island-made modern furnishings. Best of all, you can traipse across the sand to Galley Beach, one of the best restaurants around. **Pros:** Right on beach, two pools, good restaurant. **Cons:** Questionable private-beach karma, over-entitled guests, high prices. ⊠*46 Jefferson Ave., Box 449, 02554* ☎*508/228–0618 or 800/932–9645* ⊕*www.cliffsidebeach.com* ⇖*26 rooms, 3 suites, 2 apartments, 1 cottage* ⌂*In-room: safe, kitchen (some), refrigerator, DVD (some), VCR (some), no TV (some), Wi-Fi. In-hotel: restaurant, pools, gym, beachfront* ▤*AE* ⊙*Closed mid-Oct.–May* ⏐⌷⏐*CP.*

¢–$$ 🖼 **Robert B. Johnson Memorial Hostel.** One of the country's most pictur-
esque hostels, this 49-bed Hostelling International facility occupies a
former 1873 lifesaving station—known as "The Star of the Sea"—right
on Surfside Beach, a 3-mi ride from town on the bike path. Dorm
rooms (the two private rooms, one of which is wheelchair-accessible,
book quickly) are divided by gender; the common areas include a
kitchen, where a complimentary breakfast is offered. There's no lock-
out (customary at many urban hostels) and—huzzah—no curfew. Res-
ervations are always a good idea, and essential come summer. **Pros:**
Super-cheap, right on island's best beach, good company. **Cons:** Little
privacy, no frills, a long haul (3-mi public shuttle or bike ride) from
town. ⊠ *31 Western Ave., 02554* ☎ *508/228–0433* ⊕ *www.usahostels.
org/cape/hint/index.shtm* ⇋ *49 dorm-style beds* ♿ *In room: no a/c, no
phone, no TV. In-hotel: beachfront, no-smoking rooms, phone (local
calls), Wi-Fi* ⊟ *MC, V* ⊗ *Closed mid-Oct.–early May.*

NIGHTLIFE & THE ARTS

The phrase "Nantucket nightlife" verges on an oxymoron—and, dur-
ing the off-season, it's virtually a nonentity. If it's glitz and nonstop
action you're after, better stick to the mainland. On the other hand, if
you like live music, you will never go lacking—at least in season.

For listings of events, see the *Inquirer and Mirror* (⊕ *www.ack.net*),
the *Nantucket Independent* (⊕ *www.nantucketindependent.com*), and
(in season) *Yesterday's Island* (⊕ *www.yesterdaysisland.com*); the latter
two are distributed free. Posters around town announce coming attrac-
tions: check the board outside the Hub, a newsstand at the corner of
Federal and Main streets.

FILM The **Nantucket Film Festival** (☎ *508/325–6274 or 212/642–6339* ⊕ *www.
nantucketfilmfestival.org*), held each June, emphasizes the importance
of strong scripts. The final playlist—about two dozen short and fea-
ture-length films—always includes a few world premieres, and many
selections have gone on to considerable commercial success. Shows
tend to sell out, so it's best to buy online, well ahead. Informal daily
coffee-klatch discussions with directors provide the inside scoop.

The **Starlight Theatre** (⊠ *1 N. Union St.* ☎ *508/228–4435* ⊕ *www.
starlightnantucket.com*) is a small screening room appended to a
café of the same name. It presents two shows nightly in season, plus
sporadic matinees.

MUSIC The **Boston Pops** put on a blow-out concert on Jetties Beach in mid-
August to benefit the Nantucket Cottage Hospital (☎ *508/825–8250*
⊕ *www.nantuckethospital.org*).

The **Nantucket Arts Council** (⊠ *Box 554, 02554* ☎ *508/228–8588* ⊕ *www.
nantucketartscouncil.org*) sponsors a music series (jazz, country, clas-
sical) September to June.

The **Nantucket School of Music** (⊠ *11 Centre St.* ☎ *508/228–3352* ⊕ *www.
ackmusic.com*) arranges year-round choral and instrumental instruction
and sponsors and puts on concerts; choristers are always welcome.

Nantucket Musical Arts Society (☎508/228–1287) mounts concerts by internationally acclaimed musicians Tuesday evenings at 8:30 July through August. The concerts are mostly classical but sometimes venture into jazz.

The **Nantucket Park & Recreation Commission** (✉*Children's Beach bandstand, off Harbor View Way* ☎508/228–7213) hosts free jazz/pop/classical concerts (and the occasional theater production) from July 4 to Labor Day. Programs begin at 6 PM. Bring blankets, chairs, and bug repellent.

The **Noonday Concert Series** (✉*Unitarian Universalist Church, 11 Orange St.* ☎508/228–5466), Thursday at noon in July and August, brings in visiting performers and also showcases outstanding local musicians. Concerts range from bluegrass to classical.

BARS & CLUBS The **Chicken Box** (*The Box* ✉*14 Dave St., off Lower Orange St.* ☎508/228–9717) rocks! Live music—including some big-name bands—plays six nights a week in season, and weekends throughout the year. On the off nights, you can always play pool, foosball, or darts.

The **Muse** (✉*44 Surfside Rd.* ☎508/228–6873) is *the* place to catch big-name acts year-round. DJs spin between sets and on nights when there's no live act. The barnlike Muse accommodates some 370 people, who also have the option of playing pool or Ping-Pong or scarfing pies produced on-site at **Muse Pizza** (☎508/228–1471).

At the White Elephant's **Brant Point Grill** (✉*50 Easton St.* ☎508/325–1320 or 800/445–6574 ⊕*www.brantpointgrill.com*), the setting is country-elegant—Windsor chairs, varnished woodwork with huntergreen trim—and the patrons are patently moneyed, since many are hotel guests. A pianist or jazz-standards band provides atmosphere (and takes requests).

READINGS & TALKS The **Nantucket Atheneum** (✉*1 India St.* ☎508/228–1110 ⊕*www.nantucketatheneum.org*) hosts a dazzling roster of writers and speakers year-round. Except for a few big-name fund-raisers in summer, all events are free.

THEATER **Theatre Workshop of Nantucket** (✉*Methodist Church, 2 Centre St.* ☎508/228–4305 ⊕*www.theatreworkshop.com*), a semiprofessional community theater since 1956, stages plays, musicals, and readings year-round.

SPORTS & THE OUTDOORS

BEACHES A calm area by the harbor, **Children's Beach** (✉*Off Harbor View Way*) is an easy walk north from the center of town and a perfect spot for small children. The beach has a grassy park with benches, a playground, lifeguards, a café, picnic tables, showers, and restrooms. Tie-dyeing classes are offered Friday at noon mid-July through August.

Cisco (✉*Hummock Pond Rd., South Shore*) has heavy surf, lifeguards, but no food or restrooms. It's not easy to get to or from Nantucket Town, though: it's 4 mi from town, and there are no bike trails to it, so you'll have to ride in the road, walk, drive, or take a taxi. Also, the dunes are severely eroded, so getting down onto the beach can be difficult. Still, the waves make it a popular spot for body- and boardsurfers.

Dionis Beach (⊠ *Eel Point Rd.*) is, at its entrance, a narrow strip of sand that turns into a wider, more private strand with high dunes and fewer children. The beach has a rocky bottom and calm, rolling waters; there are lifeguards on duty and restrooms. Take the Madaket Bike Path to Eel Point Road, about 3 mi west of town.

★ A short bike- or shuttle-bus ride from town, **Jetties Beach** (⊠ *Bathing Beach Rd., 1½ mi northwest of Straight Wharf*) is a most popular family beach because of its calm surf, lifeguards, bathhouse, restrooms, and snack bar. It's a good place to try out water toys: kayaks, sailboards, and Day Sailers are rented in summer. On shore it's a lively scene with playground and volleyball nets on the beach and adjacent tennis courts. There is a boardwalk to the beach and you can watch the ferries pass.

> ### MICHELANGELO ON THE BEACH
>
> Buddhas, dragons, mermaids, and, of course, whales inhabit Jetties Beach during the annual Sandcastle & Sculpture Day in August. Creative concoctions emerge from the sand: porpoises, submarines, spaceships, flowers, and the famous lightship baskets are carefully and creatively crafted out of sand, shells, seaweed, and even beach litter. Anyone can stake out a patch of sand. There are prizes in several age groups and categories, so grab a shovel, bucket, and sunscreen and join in. Registration forms are available at the chamber office, 48 Main Street.

Madaket Beach (⊠ *Off Madaket Rd., Madaket*) is reached by shuttle bus from Nantucket Town or the Madaket Bike Path (5 mi from Upper Main Street) and has lifeguards, but no restrooms. It's known for challenging surf (beware the rip currents) and unbeatable sunsets.

Fodor's Choice **Surfside Beach** (⊠ *Surfside Rd., South Shore*), accessible via the Surfside
★ Bike Path (3 mi) or shuttle bus, is the island's most popular surf beach, with lifeguards, restrooms, a snack bar, and a wide strand of sand. It pulls in college students as well as families and is great for kite flying and surf casting.

BIKING The best way to tour Nantucket is by bicycle. Nearly 28 mi of paved bike paths wind through all types of terrain from one end of the island to the other; it is possible to bike around the entire island in a day. Most paths start within ½ mi of town, and all are well marked. Several lead to beaches. And if you're without your wheels, it's easy enough to rent some. The paths are also perfect for runners and bladers—but not mopeds, which are forbidden. Note that Nantucket now requires all bike riders—including adults—to wear a helmet.

The easy 3-mi **Surfside Bike Path** leads to Surfside, the island's premier ocean beach. A drinking fountain and rest stop are placed at about the halfway point.

Milestone Bike Path, a straight shot linking Nantucket Town and 'Sconset, is probably the most monotonous of the paths but can still be quite pleasant. It's about 7 mi—paired with the scenic Polpis Path, it becomes a 16-mi island loop.

At 1.2 mi, the **Cliff Road Path,** on the north shore, is one of the easiest bike paths, but it's still quite scenic, with gentle hills. It intersects with the Eel Point and Madaket paths.

The **Eel Point/Dionis Beach Path** starts at the junction of Eel Point Road and Madaket Road and links the Cliff Road and Madaket bike paths to Dionis Beach. It's less than a mile long.

The **Madaket Path** starts at the intersection of Quaker and Upper Main Street and follows Madaket Road out to Madaket Beach, on the island's west end and about 6 mi from the edge of Nantucket Town. About one-third of the way, you could turn off onto Cliff Road Path or the Eel Point/Dionis Beach Path.

Young's Bicycle Shop (⊠ *6 Broad St., Steamboat Wharf* 🕾 *508/228–1151* ⊕ *www.youngsbicycleshop.com*), established in 1931, rents bicycles, including tandems and children's equipment; weekly rates are available. The knowledgeable third-generation Young family and staff will send you off with everything you need—an excellent touring map, a helmet, and a quaint little Portuguese basket for your handlebars.

BIRD- Hundreds of species flock to the island's moors, meadows, and
WATCHING marshes in the course of a year. Birds that are rare in other parts of New England thrive here, because of the lack of predators and the abundance of wide-open, undeveloped space. Almost anywhere outside of town you're sure to see interesting bird life, not just in migratory season but year-round. Set up your spotting scope near the salt marsh at Eel Point any time of year and you're bound to see shorebirds feeding—low tide is the best time. Endangered piping plovers and least terns nest on the ocean side in spring. Folger's Marsh about 3 mi east of town and the Harbor Flats at the end of Washington Street on the eastern edge of town are also good shorebird-watching sites. Inland, a walk through Sanford Farm from Madaket Road to the south shore, traversing upland, forest, heath, and shore habitats, will bring you in range of Savannah sparrows, yellow warblers, osprey, and red-tailed hawks, the island's most common raptor. Be on the lookout for the protected Northern harrier. For woodland species, check out the trails through Windswept Cranberry Bog or the Masquetuck Reservation near Polpis Harbor.

Eco Guides: Strong Wings (⊠ *9 Nobadeer Farm Rd.* 🕾 *508/228–1769* ⊕ *www.strongwings.org*) customizes environmentally savvy birding tours based on interest and group size and, depending on your preferred degree of difficulty, can include a hike, a bike ride, or a casual stroll.

The **Maria Mitchell Association** (*MMA* ⊠ *4 Vestal St.* 🕾 *508/228–0898* ⊕ *www.mmo.org*) leads marine-ecology field trips and nature and bird walks weekly in spring and early summer and three times a week from June through Labor Day.

BOATING   During July and August, Nantucket is *the* place to study, close-up, some of the world's most splendid yachts—and the well-to-do people who own and sail them. Don't be surprised if you see yachts with piggyback motor launches, automobiles, and helicopters. Most of them spend a few days here, many from a tour that originated in the Mediterranean via the Caribbean. If you don't happen to own a floating palace, you can still hit the water—Nantucket has plenty of boat charters, rentals, and scenic cruises.

Nantucket Boat Rentals (⌖*Slip 1, Straight Wharf* ☎*508/325–1001* ⊕*www.nantucket.net/boating/boatrentals*) rents powerboats, for up to 10 passengers; security deposits are required.

Nantucket Community Sailing (⌖*4 Winter St.* ☎*508/228–6600* ⊕*www. nantucketcommunitysailing.org*) rents Sunfish sailboats, sailboards, and kayaks from Jetties Beach (Memorial Day to Labor Day); it also has youth and adult instructional sailing programs, as well as adaptive water-sport clinics for disabled athletes. NCS's Outrigger Canoe Club— a Polynesian tradition—heads out three evenings a week (depending on interest) in season.

Sea Nantucket (⌖*Washington St. Ext., ¼ mi southeast of Commercial Wharf* ☎*508/228–7499*) rents kayaks and small sailboats by the hour or half-day at the vest-pocket Francis Street Beach.

☾   The *Endeavor* (⌖*Slip 1015, Straight Wharf* ☎*508/228–5585* ⊕*www.*
★   *endeavorsailing.com*), a charter replica Friendship sloop, makes four daily 1½-hour trips out to the jetties and into the sound. Private charters and special theme trips for children—"Pirate Adventure" and "Songs and Stories of the Sea"—are available.

Shearwater Excursions (☎*508/228–7037* ⊕*www.explorenantucket. com*) mount various seaborne ecotours aboard a 50-foot power catamaran. One option is a two-hour trip to view Muskeget Island's 2,500 resident gray seals; one-hour lobster cruises to nearby Tuckernuck Island are offered on a flexible schedule out of Madaket. Sunday is for whale-watching 15 to 30 mi southeast of Nantucket; Captain Blair Perkins guarantees a sighting, which means that if no mammals show up, you can go again for free. The Shearwater is also available for private evening charters.

FISHING   Surf fishing is very popular on Nantucket, especially in the late spring when bluefish are running (the best place to go after them is Great Point). Freshwater fishing is also an option at many area ponds.

Many of the fishing charters will gladly make detours to spot whales.

Captain Peter Kaizer, a former commercial fisherman, guarantees a good catch aboard the *Althea K* (☎*508/228–3471*); he also offers whale-watching and charter cruises.

Captain Tom's Charters (⊠ *Public Landing, Madaket* ☎ *508/228–4225* ⊕ *www.captaintomscharters.com*) win consistent "best of" awards for Tom Mleczko's hands-on expertise. Choose among rips, bars, surf, open water, and flats (the latter for the added challenge of sight fishing with fly rods).

A permit is required for **shellfishing,** specifically foraging for littleneck and cherrystone clams, quahogs, scallops, oysters, steamers, and mussels. You can pick one up—along with tips on where and how to get the best catch—at the **Marine and Coastal Resources Department** (⊠ *34 Washington St.* ☎ *508/228–7261*).

HIKING   Nantucket supports approximately 1,200 species of vegetation: that's a greater variety than is found in any other area of equivalent size in the United States. It has 82 mi of beaches, and though almost 97% of the shoreline is privately owned, it's a point of pride that almost all is open for public use. There are hardwood forests, salt marshes, cranberry bogs, squam swamps, freshwater ponds, and coastal heathlands, and, with Martha's Vineyard and nearby Tuckernuck Island, the island holds more than 90% of the acreage of sandplain grassland *worldwide.* The island is home to a huge number of deer; significant colonies of harbor seals, gray seals, and harbor porpoises; turtles, frogs, rabbits, voles, and other reptiles and small field mammals. A lack of land-bound predators such as skunks and raccoons allows bird populations to thrive, and hundreds of species either live on the island or pass through on their annual migrations.

Nearly all of the 8,900 acres maintained by the **Nantucket Conservation Foundation** (⊠ *118 Cliff Rd.* ☎ *508/228–2884* ⊕ *www.nantucketconservation.com*) are open to the public; though only a few trails are marked, you can feel free to wander knowing that you can't get lost—if you keep going in one direction, you're bound to hit a road or a beach eventually. The foundation, open weekdays 8 AM to 5 PM, puts out maps and informative brochures on the most popular hiking spots. Remember that these conservation areas are set aside to preserve and protect Nantucket's fragile ecosystems—tread carefully—and also be aware that ticks are a serious problem here. Dress accordingly and carry plenty of repellent.

A 5- to 10-minute bike ride from Nantucket Town on the way to Madaket, the **Sanford Farm, Ram Pasture, and the Woods** (⊠ *Madaket Rd., between Milford and Cliff Rds.*) comprises 300 acres that were saved from developers by the Nantucket Conservation Foundation in 1971. The southern edge of the property borders the ocean.

The **Tupancy Links** (⊠ *165 Cliff Rd., 1¼ mi west of town*) runs between the Cliff Road bike path and Nantucket Sound. It's a smaller property that passes mainly through grassland populated by plants like false heather, oxeye daisy, and Queen Anne's lace, and it provides wonderful views once you reach the overlook at the water's edge. The cliff is only 42 feet above sea level, but from it you can see great stretches of the island's north shore.

PETTICOAT ROW

During the whaling era—a time, remember, when women were generally considered better seen than heard—a circumstance developed in Nantucket Town that was perhaps unique in the country: a large portion of Centre Street shops near Main Street were almost completely run by women merchants. It eventually became known as Petticoat Row, and it still exists today. Women have always played a strong role in Nantucket's history, partly because of the Quaker philosophy of sexual equality and partly because on whaling expeditions men could be gone for years at a time—and it was up to women to keep the town going. They became leaders in every arena, from religion to business.

SHOPPING

The historic center of town doubles as the commercial district: shops are concentrated primarily in the grid formed by Main, Centre, Broad, and Easy streets, with a few shops trailing off along the periphery. The former boathouses of Straight Wharf and Old South Wharf, retrofitted as shops and galleries, attract well-heeled browsers as well. The necessities of island life—hardware, office supplies, etc.—tend to be clustered mid-island, where new stores offering nonessentials are gradually making inroads as well.

Most of Nantucket's shops are seasonal, opening in time for the Daffodil Festival in late April and closing soon after Christmas Stroll in early December; a hardy few stay open year-round and often offer rather astounding bargains off-season. On summer weekends, many shops stay open late (until 9 or 10). Most galleries hold their openings on Friday evenings.

ANTIQUES **G.K.S. Bush** (⊠*13 Old South Rd.* ☎*508/325–0300*) carries ultrahigh-end American antique furniture, paintings, and decorative arts (winter headquarters are on New York's Upper East Side).

In business since 1974, **Lynda Willauer Antiques** (⊠*2 India St.* ☎*508/228–3631*) has amassed a stellar cache of American and English furniture, plus fine collectibles, including Chinese export porcelain and majolica; the shop winters in Greenwich, Connecticut.

★ **Nantucket Country** (⊠*38 Centre St.* ☎*508/228–8868* ⊕*www.nantucketcountryantiques.com*) has an especially rich inventory of quilts and flags; another specialty—in addition to maritime and "Nantucketiana"—is antique children's toys.

Nantucket House Antiques (⊠*2 S. Beach St.* ☎*508/228–4604* ⊕*www.nantuckethouse.com*) displays a wealth of well-chosen artifacts, in inspired aggregations; the owners are interior decorators.

Nina Hellman Marine Antiques & Americana (⊠*48 Centre St.* ☎*508/228–4677* ⊕*www.nauticalnantucket.com*) carries scrimshaw, whaling artifacts, ship models, instruments, and other marine antiques, plus folk art and Nantucket memorabilia. Charles Manghis, a contemporary scrimshaw artist, demonstrates and exhibits his craft here.

Fodor's Choice
★ **Rafael Osona Auctions** (⊠*American Legion Hall, 21 Washington St.* ☎*508/228–3942* ⊕*www.rafaelosonaauction.com*) holds auctions of fine antiques most Saturday mornings from Memorial Day weekend to early December; the items—furniture, decorative accessories, art, jewelry, and more—are previewable two days in advance.

Established in 1927, **Sylvia Antiques** (⊠*6 Ray's Ct.* ☎*508/228–0960* ⊕*www.sylviaantiques.com*) retains the richest stash of island-related antiquities.

ART GALLERIES   The **Artists' Association of Nantucket** (⊠*19 Washington St.* ☎*508/228–0772* ⊕*www.nantucketarts.org*) is the best place to get an overview of the work being done on-island; many members have galleries of their own.

★ At **The Brigham Galleries** (⊠*54 Center St.* ☎*508/925–2525* ⊕*www.thebrighamgalleries.com*) Sara Boyce has an entire Federal-style house in which to showcase her excellent, at times playful taste; portrait commissions are a specialty.

The **Gallery at Four India** (⊠*4 India St.* ☎*508/228–8509* ⊕*www.galleryatfourindia.com*) is a quiet, spacious refuge, with highly sought-after American and marine paintings dating from the 1850s to 1940s, plus a small sampling of contemporary realism.

★ The **South Wharf Gallery** (⊠*3 India St.* ☎*508/228–0406* ⊕*www.southwharfgallery.com*) has been showing top local work since 1978.

BOOKS   Check the Nantucket Room at the back of **Mitchell's Book Corner** (⊠*54 Main St.* ☎*508/228–1080* ⊕*www.mitchellsbookcorner.com*) for regional titles. The front is filled with an astute sampling covering a broad range of categories. Author signings are held on summer Saturdays.

Nantucket Bookworks (⊠*25 Broad St.* ☎*508/228–4000* ⊕*www.nantucketbookworks.com*) carries an extensive inventory, with an emphasis on literary works and Nantucket-specific titles, as well as children's books and gift items.

CLOTHING   **Eye of the Needle and Eye of the Needle Girls** (⊠*14–14A Federal St.*
★ ☎*508/228–1923 or 508/228–4449*) is a microcosm of urban fashion trends, playfully leavened.

She's back! The splashy resort wear so popular in the '60s is enshrined at the **Lilly Pulitzer Shop** (⊠*5 S. Water St.* ☎*508/228–0569* ⊕*www.lillyshop.com*).

Mallory Alfano (⊠*32 Center St.* ☎*508/228–0569*) combs the international boutique market to stock her namesake store with exquisite, of-the-moment accessories.

CLOSE UP

Nantucket Reds

Bermuda has its shorts, Fiji its sarongs. Nantucket's totemic clothing items are made of cotton dyed red so as to fade to a dull salmon shade. The reds were something of a secret code until they were singled out by *The Official Preppy Handbook* in 1980: "By their pink shirts ye shall know them" might be the watchwords for Nantucketers among the worldwide sailing community. Now reds are as site-specific as Martha's Vineyard's Black Dog line (attempting to compete, of late, with a satellite shop on Straight Wharf).

The principal purveyor of Nantucket reds is Murray's Toggery Shop on Main Street, which has catered to conservative dressers since the early 1900s. (Roland Macy worked here at his father's shop in the early 1800s before setting off to rewrite retailing history.) From baby togs to tote bags, you'll find everything you could want here in the way of reds. But for that weathered look that sets them off so well, you'll have to get out on the water.

Murray's Toggery Shop (✉ *62 Main St.* ☎ *508/228–0437* ⊕ *www. nantucketreds.com*) can claim credit for introducing the signature "Nantucket reds"—now available in a range of styles for men, women, and children.

Murray's Warehouse (✉ *7 New St.* ☎ *508/228–3584* ⊕ *www.nantucket reds.com*) offers discounts of up to 75% on surplus stock from Murray's Toggery Shop.

Something about the Nantucket lifestyle prompts hat hunger. **Peter Beaton** (✉ *16½ Federal St.* ☎ *508/228–8456* ⊕ *www.peterbeaton.com*) shows an international array of beauties, all customizable with special trim, along with a smattering of clothing.

Vanessa Noel (✉ *5 Chestnut St., at Centre St.* ☎ *508/228–6030*) creates ultraglam shoes—they're expensive, to be sure, but fans gladly toe the line.

Island loyalties might be tested, but the **Vineyard Vines** (✉ *2 Harbor Sq.* ☎ *800/892–4982* ⊕ *www.vineyardvines.com*) line—from flip-flops to bathing trunks, not to mention the ties that started it all—is just so irresistibly preppy, resistance is futile.

Fodor'sChoice ★ The inviting windows of **Vis-a-Vis** (✉ *34 Main St.* ☎ *508/228–5527* ⊕ *www.visavisnantucket.com*) display relaxed-luxe women's fashions amid antique home furnishings, some of which, including hooked rugs, quilts, and collectibles, are also for sale.

CRAFTS **Claire Murray** (✉ *11 S. Water St.* ☎ *508/228–1913 or 800/252–4733* ⊕ *www.clairemurray.com*) carries the designer's Nantucket-theme and other hand-hooked rugs and rug kits, quilts, and knitting and needlework kits; this little shop is where the empire got started.

Erica Wilson Needle Works (✉ *25 Main St.* ☎ *508/228–9881*) embodies the enthusiasms of the famous British-born designer, an island resident

7

since 1958. In addition to her own embroidery and needlepoint kits, the store carries winning clothing and accessories for women (look for Heidi Weddendorf's Nantucket knot jewelry), baby gifts, and appealing elements of home decor.

Since 1927, the **Four Winds Craft Guild** (⊠*6 Ray's Ct.* ☎*508/228–9623* ⊕*www.sylviaantiques.com*) has showcased local folk arts, including scrimshaw and lightship baskets (old and new), ship models, and duck decoys; the guild also offers a kit for making your own lightship basket. A satellite shop within the historic Pacific Club at 1 Main Street displays outstanding new work.

★ **Nantucket Looms** (⊠*16 Federal St.* ☎*508/228–1908* ⊕*www.nantucketlooms.com*) stocks luscious woven-on-the-premises textiles and chunky Susan Lister Locke jewelry, among other adornments for self and home.

GIFT SHOPS **Diane Johnston** (⊠*35 Centre St.* ☎*508/228–4688*) blends select clothing (hand-knit sweaters, needlepoint slippers) with antique quilts, lush rugs (from kilims to contemporary creations), and whatever else strikes the owner's fancy; the mix is magical.

Leslie Linsley Nantucket (⊠*Zero India St.* ☎*508/325–4900* ⊕*www.leslielinsley.com*), the project of a widely published crafts aficionado, carries supplies, tasteful souvenirs, and other decorative touches.

An outreach program of the Nantucket Historical Association, the **Museum Shop** (⊠*11 Broad St., next to the Whaling Museum* ☎*508/228–5785* ⊕*www.nha.org*) sells island-related books, reproduction furniture and accessories, and toys.

JEWELRY **Diana Kim England, Goldsmiths** (⊠*56 Main St.* ☎*508/228–3766 or 800/343–1468* ⊕*www.dianakimengland.com*) has created an elegant contemporary line featuring unusual gems such as tourmaline, chalcedony, and tanzanite.

The **Golden Basket** (⊠*44 Main St.* ☎*508/228–4344 or 800/626–2758* ⊕*www.thegoldenbasket.com*) was founded in 1977 by designer Glenaan M. Elliott, who fashioned the first miniature lightship basket. Other popular motifs include starfish and shells.

TOYS Carrying plenty of its namesake items in various sizes and shapes, the **Toy Boat** (⊠*41 Straight Wharf* ☎*508/228–4552* ⊕*www.thetoyboat.com*) also sells other high-quality toys for youngsters, including Nantucket mermaids, and children's books based on local themes (look for Joan Aiken's classic *Nightbirds on Nantucket*).

SIASCONSET & WAUWINET

★ *7 mi east of Nantucket Town.*

First a fishing outpost and then an artist's colony (Broadway actors favored it in the late 19th century), Siasconset—or 'Sconset, in the local vernacular—is a charming cluster of rose-covered cottages linked by driveways of crushed clamshells; at the edges of town, the former fishing shacks give way to magnificent sea-view mansions. The small town center consists of a market, post office, café, lunchroom, and liquor store–cum–lending library.

The tiny settlement of Wauwinet, a few miles north, is in a haulover–spit of land so narrow, boats can be dragged across it—leading to the immense curving sandbar of Coskata, Great Point, and Coatue.

Altar Rock. Altar Rock Road, a dirt track about 3 mi west of the Milestone Road Rotary on Polpis Road, leads to the island's highest point, Altar Rock, from which the view is spectacular. The hill overlooks open moor and bog land—technically called lowland heath—which is very rare in the United States. The entire area is laced with paths leading in every direction. Don't forget to keep track of the trails you travel to find your way back.

Nantucket Life Saving Museum. Items displayed in this re-creation of the 1874 Life Saving Service station that still stands on Surfside Beach (it's a hostel now), include original rescue equipment and boats, artifacts recovered from the *Andrea Doria* wreck, and photos and accounts of daring rescues. There are several rare pieces: for instance, one of four surviving surfboats and an equally well preserved original beach cart. ⊠*158 Polpis Rd.* ☎*508/228–1885* ⊕*www.nantucketlifesavingmuseum.com* ⊠*$5* ◷*Mid-June–mid-Oct., daily 9:30–4.*

Sankaty Head Lighthouse. The red-and-white-striped beacon overlooking the sea on one side and the Scottish-looking links of the private Sankaty Head Golf Club on the other is one of New England's many endangered lighthouses. It's not open to the public, but you can approach it, via a seashell gravel road. ⊠*Baxter Rd..*

NEED A BREAK? For a great picnic in 'Sconset, stop at **Claudette's** (⊠*Post Office Sq.* ☎*508/257–6622*) for a box lunch to go; or dig right in on the shady patio. It's open mid-May through mid-October.

Sesachacha Pond. This kettle pond (pronounced *Sah*-kah-cha) off Polpis Road is a good spot for bird-watching. It's circled by a walking path that leads to an Audubon wildlife area and is separated from the ocean by a narrow strand on its east side. It provides a good view of Sankaty Head Lighthouse.

Siasconset Casino. Despite its name, this property dating to 1899 has never been used for gambling—the meaning of "casino" was broader back when it was built—but was instead used from the beginning as a theater venue, particularly during the actors'-colony heyday, and as a gathering place. Some theater can still be seen here, but it's primarily a tennis club and informal cinema. ⊠*New St.* ☎*508/257–6661.*

Wauwinet. Now it's a hamlet of beach houses on the northeastern end of Nantucket. But early European settlers found the neck of sand above it to be the easiest way to get to the ocean for fishing. Instead of rowing around Great Point, fishermen would go to the head of the harbor and haul their dories over the narrow strip of sand and beach grass

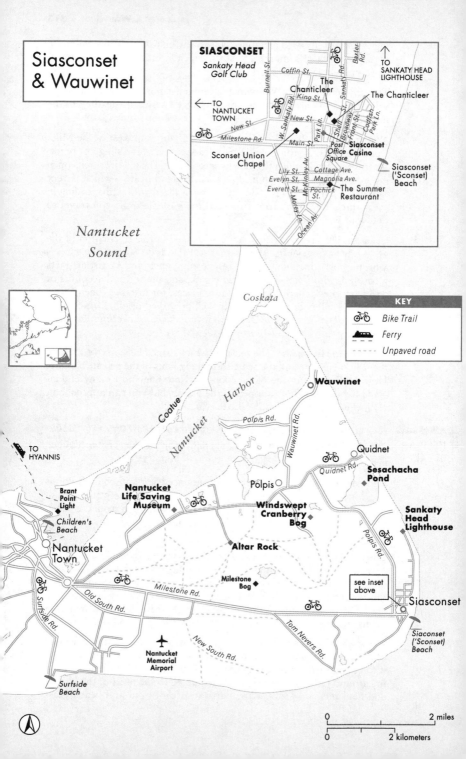

separating Nantucket Harbor from the ocean. Hence the name for that strip: the haulover.

Windswept Cranberry Bog. Throughout the year, the 205-acre conservation area off Polpis Road is a beautiful tapestry of greens, reds, and golds—and a popular hangout for many bird species. The bog is especially vibrant in mid-October, when the cranberries are harvested. (Although the weekend after Columbus Day has historically been a harvesting holiday, a glut in the market has cancelled the harvesting in recent years. Call the Chamber of Commerce for information.) A map is available from the **Nantucket Conservation Foundation** (⊠ *118 Cliff Rd.* ☎ *508/228–2884* ⊕ *www.nantucketconservation.com*).

WHERE TO STAY & EAT

$$$$ ✕**Topper's.** The Wauwinet—a lavishly restored 19th-century inn on
★ Nantucket's northeastern shore—is where islanders and visitors alike go to experience utmost luxury. Many take advantage of the complimentary launch, the *Wauwinet Lady* out of Straight Wharf, which frames the journey with a scenic harbor tour. Having traipsed past the croquet lawn, one enters a creamy-white dining room awash with lush linens and glorious flowers. David Daniel's cuisine delivers on the fantasy with a menu of intentional "simplicity"—if that's how you would describe a butter-basted lobster "surf & turf," for instance, in a carrot yuzu nage with dim sum of foie gras and Kobe (the latter elements entail a surcharge). The price scheme might seem a steal, were it not for portions that tend to tapas scale. But you can always fill up on the luscious brown bread (the sticky, molasses-infused kind so rarely encountered these days), and follow up with an exquisite, if miniscule dessert. ⊠ *120 Wauwinet Rd., Wauwinet* ☎ *508/228–8768* ⊕ *www.wauwinet.com* ⚞ *Reservations essential* ▤ *AE, D, DC, MC, V* ⊗ *Closed Nov.–Apr.*

$$$–$$$$ ✕**The Chanticleer.** Over the decades, 'Sconset's landmark restaurant had grown a bit ossified: it needed Susan Handy and chef Jeff Worster of Black-Eyed Susan's to freshen up the menu and atmosphere alike. It's still elegant—more so, really, without the attendant fussiness. Handy knows how to extend a warm (i.e., non-Gallic) welcome, and Worster has mastered the "brasserie moderne" staples, from steak frites to tarte Tatin. The all-French wine cellar is as "deep" as ever, and the porch overlooking the herb garden remains the most coveted perch. ⊠ *9 New St., Siasconset* ☎ *508/257–4499* ⊕ *www.thechanticleer.net* ▤ *AE, MC, V* ⊗ *Closed mid-Oct.–early May; no lunch Mon.*

$$$–$$$$ ✕**The Summer House Restaurant.** An integral element of the rose-canopied
★ complex of shingled shacks that epitomizes 'Sconset, the main dining room is also abloom, with lavish floral displays set against a background of pastel linen and white wicker. Here the cuisine is certainly polished, if on the sedate side; the Beachside Bistro, alongside the pool down below, goes in for splurgy dishes like a $22 Wagu Kobe–beef burger and caviar on demand. It's tempting to play favorites or, while trying to decide, bouncing back and forth. ⊠ *17 Ocean Ave., Siasconset* ☎ *508/257–9976* ⊕ *www.thesummerhouse.com* ⚞ *Reservations essential* ▤ *MC, V* ⊗ *Closed mid-Oct.–mid-May.*

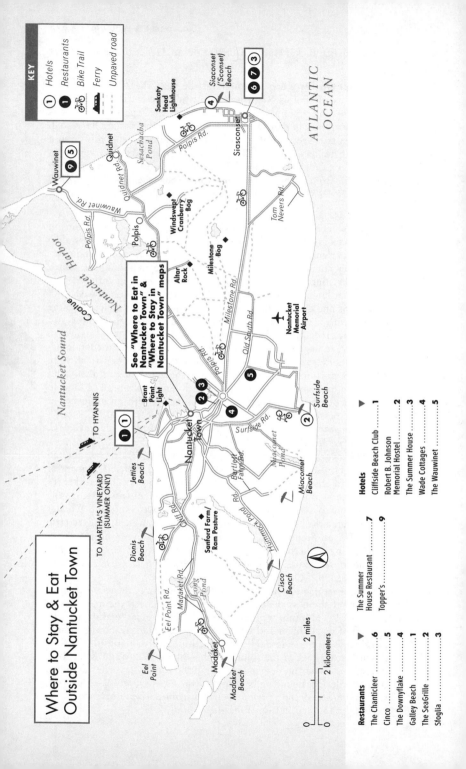

Where to Stay & Eat Outside Nantucket Town

KEY

①	Hotels
❶	Restaurants
🚲	Bike Trail
⛴	Ferry
---	Unpaved road

ATLANTIC OCEAN

Nantucket Sound

Coatue

Nantucket Harbor

TO MARTHA'S VINEYARD (SUMMER ONLY)

TO HYANNIS

See "Where to Eat in Nantucket Town" & "Where to Stay in Nantucket Town" maps

Sankaty Head Lighthouse

Siasconset ("Sconset") Beach

Siasconset

Wauwinet

Quidnet

Sesachacha Pond

Polpis Rd.

Wauwinet Rd.

Quidnet Rd.

Polpis Rd.

Polpis

Windswept Cranberry Bog

Milestone Bog

Altar Rock

Milestone Rd.

Tom Nevers Rd.

Nantucket Memorial Airport

Old South Rd.

Polpis Rd.

Brant Point Light

Nantucket Town

Jetties Beach

Dionis Beach

Eel Point Rd.

Eel Point

Madaket Rd.

Long Pond

Madaket

Madaket Beach

Cisco Beach

Sanford Farm/ Ram Pasture

Hummock Pond

Bartlett Farm Rd.

Miacomet Pond

Miacomet Beach

Surfside Rd.

Surfside Beach

0   2 miles

0   2 kilometers

Restaurants ▶

The Chanticleer **6**
Cinco **5**
The Downyflake **4**
Galley Beach **1**
The SeaGrille **2**
Sfoglia **3**

The Summer
House Restaurant **7**
Topper's **9**

Hotels ▶

Cliffside Beach Club **1**
Robert B. Johnson
Memorial Hostel **2**
The Summer House **3**
Wade Cottages **4**
The Wauwinet **5**

$$$$ 🏠 **Wade Cottages.** This 'Sconset complex of guest rooms, apartments, and cottages couldn't be better situated for beach aficionados. The buildings, in the same family since the 1920s, are arranged around a central lawn with a great ocean view, shared by most of the rooms. Furnishings tend to be of the somewhat worn beach-house school, but you'll be too busy—and happy—to waste a moment critiquing. **Pros:** Old-style Nantucket, dazzling views, compatible families. **Cons:** WASP-ily shabby (a plus in some eyes), not romantically inclined, very family-centric. ⊠*Shell St., Box 211, Siasconset 02564* 🕾*508/257–6308* 🖷*508/257–4602* ⊕*www.wadecottages.com* ⇒*8 rooms, 4 with bath; 6 apartments; 3 cottages* ⚴*In-hotel: laundry facilities, no smoking* ⊟*AE, MC, V* ⊗*Closed mid-Oct.–late May* ⏐⊖⏐*CP.*

$$$$ 🏠 **Wauwinet.** This resplendently updated 1850 resort straddles a "haulo-

Fodor's Choice ver" poised between ocean and bay—which means beaches on both

★ sides. Head out by complimentary van or launch to partake of utmost pampering (the staff-to-guest ratio exceeds one-on-one). Optional activities include sailing, water-taxiing to a private beach along Coatue, and touring the Great Point nature preserve by Land Rover. Of course, it's tempting just to stay put, what with the cushy country-chic rooms (lavished with Pratesi linens) and a splendid restaurant, Topper's. **Pros:** Solicitous staff, dual beaches, peaceful setting. **Cons:** Distance from town, overly chichi, tiny rooms on the 3rd floor. ⊠*120 Wauwinet Rd., Wauwinet* ⌓*Box 2580, Nantucket 02584* 🕾*508/228–0145 or 800/426–8718* 🖷*508/228–7135* ⊕*www.wauwinet.com* ⇒*25 rooms, 5 cottages* ⚴*In-room: safe, DVD, Wi-Fi. In-hotel: restaurant, room service, bar, tennis courts, spa, beachfront, bicycles, no elevator, con-cierge, town shuttle, no kids under 12, no-smoking rooms* ⊟*AE, DC, MC, V* ⊗*Closed Nov.–Apr.* ⏐⊖⏐*BP.*

$$$–$$$$ 🏠 **The Summer House - 'Sconset.** Perched on a bluff overlooking 'Scon-set Beach, this cluster of rose-covered cottages—cobbled from salvage in the 1840s—epitomizes Nantucket's enduring allure. The rooms, though small, are intensely romantic, with lace coverlets and pale pine armoires; most have marble baths with whirlpool tubs, and one has a fireplace. Contemplative sorts can claim an Adirondack chair on the lawn. Others may want to race down to the beach, perhaps enjoying lunch beside the heated pool en route. **Pros:** Romantic setting, beauti-ful on-site restaurants, pool right on the beach. **Cons:** 20 minutes from town, cottages snug, sounds of restaurant revelry. ⊠*17 Ocean Ave., 02564* 🕾*508/257–4577* 🖷*508/257–4590* ⊕*www.thesummerhouse. com* ⇒*10 rooms* ⚴*In-hotel: 2 restaurants, bars, pool, no elevator* ⊟*AE, MC, V* ⊗*Closed Nov.–late Apr.* ⏐⊖⏐*CP.*

NIGHTLIFE

BARS The bar at the **Summer House Restaurant** (⊠*17 Ocean Ave.* 🕾*508/257–9976*) is hands down the most romantic spot for a cocktail on-island. A pianist entertains devotees, who cluster around the bar or claim com-fortable armchairs.

FILM The **Siasconset Casino** (⊠*New St., Siasconset* 🕾*508/257–6661*) shows first-run movies, auditorium-style, Tuesday, Thursday, and Sunday evenings at 8:30, June through Labor Day. Old hands know to bring pillows.

7

SPORTS & THE OUTDOORS

BEACHES   **Siasconset Beach** (⊠*End of Milestone Rd.*) has a lifeguard (the surf runs moderate to heavy) but no facilities; restaurants are a short walk away.

BICYCLING   The 6½-mi **'Sconset Bike Path** starts at the rotary east of Nantucket Town and parallels Milestone Road, ending in 'Sconset. It is mostly level, with some gentle hills.

TENNIS   **Siasconset Casino** (⊠*10 New St., Siasconset* ☎*508/257–6585*) is a private club with 11 outdoor courts. Some nonmember court time is available; call ahead for information.

NANTUCKET ESSENTIALS

To research prices, get advice from other travelers, and book travel arrangements, visit www.fodors.com.

TRANSPORTATION

BY BOAT & FERRY

See ⇨*Boat & Ferry Travel in Essentials in the back of this book.* Nantucket has first-class marina and mooring amenities for yacht and boat owners.

Marina Contacts Madaket Marine (☎*508/228–1163* ⊕*www.madaketmarine. com*). **Nantucket Boat Basin** (☎*508/325–1333 or 800/626–2628* 🖷*508/228– 8941* ⊕*www.nantucketboatbasin.com*). **Nantucket Moorings** (☎*508/228–4472* 🖷*508/228–7441* ⊕*www.nantucketmoorings.com*).

BY BUS

The Nantucket Regional Transit Authority (NRTA) runs shuttle buses in town and to Madaket, mid-island areas (including the airport and Surfside Beach), and 'Sconset. Service is available May to late September. Fares are $1 to $2, depending on the route. Each of the routes has its own schedule (you can pick one up at the Chamber of Commerce, Visitor Services, the NRTA office, or at most any bus stop); service generally begins at 7 AM and ends at 11:30 PM. All shuttle buses have bike racks and lifts. Fares are $1 in town or mid-island; $2 to Madaket, Surfside, the airport, or 'Sconset; seniors pay half-fare and children under 7—and pets—ride free. Passes run $7 for 1 day, $12 for 3, $20 for 7, $50 for 30, and $80 for the season, with attendant discounts available. Passes for up to a week can be bought on-board; longer-term passes can be purchased at the NRTA office.

Bus Information Nantucket Regional Transit Authority (NRTA) (⊠*22 Federal St., Nantucket 02554* ☎*508/228–7025* ⊕*www.shuttlenantucket.com*).

BY CAR

The Chamber of Commerce strongly discourages bringing cars to Nantucket. They're really not needed—unless you're planning to stay a week or more, and renting far out of town, off the bus routes. The town itself is entirely walkable, and keeping a car there is not practical; the longest you're allowed to park is ½ to 1½ hours at a time ("summer specials"—supplemental police personnel—are right on it, keeping tabs by PDA). The entire island is easily accessible by bike, taxi, or public transportation.

If you're still determined to rent a car while on Nantucket, book early—and expect to spend at least $109 a day during high season.

Nantucket Agencies Nantucket Island Rent A Car (⊠ *Nantucket Memorial Airport* ☎ *508/228–9989 or 800/508-9972* ⊕ *www.nantucketislandrentacar. com*). **Nantucket Windmill Auto Rental** (⊠ *Nantucket Memorial Airport* ☎ *508/228–1227 or 800/228-1227* ⊕ *www.nantucketautorental.com*). **Young's Bicycle Shop** (⊠ *6 Broad St.* ☎ *508/228-1151* 🖷 *508/228-3038* ⊕ *www. youngsbicycleshop.com*).

BY TAXI

Taxis usually wait outside the airport, on Steamboat Wharf, and at the foot of Main Street. Rates are flat fees, based on one person with two bags before 1 AM: $6 within town (1½-mi radius), and, from town, $11 to the airport, $17 to 'Sconset, and $23 to Wauwinet.

Nantucket Taxi Companies A1 Taxi (☎ *508/325-3330*). **All Point Taxi** (☎ *508/228-5779*). **Val's Cab Service** (☎ *508/228-9410*).

CONTACTS & RESOURCES

EMERGENCIES

There is no 24-hour pharmacy on the island. Call the **Nantucket Cottage Hospital** (⊠ *57 Prospect St.* ☎ *508/825–8100* ⊕ *www.nantuckethospital.org*), in case of an emergency.

For police, fire department, or emergency medical technicians dial 911.

INTERNET, MAIL & SHIPPING

The main post office is right in the center of town; if lines are daunting, try the mid-island annex on Pleasant Street. There's a UPS Store off Surfside Road. You'll find a FedEx box (pickup is early: 4 PM) at the Steamship office, and another near the airport. The Atheneum offers free Internet access, including Wi-Fi, and the Even Keel doubles as an Internet café.

Internet Access Even Keel Café (⊠ *40 Main St.* ☎ *508/228-1979* ⊕ *www. evenkeelcafe.com*). **Nantucket Atheneum** (⊠ *1 India St.* ☎ *508/228-1110* ⊕ *www. nantucketatheneum.org*).

Mail & Shipping FedEx (☎ *800/238-5355* ⊕ *www.fedex.com*). **The UPS Store** (⊠ *2 Windy Way* ☎ *508/325-8884*). **U.S. Post Office** (⊠ *5 Federal St.* ☎ *508/228-4477* ⊠ *Annex, 144 Pleasant St.* ☎ *508/325-5682 or 800/274-8777*).

MONEY MATTERS

ATMS ATMs are ubiquitous—you'll find them at the airport, ferry terminals, and supermarkets. The following are accessible 24 hours.

24-Hour ATM Locations Fleet Bank (⊠ *Pacific National, 15 Sparks Ave.* ⊠ *Pacific Club, Main and S. Water Sts.*). **Nantucket Bank** (⊠ *2 Orange St.* ⊠ *104 Pleasant St.* ⊠ *1 Amelia Dr.*).

7

TOUR OPTIONS

ADVENTURE
TOURS
No matter what you want to do around Nantucket, be it kayaking, mountain biking, climbing, birding, hiking, snorkeling, or scuba diving, Eco Guides: Strong Wings can customize a small-group tour.

Tour Operator Eco Guides: Strong Wings (⊠ *9 Nobadeer Farm Rd.* ☎ *508/228–1769* ⊕ *www.strongwings.org*).

VAN TOURS
Sixth-generation Nantucketer Gail Johnson of Gail's Tours narrates a lively 1½-hour van tour of the island's highlights: the moors, the cranberry bogs, and the lighthouses, in addition to Nantucket Town. The 13-passenger cranberry-red van heads out at 10, 1, and 3 in season; pick-ups at in-town inns can be arranged.

Contacts Gail's Tours (☎ *508/257–6557* ⊕ *www.nantucket.net/tours/gails*).

WALKING
TOURS
Walking tours generally cover the major sights within the historic district. The Nantucket Historical Association's 90-minute Historic Nantucket Walking Tours (offered several times a day in season) provide an overview of the island's history and encompass such sites as Petticoat Row, upper Main Street, and the wharfs, churches, and library. Twelfth-generation islander Dirk Gardiner Roggeveen leads 90- to 120-minute tours in the afternoons (except Sunday); children are welcome to tag along for free.

The self-guided Black Heritage Trail tour covers nine sites in and around town, including the African Meeting House, the Whaling Museum, and the Atheneum. The trail guide is free from the Friends of the African Meeting House on Nantucket, which also leads a "Walk the Black Heritage Trail" tour by appointment in season.

Tour Operators Friends of the African Meeting House on Nantucket (⊠ *York and Pleasant Sts.* ☎ *508/228–9833* ⊕ *www.afroammuseum.org/afmnantucket. htm*). **Historic Nantucket Walking Tours** (⊠ *Whaling Museum, 15 Broad St.* ☎ *508/325–1894* ⊕ *www.nha.org*).

VISITOR INFORMATION

You can stop by the Nantucket Visitor Services and Information Bureau, open weekdays 9 AM to 6 PM year-round, to get your bearings, as well as maps, brochures, island information, and advice. The bureau is also a great resource if you need a room at the last minute—they track cancellations daily and might be able to refer you to an inn with newly available rooms. It's in the center of town, within a couple of blocks of both ferry landings, each of which also has a NVS booth in season. The Chamber of Commerce is another great place to get maps and island information; it's open weekdays 9 AM to 5 PM, year-round.

Tourist Information Nantucket Visitor Services and Information Bureau (⊠ *25 Federal St., 02554* ☎ *508/228–0925* ⊕ *www.nantucket.net/town/ departments/visitor.html*). **Nantucket Chamber of Commerce** (⊠ *48 Main St., upstairs* ☎ *508/228–1700* ⊕ *www.nantucketchamber.org*).

Cape Cod Essentials

There are planners and there are those who, excuse the pun, fly by the seat of their pants. We happily place ourselves among the planners. Our writers and editors try to anticipate all the issues you may face before and during any journey, and then they do their research. This section is the product of their efforts. Use it to get excited about your trip to Cape Cod, to inform your travel planning, or to guide you on the road should the seat of your pants start to feel threadbare.

GETTING STARTED

We're really proud of our Web site: Fodors.com is a great place to begin any journey. Scan "Travel Wire" for suggested itineraries, travel deals, restaurant and hotel openings, and other up-to-the-minute info. Check out "Booking" to research prices and book plane tickets, hotel rooms, rental cars, and vacation packages. Head to "Talk" for on-the-ground pointers from travelers who frequent our message boards. You can also link to loads of other travel-related resources.

▌RESOURCES

ONLINE TRAVEL TOOLS

For general information, visit the Cape Cod Chamber of Commerce online at ⊕*www.capecodchamber.org*. Other resources include the Cape Cod Information Center (⊕*www.allcapecod.com*) and Cape Cod Online (⊕*www.capecodonline.com*).

TRANSPORTATION

Smart Traveler (⊕*www.smartraveler.com*) provides real-time updates on traffic conditions on Cape Cod (just click on the link for Boston, and you'll find a further link to Cape Cod). You can look at live Web-cam pictures of the Bourne and Sagamore bridges at the Cape Cod USA site (⊕*www.capecodlivecam.com*), as well as Web-cam pictures of Commercial Street in Provincetown, the harbor in Hyannis, and the beach at Wellfleet.

For Cape Cod bus and trolley schedules, check with the Cape Cod Regional Transit Authority (⊕*www.capecodtransit.org*). The transportation information site of the Cape Cod Commission (⊕*www.gocapecod.org*) has links to transportation providers, updates on transportation-related construction projects, and information on bicycling and walking, including updates on the Cape Cod Rail

Trail. The Massachusetts Bicycle Coalition (⊕*www.massbike.org*) has information for bicyclists. Rails-to-Trails Conservancy (⊕*www.railtrails.org*) provides general information about rail trails, such as the Cape Cod Rail Trail.

Island ferry information and schedules are available online from the Steamship Authority (⊕*www.islandferry.com*) and from Hy-Line (⊕*www.hy-linecruises.com*). For information on the Boston to Provincetown ferries, visit the site of Bay State Cruise Company (⊕*www.baystatecruisecompany.com*) or Boston Harbor Cruises (⊕*www.bostonharborcruises.com*).

DISABILITY ACCESS

The Directory of Accessible Facilities lists accessible recreational facilities in Massachusetts (⊕*www.mass.gov/dcr/universal_access/index.htm*). Cape Cod Disability Access Directory (⊕*www.capecoddisability.org*) has useful information about facilities on Cape Cod.

VISITOR INFORMATION

Before you go, contact the state's office of tourism and the area's chambers of commerce for general information, seasonal events, and brochures. For specific information on Cape Cod's state forests and parks, the area's farmers' markets and fairs, or wildlife, contact the special-interest government offices below. You can also check Web sites on the Internet (⇨ *Web Sites*). When you arrive, stop by the local chamber of commerce for additional information—each chamber is stocked with local brochures and produces a comprehensive annual guidebook on each town.

The Army Corps of Engineers has a 24-hour recreation hotline for canal-area events, weather, and tidal and fishing information.

General Cape Contacts Cape Cod Chamber of Commerce (⊠ U.S. 6 and 132, Hyannis 02601 ☎ 508/862-0700 or 888/332-2732 🖷 508/862-0727 ⊕ www.capecodchamber. org). **Cape Cod National Seashore** (☎ 508/349-3785 ⊕ www.nps.gov/caco).

General Islands Contacts Martha's Vineyard Chamber of Commerce (⊠ Beach Rd., Box 1698, Vineyard Haven 02568 ☎ 508/693-4486 or 800/505-4815 ⊕ www.mvy.com). **Nantucket Chamber of Commerce** (⊠ 48 Main St., 2nd fl., 02554 ☎ 508/228-1700 ⊕ www.nantucketchamber.org).

Massachusetts Contacts Department of Agricultural Resources (☎ 617/626-1700 ⊕ www.state.ma.us/dfa). **Department of Conservation and Recreation** (☎ 617/626-1250 ⊕ www.mass.gov/dcr). **Department of Fish and Game** (☎ 508/626-1500 ⊕ www.state. ma.us/dfwele). **Massachusetts Office of Travel & Tourism** (⊠ 10 Park Plaza, Suite 4510, Boston 02116 ☎ 800/227-6277, 800/447-6277 brochures ⊕ www. massvacation.com).

❚ THINGS TO CONSIDER

GEAR

Only a few Cape Cod and island restaurants require a jacket and tie, as do some dinner cruises; the area prides itself on informality. Do **pack a sweater or jacket, even in summer,** for nights can be cool. *For suggested clothing to minimize bites from deer ticks and to prevent Lyme disease, see* ⇨ *Health.* Perhaps most important of all, **don't forget a swimsuit** (or two).

TRIP INSURANCE

What kind of coverage do you honestly need? Do you even need trip insurance at all? Take a deep breath and read on.

We believe that comprehensive trip insurance is especially valuable if you're booking a very expensive or complicated trip (particularly to an isolated region) or if you're booking far in advance. Who knows what could happen six months down the road? But whether or not you get insurance has more to do with how comfortable you are assuming all that risk yourself.

Comprehensive travel policies typically cover trip-cancellation and interruption, letting you cancel or cut your trip short because of a personal emergency, illness, or, in some cases, acts of terrorism in your destination. Such policies also cover evacuation and medical care. Some also cover you for trip delays because of bad weather or mechanical problems as well as for lost or delayed baggage. Another type of coverage to look for is financial default—that is, when your trip is disrupted because a tour operator, airline, or cruise line goes out of business. Generally you must buy this when you book your trip or shortly thereafter, and it's only available to you if your operator isn't on a list of excluded companies.

Expect comprehensive travel-insurance policies to cost about 4% to 7% or 8% of the total price of your trip (it's more like 8% to 12% if you're over age 70). A medical-only policy may or may not be cheaper than a comprehensive policy. Always read the fine print of your policy to make sure that you are covered for the risks that are of most concern to you. Compare several policies to make sure you're getting the best price and range of coverage available.

BOOKING YOUR TRIP

Unless your cousin is a travel agent, you're probably among the millions of people who make most of their travel arrangements online.

But have you ever wondered just what the differences are between an online travel agent (a Web site through which you make reservations instead of going directly to the airline, hotel, or car-rental company), a discounter (a firm that does a high volume of business with a hotel chain or airline and accordingly gets good prices), a wholesaler (one that makes cheap reservations in bulk and then re-sells them to people like you), and an aggregator (one that compares all the offerings so you don't have to)?

Is it truly better to book directly on an airline or hotel Web site? And when does a real live travel agent come in handy?

■ ONLINE

You really have to shop around. A travel wholesaler such as Hotels.com or Hotel-Club.net can be a source of good rates, as can discounters such as Hotwire or Priceline, particularly if you can bid for your hotel room or airfare. Indeed, such sites sometimes have deals that are unavailable elsewhere. They do, however, tend to work only with hotel chains (which makes them just plain useless for getting hotel reservations outside of major cities) or big airlines (so that often leaves out upstarts like jetBlue and some foreign carriers like Air India).

Also, with discounters and wholesalers you must generally prepay, and everything is nonrefundable. And before you fork over the dough, be sure to check the terms and conditions, so you know what a given company will do for you if there's a problem and what you'll have to deal with on your own.

■TIP➔ To be absolutely sure everything was processed correctly, confirm reservations made through online travel agents, discounters, and wholesalers directly with your hotel before leaving home.

Booking engines like Expedia, Travelocity, and Orbitz are actually travel agents, albeit high-volume, online ones. And airline travel packagers like American Airlines Vacations and Virgin Vacations—well, they're travel agents, too. But they may still not work with all the world's hotels.

An aggregator site will search many sites and pull the best prices for airfares, hotels, and rental cars from them. Most aggregators compare the major travel-booking sites such as Expedia, Travelocity, and Orbitz; some also look at airline Web sites, though rarely the sites of smaller budget airlines. Some aggregators also compare other travel products, including complex packages—a good thing, as you can sometimes get the best overall deal by booking an air-and-hotel package.

■ WITH A TRAVEL AGENT

If you use an agent—brick-and-mortar or virtual—you'll pay a fee for the service. And know that the service you get from some online agents isn't comprehensive. That said, some agents (online or not) *do* have access to fares that are difficult to find otherwise, and the savings can more than make up for any surcharge.

A knowledgeable brick-and-mortar travel agent can be a godsend if you're booking a cruise, a package trip that's not available to you directly, an air pass, or a complicated itinerary including several overseas flights. What's more, travel agents that specialize in a destination may have exclusive access to certain deals and insider information on things such as charter flights. Agents who specialize in types of travelers (senior citizens, gays and lesbians, naturists) or types of trips (cruises, luxury travel, safaris) can also be invaluable.

■ TIP→ Remember that Expedia, Travelocity, and Orbitz are travel agents, not just booking engines. To resolve any problems with a reservation made through these companies, contact them first.

A top-notch agent planning your trip to Russia will make sure you get the correct visa application and complete it on time; the one booking your cruise may get you a cabin upgrade or arrange to have bottle of champagne chilling in your cabin when you embark. And complain about the surcharges all you like, but when things don't work out the way you'd hoped, it's nice to have an agent to put things right.

Agent Resources **American Society of Travel Agents** (☎ 703/739-2782 ⊕ www. travelsense.org).

▮ ACCOMMODATIONS

Accommodations on the Cape and islands range from campsites to bed-and-breakfasts to luxurious self-contained resorts offering all kinds of sporting facilities, restaurants, entertainment, services (including business services and children's programs), and all the assistance you'll ever need in making vacation arrangements.

Because real-estate prices have skyrocketed throughout the region in the past few years, many motels and hotels have been developed into more lucrative condominiums, and quite a few B&Bs have been sold and converted back to private homes. The effect is that the Cape has fewer lodging options than it has had in years, and lodging rates have risen a bit, too. That said, there are still plenty of overnight options.

Single-night lodgings for those just passing through can be found at countless tacky but cheap and conveniently located little roadside motels, as well as at others that are spotless and cheery yet still inexpensive, or at chain hotels at all price levels; these places often have a pool, TVs, or other amenities to keep children entertained in the evening. Bear in mind that many Cape accommodations, even simple motels, have two-, three-, and even four-night minimum stays on weekends in high season, generally from around Memorial Day through Labor Day. It's still worth checking with a property to see if you can stay for fewer days, especially if you're planning to come out for a last-minute visit, but be warned that finding a single-night accommodation on a June, July, or August weekend can prove extremely challenging.

Because of extremely high demand for accommodations on the islands, it's best to reserve especially well in advance when planning a stay on Nantucket or Martha's Vineyard, especially from June through early September. If you're looking to visit during the summer months or over a popular weekend, such as the Nantucket Daffodil Festival or Christmas Stroll, it's not a bad idea to book a full year in advance. Most inns on the islands require prepayment or nonrefundable deposits as well as three-night (or more) minimums in summer. And rates can be very high, averaging $250 a night or more on Nantucket and only slightly less on Martha's Vineyard.

Families may want to **consider condominiums, cottages, and efficiencies,** which offer more space; living areas; kitchens; and sometimes laundry facilities, children's play areas, or children's programs. Especially as single-night lodging options on the Cape diminish in number, this is an increasingly popular option, although many condo and cottage rentals have one-week minimum stays, especially in summer.

The lodgings we list are the cream of the crop in each price category. We always list the facilities that are available—but we don't specify whether they cost extra: when pricing accommodations, always ask what's included and what costs extra. Properties indicated by a ✕☐ are lodging establishments whose restaurant warrants a special trip even if you are not staying at that establishment.

CATEGORY	COST
¢	under $90
$	$90–$140
$$	$140–$200
$$$	$200–$260
$$$$	over $260

All prices are for a standard double room in high season, excluding a variable state tax and gratuities. Some inns add a 15% service charge.

Most hotels and other lodgings require you to give your credit-card details before they will confirm your reservation. If you don't feel comfortable e-mailing this information, ask if you can fax it (some places even prefer faxes). However you book, get confirmation in writing and have a copy of it handy when you check in.

Be sure you understand the hotel's cancellation policy. Some places allow you to cancel without any kind of penalty—even if you prepaid to secure a discounted rate—if you cancel at least 24 hours in advance. Others require you to cancel a week in advance or penalize you the cost of one night. Small inns and B&Bs are most likely to require you to cancel far in advance. Most hotels allow children under a certain age to stay in their parents' room at no extra charge, but others charge for them as extra adults; find out the cutoff age for discounts.

■ TIP➔ Assume that hotels operate on the European Plan (EP, no meals) unless we specify that they use the Breakfast Plan (BP, with full breakfast), Continental Plan (CP, continental breakfast), Full American Plan (FAP, all meals), Modified American Plan (MAP, breakfast and dinner) or are all-inclusive (AI, all meals and most activities).

APARTMENT & HOUSE RENTALS

Many travelers to the Cape and the islands rent a house if they're going to stay for a week or longer rather than stay at a B&B or hotel. These can save you money; however, some rentals are luxury properties, economical only when your party is large. Many local real-estate agencies deal with rentals, and most specialize in a specific area; see the end of each chapter for information on agents in your area.

If you do decide to rent, be sure to book a property well in advance of your trip, as many properties are rented out to the same families or groups year after year. Rental choices are often more abundant in the smaller, quieter towns, such as Yarmouth, Chatham, Wellfleet, and Truro, or Up-Island on Martha's Vineyard.

BED & BREAKFASTS

Bed-and-breakfast inns have long been very popular on Cape Cod and the islands. Many of them occupy stately old sea captains' homes and other 17th-, 18th-, and 19th-century buildings; others are in newer homes.

In many cases, B&Bs are not appropriate for families—noise travels easily, rooms are often small, and the furnishings are often fragile—so be sure to ask. Many B&Bs do not provide phones or TVs in guest rooms, some are not air-conditioned, and nearly all prohibit smoking indoors (some allow smoking on the grounds).

In summer you should reserve lodgings as far in advance as possible—several months for the most popular inns. Assistance with last-minute reservations is available at the Cape Cod Chamber of Commerce information booths and through the chamber of commerce's Web site (⇨ *Web Sites*). Off-season, rates are much reduced, and you may find that it's easier to get to know your innkeeper.

Numerous B&B reservation agencies can aid you in choosing an inn.

Reservation Services **Bed & Breakfast.com** (☎512/322–2710 or 800/462–2632 ⊕www.bedandbreakfast.com) also sends out an online newsletter. **Bed & Breakfast Inns Online** (☎615/868–1946 or 800/215–7365 ⊕www.bbonline.com). **BnB Finder.com** (☎212/432–7693 or 888/547–8226 ⊕www.bnbfinder.com).

Reservation Services on the Cape **Bed and Breakfast Cape Cod** (☎508/255–3824 or 800/541–6226 ⊕www.bedandbreakfastcapecod.com). **DestINNations** (☎207/563–2506 or 800/333–4667 ⊕www.destinnations.com).

Reservation Services on the Islands **Martha's Vineyard and Nantucket Reservations** (☎508/693–7200 ⊕www.mvreservations.com). **Nantucket Accommodations** (☎508/228–9559 ⊕www.nantucketaccommodation.com). **Nantucket Concierge** (☎508/228–8400 ⊕www.nantucketconcierge.com).

CAMPING

There are many private and state-park camping areas on Cape Cod. For additional details on camping in specific areas, look for the 🏕 icon in that area's Dining and Lodging section.

HOME EXCHANGES

With a direct home exchange you stay in someone else's home while they stay in yours. Some outfits also deal with vacation homes, so you're not actually staying in someone's full-time residence, just their vacant weekend place.

Exchange Clubs **Home Exchange.com** (☎800/877–8723 ⊕www.homeexchange.com); $59.95 for a 1-year online listing. **HomeLink International** (☎800/638–3841 ⊕www.homelink.org); $90 yearly for Web-only membership; $140 includes Web access and two catalogs. **Intervac U.S.** (☎800/756–4663 ⊕www.intervacus.com); $78.88 for Web-only membership; $126 includes Web access and a catalog.

10 WAYS TO SAVE

1. Join "frequent guest" programs. You may get preferential treatment in room choice and/or upgrades in chains.

2. Call direct. You can sometimes get a better price if you call a hotel's local toll-free number (if available) rather than a central reservations number.

3. Check online. Check hotel Web sites, as not all travel sites list chains.

4. Look for specials. Always inquire about packages and corporate rates.

5. Look for price guarantees. For overseas trips, look for guaranteed rates. With your rate locked in you won't pay more, even if the price goes up in the local currency.

6. Look for weekend deals at business hotels. High-end chains catering to business travelers are often busy only on weekdays; they often drop rates on weekends.

7. Ask about taxes. Verify whether local hotel taxes are included in quoted rates. In some places taxes can add 20% or more to your bill.

8. Read the fine print. Watch for add-ons, including resort fees, energy surcharges, and "convenience" fees for such things as unlimited local phone service you won't use or a free newspaper in a language you can't read.

9. Know when to go. If your destination's high season is December through April and you're trying to book, say, in late April, you might save money by shifting your dates a bit. Ask when rates go down, though: if your dates straddle peak and nonpeak seasons, a property may still charge peak-season rates for the entire stay.

10. Weigh your options. Weigh transportation times and costs against the savings of staying in a cheaper but far-flung hotel.

Online-Booking Resources

CONTACTS		
Forgetaway		www.forgetaway.weather.com
Home Away	512/493–0382	www.homeaway.com
Interhome	954/791–8282 or 800/882–6864	www.interhome.us
Vacation Home Rentals Worldwide	201/767–9393 or 800/633–3284	www.vhrww.com
Villas International	415/499–9490 or 800/221–2260	www.villasintl.com

HOSTELS

Hostels offer bare-bones lodging at low, low prices—often in shared dorm rooms with shared baths—to people of all ages, though the primary market is young travelers, especially students. Most hostels serve breakfast; dinner and/or shared cooking facilities may also be available. In some hostels you aren't allowed to be in your room during the day, and there may be a curfew at night. Nevertheless, hostels provide a sense of community, with public rooms where travelers often gather to share stories. Many hostels are affiliated with Hostelling International (HI), an umbrella group of hostel associations with some 4,000 member properties in more than 60 countries. Other hostels are completely independent and may be nothing more than a really cheap hotel.

Membership in any HI association, open to travelers of all ages, allows you to stay in HI-affiliated hostels at member rates. One-year membership is about $28 for adults. Rates in dorm-style rooms run about $15 to $25 per bed per night; private rooms are more, but are still generally well under $100 a night. Members have priority if the hostel is full; they're also eligible for discounts around the world, even on rail and bus travel in some countries.

Cape Cod has some excellent hostels. In season, when all other rates are jacked up beyond belief, hostels are often the only budget-accommodation option, but you must plan ahead to reserve space. The hostel in Eastham has eight cabins that each sleep six to eight; two can be used as family cabins. In the Truro hostel, accommodations are dormitory-style. You may luck out on last-minute cancellations, but it would be unwise to rely on them. *See the lodging listings in the appropriate chapters for specifics.*

Information Hostelling International—USA (☎301/495–1240 ⊕www.hiusa.org).

▌AIRLINE TICKETS

Most domestic airline tickets are electronic; international tickets may be either electronic or paper. With an e-ticket the only thing you receive is an e-mailed receipt citing your itinerary and reservation and ticket numbers.

The greatest advantage of an e-ticket is that if you lose your receipt, you can simply print out another copy or ask the airline to do it for you at check-in. You usually pay a surcharge (up to $50) to get a paper ticket, if you can get one at all.

The sole advantage of a paper ticket is that it may be easier to endorse over to another airline if your flight is canceled and the airline with which you booked can't accommodate you on another flight.

■TIP→ Discount air passes that let you travel economically in a country or region must often be purchased before you leave home. In some cases you can only get them through a travel agent.

■ RENTAL CARS

When you reserve a car, ask about cancellation penalties, taxes, drop-off charges (if you're planning to pick up the car in one city and leave it in another), and surcharges (for being under or over a certain age, for additional drivers, or for driving across state or country borders or beyond a specific distance from your point of rental). All these things can add substantially to your costs. Request car seats and extras such as GPS when you book.

Rates are sometimes—but not always—better if you book in advance or reserve through a rental agency's Web site. There are other reasons to book ahead, though: for popular destinations, during busy times of the year, or to ensure that you get certain types of cars (vans, SUVs, exotic sports cars).

■TIP→ Make sure that a confirmed reservation guarantees you a car. Agencies sometimes overbook, particularly for busy weekends and holiday periods.

In Massachusetts you must be 21 to rent a car, and rates may be higher if you're under 25. When picking up a car, non–U.S. residents will need a reservation voucher (for prepaid reservations made in the traveler's home country), a passport, a driver's license, and a travel policy that covers each driver.

10 WAYS TO SAVE

1. Nonrefundable is best. If saving money is more important than flexibility, then nonrefundable tickets work. That said, you'll pay dearly (as much as $200) if you change your plans.

2. Comparison shop. Web sites and travel agents can have different arrangements with the airlines and offer different prices for exactly the same flights.

3. Beware the listed prices. Many airline Web sites—and most ads—show prices *without* taxes and surcharges. Don't buy until you know the full price.

4. Stay loyal. Stick with one or two frequent-flier programs. You'll rack up free trips faster and you'll accumulate more quickly the perks that make trips easier. On some airlines these include a special reservations number, early boarding, access to upgrades, and roomier economy seats.

5. Watch those ticketing fees. Surcharges are usually added when you buy your ticket anywhere but on an airline Web site. (That includes by phone—even if you call the airline directly—and paper tickets regardless of how you book.)

6. Check often. Look for cheap fares from three months out to about one month.

7. Don't work alone. Some Web sites have tracking features that will e-mail you immediately when good deals are posted.

8. Jump on the good deals. Waiting even a few minutes might mean paying more.

9. Be flexible. Look for departures on Tuesday, Wednesday, and Saturday, typically the cheapest days to travel. And check on prices for departures at different times and to and from alternative airports.

10. Weigh your options. A cheaper flight might have a long layover or land at a secondary airport, where your ground transport costs are higher.

Base rates in Boston begin at $25 to $40 a day and $170 to $250 a week for an economy car with air-conditioning, automatic transmission, and unlimited mileage; rates tend to be slightly lower out of Providence and slightly higher out of Hyannis, but much depends on availability, which changes regularly. Keep in mind that taxes and a variety of surcharges typically add 30% to 40% to your total bill.

You can book car rentals on Martha's Vineyard through the Woods Hole ferry terminal free phone. A handful of local agencies, listed below, have rental desks at the airport. The cost is $100 to $150 per day for a sedan. Renting a four-wheel-drive vehicle costs around $160 per day (seasonal prices fluctuate widely).

If you're determined to rent a car while on Nantucket, be sure to book early. Expect to spend about $100 a day during high season.

CAR-RENTAL INSURANCE

Everyone who rents a car wonders whether the insurance that the rental companies offer is worth the expense. No one—including us—has a simple answer. It all depends on how much regular insurance you have, how comfortable you are with risk, and whether or not money is an issue.

If you own a car and carry comprehensive car insurance for both collision and liability, your personal auto insurance will probably cover a rental, but read your policy's fine print to be sure. If you don't have auto insurance, then you should probably buy the collision- or loss-damage waiver (CDW or LDW) from the rental company. This eliminates your liability for damage to the car.

Some credit cards offer CDW coverage, but it's usually supplemental to your own insurance and rarely covers SUVs, minivans, luxury models, and the like. If your coverage is secondary, you may still be liable for loss-of-use costs from the car-rental company (again, read the fine print). But no credit-card insurance is valid unless you use that card for *all* transactions, from reserving to paying the final bill.

■TIP➜Diners Club offers primary CDW coverage on all rentals reserved and paid for with the card. This means that Diners Club's company—not your own car insurance—pays in case of an accident. It *doesn't* mean that your car-insurance company won't raise your rates once it discovers you had an accident.

You may also be offered supplemental liability coverage; the car-rental company is required to carry a minimal level of liability coverage insuring all renters, but it's rarely enough to cover claims in a really serious accident if you're at fault. Your own auto-insurance policy will protect you if you own a car; if you don't, you have to decide whether you are willing to take the risk.

U.S. rental companies sell CDWs and LDWs for about $15 to $25 a day; supplemental liability is usually more than $10 a day. The car-rental company may offer you all sorts of other policies, but they're rarely worth the cost. Personal accident insurance, which is basic hospitalization coverage, is an especially egregious rip-off if you already have health insurance.

■TIP➜You can decline the insurance from the rental company and purchase it through a third-party provider such as Travel Guard (www.travelguard.com)—$9 per day for $35,000 of coverage. That's sometimes just under half the price of the CDW offered by some car-rental companies.

▌VACATION PACKAGES

Packages *are not* guided excursions. Packages combine airfare, accommodations, and perhaps a rental car or other extras (theater tickets, guided excursions, boat trips, reserved entry to popular museums,

Car-Rental Resources

AUTOMOBILE ASSOCIATIONS		
U.S.: American Automobile Association (AAA)	315/797–5000	www.aaa.com; most contact with the organization is through state and regional members
National Automobile Club	650/294–7000	www.thenac.com; membership is open to California residents only
CAPE COD AGENCIES		
Rent-A-Wreck of Hyannis	508/771–9667 or 888/486–1470	www.rentawreck.com
MARTHA'S VINEYARD AGENCIES		
AAA Island	508/627–6800 or 800/627–6333	www.mvautorental.com
Adventure Rentals	Beach Rd., Vineyard Haven, 508/693–1959	www.islandadventuresmv.com
NANTUCKET AGENCIES		
Affordable Rentals	6 S. Beach St. 508/228–3501 or 877/235–3500.	
Nantucket Island Rent A Car	Nantucket Memorial Airport 508/228–9989 or 800/508–9972	www.nantucketislandrentacar.com
Nantucket Windmill	Nantucket Memorial Airport 508/228–1227 or 800/228–1227	www.nantucketautorental.com
MAJOR AGENCIES		
Alamo	800/462–5266	www.alamo.com
Avis	800/331–1212	www.avis.com
Budget	800/527–0700	www.budget.com
Hertz	800/654–3131	www.hertz.com˙
National Car Rental	800/227–7368	www.nationalcar.com

GETTING STARTED / **BOOKING YOUR TRIP** / TRANSPORTATION / ON THE GROUND

transit passes), but they let you do your own thing. During busy periods packages may be your only option, as flights and rooms may be sold out otherwise.

Packages will definitely save you time. They can also save you money, particularly in peak seasons, but—and this is a really big "but"—you should price each part of the package separately to be sure. And be aware that prices advertised on Web sites and in newspapers rarely include service charges or taxes, which can up your costs by hundreds of dollars.

■ TIP → Some packages and cruises are sold only through travel agents. Don't always assume that you can get the best deal by booking everything yourself.

Each year consumers are stranded or lose their money when packagers—even large ones with excellent reputations—go out of business. How can you protect yourself?

First, always pay with a credit card; if you have a problem, your credit-card company may help you resolve it. Second, buy trip insurance that covers default.

10 WAYS TO SAVE

1. Beware of cheap rates. Those great rates aren't so great when you add in taxes, surcharges, and insurance. Such extras can double or triple the initial quote.

2. Rent weekly. Weekly rates are usually better than daily ones. Even if you only want to rent for five or six days, ask for the weekly rate; it may very well be cheaper than the daily rate for that period of time.

3. Don't forget the locals. Price local companies as well as the majors.

4. Airport rentals can cost more. Airports often add surcharges, which you can sometimes avoid by renting from an agency whose office is just off airport property.

5. Wholesalers can help. Investigate wholesalers, which don't own fleets but rent in bulk from firms that do, and which frequently offer better rates (note that you must usually pay for such rentals before leaving home).

6. Look for rate guarantees. With your rate locked in, you won't pay more, even if the price goes up in the local currency.

7. Fill up farther away. Avoid hefty fees by filling the tank at a station well away from where you plan to turn in the car.

8. Pump it yourself. Don't prepay for rental-car gas. You won't save that much, and unless you coast in on empty you'll wind up paying for gas you don't use.

9. Get all your discounts. Find out whether a credit card you carry or organization or frequent-renter program to which you belong has a discount program. And confirm that such discounts really are a deal. You can often do better with special weekend or weekly rates offered by a rental agency.

10. Check out packages. Adding a car rental onto your air/hotel vacation package may be cheaper than renting a car separately.

Third, choose a company that belongs to the United States Tour Operators Association, whose members must set aside funds to cover defaults. Finally, choose a company that also participates in the Tour Operator Program of the American Society of Travel Agents (ASTA), which will act as mediator in any disputes.

You can also check on the tour operator's reputation among travelers by posting an inquiry on one of the Fodors.com forums.

Organizations American Society of Travel Agents (ASTA ☎703/739–2782 or 800/965–2782 ⊕www.astanet.com). **United States Tour Operators Association** (USTOA ☎212/599–6599 ⊕www.ustoa.com).

■**TIP**➔ Local tourism boards can provide information about lesser-known and small-niche operators that sell packages to only a few destinations.

TRANSPORTATION

▮ BY AIR

Most long-distance travelers visiting Cape Cod head to a major gateway, such as Boston or Providence, RI, and then rent a car to explore the region. Flying time to Boston or Providence is 1 hour from New York, 2½ hours from Chicago, 6 hours from Los Angeles, and 3½ hours from Dallas.

Boston's Logan Airport is one of the nation's most important domestic and international airports, with direct flights from all over North America and Europe (as well as other continents). Providence's efficient T. F. Green Airport receives very few international flights (mostly from Canada) but offers a wide range of direct domestic flights to East Coast and Midwest destinations; it serves the western United States to a lesser extent. Discount carrier Southwest also flies out of Providence, which helps keep fares down.

Another option is connecting from a major airport to one of the two airports on the Cape, the most popular being Barnstable Municipal Airport in Hyannis, which has direct service to Boston, Providence, and New York (La Guardia), as well as to Martha's Vineyard and Nantucket. The other, Provincetown Airport, has direct flights to Boston. Flying to either of these smaller airports can be costly, especially during busy times in summer, but it can also save you plenty of time when compared with driving to the Mid, Lower, or Upper Cape from Boston or New York City. There are also numerous flights to Nantucket and Martha's Vineyard from Hyannis, Boston, New Bedford, and Providence, and you can fly between Nantucket and Martha's Vineyard as well.

▮TIP➜ If you travel frequently, look into the TSA's Registered Traveler program. The program, which is still being tested in several U.S. airports, is designed to cut down on gridlock at security checkpoints by allowing prescreened travelers to pass quickly through kiosks that scan an iris and/or a fingerprint. How sci-fi is that?

Airlines & Airports Airline and Airport Links.com (⊕ www.airlineandairportlinks.com) has links to many of the world's airlines and airports.

Airline-Security Issues Transportation Security Administration (⊕ www.tsa.gov) has answers for almost every question that might come up.

AIRPORTS

The major gateways to Cape Cod are Boston's Logan International Airport (BOS) and Providence's T. F. Green Airport (PVD). Smaller airports include the Barnstable (HYA), Martha's Vineyard (MVY), Nantucket (ACK), New Bedford (EWB), and Provincetown (PVC) municipal airports.

▮TIP➜ Long layovers don't have to be only about sitting around or shopping. These days they can be about burning off vacation calories. Check out www.airportgyms.com for lists of health clubs that are in or near many U.S. and Canadian airports.

Airport Information Airline and Airport Links.com (⊕ www.airlineandairportlinks. com) has links to many of the world's airlines and airports. Boston: **Logan International Airport** (☎ 617/561–1806 or 800/235–6426 ⊕ www.massport.com/logan). Hyannis: **Barnstable Municipal Airport** (☎ 508/775–2020 ⊕ www.town.barnstable.ma.us). Martha's Vineyard: **Martha's Vineyard Airport** (☎ 508/693–7022 ⊕ www.mvyairport.com). Nantucket: **Nantucket Memorial Airport** (☎ 508/325–5300 ⊕ www.nantucketairport. com). New Bedford: **New Bedford Regional Airport** (☎ 508/991–6161 ⊕ www.ci.new bedford.ma.us). Providence: **T. F. Green Airport** (☎ 401/737–8222 or 888/268–7222 ⊕ www. pvdairport.com). Provincetown: **Provincetown Airport** (☎ 508/487–0241).

TRANSFERS BETWEEN AIRPORTS

Cape Destinations, Escort Coach, and King's Coach provide chartered limo service from Boston and Providence to the Cape; call ahead for reservations. Rates vary greatly, depending on your Cape destination, which airport you're flying into, and what kind of car or van you book.

Limousine Agencies Cape Destinations (☎866/760–2555 ⊕www.capedestinations. com). **Escort Coach** (☎508/548–8116 or 800/564–8116 ⊕www.whitetielimo.com). **King's Coach** (☎508/771–1000 or 800/546–6786 ⊕www.capecodlimo.com).

FLIGHTS

All of the nation's major airlines—as well as many international airlines—serve Boston's Logan Airport, and all major national carriers serve Providence. Hyannis's Barnstable Municipal Airport is serviced by US Airways Express (with service to Boston and NYC's La Guardia), Nantucket Airlines (with service to Nantucket), Island Airlines (with service to Nantucket), and Cape Air (with service to Boston, Providence, Nantucket, and Martha's Vineyard); Provincetown Airport is serviced by Cape Air (with service to Boston).

Smaller Airlines Cape Air (☎508/771–6944 or 800/352–0714 ⊕www.flycapeair. com). **Island Airlines** (☎508/228–7575 or 800/248–7779 ⊕www.islandair.net). **Nantucket Airlines** (☎508/228–6234 or 800/635–8787 ⊕www.nantucketairlines. com). **US Airways Express** (☎800/428–4322 ⊕www.usair.com).

▌ BY BOAT & FERRY

In season, ferries connect Boston and Plymouth with Provincetown.

Ferries to Martha's Vineyard leave Woods Hole year-round. In summer you can also catch Vineyard ferries in Falmouth and Hyannis. All provide parking lots where you can leave your car overnight ($10 to $15 per night). A number of parking lots in Falmouth hold the overflow of cars when the Woods Hole lot is filled, and free shuttle buses take passengers to the ferry, about 15 minutes away. Signs along Route 28 heading south from the Bourne Bridge direct you to open parking lots, as does AM radio station 1610, which you can pick up within 5 mi of Falmouth.

Ferries to Nantucket leave Hyannis year-round. In season, a passenger ferry connects Nantucket with Martha's Vineyard, and a cruise from Hyannis makes a day trip with stops at both islands. From New Bedford you can take a ferry to Martha's Vineyard from mid-May to mid-October and to Cuttyhunk Island year-round (although between mid-October and mid-April, the schedule is very limited).

FERRIES TO PROVINCETOWN

Bay State Cruise Company offers both standard and high-speed ferry service between Commonwealth Pier in Boston and MacMillan Wharf in Provincetown. High-speed service runs a few times daily from mid-May through September (with a few additional weekend runs through mid-October) and costs $69 round-trip; the ride takes 90 minutes. Standard service runs weekends from late June through early September and costs $33 round-trip; the ride takes three hours. On either ferry, the round-trip charge for bikes is $10.

Boston Harbor Cruises also offers high-speed service several times daily from mid-June to early September, with more limited service mid-May to mid-June and early September to mid-October. Rates are $70 round-trip and $10 for bikes.

Capt. John Boats runs a seasonal ferry between Plymouth and Provincetown, with daily service from late June through early September and weekend service from mid-June. The boat departs from State Pier (near the *Mayflower II*) in Plymouth and docks at MacMillan Wharf in Provincetown. The trip takes approximately 90 minutes. A round-trip ticket costs $36, the one-way fare is $21 (no one-way in July and August), and bikes cost $5 each way.

Boat & Ferry Lines **Bay State Cruise Company** (☎617/748–1428 ⊕www.baystatecruisecompany.com). **Boston Harbor Cruises** (☎617/227–4321 or 877/733–9425 ⊕www.bostonharborcruises.com). **Capt. John Boats** (☎508/747–2400 or 800/225–4000 ⊕www.provincetownferry.com).

FERRIES TO CUTTYHUNK ISLAND

The 149-passenger M/V *Cuttyhunk* runs ferries between New Bedford and Cuttyhunk Island, daily late May through September, several times a week from mid-April to late May and from early October to mid-October, and twice a week the rest of the year. Same-day round-trip fare is $30, one-way $20, bicycles $5 each way. The ride takes about an hour.

Boat & Ferry Information **M/V** Cuttyhunk (✉State Pier, New Bedford ☎508/992–0200 ⊕www.cuttyhunkferryco.com).

FERRIES TO MARTHA'S VINEYARD

The Steamship Authority runs the only car ferries, which make the 45-minute trip from Woods Hole to Vineyard Haven year-round and to Oak Bluffs from late May through mid-October. There are several runs per day, but fewer during the off-season. In summer and on autumn weekends, you *must* have a reservation if you want to bring your car (passenger reservations are never necessary). You should **make car reservations as far ahead as possible;** in season the reservations office is open daily 8 AM to 5 PM, with extended phone hours in summer and during busy times from 7 AM to 9 PM. You can also make car reservations online at the Steamship Authority's Web site. In season, standby car reservations are not available. One-way passenger fare year-round is $7 bicycles are $3. The cost for a car traveling one-way in season (April–October) is $65 (not including passengers); off-season cars cost $40.

The *Island Queen* makes the 35-minute trip from Falmouth Harbor to Oak Bluffs from late May through early October. Ferries run multiple times a day from mid-June through early September, with less frequent (but still daily) service in the spring and fall; call for schedules. Round-trip fare is $15, bikes $6. Only cash and traveler's checks are accepted for payment.

Begun in 2007, the Vineyard Fast Ferry offers high-speed passenger service from North Kingstown, Rhode Island (just a half-hour south of Providence and a half-hour northwest of Newport) to Martha's Vineyard. The ride takes 90 minutes, making this a great option for those flying in to T. F. Green Airport, just south of Providence. Service is from late May through early October and costs $46 each way ($5 for bikes).

from Falmouth Harbor to Oak Bluffs from late May through early October. Ferries run multiple times a day from mid-June through early September, with less frequent (but still daily) service in the spring and fall; call for schedules. Round-trip fare is $15, bikes $6. Only cash and traveler's checks are accepted for payment.

Hy-Line offers both high-speed and conventional ferry service from Hyannis. The conventional ferries offer a 95-minute run from Hyannis to Oak Bluffs early May to late October. One-way fare is $18.50; bicycles cost $6. The high-speed runs from from late May through late November, takes 55 minutes, and costs $31.50; it costs $6 for bikes. The parking lot fills up in summer, so **call to reserve a parking space** in high season. From June to mid-September, Hy-Line's Around the Sound cruise makes a one-day round-trip from Hyannis with stops at Nantucket and Martha's Vineyard ($73.50).

The New England Fast Ferry Company makes the hour-long trip by high-speed catamaran from New Bedford to Oak

Bluffs and Vineyard Haven from mid-May to mid-October, several times daily. One-way is $29, bicycles $5.

Boat & Ferry Information Hy-Line (✉Ocean St. dock ☎508/778–2600 or 800/492–8082 ⊕www.hy-linecruises.com). Island Queen (✉Falmouth Harbor ☎508/548–4800 ⊕www.islandqueen.com). **New England Fast Ferry** (✉State Pier Ferry Terminal ☎866/683–3779 ⊕www.nefastferry.com). **Steamship Authority** (☎508/477–8600 information and car reservations, 508/693–9130 on the Vineyard ⊕www.steamship authority.com).**Vineyard Fast Ferry** (✉Quonset Point, North Kingstown, RI ☎401/295–4040 ⊕www.vineyardfastferry.com).

FERRIES TO NANTUCKET

The Steamship Authority runs car-and-passenger ferries from Hyannis to Nantucket year-round, a 2¼-hour trip. There's also high-speed passenger ferry service, which takes only an hour, from late March through late December. Note that there are no standby car reservations on ferries to Nantucket. One-way passenger fare is $15, bicycles $6. Cost for a car traveling one-way April through October is $180 November through April, $120. One-way high-speed passenger ferry fare is $29.50, bicycles $6.

Hy-Line's high-end, high-speed *Grey Lady* ferries run between Hyannis and Nantucket year-round in an hour. Such speed has its downside in rough seas—lots of bucking and rolling that some find literally nauseating. Seating ranges from benches on the upper deck to airline-like seats in side rows of the cabin to café-style tables and chairs in the cabin front. Make reservations in advance, particularly during the summer months or for holiday travel. One-way fare is $38, bicycles $6.

Hy-Line's slower ferry makes the roughly two-hour trip from Hyannis between early May and late October. The M/V *Great Point* offers a first-class section ($24.50 one-way) with a private lounge, restrooms, upholstered seats, carpeting,

complimentary continental breakfast or afternoon cheese and crackers, a bar, and a snack bar. Standard one-way fare is $18.50, bicycles $6.

From Harwich Port, the Freedom Cruise Line runs express high-speed 75-minute ferries to Nantucket between late May and early October, allowing you to explore the rose-covered isle without having to brave the crowds of Hyannis (another plus is that for day trips to Nantucket, parking is free; it's $15 nightly, otherwise). Round-trip fare is $57 ($38 one-way), $12 for bikes. Sightseeing and seal cruises are also offered daily.

Boat & Ferry Information Freedom Cruise Line (✉Saquatucket Harbor, Harwich Port ☎508/432–8999 ⊕www.nantucketislandferry. com). **Hy-Line** (✉Ocean St. dock ☎508/778–2600 or 800/492–8082 ⊕www.hy-linecruises. com). **Steamship Authority** (✉South St. dock ☎508/477–8600, 508/495–3278 on Nantucket for reservations ⊕www.steamship authority.com).

▌BY BUS

The Cape Cod Regional Transit Authority operates several bus services that link Cape towns. All buses are wheelchair accessible and equipped with bike racks. The SeaLine runs along Route 28 Monday through Saturday between Hyannis and Woods Hole (one-way fare $3.50, from Hyannis to Woods Hole; shorter trips cost less), with stops including Mashpee Commons, Falmouth, and the Woods Hole Steamship Authority docks. The SeaLine connects in Hyannis with the Plymouth & Brockton line as well as the Barnstable Villager, another bus line that runs along Route 132 between Hyannis and Barnstable Harbor, stopping at the Cape Cod Mall. It also connects with the Hyannis Villager, which runs through Hyannis. The driver will stop when signaled along the route.

The H2O Line offers daily regularly scheduled service year-round between Hyannis and Orleans along Route 28. The Hyannis–Orleans fare is $3.50; shorter trips are less. Buses connect in Hyannis with the SeaLine, the Barnstable Villager, and Plymouth & Brockton lines.

The b-bus is composed of a fleet of minivans that will transport passengers door to door between any towns on the Cape. You must register in advance to use the b-bus service (you pay in advance by a prepaid account system); phone the Cape Cod Regional Transit Authority 11 AM to 5 PM on weekdays to sign up. You must also make advance reservations when you want to ride the b-bus. After you are enrolled, call for reservations 8 AM to 5 PM 5 on weekdays; reservations may be made up to a week in advance. Service runs seven days a week, year-round. The cost is $2.50 per ride plus 10¢ per mi.

The Flex bus runs between Harwichport Chamber of Commerce and Shore and Highlands roads in Truro (from which free transfers are available to Provincetown, late May through mid-October), with stops in Brewster, Orleans, Eastham, and Wellfleet. Riders can also schedule additional off-route stops by calling the Cape Cod Regional Transit Authority. All one-way fares are $1, and buses run Monday to Saturday year-round.

The Cape Cod Regional Transit Authority also runs the seasonal trolleys in Falmouth, Mashpee, Hyannis, Yarmouth, and Dennis. Fares and times vary; call for more information.

On the Outer Cape, Cape Cod Regional Transit Authority's Provincetown Shuttle serves North Truro and Provincetown daily from late May through mid-October, with more-limited service during the late fall and early spring, and no service in winter. The route begins at Dutra's Market in Truro and continues to Provincetown along Route 6A; it stops wherever a passenger or roadside flagger dictates. Once in Provincetown, the shuttle continues up Bradford Street, with alternating trips to Herring Cove Beach and Pilgrim Park as well as summertime service up to Provincetown Airport and Race Point Beach. It runs every 20 minutes and is outfitted to carry bicycles. The service is popular and reasonably priced ($1 for a single fare, $3 for a day pass).

The big buses of the Martha's Vineyard Transit Authority (VTA) provide regular service to all six towns on the island, with frequent stops in peak season and quite limited service in winter. The fare is $1 per town, including the town of departure. One-day ($6), three-day ($15), and one-week ($25) passes can be purchased on the bus and at Steamship Authority terminals.

The Nantucket Regional Transit Authority (NRTA) runs shuttle buses in town and to Madaket, mid-island areas (including the airport, 'Sconset, Surfside Beach, and Jetties Beach). Service is available late May to early September. Fares are $1 to $2, depending on the route passes cost $7 for one-day, $12 for three days, and $20 for one week.

Bus Information Cape Cod Regional Transit Authority (☎508/790–2613 or 800/352–7155 ⊕www.capecodtransit.org). **Martha's Vineyard Transit Authority (VTA** ☎508/693–9940 ⊕www.vineyardtransit.com). **Nantucket Regional Transit Authority (NRTA)** (✉22 Federal St., Nantucket 02554 ☎508/228–7025 ⊕www.shuttlenantucket.com). **Plymouth & Brockton Street Railway** (☎508/746–0378 ⊕www.p-b.com).

BUS TRAVEL TO & FROM CAPE COD

Greyhound serves Boston and Providence from all over the United States; from there you can connect to Greyhound's affiliate, Peter Pan Bus Lines, which serves Barnstable, Bourne, Falmouth, Hyannis, Otis Air Base (in Sandwich), Sagamore Circle, and Woods Hole on the Cape, plus nearby Fall River, New Bedford, and Plymouth. The Plymouth & Brockton Street Railway buses travel all the way to Provincetown from Boston and Logan Airport, with stops en route at a number of towns throughout the Cape, including Plymouth, Sagamore, Barnstable, Hyannis, Orleans, Eastham, Wellfleet, and Truro.

Bus Information Greyhound (☎800/231-2222 ⊕www.greyhound.com).**Peter Pan Bus Lines** (☎508/548-7588 or 888/751-8800 ⊕www.peterpanbus.com).**Plymouth & Brockton Street Railway** (☎508/746-0378 ⊕www.p-b.com).

∎ BY CAR

To reach Cape Cod from Boston (60 mi), take Route Interstate 93 south, then Route 3 south, and cross the Sagamore Bridge, which puts you onto U.S. 6, the Cape's main artery, leading toward Hyannis and Provincetown. From western Massachusetts, northern Connecticut, and upstate New York, take Interstate 84 east to the Massachusetts Turnpike (Interstate 90) and take Interstate 495 south to the Bourne Bridge. From New York City and southern Connecticut and Rhode Island, take Interstate 95 north toward Providence, where you pick up Interstate 195 east (toward Fall River–New Bedford) to Route 25 east to the Bourne Bridge. From the Bourne Bridge you can take Route 28 south to Falmouth and Woods Hole (about 15 mi), or—as you approach the Bourne Bridge—follow signs to U.S. 6 if you're headed elsewhere on the Cape.

Driving times can vary widely, depending on traffic. In good driving conditions you can reach the Sagamore Bridge from Boston in about 1½ hours, the Bourne Bridge from New York City in about 5 hours.

On summer weekends, when more than 100,000 cars a day cross each bridge, **make every effort to avoid arriving in late afternoon,** especially on holidays. And be sure to give yourself extra time if you're driving to any of the ferry terminals to Nantucket and Martha's Vineyard. U.S. 6 and Route 28 are heavily congested eastbound on Friday evening, westbound on Sunday afternoon, and in both directions on Saturday (when rental homes change hands). On the north shore, the Old King's Highway—Route 6A—parallels U.S. 6 and is a scenic country road passing through occasional towns.

When you're in no hurry, use back roads—you won't get there any faster, but they're less frustrating and much more rewarding. Heading from the Bourne Bridge toward Falmouth, County Road and Route 28A are prettier alternatives to Route 28, and Sippewisset Road meanders near Buzzards Bay between West Falmouth and Woods Hole. Just remember that some of these roads travel through residential areas, so keep your speed down.

Driving to Provincetown from other points on the Cape is mostly a scenic adventure. The wooded surrounds of Truro break into a breathtaking expanse of open water and sand dunes, with the skyline of Provincetown beyond. The busiest time is early morning—especially on days when the sun is reluctant to shine—when it seems that everyone on Cape Cod is determined to make it to Provincetown. Traffic is heaviest around Wellfleet, and because the road is just two lanes until North Truro, it can be slow going. Except during the traffic-heavy season, you'll find the drive from Wellfleet to Provincetown beautiful and only 25 minutes in duration.

Traffic delays often result from congestion at the Sagamore and Bourne bridges, but in 2007 a "flyover" road was built connecting the Sagamore Bridge directly to Route 3 and thus greatly reducing the traffic jams that used to result from the much-despised and now-replaced traffic rotary on the mainland side of the bridge. This development has cut travel time onto the Cape by as much as 20 minutes on busy days.

Traffic can be a challenge on the islands, especially in season. Nantucket is small enough that you can easily get around on foot or by public transportation, but on Martha's Vineyard, it can be handy to have a car if you really want to see the whole island and travel freely among the different towns. Bringing a car over on the ferry in summer requires reservations far in advance, costs almost double what it does off-season, and necessitates standing in long lines—it's sometimes easier and more economical to rent a car once you're on the island, and then only for the days you plan on exploring. And consider public transportation and taxis if you're only making a few trips to different parts of the island, which has very good bus service that can get you to just about every major sight, village, and beach. Where you stay and what you plan on seeing can greatly influence your transportation plans. As soon as you've booked a room, discuss the different options for getting around Martha's Vineyard with your innkeeper or hotel staff.

PARKING

Parking, in general, is a great challenge across much of Cape Cod and the islands from mid-June through early September, although many towns have metered lots and street parking or flat-fee or hourly pay lots. Popular and congested downtowns such as Falmouth, Provincetown, Hyannis, Oak Bluffs, Nantucket Town, and Chatham tend to prove especially tough. A number of smaller communities even have free street parking and municipal lots. In general, however, anytime you can walk, bike, or cab it somewhere, or you're able to travel in one car instead of two or more, do so. Off-season, parking is rarely a problem anywhere on the Cape or islands.

RULES OF THE ROAD

In Massachusetts, highway speed limits are 55 mph near urban areas, 60 or 65 mph elsewhere. Speed limits on U.S. 6 on the Cape vary as it changes from four lanes to two lanes. Radar detectors are legal in Massachusetts.

Massachusetts permits a right turn on a red light (*after* a full stop) unless a sign says otherwise. Also, when you approach one of the Cape's numerous rotaries (traffic circles), note that the vehicles already in the rotary have the right of way and that those vehicles entering the rotary must yield. Be careful: some drivers forget (or ignore) this principle.

Massachusetts law requires that drivers **strap children under age five (or under 40 pounds) into approved child-safety seats.** Kids ages 5 to 12 must wear seat belts. Drivers (but not other passengers over age 12) are legally required to wear seat belts, but they can only be ticketed for not wearing them if they're pulled over for some other reason.

ON THE GROUND

■ BEACHES

In season, you must pay to park at public beaches. Parking at "restricted" beaches is available only to residents and to visitors with permits. If you're renting a house, you can purchase a weekly beach permit; contact the local town hall for details. Walkers and cyclists do not need permits to use restricted beaches. The official season generally begins the last weekend in June and ends on Labor Day. Note that the lots are often open to all early in the morning (before 8) and late in the afternoon (after 4 or 5), even at resident beaches in season.

■ BIKE TRAVEL

Biking is very popular on Cape Cod and the islands, which have an abundance of excellent bike trails, some of them as busy as the region's roads in summer. Note that Massachusetts law requires children under 13 to wear protective helmets while riding a bike, even as a passenger. *For information on trails, maps, and rentals, see listings for specific towns.*

Bike Maps **Rubel Bike Maps** (⊠ Box 401035, Cambridge, MA02140 ⊕www.bikemaps.com).

■ BUSINESS HOURS

Hours on the Cape and the islands can sometimes differ from those elsewhere in New England, as many businesses and attractions are open only seasonally or have limited hours during the quieter months, from mid-fall to mid-spring. Within the region, shops and other businesses in the towns near the Cape as well as on the Upper Cape and even as far out as Barnstable and Hyannis tend to be less seasonal, catering to the larger year-round populations in those areas. The farther out you go, toward the Lower Cape and Outer Cape and on the islands, the more likely you are to encounter businesses that close or keep shorter hours off-season.

■ DAY TOURS & GUIDES

BOAT TOURS

Cape Cod Canal Cruises (two or three hours, narrated) leave from Onset, just northwest of the Bourne Bridge. A Sunday jazz cruise, sunset cocktail cruises, and Friday and Saturday dance cruises are also available. Children 12 and under cruise free on Family Discount Cruises, Monday through Saturday at 4. Cruises cost between $11 and $18.

Patriot Boats has two-hour day and sunset cruises from Falmouth Harbor on the 74-foot schooner *Liberté II* in July and August. Another sunset cruise, which operates on Friday and Saturday evenings, passes six lighthouses in the Falmouth area. Fishing charters are also available.

Hy-Line runs one-hour narrated boat tours of Hyannis Harbor, including a view of the Kennedy compound. On Sunday, you can embark on a Ben & Jerry's make-your-own-sundae "ice-cream float" through Lewis Bay; ticket prices for all tours range between $14 and $15.

The gaff-rigged schooner *Bay Lady II* makes two-hour sails, including a sunset cruise, across Provincetown Harbor into Cape Cod Bay; fares are $18 to $24. Private charters are also available.

Fees & Schedules **Bay Lady II** (⊠ MacMillan Wharf, Provincetown ☎508/487–9308 ⊕www.sailcapecod.com). **Cape Cod Canal Cruises** (⊠ Onset Bay Town Pier, Onset ☎508/295–3883 ⊕www.hy-linecruises.com). **Hy-Line** (⊠ Ocean St. dock, Pier 1, Hyannis ☎508/778–2600 or 800/492–8082 ⊕www.hy-linecruises.com). **Patriot Boats** (⊠ 227 Clinton Ave., Falmouth ☎508/548–2626 or 800/734–0088 ⊕www.theliberte.com).

TRAIN & TROLLEY TOURS

The Cape Cod Central Railroad offers two-hour, 42-mi narrated rail tours from Hyannis to the Cape Cod Canal (fare $18) from late May through October; trains generally run daily, but call for a schedule. You can have your fill of cranberry bogs, marshes, and woodlands, as well as such unusual sights as the Barnstable House of Corrections, where you'll spot inmates farming in the fields. From Hyannis, sit on the right side of the train for the best views. The second hour and its narration are a bit subdued, as you're traveling back the way you came, but the scenery and loud whistle blasts ought to keep you alert and engaged. You can also opt for the rail-sail option, which combines this trip with a Hy-Line Cruises *(see above)* harbor tour; the cost is $25 per person. There's also a three-hour, adults-only dinner train where you can settle back and watch the scenery as you nosh; it runs Thursday through Saturday in summer and less frequently spring and fall. The cost is $64.95 per person. Another dinner train, geared toward families, with a kids' menu and activities, runs on Monday through Wednesday evening and costs $39.95 for adults and $25.95 for kids under 12. A lunch train operates midweek from June through October and costs $39.95 per person.

The Provincetown Trolley offers 40-minute narrated tours of Provincetown, leaving from outside town hall every 30 minutes daily 10 to 4, and every hour daily 5 to 7 PM. The ride takes you through downtown, out to the Provincetown Monument, and by the beaches. The fare is $10.

Fees & Schedules Cape Cod Central Railroad (✉ Hyannis Train Depot, 252 Main St., Hyannis ☎ 508/771–3800 or 888/797–7245 ⊕ www.capetrain.com). **Provincetown Trolley** (☎ 508/487–9483 ⊕ www.provincetowntrolley. com).

WALKING TOURS

Colonial Lantern Tours offers guided evening walking tours April through November of the original Plymouth plantation site and historic district, as well as the nightly "Ghostly Haunts and Legends" tour highlighting Plymouth's more macabre history. The cost is $15.

Liz Villard's Vineyard History Tours leads walking tours of Edgartown's "history, architecture, ghosts, and gossip," including a stop at the Vincent House. Tours are run from April through December; call for times. Liz and her guides also lead similar tours of Oak Bluffs and Vineyard Haven. Walks last a little over an hour. Sixth-generation Nantucketer Gail Johnson of Gail's Tours narrates a lively 1½-hour van tour of the island's highlights.

Fees & Schedules Colonial Lantern Tours (✉ 5 North St., Plymouth ☎ 508/747–4161 or 800/698–5636 ⊕ www.plimouth.com). **Gail's Tours** (☎ 508/257–6557 ⊕ www.nantucket. net/tours/gails). **Vineyard History Tours** (☎ 508/627–8619 ⊕ www.mvpreservation. org/tours.html).

▌EATING OUT

The restaurants we list are the cream of the crop in each price category. Note that ordering a lobster dinner, which can be far more expensive than other menu items, may push your meal into a higher price category than the restaurant's price range shows. Properties indicated by a ✕🏠 are lodgings with exceptional restaurants.

CATEGORY	COST
¢	under $10
$	$10–$16
$$	$16–$22
$$$	$22–$30
$$$$	over $30
Per person for a main course at dinner	

CUTTING COSTS

Even the best of the region's restaurants offer slightly scaled-down portions of pricier dinner menus during lunchtime. Any time of day, you can indulge in fresh local seafood and clambakes at **seat-your-self shanties** for a much lower price than their fine-dining counterparts. Often the tackier the decor (plastic fish on the walls), the better the seafood. These laid-back local haunts usually operate a fish market on the premises and are in every town on the Cape.

Bear in mind that Cape Cod waters are occasionally plagued by red tide, an insidious algae that infests shellfish; 2005 saw a particular bad strain, which led to skyrocketing prices for fried whole-belly clams, but area waters have been largely back to normal ever since. During periods of red tide, you can still usually find most shellfish on menus, as it's easily brought in from other parts of the country, but whole-belly clams are expensive when shipped in from elsewhere, and menu prices reflect this.

WINES, BEER & SPIRITS

Massachusetts is not a major wine-growing area, but Westport Rivers Winery in Westport and the Cape Cod Winery in East Falmouth produce respectable vintages. The family that owns Westport Rivers also runs the local Buzzards Bay Brewing Co. Wines from Truro Vineyards of Cape Cod are local favorites.

In Massachusetts, you can generally buy alcoholic beverages (wine, beer, and spirits) in liquor stores, known locally as package stores. A few exceptions allow some grocery stores to sell wine and beer. All of the towns on Martha's Vineyard except Oak Bluffs and Edgartown are "dry" and don't sell alcohol, although as of this writing, the town of Vineyard Haven was considering allowing the sale of alcohol in restaurants.

▌ EMERGENCIES

Cape Cod Hospital has a 24-hour emergency room. For rescues at sea, call the Coast Guard. Boaters should use Channel 16 on their radios.

Emergency Services Ambulance, fire, police (☎911 or dial township station). **Coast Guard** (☎508/888–0335 in Sandwich and Cape Cod Canal, 508/945–0164 in Chatham ⊕www.uscg.mil).

Hospitals Cape Cod Hospital (✉27 Park St., Hyannis ☎508/771–1800 or 877/227–3263 ⊕www.capecodhealth.org). **Falmouth Hospital** (✉100 Ter Heun Dr., Falmouth ☎508/548–5300 or 877/227–3263 ⊕www.capecodhealth.org). **Jordan Hospital** (✉275 Sandwich St., Plymouth ☎508/746–2000 ⊕www.jordan.org). **Martha's Vineyard Hospital** (✉Linton La., Oak Bluffs ☎508/693–0410 ⊕www.marthasvineyardhospital.com). **Nantucket Cottage Hospital** (✉57 Prospect St., Nantucket ☎508/825–8100 ⊕www.nantuckethospital.org). **St. Luke's Hospital** (✉101 Page St., New Bedford ☎508/679–3131 ⊕www.southcoast.org/stlukes).

24-Hour Pharmacies CVS Falmouth (✉105 Rte. 28, Falmouth ☎508/540–4307). **CVS Hyannis** (✉176 North St., Hyannis ☎508/775–8462). **CVS Plymouth** (✉8 Pilgrim Hill Rd., Plymouth ☎508/747–1465).

Late-Night Pharmacy Leslie's Drug Store (✉65 Main St., Vineyard Haven ☎508/693–1010).

GAY & LESBIAN TRAVEL

Provincetown, at the tip of the Cape, is one of the East Coast's leading lesbian and gay seaside destinations, and it also has a large year-round lesbian and gay community. Dozens of P-town establishments, from B&Bs to bars, cater specifically to lesbian and gay visitors, and all of the town's restaurants are gay friendly; many are gay-owned and -operated. Hyannis has Cape Cod's sole gay bar outside P-town, but attitudes throughout Cape Cod tend to be extremely accepting and tolerant toward gays and lesbians. Martha's Vineyard, although lacking any gay-specific nightlife, has a number of gay-friendly businesses and accommodations and has become increasingly popular as a gay vacation spot in recent years. Nantucket is also quite tolerant but has less of a gay following than the Vineyard.

Gay- & Lesbian-Friendly Travel Agencies
Different Roads Travel (☎760/325–6964, 800/429–8747 Ext. 14 ✎ lgernert@tzell.com). **Kennedy Travel** (✉130 W. 42nd St., Suite 401, New York, NY 10036 ☎800/237–7433 or 212/840–8659 📠212/730–2269 ⊕www.kennedytravel.com). **Now, Voyager** (✉4406 18th St., San Francisco, CA 94114 ☎415/626–1169 or 800/255–6951 📠415/626–8626 ⊕www.nowvoyager.com). **Skylink Travel and Tour/ Flying Dutchmen Travel** (☎707/546–9888 or 800/225–5759) serving lesbian travelers.

HEALTH

LYME DISEASE

Lyme disease, so named for its having been first reported in the town of Lyme, Connecticut, is a potentially debilitating disease carried by deer ticks, which thrive in dry, brush-covered areas, especially on Cape Cod. Always **use insect repellent**; it's imperative that you protect yourself from ticks from early spring through summer. To prevent bites, **wear light-colored clothing and tuck pant legs into socks.** Look for black ticks about the size of a pinhead around hairlines and the warmest parts of the body. If you have been bitten, **consult a physician, especially if you see the telltale bull's-eye bite pattern.** Influenza-like symptoms often accompany a Lyme infection. Early treatment is imperative.

PESTS & OTHER HAZARDS

Cape Cod's greatest insect pest is mosquitoes, which are at their worst after snowy winters and wet springs. The best protection is **repellent containing DEET.** A particular pest of coastal areas, especially salt marshes, is the greenhead fly. Their bite is nasty, and they are best repelled by a liberal application of Avon Skin So Soft.

Poison ivy is a pervasive vinelike plant, recognizable by its leaf pattern: three shiny green leaves together. In spring new poison-ivy leaves are red; likewise, they can take on a reddish tint as fall approaches. The oil from these leaves produces an itchy skin rash that spreads with scratching. If you think you may have touched some leaves, **wash as soon as you can** with soap and cool water.

SHELLFISHING

Cape Cod attracts seafood lovers who enjoy harvesting their own clams, mussels, and even lobsters; permits are required, and casual harvesting of lobsters is strictly forbidden. Amateur clammers should be aware that New England shellfish beds are periodically visited by red tides, during which microorganisms can render shellfish (excluding lobsters, scallops, and all fin fish) poisonous. To keep abreast of the situation, inquire when you apply for a license (usually at town halls or police stations) and pay attention to red-tide postings as you travel.

Lyme Disease Info Massachusetts Department of Public Health (☎508/947–1231, 866/627–7968 public health hotline ⊕www.state.ma.us/dph). **National Centers for Disease Control and Prevention** (☎888/232–3228 general information, 877/394–8747 travelers' health line, 800/311–3435 public inquiries 📠888/232–3299 ⊕www.cdc.gov).

▮ SPORTS & THE OUTDOORS

For further details on enjoying the outdoors, including water sports, see ⇨ *the appropriate regional chapter.*

BASEBALL

The Cape Cod Baseball League, considered the country's best summer league, is scouted by all the major-league teams. Ten teams play a 44-game season from mid-June to mid-August; admission is free to games at all 10 fields, although donations are accepted. The teams also conduct baseball clinics for children and teens.

Contact Cape Cod Baseball League (☎508/ 432–6909 ⊕www.capecodbaseball.org).

BICYCLING

In the Plymouth area, the Myles Standish State Forest has 15 mi of bike trails. Fall River and New Bedford are predominantly urban areas that are not well suited for cyclists, but nearby, many local roads in Westport and South Dartmouth are pleasant biking spots. In the New Bedford suburb of Fairhaven, the Phoenix bike trail is a 3.3-mi rail trail that begins at the intersection of Ferry and Main streets. It runs east to the Mattapoisett town line.

Despite the heavy summertime traffic, the Outer Cape is quite blessed with bike trails. Off-road, the sandy, pine needle–covered trails of miles of fire roads traverse the National Seashore on the ocean side, from Wellfleet all the way on up to Truro. Bikers with thick wheels, stamina, and ambition will find hours of uninterrupted time with which to ride these trails, coming upon little other life than squirrels, birds, and the occasional deer. Provincetown is very bike friendly, as cycling is a far better way to get around than driving in summer. There are several stunning trails within the grounds of the Province Lands that will take riders through dunes and forest and alongside salt marshes.

Martha's Vineyard has superb terrain for biking—you can pick up a map that shows the island's many dedicated bike paths from the chamber of commerce. Several shops throughout the island rent bicycles, many of them close to the ferry terminals.

FISHING

Charter boats and party boats (per-head fees, rather than the charters' group rates) fish in season for bluefish, tuna, marlin, and mako and blue sharks. Throughout the year there's bottom fishing for flounder, tautog, scup, fluke, cod, and pollack.

The Cape Cod Chamber of Commerce's *Sportsman's Guide* provides fishing regulations, surf-fishing access locations, a map of boat-launching facilities, and more. The state Division of Fisheries and Wildlife has a book with dozens of maps of Cape ponds; the maps are also available on the Division's Web site. Remember, you'll need a license for freshwater fishing, available for a nominal fee at bait-and-tackle shops. Molly Benjamin's fishing column in the Friday *Cape Cod Times* gives the latest information about fishing on the Cape—what's being caught and where.

GOLF

The Cape Cod Chamber of Commerce produces a "Golf Map of Cape Cod," locating dozens of courses on the Cape. Summer greens fees range from $25 to about $100.

▮ TAXES

The state hotel tax varies from town to town but never exceeds 9.7%.

SALES TAX

Massachusetts state sales tax is 5%.

INDEX

PHOTO CREDITS

ABOUT OUR WRITERS

Former Fodor's staff editor and longtime Cape Cod contributor Andrew Collins updated the Outer Cape and Martha's Vineyard chapters for this edition, as well as the information in the front of the book. Andrew grew up in New England and has visited Cape Cod for many years, writing about it for *Fodor's Gay Guide to the USA*, several other Fodor's titles related to New England, and a number of newspapers and magazines. He has contributed to *Fodor's New Mexico, Travel & Leisure, Out Traveler, Sunset,* and *New Mexico Magazine,* and teaches a course on travel writing for New York City's Gotham Writers' Workshop.

Nantucket resident Sandy MacDonald is a seasoned travel writer who has written several New England guidebooks and contributed to others. She has also written about the island for publications such as *Boston Magazine* and *New England Travel & Life.* For this book, she covered Nantucket's good life—including dining, lodging, nightlife, the arts, and shopping.

Laura V. Scheel updated the Approaching Cape Cod, Upper Cape, Mid Cape, and Lower Cape chapters of this edition. She has written frequently for Fodor's, contributing to titles such as *Fodor's Maine Coast* and *Fodor's The Thirteen Colonies.* When not writing about travel, history, and the arts, she raises oysters in Wellfleet on the Outer Cape.